PERSONAL FINANCE

FOR CANADIANS

KATHLEEN H. BROWN

Prentice Hall Canada Inc.
Scarborough, Ontario

Canadian Cataloguing in Publication Data

Brown, Kathleen H. (Kathleen Helen), 1926-
    Personal finance for Canadians

5th ed.
ISBN 0-13-063876-5

I. Finance, Personal – Canada. 2. Consumer credit –
Canada. 3. Financial security. I. Title.

HG179.B78 1994 332.024 C93-094685-5

Prentice-Hall, Inc., Englewood Cliffs, New Jersey
Prentice-Hall International (UK) Limited, London
Prentice-Hall of Australia, Pty. Limited, Sydney
Prentice-Hall Hispanoamericana, S.A., Mexico City
Prentice-Hall of India Private Limited, New Delhi
Prentice-Hall of Japan, Inc., Tokyo
Simon & Schuster Asia Private Limited, Singapore
Editora Prentice-Hall do Brasil, Ltda., Rio de Janeiro

ISBN: 0-13-063876-5

Acquisitions Editor: Suzanne Tyson
Developmental Editor: Linda Gorman
Copy Editor: Chelsea Donaldson/Leah Johnson
Production Editor: Kelly Dickson
Production Coordinator: Anna Orodi
Cover and Interior Design: Carole Giguère
Cover Image: Valerie Sinclair
Page Layout: free&Creative

2 3 4 5 GI 98 97 96 95

Printed and bound in Canada.

Every reasonable effort has been made to obtain permissions for all
articles and data used in this edition. If errors or omissions have
occurred, they will be corrected in future editions provided written
notification has been received by the publisher.

CONTENTS

PREFACE

Changes in the Fifth Edition

The fifth edition of Personal Finance for Canadians, follows the same basic structure as previous editions but with substantial updating and revision of the content to reflect recent changes in our economic and financial environment. Examples and figures have been updated and new ones added and, in some chapters, the content reorganized somewhat. In Chapter 1, there are new sections on two-income families, and women and financial independence. A major section on bankruptcy, summarizing some aspects of the new legislation, was added to Chapter 17.

Thesis

Beginning with the first edition, the thesis of this book has been that, under dynamic conditions, memorizing many details has limited long-term value, and that the best preparation for taking control of personal financial affairs is a thorough understanding of basic principles, concepts, and vocabulary. With these skills, a person will be able to adjust to changing situations, recognizing the ways in which a new practice or financial instrument relates to previous ones, and to evaluate its usefulness. Although there is much readily available information about financial matters, many people fail to make maximum use of it. Either they do not know where to find it, or they do not know how to understand and use it. The purpose of this book is to assist readers in comprehending and making use of the constant flow of financial information. A competent financial manager should be able to ask meaningful questions before completing a transaction, but to do so requires knowledge of basic vocabulary and principles.

Organization and Approach

The chapter format is unchanged from previous editions: each begins with educational objectives to guide the learner followed by a brief introduction and many examples, case studies, tables, figures, and contracts to illustrate the subject matter. A set of problems, which offer opportunities to apply the material studied in the chapter to a variety of situations, and a list of references complete each chapter. Instead of a glossary, care was taken when preparing the index to indicate where to find definitions of new terms.

The topics included in this text, chosen to provide beginners with a comprehensive introduction to the field of personal finance, vary in depth of coverage. This was determined to some extent by the availability of other source material. For instance, there are many publications with detailed information about income tax and specific investments, but fewer that treat in any depth either consumer credit or general insurance. Therefore, income tax is not treated in depth in this book but, instead, an overview of the tax system is presented to guide readers in the use of more specific or technical publications. The chapters on investments explain the basic types of securities and how they are bought and sold. For further study, readers are directed to the references listed at the end of each chapter.

This text is divided into three parts: financial planning, financial security and credit. Part I, Financial Planning, explains how to make financial plans for spending and saving, the functions of wills in planning for the distribution of an estate after death, and the basic structure of the tax system. Part II, Financial Security, begins by identifying economic risks that threaten individuals. The following chapters address ways to minimize risk by insuring personal possessions or the life of a breadwinner, or investing successfully to increase net worth. Finally, Part III, Credit, examines in some depth the many complexities of obtaining consumer credit, credit reporting, collecting practices, and overindebtedness as well as home mortgages.

The dilemma faced by authors of books on personal finance is how to handle the ever-changing nature of the information. Some respond by keeping their books very general, others by producing revised editions annually. The solution chosen here is to present reasonably complete information, available at the time of writing, to allow the reader to become familiar with a wide variety of information, while making it clear how necessary it is to keep up-to-date and be aware of changing conditions.

In spite of great care, it is difficult to ensure that there are no errors in this text and, therefore, it would be helpful to hear from anyone who finds mistakes.

K.H.B.

ACKNOWLEDGEMENTS

The preparation of this book required the generous help and cooperation of a number of people. In addition to those who assisted with previous editions, particular credit is given to the following technical reviewers who kindly read portions of the manuscript of this edition and made helpful suggestions. They were: Sharon Brown, tax accountant with Deloitte Touche; Theodore Farley, lawyer with Moon, Heath; Delores Vokey, personal property manager with The Cooperators; Deborah Blewett, automobile manager with The Cooperators; Nazir Damji, underwriting executive with The Mutual Group; Kevin Simpson, investment counsellor with Richardson Greenshields; Marilyn Benson, marketing manager with Guelph Wellington Credit Union; Linda Routledge, advisor for consumer affairs with the Canadian Bankers Association; Donald McClure, senior account manager at Canada Trust; Hugh Ferguson, president of Collectrite Ontario; Lawrence Brown, director of quality assurance for Equifax Canada; David Stewart, assistant superintendent in Hamilton of the Bankruptcy Branch; Patricia Liptrap, special projects manager for The Ontario Association of Credit Counselling Services. Robert Bothwell of Bothwell Insurance kindly provided insurance and annuity quotations. Craig Hurl, of the Index Section of the Toronto Stock Exchange, provided data for the graphs of the TSE index.

Considerable use was made of data from Statistics Canada who have requested readers be informed that copies of their publications may be obtained by writing Publication Sales, Statistics Canada, Ottawa, Ontario, K1A 0T6 or by calling 1-613-951-7277 or 1-800-267-6677. Their facsimile number is 1-613-951-1584.

My research assistant, Ilona Dobos, helped in every possible way. She visited financial institutions to collect new contracts, prowled in libraries for new information, proofread many pages, checked and re-checked graphs, tables, and examples, and cheerfully carried out various other tasks. Many thanks to her.

PART ONE

FINANCIAL PLANNING

Contemporary interest in financial planning has generated increasing numbers of books and articles on the subject and a developing profession dedicated to helping people solve their financial problems. But what is financial planning? It can be whatever you want it to be: a tax plan, an investment strategy, a life insurance needs assessment, or a comprehensive financial appraisal. Analyzing or forecasting almost any personal financial activity may be labelled financial planning; consequently, the results can range in scope from a very specific tax plan to a complete strategy covering all personal financial affairs.

In Chapter 1 the general process of making financial plans is explained, including why future cash flow projections should be based on identification of future goals and knowledge of present resources. Most financial planning involves some understanding of basic tax concepts which are outlined in Chapter 2. After this introduction to the topic, income tax will come up again in later chapters dealing with retirement income, savings, and investments.

Financial planning is not only important in directing the management of resources during our lives but also in preparing for the disposition of our estate after death. Therefore, this section includes a chapter on wills and planning for the distribution of estates.

CHAPTER ONE

Financial Planning

OBJECTIVES

1. To explain how the use of economic resources can be improved by financial planning.

2. To examine reasons for taking a lifetime perspective in personal financial planning.

3. To demonstrate how a financial plan can influence decisions about spending, income tax, insurance, and investments.

4. To explain the basic principles of financial planning.

5. To identify the functions of net worth statements, expenditure records, and budgets in the financial planning process.

6. To evaluate a net worth statement.

7. To distinguish between income and wealth.

8. To evaluate various methods of controlling expenditures, and to identify obstacles to successful control.

9. To identify behaviours with a psychological or social origin that may interfere with successful implementation of a financial plan.

10. To examine the costs and benefits of various models for handling finances in a two-income family.

11. To identify reasons why women face greater economic risks than do men.

12. To examine the status of the new financial planning industry.

Introduction

Money means a great deal to most of us. And while a minority are obsessed with it and some try to disregard it as much as possible, most of us fall between these extremes. Not only do we depend on money to get the goods and services we want, but we often look upon money as an indicator of our material success. Perhaps because it is so important, our emotional relationship with money, shaped by cultural and family influences, is not something we want to talk about. Nonetheless, the way we spend money is a reflection of our most important values. The emotions of greed, fear, anger, pride, and guilt may all play a part in our financial decisions.

Financial behaviour, like other types of behaviour, is determined by personality as well as influences from our social and economic environments. Whether you are a tightwad or a spendthrift, see money as basic to your self-esteem and security, or use money to control and dominate others, it is a part of your psychological make-up. Established social norms also dictate many aspects of financial behaviour, such as how much money you consider essential for an acceptable lifestyle. Since your desires and wants usually exceed your resources, your economic behaviour is also determined by your actual economic situation, which forces you to make choices.

While this text is written from an economic perspective, it recognizes that psychological and social influences have a powerful effect on financial management, and must not be ignored. You may have a clear understanding of financial planning at the cognitive level, but be unable to implement your plan successfully because of conflicting underlying forces in your personality or social environment. To help you to understand your own financial behaviour you are referred to the publications on the psychology of money listed at the end of this chapter. This reference list includes much diversity. You will notice that psychologists tend to explore the reasons for financial behaviour while economists explain financial institutions and practices and how to make rational choices among competing demands.

Why do the people who say they are in favour of financial plans far outnumber those who actually make plans? The reasons are many and varied. While the idea of being in control of money and financial affairs is widely appealing, it is easy to feel overwhelmed by the process and intimidated by perceptions of its restrictiveness. You may be fearful that financial planning may prove too constricting on your lifestyle, believe you don't have enough money to make any plans, be hesitant to make commitments to the future, be reluctant to spend the time, or be unaware of how to make plans. However we rationalize it, most of us procrastinate and feel guilty about it. This chapter explains how to make financial plans and suggests that psychological aspects of behaviour play a very significant part in their implementation.

How do you make financial decisions? Do you decide on impulse? Do you leave things to chance? Do you make decisions by default or do you make deliberate financial choices in the context of an overall plan? It is said that there are two types of financial plans: those you make and those forced on you by circumstances. In reality, the way you handle financial matters has a significant impact on the quality of your life. If your decisions are guided by a financial plan the probability of your goals being achieved increases. If, instead, you make hasty *ad hoc* choices, isolated from any long-term strategy, the best use of your resources may be impossible.

You can increase your wealth, achieve financial security, and gain economic independence if you identify definite goals and create strategies to achieve them. To do so, you must be clear about your objectives, be prepared to make plans, and be willing to give close attention to your financial affairs. Generally, we put a great deal of time, effort, and money into developing skills needed to earn money, but very little into its management after we get it.

As most topics in financial planning are interrelated, it is impossible to avoid mention in this chapter of some terms and concepts that will be explained fully later. For this reason, you may want to review Chapter 1 after reading the rest of the book.

NEED FOR FINANCIAL PLANS

What is a Financial Plan?

A **financial plan**, like any other kind of plan, begins with goals that indicate what is to be achieved. After available resources are identified and assessed they are allocated to the desired objectives. Finally, a strategy is developed to ensure that goals are reached. Although the procedure for making a plan is straightforward, implementing it is quite another matter, especially if some change in behaviour is required.

Financial plans come in many degrees of completeness and complexity. A small plan might be devised to control spending on entertainment and recreation; such a plan would include specific goals, a set limit for this category, and some ways to ensure that you do not overspend. At the other extreme, a very comprehensive financial plan can include all aspects of a person's financial affairs, starting with financial objectives and including current spending and saving projections, investment strategies, income tax plans, estate plans, and schemes for financing specific goals including retirement. In most cases, people make financial plans that fall somewhere between these two extremes of complexity. Several examples of financial plans are included later in this chapter.

Why Plan Financial Affairs?

Planning makes it possible for you to live within your income, save money for short-term and long-term goals, and reduce financial worries and stresses in the household. Do you hope to purchase expensive goods, take a big trip, buy a house, send your children to university, or just make ends meet? Do you want to achieve financial independence and have a comfortable retirement? Do you wish to leave your dependents well provided for if something should happen to you? A financial plan will help you to take control of your finances and attain these goals.

There are both non-economic and economic reasons for making financial plans. Taking control of your finances can reduce anxiety, raise self-confidence, and increase satisfaction. In addition to feeling much better about yourself and your finances, there are a number of economic goals that can be accomplished by planning:

(a) balancing cash flows,

(b) accumulating funds for special goals,

(c) adjusting lifetime earnings to expenses,

(d) meeting the needs of dependents in case of death or disability,

(e) minimizing income taxes,

(f) maximizing investment returns.

BALANCE CASH FLOWS   Everyone faces the necessity of ensuring that current income is adequate to cover expenses, a task otherwise known as making ends meet. Those with financial plans are in a better position to balance receipts and expenditures because of their overall view of the situation. Some non-planners go through cycles of feast and famine, spending money when they have it and doing without when it is gone. Others have a sufficient margin between income and expenses so the problem does not arise. Taking control of current cash flows leads to peace of mind and greater success in achieving financial goals.

SPECIAL GOALS   We all dream of things we would like to do or buy but know the cost is too much to handle on our current income. We have a choice: to wait until we have saved enough or to do it now and pay later. Each option has costs and benefits. Is it better to submit to the discipline of waiting and saving, or to pay the extra costs of using credit? If the expenditure can be postponed, there is much to be said for selecting a savings target and gradually accumulating the needed funds. This way, you earn interest while waiting instead of paying it to someone else as a credit charge. Good money managers try to receive interest, not pay it. It is usually worthwhile to save before buying a house because a large down payment substantially reduces interest costs. The key point is that your goals will be more easily reached if you have a plan for achieving them.

THE CREDIT TRAP

Marie and Henry find themselves on a treadmill. In addition to having very little income, they have a short time horizon and a great fascination with consumer durables. Their old car gave out before it was paid off: but since they preferred using a car to taking the bus they persuaded a bank to increase their loan so they could get another car.

Meanwhile, easy credit made it possible to add to their home entertainment centre: a second television for their daughter's room, new videotapes, a compact disk player and disks, etc.

Henry works at a factory that has a layoff for at least six months every year and Marie is at home looking after little Gina. During layoffs, Henry finds that most of his unemployment benefits cheque goes for debt repayment and rent.

This family, which can so ill afford it, is paying high rates of interest for consumer debt, living from hand to mouth, and accumulating no reserve funds.

LIFETIME PERSPECTIVE   A planner has a long time horizon, looking ahead to future years and not just this month or year. For instance, most people can expect the relation between their income and expenses to vary over their life span: generally, living expenses will be more stable than employment earnings. Living costs tend to rise somewhat as our expectations increase and definitely expand when children join the family. Earnings, on the other hand, may be very small or nonexistent for a student, take a jump with labour force involvement, increase gradually with experience, and reach a peak just before terminating at retirement.

In the early stages of family formation, it is not unusual to find expenses exceeding income with a consequent dependence on consumer credit. In middle age, as the children leave home and earnings are reaching a peak, opportunities to save may be particularly good. At retirement, there may be income from deferred earnings in the form of pensions, but often this is inadequate to support your accustomed lifestyle. At this stage, investment income can make life much more comfortable. In summary, an important planning task is to develop a way of distributing resources to support a fairly stable consumption level throughout the life span. A lifetime perspective on income and expenses is suggested in the diagram in Figure 1.1.

NEEDS OF DEPENDENTS   If you have dependents you will want to consider the economic consequences of your untimely death. Should you die tomorrow, would there be enough money to support your dependents for as long as needed? Young families, who usually lack enough wealth to cope with such situations, buy life insurance to fill the gap. Another aspect of planning is to make a will to ensure that funds will be distributed as you intend after your death.

MINIMIZE INCOME TAX   The income tax system has become very complex. While there are ways to minimize your tax bill, the responsibility is yours to know and take advantage of all the possibilities. By tax filing time in April, it is usually too late to implement most tax-saving strategies. Plans must be made well in advance.

FIGURE 1.1   INCOME AND LIVING COSTS: AVERAGE LIFETIME PROFILE

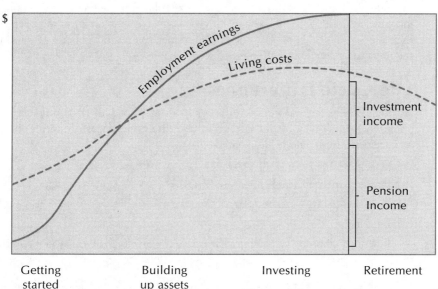

STAGES IN THE FINANCIAL LIFE CYCLE

MAXIMIZE INVESTMENT INCOME   Some people who are good savers have no idea how to go about investing. They find the subject of investments so overwhelming that they leave too much money in low-yielding securities. If increasing wealth is a goal, it is necessary not only to save but also to invest prudently.

When to Start Planning

Planning is best not postponed on the assumption that there will be more money in the future. Start right now to make the best use of what you have. You can achieve financial independence if you are determined to do so. It will mean taking deliberate control of your own financial affairs, rather than delaying decisions, letting things drift, and becoming a victim of circumstances. Many opportunities have been missed by those who considered financial matters beyond their control. Numerous people have retired with insufficient funds for a comfortable life because they did not save and invest during their working years.

Reaching Financial Independence

The way to financial independence is to spend less than you earn and to invest the savings. As your wealth gradually grows you will be able to achieve more of your financial goals and perhaps retire earlier. The key is to increase your wealth steadily so that eventually investment income can replace or augment your employment income. Naturally, it helps to have a high income but many highly paid people spend their money as quickly as they get it. The sooner you begin to plan, save, and invest, the more time the money will have to grow.

Life Cycle Differences

Although there are individual differences, most of us will go through a series of phases in our lifetimes. Sociologists call these "**life cycle stages**." In terms of financial management they could be designated:

(a) getting started (to mid-thirties),

(b) building up assets (mid-thirties to fifties),

(c) investing (fifties to retirement),

(d) retirement.

Financial planning is dynamic. Expect your plans to change as you move through the life cycle.

GETTING STARTED   Students are naturally concerned with educational and living costs and obtaining a job in a chosen field. It is wise to invest money saved from summer employment in secure, short-term deposits (savings account, term deposit, Canada Savings Bonds) to generate as much interest as possible. Careful spending plans can be helpful in ensuring that funds last until the end of term. Perhaps you have noticed that for some students the money ends before the term does. There are others who manage to put themselves through college or university and still have a nest egg at the end of it all. Why the difference? Could it be planning?

After graduation, high priority will be given to career advancement, saving for an emergency fund, perhaps buying a house, and starting a modest investment portfolio. If you are raising a family, life insurance may be needed to cover the risk that you might die while supporting dependents. The funds available to do all these things will usually come from earnings, since there has not been time to build up wealth to generate investment income.

BUILDING UP ASSETS   The middle years are the time to concentrate on paying off the mortgage on the house, increasing savings and investments, and giving some thought to retirement planning.

INVESTING   In middle age most people have the best opportunity to save and acquire a variety of assets. Obligations to children usually diminish, the house becomes mortgage-free, and income is at or near its peak. This is the time to give a high priority to increasing assets for an adequate retirement income.

RETIREMENT   After retirement, your opportunities to increase wealth will be much diminished. Your attention will be focused on sound management of previously acquired assets and changing the mix of assets to emphasize income rather than growth.

This review of changes in financial management as one moves through the life cycle demonstrates that long-term planning is essential. A small investment left to grow for many years will take advantage of the time effects of compounding, but those who wait until age 55 to start saving for retirement will have to save more to compensate for the shorter time for growth. Since we all want to achieve financial independence we must be willing to pay the price in time, effort, and self-discipline.

WHEN TO START SAVING FOR RETIREMENT?

Yolanda and Dan were debating when they should start saving for their retirement. Yolanda thought that if they put away $1000 each year for the next 30 years they would have a useful sum when they turned 65. Dan, however, argued that with a young family it would be too hard for them to do without $1000 now. He said that if he started at age 55 and saved $3000 a year he would be just as far ahead as Yolanda. Either way they would be saving the same amount—$30 000. To support her position, Yolanda decided to look up some compound interest tables. Assuming an average return of 7% compounded annually she found that in 30 years her savings would have grown to $101 073. With ten years of investment, Dan's $30 000 would become only $44 352. The results are shown in Figure 1.2.

THE FINANCIAL PLANNING PROCESS

Financial planning is the currently-popular name for an age-old process, usually known as "budgeting." However, financial planning sometimes means a more comprehensive plan than the traditional budget. A word here about terminology: the word "budget," which has a strict technical meaning, is often misused. A **budget** is a plan for using financial resources, a projection for the future. It is not a record of what was spent last year. Very often "budget" is used to imply thrift, scrimping, or lower quality. This book adheres to the technical definition of a budget.

The basic principles of management apply just as much to handling financial affairs as to any other kind of activity. In this section, a general overview of the financial planning process will be followed by more detailed discussion of each component. The time span used for financial planning is entirely personal, but for simplicity we will assume that the planning period is one year. During that time, most kinds of expenses and income will have occurred at least once.

FIGURE 1.2 VALUE OF ANNUAL DEPOSITS OF $1000 FROM AGE 35–64 AND $3000 FROM AGE 55–64 AT 7%

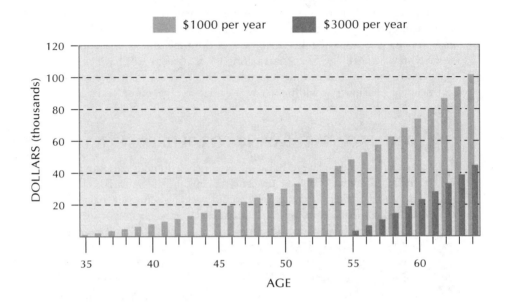

The first principle of financial management—as with any other type of management—is that goals must be identified before they can be achieved. Because it is usual to have more objectives than financial resources, priorities must be attached to goals to reflect their relative importance. The second principle is that an analysis of present financial resources is basic to future planning. Assemble all records of income and expenses for the past year, as well as a list of your assets and debts.

The third principle is that successful planning requires balanced cash flows. Refer to past spending records as a basis for estimating the cost of accomplishing your objectives. Draw up a plan or forecast for a specific period, perhaps a year, which includes a statement of your anticipated financial resources and their allocation; this plan is called a budget.

Fourth, strategies for the implementation and control of the plan are essential. Plans are intended to direct some action and to manage changes as they occur. The fifth and final principle is that effective financial management requires the ongoing evaluation of plans and implementation strategies to keep the plan relevant and effective. A summary of the process is shown in Figure 1.3.

FIGURE 1.3 STEPS IN THE FINANCIAL PLANNING PROCESS

> 5. EVALUATE PROGRESS
> 4. DEVELOP IMPLEMENTATION & CONTROL STRATEGIES
> 3. BALANCE FUTURE CASH FLOWS
> 2. ASSESS RESOURCES
> 1. IDENTIFY GOALS & SET PRIORITIES

IDENTIFY VALUES, GOALS, PRIORITIES

What is meant by a financial goal and how does it differ from a personal goal? Personal goals tend to be more global and depend on a range of resources; a personal goal to have a happy, satisfying lifestyle requires other resources in addition to money and may be accomplished through a number of intermediate goals. The desire to buy a house is a goal with a financial component, which might contribute to the larger personal goal of obtaining a certain lifestyle. In this book the focus tends to be on the financial aspects of goals, sometimes referred to as financial goals.

Three major areas in which many people have goals with financial elements are: (i) level of living, (ii) financial security, and (iii) estate planning. In allocating financial resources, each individual creates his or her own balance among desires for comforts and amenities at present, developing a reserve of funds to be used in emergencies and on retirement, and amassing an estate to bequeath to others.

Establishing financial goals is a very personal matter. A counsellor or advisor can ask questions to help you identify goals and the priorities you place on them, but cannot and should not attempt to decide what your goals are. Once the goals and their attached priorities are made explicit, a financial adviser can assist you to learn the management process necessary to reach the goals.

Conflicts in Goals and Values

Unfortunately, it is a common family problem that people sharing economic resources do not always share financial goals. For example, one partner may want to save as much as possible for a down payment on a house, while the other has a strong need to pursue an expensive hobby or other recreation. With limited resources, this couple will have difficulty in reaching both goals. Furthermore, they will likely have problems in their relationship until they settle their differences. Recognizing that a difference in values is at the root of their problem is an essential first step in resolving these difficulties.

Financial management may sound easy, but it can be difficult to accomplish because conflicts in attitudes, beliefs, and values continually intrude. As you would expect, the greater the number of individuals involved in the financial management of a common set of resources, the greater the potential for conflict. One might think that a person who lives alone and who does not have to share resources or cooperate with others in determining goals would have no problems. Not so. Single individuals often experience financial difficulties because of a lack of clarity in goals, unresolved conflicts in priorities, lack of self-discipline, and poor methods of control. You may wish to do further reading about clarifying values and handling interpersonal conflicts; here it is emphasized that attitudes, values, and motivation are probably the most important components in the financial management process. Books, courses, and financial advisers can tell you how to manage your money, but only you can decide whether to act.

ASSESS RESOURCES

Once you are clear about goals and priorities, the next step is to take an inventory of the resources you have, or can expect to receive, that may be used to achieve these goals. There are two components to this resource assessment: (i) an inventory of assets called a net worth statement, and (ii) an income statement. The distinction between income and wealth is important. A net worth statement shows the stock of assets and the amount of liabilities at a specific time or your net **wealth. Income,** which is not a stock but a flow of resources over a period of time, is usually expressed as an amount per week, per month or per year. An analogy may help to clarify this point. Think of income as the rate at which water flows into a pond, and net worth as the amount of water in the pond (Figure 1.4). Those people who do not let some water stay in their ponds will find that their net worth fails to grow.

Net Worth

An essential requirement for financial planning is knowledge of exactly what you own and what you owe. Begin by making a list of all your assets and liabilities, or a net worth statement. Subtract the liabilities from the assets to find your actual **net worth,** or wealth. Those who make a wealth inventory are usually surprised by what they find. They may have more assets than they thought, or more debts than they imagined, or find that their assets are not sufficiently diversified.

MEASURE OF ECONOMIC PROGRESS If your goal is to increase wealth for financial security and independence, you must have some way to measure your progress. A series of annual net worth statements will reveal the rate at which your wealth is growing, and indicate whether you should make changes in your saving or investing practices. Think of a net worth statement as a snapshot of wealth on a given day; since it may be larger or smaller at another time, it should always be dated.

FIGURE 1.4 ECONOMIC RESOURCES OF THE HOUSEHOLD: FLOWS AND STOCK

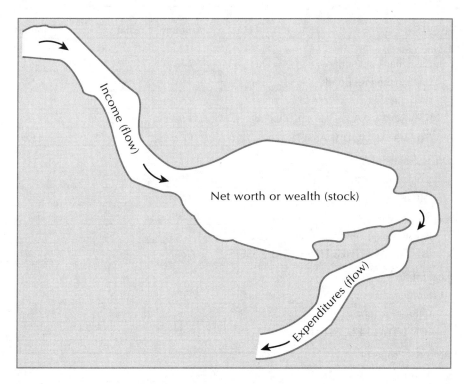

NET WORTH STATEMENT   When making a net worth statement, list all your assets at their current value and the total amounts presently outstanding on all existing liabilities, as shown in Table 1.1. Assets that are not fully paid for, such as a house or car, are listed at their present market value in the asset column, and the amount owing is listed under liabilities. Total each column and find the difference between the two. If your assets exceed your liabilities you have a positive net worth. Many people start their working lives with a negative net worth, but expect a growing positive net worth as middle age nears. In summary:

Net worth = total assets − total liabilities

TABLE 1.1   NET WORTH STATEMENT

	Self or joint		Spouse	
ASSETS	**Amount**	**% of total**	**Amount**	**% of total**
Liquid Assets				
Cash, bank accounts	1 200			
Canada Savings Bonds	3 000		2 500	
Term deposits	1 500			
Life insurance (cash surrender value)	3 500		1 450	
(A) **TOTAL LIQUID ASSETS**	9 200		3 950	
Other Financial Assets				
Stocks and bonds	2 500			
GICs	1 500		2 000	
RRSPs	7 500		5 000	
Pension plan credits				
(B) **TOTAL OTHER FINANCIAL ASSETS**	11 500		7 000	
Real Estate				
Home	135 000			
Other real estate				
(C) **TOTAL REAL ESTATE**	135 000			
Personal Property				
Vehicles	13 000		18 900	
Furnishings, jewellery			9 500	
(D) **TOTAL PERSONAL PROPERTY**	13 000		28 400	
(E) **BUSINESS EQUITY**				
(F) **TOTAL ASSETS**	168 700		39 350	
Add subtotals (A), (B), (C), (D), (E)				
LIABILITIES				
Short-Term Debt				
Loans, instalment contracts	8 000		12 000	
Credit card debts	450		1 000	
Life insurance loans				

(continued)

TABLE 1.1 NET WORTH STATEMENT (CONTINUED)

ASSETS	Self or joint Amount	% of total	Spouse Amount	% of total
Long-Term Debt				
Mortages	110 000			
Other debts				
Total Liabilities	118 450		13 000	
TOTAL ASSETS (F)	168 700		39 350	
Assets – Liabilities = NET WORTH	50 250		26 350	
COMBINED NET WORTH OF SELF AND SPOUSE $		76 600		
DATE January 31, 1994				

Use the sample net worth statement in Table 1.1 as a guide in preparing your own. A couple is advised to make individual net worth statements as well as a joint one. Since Canadians prepare individual tax returns, it is helpful for tax planning to be able to analyze the assets of each partner separately. For instance, a family might decide that the spouse with the lower income will own those assets that generate the most income. For later analysis, calculate what proportion of the total is represented by each asset.

WHAT TO INCLUDE   What to include in a net worth statement will depend on how you intend to use it. Be consistent in your choice of items in annual net worth statements used to measure economic progress, so you can compare your results from year to year. You may decide that household furnishings and clothing are fairly constant and can be excluded. On the other hand, if you need to monitor the growth in your personal household capital goods, you may decide to include specific items. When an estate is being settled, a very detailed net worth statement may be required which includes all the personal possessions of the deceased. For loan applications, the credit manager might ask enough questions to estimate the borrower's net worth, with emphasis mainly on liquid assets and real property. When preparing a net worth statement for retirement planning, the attention will be on assets that have income-producing potential.

USES FOR NET WORTH STATEMENTS   What uses are there for net worth statements, other than to measure economic progress, obtain a loan, or settle an estate? An analysis of assets and debts can help determine if the asset mix is appropriate and whether the debt/asset ratio is satisfactory. When making plans for retirement, you will want to know what wealth you have available to generate future investment income. Should you need to draw on net worth in a time of crisis, it will be helpful to have a clear idea of what your resources are. If you are trying to decide whether you need life insurance, the net worth statement can be examined to see if there is a gap between the resources the dependents would need and what the family already has.

ANALYZE NET WORTH   Once made, a net worth statement should be analyzed, not just filed. Use Table 1.2 and the following questions as a guide for evaluating net worth.

(a) **Has your net worth grown faster than inflation in the past year?**

If not, assets have been losing purchasing power. Look for a minimum long-term growth of about three percent after inflation. For instance, if net worth increased eight percent in a year when inflation was five percent, there would be a net change of three percent after inflation, also known as the **real rate of return**. Next, check if all the growth has been in the value of your home. If so, this may be overshadowing a lack of growth in other assets.

(b) **What is the ratio of liquid assets to total assets?**

In order to answer this question, you need to know that **liquid assets** are those which can be converted to cash readily without loss of principal, such as bank deposits or Canada Savings Bonds. Too much or too little liquidity can be unwise, as will be discussed in the chapter on investments. Some liquid assets, perhaps the equivalent of three months' wages, may be reserved for emergencies. However, since liquid assets tend to earn less than other investments, an over-emphasis would mean a loss of potential income. Many people have too large a proportion of their assets in liquid form.

(c) **What is the ratio of short-term debt to liquid assets?**

A high ratio indicates a precarious position if anything should happen to income. Is the ratio appropriate for your stage in the life cycle? Normally, the debt/income ratio will decrease with age.

(d) **What is the ratio of investment assets to investment debt?**

After purchasing a house with a large mortgage, this ratio may be low, but with time, it should increase.

(e) **What is the ratio of short-term to long-term liabilities?**

Short-term debt should not be greater than long-term debt. Are you using most of the long-term debt to acquire assets? Is your short-term debt for living expenses? Borrowing to buy assets such as property makes sense, but too much dependence on credit for day-to-day living costs is a drain on resources and impedes the growth of wealth.

TABLE 1.2 ANALYSIS OF NET WORTH

1. ANNUAL GROWTH IN NET WORTH

Present net worth	$	76 600
Previous net worth (year ago)	$	69 700
Change in net worth (+ or –)	$	6 900
Percentage change in net worth		9.9%
Inflation rate for same period		5.3%
Net change after inflation		4.6%

2. LIQUIDITY

Total liquid assets	$	13 150
Total assets	$	208 050
Liquid assets/total assets ratio		0.06

3. DEBT RATIOS

Total short-term debt	$	21 450
Liquid assets	$	13 150
Short-term debt/liquid asset ratio		1.63
Total asset in property, and other investments	$	153 500
Total debts for property and other investments	$	110 000
Investment asset/debt ratio		1.39
Total short-term debt	$	21 450
Total long-term debt	$	110 000
Short-term long-term debt ratio		0.19

4. DIVERSITY

Deposits and other loans (Debt securities)	$	13 150
Total liquid assets	$	3 500
Total RRSPs	$	12 500
Bonds other than CSBs	$	
Other loans (you are the lender)	$	
Total debt securities	$	29 150
Ownership (Equities)	$	
Total stocks	$	2 500
Total equity in property	$	25 000
Total business equity	$	
Total equity securities	$	27 500
Debt securities/equity securities ratio		1.06

(f) **How diversified are the assets?**

Add up all the assets that are deposits, bonds, or other loans, also referred to as debt securities. These assets are usually low risk, and pay interest income.

Compare this total with those assets which you own, such as property or stocks. These are called equity securities. What is the ratio of debt securities to equity securities? Are the various kinds of risks balanced? What might happen to the purchasing power of assets if we have a period of high inflation? Generally, debt securities lose purchasing power in periods of inflation and equity securities are more likely to appreciate. How much is exposed to market risk, as in a business or the stock market? Different types of risks are explained in Chapter 9.

Income

The second task in assessing financial resources is to predict your income for the planning period by examining past income records. Use Table 1.3 to record your income for the last calendar year. Income tax records can be helpful for this. Enter your gross income before any deductions, not your take-home pay. All deductions, including income tax, will be shown in the expenditure record.

OTHER RESOURCES   Include in the income statement any other resources you used last year to cover living expenses, such as savings, credit, or gifts if you expect to use them in the next planning period.

Expenditures

ESTIMATE LIVING COSTS   Before making plans for next year, it is best to have the most complete information possible about current living costs. Those who have been keeping records will have a great advantage here. Otherwise, make the best and most detailed estimates possible of your costs for the past year, using Table 1.4 as a guide. Try to reconstruct the outward cash flow, using cheque stubs, receipts, and any records available. Anyone who feels overwhelmed by the detail required in Table 1.4 can skip to the end and use the summary part only. This may be quicker but you will recognize that these estimates may not be as accurate.

TABLE 1.3 ESTIMATED ANNUAL INCOME

Source	Self	Spouse
Employment		
Gross income from employment	56 900	25 000
Other (bonuses, etc.)		
(A) TOTAL EMPLOYMENT INCOME	56 900	25 000
Government Payments		
Unemployment Insurance		
Workers' Compensation		
Pensions (Veteran's, CPP, Old Age Security, other)		
Welfare, family benefits		
(B) TOTAL GOVERNMENT PAYMENTS		
Investment		
Interest and dividends	450	
Rent (net income)		
Capital gains/profit		
Annuities		
Other		
(C) TOTAL INVESTMENT INCOME	450	
Other Income		
(D) TOTAL OTHER INCOME		
Total Annual Income	$ 57 350	$ 25 000
[(a) + (b) + (c) + (d)]		
Total Family Income		$ 82 350
Other Resources Used		
Savings spent		
Money borrowed		
Gifts received		
Total Other Resources	$	$

Date   _January 31st, 1994_

TABLE 1.4 ESTIMATED ANNUAL EXPENSES

Expense Item	Per wk.	Per mo.	Per yr.	Check fixed expenses
Deductions from pay				
Income tax (include with taxes and security at the end)				
Canada Pension Plan		88.55	1 062.60	✓
Unemployment Insurance		109.27	1 311.24	✓
Parking		24.00	288	✓
Company pension		367.26	4 407.12	✓
Association/union dues		35	420	✓
Health insurance		0	0	✓
Group life insurance		10.00	120.00	✓
Long-term disability insurance		10.00	120.00	✓
Dental plan		12.51	150.12	✓
Extended health insurance		0	0	✓
Other		.10	120.00	✓
TOTAL DEDUCTIONS			7 999.08	
Food				
Groceries	180.00		9 360.00	
Eating out		60.00	720.00	
TOTAL FOOD			10 080.00	
Housing				
Rent or mortgage		929.00	11 148	✓
Real estate taxes		125	1 500	✓
Hydro, water		60	720	✓
Heat		75	900	✓
Telephone		40	480	
Cable TV		40	480	✓
Household operation and help				
Home maintenance		58.33	700	
Purchase of furniture and appliances			1 000	
Home insurance			360	✓
TOTAL HOUSING			17 288	

(continued)

TABLE 1.4 ESTIMATED ANNUAL EXPENSES (CONTINUED)

Expense Item	Per wk.	Per mo.	Per yr.	Check fixed expenses
Medical				
Insurance premiums				
Dental			230.00	✓
Drugs		10.00	120.00	✓
Optical (annual average)			100.00	✓
Other				
TOTAL MEDICAL			450.00	
Transportation				
Car/Vehicle purchase or payments		260.00	3 120.00	✓
Vehicle insurance		42.5	510.00	✓
Operation (including gas, oil licence, parking)			1 200.00	✓
Vehicle maintenance			500.00	✓
Travel and public transportation		10.00	120.00	✓
TOTAL TRANSPORTATION		312.50	5 450.00	
Personal needs				
Pocket money		100.00	1 200.00	
Personal care		45.00	540.00	
TOTAL PERSONAL NEEDS		145.00	1 740.00	
Gifts and Donations				
Gifts			1 500.00	
Charitable donations		53.33	640.00	
Religious contributions		190.00	2 288.00	
TOTAL GIFTS AND DONATIONS			4 428.00	
Clothing				
Wife			450.00	
Husband			400.00	
Other family members			600.00	
Laundry and cleaning			100.00	
TOTAL CLOTHING			1 550.00	

(continued)

TABLE 1.4 ESTIMATED ANNUAL EXPENSES (CONTINUED)

Recreation and Entertainment

Hobbies		1 500,00
Liquor, tobacco		
Books, subscriptions, records tapes, etc.		520,00
Other: *travel*		1 000,00
TOTAL RECREATION		3 020,00

Security and Taxes

Life insurance	98,00	1 176,00	✓
Annuities, RRSPs	50,00	600,00	
Regular savings	300,00	3 600,00	
Income tax		18 904,60	✓
TOTAL SECURITY AND TAXES		24 280,60	

Other expenses

TOTAL OTHER EXPENSES	800

Debt repayment

TOTAL DEBT REPAYMENT	3120	*included in transportation*

Summary of expenses

Expense Item	Per yr.	
1. Deductions	7 999,08	
2. Food	10 080,00	
3. Housing	17 288,00	
4. Medical	450,00	
5. Transportation	5 450,00	
6. Personal needs	1 740,00	
7. Gifts and donations	4 428,00	
8. Clothing	1 550,00	
9. Recreation and entertainment	3 020,00	
10. Security and taxes	24 280,60	
11. Debt repayment		
12. Other	800,00	
TOTAL EXPENSES	77 085,68	
TOTAL FIXED EXPENSES	48 967,68	
TOTAL SAVINGS	3 600,00	4.4% of income

Note that in Table 1.4 a check mark is to be placed beside all expenses that are considered fixed. It is helpful in planning to distinguish between **flexible expenses** (which can be altered if needed) and **fixed expenses** (which are difficult to change in the short term). In the long run, of course, all expenses can be altered. Whenever quick adjustments are required, it will probably have to be in the flexible expenses. Enter expenses by week or month as convenient, then convert all to annual amounts.

ANALYZE EXPENSE RECORD   Review the expense record to discover whether there is consistency between the way money has been spent and the statement of goals and priorities. Quite often we say one thing but do another. Identify spending categories that may need better methods of control. Is debt repayment too large a proportion of expenses? Will next year's expenses be about the same as the last, or are changes expected?

SAVING   What proportion of income was saved last year? Is this satisfactory or could it be increased? A discussion of savings strategies may be found in Chapter 9.

BALANCE FUTURE CASH FLOWS

Income

Based on the data you have assembled, estimate your income for next year. If you are at all unsure that you will receive some income, do not include it. There will be fewer unpleasant surprises if you are conservative in predicting income, but generous in estimating expenses. Enter the amounts in Table 1.5.

IRREGULAR INCOME   When income is irregular it is harder to make a forecast, unless there are adequate records from past years. Make the best estimate possible of next year's income, but be restrained. Since expenses are likely to be more regular than income, divide total expenses by 12 and allocate this amount for monthly living expenses and savings.

Other Resources

If you expect that your income will not be high enough to cover your expenses, list the other resources that you will use, such as savings, borrowed funds, and gifts from others. Such resources may be needed by students, the unemployed, or the retired if they have insufficient income to support their living costs. At other times in the life cycle, it should be possible to add to savings rather than use them. It has been observed, however, that those who have been good savers all their lives are often reluctant to use these assets to support their lifestyle when they are old. They have saved for a rainy day and they are concerned that things may be worse in the future. Sometimes it is difficult to decide whether you have arrived at a rainy day!

TABLE 1.5 THE BUDGET

Planning period from   *January 1st, 1994*   **to**   *December 31st, 1994*

Available Resources

Income		$ *82 350*
Savings		
Borrowing		
TOTAL RESOURCES AVAILABLE		$ *82 350*

Allocation of Resources

Savings

Emergency funds	*1 000,00*		
Short-term goals	*1 400,00*		
Long-term goals	*1 200,00*		
TOTAL SAVINGS		$ *3 600,00*	

Expenses

TOTAL EXPENSES		$ *77 085,68*	
TOTAL SAVINGS AND EXPENSES		$ *80 685,68*	$ *80 685,68*
Difference between total resources and total savings and expenses			$ *1 664,32*

Savings

Plan your savings for the year first; don't just hope that some money will be left over. How much must be saved to meet various long-term and short-term objectives? For instance, if you are planning a large purchase in four years, determine how much you must save each year. Is there enough in the emergency fund? What part of the savings is going towards a retirement fund? Keeping in mind goals and annual resources, decide how much would be realistic to save for the year. This subject is explored in more detail in Chapter 9.

Living Expenses

How much does it cost to run a household, to clothe and feed family members, to take an annual holiday? How much will be needed for those desired expensive items, or the down payment on a house? Past records of expenditures will be helpful in predicting regular costs.

If you lack adequate records, or expect that next year will be very different from the last, it may be difficult to make realistic projections. Allow for flexibility in your plan. Estimate your total expenses for the year to come using a table similar to the summary part of Table 1.4 and enter total predicted expenses in Table 1.5.

PERSONAL ALLOWANCES   Designate a sum of money for each individual in the family to use without having to give account to others. This will simplify record-keeping and also enhance family harmony. Obviously, you will need to reach some agreement about what sort of expenditures will be covered by these personal allowances.

Balance Income and Expenses

Use Table 1.5 as a guide for comparing total budget figures. Will the financial resources you expect to have available during the budget period cover predicted saving and spending? It is not unusual at this stage to find that there is not enough money for everything and that adjustments are needed. To balance the budget, you have the choice of increasing resources, reducing wants, or doing some of both. This balancing step is a critical one in financial management because goals, priorities, and the total expected financial situation for a year (or other period) are being taken into consideration. A calm look at the overall plans will lead to more careful, rational allocation of resources than hasty *ad hoc* decisions made while shopping.

When trying to make a budget balance, review estimates to ensure that they are as accurate as possible. Has uncertain income been included? Are the expenditure estimates inflated? What has been included that is not essential or important? Could better use be made of the money?

DEVELOP IMPLEMENTATION AND CONTROL STRATEGIES

A critical part of the planning process is controlling the plan. Many splendid budgets have been prepared and filed away by their creators who thought the task was finished. In fact, a plan for any type of activity is ineffective until it is put into action. Once the saving and spending estimates have been balanced with expected resources, consider how you can make the plan work.

The following generalizations summarize key points about controlling financial plans:

(a) All those handling the money share a commitment to the plan.

(b) The control system is compatible with an individual's personality and habits.

(c) Controlling a plan requires that someone knows where the money is going.

(d) The funds for major groups of expenditures are segregated in some way to prevent overspending.

Shared Commitment

All those who are sharing income and expenses and have a common budget must not only be informed about the budget but also be committed to it. Any plan not supported by all those concerned is doomed at the outset. For instance, a family argument may result in one person using money to punish the other by running up large bills on a spending spree. Such a family relations problem must be dealt with before any budget can be effective. Ideally, all those in the spending unit will work together in preparing the financial plan, taking time to resolve conflicts in values as they arise.

A System to Suit Your Personality

It is impossible to prescribe a system of control for another's financial affairs; we can only suggest possible alternatives. People differ too widely in their styles of handling money and in their willingness to maintain written records. Consider your own habits and personality, and develop ways to ensure that your money will be spent or saved as planned. If money burns holes in your pockets, you will need to do something to curb your impulsiveness.

Know Where the Money is Going

This involves some kind of record-keeping, but keep the system simple enough that it does not become onerous and thus neglected. Decide how much detail is needed or wanted and proceed accordingly. Often the act of recording expenditures in itself serves as a control on spending because having to write down what you spend tends to encourage reflection on your financial habits.

Control the Allocations

There are several ways this can be done. The simplest method is to operate strictly on a cash basis, putting the allocated amounts in envelopes, purses, or sugar bowls. During a specific period, spending is restricted to the sum in each container. This is not a practical system for many people because of the danger of theft and loss, and the inconvenience of handling complex affairs this way. However, this concrete approach is useful for people who have difficulty with abstract thinking. At the opposite extreme is the completely abstract method of control by double entry bookkeeping, which can be very effective if you are committed to the system.

A possible compromise is to establish several levels of control by opening a number of savings and chequing accounts. For example, you could have one account for long-term savings, one for short-term goals, one for irregular expenditures, and one for regular living expenses. These accounts serve the same function as the envelopes or sugar bowls mentioned above. Decide which expenditures can be handled by the same account and deposit the planned amount each time a paycheque is received. To make certain that this system will work, cheques must be written on the appropriate account and cheque records kept up-to-date. If you have a joint account, each user must inform the other of deposits and withdrawals.

Actions or Events That Jeopardize Plans

UNEXPECTED EXPENSES As many will attest, unexpected expenses occur just about every month, so you may as well plan for them. Add such a category to the budget to prevent frustration when the unforeseen occurs. It is virtually impossible to plan spending exactly to the last dollar, but with experience it becomes easier to approximate how much to allow for the unexpected.

USE OF CREDIT   How does the use of credit cards affect the control system? If purchases are charged as a convenience and you pay off the total bill monthly, they can be treated in the same way as other bills. However, if you are susceptible to the impulse buying that credit cards encourage, you will need to develop restrictions on having or carrying credit cards. If charge account balances are growing because you pay only a portion of the total each month, consider how much you are spending on costly credit charges and also whether you have a tendency to overspend.

IRREGULAR EXPENSES   Everyone has irregular large bills that cannot be paid from the monthly allocation without planning for them. Using last year's records as a guide, find the annual total of expenses such as insurance, taxes, auto licence and maintenance, and income tax. Divide the total by the number of pay days and deposit the appropriate amount in the account earmarked for these bills.

UNREALISTIC PLAN   If your plans never seem to materialize, it could be because they are unrealistic. The first time you make a budget, lack of experience and inaccurate records may result in poor plans. Do not give up, but expect to make adjustments to your plans. Remember that you can change the plan at any time, and that as time goes on, your plans will become more realistic.

A budget may be most needed just when predictions are most difficult to make. For instance, when there is a change in living arrangements or in household composition, or a drop in income, it is evident that things are going to be different but it is hard to know how different. A couple establishing a new household will have no past records to refer to. They will have to make the best estimates they can for a few months, then review them and make a better plan. Likewise, the arrival of a child will add to costs, but new parents lack data to make forecasts.

INFLEXIBLE PLANS   Do not consider plans to be unchangeable. A plan is a device to help achieve goals, not a straitjacket. If it becomes inappropriate for some reason, it can be revised. Consider plans to be your servants, not your masters.

TOO MUCH PRECISION EXPECTED   Decide how precise financial plans and records must be to achieve the desired goals, and proceed accordingly. Do not make the mistake of embarking on a first financial plan with unrealistic notions of how much record-keeping will be done and how precisely the actual expenses must match the budgeted amount.

USING A FINANCIAL PLAN TO REFORM BEHAVIOUR   If you are feeling guilty about the way you are now spending money, you might want to make a plan on the assumption that certain vices will be cut out. How successful will that plan be? Reforming yourself may be a good idea, but it would be best to separate that goal from financial planning. We need to accept the fact that changing behaviour, even our own, is difficult. Anyone who intends to change their spending habits, their record-keeping practices, or their savings goal, must plan for a series of small changes, not a large one. Success with each small change achieved will be motivation to undertake another modification. Attempts to make too big a change usually result in failure.

SIMPLE RECORD-KEEPING AND CONTROL

Bill wants to be in control of his finances, but after a demanding day at work he is just too tired to get involved with detailed recording of his finances. He and Helen have developed a simplified process that meets their needs. They have set up a number of bank accounts that keep track of and control gross spending; they have decided not to bother with details. These are their accounts:

(a) Personal accounts for each person for their own expenditures, including clothing, personal care.

(b) Family living account for regular living costs, including housing, utilities, food, entertainment.

(c) Irregular payments account for periodic expenses, such as insurance, taxes.

(d) Holiday account to accumulate funds for future trips.

(e) Savings account to accumulate funds for various objectives, such as education, investment, new car, retirement.

Helen is responsible for allocating all family income among these various accounts and balancing the cheque books monthly. It is Bill's task to make out cheques for family expenses and to analyze the monthly statements to ensure that the allocations are appropriate and spending control is maintained.

EVALUATE PROGRESS

Since the purpose in making a budget is to have a blueprint to guide financial decisions, there must be a mechanism for measuring progress. Periodically, compare what is happening with the plan. Are goals being met? If what is happening does not correspond very well with the plan, ask why. Was the plan unrealistic because it was based on wrong assumptions or on incomplete data? Is the problem with the methods of control? Do not expect too perfect a match between the actual and the budgeted amounts for each category of spending. Rather, look for a balance in overall cash flow, and check if any particular category is out of line.

Develop some system to simplify comparisons between the amounts budgeted and actual cash flow, and check on this often enough to prevent things getting out of control. An annual review of changes in net worth should be adequate but allocations for saving and living expenses need a closer watch, perhaps monthly or at least quarterly. Successful monitoring and review of budgets requires a system of records.

Financial Records

CASH FLOW CONTROL WORKSHEET   There are three steps in this record-keeping task:

(a) collecting the data,

(b) summarizing or finding monthly and annual totals,

(c) analyzing the results.

Some may get stuck at the first step because they have no system for recording what they have spent. It may help to begin by concentrating on the regular, fixed expenses that are usually well known, or are recorded in cheque books. Once all the information on the fixed expenses has been obtained, the flexible expenses can be added.

Develop a method that suits you and provides enough information for your purposes. Do not attempt too ambitious a scheme, which may be neglected because it is too time-consuming. Some people use a ledger book, or ruled loose-leaf pages, with columns for all the expense categories. Enter each expense, as it occurs, under the appropriate column. Others carry a small notebook to record expenditures as they occur, and later transfer the information to a ledger.

Analyze the results by comparing the actual monthly totals with the budgeted amounts. This can be done on another summary sheet that has space for 12 months.

A microcomputer can be helpful for record-keeping. A number of commercial software programs have been developed for this purpose, but they do not eliminate the task of collecting the data. What they do well is categorizing entries, creating totals, and calculating percentages that make it much easier to summarize and analyze the data. If you find the computer more fun than working with pencil and paper, use it for your record-keeping and analysis.

STRATEGIES FOR TWO-INCOME HOUSEHOLDS

Changing Family Patterns

Among the many dramatic changes in family structure we have witnessed in recent decades, the increasing number of women in the labour force is one that has had an impact on the household's finances. In the late sixties, women with young children or with high-earning husbands tended not to take paid employment, but that is no longer true. Figure 1.5 illustrates the changing pattern of dual earners by the husband's earnings. It is clear that nowadays dual-earner families have become the most common type, even when the husband receives a high income.

FIGURE 1.5 Percentage Distribution of Families with Both Spouses Working, by Husbands' Earnings, Canada, 1967 and 1989

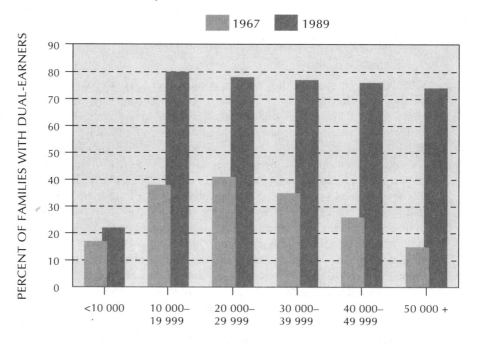

Source: Raj K. Chawla, "The Changing Profile of Dual-earner Families," *Perspectives on Labour and Income*, Summer 1992, Vol. 4, No. 2, Table 1 (pp. 22–29). Statistics Canada. (Catalogue No.75-001.) Reproduced with the permission of the Minister of Industry, Science and Technology, 1993.

The increasing proportion of all families that have two earners (from about one-third in 1967 to nearly two-thirds by 1989) has implications for the way finances are managed within the household. A strategy that may have been reasonable for a one-earner family, such as pooling all resources, may be less appropriate when there are two earners. Some models used by dual-income families to organize their finances are outlined below.

(a) Pooled funds—All income is combined and expenses paid from this pool. This requires frequent discussion to achieve shared values and goals.

(b) Equal split—Each partner puts the same amount into a common pool to cover specified joint expenses. They also have separate personal and savings accounts. This works best if both earn about the same amount.

(c) Proportionate contributions—When one partner earns more than the other, their contributions to the common pool are based on agreed proportions of their incomes to make it more equitable.

(d) Dividing the bills—Instead of pooling funds, each person agrees to handle certain expenses.

When deciding what model to try, a couple should take stock of their personalities and values. Some systems require more discussion and agreement then others. The pooled fund system works best if both share values and attitudes towards money. When one partner is a spendthrift and the other a tightwad it might work better to have each individual handle more of their money on a personal basis.

REASONS FOR NOT MAKING PLANS

Although almost anyone will tell you that it is a good idea to make a financial plan, fewer people actually do much planning. Why the discrepancy? Making and using a financial plan requires motivation, knowledge, time, effort, and finally, discipline and persistence. Planning is easily postponed in favour of more interesting or more pressing activities. This chapter, as well as other sections of this book, are intended to increase your motivation to take control of your personal financial affairs and to show how to do it, but it is up to you to provide the other necessary components.

Those who think they ought to do some financial planning but don't should ask themselves what obstacles are preventing them from taking greater control of their finances. Is it lack of motivation or lack of a reason for getting involved? Is it not knowing how to get started? Is it a perceived lack of time? Or, is it a general distaste for financial matters? Once the reason for not doing more planning has been identified, steps can be taken to improve matters. You may choose to learn how, to delegate planning to someone else in the family, or to hire assistance.

People have a variety of reasons for not making financial plans. Some people say that their income and expenses are too unpredictable to plan anything; others feel that plans are much too confining, or that planning takes all the fun out of spending. Discouragement with a plan that did not work effectively may be the result of unrealistic estimates, or inadequate methods of controlling the plan. It would be better to try again than to abandon all plans.

A PLAN THAT WORKS FOR THEM

Ilona and Peter belong to the ranks of people who don't like to keep a regular account of their expenses and who prefer to plan their budget in their heads. However, now that their children have reached university age, they find that they need to maintain a reserve fund to cover some of the boys' expenses. Also, they want to be able to finance the family's hobbies of cycling and cross country skiing, both of which are becoming more expensive with each new high-technology development. To find the least demanding and tiresome method of financial planning, they attended a one-day workshop that also included planning for retirement.

After brief deliberation, they decided that the best method for them was to create a budget around their current spending habits. To start, they needed to estimate their expenses for the next year. This involved figuring out how much they would spend on three major categories: (i) the house (mortgage, electricity, taxes, insurance, telephone, water softener, landscaping, repairs and maintenance), (ii) personal/discretionary (groceries, drugstore, cosmetics, clothing, medical, non-essentials for the house, gifts, books, ski and bicycle accessories, race fees, boots), and (iii) savings and investment (RRSPs, mutual funds, Canada Savings Bonds, savings account).

Their paycheques, with combined earnings of $83 000 per year, are deposited into their personal chequing account. Automatic monthly transfers of funds have been arranged for RRSPs, investments, life insurance, mortgage payments, and to the savings account. To avoid recording detailed grocery expenditures, a sum of $850 per month is set aside for this purpose, or $180 for a week.

Once a month, Ilona and Peter spend a few hours recording the cash flows of the previous month. They use a transaction log to record all deposits, automatic monthly transfers, cheques, cash withdrawals (automatic teller), and any other transactions. From Visa statements and cheque-book records they are able to categorize all expenses according to their two major categories: personal/discretionary and house. Next, the amounts for each category are totalled and entered on the monthly budget page and also on a year-to-date statement.

Like everyone else, they find that there are times when there has been overspending in one or more categories. They are able to bring the budget in line over the next several months by spending less in each category or skipping a category (for example, no new cycling shorts and jerseys, renting videos instead of going to the movies).

By choosing a budget method that suits their personalities, Ilona and Peter have been able to gain control over their expenses without drastically changing their lifestyles and without feeling bound by too stringent a system. In their case, flexibility and ease of administration were the key factors that made their financial planning successful.

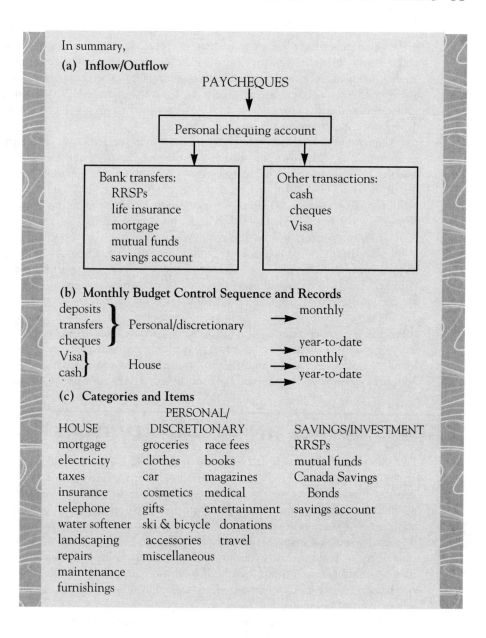

In summary,

(a) Inflow/Outflow

PAYCHEQUES

↓

Personal chequing account

↓   ↓

Bank transfers:
  RRSPs
  life insurance
  mortgage
  mutual funds
  savings account

Other transactions:
  cash
  cheques
  Visa

(b) Monthly Budget Control Sequence and Records

deposits ⎫
transfers ⎬ Personal/discretionary ➜ monthly
cheques ⎭
                                     ➜ year-to-date
Visa ⎫   ➜ monthly
cash ⎭ House   ➜ year-to-date

(c) Categories and Items

	PERSONAL/	
HOUSE	DISCRETIONARY	SAVINGS/INVESTMENT
mortgage	groceries race fees	RRSPs
electricity	clothes books	mutual funds
taxes	car magazines	Canada Savings
insurance	cosmetics medical	Bonds
telephone	gifts entertainment	savings account
water softener	ski & bicycle donations	
landscaping	accessories travel	
repairs	miscellaneous	
maintenance		
furnishings		

WOMEN AND FINANCIAL INDEPENDENCE

Women often face higher economic risks than men for several reasons. Women's economic well-being often depends on their relationships with men and any time the relationship breaks down, their finances may be in jeopardy. Women tend to have less regular labour force attachment than men because of family responsibilities to children and older relatives, they usually earn less than men, and they generally live longer than men. As a result, they have less opportunity to acquire personal financial assets or to accumulate pension credits with Canada Pension Plan or employer-sponsored pension plans. When families break up women are often left with dependent children and uncertain child support.

Many women, who will probably spend years living on their own, will encounter economic uncertainty in their old age because they do not have enough personal assets or pension credits. What steps can younger women take to ensure their future financial security? Perhaps the most important thing is to have a long planning horizon so that current decisions are taken with reference to future implications. Women who have a marketable skill and who keep it up-to-date will have more economic independence than those who do not. Those who establish a savings account in their own name and keep adding to it will have a nest egg. Anyone who has personal assets before marriage may do well to get advice about a marriage contract. Family laws in various provinces differ in how matrimonial property is divided up after a separation, and it is wise to know your rights.

Planning for economic self-sufficiency is not always easy. It seems disloyal to be thinking about independence while in a happy marriage. Nevertheless, those women who are informed about financial affairs, have some personal assets, avoid co-signing loans with spouses, have a marriage contract, and maintain a paper trail of any personal gifts and inheritances will have an advantage if the unthinkable happens.

PROFESSIONAL FINANCIAL ADVISERS

Professional advice on personal financial affairs has long been available to certain segments of society. The wealthy pay investment counsellors for advice on investments and tax planning. The overindebted go to publicly-supported credit counsellors, who suggest ways of coping with too much debt. Where do the rest of us go for advice? There is no shortage of those who want to advise us—to invest in term deposits, guaranteed investment certificates, Canada Savings Bonds, mortgages, real estate, stocks, bonds, mutual funds or to buy insurance. Each advisor has a special interest in promoting ways to invest our spare cash, and each is knowledgeable in a special area. Since many of these sales people depend on sales commissions, their advice may not be unbiased.

The various kinds of financial advisers may be categorized as:

(a) investment counsellors,

(b) credit counsellors,

(c) officers and salespersons of financial institutions (e.g., bankers, trust company officers, life insurance agents, brokers, mutual fund agents),

(d) financial planners,
   — fee-only
   — commissions only (may be the same as (c), above)
   — mixture of commission and fees.

Investment Counsellors

For years, professional **investment counsellors** have advised the wealthy on how to handle their finances, with special attention to minimizing income tax and maximizing investment return. Many of these will invest funds and handle all the day-to-day decisions for their clients, although some investment counsellors are not interested in clients with less than $200 000 or even $500 000. For ongoing investment services, the management fee may be based on a percentage of assets. Clearly, the assistance of these investment counsellors is beyond the reach of most families.

Credit Counsellors

At the other end of the financial spectrum are the overindebted, who often, although not always, have low incomes. In times of debt crises, they turn to **credit counsellors** for help in reducing the pressure from creditors and debt collectors. Every effort is made to find ways to help families and individuals cope with the presenting crisis. Others, not yet overindebted, may come for information and assistance in financial management. This service, now available in most major communities, may or may not be free to clients. There is more about credit counselling in Chapter 17.

Financial Advice for the Majority

Generally, the majority of citizens, who are neither very wealthy nor overindebted, lack independent financial counsellors to turn to for help. If they want to know more about financial management, they have to read books, take courses, or consult those selling various financial products. The high cost of providing advice, and the reluctance of people to pay for this kind of service, means that independent financial advisers have not been widely available to the middle class.

By the 1980s, both the availability of microcomputers and greater family affluence (partly the result of two-earner households) caused some changes. As the sums of money families handled increased and the services and products offered by financial institutions became ever more complex, the demand for information and help with financial management grew. This need was recognized by publishers, who rapidly expanded the number of books and articles on personal finance, and by companies selling such products as mutual funds, stocks, life insurance, annuities, and RRSPs. The offer of some financial planning became a new marketing tool for a variety of companies. Large financial institutions, such as banks and trust companies, began to offer financial planning without charge, to entice customers. Computers made the planning process quicker and cheaper.

Financial Planners

Financial planners may be categorized in three groups, based on the source of their remuneration. Many of those who call themselves financial planners sell financial products, such as mutual funds, guaranteed investment certificates, life insurance, bonds, and stocks, and gain their incomes from sales commissions. A much smaller number are fee-only planners who depend solely on client fees and sell no financial products. The third group are planners who combine characteristics of the other two: they charge fees for financial planning and receive commissions on the products sold.

A big issue is the potential conflict of interest that arises when a financial adviser does not charge for advice but gains his or her income from product commissions. It would be natural for such a planner to find that a client's solutions included some of the products he or she is particularly well informed about and is licensed to sell.

Financial planning, a rapidly growing business in the United States and Canada, may soon become an accepted profession, but in the meantime, efforts are being made to reduce the confusion resulting from its rapid expansion. It has been a largely unregulated activity to date, but is under review by securities branches in several provinces where discussions are going on about establishing standards for education, liability insurance coverage, and ethics. In 1989, Quebec became the first province to pass legislation linking the use of the term "financial planner" with specific educational criteria and mandatory registration. Other provinces are studying the matter and some are expected to take similar action soon. Until then, anyone can call themselves a financial planner, financial consultant, or financial adviser.

The Canadian Association of Financial Planners, founded in 1983, is anxious to solve the problems of educational requirements and certification. Those with three years' practice who pass a one-day examination may use the designation "Registered Financial Planner" and those with two years' experience who complete six correspondence courses become "Chartered Financial Planners."

Meanwhile, a number of competing groups are offering educational programs in financial planning. Those who successfully complete these programs are given a special designation such as certified financial planner or chartered financial planner, and may add the appropriate initials to their business cards. All this activity seems to indicate the emergence of a new profession that may eventually become standardized and regulated.

COMPUTER PROGRAMS FOR FINANCIAL PLANNERS Since it may take a financial planner up to 40 hours to create a comprehensive financial plan for a family, and cost as much as $3000–$4000, a way was needed to deliver financial planning to clients more cheaply. The solution was found in computers. Software programs have been developed that will use the data provided by a client to generate a financial plan fairly inexpensively. The programs vary widely in the extent to which they make adjustments for personal habits and preferences, and the assumptions they use. The expansion of financial planning coincided with the availability of microcomputers and suitable programs, and most financial planners now depend heavily on computers.

Choosing a Financial Adviser

It is wise to make some inquiries before entrusting your financial affairs to an unknown adviser.

(a) Find out how the financial planner is paid. Is it from fees only, fees and commissions, or commissions only?

(b) Inquire about the planner's qualifications. What educational background, experience, and licences does the person have?

(c) Does this planner have certain areas of specialization?

(d) What sort of planning is he or she offering? Is it a very detailed, comprehensive plan, or the solution to a specific problem? Will there be a written report with recommendations? Does the planner have a sample plan to show you?

(e) Will the planner provide an analysis of the costs and benefits of the various alternatives suggested?

(f) What will the cost of the plan be?

Summary

We have examined reasons why individuals should take control of their own financial affairs, rather than let them drift. Those who take control will increase their chances of reaching their financial goals and improving their quality of life. Although money is not everything, it is the means of achieving many desires. The process of planning and managing finances begins with specifying definite goals, and assessing what resources are available to reach them. With this information, a plan can be made for the next year or other time period. To ensure that the plan becomes reality, means must be designed to implement the plan and control spending behaviour. Periodic review of the process will reveal whether progress is satisfactory.

Financial planning requires some record-keeping. In this chapter we presented sample forms for assessing and analyzing net worth, assessing income, summarizing expenditures, and creating a one-year budget. We used several examples to illustrate less complex ways of planning and controlling expenditures.

Women have special economic problems because of social attitudes or interrupted labour force involvement and should give thought to ways of ensuring their personal economic security.

Financial planning is an emerging profession. Financial planners offer advice on personal financial affairs, sometimes for a fee. Those who do not charge fees for their advice depend on commissions from the sale of financial products, such as mutual funds, life insurance, stocks, bonds, annuities, and RRSPs.

Vocabulary Review

budget (p. 9)

credit counsellor (p. 35)

financial plan (p. 4)

financial planner (p. 36)

fixed expenses (p. 23)

flexible expenses (p. 23)

income (p. 12)

investment counsellor (p. 35)

life cycle stage (p. 8)

liquid assets (p. 16)

net worth (p. 12)

real rate of return (p. 16)

wealth (p. 12)

Problems

1.

WHERE DOES ALL THE MONEY GO?

Jan and Dave, a couple in their early thirties, have recently purchased a new house in Vegreville, Alberta. The purchase price of $145 000 was a little more than they anticipated, but they love the life in this small town. Dave is able to commute to his office in Edmonton where he works as a sales manager for a scientific supply company. Jan, an elementary school teacher, is just getting back into the work force now that eight-year-old Brent and six-year-old Karen both attend school. Since she is working as a substitute teacher until a full-time position becomes available, her income is quite uncertain and irregular.

With a down payment of $46 000 from the sale of their old home, the mortgage of $96 000, to be paid off in 25 years, costs them $748.80 a month. In the excitement of buying the new house, they forgot to allow for legal bills, moving costs, and the need for new draperies so they had to get a personal loan of $3000, with a two-year term. Recently, they purchased a new car for Jan, costing $12 500, financed with a loan of $10 000, with monthly payments of $308.32.

They have $1500 in Canada Savings Bonds (a gift from Jan's grandmother), $355 in Jan's savings account, and about $456 in their joint chequing account. Last year they received about $82.50 in interest from Canada Savings Bonds. Except for a pension plan refund put into an RRSP a few years ago when Dave transferred from another company, which is now worth about $3755, their only major asset is their home.

When they married, Jan and Dave each bought a $100 000 life insurance policy. If they were to cash in these policies, each would have a cash surrender value of $2000.

They rely on a line of credit from the bank for emergencies, but apart from this have very little flexibility if Dave should be off work for any length of time. He does have insurance coverage at work which would pay about half of his usual wages if he should become disabled longer than three months. During the three-month waiting period, there would be a small unemployment insurance benefit and a few days' sick leave with pay.

Dave's benefits at work include the use of a leased car and an expense account for lunches and the occasional dinner. He also has comprehensive dental, drug, and vision care plans, and some group life insurance coverage.

Fortunately, there seems to be little need for maintenance work on their new house, but Jan and Dave would like to start fixing up the basement. They are hoping that Jan will get full-time work soon so that they will be able to clear some debts and be able to start on the basement.

Dave feels that with his relatively high income of $55 000 a year, including commissions, they should not have the money worries they are currently experiencing and should be in a better position to invest some funds in RRSPs to save for the future and take advantage of the tax saving, but at the moment he does not see how he can afford to do so.

Jan confesses that before the children came along they were used to spending quite freely since both were earning good wages. Now, with no established management pattern, the money just seems to disappear.

Following is the list Jan and Dave made of their monthly income and expenses. They do not keep records, so these are their best estimates. The income figures are net of deductions at the source, such as income tax, Canada Pension and Unemployment Insurance premiums, and registered pension plan contributions.

Income	Per month
Dave's take home pay	$2909
Jan's average salary	600
TOTAL	$3509

Short-term debt repayment	
Bank loan for car	$308.33
Bank loan	134
TOTAL	$442
Expenses	
Mortgage	$748
Heating	90
Electricity and water	115
Telephone	35
Home insurance	25
Property taxes	120
Food	650
Entertainment	120
Clothes	200
Babysitter	40
Expenses (continued)	
Books, magazines, records	35
Gifts	100
Life insurance	110
Transportation (Jan's car)	200
Miscellaneous	300
TOTAL	$2888

(a) Make a net worth statement for this couple.

   Analyze their net worth position and make a list of issues you would raise in a discussion with them if you were their financial counsellor.

(b) Make a summary cash flow statement for Jan and Dave, noting which expenditures are fixed and which flexible.

   Analyze their cash flow situation. Are there some expense categories that seem to be missing?

(c) Evaluate the financial security of this couple. How well prepared are they for a financial emergency?

(d) Do you think this couple ought to be saving more? What do you suggest? What future difficulties do you foresee for them if they continue as at present?

(e) Evaluate the financial management strategies of this couple in terms of the basic steps of financial planning. If they are really motivated to make a change, where might they begin?

2. Decide whether you AGREE or DISAGREE with each of the following statements:

(a) Making a financial plan and sticking to it is easier if some rewards are built into the system.

(b) A budget takes all the fun out of spending.

(c) Financial planning makes more sense for those with a good income; for those who are poor, planning is impossible.

(d) If you and your spouse cannot agree on some financial goals, perhaps the solution is to handle your money separately instead of pooling it.

(e) If your financial affairs have been stable for some years and you have reached a comfortable agreement with your spouse about who pays for what and how much to spend on various things, your need for detailed budget analysis may be less than for a couple recently married.

(f) Students can't really make spending plans because they have no regular income.

(g) If your income is very irregular, your spending must necessarily be adjusted to the fluctuations of your income.

(h) It is impossible to make a budget work because of all the unexpected expenses that occur.

(i) The reason there is more belief in the value of budgets than in actually making them is the amount of paperwork involved.

3. Explain the difference between these pairs of terms:

(a) budget and expenditure record.

(b) assets and liabilities.

(c) net worth (wealth) and income.

(d) credit counsellor and financial planner.

(e) investment counsellor and financial planner.

(f) cash flow control worksheet and net worth analysis.

(g) budget and methods of control.

4. Julie was taught that responsible financial management required that a record be kept of every penny she spent. She has continued to do this throughout her life. She keeps this in a running diary without any expenditure categories, and does not total the figures or do any analysis. What value does this record-keeping probably have for Julie? What is your opinion of its usefulness?

5. How important is it to have an emergency fund when you do not know if you will ever need it, and you feel that you could always borrow in a pinch?

6. Suggest reasons why people get into a position where their income does not cover expenses.

7. Refer to the example, "The Credit Trap." Why do you think this family got caught in this trap? Is this mostly a problem for low income families?

8. How did your parents teach you how to handle money? Will you do things differently with your children?

9. Some people say that the only way to teach children responsibility in handling money is to give them an allowance. What is your opinion?

10. Refer to Figure 1.2. Why did Yolanda's $30 000 grow to a larger sum than Dan's?

11. Mario and Kim always ran out of money before their next pay day arrived. Eventually, they became so frustrated with the frequent crises that they decided to seek help from a financial counsellor. As the interview progressed, it became apparent that Mario was in a job that involved much entertaining of clients. Somehow this had led to more and more partying, until he felt he needed quite a bit of money to pay his share when out with others.

    Kim was working full-time, but they both intended that she would stop soon to have a family. Her complaint was that there was no way they could make the payments on the mortgage and the car loan, and support Mario's social life on his salary alone. She had wanted a cheaper house and a smaller car, but Mario felt the need to keep up a fairly expansive lifestyle. She blames Mario for spending more money than they can afford and making it impossible to save. He says that if she will be patient, he will soon be earning more.

    What would you say to this couple if you were their counsellor?

12. Lucy called a financial adviser, saying she did not know how to cope with her financial affairs. She never had to give money a thought before her recent divorce from a well-to-do businessman. When she decided to look for work, she was at a disadvantage without previous work experience. However, she found a job in a women's clothing store where she enjoyed selling clothes and getting things for herself at a discount. She loves clothes and always dresses well. Her two children are grown and independent and she owns a spacious condominium apartment in a good part of town.

    Lucy was trying to maintain her accustomed level of living but found that she had to dip into her divorce settlement funds to make ends meet. Also, she was having trouble with a trust company over the way her money was being handled and was quite confused about what kinds of accounts she had. Now in her late forties, Lucy has been too absorbed in recent family crises to give thought to her own future. She was not too enthusiastic about the adviser's suggestion that they make a long-term financial plan for her. She wanted an immediate solution and freedom from financial stress.

    (a) If you were in Lucy's shoes what would you do now?

    (b) Identify factors that have created Lucy's current problems.

    (c) What sources of income will Lucy probably have when she turns 65?

References

BOOKS

AMLING, FREDERICK and WILLIAM G. DROMS. *The Dow Jones-Irwin Guide to Personal Financial Planning*. Second Edition. Homewood, Illinois: Dow Jones-Irwin, 1986, 549 pp. Although written for American readers, much of the discussion of financial planning, life insurance, retirement planning, and investments is relevant for Canadians.

BELAND, PAUL and ISAAC CRONIN. *Money Myths and Realities*. New York: Carroll and Graf, 1986, 205 pp. Popular book that attempts to dispel widely held myths about money.

BIRCH, RICHARD. *The Family Financial Planning Book, A Step-by-Step Moneyguide for Canadian Families*. Revised Edition. Toronto: Key Porter, 1989, 216 pp. An easy-to-read guide to taking control of your personal finances that discusses budgets, income tax, insurance, RRSPs, mortgages, and investments.

BUDD, JOHN, CLAUDE RINFRET, RICHARD DAW, and DANIELLE BRIEN. *Canadian Guide to Personal Financial Management*. Scarborough, Ontario: Prentice-Hall Canada, annual, 231 pp. Accountants provide guidance on a broad range of topics, including planning finances, estimating insurance needs, managing risk, and determining investment needs. Instructions and the necessary forms for making plans are provided.

CHILTON, DAVID. *The Wealthy Barber, The Common Sense Guide to Successful Financial Planning*. Toronto: Stoddart, 1989, 201 pp. In a chatty style, a financial planner advises how to organize your personal finances.

COHEN, DIAN. *Money*. Scarborough, Ontario: Prentice-Hall Canada, 1987, 270 pp. An economist suggests strategies for coping with personal finances in the context of changing economic conditions. Topics include financial plans, buying a home, insurance, income tax, retirement, estate planning, and investments.

CÔTÉ, JEAN-MARC, and DONALD DAY. *Personal Financial Planning in Canada*. Toronto: Allyn and Bacon, 1987, 464 pp. A comprehensive personal finance text that includes financial planning, income tax, annuities, pensions, investments, credit, mortgages, and wills with particular attention to the banking and insurance industries.

DOMINGUEZ, JOE, and VICKI ROBIN. *Your Money or Your Life, Transforming Your Relationship with Money and Achieving Financial Independence*.New York: Viking, 1992, 350 pp. The authors chose to give up the pressure to earn as much as possible in order to buy as much as possible, and instead to live more economically and peacefully.

FORMAN, NORM. *Mind Over Money, Curing Your Financial Headaches with Moneysanity*. Toronto: Doubleday Canada, 1987, 248 pp. A psychologist examines the effects money has on behaviour, looking at the origin of money problems and suggesting therapies to help us to better understand ourselves.

GOHEEN, DUNCAN. *Planning for Financial Independence, Choose Your Lifestyle, Secure Your Future*. Vancouver: International Self-Counsel Press, 1988, 128 pp. Detailed guidance for making a financial plan, including the necessary charts and tables.

GOLDBERG, HERB and ROBERT T. LEWIS. *Money Madness, The Psychology of Saving, Spending, Loving and Hating Money*. New York: William Morrow, 1978, 264 pp. Two psychologists explain, in non-technical terms, how to become disentangled from our self-destructive money behaviours.

KNIGHT, JAMES. *For the Love of Money, Human Behavior and Money*. Philadelphia: Lippincott, 1968, 184 pp. Addresses psychological meanings of money, including its uses and misuses; children and money; and family ties and money.

LINDGREN, HENRY CLAY. *Great Expectations, The Psychology of Money*. Los Altos, CA: William Kaufmann, 1980, 246 pp. A classic, but non-technical book, which explores how money motivates our behaviour.

MACFARLANE, LYNNE. *Double Income Families, Money Management for Working Couples*. Toronto: Key Porter Books, 1990, 291 pp. A non-technical book that addresses a significant issue. Standard personal finance topics are considered in the context of the two-income family.

MATTHEWS, BETSY and RICHARD BIRCH. *Taking Care of Tomorrow, The Canadian Money Book for Prime Time Women*. Toronto: McGraw-Hill Ryerson, 1992, 230 pp. Written for women aged 45 and over who often face their later years with inadequate financial security. Designed to help such women make plans that will help to prevent impoverished later years.

PAPE, GORDON. *Building Wealth in the '90s*. Scarborough, Ontario: Prentice-Hall Canada, 1992, 294 pp. An easy-to-read guide for the novice financial manager and investor. Considers interest rates, credit cards, mortgages, RRSPs, mutual funds, and the stock market.

VAN ARSDALE, MARY G. *A Guide to Family Financial Counseling, Credit, Debt and Money Management*. Homewood, Illinois: Dow Jones-Irwin, 1982, 381 pp. Provides guidance for financial counsellors on such topics as building the relationship, obtaining client information, diagnosis, generating alternatives, and evaluation of results.

WEINSTEIN, BOB. *Money Hang-ups*. New York: Wiley, 1982, 157 pp. A financial journalist examines our attitudes towards money and their origins, and suggests coping strategies.

WYATT, ELAINE. *The Money Companion, How to Manage Your Money and Achieve Financial Freedom*. Revised Edition. Markham, Ontario: Penguin Books, 1991. A guide to personal financial management that focuses on planning, investment strategy and retirement needs.

ARTICLE

CHAWLA, RAJ K. "The Changing Profile of Dual-earner Families," *Perspectives on Labour and Income*, Summer 1992, Vol. 4, No. 2. Statistics Canada (Catalogue No. 75-001).

PERIODICALS

The Financial Post. Daily and weekly. The Financial Post Company, 777 Bay Street, Toronto, Ontario, M5G 2E4. Often contains articles on financial planning, income tax, insurance, investing, and retirement planning.

Report on Business. Daily. A section of The Globe and Mail. Frequently has articles on personal finance.

CHAPTER TWO

Introduction to Personal Income Tax

OBJECTIVES

1. To explain how the following elements fit into the basic structure of the Canadian personal income tax system: gross income, deductions (exemptions), taxable income, tax rates, and tax credits.

2. To distinguish between the following pairs of concepts:

    (a) gross income and net income,

    (b) average tax rate and marginal tax rate,

    (c) progressive tax rate and marginal tax rate,

    (d) wealth and capital gain,

    (e) before-tax and after-tax dollars,

    (f) tax-exempt income and tax-sheltered income,

    (g) tax avoidance and tax evasion,

    (h) income exemption and tax credit,

    (i) capital gain and taxable capital gain,

    (j) refundable and non-refundable tax credit,

    (k) RRSP and RESP,

    (l) tax avoidance and tax deferment.

3. To outline some approaches to tax planning, including income deferment, income splitting, and transfer of tax credits.

4. To explain the principle of attribution.

Introduction

The intent of this chapter is to provide an overview of the personal income tax system, rather than an in-depth treatment of a very large and complex topic. This explanation of basic terminology with a simplified framework that shows the relationships among a few key concepts should make it easier for you to understand the many articles and books on personal income tax. In addition to the discussion in this chapter, you will find income tax mentioned in relation to other topics, especially retirement income and investments.

In the late 1980s the federal government made major revisions to the income tax system, reducing the kinds of allowable deductions, increasing tax credits, changing tax rates, and shifting some taxation from income to expenditures. To keep up-to-date with the details of our ever-changing tax rules, it is necessary to follow the financial press or read some of the annually revised tax guides.

THE TAX BURDEN

Personal income tax has become an increasing burden. The $101 billion in income taxes Canadians paid to federal and provincial governments in 1992 works out to about $3711 for each man, woman, and child. Since 1946, our income tax burden has been steadily increasing, as shown by the per capita data in Figure 2.1. Note that these data have been adjusted for the effects of inflation by converting all values to 1981 dollars using the Consumer Price Index. Thus, it is possible to see the trend in the income tax burden while holding population increase and inflation constant.

Income tax was introduced in 1917 as a temporary measure to pay the costs of World War I. It has been continued ever since to meet governments' ever increasing need for funds. We have become accustomed to a wide variety of government-provided services and comprehensive income security programs that require large amounts of public funds. Therefore, it is not surprising to find that we are paying increasing amounts of income tax.

THE PERSONAL INCOME TAX SYSTEM

Who Pays Income Tax?

All Canadian residents with incomes above a certain level are taxed on their Canadian income as well as any received from outside the country. Each of us must file an individual income tax return; spouses cannot file a joint return as in the United States.

FIGURE 2.1 **INCOME TAX PER CAPITA (1981$),**
CANADA, 1946 – 1992

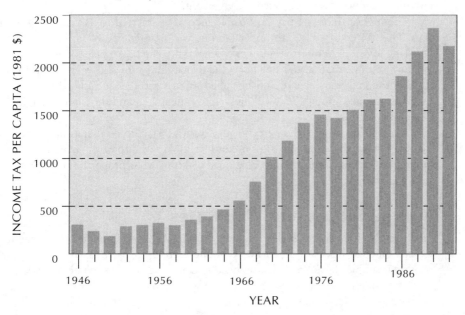

SOURCES OF DATA: *Canadian Economic Observer, Historical Statistical Supplement,* 1991/92.
Ottawa: Statistics Canada, 1990, Table 1.5 (p. 10); Table 3.2 (p. 51); Table 11.1 (p. 98).
(Catalogue No. 11-210.) *Canadian Economic Observer,* April 1993. Ottawa: Statistics Canada,
Table 1.5 (p. 5.7); Table 3.2 (p. 5.41); Table 11.1 (p. 5.94). (Catalogue No. 11-010.) Reproduced
with the permission of the Minister of Industry, Science and Technology, 1993.

Federal Income Tax Rates

In Canada, we use a **progressive tax rate** system, which means that as taxable income
increases, the tax rate increases. Taxable income is calculated by subtracting certain
deductions from gross income (more about this later). The diagram below illustrates the
progressive nature of federal income tax (using taxable income and 1992 tax rates).

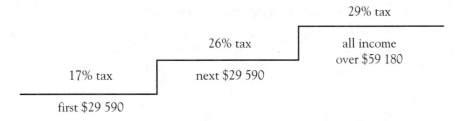

This means that taxable income of $29 590 or less is taxed at 17 percent. If you have more taxable income than this, the next $29 590 is taxed at 26 percent, and anything beyond $59 180 is taxed at 29 percent.

The highest rate you pay on taxable income is referred to as your **marginal tax rate**. This concept is basic to understanding the significance of tax shelters and to choosing investment alternatives. For example, if you paid 26 percent as your highest federal tax rate, that would be your federal marginal rate and each extra dollar of taxable income you receive will be taxed at this rate. Obviously, if your taxable income increases enough, you will move to the next step and the higher marginal tax rate of 29 percent.

Average tax rate is the percentage of your gross income that is paid in income tax. Generally, this concept is less useful in tax planning than the marginal tax rate, although occasionally there may be a need to know what proportion of your income was paid in taxes.

Provincial Income Tax Rates

Although all the provinces levy income taxes as well as the federal government, all except Quebec have arranged for Revenue Canada to collect the tax for them, making it simpler for taxpayers, who need to complete only one combined tax return. Quebec residents file separate provincial returns. Provincial tax rates, expressed as a percentage of federal tax payable, change from time to time, but in 1993 they were:

British Columbia	52.5%	Nova Scotia	59.5%
Alberta	45.5	Prince Edward Island	59.5
Saskatchewan	50.0	Newfoundland	69.0
Manitoba	52.0	Yukon	45.0
Ontario	58.0	Northwest Territories	45.0
New Brunswick	60.0		

After calculating the amount of your federal tax you must add on the provincial tax. For example, if your federal taxes were $2000 and you lived in New Brunswick, you would add 2000 × .60 = $1200, making your combined tax a total of $3200.

Combined Marginal Tax Rate

To find your **combined marginal tax rate** multiply the federal rate by the provincial rate and add this amount to the federal rate. Assume, for example, that you have a federal marginal tax rate of 26 percent and your provincial rate is 52 percent of federal tax. Your combined marginal tax rate would be 26 + (.52 × 26) = 39.5 percent.

How Much Tax to Pay

Stripped of detail, the process of calculating the amount of federal income tax payable can be summarized in three steps:

(a) Total relevant income   –   Deductions   =   Taxable income

(b) Taxable income   ×   Tax rate   =   Total tax

(c) Total tax   –   Tax credits   =   Tax payable

If you analyze the articles on income tax in the financial press, you will find that much of the content has to do with these three issues:

(a) What is counted as relevant income for tax purposes,

(b) Which deductions can be used to reduce taxable income,

(c) How to make use of tax credits.

Each of these will be examined in turn.

WHAT IS INCOME?

Gross and Net Income

Gross income is all the income before anything has been subtracted. Wage rates are usually quoted as gross income. **Net income** is less precise; it indicates that something has been subtracted. Any use of this term should be accompanied by information about what the income is net of; for instance, it may be net of deductions by the employer or net of income tax.

Legislative Concept of Income

Income can be quite difficult to define. In economic terms, **income** is a flow of economic resources over a specified time period, usually referred to as a rate per hour, per day, per week, per month, or per year. The *Income Tax Act* uses a legislative concept of income for the purposes of taxation, and does not necessarily define income in the way economists do. Therefore, we find that some income is presently subject to income tax, and some is not. An abbreviated list of some forms of income which are taxable and some which are not is given here:

Income Subject to Tax

Income from employment

- wages, salaries
- net income from self-employment
- value of employment benefits

Pensions and social security

- Canada/Quebec Pension Plan
- Old Age Security
- Unemployment Insurance
- employment-related retirement pensions
- annuity income bought with RRSP funds

Income Exempt from Tax

Income support payments

- Guaranteed Income Supplement
- Spouse's Allowance
- Workers' Compensation
- welfare

Investment income

- interest
- dividends
- rent
- net profit
- withdrawals from RRSPs

EMPLOYMENT BENEFITS   In addition to income, employees may receive taxable benefits that are added to income for tax purposes. Some examples are employee loans, personal use of a company car, medical care plans, and travel benefits. Some other benefits are exempt from taxation, such as employers' contributions to employee pension plans or group insurance.

Capital Gain or Loss

In addition to taxing income, governments may tax changes in wealth. In the past, there have been taxes on estates, inheritances, and gifts, but these have been discontinued. Currently there is taxation of capital gain. **Capital gain** is not income but a change in wealth, or the windfall accruing to an owner because property or possessions have increased in value. In simple terms, capital gain is the difference between original cost and selling price. The income tax literature makes a distinction between capital gain and **taxable capital gain** because only a portion of any capital gain (e.g., three-quarters) is considered to be taxable.

DEDUCTIONS FROM INCOME

Once income and the changes in wealth that are subject to tax have been identified and listed, the next step is to examine what deductions may be used to reduce taxable income. (Note that, although technically there may be a difference between an exemption and a deduction, both serve to reduce taxable income, and the terms are often used interchangeably.) The exact nature and amounts of deductions allowed may change whenever the federal government amends The Income Tax Act. Deductions from income may be classified in three categories, with the specific examples changing from time to time. In many cases there are limits on the amounts that may be deducted.

    (a) Contributions to retirement pension plans

- registered pension plan (RPP)
- registered retirement savings plans (RRSP)

    (b) Specified expenditures associated with:

- earning a living

       – union and professional dues

       – moving expenses

       – child care

- investing

       – interest on money borrowed to invest

       – rent of safety deposit box

       – accounting fees

       – investment counsel fees

- family support

       – alimony

(c) Capital gains exemption

- net capital gains

Contributions to Retirement Plans

Encouraging Canadians to save for their retirement has been a matter of public policy implemented through the income tax system. Therefore, contributions to employer-sponsored registered pension plans (RPP) and registered retirement saving plans (RRSP) have been exempt from tax, within limits. Since money goes into these plans tax-free and any return generated within the tax shelter is not taxed, they are **tax-sheltered funds**. However, when they are withdrawn or turned into retirement pensions, they come out of the shelter and become fully taxable. A major reason for putting money in a tax shelter is to defer taxes until a time, such as retirement, when you expect to have a lower marginal tax rate.

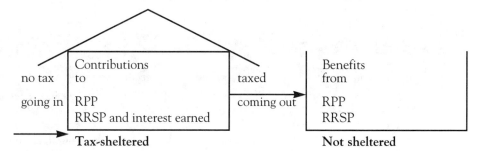

Specified Expenditures

Within limits, a few types of expenditures are exempt from tax, including some associated with earning a living, investing, and family support. Some examples were listed in the section, "Deductions from Income."

Capital Gains Exemption

The opportunity to make a capital gain is always associated with the possibility of having a capital loss. Therefore, for tax purposes, capital losses are subtracted from capital gains, to get **net taxable capital gains**. These terms and relationships are summarized in the following diagram.

Sale price	–	Purchase price	= Capital gain
Capital gain	–	Capital loss	= Net capital gain
Net capital gain	×	.75	= Net taxable capital gain

PRIMARY RESIDENCE   Capital gain realized on the sale of your home is not subject to tax, but there are limits on this: you (and your spouse) can have only one primary residence at any one time.

LIFETIME EXEMPTION   Since 1985 there has been a lifetime exemption for each taxpayer of $100 000 net capital gain. (There is a larger exemption for qualified farm property or shares in a small business corporation.) That means that during your lifetime you can receive a total of $100 000 in capital gains (net of capital losses) without paying tax. The tax department will keep a record of the amounts you have claimed, and you should do likewise.

The calculation of capital gains and losses has become quite complex in recent years; consult books on income tax if you want more information.

NON-TAXABLE CHANGES IN WEALTH   If you receive an inheritance, win a lottery or make a gain from gambling, these increases in your wealth are not subject to income tax. In the case of an inheritance, any taxes owing on the estate of the deceased will have been paid before the estate was distributed.

TAX CREDITS

After calculating your total federal income tax, determine your eligibility for certain tax reductions, called tax credits. A **tax credit** is subtracted after total tax has been determined. Because deductions tend to be of greater benefit to those with higher incomes, many income deductions were replaced with tax credits in the tax reform of 1988. To illustrate how tax credits make the tax burden more equitable, under the previous rules a person with a combined marginal tax rate of 54% and a $1000 deduction would save $540 in taxes while another one with a marginal rate of 32% and the same deduction would save only $320. However, if both persons were eligible for the same tax credit they would have an identical benefit, unrelated to income.

As most tax credits are not refundable, they are not useful unless you have some taxable income. If, for example, you calculated that your federal tax was $5000 and your tax credits $1000, your federal tax would be reduced to $4000. If, on the other hand, your taxable income were so low that you owed no tax, a non-refundable tax credit would be of no use.

Some tax credits, such as the basic personal amount and the married amount, are partially indexed or adjusted for part of the annual change in the Consumer Price Index. If the price index rose more than three percent in the previous year, these amounts would be increased by the difference between the inflation rate and three percent. For instance, an annual inflation rate of 5.5 percent would mean an increase of 2.5 percent in certain tax credits.

INDEXATION OF PENSIONS

Marina's CPP retirement pension, which was $540 a month last year, will be revised in January to take account of the inflation rate. Since prices rose an average of 4% the previous year, her pension will be increased by 4%: $540 + (540 × .04) = $561.60. This is an example of **full indexation.**

Unfortunately for her, the pension from her previous employment is only partially indexed, with adjustments made for inflation greater than 3%. Thus, with **partial indexation**, the pension of $750 a month was adjusted as follows: $750 + (750 × [.04–.03]) = $757.50.

REFUNDABLE TAX CREDITS   Sometimes the federal income tax system includes **refundable tax credits** and sometimes it does not. Persons eligible for a refundable tax credit may be divided into two groups. Those with no taxable income can claim the tax credit and it will be paid to them by cheque. Those with taxable income can use a tax credit to reduce taxes. An example of a refundable tax credit is Ontario's provincial sales tax credit. It is designed to provide benefits for low income individuals and therefore is negatively related to taxable income.

NON-REFUNDABLE TAX CREDITS   Most tax credits are in this category. A partial list of **non-refundable tax credits** follows:

Basic personal amount	Age amount
Married amount	Dependent children
Pension income	Disability
Tuition fees	Medical expenses
Charitable donations	Donations to political parties

Dividends

Canada or Quebec Pension
   contributions

Unemployment Insurance
contributions

The specifics of each of these tax credits are subject to change, and will not be discussed here. Instead, you are referred to current income tax books. However, because of its significance for investment planning, the dividend tax credit will be explained in detail in the chapter on stocks and mutual funds.

TAX PLANNING

The aim of personal tax planning is to pay no more taxes than necessary at present and, whenever possible, to defer tax to a future time when your marginal rate may be lower. Effective tax planning cannot be done each April, when you are completing your tax return, but should be an ongoing process. Most tax planning possibilities may be classified as either: (i) tax avoidance, or (ii) tax deferment. A few examples to be discussed here include avoiding tax by income splitting and transfer of deductions or credits, and deferring tax with registered retirement savings plans or registered educational savings plans.

Tax Avoidance

Arranging one's affairs to minimize income tax is considered perfectly acceptable and is called **tax avoidance**. Many Canadians pay more tax than necessary through ignorance of the tax rules and failing to report deductions or tax credits for which they are eligible. This is quite understandable given the increasing complexity of our income tax system. The solution is either to become knowledgeable yourself by following the financial press, or to obtain advice from a tax accountant.

Deliberate **tax evasion**, on the other hand, is a violation of the law. Our system depends on voluntary compliance which is encouraged by unannounced audits of a sample of taxpayers each year, involving examination of records, receipts, cancelled cheques, bank statements, etc. It is in your own interest to keep your records in good order. Less complex than a tax audit is a tax reassessment. Revenue Canada may conduct a reassessment of your taxes for any year within the past three, which may involve a request for more information to support your claims.

INCOME SPLITTING A family unit that is pooling income and expenses may have some members who earn a great deal more than others; nevertheless, each must file an individual tax return. Tax planning aims to shift some of the income from high earners to low earners with lower marginal tax rates and thus reduce the family's total income tax. This is a complicated matter for which professional advice is best.

A basic principle to be considered when contemplating intrafamilial transfers of funds is that of **attribution of income**. Under income tax legislation, reported income must be identified with a specific earner. In most cases, the person who earned the income also received it. However, if one person (A) earns revenue but arranges that it be received by another (B), such income is generally "attributed" to the earner (A) who is liable for the tax on it. Attribution rules are designed to discourage income splitting.

ATTRIBUTION OF INCOME

Keith has a higher income than Sarah, his wife. The couple wants to reduce the family's income tax burden. Keith thought that if he gave Sarah $20 000 in Canada Savings Bonds she could receive the interest of about $1000 and report this revenue on her income tax return. By reducing his income and increasing hers he hoped to minimize family tax.

Unfortunately, Keith did not understand the attribution rules that apply to any loans or transfers of property to a spouse. The $1000 in interest will be attributed to Keith and taxed as his income. However, if Keith pays the tax but Sarah keeps the $1000 and invests it, any yield she gets from the $1000 will not be attributed back to her husband. Generally, there is no attribution of income earned on attributed income. Therefore, it may be to their advantage to make this transfer if they take a long-term perspective, because over time Sarah will have a growing asset. The bookkeeping will be simplified if they keep the principal of $1000 in a separate account from the yield this sum generates.

With professional advice, some income splitting can be achieved. For instance, attribution rules do not generally apply to business income earned by a spouse or child from funds lent or transferred to them. Funds may be contributed to a spouse's RRSP, which will be discussed further in Chapter 7. As a gift, the higher income spouse may pay the income tax of the lower income spouse as a way of transferring funds. Or, if one spouse has more income than the other, the higher income earner can pay as many of the family expenses as possible, leaving the other to invest his or her personal income. For example, if Joan has a higher income than John, she could pay more than her share of expenses. John would then invest much of his income. Thus, the family's investment income would be reported by the lower income spouse and thus attract less tax. Another possibility is that a spouse or child may be paid an income for work performed in the family's business.

If family benefit cheques are put into an account or investment for the child, the income earned will not be attributed back to the parent. For those receiving the benefit this may be an effective way of splitting income and building an asset for the child.

TRANSFER OF TAX CREDITS   If your spouse cannot use all the eligible tax credits, they can be transferred to you. For instance, if one spouse is eligible for but cannot use certain tax credits, such as the age amount, pension income amount, or tuition fees, they may be transferred to the other spouse.

Tax Deferment

With careful planning, you may be able to defer income tax by arranging for some income not to come into your hands until a later time, such as retirement, when you expect to have a lower marginal tax rate.

REGISTERED RETIREMENT SAVINGS PLANS   **RRSPs** are good examples of tax deferment. While you are earning wages you can shift some funds into a tax shelter or RRSP without paying any tax and the money will grow, sheltered from tax, until you deregister the plan. Of course, when you take the funds out of the RRSP you will pay income tax, but at a lower rate if you choose a year when you have less income. Even if your marginal tax rate is not expected to be lower in the future, funds in a tax shelter will grow faster than unsheltered funds. This point is illustrated in the example, "Should She Use a Tax Shelter?"

Whenever you have income that you do not currently need, give some thought to ways of deferring it. Situations to consider are pension plan refunds when you change jobs and retirement allowances. You may be able to transfer these funds directly from your employer to your RRSP.

REGISTERED EDUCATION SAVINGS PLANS   To create a fund to support a child's post-secondary education and to defer tax on investment income, you might enrol in an **RESP**. The money put into an RESP is not tax deductible, but the interest earned while it is in the plan is tax-sheltered. If the child pursues post-secondary education, the money will be paid to the child and taxed in his or her hands, presumably at a lower marginal rate than the parents'. There may be a disadvantage in this plan, in that if the child does not continue past the secondary level of education, and no other children in the family continue either, the interest earned in the fund may be forfeited; the invested capital would be refunded to the parents. However, some plans permit the funds to be paid to almost any designate attending a post-secondary educational program.

Before-Tax and After-Tax Dollars

Articles on tax planning or investing often mention the terms before-tax and after-tax dollars. It is important to make a distinction between funds on which income tax has already been paid, or **after-tax dollars**, and money received on which no tax has been paid, or **before-tax dollars**. The following example illustrates the difference.

SHOULD SHE USE A TAX SHELTER?

Maya has $1000 (before tax) to invest and she is wondering whether to put the money in an RRSP or buy a guaranteed investment certificate without the restrictions of a tax shelter. Her combined federal and provincial marginal tax rate is 39% and the interest rate on the certificate is 7%. When she worked out the return over 5 years for each alternative, her results were as follows:

Alternative 1: put $1000 in tax shelter

Amount invested	$1000.00 before-tax dollars
Future value (7%, 5 years) [Table 8.1]	1400.00 before-tax dollars
Interest (5 years)	400.00 not taxed

Whenever she takes the money out of the tax shelter, these before-tax dollars will become subject to income tax. If she takes them out when her marginal rate is 39% she would pay $546 in taxes and have $854 left. However, if she can leave the funds in the tax shelter until some time when her income is lower, the tax will be lower.

Alternative 2: invest $1000 not tax-sheltered

Amount available	$1000.00 before-tax dollars
Income tax payable	390.00
Amount to invest	610.00 after-tax dollars

Year 1

Interest @ 7% on $610	42.70 before tax
Income tax on interest @ 39%	16.65
Net yield (42.70 – 16.65)	26.05 after tax

Year 2

Interest on $636.05 (610 + 26.05)	44.52 before tax
Tax on interest (.39 × 44.52)	17.36
Net yield (44.52 – 17.36)	27.16 after tax

Year 3

Interest on $663.21	46.42 before tax
Tax on interest	18.11
Net yield (46.42–18.11)	28.31 after tax

Year 4

Interest on $691.52	48.41 before tax
Tax on interest	18.88
Net yield (48.41–18.88)	29.53 after tax

Year 5

Interest on $721.05	50.47 before tax
Tax on interest	19.68
Net yield (50.47–19.68)	30.79 after tax
Total value of investment	751.84 after tax

Comparison of the Alternatives

	Alternative 1 (tax-sheltered)	Alternative 2 (not sheltered)
Amount invested	$1000.00	$610.00
Total interest earned	400.00	232.52
Income tax paid	nil	480.68
Asset value after 5 years	1400.00	751.84
Income tax due if taken out of shelter	546.00	nil
After-tax value	854.00	751.84

Summary

This chapter presented a simplified framework for understanding personal income tax, which sets the stage for further study of the subject. Knowing how key concepts are related is basic to understanding the current information on tax planning in the financial press.

Canadian income tax rates are progressive; that is, they increase as taxable income rises. Taxable income is gross income minus deductions. Once you have determined your taxable income, you can determine your total tax by multiplying by the tax rate. Tax credits are deducted directly from total tax owed, thereby reducing your actual tax payable. In addition to income, some increases in wealth or capital gains are also subject to taxation.

Tax planning is a year-round activity. It is important to pay attention to your marginal tax rate, or the rate applicable to your last dollar of income, and to distinguish between before-tax and after-tax dollars. Much tax planning involves either avoiding income tax or deferring tax until a time when your marginal tax rate may be lower. While couples may wish to avoid taxes by income splitting—shifting some of the income of the higher paid spouse to the lower paid spouse—attribution rules must be considered.

Vocabulary Review

attribution of income (p. 54)	non-refundable tax credit (p. 53)
average tax rate (p. 48)	partial indexation (p. 53)
after-tax dollars (p. 56)	progressive tax rate (p. 47)
before-tax dollars (p. 56)	refundable tax credit (p. 53)
capital gain (p. 50)	RESP (p. 56)
combined marginal tax rate (p. 48)	RRSP (p. 56)
full indexation (p. 53)	tax avoidance (p. 54)
gross income (p. 49)	tax credit (p. 52)
income (p. 49)	tax evasion (p. 54)
marginal tax rate (p. 48)	tax-sheltered funds (p. 51)
net income (p. 49)	taxable capital gain (p. 50)
net taxable capital gain (p. 52)	

Problems

1. If you received any of the following, should they be reported as income on your tax return?

    (a) an inheritance from your grandfather's estate

    (b) a lottery winning

    (c) the old age security pension

    (d) capital gain from selling your principal residence

    (e) Unemployment Insurance benefits

2. If you have dependent children, can you claim a deduction for them, a tax credit, or both? Explain.

3. Decide whether you AGREE or DISAGREE with each of the following statements:

(a) The money put into a tax shelter would be classed as after-tax dollars.

(b) The proportion of taxable income on which tax is paid is called the marginal tax rate.

(c) To find your taxable income, you would deduct from gross income any applicable tax credits.

(d) Capital gain is a change in wealth rather than income.

(e) Persons over the age of 65 are allowed special tax credits.

(f) On a per capita basis, the federal income tax burden has not changed significantly over the past 25 years.

(g) Spouses have a choice whether to file individual or joint income tax forms.

(h) Interest income is deductible from gross income.

(i) Capital loss is deducted from capital gain before determining net taxable capital gain.

(j) RRSPs are tax shelters because the funds put in are not taxed, even though the income gained while in the shelter is taxed.

4. Jean, who lives in Manitoba, has determined that she owes $8997 in federal income tax. How much provincial tax does she owe? Find the current tax rate for Manitoba, or use the rates given in this chapter.

5. Assume that you have a mortgage at 8 percent and also have $6000 that can be used either to reduce the mortgage or to invest at 7 percent. Should you (i) reduce your mortgage by $6000 and borrow money to invest, or (ii) simply invest the money?

   Assumptions: the mortgage company will not charge a penalty if you decide to reduce your mortgage; your combined federal and provincial marginal tax rate is 39 percent; if you borrow money to invest, the interest will be a tax deduction, but the interest paid on your mortgage is not deductible.

6. Obtain a current income tax form and complete it for Vivian, aged 45, who lives in Vancouver, is employed full-time, and has no dependents. She has never before reported any capital gains. The information she provides is as follows:

Employment income	$34 540
Interest income	1 875
Net capital gain from selling property (not her home)	9 600
Contributions to	
Unemployment Insurance	1 162
Canada Pension Plan	752
RRSP	1 500
registered pension plan	2 000

professional dues	350
Charitable donations	950
Rent on safety deposit box	20
Accountant's fee	150
Donation to the federal Liberal party	250

(a) Find Vivian's

   — taxable income

   — federal tax

   — provincial tax

(b) What is her federal marginal tax rate?

(c) Does Vivian have any tax credits? If so, which?

7. What is a significant difference between an RRSP and an RESP?

8. Suggest some ways of reducing a family's income tax. Would they be considered tax avoidance or tax evasion?

References

BOOKS

BEACH, WAYNE and LYLE R. HEPBURN. *Are You Paying Too Much Tax?* Toronto: McGraw-Hill Ryerson, annual, 206 pp. A tax planning guide for the general reader that includes a discussion of capital gains, RRSPs, and investment income.

BIRCH, RICHARD. *The Canadian Price Waterhouse Personal Tax* Advisor. Toronto: McClelland-Bantam, 1991, 199 pp. A non-technical guide prepared by tax accountants that outlines how the tax system works and explains the basics of personal income tax, including RRSPs.

BUDD, JOHN, CLAUDE RINFRET, RICHARD DAW, and DANIELLE BRIEN. *Canadian Guide to Personal Financial Management*. Scarborough, Ontario: Prentice-Hall Canada, annual, 225 pp. Accountants provide guidance on a broad range of topics, including planning finances, estimating insurance needs, managing risk, and determining investment needs. Instructions and the necessary forms for making plans are provided.

COSTELLO, BRIAN. *Your Money and How to Keep It*. Fifth Edition. Toronto: Stoddart, 1990, 248 pp. Particular emphasis on investments and income tax.

DELOITTE AND TOUCHE. *How to Reduce the Tax You Pay*. Toronto: Key Porter, annual, 223 pp. A non-technical guide, prepared by tax accountants, that explains the basics of personal income tax.

DRACHE, ARTHUR B. C., editor. *The Canadian Taxpayer*. Toronto: Richard De Boo Publishers, bi-monthly. A newsletter with up-to-date income tax information. Includes articles on tax cases, relevant political events, recent changes to regulations and other tax planning topics of interest.

DRACHE, ARTHUR B.C., editor. *Canada Tax Planning Service*. Toronto: Richard De Boo Publishers, subscription service. A detailed professional reference that is kept up-to-date by regular mailings of replacement pages. Four-volume looseleaf set.

GRENBY, MIKE. *More Best of Mike Grenby: A Year-Round Guide to Managing Your Money*. Vancouver: International Self-Counsel Press, 1990, 192 pp. A quick reference on how to reduce your income tax.

HOGG, R. D. *Preparing Your Income Tax Returns*. Toronto: CCH Canadian, annual, 589 pp. A complete and technical guide to income tax preparation.

JACKS, EVELYN. *Jacks on Tax Savings*. Toronto: McGraw-Hill Ryerson, annual, 228 pp. Explains the current tax rules and demonstrates how to prepare a tax return.

MACINNIS, LYMAN. *Get Smart! Make Your Money Count in the 1990s*. Second Edition. Scarborough, Ontario: Prentice-Hall Canada, 1989, 317 pp. A book for the general reader that includes financial planning and income tax principles, but gives major attention to investing in the stock market.

WYATT, ELAINE. *The Money Companion, How to Manage Your Money and Achieve Financial Freedom*. Markham, Ontario: Penguin Books, 1991. A guide to personal financial management that focuses on planning, investment strategy, and retirement needs.

ZIMMER, HENRY B. *The Canadian Tax and Investment Guide*. Toronto: McClelland and Stewart, 1993, 301 pp. Comprehensive treatment of income tax as it relates to such topics as RRSPs, investment income, separation and divorce, retirement and estate planning.

PERIODICALS

Financial Times. Weekly. Suite 500, 920 Yonge Street, Toronto, Ontario, M2W 3L5. Provides current information on a range of business and economic topics.

Report on Business. Daily. A section of The Globe and Mail. Important source of information on the financial markets.

The Financial Post. Daily and weekly. The Financial Post Company, 777 Bay Street, Toronto, Ontario, M5G 2E4. Up-to-date information on business, economics, income tax, and investments.

CHAPTER THREE

Wills: Planning for the Distribution of Assets

1. To explain how wills fit into comprehensive financial planning.

2. To differentiate among the responsibilities involved in:

    (a) drawing a will,

    (b) witnessing a will,

    (c) acting as executor of an estate.

3. To compare the effects on the settling of an estate of:

    (a) the existence of a valid will,

    (b) no will.

4. To identify assets that are not distributed by a will.

5. To explain the purpose of probate.

6. To explain the distribution of an estate in the case of intestacy.

7. To evaluate the legal position of dependents who are not provided for in the will.

8. To distinguish between the following pairs of terms:

    (a) testator and testatrix,

    (b) executor and administrator,

    (c) bequest (or legacy) and beneficiary (or legatee),

    (d) codicil and holograph will,

    (e) joint tenancy and tenancy in common.

9. To explain these terms: letters of administration, letters probate, preferential share, testamentary trust, power of attorney.

10. To explain how the transfer of ownership of assets underlies most of the formalities associated with wills and the settling of estates.

Introduction

The general discussion of financial planning in Chapter 1 focused on the maximization of resources during one's lifetime. Persons with assets also need to make provision for the distribution of their estate after death, but estate planning is often postponed because there is no sense of urgency. Unfortunately, those who die leaving no legal statement of how they wish to dispose of their possessions and assets often create difficulties for the surviving family members. In such cases, as we shall see, provincial laws direct how the estate is distributed.

A will provides an orderly procedure for changing the ownership of assets after a death, indicating which assets should be transferred to which people. When a person dies without a will, the assets are distributed according to the law of the province, which may or may not coincide with the desires of the deceased. A comprehensive financial plan includes a will to ensure the orderly transfer of assets at death.

Some of the general procedures and terminology associated with wills and estates are introduced in this chapter. Although they may seem confusing at first, there is a logic in the process which, once identified, makes it quite understandable.

After death, the person named to act in your place—the executor—gets the power to do so from the will. Often the will is submitted to a special court to verify that it is valid. Then the executor proceeds to make a list of the assets of the deceased, pay the bills, and distribute the estate according to the will. Much of the legal formality associated with wills is concerned with transferring ownership of assets from the deceased to other people.

NEED FOR A WILL

What is a Will?

A **will** is a legal document that gives someone the power to act as your financial representative after your death and directs how your assets should be distributed. The person named in the will to act as your agent is called an **executor** if a man, or an **executrix** if a woman. A will has no effect or power during your lifetime; while you are alive you can change your will as often as you wish, give away the possessions listed in your will, or write new wills. A will takes effect on the death of the **testator,** or the one who signed the will. A woman who makes a will is a **testatrix.**

Who Needs a Will?

Most adults should have a will for two reasons: it ensures that their estate is distributed according to their wishes, and by naming an executor, the handling of the estate is simplified. Most people have a larger estate than they realize because they tend to forget about those assets that do not form part of their estate until they die, such as the proceeds from life insurance, the lump-sum death benefit from the Canada Pension Plan, group life insurance plans in connection with their employment, registered retirement savings plans, and credits in company pension plans. All of these assets become part of your estate at death, even though some may not be accessible during your lifetime.

Legal Capacity to Make a Will

To make a valid will, the testator must be:

(a) of the age of majority (17 in Newfoundland; 18 in Alberta, Manitoba, Ontario, Quebec, Prince Edward Island, and Saskatchewan; 19 in New Brunswick, the Northwest Territories, Nova Scotia, British Columbia, and the Yukon). A person is permitted to make a legal will before the age of majority if he or she is married or a member of the military.

(b) of sound mind, i.e., he or she must understand what is being done. People who are mentally unfit may not meet this requirement. This is a particular concern with those who may have some degree of senility, or anyone who is undergoing psychiatric treatment. If the will is contested (disputed before a court) after their death, and it can be shown that the person signing it was not of sound mind, the will may be considered invalid.

(c) free of undue influence by another person. A will should not be signed under conditions of coercion or persuasion, or there may be a basis for contesting it.

DRAWING UP A WILL

How to Begin

First, take stock of possessions, assets, and any other moneys that would form part of your estate. Next, decide how you want to allocate this estate. If you take this list to a lawyer along with the name of your executor, a will can be drafted for you. The lawyer's role is to translate your wishes into legal language and suggest ways to allow for various contingencies that you may not have considered, such as naming an alternate executor, including a common disaster clause in case husband and wife are killed in a common accident, and allowing for children yet unborn.

It is not essential that a will be drawn up by a lawyer. The law does not require any special format, or legal words, or typing. You can write a will in your own words or use a standard form bought at a stationery store. However, if you are not experienced in writing wills, you may not make your intentions perfectly clear by your choice of words, and you may forget important clauses. Lawyers charge nominal fees to draw up wills and it is worthwhile to have their assistance.

What to Include in a Will

A will usually includes the following information:

(a) the domicile of the testator.

(b) a statement that previous wills made by the testator are revoked.

(c) direction to pay funeral expenses, debts, and taxes before distributing the estate.

(d) possible specific bequests (or legacies) of certain possessions or moneys to named persons.

(e) a clause to dispose of the residue of the estate, e.g., one or more persons who may be named as **residual legatees** to receive any balance remaining after debts, taxes, and specific bequests.

(f) the appointment of an executor and possibly an alternate executor.

(g) the naming of a guardian if there are minor children.

(h) possibly, a common disaster clause to cover a situation such as the death of a couple as a result of one event.

A person who benefits from a will is called a **beneficiary,** and an asset or possession left to this person is called a **bequest** (or **legacy**) or, if real property, a **devise.**

Guardians for Children

A guardian for children is often designated in a will, but the testator does not have the final word on this decision. After the death of their parents the court appoints a guardian for the children; in many cases the guardian named in the will is appointed by the court if that person is agreeable and able to act. Not being bound by the terms of a will, the court has the flexibility to make the most appropriate decision about guardianship at the time of death.

Can the Family be Disinherited?

There is no legal requirement that a person leave his or her estate to family members, contrary to the hopes of some children. However, if a spouse or children who were financially dependent on the deceased at the time of death are disinherited, these survivors may have a basis to contest the will under provincial legislation. If they can show that they have financial needs, the court may award them a share of the estate. The relevant acts are:

Alberta, Newfoundland	*Family Relief Act*
British Columbia	*Wills Variation Act*
Manitoba, New Brunswick, Nova Scotia	*Testator's Family Maintenance Act*
Ontario	*Succession Law Reform Act*

| Prince Edward Island | *Dependents of a Deceased Person Relief Act* |
| Saskatchewan, Yukon, Northwest Territories | *Dependents' Relief Act* |

Recent changes in family law acts regarding the division of family property (after family break-up or death) can have an effect on the spouse's share of an estate. For instance, under *The Ontario Family Law Act* of 1986, a spouse may choose between the provisions under the will or a half share of the net family property calculated according to this act. Certain property of the deceased, such as a prior inheritance, may be excluded from net family property. This legislation has implications for wills written before 1986. For instance, a will that leaves an estate in trust for a spouse during that person's lifetime, with the balance going to a third party after the spouse's death, may be put aside if the spouse elects to take one-half of the net family property.

Signing and Witnessing a Will

A will must be signed at its end almost simultaneously by the testator and two witnesses; all three must be present together. By their signatures, the witnesses attest that they watched the testator sign this will, but they need not read the will or know the contents. It is advisable that neither a spouse nor a person who is to benefit from a will be a witness to that will. This could result in any gift to that person being declared void. Check provincial legislation on this point.

A person named in a will as executor may also be, and very often is, a beneficiary. For instance, if a man names his wife as executrix and leaves his estate to her, this should present no difficulty; however, it would be preferable that she not be a witness.

How to Choose an Executor

When selecting an executor, consider the person's age, willingness to handle your business, and capability of doing so. It is wise to appoint an executor who may be expected to survive you. Often close relatives are appointed executors, but in cases of large and complex estates, a trust company may be appointed sole executor or joint executor with a family member. If, for instance, the testator considers that the management of the estate may be a burden for the survivor, the spouse may be appointed a **co-executor** with a trust company. This would allow the spouse to be involved in settling the estate and aware of what is being done without taking the sole responsibility. However, trust companies are not very interested in small estates because of the limited revenue generated.

An executor named in a will is not bound to accept this appointment and may refuse if unable or disinclined; therefore, it is wise to determine your nominee's preference in advance. The executor need not see the will, but he or she would find it helpful to know where it is kept. More than one executor can be named to act as co-executors, although for small estates this can be an unnecessary complication. It can be inconvenient if the signatures of several people are required to implement each action when settling an estate,. However, it is wise to name an alternative executor who would act if the one originally selected is unwilling or unable to act, or has died.

Where to Keep a Will

A will should be kept in a safe spot, but where the survivors can find it. The main alternatives are to leave it with a trust company or lawyer to keep in their vaults, or put it in a safety deposit box. There is only one signed copy of a will, but the unsigned duplicate could be kept at home with other personal papers.

Disposing of Small Personal Possessions

People often change their minds about which relative should receive the grandfather clock or the antique rocker, but it may be inconvenient and expensive to have a new will drawn to accommodate each change. One solution is to attach a memorandum to the will listing such possessions and who should receive each. The list can easily be changed because it is not part of the will, and if there is harmony in the family, the executor is likely to follow these instructions. However, remember that such a memorandum carries no legal weight and if the will were contested, such a list might not be followed. Although it has no legal weight, it is wise to make reference to the memorandum in the will.

Instructions About Funeral Arrangements

These instructions do not need to be included in a will because after death the body belongs to the next of kin, who decide on its disposition. Nevertheless, in most cases relatives try to follow the wishes of the deceased. Such instructions can be filed with the will if desired, but it is important that others know about such instructions or they may not be found until it is too late to act on them.

Marriage and Wills

Usually a will made prior to marriage is void unless the spouse elects in writing to uphold it after the testator's death. To avoid having to make a will on your wedding day, you may write a will in contemplation of marriage that takes effect after the marriage. It states that it was written in contemplation of marriage and names the expected spouse.

Revoking or Altering a Will

While you are alive you can alter your will or make new ones as often as you wish because the document has no power until after death. A will may be cancelled or revoked by (i) destroying it, (ii) writing a new will that expressly states that previous wills are revoked, or (iii) getting married. If you want to change your will after it has been drafted but not yet signed, alterations may be made as long as each change is signed and witnessed. If you want to alter an existing will without writing a new one, add a codicil. A **codicil** is a postscript to a will, although it is really a separate document. It must contain a reference to the will to which it is appended and must be dated, signed, and witnessed.

Some lawyers feel that it is better to rewrite a will than to add a codicil. However, if there is any doubt as to the testator's mental capacity at the time the new will is made, it might be better to add a codicil. Better that the codicil should fail than that the entire will be declared invalid.

The Holograph Will

A will entirely in the handwriting of the testator, dated and signed, but not witnessed, is called a **holograph will** and is valid in some provinces (e.g., Ontario if the will was written after 1978, Quebec, and Saskatchewan). Note that a will on a stationery store form where the testator fills in the blanks is not a holograph will and therefore must be properly witnessed. Holograph wills are not valid in British Columbia, Nova Scotia, and Prince Edward Island, which require that the testator's signature be witnessed. An example of a holograph will is shown in Figure 3.1.

SETTLING AN ESTATE WITH A WILL

Finding the Will

After a death the first and obvious step in settling the estate is to find the most recent will. A thorough search of the deceased's home, safety deposit boxes, and appropriate lawyers' offices must be conducted before concluding that there is no will.

Duties of the Executor

A will usually names one or more persons to act as executors or as the personal financial representatives of the deceased. The executor is charged with a variety of duties which may be categorized as:

(a) proving the validity of the will,

(b) assembling and administering the assets of the estate in trust,

(c) distributing the estate to the heirs.

If no executor was named, if the named executor is deceased, unable, or unwilling to act, or if the deceased died without a will, someone with a financial

FIGURE 3.1 MRS. HASTINGS' HOLOGRAPH WILL

> For Winston
> In case I should be taken before Cedric R.M. Hastings
>
> July 30, 1933
>
> If my brother, Winston, should outlive me, there are a few things that I wish he would attend to, viz:-
>
> If my Husband, Cedric Hastings outlives me and there is any of my property left, please see that he is provided for.
>
> I should like to see my personal property such as the family silver, bedding, and my trinkets, brooches etc. divided among my nieces Camille, Mabel and Beatrice. Likewise, the furniture that was mine at the time of our marriage. I should like Cedric to have the gold (Howard) watch that Dad gave me. The books and pictures are left for Winston to dispose of as he sees fit. If there is any items that Cedric particularly wished to keep, please see that he has it.
>
> Rebecca Maud Hastings

interest in the estate must apply to the Surrogate Court for **Letters of Administration** which appoint an administrator to act for the deceased. The **Surrogate Court** is the provincial court that arbitrates matters relating to wills and the settling of estates. Once appointed, an **administrator** has the same duties and responsibilities as an executor. The only difference between an executor, named by a will, and an administrator, given authority by the Surrogate Court, is in the manner of their appointment and the possible requirement that the administrator be bonded. A bond, equivalent to the value of the estate, can be posted by paying a fee to a bonding company to insure that the administrator is trustworthy in carrying out his or her duties. Bonding, of course, represents an additional cost to the estate. Clearly, having an administrator appointed means additional steps before the settling of the estate can begin.

Proving the Will

A will is submitted to the Surrogate Court for **probate**, a process whereby the Court verifies the authenticity of the will and the appointment of the executor. The confirming document is called **Letters Probate**. In the subsequent steps of assembling the assets and paying the taxes, the Letters Probate are used to support the authority of the executor to conduct these transactions.

Some wills are not probated, especially when the estate is small and uncomplicated. The legal transfer of ownership of assets from the name of the deceased to the names of the heirs, the crucial task in settling an estate, is sometimes accomplished without probate. However, the financial institutions involved require adequate documentation if there are no Letters Probate.

Administering the Estate in Trust

After the testator's death, the property included in the will comes under the authority and control of the executor, whose duty it is to implement the provisions of the will. An executor usually engages a lawyer, and delegates to this person certain tasks in fulfilling the legal formalities involved with the estate. Final responsibility, however, rests with the executor. The extent of the executor's task depends on the complexity of the deceased's estate and whether or not it was left in good order.

ASSEMBLING THE ASSETS   Once the executor's or administrator's authority to proceed has been established, the next task is to compile an inventory of the deceased's assets and liabilities. In the process of doing so, the executor informs all financial institutions holding these assets of the testator's death. The executor opens a trust account into which funds belonging to the deceased may be deposited temporarily. This account is needed to handle the business of the estate, including the payment of bills and the final distribution to beneficiaries.

PAYING THE DEBTS   Once the financial institutions holding accounts in the name of the deceased are given proof that the person has died and that the executor is empowered by the will to act, funds are usually released. During the time the estate is being settled, the assets may be generating income in the form of interest, dividends, rent, and profit. For income tax purposes, the executor must keep a record of the income received by the estate during the time it was held in trust.

Before the estate can be distributed, all debts must be paid, with taxes and funeral expenses taking first priority. (Note that there are no longer any succession duties or estate taxes in Canada, but when there were all assets were frozen until the taxes had been assessed.) Should the debts of the deceased exceed the assets, the executor must devise a way to distribute what there is among the creditors, perhaps on a pro rata basis.

The executor has to pay income tax due on (i) any income the deceased received from January 1 until the date of death, and (ii) any income generated by the estate between the date of death and the date of distribution. An executor should contact the local office of Revenue Canada Taxation for instructions about income tax for deceased persons and estates. Essentially, the first task is to complete an income tax return for the portion of the year that the deceased was alive. The executor must pay whatever income tax is owing from the estate funds being held in trust. Just before distributing the estate, another income tax return must be completed reporting any estate income and paying the appropriate tax. This process is summarized in Figure 3.2.

FIGURE 3.2 Income Tax Returns for Deceased Persons

Return I	Return II
INCOME RECEIVED WHILE THE PERSON WAS ALIVE	INCOME RECEIVED BY THE ESTATE WHILE IT WAS HELD IN TRUST
January 1 until date of death	Date of death until the estate is distributed

RECORDING THE ACCOUNTS   The executor is responsible for maintaining a record of accounts showing all receipts and disbursements, but this task may be delegated to a lawyer. Beneficiaries with questions may wish to see the accounts, and if there is concern about the misuse of funds, the court may require that the accounts be submitted, a process known as **passing the accounts**.

Distributing the Estate

When the executor has paid the deceased's debts, filed an income tax return, and paid the legal fees, the estate may be distributed to the beneficiaries according to the will. In some instances it may be necessary to sell certain assets in order to pay debts and make the distribution; other assets may be transferred to new owners. Whether all assets must be converted into cash or whether some may be transferred in their present form depends on the instructions in the will and the wishes of the beneficiaries.

In some cases, the executor may have to sell property in order to divide the estate among several people. For instance, if the chief asset in the estate is a house and there are three beneficiaries, the house could be sold and the proceeds divided, or one of the heirs could buy the house by paying the other beneficiaries their shares. In cases where a division of the asset is not necessary, the executor may simply transfer ownership of the property.

The demands on the executor at this stage depend on the complexity of the deceased's estate. A lawyer can help with the legal formalities of transferring various forms of property.

FEES FOR SETTLING AN ESTATE   Settling an estate involves two sets of fees: one for the services of a lawyer and one for the executor. Lawyers prepare applications for probate, and there is usually a Surrogate Court tariff setting the fee (not including disbursements) for an estate of average complexity, e.g., $5 per $1000 of value for the first $50 000 and $15 per $1000 of value over $50 000.

Executors are responsible for all the other work involved in settling the estate and are entitled to fees based on its complexity and on the time and effort they have expended. This fee is usually around four to five percent of the value of the estate. If the executrix wants the lawyer to do her work, the lawyer charges the executrix, who pays the lawyer from the moneys due to her as executrix. If several executors are involved, the fee is divided among them. Frequently, family members act as executors without taking any fees from the estate.

Legal fees depend on the amount of work the lawyer has to do for the estate. Fees may be based on the time he or she spends or on a percentage of the assets. The executor should discuss the fee schedule with the lawyer before work on the estate begins. Legal fees can be reduced if the executor decides to do some tasks, such as assembling the assets and paying debts. These fees are paid from estate funds held in trust before the distribution of the estate.

SETTLING AN ESTATE WITHOUT A WILL

It is not uncommon to discover that there is no will; many people who are fond of talking about their wills and their plans for disposing of their possessions have never made a will at all. It is something we tend to postpone, thinking it is not an urgent matter. Also, we are reluctant to contemplate our mortality. However, before concluding that no will was left, a thorough search must be made.

If the relatives think that a will existed at some time, but it cannot be found, the will is presumed to have been revoked unless contrary evidence can be discovered. Should a will be found subsequent to the distribution of the estate, it may be very difficult or impossible to make any alteration in the distribution.

Naming the Administrator

If you die without a will, or **intestate,** someone with a financial interest in your estate must apply to court to be appointed administrator. If family members do not do so, a creditor, such as the funeral director, may press for action. The application includes an inventory of the estate's assets and debts, a list of close relatives, and an affidavit stating that the deceased left no will. As previously mentioned, the applicant may also be asked to post a **bond of indemnity** with the court so that the estate is protected should the administrator be dishonest. If the administrator absconds with the assets or dissipates the estate and fails to render a true accounting to the court, beneficiaries can call upon the bond of indemnity to protect their financial interests. A fee also must be paid to the Surrogate Court. After the applicant receives Letters of Administration he or she can begin to settle the estate.

WILL BUT NO EXECUTOR   If there is a will but no executor prepared to act, someone must apply to the court for Letters of Administration and the appointment of an administrator. In such a case, the situation is referred to as an **administration with will annexed**.

The Administration

The administrator carries out the same duties as an executor, but may be required to withhold distribution of the assets of the estate until one year after the deceased's death, unless there has been an advertisement for creditors. This requirement does not apply to an executor, but it is often done for convenience, and for the protection of the executor; an executor can be held personally liable if the estate is distributed to beneficiaries without prior repayment of debts. The one-year waiting period is one way to ensure that all creditors are informed of the death and have an opportunity to submit any outstanding bills.

Distributing the Intestacy

When there is no will (an *intestacy*), the estate is distributed according to the provisions of the appropriate provincial law. An outline of some rules regarding intestacy is shown in Table 3.1. For greater accuracy and completeness you should consult the appropriate provincial statute. You may note a reference to **preferential shares** in this table, which means that the spouse gets a specified share before any other beneficiary. For example, if the spouse's preferential share is $50 000, this must be paid to the spouse before anyone else gets anything. If the estate is less than $50 000, then the spouse gets it all.

GEORGE LEFT NO WILL

George always intended to write a will, but like many people, he never got around to it. After his death, his wife Alma, who was appointed administrator, discovered that his estate totalled about $105 000. According to Ontario law the estate was to be divided as follows:

To Alma, preferential share of $75 000 plus
one-third of the balance, making a total of $85 000
Two-thirds of the balance to the children:

Son, Simon	$6666
Son, Richard	$6666

Deceased son Henry's children:

Lisa	$3333
Sam	$3333

TABLE 3.1 PROVINCIAL LEGISLATION REGARDING INTESTATE SUCCESSION

Although legislation governing intestate succession varies from province to province, there are a number of aspects which are the same in all 10 jurisdictions. Similarities will be outlined first with differences listed below.

(i) General Rules for Intestate Succession

If the deceased left	the estate goes
spouse, no children	all to the spouse
spouse and 1 child*	preferential share to spouse; excess split 50/50 between spouse and child
spouse and 2 or more children*	preferential share to spouse; excess split 1/3 to spouse and 2/3 shared equally among children
no spouse, but children	all to children, shared equally
no spouse or children	all to parents
no spouse, children or parents	all to brothers and sisters

(ii) Intestate Succession and Variations from General Rules

Province	Relevant Legislation	Variations from General Rules
Alberta	Intestate Succession Act	• spouse's preferential share is $40 000
British Columbia	Estate Administration Act (Pt. 7)	• spouse's preferential share is $65 000
Manitoba	Intestate Succession Act	• spouse's preferential share is $50 000 • spouse gets 1/2 excess regardless of number of children
New Brunswick	Devolution of Estates Act	• no preferential share to spouse
Newfoundland	Intestate Succession Act	• no preferential share to spouse
Nova Scotia	Intestate Succession Act	• spouse's preferential share is $50 000
Ontario	Succession Law Reform Act	• spouse's preferential share is $75 000
Prince Edward Island	Probate Act (Pt. 4)	• spouse's preferential share is $50 000
Quebec	Civil Code of Quebec	• no preferential share to spouse • spouse gets 1/3 of estate; children get 2/3
Saskatchewan	Intestate Succession Act	• spouse's preferential share is $40 000

*predeceased children are "represented" by their surviving children

CONSANGUINITY There is a method of classifying relatives according to their nearness to the deceased. To illustrate how the system works, an abbreviated table of **consanguinity** (blood relationships) is shown in Table 3.2. Relatives beyond the nuclear family are grouped in classes. Should the deceased die intestate leaving no spouse or children, the estate may be divided equally among the next-of-kin in the class closest in blood relation. If there are no relatives in Class I, the estate is divided equally among all those in Class II. When there is even one relative in a class, that person gets the whole estate, and the distribution does not continue to the next class. If the deceased leaves grandchildren, but no living children, the estate goes to the grandchildren through a process called **representation**, because they receive their parents' share.

TABLE 3.2 ABBREVIATED TABLE OF CONSANGUINITY

All blood relatives, beyond children, are classified into numbered classes as follows:

Class I	father, mother, brother, sister
Class II	grandmother, grandfather
Class III	great grandmother, great grandfather, nephew, niece, uncle, aunt
Class IV	great-great grandfather, great-great grandmother, great nephew, great niece, first cousin, great uncle, great aunt
Class V	great-great uncle, great-great aunt, first cousin once removed, etc.

COMMON-LAW SPOUSES The status of common-law spouses is changing gradually, but at this time there is no generally accepted treatment of such spouses under all conditions. While the Canada Pension Plan, as well as some other pension plans, may provide benefits to a common-law spouse, provincial statutes have not considered them to be legal spouses in cases of intestacy. Therefore, it is difficult to generalize about their rights. At the time of writing, common-law spouses do not automatically receive a share of an intestacy, but may go to the court to argue for a portion because of financial dependency. Of course, if there is a will, a common-law spouse can be named a beneficiary.

TRANSFERRING OWNERSHIP OF ASSETS

The main purpose of settling an estate is to transfer ownership of assets from the deceased to designated beneficiaries, and the various formalities are necessary to ensure that this is correctly done. The diagram in Figure 3.3 summarizes the transfer of the ownership from the deceased to the executor (administrator) in trust, and finally to the beneficiaries.

FIGURE 3.3 Transfer of the Deceased's Assets

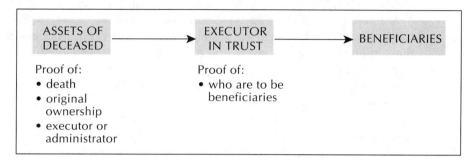

ESTATE ASSETS NOT DISTRIBUTED BY THE WILL

There are two situations in which the deceased's assets go directly to a beneficiary, independently of the will, by contract and at law. Certain financial assets—such as life insurance, annuities, and registered retirement savings plans—may have a designated beneficiary named in the contract by the deceased during his or her lifetime. On proof of death, the financial institution holding these assets automatically transfers ownership to the beneficiary; the will is not involved. If the named beneficiary has predeceased the testator, the assets will probably be paid into the estate unless an alternate beneficiary was named.

Other assets that are not distributed by the will are those held in **joint tenancy**, a situation that confers the right of survivorship. For instance, if a couple has a joint bank account, the wife, through right of survivorship, becomes the sole owner of the account on her husband's death. Real property held in joint tenancy is handled similarly. Note that joint tenancy is not the same as **tenancy in common**. In this latter instance, each owns an undivided share of the asset. If a couple owns the family house as tenants in common, on the death of one partner one-half of the value of the house would form a part of the deceased's estate and one-half would continue to belong to the survivor. However, if the house was held in joint tenancy, the ownership of the house would pass to the survivor.

TESTAMENTARY TRUSTS

A will may state that particular assets or property are to be held in trust for some person or persons. This is called a **testamentary trust** because the trust is established by a will, in contrast to a **living trust,** which becomes operative during the lifetime of the person who established it. A testamentary trust must be managed by an appointed trustee. Usually the trustee (and perhaps an alternate) is named in the will. Trust companies specialize in this service, with trust departments that offer advice in planning the trust. The company acts as trustee when the trust becomes operative. When trust companies are involved in planning an estate, with or without a trust, they usually insist that the company be named executor or co-executor of the will. If there is to be a trust, the company may be named the trustee. Trust companies, obviously, charge a fee for managing assets for others. In fact all trustees, whether corporations or individuals, are entitled to charge a fee, subject to review by the court. In some situations the executor may also be the trustee and decide to appoint someone to carry out the management of the trust property. In such a case, the executor retains ultimate responsibility.

It is wise to select a trustee who does not have a conflict of interest. As an example, Jane has been named the trustee of funds for her disabled brother, John. The will states that the income from the estate is to be used for John, and after his death the balance of the estate goes to Jane. There can be a conflict of interest in such a situation; if Jane restricts the money available for her brother she may inherit a larger estate. A trustee, however, is obliged to be even-handed in dealing with the interests of beneficiaries. Consideration must be given to the life interest of one beneficiary as well as the ultimate interest of the other.

POWER OF ATTORNEY

Another aspect of financial planning is making provision for the possibility of becoming incapacitated through accident or disease. As has been explained in this chapter, there is a process for handling the affairs of a deceased person. An incompetent person presents different problems. Unless the client has a legally appointed representative, officers of financial institutions have no choice but to follow the client's instructions, regardless of his or her competency level. Family members are helpless to intervene unless a prior power of attorney has been signed or they initiate the slow and painful court process of having the person ruled mentally incompetent and naming a legal representative. In some situations, a joint bank account for depositing income and paying expenses may be a practical and informal alternative, at least for a time.

A **power of attorney** is a legal document that names someone to handle your finances under certain conditions. It is a wise precaution to assign power of attorney to a trusted person who can handle your financial affairs if necessary. Generally, it is also advisable to name an alternate in case your first choice is unable to act. There are various ways to make a power of attorney restrictive enough that you do not lose control of your affairs prematurely. For instance, the family lawyer can keep the document and release it only when two doctors have stated in writing that the person can no longer handle his or her own affairs.

It is easier, cheaper, and less cumbersome for the family if a power of attorney is signed when the individual is capable. However, additional safeguards are built into the more complex court process of determining incompetency. The person named by the court to manage assets has to submit regular detailed reports to the court for approval.

Summary

Most adults should have a will, and generally should obtain help from a lawyer in drawing it up. A trusted, capable, and willing person should be named executor or executrix, with a second person as alternate. It is wise to review and revise your will periodically to reflect any changes in your financial resources or family composition. A will is not operative until death, when it becomes the plan for disposing of the estate. The executor has responsibility for carrying out the provisions of the will. The estates of those who die intestate are disposed of according to provincial law. The status of common-law spouses is changing in Canada, but in most jurisdictions they are not given spouse status in cases of intestacy.

There are sound arguments for giving power of attorney to someone to act as your representative if you should become incompetent to handle your own financial affairs.

Vocabulary Review

administration with will annexed (p. 74)

administrator (p. 70)

beneficiary (p. 66)

bequest (p. 66)

bond of indemnity (p. 73)

codicil (p. 69)

co-executor (p. 67)

consanguinity (p. 76)

devise (p. 66)

executor (p. 64)

executrix (p. 64)

holograph will (p. 69)

intestate (p. 73)

joint tenancy (p. 77)

legacy (p. 66)

Letters of Administration (p. 70)

Letters Probate (p. 71)

living trust (p. 77)

passing the accounts (p. 72)

power of attorney (p. 78)

preferential shares (p. 74)

probate (p. 71)

representation (p. 76)

residual legatee (p. 66)

revoke (p. 69)

Surrogate Court (p. 70)

tenants in common (p. 77)

testamentary trust (p. 77)

testator (p. 64)

testatrix (p. 64)

will (p. 64)

Problems

1.

A CASE OF INTESTACY

At his death, Eugene Markotic who was living with his common-law wife Mrs. Anna Pavlicek and her children, was operating a successful pig-raising business with the help of Anna's son, Larry. Because Mr. Markotic left no will, there was much uncertainty about who should look after his affairs, including the growing pigs. Mr. Markotic was divorced, had no children, and his parents were deceased; by the rules of intestacy the collateral relatives would be the heirs, in this case his three brothers. It was agreed that one brother, Tom, would apply to be the administrator of the estate.

Initially, Mr. Markotic's affairs appeared quite straightforward. He left two rented barns full of pigs, a truck, some supplies and equipment, personal belongings, and a bank account. A search of his apartment revealed seven burlap bags of personal papers dating from the late 1940s. Tom found that his brother held two mortgages, several bank accounts, stocks, bonds, and two life insurance policies with named beneficiaries, in one case his deceased mother and in the other his divorced wife.

Mr. Markotic had lived with Mrs. Pavlicek for a number of years, treating her family as his own. However, Mr. Markotic's brothers did not approve of this situation and had kept their distance. Gradually it was revealed that Mr. Markotic had had plans for the disposition of his estate, which he had not put in writing. He had often mentioned taking Larry into partnership in the business, and he had always meant to change his life insurance policies to name Anna as beneficiary, and also to cancel the mortgage he held for her daughter and son-in-law. His lawyer knew of his intention to make a will naming one brother as executor and recipient of 60 percent of the estate, with the remaining 40 percent to be divided, one half to Anna and one-half between the other two brothers. Unfortunately, he died before making such a will; therefore his plans could not be implemented.

(a) Would probate be involved in settling Mr. Markotic's estate?

(b) Since Mr. Markotic did not leave a will, what steps would be necessary to have Tom appointed to handle his estate?

(c) Would there be any additional costs or delays incurred because Mr. Markotic did not name an executor?

(d) Who would receive the benefits of the two life insurance policies?

(e) What was the name of the law that specified how Mr. Markotic's estate would be distributed?

(f) Assuming that this situation occurred in your province, estimate the share Anna Pavlicek would receive under the intestacy law.

(g) Make a list of things that would probably have turned out better if Mr. Markotic had written a will.

(h) Do you think the common-law wife should investigate the possibility of making a claim as a dependent? What law would be involved?

(i) Does Larry Pavlicek have a basis for contesting the distribution of this estate?

2.

WILLS OF ALL SORTS

When Mrs. Hastings died in 1972 at the age of 94, her family began the search for her will. Someone remembered that there was a letter in her brother's desk, which had been there for years, with instructions to open it after her death. That turned out to be the holograph will reproduced in Figure 3.1. The search did not end there, because someone thought that Mrs. Hastings had once said something about keeping her will at a certain bank. A search of several banks revealed some Canada Savings Bonds, a life insurance policy belonging to her husband, and his will.

After the funeral, a careful search of her room uncovered a second will that had been drawn by a lawyer in 1939 (Figure 3.4). Note that Mrs. Hastings made some revisions to this will nine years later when she cut out sections and pasted in changes. Finally, the matron of the nursing home where Mrs. Hastings had been living produced yet another will, which was on a stationery store form (Figure 3.5). This last will was the most recent, and it was submitted for probate.

FIGURE 3.4 MRS. HASTINGS' SECOND WILL

ON THIS twenty first day of the month in February, in the year one thousand nine hundred and thirty nine, at the Village of Rockport, County of Crompton, District of St. francis, and Province of Quebec:

Before the undersigned Witnesses, Catharine Ross, Advocate, and Mary Goodman, Accountant, both of the Village of Rockport, said County, District and Province,

CAME AND APPEARED

REBECCA M. HASTINGS (nee Cassells), of the Township of Smithton, said District and Province, who being of sound mind, memory and understanding, has declared the following to be her Last Will and Testament:

1. I commend my soul to Almighty God.

2. Hereby revoking any and all former Wills, I hereby will, devise and bequeath any and all property, real and personal, which is now own, or may own or possess at the time of my death, in the following manner:

November 25, 1948

If my good and faithful husband, Cedric Hastings outlives me, I wish what property is left to be used for his benefit as my dear brother Winston Cassells sees fit. Also that the Sun Life Insurance money be used for Cedric's benefit.

I should like a double tombstone erected for both of us, whenever seems most suitable, the cost thereof to come out of our estate. I wish Cedric to have my large trunk and the best black suitcase. Also Dad's gold "Howard" watch. Will Winston and Camille please be my executors?

D. I desire my niece Camille H. Cassells to have Blue and White bedspread woven by her Grandmother. And my niece Mabel Cassells to have the White bedspread with "Theresa A. Green" woven thereon. And to my niece Beatrice Cassells the silk quilt.

E. I desire my furniture, books, pictures, silverware, and household effects generally, to be divided between my three nieces, Camille, Mabel and Beatrice Cassells abovementioned, as my Executrix may see fit.

After due reading of this Will by the Testatrix, she has signed the same in presence of the Witnesses, who have also signed in her presence and in presence of each other.

WITNESSES

Rebecca M. Hastings

Catherine Ross

Mary Goodman

FIGURE 3.5 MRS. HASTINGS' LAST WILL

THIS IS THE LAST WILL AND TESTAMENT OF ME, Rebecca Maud Cassells Hastings, at present residing at Eliza Gregson Home, in the Township of Smithton, in the District of St. Frances, retired.

I hereby revoking all former wills and testamentary dispositions heretofore made by me.

I NOMINATE AND APPOINT my brother, Winston Charles Cassells, farmer, residing on Rural Route 4, Crompton, Quebec, and my nieces, Camille Cassells, teacher, residing in Perth, Ontario, and Mabel Cassells, nurse, residing in Toronto, Ontario, and the survivor of them, to be the Executors and Trustees of this, my Will.

I GIVE, DEVISE AND BEQUEATH all the Real and Personal estate of which I shall die possessed or entitled to unto my said Executors and Trustees hereinbefore named, in Trust for the purposes following:

Firstly, to pay my just debts. Secondly, to pay the expenses of my burial which I wish to have undertaken by L.O. Cass and Son, Ltd., funeral directors, of Crompton, Que. Thirdly, to provide for the erection of a modest headstone over the grave of my husband and myself, and to cover all testamentary expenses. Fourthly, to pay to Eliza Gregson Home in the Township of Smithton, Que., whatever may be required for the maintenance of my husband, Mr. Cedric Hastings, during his lifetime. Fifthly, to divide between my nieces, Camille Cassells and Mabel Cassells (aforementioned) and Beatrice (Mrs. B.M. Thomas), my pictures, trinkets and personal things. All the rest and residue of my estate both Real and Personal, I GIVE, DEVISE AND BEQUEATH unto Eliza Gregson Home in the Township of Smithton in the Province of Quebec absolutely.

With full power and authority to my Executors and Trustees to sell and dispose of all or any part of my Real or Personal estate, where necessary for the carrying out of the purpose of this my will, and to execute any and all documents that may be necessary for so doing.

IN WITNESS WHEREOF I have subscribed these presents at Eliza Gregson Home in the Township of Smithton, this 14th day of September, Nineteen hundred and sixty-five.

SIGNED published and declared by the above-named testatrix as and for her last Will and Testament in the presence of us both present at the same time, who at her request and in her presence have hereunto subscribed our names as witnesses.

Rebecca M. Hastings

(Witnesses)

Name   *Terry Petrie*

Address   *290 Oba St. Sherbrooke*

Name   *Miss Betty McDonald*

Address *Eliza Gregson Home*

(a) When Mrs. Hastings died, her holograph will, written in 1933, would have been valid in Quebec if she had not written later wills. Would it be acceptable now in British Columbia or Ontario?

(b) What is your opinion of the way Mrs. Hastings revised her second will? Do you think the entire will would be valid or only a part of it? If your will needed revision, how would you do it?

(c) Changes occurred during Mrs. Hastings' long life, and some personal possessions listed in her various wills were disposed of before she died. In your opinion, how might this matter of designating the distribution of personal possessions be handled?

(d) How many executors did Mrs. Hastings name in her third will? Were they to act as co-executors or were some of them alternates in case the others were unable or unwilling to act? How many executors and alternates would you suggest that she needed for a very small estate?

3. Ted Andrachuk died without a will, leaving an estate of approximately $65 000. His nearest relatives are his parents, his wife, and his three children.

(a) How would his estate be divided?

(b) His wife is the beneficiary of a $40 000 life insurance policy. Would this be distributed as part of the estate?

(c) He and his wife had a joint bank account. Would this form part of his estate?

(d) He and his wife owned their house as tenants in common. Would all, a part, or none of the house be considered part of his estate?

4. Marie, who lived common-law for 15 years, tells this story:

INTESTACY AND COMMON-LAW SPOUSES

My common-law husband was a wonderful man, but although I tried and tried to get him to make a will, he said he considered wills meaningless pieces of paper. As the years went by, I worried less about this and concentrated on planning our future together. I never gave up my well-paying job because we needed the money. We pooled all our finances to pay current expenses as we raised his three daughters, bought a house, and established a retirement fund.

Suddenly, my husband died, leaving me not only grief-stricken but also penniless. Here I am living alone in a nearly empty apartment with very few of the lovely things we had over the years. Our house is for sale and the antique furniture that I collected as a hobby has been distributed among my husband's grasping family, who never approved of our relationship. I never thought my stepchildren would show such disloyalty to their father that they would do things he never would have wanted.

(a) What can a common-law wife like Marie do to protect her financial security?

(b) Do you think she has a strong case for contesting the distribution of this estate?

(c) If a person dies without a will in your province, does a common-law spouse automatically get a preferential share? Does the length of time the couple have been living common-law make any difference?

5. Mrs. DeMelo has a dependent daughter who is severely handicapped and has a limited capacity to handle financial affairs. Mrs. DeMelo's will leaves her estate in equal shares to this daughter and to her son, but she is wondering whether she should revise her will to establish a testamentary trust for the daughter. Because her son is financially independent and her daughter is not, Mrs. DeMelo proposes leaving her total estate in trust for her daughter, with the residue to go to her son after her daughter's death.

(a) List some factors to be considered in deciding whether to leave the estate in trust for the daughter.

(b) Do you think a testamentary trust would be a wise decision in this case?

(c) Do you see a potential conflict of interest for the son if he is made a trustee?

6. Mr. Schwartz left a will which stated that his estate was to be divided equally among three of his four children. His youngest son George, now 32, with whom he had been on bad terms for some years, was left out of the will. Does the fact that George was the only child excluded from the will form a good basis for him to contest the will?

7. (a) Why does an executor need a trust account?

(b) The main task of an executor is to assemble the assets of the deceased and distribute them to the designated beneficiaries. Why is there so much formality associated with transferring the assets?

(c) If the beneficiaries suspect that an executor is not acting in their best interests, what can they do to check on this?

8. When Mrs. Singh died at an advanced age, it was discovered that her will named her deceased husband as executor. How would this estate be settled, when there is a will but no executor?

9. Maisie had often talked about how she would leave her estate, but after her

death no will could be found. As a result, her estate had to be treated as an intestacy and was administered by her cousin John. Maisie's estate included the following assets:

Cash and deposits of $26 000

House valued at $185 000 which she owned as a tenant in common with her estranged husband

Canada Savings Bonds, worth $5000

Car valued at $8000

Life insurance policy with face value of $38 000, which named her husband as beneficiary

RRSP of $3600

Pension plan credit of $6849

In addition to her estranged, but never divorced, husband, Maisie left a mentally disabled daughter and an elderly mother.

(a) Make a list of the assets that would form part of Maisie's estate.

(b) Using the rules for intestacy for your province, show how this estate would be divided.

(c) Might there be a reason for an application to the Surrogate Court for a change in this division to favour the daughter who is mentally disabled? What information about the family would you need to know to determine if there is a case to be made?

(d) If the husband wanted the house, would it have to be sold or could it go to him?

10. Arrange for a debate on the resolution:

"Resolved that a young couple without children does not need a will."

References

BOOKS

BUDD, JOHN, CLAUDE RINFRET, RICHARD DAW, and DANIELLE BRIEN. *Canadian Guide to Personal Financial Management*. Scarborough, Ontario: Prentice-Hall Canada, annual, 225 pp. Accountants provide guidance on a broad range of topics, including planning finances, estimating insurance needs, managing risk, and determining investment needs. Instructions and the necessary forms for making plans are provided.

COHEN, DIAN. *Money*. Scarborough, Ontario: Prentice-Hall Canada, 1987, 270 pp. An economist suggests strategies for coping with personal finances in the context of changing economic conditions. Topics include financial plans, buying a home, insurance, income tax, retirement, estate planning, and investments.

DRACHE, ARTHUR B. C. and SUSAN WEIDMAN SCHNEIDER. *Head and Heart, Financial Strategies for Smart Women*. Toronto: Macmillan, 1987, 348 pp. Recognizing the needs and perspectives of women, a tax lawyer and journalist have collaborated to present basic financial information, taking into account women's concerns at different stages in their lives.

FORMAN, NORM. *Mind Over Money, Curing Your Financial Headaches with Moneysanity*. Toronto: Doubleday Canada, 1987, 248 pp. A psychologist examines the effects money has on behaviour, looking at the origin of money problems and suggesting therapies to help us to better understand ourselves.

GEORGAS, M. STEPHEN. *Power of Attorney Kit*. Fourth Edition. Vancouver: International Self-Counsel Press, 1991, 40 pp. Instructions and forms for drawing up a power of attorney.

GOTTSELIG, CHERYL. *Wills for Alberta*. Eighth Edition. Vancouver: International Self-Counsel Press, 1992, 128 pp. A lawyer explains the hows and whys of writing a will and some pointers on estate planning.

KRUZENISKI, RONALD and JANE E. GORDON. *Will/Probate Procedure for Manitoba & Saskatchewan*. Fourth Edition. Vancouver: International Self-Counsel Press, 1990, 96 pp. A basic explanation of the terminology and procedures involved in drawing or probating a will.

MACINNIS, LYMAN. *Get Smart! Make Your Money Count in the 1990s*. Second Edition. Scarborough, Ontario: Prentice-Hall Canada, 1989, 317 pp. A book for the general reader that includes financial planning, and income tax principles, but gives major attention to investing in the stock market.

WONG, STEVEN G. *Wills for British Columbia*. Fifteenth Edition. Vancouver: International Self-Counsel Press, 1991, 112 pp. Gives the general reader an explanation of basic processes involved with wills.

WYATT, ELAINE. *The Money Companion, How to Manage Your Money and Achieve Financial Freedom*. Markham, Ontario: Penguin Books, 1991. A guide to personal financial management that focuses on planning, investment strategy, and retirement needs.

WYLIE, BETTY JANE and LYNNE MACFARLANE. *Everywoman's Money Book*. Fourth Edition. Toronto: Key Porter, 1989, 223 pp. A journalist and a stock broker have collaborated on this wide-ranging treatment of a variety of personal finance topics, including women and credit; the budget; insurance; retirement; children; and money.

PART TWO

FINANCIAL SECURITY

The processes of making financial plans to maximize the use of resources during one's lifetime and afterwards were the focus of Part I. An integral part of financial planning is to ensure financial security for oneself and one's dependents. The objective of Part II is to examine, in some depth, a variety of ways to protect financial security, such as buying insurance or increasing net worth. Before becoming too involved with specific information about insurance, pensions, annuities, bonds, and stocks, it is essential to reflect on the necessity for any of them.

Part II begins with an introductory chapter that explains financial security and identifies economic risks; the rest of the chapters in this section are concerned with ways of enhancing financial security by reducing risk. Two chapters explain which risks can be handled by general and life insurance. Next, retirement income, an important aspect of financial security, involves social security programs and private savings, including annuities and registered retirement savings plans. The three final chapters are concerned with saving and investing—indispensable ways of increasing financial security.

CHAPTER FOUR

Economic Risks and Financial Security

1. To explain what is meant by financial security.

2. To explain how the need for financial security affects decisions about the use of economic resources, e.g., saving for the future or selecting insurance.

3. To identify events that pose economic risks for individuals or families.

4. To differentiate between assuming risk and sharing risk.

5. To distinguish between steps an individual can take to enhance financial security and the means provided by society to do so.

6. To identify: (i) threats to financial security posed by a serious disability, and (ii) ways to alleviate the consequences of disability.

7. To analyze the meaning of disability as defined by various insurers.

8. To identify important features in disability insurance coverage.

Introduction

Maintaining a feeling of financial security, or assurance that we can cope with whatever may happen, is of prime concern to everyone. This feeling of security can be enhanced if we know what our economic risks are, and can take steps to reduce their consequences. Life is full of economic risk, but sometimes we fail to recognize the particular risks that most threaten our economic well-being. Perhaps that explains why some people buy life insurance regardless of whether they need it, and why others who really need the protection fail to buy it. This chapter helps to identify those economic risks that pose the greatest threats to personal welfare, and suggests ways to minimize them. Certain risks, such as the untimely death of a person with dependents, or theft or damage of personal property, may be shared through the purchase of insurance. We have social programs (e.g., Old Age Security, Canada/Quebec Pension Plan, Unemployment Insurance, welfare) to minimize the effects of some events, such as loss of income. The risk of becoming disabled and unable to earn a living is a serious one that is too often ignored.

The chapters that follow this one consider in some detail several important ways to reduce economic risk, such as insuring your possessions or your life, planning for retirement income, and saving and investing to build up your net worth.

FINANCIAL SECURITY

What do we mean by financial security? You will experience a feeling of **financial security** if you are confident that you will have the economic means to meet your needs in the present and in the future. As there are many conceptions of what is needed for a satisfactory level of living, so there are many notions of what constitutes financial security. Your feelings about risk as well as your economic situation will have much to do with the nature of your concerns about financial security. For instance, a family living on welfare may well consider that having enough money to pay the current bills for food, shelter, and clothing represents financial security for them, while a family living in affluent circumstances may have much more expansive ideas about what is required to maintain their financial security. The latter may feel economically threatened if they have to give up a vacation home, regular holidays, or restaurant meals.

If you feel financially secure, it may be assumed that you feel confident that you will be able to handle the following needs: (i) maintaining your accustomed level of living, (ii) coping with financial emergencies or unusual expenses, and (iii) making provision for loss of income resulting from illness, unemployment, retirement, aging, or disability. By knowing that you are protected from financial threats, you can feel reasonably secure about the future. But is this true for many of us? Who can be certain what our future needs will be or what resources we will have as we move through the various stages in our life cycle?

Both as individuals and as a society, we have taken an increasing interest in ensuring financial security. For one thing, we have become used to a complex level of living with more to protect. For another, our society has changed within a few generations to less economic self-sufficiency and more economic interdependence. In an agrarian society, many families can supply more of their needs outside the market than is possible today. We rely, for the most part, on money income rather home production to support our desired lifestyle; anything that interrupts or halts the flow of income is a serious threat. In response to social changes, government-sponsored programs have been instituted to provide partial financial security for the young, the old, the disabled, the unemployed, and the poor. Since most of us want more than partial financial security, we must take steps to protect ourselves against a variety of economic risks.

ECONOMIC RISKS

Before we can make any plans to enhance our financial security we must first identify what events pose economic risks for us. The list of risks will not be identical for everyone, nor the same at all stages of our lives. If you do not own a house, you will not face the risk of it burning down; if you do not have dependent children, you will not have to worry about the risk of being unable to support them; if you do not own a car, damage to it is not one of your risks. It is essential to remember that economic risks and our ideas about financial security are changing constantly as our lives change. Most of our economic risks can be categorized as:

(a) loss of income

    —destruction of earning capacity

    —loss of market for your services

(b) unexpected large expenses

    —destruction of property

    —illness or death

    —personal liability

(c) loss in value of capital

    —drop in market value

    —inflation

Loss of Income

Anything that causes the income stream to stop poses a very serious threat to economic security. As long as your income continues, there is some possibility of coping with unexpected expenses or loss of capital, but without a regular income it is difficult to obtain enough resources. The reasons for termination of income are usually either the destruction of your earning capacity or the disappearance of the market for your services.

DESTRUCTION OF EARNING CAPACITY   Ability to earn income may be lost temporarily through illness, or permanently through disability, aging, or death. Of these, permanent disability presents a particularly serious risk. Not only would you be unable to work, you would have to be supported and might also need expensive care. Our social mechanisms for this financial burden have not been as fully developed as those for aging or death, perhaps because we all expect to get older and to die, but not to be disabled.

LOSS OF MARKET FOR YOUR SERVICES   The self-employed must consider the prospect that the market for their goods or services may disappear, leaving them without income. If at all possible, they will need to change what they produce. Employees may find that their services are no longer needed because the demand for particular skills has fallen, because economic conditions have reduced economic activity, or for a number of other reasons. Employees, like the self-employed, may have to acquire new skills to fit into the labour market again.

Unexpected Large Expenses

Many kinds of unexpected large expenses that may threaten financial security, but only three will be discussed here:

(a) destruction or loss of personal property,

(b) illness and death,

(c) personal liability.

DESTRUCTION OF PROPERTY   The more we own, the greater the risk of loss or destruction of our possessions. Loss can be the result of many factors, such as theft, fire, or weather. Should a family lose their house and all the contents through fire, they would probably be unable to replace everything from their own resources; for this reason they buy home insurance.

ILLNESS AND DEATH   Many, but not all, of the large expenses associated with illness and death have been shared through our health insurance program. However, the home care of a person who is ill for a long time can be very expensive and some or all of this expense may have to be borne by the family. Therefore, some personal resources may be needed in addition to health insurance and other social programs.

PERSONAL LIABILITY   Any one of us could face a very large unexpected expense if found liable for damage or injury because of negligence. We are probably most aware of this in relation to our cars, because of the potential for destruction and death from a moment's inattention while driving. This concept will be more fully developed in the chapter on general insurance.

Loss in Value of Capital

Things you own can lose value because of a reduction in the demand for them. If a highway is built close to your house, if interest in a certain artist wanes, or if no one wants your mining stocks, your capital—in the form of a house, painting, or shares—diminishes through no action of yours.

Inflation affects various assets differently; some lose value and others gain it. The value of money saved in deposits tends to suffer substantial loss during inflationary times. For instance, a dollar earned in 1970 and saved (ignoring interest) until 1990 would buy only 26 percent of what it had 20 years earlier, a loss of about three-quarters of its purchasing power. That is why it should have been invested to earn a return at least as great as the inflation rate, and preferably greater. Real property, on the other hand, appreciated greatly during this inflationary period.

What Are Your Economic Risks?

Make a list of economic risks that could threaten your financial security this year. Which events might cause a loss of income, even for a time? What are some unexpected large expenses that would create hardship? How much of your net worth is at risk from price changes? Next, assign priorities to your list so that you can make plans to handle these risks.

Second, make a list of future economic risks—issues that are not current concerns but may be at another time—such as insufficient retirement income and inability to support children or other relatives.

Need for Savings

Even if you are fortunate enough to go through life without a disability, a major illness, or unemployment, you will probably retire sometime. When you do, your employment income will stop and you will become dependent on pensions and investment earnings. Unless you spend your work years with the same employer, preferably a government or large and successful company, you may find that your work pension will not support you in the style you would wish. Public pensions will help, but many people find retirement much more comfortable if they have private investment income as well. However, before you get any investment income, you have to save some money and invest it.

HANDLING RISK

Having identified your economic risks, the next step is to decide what to do about them. Essentially there are three possibilities:

(a) try to prevent the event from happening,

(b) assume the risk yourself,

(c) share the risk with others.

The task of thinking of ways to reduce or prevent risks is left to you. Some possibilities for assuming and sharing risk are outlined here, but the concept will be more fully developed in subsequent chapters on general insurance, life insurance, and annuities.

Assuming Risk

If you have enough financial resources, you can assume your own risks; that is, you can handle unfortunate events without jeopardizing your level of living. You expect to have the funds to cope with unemployment, an unexpected large expense, illness, or retirement. Accumulating net worth is clearly one way of preparing to handle whatever risks come your way. That is why all advice on financial planning stresses saving for unforeseen needs, emergencies, and retirement.

Another way a family can assume risk is to expect individuals to help each other. When one earner is unable to work, someone else in the family may be able to support the household. Two-income families have spread the risk of something happening to the income stream. Nevertheless, most of us are unable to assume all potential risks, and must depend on some risk-sharing.

Sharing Risk

When a risk is too much for individuals or families to bear alone, it may be shared through private insurance or social income security programs. By collecting small contributions from many people, a fund is created sufficient to compensate those few people who experience the unfortunate event. For example, all car owners contribute to car insurance, but only those who have accidents draw on the fund. Participants in risk-sharing programs enhance their financial security by the knowledge that compensation is available if they should require it.

PRIVATE EFFORTS   Through general insurance, the risks of loss or damage to personal property, as well as personal liability, are shared. Life insurance is designed to protect against the risk of the premature death of a person with dependents. Annuities, by turning capital into an income stream guaranteed for life, protect against the risk of living so long that there are no savings left.

PUBLIC PROGRAMS   Our public income security programs are based on risk-sharing, one way or another. The Canada and Quebec Pension Plans and Unemployment Insurance are social insurance programs to which most employed people make contributions, and eligibility for benefits depends on having been a contributor. These programs offer protection against the risks of unemployment, disability, aging, and death. There are others, such as Old Age Security and social welfare, which we fund through taxes rather than direct contributions. In this way, those in the labour force provide support for those who are old, or are unable to work.

In addition to these income security programs, society takes other steps to help us plan for our own financial security. The income tax system encourages retirement planning by offering tax deductions if we invest in RRSPs and contribute to employment-related pension plans.

DISABILITY — A SERIOUS RISK

In this chapter, brief mention will be made of personal disability, a very significant economic risk that we too often ignore. A common hazard is the loss of our ability to earn a living because of temporary or permanent disability due to an accident or an illness. The following case study, based on a real situation, illustrates the disastrous effect that permanent disability can have on a family's financial security.

HIS LIFE WAS CHANGED BY A FALL

Simon, a self-employed mason, fell 15 metres from a scaffold, injuring himself so badly that after months in hospital he still lives in constant pain and walks with difficulty. He can't lift or carry anything. Fortunately, he was covered by Workers' Compensation, which entitles him to a small pension, but inexplicably he was classified as 25 percent disabled. Two years after the accident, Simon was still negotiating with Canada Pension about the extent of his disability. His first application was rejected because of the possibility that he might be able to return to work. He has now applied again.

At 40, Simon is unable to work to support his wife and three teen-aged children. He gave up his business, sold the house, and they lived on their savings as long as they lasted. The cheque from Workers' Compensation is just large enough to pay the rent on a subsidized apartment. The small amount Simon gets from welfare is insufficient to buy the family's food. Applying for disability benefits involves considerable red tape and waiting, as Simon has discovered. Simon's fall drastically changed life for himself and his family.

Although the probability of suffering a disability is greater than that of dying for those under the age of 65, people are more likely to have life insurance than disability insurance. The gender differences in the probability of being disabled for more than six months between the ages of 25 and 55 are illustrated in Figure 4.1. Females in this age group face a significantly greater risk of being disabled than dying, but have a lower mortality rate than males of the same age. Experience has shown that anyone

FIGURE 4.1   PROBABILITY OF DEATH OR LONG-TERM DISABILITY (OVER SIX MONTHS) OCCURRING WITHIN A YEAR, BY GENDER

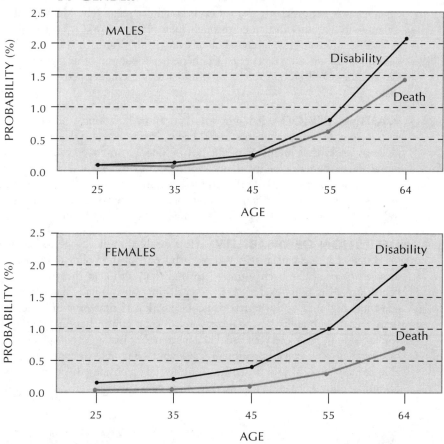

SOURCE: Mutual Life's group insurance data. Reproduced with the permission of Mutual Life of Canada.

who is disabled for more than three months will probably still be disabled five years later. The risk of becoming disabled is one that most of us are financially unable to assume alone. How many young people, or even older ones, have enough savings to support themselves for a year or more?

To protect ourselves against the risk of becoming disabled we can purchase **disability insurance**, sometimes called income replacement insurance. Otherwise we will have to depend on others to support us—our families or the social welfare system.

Disability Insurance

Disability insurance may be purchased privately, or more cheaply through a group policy. When an insurance company insures a group of employees in one policy, the coverage will be less costly than if each bought it separately. Many employees have some group disability insurance through their place of work. It is critical to find out exactly what coverage you have. Policies vary in the waiting period, the definition of disability, the amount of benefits, the benefit period, and other options. The cost of the coverage will be dependent on the features included; better benefits will cost more.

WAITING PERIOD   It is important to know how long you must be unable to work before disability payments would begin. If you have sick-leave coverage at your place of work, that might or might not be enough to cover you until the income replacement benefits begin. If not, you may have to wait several months before receiving any payments. Policies can have waiting periods as short as one week or as long as four months. Consider how long you could survive before benefits started and, to keep the premium cost down, choose the longest waiting period you could manage.

DEFINITION OF DISABILITY   How disabled must you be to become eligible for benefits? It is essential that you read this part of the policy very carefully; many disabled people have been surprised to find that, although they had insurance, the definition of disability excluded them. A distinction is usually made between partial and total disability, and whether you could work part-time or at an occupation other than your usual one. By paying more you can get a policy that provides benefits until you are able to return to your usual occupation. For instance, consider a teacher who has suffered some voice impairment. He might be unable to continue teaching, but able to do a clerical job. Since he would not be considered totally disabled, some disability policies would not provide support for him because he appears able to handle different work.

COLLECTING DISABILITY BENEFITS CAN BE DIFFICULT

A decade ago, Karen was happily employed as a nursing assistant in a Nova Scotia hospital when disaster struck. While she was lifting a heavy patient she had a heart attack that left her with a poorly functioning heart. Various medications and treatments added to her miseries and disability. After a 27-year career, Karen was no longer able to work as a nursing assistant.

She applied for benefits under her income replacement group insurance. To her surprise, the insurance company refused her claim on the grounds that she did not qualify as totally and permanently disabled so as to be unable to work at some occupation, not necessarily nursing. She took her case to court and eventually received a settlement.

AMOUNT OF BENEFITS   Even if you obtain the most coverage you can afford, at best it will probably amount to only 60–70 percent of your usual income. No insurance company will offer a policy that would make it profitable for anyone to become disabled. For an additional premium, it may be possible to have a policy that would index benefits to inflation.

BENEFIT PERIOD   What limits are there on the benefit period? Policies may restrict benefits to a few weeks, one year, or until reaching age 65. Again, you will want the longest benefit period you can afford.

RENEWABILITY   Is there a clause in the policy that guarantees that it is non-cancellable or renewable? You would not want to find, as you get older, that the company will not renew your policy.

Social Support for the Disabled

Are there social programs for which you might be eligible if you became disabled? Eligibility requirements may be that you contributed to the program previously or the disability resulted from an injury on the job or during military service. Following is a list of the major social supports for disability:

(a) **Unemployment Insurance**—a federal program that provides short-term benefits to contributors.

(b) **The Canada and Quebec Pension Plans**—a disability pension for contributors with a severe or prolonged disability, and their dependents and survivors.

(c) **Workers' Compensation**—provincial plans that offer medical, financial, and rehabilitative assistance to workers who become disabled by accidents or illness related to their jobs.

(d) **Short-term or Long-term Welfare**—municipal and provincial programs for those with few other resources.

Summary

Financial security is something we take for granted when things are going well, actively endeavour to protect if threatened, and vigorously try to regain if lost. It is a feeling of assurance that we have the capacity to maintain our desired level of living. Prudent people take steps to protect their financial security as much as possible from those economic risks that can result in loss of income or unexpected large expenditures. This can be done by trying to reduce some risks, assuming others, and sharing the largest risks with a group. The latter is the underlying principle of all forms of insurance. A serious, but much neglected, risk is the possibility of becoming disabled.

This chapter has perhaps alerted you to economic risks that could be threatening to your financial security at some time in your life, but has not specified exactly what you can do to protect yourself. Subsequent chapters will address in detail the protection offered by general insurance and life insurance, private and public pensions, and annuities. Net worth, which is helpful in any financial crisis, is achieved by regular saving and wise investing.

Vocabulary Review

disability insurance (p. 97)   financial security (p. 91)

Problems

1.

WHEN DISASTER STRUCK

Six years ago, Luke and Vera never imagined that they would be in such dire straits financially as to have to apply for welfare. He was a self-employed, skilled construction worker who was making a good income when suddenly he developed a heart condition that required open-heart surgery. Complications developed, and after extended hospitalization Luke went home, but was not well enough to work. His doctor advised him that any physical activity could cause a coronary.

The stress of Luke's illness, the financial problems, and having to look after the home and children on her own caused a gastric condition that made Vera miserable and not well enough to go out to work. If she did, who would look after the children, who were 5, 4 years, and ten months old?

When Luke stopped working they had $2000 in the bank, and had built up about $10 000 equity in the semi-detached home they were buying. They did not apply for welfare because they were afraid they would have to sell their house and car, so they lived on their savings as long as they could. Being self-employed, Luke was not covered by Unemployment Insurance, but he had been paying into the Canada Pension Plan. He had once thought about disability insurance but decided against it because of the high premiums. In addition to regular living expenses, costly drugs were needed for Luke, and a special formula for the baby, who was allergic to milk.

Finally this family became so desperate that they called Social Services. They were immediately put on short-term welfare that included a waiver of their health insurance premium, free prescription drugs and dental care, and an allowance for the special diet. They were advised to see their bank about the mortgage payment that was one month in arrears to ask that it be deferred and the mortgage extended a month. They discovered to their surprise that welfare applicants are allowed to have a car and a few assets, and that if they had applied sooner, they could have kept their savings in the bank.

    (a) Can you think of anything this family could have done to be better prepared for such an economic disaster?

    (b) Should they be applying for disability benefits from the Canada Pension Plan?

    (c) Do you have any other suggestions for ways they could obtain more resources?

2. Interview people you know and compare two families who have quite different ideas of what financial security means to them.

3. At what stage in the life cycle do you think economic risks are most threatening?

4. Make a list of four or five economic risks that could threaten your financial security right now. What changes in your economic risks do you foresee occurring over the next five years?

5. Make a list of several features that it would be desirable to include in a disability insurance policy. Which of these would add to the premium cost?

6. Why do you think people tend to neglect protection for the risk of becoming disabled?

7. In this chapter we have mentioned a variety of economic risks, and suggested various ways to minimize the effects of each. As an aid in summarizing this information, complete the following chart. In addition to the material in this chapter you should be able to draw on your general knowledge. The first and last lines have been filled in as examples.

Economic risks	Ways To Handle Economic Risks		
	As an individual or family member	As an employee	As a citizen
A. LOSS OF INCOME			
1. Earning capacity destroyed (a) temporarily (e.g., illness)	*Use savings. Income of another family member.*	*Sick leave with pay*	*Health insurance*
(b) permanently —disability			
—aging			
—death			
2. Market for earner's services destroyed (a) unemployment			
(b) fall in profits for self-employed			
B. UNEXPECTED LARGE EXPENSES 1. Destruction or loss of personal property			
2. Illness, death			
3. Personal liability			
C. LOSS OF VALUE OF CAPITAL 1. Drop in market value (e.g., house, stock)	*Diversify assets*	*n/a*	*n/a*
2. Price changes (e.g., inflation)	*Diversify assets*	*n/a*	*n/a*

8. Evaluate the following long-term disability plan, which covers one group of employees. How effective do you think it will be in meeting the needs of employees who become disabled?

Benefits: 66 2/3 percent of basic monthly earnings, to a maximum of $3500. This will be reduced by any amount to which you are entitled from Workers' Compensation or Canada Pension (benefits for dependents are excluded). The employer will supplement this at 13 1/3 percent of the basic salary for a period of 4 months, to a maximum of 80 percent of your basic earnings.

Waiting Period: Benefits begin on the 91st consecutive day of total disability.

Benefit Period: until age 65 for total disability; two years for a temporary disability that prevents you from performing the duties of your occupation. Benefits are payable beyond two years if you are disabled to the extent that you cannot engage in any occupation for which you are or could reasonably become qualified as determined by your doctor.

9. Decide whether you AGREE or DISAGREE with each of the following statements.

(a) What you already possess affects your concept of financial security.

(b) Unemployment Insurance protects against the risk of personal liability.

(c) You have to contribute to the Canada/Quebec Pension Plan or Unemployment Insurance to become eligible for disability benefits.

(d) Unemployment Insurance will assist a family when the breadwinner dies suddenly.

(e) For those aged 30, the probability of becoming disabled (for more than three months) is greater than the probability of dying.

(f) Social programs tend to provide income support for those unable to work, but leave individuals to arrange their own protection for risks to property or capital.

10. Try to find out the cost of buying disability insurance privately for 25-year-old employed males and females. If possible, compare this to the cost of group protection.

References

BOOKS

BUDD, JOHN, CLAUDE RINFRET, RICHARD DAW, and DANIELLE BRIEN. *Canadian Guide to Personal Financial Management*. Scarborough, Ontario: Prentice-Hall Canada, annual, 225 pp. Accountants provide guidance on a broad range of topics, including planning finances, estimating insurance needs, managing risk, and determining investment needs. Instructions and the necessary forms for making plans are provided.

COHEN, DIAN. *Money*. Scarborough, Ontario: Prentice-Hall Canada, 1987, 270 pp. An economist suggests strategies for coping with personal finances in the context of changing economic conditions. Topics include financial plans, buying a home, insurance, income tax, retirement, estate planning, and investments.

MATTHEWS, BETSY and RICHARD BIRCH. *Taking Care of Tomorrow: The Canadian Money Book for Prime Time Women*. Toronto: McGraw-Hill Ryerson, 1992, 230 pp. A practical guide that deals with financial needs and realities of women in different social and financial circumstances.

WYATT, ELAINE. *The Money Companion, How to Manage Your Money and Achieve Financial Freedom*. Markham, Ontario: Penguin Books, 1991. A guide to personal financial management that focuses on planning, investment strategy, and retirement needs.

CHAPTER FIVE

General Insurance

OBJECTIVES

1. To identify:

   (a) the major financial risks associated with owning a house and its contents, personal possessions, or an automobile,

   (b) the appropriate type of insurance coverage for each risk.

2. To understand and demonstrate applications of the following basic insurance principles:

   (a) sharing risk,

   (b) indemnification,

   (c) subrogation,

   (d) co-insurance.

3. To distinguish between:

   (a) pure cost of insurance and loading charge,

   (b) premium and policy,

   (c) insurable interest and insurable risk,

   (d) insured and insurer,

   (e) actual cash value and replacement value,

   (f) deductible and policy limits,

   (g) scheduled property rider and clause covering possessions taken from home,

   (h) named-peril and all-risks coverage.

4. To explain the different functions of an:

   (a) actuary,

   (b) insurance agent,

   (c) insurance broker,

   (d) adjuster,

   (e) claims department.

5. To ascertain, from reading an insurance policy, the risks that are:
   (a) covered, and (b) excluded.

6. To identify some of the factors insurers consider when settling claims.

7. To explain how the concept of negligence affects insurance claims.

8. To explain these terms: depreciation, rider or endorsement, short rate, accident benefits.

Introduction

The analysis of financial security in Chapter 4 led to the conclusion that some risks can be minimized by purchasing insurance. This chapter identifies economic risks that are of concern to anyone owning real property or personal possessions, explains the basic concepts and principles of general insurance, and examines in detail three types of general insurance: property insurance, personal liability insurance, and automobile insurance. Life insurance, which is not considered a type of general insurance, is discussed in the next chapter.

THE ECONOMIC RISKS OF OWNERSHIP

Two types of risk are associated with ownership: (i) the property itself may be damaged, destroyed, or lost, and (ii) anyone may be held responsible for damage or injury to others or their possessions because of what they do or own. Fire and theft are examples of the first type of risk. The second type of risk is known as a personal liability risk, and is perhaps less easily understood than the former. A person may have a financial responsibility (or liability) if their car, dog, or broken steps cause damage or injury, although it is usually necessary for those making the claim to prove that there was negligence. Liability risks need not be related to ownership; careless behaviour can also create liability.

Damage or Loss of Property

Both tenants and home owners must consider the risk that their furnishings and other possessions may be stolen or damaged by fire, and owners must consider the possibility that their houses may burn. Damage to or loss of a car is another risk to consider, but a less serious one than being responsible for injury to other people. At the very worst one would be left without a car, but not burdened with a monstrous debt for many years.

Liability for Damages

Being found responsible, because of negligence, for damage to the lives or property of others is one of the risks anyone may be exposed to. Here we are not speaking about damage to yourself or your possessions, but claims against you by others for their losses. A tenant may be held responsible for damage to rented premises. If, for instance, the tenant's careless smoking or forgetfulness in using a cooking or heating appliance was the cause of an apartment fire, the landlord's insurer would reimburse the landlord for the damage to the building, but would probably bill the tenant for the cost of the repairs. The extent the tenant's liability would depend on the circumstances.

A home owner faces the risk that his walks, yards, trees, and so on may cause injury. His tree may fall on the neighbour's car, or someone may fall on his broken steps. An automobile owner faces the serious risk of being liable for a death or an injury, with enormous financial consequences. Recent Canadian settlements for personal injury in automobile accidents have been as high as several million dollars. Cars can also damage other people's cars or property, but these claims are usually less than those for personal injury.

Most of us consider the risks outlined above to be too great to accept entirely on our own, and therefore we buy insurance to share the risks with others. In fact, society considers the liability risks associated with car ownership so serious that insurance coverage is often mandatory. Before going on to examine various types of insurance, it is necessary to understand a few basic insurance concepts and principles.

BASIC CONCEPTS AND PRINCIPLES

The Insurance Principle

Since a major fire or auto accident can financially cripple an individual or family, methods have been devised to spread the risk. If a large number of people who face a common risk pool their money, there will be sufficient funds to compensate the few who actually experience the disaster. This sharing or **pooling risk** is the basic principle on which all types of insurance are based. However, it depends on the law of large numbers and will not work for a small group. The insurance companies that collect, manage, and disperse the pooled funds employ specialized mathematicians called **actuaries** to predict the probability of a particular event occurring per 1000 people. These predictions can be fairly accurate for large numbers of people or events, but they cannot, of course, identify which persons will be affected in a particular year. The amount each person contributes to the insurance pool or fund depends on:

(a) the probability of the event occurring,

(b) the cost of compensation,

(c) the number sharing the risk.

The following simplified example illustrates this principle.

SHARING THE RISK

In the town of Bayfield there are 1000 houses, all wooden and of approximately equal value. Past records reveal that, on average, one house burns down each year, and that the cost of rebuilding a house is approximately $100 000. It is not necessary to take into account the value of the land on which the house stands because fire does not destroy the lot.

The loss of a house is such a serious disaster that the community does not expect the affected family to cope alone. In the nineteenth century it was customary for neighbours to come to the rescue, providing temporary shelter for the homeless family while they felled logs and sawed boards to construct a new house. Now the scarcity of trees and the complexity of house construction has caused the house-building bee to be abandoned in favour of property insurance.

How large a fund will be needed in Bayfield to cover the fire losses to houses?

Number of home owners sharing the risk:....................1000
Probability of fire: ....1 per 1000/year
Cost of compensation: $100 000

If each owner contributes $100 per year, there will be a fund of $100 000. At the end of a typical year, with one claim for $100 000, the fund will be exhausted.

To summarize, the principle of sharing risk works when a large number of people are willing to pay a regular fee that is certain, in exchange for protection against a hazard that is uncertain. This means that those who experience a loss will be compensated and that those fortunate enough not to have had a loss will not need to claim anything from the insurance fund. Nevertheless, all will have enhanced their financial security by having insurance.

Factors Affecting Cost

The cost of property insurance, as we have said, depends on the probability of a particular peril occurring, the cost of compensation, and the number of people sharing the risk. In practice, actuaries take into consideration more complex factors than those in the above example. The probability of fire and the extent of damage are affected by the availability of fire-fighting facilities, the proximity of hazards such as paint factories or oil storage tanks, and the inflammability of the house. The cost of compensation depends on the value of the property to be repaired or replaced, which can vary considerably in the case of houses.

Once the probability of the event occurring has been established and the cost of compensation estimated, an actuary can determine the cost of covering this risk, which is called the **pure cost of insurance**. To this amount will be added a **loading charge** to cover the costs the insurance company incurs in collecting and managing the insurance funds, settling the claims, and returning profits to the company's shareholders. Not surprisingly, the estimates of all these costs vary from company to company. The charge to insure a property, called a **premium**, will be paid at regular intervals to keep the insurance in force.

Risk Management

INSURABLE INTEREST It is impossible to buy insurance against a risk unless it can be shown that the buyer has an **insurable interest** in the risk in question. In other words, would the buyer suffer a financial loss if the event occurred? An owner of property has an insurable interest in the possibility of it being stolen or destroyed, but a relative or friend who has no legal relation to the property cannot insure it. This principle applies to all types of insurance, including life insurance.

INSURABLE RISKS Insurance is concerned with **insurable risks** only; these risks result from chance events and are not caused by deliberate action on the part of the person insured. If a fire starts because of lightning, it is a chance risk, but if the fire was started by the property owner, it is not. Insurance companies have to be sure of the cause of the damage before settling the claim.

HANDLING RISK Three possible ways of dealing with insurable risks are:

(a) taking steps to eliminate or reduce the risk,

(b) preparing to handle the loss oneself,

(c) sharing the risk with others.

An example of reducing risk of injury from fire would be to install smoke detectors in the home. The risk of theft could be reduced by improving the locks on the doors and windows. Some people decide to handle some risks themselves if the risk is not too high and their financial resources are adequate. A person who decides not to buy collision coverage on an old car is accepting the risk of destruction of the car instead of sharing it by buying insurance. Sharing risks through insurance is prudent whenever the possible loss would be too heavy to handle alone. In planning for financial security, it may be wise to use a combination of these three options. Most people probably need some insurance, but they may be able to reduce the cost if they take steps to minimize the risk and assume some portion of the risk themselves.

The Insurance Contract

A person deciding to purchase insurance may contact an **agent** who represents a single insurance company or a **broker** who represents several companies. The broker is able to do comparison shopping for the client among the several companies he or she represents to find the most economical and most appropriate coverage.

A buyer applying for insurance completes an application form and receives an explanation of the policy from the agent. Generally, purchasers are more likely to be given a complete copy of a home insurance policy than an automobile policy.

Perhaps that is because, in some provinces, there is a standard car insurance policy for the whole province, irrespective of insurance company.

The legal contract or agreement between the person buying insurance, the **insured,** and the insurance company, the **insurer,** is called a **policy.** Traditionally, policies have been written in legal language that is difficult to understand, but some insurers are now writing their policies in a more simplified form. Find a home insurance policy for practice reading. A policy will seem less daunting if you begin by identifying the following main components:

(a) preamble or declaration sheet,

(b) insuring agreement,

(c) statutory and policy conditions,

(d) endorsements or riders.

INSURANCE TERMINOLOGY

Policy—the contract between the insured and the insurance company that specifies the terms of the agreement.

Premium—the regular payment made for insurance coverage.

Insured—the person whose risks are covered by the insurance, usually the purchaser.

Insurer—the insurance company.

Peril—a risk of some damage or injury.

Endorsement or **rider**—a statement appended to an insurance policy that may specify additional coverage and a change in ownership or in risk.

DECLARATION SHEET   The preamble, or declaration sheet, is a separate page that is filled in for each insurance buyer, giving the names of insurer and insured, the dates the insurance will be in effect, the amounts paid, and the risks to be covered in the agreement. Without this sheet, it is impossible to know what coverage the insured has bought. The page can be easily identified because the spaces in it have been filled in by writing or typing.

The rest of the policy consists of several printed pages that the company routinely uses for all similar risks. For instance, the company may have a standard fire insurance policy that can be adjusted to fit individual requirements by the selections made on the declaration sheet. If the space beside a risk on the declaration sheet is not filled in, that risk is not covered in that particular agreement. When reading a policy, first determine what coverage is on the declaration sheet, and then locate the sections of the policy's printed portion that are relevant.

INSURING AGREEMENT The printed part of the policy will contain an insuring agreement, setting out which kinds of property are covered, which perils are insured against, the exclusions or situations not covered by the policy, and the circumstances under which insurance settlements are made.

POLICY CONDITIONS Statutory and policy conditions include statements about the responsibilities of the insurer and the insured, including misrepresentation, termination of the policy, requirements after a loss, and fraud.

ENDORSEMENTS Insurance policies may be modified by the use of an **endorsement** or **rider**, which is a statement appended to the contract. Some examples of possible riders include a change in the ownership of the property, a change in the risk situation of the property owner, or an additional coverage.

HOW TO READ A POLICY

Examine a home insurance policy to find the answers to these questions.

1. *Who* is covered?
2. *What* property is covered?
3. What *perils* are covered?
4. *Where* does the coverage apply?
5. What are the *exclusions*? (These may apply to who is covered, the perils not covered, or the location where coverage applies.)
6. What are the *extensions* of the coverage?
7. What are the *conditions* of coverage? For example:
   (a) What must the insured do to have coverage continue?
   (b) What must the insured do if there is a loss?
   (c) What must the insured do to recover a loss?

CANCELLATION The insured, may cancel a policy at any time, but the insurer may choose to retain a portion of the premium calculated at the **short rate.** This means that the insurer keeps more than the prorated share of the premium. For instance, if a one-year policy was cancelled after six months, the refund would be less than one half of the premium paid.

Insurance Settlements

CLAIMS PROCESS After a loss has occurred, it is the insured's responsibility to provide proof of the loss. Specialists called **adjusters,** who are either on the regular staff of the insurance company or working independently for a number of companies, immediately go to the scene of the misfortune to begin estimating the extent of the damage. They report their results to the claims department of the insurance company, which negotiates a settlement. It should be noted that agents and brokers have little, if any, part in the claims procedure.

There are two approaches to determining the amount of an insurance settlement: (i) actual cash value (indemnification), or (ii) replacement value. Traditionally, most claims were settled using the principle of cash value or indemnification but in recent years insurers have offered replacement value coverage. Actual cash value coverage will be considered first.

ACTUAL CASH VALUE   Property insurance, but not life insurance, is based on the principle of indemnifying the insured for a loss. **Indemnification** is compensation for the insured at such a level that the insured will be returned to approximately the same financial position enjoyed before the loss, because it is not intended that anyone should profit from an insurance settlement. The concept of indemnification sounds simple, but in practice it may not be easy to determine exactly what the previous financial position of the insured was in regard to the lost or damaged property.

Some property insurance policies promise to indemnify on the basis of the **actual cash value** of the property at the date of the loss, which is the cost of replacing it less the use already received from it. Therefore, it is the cash value when the loss occurred that is significant, not the value of the property when it was bought, or when it was insured.

There are various methods of arriving at the actual cash value, but a common one is to determine the **replacement value** of the loss and then deduct any accumulated depreciation. The replacement value of a house is the cost of rebuilding it, not what it might have sold for. The replacement value of a household possession is the cost of buying a similar new one. **Depreciation** is the monetary value that has been used up since the item was new. Different objects wear out at different rates because of characteristics of the object or the way it was used or cared for. Insurance companies have tables of standard rates of depreciation for many household goods. The adjusters may adapt these rates somewhat to allow for especially good care or very hard usage. The well-established rates of depreciation of cars are found in tables possessed by most automobile dealers. The way to calculate actual cash value is shown in the example, "Actual Cash Value."

ACTUAL CASH VALUE

A small fire in Vickie's living room damaged her sofa and some chairs beyond repair. When she bought the furniture five years ago, she paid $800, but to replace it now would cost about $1200. The insurance adjuster explained to her that the actual cash value of her loss would be calculated as follows:

Actual cash value = replacement cost – depreciation
$$= \$1200 - (.30 \times \$1200)$$
$$= \$1200 - \$360$$
$$= \$840$$

Vickie was surprised to discover that the insurance settlement would be too small to replace her furniture. When she complained to the adjuster that this furniture had been perfectly good before the fire, she was told that she was not making allowance for the five years' use she had already had from it.

The insurance adjuster had allowed 10 percent depreciation the first year and 5 percent each subsequent year. Vickie's policy promised that she would be indemnified for a loss, which does not mean replacing used furniture with new.

The insurer has the option of offering:

(a) a cash settlement,

(b) a similar article to replace the damaged one,

(c) to repair the damaged article.

If the repair results in an improvement of the property, the value of the betterment is charged to the insured. In addition to the factors mentioned, the condition of the property and the standard of maintenance affects the estimated cash value. In the case of a building that has been destroyed or damaged, the insurer usually settles by paying for the repair or rebuilding, but does not take possession of the property.

In cases of partial loss, the insured might be reimbursed for a total loss but any **salvage value** of the damaged property belongs to the insurance company. For instance, if a heavily damaged car is replaced by the insurer, the owner would have no claim on the remnants of the smashed car; it would belong to the insurance company as salvage. To retain the salvage, the owner must pay the insurer for it.

REPLACEMENT VALUE INSURANCE Although it has been traditional to indemnify the insured on the basis of actual cash value, in recent years insurers have offered replacement value insurance, agreeing to replace used possessions with similar new ones. This practice increases the cost of compensation and consequently the premium charged. Replacement value insurance does not follow the classical principle of indemnification of losses because the replacement of used furniture with new may leave the insured in a better position than before the loss. Replacement value insurance is now very popular and some companies report that it predominates over actual cash value coverage. Claimants, pleased to receive settlements that enable them to replace lost articles without considering depreciation, are willing to pay the higher premiums.

INSURER'S LIABILITY   The insured is entitled to compensation for personal loss, but this amount can never be greater than the **policy limits** purchased. A $80 000 fire insurance policy limits the insurer's liability on this contract to $80 000. For any claim, the insurer will pay the lesser of the policy limits, the actual cash value of the loss, or the cost of repairs. If it is a replacement value policy, the insurer will pay the lesser of the policy limits or the replacement value. A person who had a loss valued at $7000 but with a policy limit of $5000 would receive $5000. In the case of automobiles, the insurer's liability is the lesser of the actual cash value or the cost of repairs.

Small claims are expensive for an insurance company to handle, and it is customary to offer the insured the opportunity to pay a lower premium and carry a certain amount of the risk himself. If the insured agrees to assume responsibility for the first $200 of damages, this contract is said to have a **deductible clause** of $200. Obviously, the higher the deductible the lower the premium.

SUBROGATION   When an insurer indemnifies a claimant for a loss, the insurer is entitled to attempt to recover damages from any other persons who may have been responsible for the loss—a procedure called **subrogation.** For instance, if a tenant is responsible for fire damage in an apartment, the insurer of the building may indemnify the landlord and then by subrogation attempt to collect from the tenant who caused the damage.

PROPERTY INSURANCE

In the interests of clarity, this discussion of property insurance will be limited to coverage on personal possessions, houses, and liability, and will look at each type separately. However, in practice, coverage for several risks is often combined in one policy, as for example home owners' or tenants' policies.

The Risks

The many perils that may befall a house or its contents can be categorized as either: (i) accidental, or (ii) the result of criminal actions. Such perils as fire, smoke, water, windstorm, and falling objects are accidental damage; vandalism and stealing are criminal actions. Defining perils and specifying exclusions not covered in the contract can be quite complex. For example, stealing is classified as theft, burglary, or robbery. Theft means the loss of property by stealing without violence against persons or forced entry. Burglary involves theft and forcible entry that leaves visible marks on the premises. Robbery is theft accompanied by violence or the threat of violence to a person.

Coverage

Most insurance companies sell two types of home owner coverage: (i) **named-peril** that provides protection for losses from a list of perils named in the contract, or (ii) **all-risks** that covers all risks except for those specifically excluded. The more comprehensive coverage may be limited to the house, with the contents covered for named perils only.

It is possible to insure certain possessions against all risks by having an endorsement or rider added to the policy. This coverage would include all kinds of risks associated with direct physical loss or damage, limited only by the exclusions listed. It is usually specified that the damage be accidental and not due to the nature of the property itself, for example, rust or age. When the all-risks coverage is bought for such items as cameras, furs, jewellery, and collections, these items are listed as scheduled property.

The **scheduled property rider,** also called the **valued contract endorsement,** lists the items covered with their value, and includes identifying information such as descriptions and serial numbers. To confirm the value, the insurer will require a bill of sale for a recently acquired item, or an official appraisal for a previously purchased article. In the event of loss or damage, the insurer's maximum liability is the value placed on the property when it was insured. Such contracts are generally used to insure items whose true value is difficult to determine after a loss, such as jewellery, works of historic value, antiques, and stamp and coin collections. Unfortunately, in periods of rapid inflation the maximum liability established when the insurance was bought can become outdated quickly. Unless the insurance company offers automatic adjustment for inflation, the owner should have new appraisals done periodically.

SCHEDULED PROPERTY RIDER

Sandra insured her diamond ring and gold necklace for $1000 on a valued contract or special items endorsement. Before insuring them, they were appraised by a qualified jeweller who estimated their worth to be $1000; this information was given to the company. Six years later her jewellery was stolen when thieves broke into her home. Although her ring and necklace now had a replacement value of $1350, the insurance settlement was for $1000—the maximum liability assumed by the company on this contract. If she had wanted to be more fully insured, she should have had her jewellery appraised more frequently. The insurer requires an expert appraisal each time the limits are changed.

PERSONAL PROPERTY TAKEN AWAY FROM HOME   Policies often contain a personal property clause that covers personal items taken away from home temporarily. The key word is temporarily; possessions taken on a trip, to a summer cottage for a few weeks, or by a student to a college residence would be considered temporarily away. The amount of coverage for these possessions will vary with the policy. For instance, if the policy states that possessions taken away from home are covered for 10 percent of the total coverage on all personal possessions, and if the household contents were insured for $30 000, there would be coverage of $3000. Read the policy to find out the extent of insurance coverage.

Co-insurance

Actuaries base the premium structure on the assumption that property owners will carry sufficient insurance to cover a total loss of the building. In fact, very few buildings burn completely and most claims are for damage costing a few thousand dollars. Knowing this, the insured may decide to buy a policy with very low limits. If this were to happen, insurance funds would be insufficient to provide compensation for all claims. To prevent such under-insurance, many companies include a co-insurance clause in the policy, which applies to the building, but not to the contents.

The **co-insurance** clause states that the insured must carry policy limits to a level considered adequate by the company. An adequate level may be, for example, 80 percent or 100 percent of the replacement value of the building. If the owner fails to carry sufficient insurance, any claims made for damage to the building will be prorated. For instance, if the policy limits are one-half what is considered to be adequate, the claim for a small fire will be reduced by one-half. The example, "Under Insured," illustrates how a claim is prorated if the insured does not carry sufficient insurance. The purpose of the co-insurance clause is to encourage the purchase of adequate limits. Those who do not do so share the risk with the company, hence the term co-insurance.

UNDER-INSURED

The Hills bought a policy on their house with limits of $80 000. A few years later they had a bad fire, that resulted in damage valued at $40 000. At that time, their house was estimated to have a replacement value of $140 000. Their policy had a co-insurance clause which required that they have coverage for 80 percent of the replacement value.

Policy limits . . . . = $80 000
Replacement value . . . = $140 000
Adequate coverage . . . = 80% of replacement value

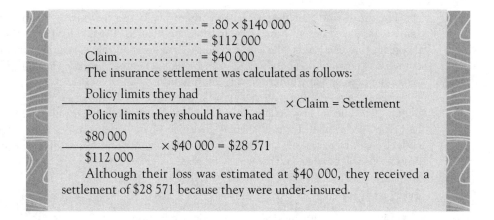

```
...................... = .80 × $140 000
...................... = $112 000
Claim................ = $40 000
```

The insurance settlement was calculated as follows:

$$\frac{\text{Policy limits they had}}{\text{Policy limits they should have had}} \times \text{Claim} = \text{Settlement}$$

$$\frac{\$80\ 000}{\$112\ 000} \times \$40\ 000 = \$28\ 571$$

Although their loss was estimated at $40 000, they received a settlement of $28 571 because they were under-insured.

Property Insurance and Mortgages

Property insurance may include a mortgage clause, which recognizes that there is a mortgage on the property and specifies the rights and obligations of both lender and insurer. The effect of this clause is to express an agreement between the mortgage lender and the insurer that is independent of the agreement between the insurer and the insured, even though this clause is attached to the insured's policy.

The lender has the right to share in any insurance settlement on the property as long as the insured still has an outstanding balance owing. Once the mortgage is completely repaid, the mortgage lender has no claim. The mortgage clause entitles the lender to receive a loss payment regardless of any act or neglect of the home owner or borrower. For example, the insured may breach a condition of the contract with the insurance company, making the claim for damages void; nevertheless, the lender would still be entitled to compensation. An insured who committed arson could not collect insurance, but the lender could.

The mortgage lender has the obligation of informing the insurer of any factors that may change the risk situation. If the risk should increase, and the insured does not pay the additional amount required, the lender is responsible for this amount. The lender's rights in an insurance settlement would take into account the amount still owing on the property at that time.

The Inventory

When a loss is experienced, it is necessary to produce proof of what was lost. In some instances, there may be enough evidence remaining for the adjusters to see what sort of possessions the insured had; at other times, little may be left. It is best to be prepared by keeping an up-to-date inventory of possessions in a secure place away from the house, such as in a safety deposit box. It will not be of much help if the inventory burns up.

For those who feel that a written inventory is too tedious, a camera, video camera, tape recorder, or some combination can be used. With video camera or tape recorder, someone can go through the house describing all that is seen, including the contents of cupboards. These records may be supplemented with sales receipts, lists of serial numbers, and any other relevant information.

Preparing a detailed inventory and attaching current values to each item will help in determining how much insurance coverage is required. Consideration should be given to the need for any special coverage of such items as jewellery, special collections, or antiques. Doing this inventory is not a one-time event; the list of possessions will change, and some may increase in value.

Inflation

If the insurance company does not automatically adjust policy limits in relation to changes in general price levels, the policy holder may have to review his or her coverage regularly. In periods of inflation, replacement costs tend to increase making policy limits are too low to cover a total loss. Many home owners' policies now contain an automatic inflation clause, particularly for the coverage on the building.

PERSONAL LIABILITY INSURANCE

The Risks

Anyone's financial security may be jeopardized if they should be found responsible for damage to someone else's property or for an injury to another person. However, the person claiming damages would have to prove that the loss or damage was caused by negligence. Negligence is defined as either failing to do what a reasonable and prudent person would do in such a situation, or doing what a prudent person would not do. Everyone lives under a legal requirement not to cause harm to others or their property and to take reasonable steps to preserve the safety of others. In addition to being held liable for our own negligent acts, those with employees are also responsible for their work-related actions. Each of us is responsible for losses caused by our animals and, to some extent, for our children's carelessness. The examples below illustrate some types of claims that have been made.

PERSONAL LIABILITY INSURANCE CLAIMS

1. Ten-year-old Rosa, whose broken leg was in a cast, was sitting in an ice cream parlour with her friends when an elderly woman walking down the aisle tripped and fell over Rosa's cast. The woman broke her leg and claimed $10 000 for damages. Rosa's father's insurance

company investigated the circumstances, found that the woman's companion, who had preceded her down the aisle, had manoeuvred safely around the cast, and decided that there was not a strong case for finding Rosa negligent. Rather than go through the expense of a suit, the company paid the woman $2000 *ex gratia*, without admitting any liability. The settlement was made under Rosa's father's personal liability insurance.

2. Alan's son broke a neighbour's window while playing baseball. Alan's insurance company paid the neighbour for the window.

3. A child visiting the Duval family fell while playing on their back deck and required root canal work on a tooth. The Duval's insurer paid the dentist.

4. At a campground, a girl broke her neck by diving into water only 1.2 metres deep. She eventually recovered with a 20 percent disability. Because she had various Red Cross swimming certificates, it was established that she was 25 percent at fault for not investigating the water depth, and the campground owner was held to be 75 percent at fault. His insurer paid the girl $50 000.

5. Mr. Nielsen, an independent handyman, was called to a commercial building to check the plumbing. He proceeded to thaw frozen pipes with a blow torch and succeeded in igniting the whole building, resulting in a total claim in excess of $500 000. His liability coverage was $100 000, leaving him responsible for the difference.

Coverage

Liability insurance, sometimes called legal liability covers the risk of being found responsible for damage caused by the negligence of oneself, one's family members, employees, animals, and so on. This is third party insurance because it involves the insured, the insurer, and some third party who is seeking compensation for a loss. The need to establish who was at fault makes liability insurance claims more involved with legal matters than other kinds of insurance.

Under liability insurance coverage, the insurer agrees to pay for damages attributed to the policyholder, including costs of a court defence, interest, and reimbursement for some immediate expenses. Because the insurance company defends the insured in a liability suit, it is important that there be no admission of liability or offer to make payments, because such actions or statements could prejudice the defense. In some situations there must be a court case to prove negligence, in others an out-of-court settlement may be reached. Before the insurance company will settle a liability claim, it must be satisfied that the insured was legally liable in this instance and that the policy covers this particular liability.

Liability insurance may be bought separately or, more commonly, as a part of another policy, such as home or auto insurance. A home owner or tenant policy that includes comprehensive personal liability may cover damage to property or injury to people as a result of use or maintenance of property, personal acts of the insured, ownership of animals, ownership of boats, and children's carelessness. It may cover the insured's legal liability for fire, explosion, and smoke in rented premises. In addition, some policies may include a small amount of coverage for damage caused by the insured without reference to negligence. Subject to a list of exclusions, the coverage applies wherever the insured is engaged in normal activities as a private individual; business pursuits are commonly excluded in personal liability policies. Personal liability insurance is a quite inexpensive way to protect yourself against risks that may have a low probability of occurring but that can be extraordinarily costly if they do happen.

AUTOMOBILE INSURANCE

This section is intended to provide an understanding of basic principles and concepts associated with auto insurance, not to supply the details of coverage available in each province. The social and financial risks associated with automobiles, considered too significant to be left to personal discretion, are protected to some degree by minimum insurance requirements legislated by each province or territory. Three major categories of risks will be identified and the relevant types of insurance protection explained. With this basic knowledge you will be prepared to investigate the specific arrangements for auto insurance in your province. There is too much variation to go into all the features here.

Two distinguishing points among provincial arrangements for automobile insurance are: (i) who supplies the insurance coverage—whether a public body, private companies, or a public-private combination, and (ii) how fault is handled. It will be more meaningful to leave the discussion of fault until after identifying the risks associated with car ownership and explaining the basic types of insurance protection.

Insurance Providers

In British Columbia, Manitoba and Saskatchewan, basic automobile insurance coverage is government-provided, with extra insurance available from private insurers. Quebec splits auto insurance coverage between government and private companies, and the other provinces and territories leave insurance provision to private companies. Wherever auto insurance is publicly provided, there is one price and one place to get coverage; where insurance is offered by private enterprise, there may be many competing suppliers.

The Risks

As noted, car ownership poses such a significant threat, not only to the financial security of individuals but also to society, that a minimum amount of public liability and accident benefits coverage is mandatory. Three major categories of financial risks that a car owner assumes and the basic types of protection, are as follows:

Risk	Insurance Coverage
1. Liability to others for injury, death, or property damage	Public liability (third party)
2. Injury to or death of self or passengers	Accident benefits
3. Damage to insured's vehicle	Physical damage (e.g., collision, comprehensive)

Liability to Others

Anyone who drives or owns a car faces the risk that, because of negligence, they will be held financially responsible for injuries to others or damage to their property. When assessing liability risk, reflect on the high probability of being involved in a car accident at some time, simply because of the large number of vehicles on our roads. Despite our best intentions, a little mistake can cause a serious accident. The consequences of severely injuring one or more persons could be financially disastrous; the courts have been awarding increasingly large settlements, sometimes as high as several million dollars. The rising costs of car repair, medical care, and income replacement for killed or injured persons have increased settlements to the point where some insurers are now advising their customers to have at least $1 000 000 in liability coverage.

POLICY LIMITS   As with most types of insurance, the liability policy limits determine the maximum that the insurer will pay on a claim. It may not always be understood that a court can award a settlement to an accident victim that exceeds the policy limits. In such a case, the insured is responsible for paying the difference, unless the policy includes specific coverage for such situations.

NEGLIGENCE   Public liability insurance does not apply to damage to one's own car or injury to oneself, but is limited to situations where others have suffered loss due to your negligence. Because liability claims depend on proving negligence, it is important to give some thought to the legal concept of negligence. Sometimes distinctions are made between ordinary negligence and gross negligence. Ordinary negligence is the failure to do what a reasonable person would do, or doing what a reasonable person would not do. Gross negligence, on the other hand, is considered to be reckless, wanton, and wilful misconduct in which the person has failed by a wide margin to exercise due care, thereby reflecting an indifference to the probable consequences.

The basic rule in our society is that each of us has the duty to take proper care no matter what we are doing, and must take responsibility for any injury caused by our carelessness. Motorists can be held negligent for not keeping a proper look-out or for failing to have their vehicles under complete control at all times. Icy roads or storms are not an excuse; drivers are supposed to adjust their driving to suit conditions. In some jurisdictions, a car owner is responsible for the consequences of any negligence on the part of persons who drive his or her car with consent. When a friend borrows a car and has an accident with it, liability or collision claims may be handled by the owner's insurance. It is well to know the terms of the policy when lending a car. If the owner is liable, the claim will be submitted to his or her insurer, who in turn may raise future premiums if the friend was at fault.

HIGHWAY TRAFFIC ACT   If there is an infraction of a traffic regulation in a highway accident, the insurer may use this information when determining negligence. However, not being found guilty of a traffic offense does not necessarily mean absolution of negligence as far as the insurance company is concerned.

PROVING FAULT   A serious problem for insurance companies is the difficulty of proving negligence in auto accidents, where events happen very fast and there may be no witnesses. If there is uncertainty about who was at fault, the issue can be decided in court, or the two insurers may reach an out-of-court agreement in which the responsibility for the accident is divided between them. For instance, a 60/40 split would mean that 60 percent of all the damages resulting from the accident would be assessed to one driver and 40 percent to the other, both of whom would in turn refer the claims to their respective insurance companies as third party liability claims. High legal costs, prolonged court processes, and the difficulty of determining fault have created so many problems that some measures have been devised to expedite certain types of claims by not requiring that fault be established. In a later section we will examine so-called "no-fault" auto insurance, but first we will consider the two other categories of risks faced by motorists.

QUESTIONS TO ASK ABOUT YOUR LIABILITY COVERAGE

1. **Who is covered by this part of the policy and in which situations?** There should be protection for you, the car owner, and persons using the vehicle with your consent, if the driver's negligence caused injury, death, or property damage to others. Find out if you are covered when driving cars that you do not own or use regularly, such as temporary substitute cars or uninsured cars. Whose insurance will cover you if you were found negligent in an accident while driving a friend's car? Does your liability coverage protect you if family or passengers sue you for negligence?

2. **How much liability coverage do you need?**
   Inquire about the size of recent liability settlements to get an idea of the amount of coverage you need.
3. **What is not covered by your liability insurance?**
   It does not cover injury to or death of yourself, damage to your own car or to property carried in or on it.
4. **What other things does your insurer agree to do?**
   In addition to paying claims resulting from negligence, the insurer may cover the costs of investigating the accident, negotiating a settlement, settling a claim, and defending you in court. Also, the insurer may reimburse you for out-of-pocket costs for immediate expenses associated with the accident, and pay court costs and interest on the insured portion of settlements charged to you. These costs are in addition to the liability limit of your policy.

Personal Injury or Death

The second major risk is that the driver or passengers will be injured. Medical insurance or accident benefits coverage is designed to provide benefits in case of bodily injury to the occupants of the vehicle, or to anyone struck by it. Note that the term **accident benefits** refers to insurance coverage for personal injury or death. Payment of claims for accident benefits is without reference to fault, and claims are made to the policyholder's insurance company. All provinces, except Newfoundland, require compulsory accident benefits coverage as part of auto insurance. There is some variation by province, but essentially, accident benefits cover, to defined limits, such things as medical payments, disability income, death payments, and funeral expenses. Find out what the accident benefits are where you live.

Damage to Your Vehicle

The least serious risk drivers face is that their cars may be stolen or damaged and insurance coverage is generally not mandatory for this risk (with the exception of Saskatchewan and Manitoba). Physical damage coverage does not have a dollar limit, but is based on the actual cash value of the car at the time of the loss. Because of the rapid rate at which cars depreciate, it is best to review physical damage insurance from time to time; the coverage may be dropped when the premium is too high in relation to the size of the risk being covered. For instance, if an old car has an actual cash value of a few hundred dollars, that would be the maximum settlement in the event of a total loss of the car. How much is it worth in annual premiums to protect this small amount of capital in the car?

Coverage for physical damage to a car is often subject to some deductible amount. The deductible is the amount of each claim that the insured pays; for instance, collision coverage with $250 deductible means taking responsibility for paying the first $250 in damages. By sharing the risk with the company, insurance costs are lowered.

Most insurance companies will offer a choice of physical damage coverage, such as: (i) all perils, (ii) specified perils, (iii) collision, and (iv) comprehensive. All perils is the broadest, covering everything included in the other three categories and possibly more. The policy should be examined to find out what is excluded, because everything else will be covered. By contrast, specified perils includes only named risks. The two other coverages, collision and comprehensive, are widely used.

COLLISION   Collision covers a collision between a car and another object. Usually a collision involves the car striking or being struck by another car, but it also includes the one-vehicle accident in which the car strikes a tree, guard rail, another object, or the surface of the ground.

If a collision that was caused by the negligence of another, the car owner's insurer will pay the damage claim if it is greater than the deductible and then, by the right of subrogation, will endeavour to collect from the person responsible for the accident. The insurer has agreed to indemnify the owner under the collision coverage whether or not the driver was at fault. If the insurer is successful in collecting from the third party, the policyholder will be reimbursed for the deductible amount.

COMPREHENSIVE   This covers perils, other than collision, that may happen to a car. The distinction between collision and comprehensive coverage sometimes seems confusing. If a loss is specifically excluded under collision, it may be covered under comprehensive. Some of the perils included in comprehensive coverage are: theft, vandalism, fire, lightning, windstorm, hail, and damage caused by falling or flying objects. This section is usually subject to a deductible amount, but the deductible may not apply in some situations, such as when the entire auto is stolen.

Mandatory Provincial Coverage

A summary of how auto insurance is provided and what coverage is mandated in various provinces and territories is presented in Table 5.1.

Factors Affecting Insurance Rates

Usually we pay more to insure our cars than our much more valuable houses because cars pose a greater risk to financial security. The increasing number of accidents and the rising cost of settlements have caused car insurance premiums to escalate. Auto insurance premiums reflect not only the coverage requested, but possibly a number of other factors, grouped according to: (i) personal characteristics, (ii) type of car, (iii) use made of the car, and (iv) region.

TABLE 5.1 AUTOMOBILE INSURANCE PROVIDERS AND MANDATED COVERAGE BY PROVINCE, CANADA, 1992

Province/ Territory	Public liability minimum	Mandatory accident benefits	Mandatory collision coverage
Public Insurer			
B.C.	$200 000	X	
Sask.	$200 000	X	X
Man.	$200 000	X	X
Public & Private Insurers			
Que.	$50 000	X	
Private Insurers			
Alta.	$200 000	X	
Ont.	$200 000	X	
N.B.	$200 000	X	
N.S.	$200 000	X	
P.E.I.	$200 000	X	
Nfld.	$200 000		
Yukon	$200 000	X	
N.W.T.	$200 000	X	

* Quebec residents are compensated for injury without regard to fault. Liability limits are $50 000 for property damage claims within Quebec, and personal injury and property damage claims outside the province.

SOURCE OF DATA: Insurance Bureau of Canada, Toronto.

PERSONAL CHARACTERISTICS Traditionally, statistics linking accident frequency to personal characteristics, such as age, gender, and marital status, have been used in determining rates for individuals. Although there has been discussion of eliminating these criteria, not all provinces have yet done so. Modifications to the risk-according-to-age method may be made in the case of young people who have had driver training; they are considered to present less risk to the insurer. Likewise, a driver who has had no accidents for several years is considered a much better risk than one with accidents or traffic violations on their record. After an accident, insurers reassess the risk classification and usually increase the premium if the insured was at fault.

TYPE OF CAR   The type of car will have an obvious effect on the cost of collision and comprehensive coverage because of repair cost. In addition, insurers may increase liability and accident benefits premiums for powerful cars because of their potential for causing substantial damage.

USE OF CAR   The number of kilometres driven in a year and the number of people who normally drive a particular car affect the risk situation. The more a car is driven, the more the driver is exposed to risk. Whether or not the car is used to drive to work is also a consideration.

REGION   More accidents occur in certain regions of the country, usually because of population density or adverse driving conditions due to weather.

PROVINCIAL DIFFERENCES   Provinces differ in the factors used for determining premium rates. Quebec, for instance, has a set premium for a given class of vehicle, regardless of the risk presented by the individual. In Manitoba, rates are based on the make and model of vehicle, use, geographical location and driving record with no discrimination based on age, sex, or marital status. British Columbia drivers pay premiums determined by the value of the vehicle, use, geography and their claims experience.

COMPARISON SHOPPING FOR INSURANCE

If you want to find the best rates for car or home insurance you have a number of choices. You can get prices from a number of agents, which can be time-consuming. Or, you can consult an insurance broker who represents a number of companies. However, a broker who subscribes to a computerized rating service will give you access to the broadest rate comparison.

Insurance for High-Risk Drivers

There are some drivers whose accident records or other characteristics make them very high risks and thus unacceptable to insurers. However, if they are able to get a driver's license, and car insurance is mandatory, there must be some way to insure them to protect society as well as themselves. The insurance industry solved this problem by creating an arrangement whereby insurers pool the high risks, making it possible to cover all licensed drivers and registered owners. The high-risk driver makes application for auto insurance in the same way as anyone else, but the policy is then transferred to the insurance pool which in turn assigns these high-risk cases to companies in proportion to their share of auto insurance in each province. Thus, no single company will receive more than its share of bad risks, and all those who want insurance will obtain it. Naturally, the premiums paid by high-risk drivers are very high. Claims made on these policies are handled in the usual way by the insurer concerned.

Responsibility of the Insured

The agreement with the insurer requires that the policyholder give written notice with details of the accident as soon as possible after it occurs. At the scene of an accident, information about the other driver, including his or her name, address, insurance company, and car license number should be collected. Names and addresses of passengers and other witnesses may be useful later. The driver should not assume any obligation or accept any responsibility for the accident or make any payment to the victims.

After the accident, the car owner must cooperate with the insurer by providing information as needed, forwarding all summonses, notices of suit, and other correspondence received, and appear in court if required. The victim's claims are being made against the car owner, not the insurer. If there is a court case, it will be the case of Smith v. the owner, not Smith v. the owner's insurer. The insurer's responsibility is to help in resolving the problem, not to take it over entirely.

DAMAGE TO RENTAL CARS

Denise and her friend plan to rent a car for the two weeks they will be on holiday. A friend pointed out to them that they would be signing a rental agreement stating they are responsible for returning the car in the same condition as they took it, meaning that the risk of any damage is theirs. When Denise made inquiries about supplementary insurance for rented cars she found three alternatives. The first option was to buy the extra coverage offered by the rental companies. One firm offered a damage waiver for about $10 a day that protected customers against damage to the vehicle from just about any cause, including collision, vandalism, falling trees, etc., with no deductible. Another company offered a waiver that covered damage from a collision only. Clearly, it is important to read the rental contract before signing.

Next, Denise checked her own car insurance policy to see if it had a clause regarding rental cars. She found that she could buy additional coverage for the duration of her holiday for a small fee ($15 to $20), but that her own deductible amounts would apply if there was a claim. Furthermore, if she decided to have her own insurance company protect her against damage to a rented car, she would be required by the rental company to provide written documentation of that coverage.

Denise's third option was to use her premium credit card. The card, which costs her over $100 a year for a variety of services, provided the same protection as that sold by the rental companies—broad damage coverage with no deductible.

NO-FAULT AUTOMOBILE INSURANCE

The Fault System

Under the law of torts, which has descended to us from the English common law system, each person has a basic duty to take care not to harm other people or damage their property, either intentionally or unintentionally. When applied to car accidents, this system has created problems because in many instances it is difficult to clearly establish fault. In addition to driving errors, accidents are caused by adverse road or weather conditions, or by cars or pedestrians not involved in the crash. Naturally, the more extensive the injuries and damage, the greater the need to establish fault in order to receive compensation, but such cases often take years to settle because of long delays in getting court hearings. Some people are never compensated because no one can be shown to have been negligent.

No-Fault Insurance

Claims under accident benefits and physical damage to one's own car have usually been paid without regard to fault. Much of the discussion surrounding no-fault insurance has been in relation to third party liability claims. In a pure no-fault system, proof of fault would not be required in order to settle claims for injuries and damages resulting from car accidents. Instead, each person would claim damages from their own insurer, thus saving litigation costs and considerable time, and also ensuring that all claims are paid. However, this simple idea raises some important questions. Should the insurance premium be raised because the policyholder was paid a large settlement for damages caused by another? Should a consistently bad driver continue driving without penalty? Should those seriously injured be deprived of the right to sue for damages?

Many modifications of the basic no-fault idea have been tried in a number of provinces and states, with the result that we have now reached a state of terminological confusion. The term no-fault has been applied to so many versions of the basic idea that it is no longer meaningful. For example, a partial no-fault scheme may pay claims without regard to fault up to some maximum amount, but permit claimants to sue for further damages in court.

Quebec No-Fault Insurance

BODILY INJURY   In 1978, Quebec completely abolished the fault system of compensating accident victims for bodily injury. Instead of public liability insurance and the right to sue, there are two forms of coverage: (i) a basic compulsory public plan that pays unlimited sums for medical and rehabilitation costs and limited amounts for injuries, and (ii) a supplementary elective private plan to provide no-fault insurance for those who want additional coverage. Under these plans, no legal action may be taken. If the insured disagrees with the decision, application may be made to a tribunal to have the claim reviewed.

PHYSICAL DAMAGE   A compulsory, partial no-fault system for property damage that eliminates third-party compensation is administered by private insurers. Car owners are required to purchase property damage insurance to cover damage to vehicles other than automobiles caused by the driver, and to compensate the driver who is not at fault for damage to his or her own vehicle. When the driver is deemed at fault, based on a simplified fault determination process, he or she must compensate the other driver for damages; collision coverage for this situation is available, but not compulsory.

Ontario Partial No-Fault Insurance

BODILY INJURY   In 1990, Ontario introduced limited no-fault insurance that permits lawsuits against those who cause accidents only when the personal injuries are severe or fatal. The mandatory accident benefits coverage, payable without proving fault, provides immediate payments for the driver, passengers, or injured pedestrians. Claims must be paid within 30 days. It is estimated that this new plan will handle 90 percent of claims, while remaining claimants retain the option of suing for damages.

PHYSICAL DAMAGE   If the driver is not at fault, damage to the car and its contents will be recovered from his or her own insurance company. However, a driver who is at fault or partially at fault is responsible for paying all or a portion of the costs, unless covered by optional collision coverage.

Summary

This chapter introduced the insurance principle, and explained its application to risks associated with ownership of property. The importance of identifying risk exposure before selecting insurance coverage has been emphasized. The concepts of indemnity, depreciation, subrogation, and co-insurance were illustrated in relation to property insurance. Car owners face a number of risks, the most significant being their liability to others. It cannot be too strongly emphasized that adequate liability coverage for car owners is most essential. The age and condition of the car has little to do with the risk of causing damage or injury. Physical damage to a car presents a smaller risk; by accepting some of this risk oneself through a larger deductible amount, the cost of insurance can be reduced.

Although there has been much discussion of the merits of a truly no-fault auto insurance system, problems have prevented its implementation. However, modified versions are now in use in several provinces. Modest coverage for personal injuries, where proof of fault is not required for compensation, is mandatory in most provinces.

Vocabulary Review

accident benefits (p. 123)

actual cash value (p. 112)

actuary (p. 107)

adjuster (p. 111)

agent (p. 109)

all-risks coverage (p. 115)

broker (p. 109)

co-insurance (p. 116)

deductible clause (p. 114)

depreciation (p. 112)

endorsement (rider) (p. 111)

indemnification (p. 112)

insurable interest (p. 109)

insurable risk (p. 109)

insured (p. 110)

insurer (p. 110)

liability insurance (third party insurance) (p. 119)

loading charge (p. 108)

named-peril coverage (p. 115)

policy (p. 110)

policy limits (p. 114)

pooling risk (p. 107)

premium (p. 109)

pure cost of insurance (p. 108)

replacement value (p. 112)

salvage value (p. 113)

scheduled property rider (valued contract endorsement) (p. 115)

short rate (p. 111)

subrogation (p. 114)

Problems

1. To answer this question, you need to obtain a property insurance policy.

    (a) Look for the answers to the questions posed in the box, "How to Read a Policy."

    (b) Is there any automatic inflation adjustment of the policy limits? If so, does it apply to both the house and the contents?

    (c) How much coverage is there for personal property taken away from home?

    (d) Does the policy include coverage for personal liability? If so, what is the liability limit?

    (e) If the owner of this policy lost all of his or her personal possessions in a fire, would the maximum settlement be the actual cash value of the loss or the policy limits?

    (f) Does this policy cover a theft that occurred while the family was away?

    (g) Are there any riders or endorsements attached to the policy?

    (h) Is this an all-risks policy or a named-perils policy?

    (j) Is there a co-insurance clause? If so, what is the policyholder's responsibility?

2.   The Sawchuks came home to find the fire department extinguishing a fire in their living room. The fire had started from a cigarette carelessly left near some papers. The carpet, walls, and ceiling of the living room of their rented apartment were damaged, as well as some of their furniture. The landlord is claiming damages to his building, the Sawchuks are claiming damages to their possessions, and the landlord's insurer is making claims against the Sawchuks. The Sawchuks' contents policy was for actual cash value coverage, with $50 000 personal liability.

    (a) Who pays for what in this case?

    (b) Is there a possibility that the principle of subrogation might be applied in the Sawchuks' situation? If so, who would do what?

    (c) Would the Sawchuks receive a settlement large enough to replace the damaged furniture? How would allowances for inflation in furniture prices and depreciation be taken into account?

3.   The Arbics have just bought their first home for a price of $170 000. The house alone is estimated to have a replacement cost of $120 000.

    (a) Do they need $170 000 insurance coverage on the house? Explain.

    (b) The Arbics decided to save money for a year or two by buying home insurance with policy limits of $50 000, but during this time they had a fire. The claims manager from the insurance company said that the Arbics are under-insured and that the amount they will recover will be determined by the co-insurance clause that requires 80 percent of replacement value. Calculate the amount of the settlement they will receive for damages valued at $9000.

4.   (a) What are the pros and cons of buying a replacement value insurance policy on your household effects?

    (b) How does replacement value insurance alter the basic principle of indemnification?

5.   Obtain an automobile insurance policy and examine it to find answers to the following questions.

(a) If you or your passengers should be injured and unable to work, would there be any income replacement payments? How much? For how long?

(b) If one of your passengers was killed, would there be any compensation for funeral costs?

(c) If your injuries included some that were not covered by the provincial health insurance, would the accident benefits portion of your car insurance policy provide some help? Is there any limit on the amount?

(d) Do you have collision coverage? What is the deductible?

(e) Is there a deductible amount on the comprehensive coverage?

(f) Are there any exclusions to the coverage for damage to the insured's automobile?

6. When Dave Hill's father was buying a new car, he found that his old one was valued at $1900 as a trade-in. He offered it to 19-year-old Dave on condition that Dave handle all the operating costs and insure it. Dave was delighted—he would have his own car at last. The insurance agent was happy to help him arrange suitable coverage for the car, but Dave was dismayed to find that the premium would be higher than his father had been paying. To economize, he thought that he could cut down on some parts of the insurance. He told the agent that he would take collision coverage but drop the third party liability because the car was getting old; he certainly wanted coverage for theft and fire.

Consider each of the following statements in relation to Hill's case and decide whether you AGREE or DISAGREE.

(a) If Dave doesn't buy public liability coverage, he will not be able to register his car.

(b) If Dave buys an automobile insurance policy, he is required to have at least $100 000 public liability.

(c) In Dave's case, it is probably a good idea for him to skip the public liability coverage because it wouldn't be a great disaster if the old car was wrecked.

(d) If Dave takes out a policy with $250 deductible collision coverage and then runs into a bridge, completely demolishing his car, he would have to pay the first $250 of damages, but his insurance company would pay him $1650 to buy another car.

(e) Dave is wise to insist on coverage for fire and theft even if he has to do without some other coverage.

(f) Because of the province's mandatory no-fault accident benefits insurance coverage, Dave would not be held accountable if he injured another person in an auto accident.

7. Analyze the following complaints from car owners regarding insurance claims and note how you would explain the situation to each.

(a) Sam writes, "under conditions of icy roads and high winds, our car was blown off the road. When I presented a claim for damage to my car, I was told that my policy did not include collision coverage. On reading the policy I find that we are covered for windstorm damage. The company still insists that they have no responsibility for paying my car repairs."

(b) The summer before last Bob was in a head-on collision with a car that suddenly appeared on his side of the road. Because he had no collision coverage, he was advised to settle on a 50/50 basis since it would cost too much to prove he was in the right. His lawyer will not take the case because she says it will cost more to fight the case than the car is worth. Bob wonders what to do.

(c) Sophie had considered her car insurance quite adequate, as she has collision, comprehensive, and public liability coverage. An unknown driver damaged her car when it was parked legally on the street. She assumed such damage would be covered under the comprehensive clause (with only $50 deductible), since collision must involve her car colliding with another vehicle or some object. The insurer says that since her car was hit by a car, rather than a stone, the accident is classified as a collision. To her, this seems to be an impossibility because she was not even in the car, nor was the car moving. She thinks collision coverage should pay for damage due to her own carelessness, not someone else's. She says comprehensive covers vandalism. The insurer company wants her to pay for the damage because it amounted to less than her deductible amount under collision coverage. Is this right?

8. What is the extent of no-fault auto insurance coverage where you live?

9.

ONE MAN DEAD, ANOTHER PARALYZED IN TWO-CAR CRASH

The foggy wet weather and poor driving conditions on Saturday evening accounted for a head-on collision involving cars driven by Richard Chaney and Russell Talcott. Police reports indicate that Chaney's car went out of control on the northbound lane and crossed the slippery pavement into the southbound lane, where it collided with the vehicle driven by Talcott. On arrival at the General Hospital, Russell Talcott was pronounced dead. He is survived by his wife Mary and their young son Jason. At present Richard Chaney is reported to be in critical condition as a result of a serious spinal injury. No charges were laid in this case.

Assume the following information about the insurance and other security plans of these men:

	Chaney	Talcott
Health insurance	covered	covered
Canada Pension	contributor	contributor
Group life insurance	$70 000	$35 000
Personal life insurance	$75 000	$150 000
Disability insurance	none	pays 1/2 salary
Auto insurance:		
Collision insurance	none	$250 deductible
Comprehensive	none	$50 deductible
Accident benefits	yes	yes
Public liability	$200 000	$300 000

(a) Identify by check marks the areas of probable financial need of each family as a result of this accident.

	Chaney	Talcott
Personal injury		
Funeral expenses		
Property damage		
Liability to others		
Loss of income		
Other		

(b) Using the chart below, note the resources these families could call on and what each would cover.

	Chaney	Talcott
Health insurance		
Canada/Quebec Pension		
Group insurance		
Personal life insurance		
Disability insurance		
Auto insurance:		
Collision		
Comprehensive		
Public liability		

Note: Assume that the accident happened in your province when answering the following questions.

(c) Will Chaney's insurer immediately authorize repairs to his car, and look after the bill? Would you expect Talcott's company to do this? Explain.

(d) Both of these drivers had third-party liability. Explain how claims against this portion of their coverage would proceed. Does the case necessarily have to go to court? What would the claims be for?

(e) If the case did go to court and Chaney was declared to be more than 50 percent responsible for the accident, will Chaney receive any compensation for his disability from Talcott's insurer?

(f) From information provided, which of the two families seems to be in the worse financial position as a result of this accident?

(g) Does the fact that the police did not press charges under the Highway Traffic Act mean that the insurer will not make any settlement under the liability coverage?

References

BOOKS

BUDD, JOHN, CLAUDE RINFRET, RICHARD DAW, and DANIELLE BRIEN. *Canadian Guide to Personal Financial Management.* Scarborough, Ontario: Prentice-Hall Canada, annual, 225 pp. Accountants provide guidance on a broad range of topics, including planning finances, estimating insurance needs, managing risk, and determining investment needs. Instructions and the necessary forms for making plans are provided.

FLEMING, JAMES. *Merchants of Fear, An Investigation of Canada's Insurance Industry.* Markham, Ontario: Penguin Books Canada, 1986, 409 pp. An investigative report on the life and general insurance industries.

INSURANCE BUREAU OF CANADA. *Facts.* Toronto: Insurance Bureau of Canada, annual, 58 pp. Annual summary of industry statistics.

ONTARIO TASK FORCE ON INSURANCE. *Final Report of the Ontario Task Force on Insurance.* Toronto: Ministry of Financial Institutions, 1986, 384 pp. Summarizes findings about property and casualty insurance, particularly in Ontario, and makes recommendations. A summary of the Quebec automobile insurance system is included in an appendix.

QUEBEC CONSUMERS' ASSOCIATION. *The Canadian Insurance Guide.* Montreal: Quebec Consumers' Association, 1988, 126 pp. Explains how to determine home and automobile insurance needs and how to select an insurer; gives most attention to evaluating the solvency of insurers.

CHAPTER SIX

Life Insurance

1. To explain the function of life insurance in enhancing financial security.

2. To relate the need for life insurance to changing life cycle requirements.

3. To analyze arguments for and against the use of life insurance as a savings vehicle.

4. To explain the principles of:

   (a) pooling risk,

   (b) pure cost of life insurance,

   (c) level premium.

5. To demonstrate how the basic types of life insurance policies differ with respect to:

   (a) policy reserves,

   (b) duration of insurance protection,

   (c) insurer's liability.

6. To explain how the following policy variations serve specific needs:

   (a) decreasing term,

   (b) limited-payment life,

   (c) family policy,

   (d) family income policy,

   (e) universal life insurance.

7. To identify the insured's options for using:

   (a) the cash surrender value of a policy,

   (b) dividends.

8. To assess the merits of these options:

   (a) renewability,

   (b) convertibility,

   (c) waiver of premium,

   (d) guaranteed insurability,

   (e) accidental death benefit.

9. To ascertain from an insurance policy the main features of the agreement.

10. To formulate generalizations about:

    (a) trends in per capita insurance coverage,

    (b) reasons for termination of policies,

    (c) trends in ownership of group and individual life insurance,

    (d) the influence of gender, age, and income on the decision to buy individual policies.

11. To explain these terms: face amount, premium, beneficiary, policyholder, insurable interest, paid-up policy, dividend, participating policy, group insurance, endorsement or rider, settlement option, loading charges, front- and back-loaded.

Introduction

The intent of this chapter is to help you to take control of another aspect of your financial affairs. Most Canadians think they ought to have some life insurance, but are bewildered by the process of making a choice. In addition to a natural reluctance to think about their mortality, many people are dubious about insurance agents and unable to evaluate the sales presentation. Their perplexity stems from a lack of understanding of life insurance principles and concepts and is compounded by the terminological confusion engendered by the industry. Since there is, unfortunately, no established standard nomenclature for life insurance policies, companies adorn their offerings with a wide variety of names. Much of the confusion felt by buyers can be traced to the naming of policies, varied financing methods, and the multiplicity of renewal provisions. You may be encouraged to learn that there are only two fundamental types of life insurance. The confusion arises because of the numerous modifications and combinations of the basic types, named as companies see fit. If you have an understanding of basic principles and terms you will be in a better position to determine your own insurance requirements and to make rational choices.

THE ECONOMIC RISK OF DYING TOO SOON

If you died tomorrow, would your death create economic hardship for anyone? If the answer is yes, you will want to consider insurance on your life as one way of improving financial security for your dependents. If, as far as you can foresee, the answer is no, you probably do not need life insurance. The primary purpose of life insurance is to protect an income stream for dependents should the breadwinner die prematurely. Another use of insurance, important in certain cases, is to provide liquidity for an estate at death. When ready cash is needed by the survivors but most of the assets are tied up in property or securities that take time to sell, a lump-sum insurance settlement can be helpful. This chapter concentrates on the use of life insurance to protect a family's income stream and does not address other possibilities.

Financial Responsibility of Parents

Raising children creates a financial risk that peaks on the day the last one is born; at that time the family has its maximum number of children with the longest period of dependence ahead. As the children grow and the time left to support them decreases, this economic risk lessens. Consequently, the funds that would be needed to support children until they become independent becomes less each year. This changing risk is represented in Figure 6.1 by a hypothetical curve; for comparison, the average profiles of family income and wealth over the life cycle are superimposed.

FIGURE 6.1 RESOURCES AND ECONOMIC RISKS OF PARENTHOOD BY LIFE CYCLE STAGE

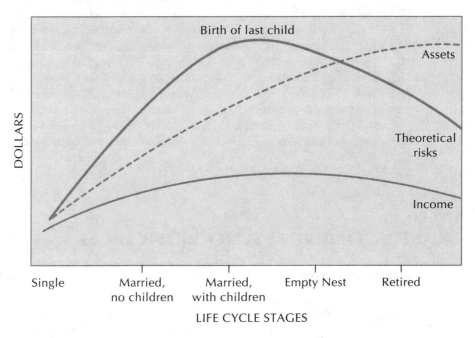

For many families, the financial risk associated with parenthood does not correspond very well with their economic resources. Their financial risk tends to peak before their income or assets reach their highest levels. On average, a family can expect their income to increase until at least middle age, and assets to grow until retirement or after, with the period of greatest wealth occurring after the children have left home. This discrepancy, which can pose a significant threat to the financial security of young families, may be minimized by life insurance.

WHEN INSURANCE IS NEEDED

Neither Sue nor Pete had any life insurance when they married, but after baby Daphne's arrival they became aware of their responsibility to support her for at least 18 years. Since both were employed, they decided each should have some life insurance coverage, and they bought two policies. The birth of Adam two years later increased their financial commitments. Now that they were responsible for supporting Daphne for at least 16 years and Adam for 18, or the equivalent of 34 child-years, an increase in their insurance coverage was needed.

Will Sue and Pete need to carry the same amount of life insurance throughout their lives? Assuming that they have no more children, the economic risk of parenthood will decline each year, going from the peak of 34 child-years to 32 at the end of the next year, then to 30, and so on to zero when they stop supporting the children. After the child support years and before their retirement they should be building their net worth for their non-earning years. Thus, their need for life insurance may slowly decline to a point where they may need none or very little.

BASIC CONCEPTS AND PRINCIPLES

Terminology

When you buy life insurance, the company provides an agreement or contract, called a **policy,** that states the risks the company has agreed to assume. This policy specifies in detail all aspects of the agreement, including the maximum liability the company will assume, known as the face amount or face value. A policy with a **face amount** of $100 000 is an agreement that the insurance company will pay your beneficiaries $100 000 on your death. A **beneficiary** is the person named in the policy to receive the proceeds. The regular payments required to keep the policy in force are called **premiums.** Insurance premiums may be paid monthly, semi-annually, or annually, depending on the arrangement with the company, and generally are paid throughout the period the coverage is in force.

As with any type of insurance, a policy cannot be purchased unless there is an **insurable interest,** or a relationship between the insured and the event being insured against. You do not have an insurable interest in the life of another person unless that person's death would have a financial impact on you. Usually, a person is considered to have an insurable interest in his or her own life and in the life of a spouse, child, grandchild, employee, or any person on whom he or she may be wholly or partially dependent. For example, a creditor has an insurable interest in the lives of his debtors.

Basic Principles

Three basic principles of life insurance to be discussed here involve:

(a) pooling risk,

(b) the pure cost of life insurance,

(c) the level premium.

POOLING RISK   Life insurance, like general insurance, is a method of pooling small contributions from many people to compensate those who experience a loss. Actuaries use mortality tables drawn from death records over many years to predict the number of persons of any given age who can be expected to die within the year. Their predictions, quite accurate for large numbers, cannot forecast which persons will die in a given year—only how many. Once the number of expected deaths is known for a specific population, as well as how much money is to be given to the dependents of each, it is possible to determine the size of fund required to make the payments. The over-simplified example, "Pooling the Risk" illustrates this point.

POOLING THE RISK

Population of men aged 30 . . . . 200 000

Amount to be paid per deceased $50 000

Mortality rate for males aged 30 . . . . 2.13/1000

Number of deaths expected in the year in this population:

$$200\ 000 \times \frac{2.13}{1000} = 426$$

Fund for dependents: $426 \times \$50\ 000 = \$21\ 300\ 000$

Cost per man:

$$\frac{21\ 300\ 000}{200\ 000} = \$106.50 \text{ for the year}$$

At the end of the year, the fund would be exhausted and more contributions would be needed.

THE PURE COST OF LIFE INSURANCE   As you can see from Figure 6.2, the one-year mortality rate rises with age and is higher at any given age for males than females. The cost of insuring a life for one year is based on the mortality rate for persons of the same age and gender and is called the pure cost of life insurance. Therefore, the **pure cost of life insurance** follows the mortality curve, becoming more expensive each year as one ages, but is less costly for females.

FIGURE 6.2   PROBABILITY OF DYING WITHIN THE YEAR, BY AGE AND GENDER

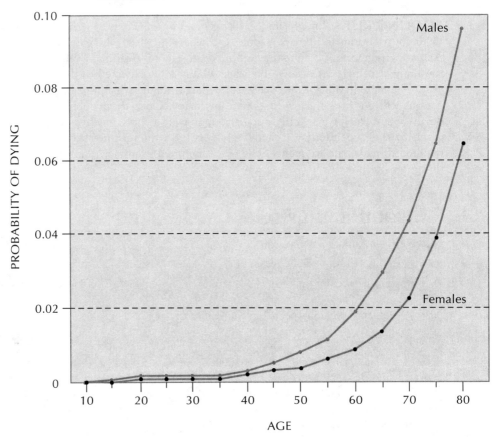

SOURCE OF DATA: *Canada Year Book,* 1978–79. Ottawa: Statistics Canada, 1978, Table 4.45 p. 180. (Catalogue No. 11-202), Reproduced with the permission of the Minister of Industry, Science and Technology, 1993.

THE LEVEL PREMIUM   In response to buyer resistance to paying higher premiums each year, insurance companies have devised the level premium. This is the way it works: rather than charge the pure cost of insurance each year, they establish a constant or **level premium** when a life insurance policy is bought; the policyholder pays this amount regularly for the duration of the policy, whether it be five years or 50. If we superimpose the amount of the level premium on the curve of risk, or the pure cost of insurance, it is obvious that in the early years of the contract the premium is higher than the pure cost, but in later years it is lower (Figure 6.3). The reserve accumulated from the over-payment at the beginning, together with the interest it generates, helps to meet the higher cost of coverage in the later period.

FIGURE 6.3 OVER-PAYMENT AND UNDER-PAYMENT TO SUSTAIN A LEVEL PREMIUM

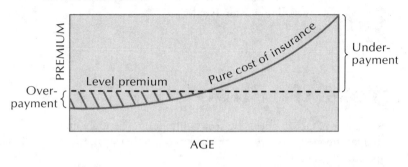

A company that writes an insurance policy to cover an individual for his or her entire life has assumed a liability that is certain. It has promised to pay a specified sum when the person dies—a situation with 100 percent probability and an important feature distinguishing life insurance from other forms of insurance. Many policies on homes, cars, and personal liability do not result in claims, and of those that do, few are for the maximum coverage. When an insurer establishes the premium for a policy to cover a person for life, it must be set at a level that will accumulate enough reserves in the early years to pay the certain claim later on.

The level premium and the policy reserves are established to ensure that there will be enough money to pay the face amount to the beneficiary at some future date. However, if the policyholder decides to cancel the policy, the insurance company is relieved of the promise to pay this amount, the reserve fund will not be needed and, therefore, can be refunded to the policyholder.

It is unfortunate that so much of the life insurance literature (and sales pitch) refers to policy reserves as the savings feature. The policy reserves are available to the policyholder only if the policy is cancelled or the coverage reduced; it is impossible to have both full life insurance coverage and access to the policy reserves at the same time. Life insurance will be easier to understand if you remember that the cash value of a policy is the reserve required to cover the certain liability that the company has assumed.

DAVID CANCELS HIS POLICY

When he was 25, David decided to buy a whole life policy with a face amount of $50 000. The premium of $554.50 was payable once a year for the rest of his life.

By the time he was 40 he was divorced, without children or other dependents and saw no need to continue this policy. He informed the insurance company that he wished to cancel his insurance and have a refund of the policy reserves, that had grown to $5950. This cancellation meant that David was no longer insured and the company had no further liability.

FACTORS AFFECTING COST

A number of factors affect the cost of life insurance, including mortality rate, loading charges, frequency of premium payments, whether or not it is a participating policy, and the type of policy.

Mortality Rate

Mortality rate is the primary determinant of the price you will pay for life insurance. To estimate your mortality risk, an actuary would need to know your age and gender, the state of your health, and whether you engage in any hazardous activities. Your cost will be raised by anything that increases the risk of death (for instance, smoking). Should the insurance company consider the probability of your dying soon to be too high, it will not insure your life. Fortunately, the proportion of applicants rejected is very small (about two percent) but some people, classified as higher than average risks, have to pay larger premiums.

Loading Charges

In addition to the pure cost of insuring a life, an amount called the loading charge is included in the premium. The company's **loading charge** includes administrative costs, commissions to sales people, and profit for shareholders. The largest component in loading charges is a commission to life insurance agents, which may be from 25 percent to 85 percent of the first year premium. On renewals, the commission may be from 2 to 15 percent. Individual life insurance policies are sold by sales agents who depend on commissions for income and must search energetically for clients, a very expensive method of selling. Other financial institutions—especially banks and trust companies—are now interested in selling insurance at their offices, probably more cheaply. It will be interesting to watch developments.

Offsetting these loading costs to some extent is the interest that may be earned on the pooled funds, which the company can invest until claims are made. Life insurance companies, as managers of the pooled insurance funds, usually collect more than they expect to pay out in claims, not just to establish policy reserves, but also to set up special reserve funds in case their estimates are too low.

Frequency of Premium Payments

Your total cost per year will vary slightly depending on the frequency with which the premiums are to be paid. If you pay annually, the total cost will be lower than if you pay semi-annually or monthly. The basis for these differences is the amount of interest the company can obtain by investing the premium funds.

Participating and Non-Participating Policies

The difference between participating and non-participating policies lies in the way the premiums are calculated. Premiums for **non-participating policies** are estimated as accurately as possible and cannot be increased by the company. If the company under-estimated or over-estimated the cost, the difference is met from the company's funds or a change in premium rates on policies sold in the future. For **participating policies**, the premiums are usually set somewhat higher than for non-participating ones, but the policyholder will receive a refund on any excess. These refunds are called **dividends**, but the term is confusing since they are not a form of income such as stock dividends. Because they are refunds, they are not subject to income tax. In other words, insurance dividends are a return of after-tax dollars.

In any one year, the dividend amount will depend on such factors as the company's efficiency, its return on investments, the amount paid out in claims, and the number of policies cancelled. Dividends may be taken in cash, used to pay the next premium, used to buy more insurance, or left on deposit to earn interest. Although dividends are not considered taxable income, any interest they generate will be taxable.

BASIC TYPES OF LIFE INSURANCE

Distinguishing Features

A life insurance policy, however it may be labelled to interest prospective buyers, is almost always one or a combination of two basic types—term or whole life. The inventiveness of companies in naming their many elaborations has led to unnecessary confusion.In spite of a lack of uniform terminology, it is usually possible to identify the fundamental policy type if you have a good understanding of the distinguishing features of each. Two important characteristics to consider are whether or not:

(a) the coverage is for life,

(b) the policy accumulates a cash value.

Term insurance is coverage for a specific period, without cash value, while whole life provides life-long protection, with cash value.

Term Insurance

Like fire or auto insurance, **term insurance** provides protection against a specified risk for a definite length of time. At the end of that time, or term, the insurance lapses unless renewed. The important characteristic of term insurance is that it is protection for a designated period—not for life. Term insurance may be purchased for periods of various length: one, five, and ten years are common. It is also possible to buy term to age 65 years, or even to 100. A product called "term to 100" adds to the confusion by offering coverage for life with no cash value.

Because most buyers of term insurance have a fairly low probability of dying in the near future—they are usually under 65 years of age—and because the company does not assume coverage for life, the cost of term insurance is lower than for other types. The premium is made level for the term of the policy and any reserves

FIGURE 6.4 PREMIUM LEVELS FOR FIVE-YEAR RENEWABLE TERM INSURANCE BY GENDER AND AGE

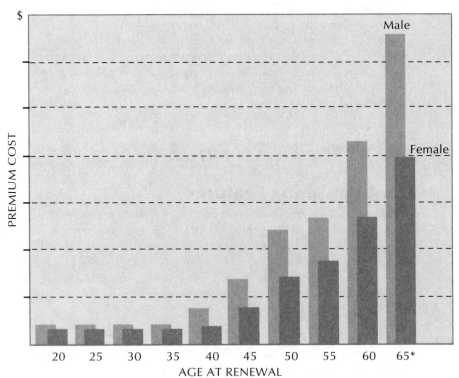

accumulated are relatively small and will be used up during the term. For these reasons, no cash value is available to the policyholder. As with all life insurance, the face value will be paid to the beneficiary if the insured dies while the policy is in force. However, from the company's point of view, the probability of paying claims on term insurance is low; they have not taken on the sure liability they assume in policies with lifelong coverage.

Although the premium for term insurance is level for the specified term, at the next renewal the premium must necessarily be raised, since the insured has aged and the probability of dying has increased. Figure 6.4 illustrates the changes in premium at each renewal as the pure cost of life insurance rises. By age 65, the pure cost of life insurance becomes very high, and few term policies are offered because of the limited market at that price.

Term insurance offers the most face value per premium dollar of any type of life insurance because it does not give protection at advanced ages, when the cost of insurance is high. As illustrated in Figure 6.5, for every $100 that you can afford to spend each year on life insurance, you will obtain more face amount (life insurance coverage) with term insurance than other types of policies. Although this is a useful comparison, there are two caveats. First, the insurer's liability is not the same with each type of policy shown, varying from five years to life. Second, the premiums shown in this comparison have been made level for different periods, involving varying amounts of reserve funds. Looked at in another way, for a given amount of life insurance, the annual cost will be lowest for term coverage.

DECREASING TERM INSURANCE   Thus far we have discussed term insurance with a face amount that is constant throughout the term. However, it is also possible to buy term insurance with a decreasing face amount. This variant is useful when the risk being covered is expected to diminish. It is often used as mortgage insurance by persons who wish to leave dependents a debt-free home in the event of their death. At the outset, the face amount is equal to the outstanding debt on the house, but decreases at a rate roughly equal to that at which the debt is expected to be reduced. If the insured dies during the term, the face amount of the policy should be adequate to pay the outstanding balance on the mortgage. The beneficiary is, of course, under no obligation to use the death benefit for this purpose. It is simply a life insurance policy that will pay a certain sum to the beneficiary when the insured dies. One may argue that special mortgage insurance is unnecessary if overall life insurance coverage is adequate.

Another use for decreasing term insurance is income protection for a young family. Many people feel it is wise to arrange their insurance coverage to match the period of highest financial risk so that coverage is at a maximum when the children are very young. As the children grow, the risk decreases, and so may the need for life insurance. Reducing term insurance is appropriate for such a situation.

FIGURE 6.5 Face Amount by Policy Type for a Given Premium

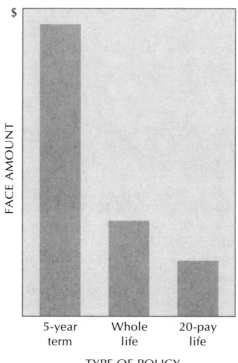

The face amount of a decreasing term policy falls to zero at the end of the term, with downward adjustments monthly or annually. Premiums, however, are level for the term, probably to discourage policyholders from cancelling the policy when the coverage becomes low. Some companies set a level premium for a period shorter than the entire term; for instance, the premiums on a 20-year decreasing term policy might be paid up in 16 years. Term and decreasing term insurance are compared in Figure 6.6.

GROUP LIFE INSURANCE   Life insurance may be purchased by individuals or groups. In its most common form, group insurance is bought by employers to cover the lives of a large group of employees. Payment for this insurance may be shared by employer and employee, or alternately, one or the other may pay the entire amount. In any event, one policy covers a group of lives. No medical examinations are required as evidence of insurability, but there are some rules intended to avoid a selection of risks that might be adverse to the insurance company. For instance, all employees may be required to join the group plan, or, if there is a choice, employees may be required to join at a specific time, perhaps when they begin employment. In

FIGURE 6.6 TERM AND DECREASING TERM INSURANCE

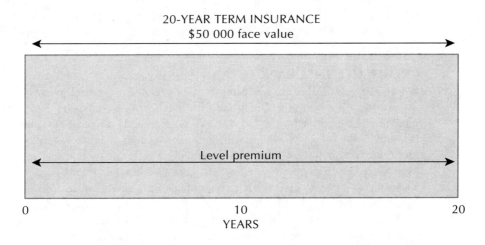

20-YEAR TERM INSURANCE
$50 000 face value

Level premium

0   10   20
YEARS

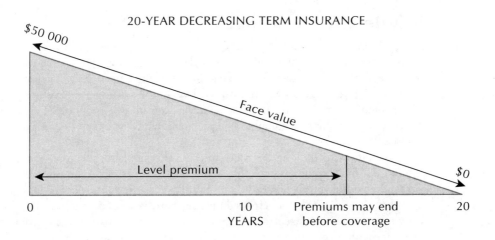

20-YEAR DECREASING TERM INSURANCE

$50 000

Face value

Level premium

$0

0   10   Premiums may end   20
         YEARS   before coverage

any case, it will be arranged so that most employees cannot avoid being insured. The amount of coverage will also depend on a rule: the face amount may be some multiple of the employee's annual salary, or all employees may be covered for the same amount.

Group insurance is most often one-year renewable term, but it may also be whole life insurance. Since employees of all ages pay the same premium, group coverage can be a bargain for the older worker. The coverage usually ends whenever an employee terminates employment, but there may be an option of converting, within a month, from the group policy to individual term or whole life. The premiums for group policies are usually lower than for similar insurance bought individually because selling and administration costs are decreased when a single policy covers a large group of lives. The employer collects the premiums and pays the insurer for the group.

CREDIT LIFE INSURANCE A specialized version of group term insurance, known as **credit life insurance,** is purchased by lenders to cover the lives of a group of borrowers. If a borrower should die with a debt still outstanding, the insurer will reimburse the creditor for the balance owing. Ultimately, the cost of such insurance is borne by the borrower, who may or may not be given a choice in having the loan life insured. This type of insurance is certainly of interest to creditors who are not keen to see debt repayments cease when a borrower dies, and can be useful to anyone who is anxious not to leave a debt to be paid out of his or her estate.

In summary, credit life insurance is a type of group coverage arranged by the lender and the benefits must be used to discharge the debt. Alternatively, decreasing term insurance to insure a person who has a mortgage may be arranged privately and need not be used to pay off the mortgage.

Whole Life Insurance

A type of insurance commonly bought by individuals is **whole life insurance** (also called straight life or ordinary life). It provides insurance protection from the time of purchase until death (Figure 6.7). To maintain this lifelong coverage, premiums must be paid each year as long as the insured lives—unless the premiums are prepaid. Some companies terminate the policies at very advanced ages, such as 95, and pay the policyholder the face amount. The premium, which is established at the time of purchase, is level for life.

In addition to its long duration, another distinguishing feature of whole life insurance is the accumulation of policy reserves, also known as **cash reserves** or **cash surrender value.** From Figure 6.3, you will recall that in order to have a level premium, the policyholder overpays during the early years and underpays later. These early payments, which exceed the pure cost of insurance, create a reserve that grows over time as more premiums are paid and the reserve funds earn interest.

Any cash reserves created in the first year or two are used for the company's selling and issue expenses, including commissions, and therefore the policy has no cash value at first. A sample whole life policy is reproduced in Figure 6.8. This policy has a table showing cash values each year the insurance is in force. To read the table, find the column headed by the policyholder's age at time of purchase, which in this case was 25. Assume that you wish to know the cash value five years later. The entries in the table are per $1000 of face value. This policy was for $50 000, therefore the cash value after five years would be 18 × 50 = $900. Each year the reserves continue to grow until around age 100, when the cash value will equal the face amount (Figure 6.7).

FIGURE 6.7 TYPES OF LIFE INSURANCE

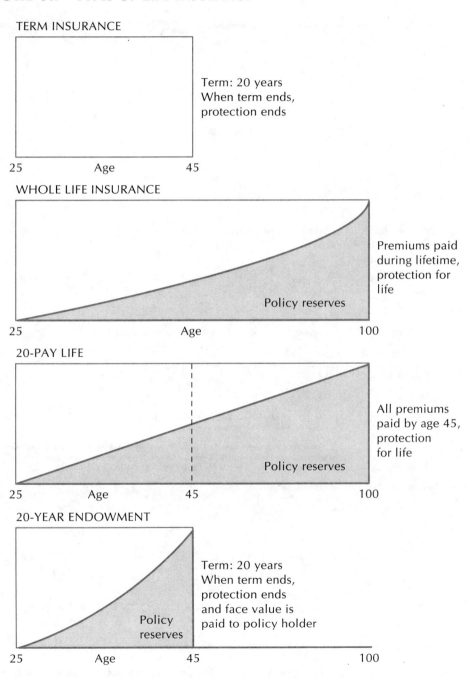

TERM INSURANCE

Term: 20 years
When term ends,
protection ends

25   Age   45

WHOLE LIFE INSURANCE

Premiums paid
during lifetime,
protection for
life

Policy reserves

25   Age   100

20-PAY LIFE

All premiums
paid by age 45,
protection
for life

Policy reserves

25   Age   45   100

20-YEAR ENDOWMENT

Term: 20 years
When term ends,
protection ends
and face value is
paid to policy holder

Policy
reserves

25   Age   45   100

FIGURE 6.8 SAMPLE LIFE INSURANCE POLICY

Policy Data

POLICY NUMBER   *346238*

POLICY DATE   *August 7, 1986*

LIFE INSURED   *David Gerald Hill*

AGE OF LIFE INSURED   *25*

OWNER   *David Gerald Hill, the life insured*

BENEFICIARY   as stated in the application unless subsequently changed

PLAN OF INSURANCE   Whole Life

FACE AMOUNT $ *50,000.00* **

PREMIUMS   Amount $ *554.50*

The first premium is due on the policy date. Premiums are payable every *twelve* month(s) while the life insured is living.

If this policy includes any Additional Benefits, the premium above includes the premiums for such benefits. When the premium for any Additional Benefit is no longer payable, the premium for the policy will be reduced accordingly.

Additional Benefits included in this policy are:

Policy Data   **SPECIMEN**

FIGURE 6.8 SAMPLE LIFE INSURANCE POLICY (CONTINUED)

General Provisions

The Contract

The policy and the application are part of the contract. The contract also includes documents attached at issue and any amendments agreed upon in writing after the policy is issued. The policy may not be amended nor any provision waived except by written agreement signed by authorized signing officers of the Company.

Owner

While the life insured is living, all benefits, rights and privileges under the contract belong to the owner.

Beneficiary

The owner may appoint a beneficiary. The owner may change the beneficiary unless the appointment was irrevocable. If there is no beneficiary living when the life insured dies, the owner or the estate of the owner is the beneficiary.

Payment of Premiums

Premiums are due on the dates indicated on the policy data page. If any cheque or other instrument given for payment is not honoured, the premium remains unpaid.

If a premium remains unpaid by the end of the days of grace, dividend accumulations will automatically be applied towards paying the premium. Any portion of the premium still remaining unpaid will be automatically paid by a loan on the policy, subject to the terms of the Automatic Premium Loan clause. If the premium remains only partially paid after the application of dividend accumulations or by payment by an automatic premium loan or both, the policy will stay in force for a pro-rated part of the premium period. This is the only condition under which we will accept a premium payment for less than the amount due.

Currency and Place of Payment

All amounts payable to or by us will be payable in Canadian dollars at any of our offices.

Days of Grace

Thirty-one days of grace are allowed for payment of each premium except the first. During this time, the policy will stay in force. If the life insured dies during this time, any premium due but unpaid will be deducted from the amount payable.

Lapse

This contract will lapse and our liability will cease:

— at the end of the days of grace of an unpaid premium unless:

  i. the premium or part of it is advanced by dividend accumulations or by automatic premium loan, as described in the payment of premiums provision; or

  ii. the policy is changed to Reduced Paid-Up Life Insurance; or

— at the end of a pro-rated part of a premium period, if part of a premium has been advanced by dividend

accumulations or by an automatic premium loan, or both; however, the policy will not lapse before the end of the days of grace for an unpaid premium; or

— when the indebtedness equals or exceeds the cash value.

Assignment

We will not recognize an assignment until we receive written notice of it at our Head Office. We are not responsible for the validity of any assignment.

Misstatement of Age

If the date of birth of the life insured or any other person insured under this policy has been misstated, the amount payable shall be increased or decreased to the amount that would have been provided for the same premium at the correct age or ages.

Validity

We may contest the contract if any statement or answer on any application misrepresents or fails to disclose any fact material to the insurance. We shall not contest the contract for these reasons after it has been in force during the lifetime of the life insured for two years from the date it takes effect, either on issue, on reissue for an increased amount or on reinstatement. However, in cases involving fraud, we may contest the contract at any time.

Reinstatement

This contract may be reinstated within three years of lapse. Reinstatement is not allowed on policies where the cash surrender value has been paid or the policy has been changed to Reduced Paid-Up Life Insurance.

Reinstatement requires:

— a written application; and

— evidence which satisfies us that the life insured and any other person insured under this policy is an acceptable risk; and

— all overdue premiums and the indebtedness outstanding at the lapse date must be paid with interest at the yearly rate determined by us.

This policy shall not be deemed to be reinstated until our official notification of reinstatement has been issued.

Self-Destruction

If the life insured dies from suicide or self-inflicted injuries, while either sane or insane:

— within one year of the date of Part 1 of the application for this policy, the amount payable is limited to the premiums paid;

— within one year of the date of the application for any Additional Benefit under this policy, the amount payable in respect of the Additional Benefit is limited to the premiums paid for the Additional Benefit;

— within one year of the date of the application for any reinstatement of this policy, the amount payable is limited to the premiums paid since the date of the last reinstatement.

General Provisions **SPECIMEN** LIR 709 508

FIGURE 6.8 SAMPLE LIFE INSURANCE POLICY (CONTINUED)

Benefit Provisions

Insuring Clause

We agree that the amount payable under the terms of this policy will be paid on the death of the life insured. Death must occur while this policy is in force.

Benefit Clause

Subject to the terms of this policy, the amount payable will include the face amount, dividends, any Additional Benefit payable on death, less any indebtedness.

Definitions

"Indebtedness" means any policy loans and premium loans and overdue premiums and includes accrued interest.

"Tabular Cash Value" means the value determined in accordance with the "Table of Guaranteed Values".

"Cash Value" means the tabular cash value plus the surrender value of any paid-up additions purchased by dividends. This surrender value will be determined using the same mortality table and rate of interest as used in calculating the "Table of Guaranteed Values".

"Cash Surrender Value" means the cash value plus dividend accumulations less any indebtedness.

"Loan Value" means the cash value less one year's interest, at our current loan interest rate, on the cash value.

"Policy Date" is the date used to determine premium due dates, policy anniversaries and policy years.

"We", "our", and "us" refer to the Co-operators Life Insurance Company.

Payment on Death

The amount payable on the death of the life insured will be paid when sufficient evidence is received as to the death, the age of the life insured, the right of the claimant to be paid and the identity and age of the beneficiary (if any).

Dividends

This policy participates in the surplus distribution of the Company. Our Board of Directors determines the owner's share and we credit it to the policy as a dividend at the end of each policy year. Dividends are applied under the option the owner has elected from those available on this policy. This option remains in effect unless we agree to a change.

Policy Loans

We will grant a loan on the security of the policy. The maximum loan available will be the loan value less any indebtedness. We may require completion of a loan agreement. Interest will accrue from day to day on any loan, whether granted under this clause or under the Automatic Premium Loan clause. The interest rate will be determined by us from time to time. Interest not paid by the end of each policy year will be added to the principal of the loan and will bear interest.

Automatic Premium Loan

We will automatically make a policy loan to pay for any premium not paid by the end of the days of grace. If the loan available is less than the unpaid premium, the loan will be used to keep the policy in force for a pro-rated part of the premium period. Such loans shall bear interest from the end of the days of grace.

Reduced Paid-Up Life Insurance Option

The owner may elect to change this policy to paid-up whole life insurance provided that the new face amount is greater than a minimum value set by us. The new face amount will be the amount provided by the cash value less any indebtedness applied as a single premium and premium payments will cease.

Cash Surrender Option

While this policy has a cash surrender value, it may be surrendered for cash.

On surrender, we will pay the cash surrender value and our liability will cease. Evidence as to the age of the life insured and the right of the claimant to be paid is required on surrender.

Settlement Options

The amount payable on the death of the life insured or on surrender of the policy may be paid in cash, left on deposit at interest, used to provide an annuity or settled on any other agreed basis.

The choice of settlement may be made by the owner. If the owner does not make a choice, the beneficiary shall make the choice of settlement. With our consent, the beneficiary may change a settlement chosen by the owner, unless the owner has specified otherwise.

Details of the options and the conditions under which they are available will be provided on request.

SPECIMEN

Benefit Provisions

FIGURE 6.8 SAMPLE LIFE INSURANCE POLICY (CONTINUED)

Excerpt from a Table of Guaranteed Values

Tabular cash values and paid-up whole life insurance values, per $1000.00 of the face amount, are shown in this table. The values applicable to this policy are those for age shown in the policy data page as Age of Life Insured.

END OF POLICY YEAR	AGE 21 CASH VALUE	AGE 21 PAID-UP VALUE	AGE 22 CASH VALUE	AGE 22 PAID-UP VALUE	AGE 23 CASH VALUE	AGE 23 PAID-UP VALUE	AGE 24 CASH VALUE	AGE 24 PAID-UP VALUE	AGE 25 CASH VALUE	AGE 25 PAID-UP VALUE	AGE 26 CASH VALUE	AGE 26 PAID-UP VALUE	AGE 27 CASH VALUE	AGE 27 PAID-UP VALUE	END OF POLICY YEAR
1	–	–	–	–	–	–	–	–	–	–	–	–	–	–	1
2	–	–	–	–	–	–	–	–	–	–	–	–	–	–	2
3	–	–	–	–	–	–	–	–	1	6	1	6	2	11	3
4	5	33	6	39	7	44	8	48	9	52	10	56	11	59	4
5	12	78	14	87	15	90	17	98	18	100	19	102	21	109	5
6	20	125	22	132	24	139	25	139	27	145	29	150	31	155	6
7	28	168	30	173	32	178	34	183	37	191	39	194	41	197	7
8	36	208	39	217	41	220	44	228	46	229	49	235	51	236	8
9	45	250	48	257	51	264	54	269	56	269	59	273	62	276	9
10	54	290	57	295	60	299	64	307	67	310	70	310	74	318	10
11	62	320	66	329	69	331	73	337	77	343	80	343	84	348	11
12	71	353	75	360	79	365	83	370	87	373	91	376	95	379	12
13	80	383	84	388	88	392	93	399	97	401	102	407	106	407	13
14	89	411	94	418	98	420	103	426	108	430	113	434	118	437	14
15	98	436	104	446	109	450	114	454	119	457	124	459	130	465	15
16	108	463	114	471	119	474	125	480	130	482	136	486	142	490	16
17	118	488	124	494	130	499	136	504	142	507	148	510	155	516	17
18	129	514	135	519	141	522	148	529	154	531	161	536	168	540	18
19	139	534	146	541	153	547	160	552	167	556	174	559	181	562	19
20	151	559	158	565	165	569	172	572	179	575	187	580	194	582	20
Age 60	416	833	413	827	410	821	406	813	402	805	398	797	394	789	Age 60
Age 65	497	874	494	869	491	864	488	858	484	851	481	846	477	839	Age 65

END OF POLICY YEAR	AGE 28 CASH VALUE	AGE 28 PAID-UP VALUE	AGE 29 CASH VALUE	AGE 29 PAID-UP VALUE	AGE 30 CASH VALUE	AGE 30 PAID-UP VALUE	AGE 31 CASH VALUE	AGE 31 PAID-UP VALUE	AGE 32 CASH VALUE	AGE 32 PAID-UP VALUE	AGE 33 CASH VALUE	AGE 33 PAID-UP VALUE	AGE 34 CASH VALUE	AGE 34 PAID-UP VALUE	END OF POLICY YEAR
1	–	–	–	–	–	–	–	–	–	–	–	–	–	–	1
2	–	–	–	–	–	–	–	–	–	–	–	–	–	–	2
3	2	11	3	16	3	15	4	19	4	19	5	22	5	22	3
4	12	62	13	65	14	67	15	70	16	72	17	73	18	75	4
5	22	110	23	111	25	116	26	116	28	121	29	120	30	120	5
6	32	154	34	158	36	161	38	163	40	166	42	168	44	170	6
7	43	199	45	201	47	202	50	207	52	208	54	208	57	212	7
8	54	241	56	241	59	244	62	248	65	250	68	253	71	254	8
9	65	279	68	282	71	283	75	289	78	290	81	290	85	294	9
10	77	319	80	319	84	323	88	327	91	326	95	328	99	330	10
11	88	351	92	354	96	356	100	358	104	359	109	363	113	364	11
12	99	381	103	382	108	386	113	390	118	393	122	392	127	395	12
13	111	411	116	415	121	418	126	420	131	421	136	422	142	426	13
14	123	440	128	442	134	446	138	447	145	450	151	453	157	455	14
15	135	466	141	469	147	472	153	475	159	477	165	478	172	482	15
16	148	493	154	495	161	500	167	501	174	504	180	505	187	507	16
17	161	517	168	521	174	522	181	525	188	527	196	532	203	533	17
18	174	540	181	543	189	548	196	549	203	551	211	554	219	557	18
19	188	564	195	565	203	569	211	572	219	575	227	577	235	578	19
20	202	586	210	589	218	591	226	593	234	595	243	598	251	599	20
Age 60	389	779	384	769	378	757	373	747	367	735	360	721	354	709	Age 60
Age 65	473	832	468	823	464	816	459	807	454	798	448	788	442	777	Age 65

END OF POLICY YEAR	AGE 35 CASH VALUE	AGE 35 PAID-UP VALUE	AGE 36 CASH VALUE	AGE 36 PAID-UP VALUE	AGE 37 CASH VALUE	AGE 37 PAID-UP VALUE	AGE 38 CASH VALUE	AGE 38 PAID-UP VALUE	AGE 39 CASH VALUE	AGE 39 PAID-UP VALUE	AGE 40 CASH VALUE	AGE 40 PAID-UP VALUE	AGE 41 CASH VALUE	AGE 41 PAID-UP VALUE	END OF POLICY YEAR
1	–	–	–	–	–	–	–	–	–	–	–	–	–	–	1
2	–	–	–	–	–	–	–	–	–	–	–	–	–	–	2
3	6	25	6	24	7	27	8	30	8	29	9	31	9	30	3
4	19	76	20	77	21	78	22	79	23	80	24	81	26	85	4
5	32	124	34	127	35	126	37	128	39	131	40	130	42	132	5
6	46	171	48	172	50	173	52	174	55	178	57	178	59	178	6
7	60	215	62	215	65	217	68	220	71	222	74	223	77	225	7
8	74	256	77	257	80	258	84	262	87	262	91	265	95	268	8
9	89	297	92	296	96	299	100	301	104	303	108	304	113	308	9
10	104	335	108	336	112	337	117	340	121	340	126	343	131	345	10
11	118	367	123	369	128	372	133	374	138	375	143	376	149	380	11
12	133	399	138	400	143	401	149	405	155	407	161	410	167	412	12
13	148	429	153	429	159	432	166	436	172	438	178	439	185	442	13
14	163	457	169	458	176	462	182	463	189	465	196	468	204	472	14
15	179	485	185	486	192	488	200	492	207	494	214	495	222	499	15
16	194	509	202	513	209	514	217	518	224	518	232	521	240	524	16
17	210	534	218	537	226	539	234	542	242	544	250	545	259	549	17
18	227	559	235	561	243	562	252	566	260	567	269	570	278	573	18
19	243	580	252	583	261	586	269	587	278	589	287	591	297	595	19
20	260	602	269	604	278	606	287	608	296	610	306	613	316	616	20
Age 60	347	695	339	679	332	665	324	649	315	631	306	613	297	595	Age 60
Age 65	436	767	430	756	423	744	416	732	409	719	401	705	393	691	Age 65

It is impossible to have the use of the cash reserves and also maintain full insurance coverage. The policy states that if the insured person dies, the full face amount of the policy will be paid to the beneficiary. Whenever that happens, the policy terminates and so does the cash value. However, during his lifetime, the insured can make use of the cash reserves if he or she is willing to diminish the coverage accordingly. A number of uses for the cash reserves will be outlined in a later section.

LIMITED PAYMENT LIFE INSURANCE   A variation of whole life insurance is the **limited payment policy** that, as the name indicates, is completely paid for during a specified period. Instead of paying premiums for life, the insured pays higher premiums for a shorter time, usually 20 years or to age 65. After it is paid up, the policy remains in force for the rest of the life of the insured. This type of policy is selected when the insured expects to be able to pay for insurance more readily early in life, and thus may be appropriate for people who expect high incomes for a short time, such as professional athletes. However, for most families this type of policy cannot provide sufficient coverage when it is most needed.

The more rapid rate of payment with limited payment insurance causes the cash surrender value to increase faster than with whole life. After the payment period ends, the cash surrender value continues to grow (Figure 6.7). Except for the shorter payment period, limited-pay life is similar in most respects to whole life insurance; the cash surrender value can also be used in the same ways.

COMBINATION POLICIES

There are too many variations and combinations of the two basic types of life insurance to consider them all here. As well, the industry is constantly inventing new versions. The four combination types selected for discussion here are: endowment life, universal life, family income policy, and family policy.

Endowment Life Insurance

Endowment life insurance, a policy type rarely sold nowadays, provides coverage for a specified period, at the end of which the insurer promises to pay the face amount. The insurance company accepts a liability that is 100 percent certain: the face value must be paid if the insured dies during the term or if the insured is alive at maturity. Therefore, the policy reserves must be built up rapidly (Figure 6.7) resulting in higher annual premiums than are required for other types of insurance. While the policy is in force, the cash surrender value may be used by the insured in the same ways as whole life. Endowment insurance shares characteristics with both term and whole life: it is for a term but it has a cash value. However, it is not an effective way either to build up savings or obtain life insurance coverage.

Universal Life Insurance

The rigidity of a fixed premium for life with an inflexible face amount to be paid many years later have not always been attractive to insurance buyers. For instance, in inflationary periods, insurance coverage once thought to be sufficient for dependents may become inadequate because of lost purchasing power. Those who want to invest their savings with an insurance company may prefer to have insurance coverage and savings kept separate. **Universal life insurance,** invented to offer buyers such flexibility, is a combination of term insurance and a savings account.

The distinctive features of universal life are: (i) the flexibility in payments, (ii) the opportunity to withdraw funds, (iii) the freedom to alter the amount of insurance coverage at any time, and (iv) the regular disclosure of fees, interest earned, and other information. These features contrast with traditional policies where the buyer does not know how the premiums are divided among the pure cost of insurance, reserves, and loading charges, or what rate of interest is being credited on the reserves.

FLEXIBLE PAYMENTS   The payment of money into a universal life policy is voluntary within prescribed limits. The money is used to create a fund from which the company deducts the cost of insurance protection—which is rather like term coverage—and a loading charge. The balance is credited with interest and treated as a sort of investment fund from which the policyholder may make withdrawals. The policyholder can choose how much to put in each year, but if no payment is made for a time, the insurance cost will be deducted from any balance in the fund. If the company is deducting the pure cost of insurance each year, you can expect this amount to increase as you grow older.

WITHDRAWAL PRIVILEGES   The funds in the cash account are available for you to withdraw or borrow against as you wish. If you leave the money in the account, you will draw interest at current rates. A minimum rate may be guaranteed for a year.

FLEXIBLE COVERAGE   There may be possibilities for changing your coverage, within limits, as your needs change. The flexibility in premiums may lead the buyer to forget payments, with consequent loss of coverage.

REGULAR STATEMENTS   You will receive regular statements showing all the transactions in your account. These statements will keep you informed about your coverage and its cost, loading charges, and the return on the cash account.

CAVEATS FOR BUYERS   Prospective buyers of universal life insurance need to become informed about all the charges that will be assessed, such as one-time administrative fees, loading charges, and surrender charges. Buyers should also know how the loading charges will be distributed. Some companies deduct loading charges before depositing the premium in the account, while others credit the premium, then deduct charges. Some may charge an initial fee and then a loading charge of 5 to 10 percent, and a fee for each withdrawal. Loading charges may be a constant proportion of each premium, front loaded, or back loaded. If in the early years of the policy a larger share of the premium is used for loading charges, the policy is referred to as **front-loaded.** When little is deducted from the premiums at the outset for loading charges, but a disproportionate share is added when a policy is surrendered, the policy is **back-loaded.** Some companies may charge very high surrender charges if the policy is cancelled within a few years. However, if the policy remains in force for some time, the surrender charges diminish.

Other aspects to investigate include the tax treatment of interest, buried fees, and the costs and benefits of having insurance coverage combined with a savings account. The tax treatment of interest and the payments to beneficiaries should be inquired into, along with the nature of the various fees. It is also possible that some charges may be buried in changed rates for the "pure cost of insurance." Companies may use high interest rates to attract buyers, but decrease them later, or project unrealistic future interest rates. Thought should be given to the wisdom of having a term life policy and investment fund combination in one contract, instead of separate arrangements for each.

Family Income Policy

Term and whole life insurance are combined in various ways to make a **family income policy** (Figure 6.9). The person insured is usually the family's principal income earner. The whole life portion of the policy covers the insured for life, paying a specified amount on his or her death, whenever it may occur. The term portion provides coverage for a definite period, for example, 20 years. If the insured dies during the term, the policy will provide an income for dependents that will continue for the remainder of the term. If the insured lives more than 20 years after buying the policy, the term coverage will have expired, but the whole life insurance will continue.

Family Policy

Some insurers may offer a **family policy** that is a package with separate coverage for the husband, the wife, and each present and future child. This policy may be term insurance only, or a combination of term and whole life. In the latter instance, the whole life coverage would probably be on the life of the principal earner. If any family member should die during the term of his or her coverage, the insurer will pay the coverage for that individual, but the package will continue to cover the lives of the survivors. The buyer should evaluate the risks to the family's economic situation of the death of each family member.

FIGURE 6.9 FAMILY POLICY AND FAMILY INCOME POLICY

FAMILY POLICY

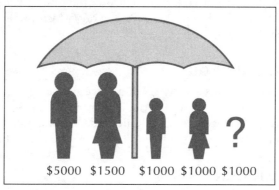

$5000 $1500 $1000 $1000 $1000

FAMILY INCOME POLICY

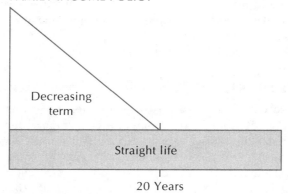

THE INSURANCE POLICY

A life insurance policy is the contract between the insuring company and the policyholder. Some aspects of this complex legal document will be outlined here. A life insurance contract is not a contract of indemnity as is property insurance, where the insured is to be indemnified or returned to the financial position he or she would have been in had the loss not occurred. With a life insurance policy, a predictable sum of money is payable by the insurer—an important distinction. A sample whole life policy is shown in Figure 6.8.

Description of Policy

Near the beginning of the policy there should be such basic information as: the face amount, the type of policy, the name of the insured person, the insured's age, the date the coverage begins, the period during which the insurance is to be effective, and the amount of the premium.

Grace Period

The policyholder is usually given a **grace period** of one month after the date the premium is due, during which the insurance remains in force and the premium may be paid without penalty. If the insured should die during the grace period, the beneficiary will receive the face value less the amount of the unpaid premium.

Dividends

The dividend clause in a participating policy covers the details of the company's payment of dividends and describes the various options available to the policyholder. The insured may take the dividends in cash, use them to reduce the premium, use them to purchase paid-up additions to the life insurance in force or one-year term additions, or leave them on deposit with the company to earn interest. The range of options available is determined by the company.

Incontestability

To protect themselves from future legal actions arising from alleged misrepresentations by the insured, life insurance companies have inserted an **incontestability clause,** stating that after two years in force, the policy will not be invalidated by any non-disclosure or misrepresentation that may be discovered, with the exception of fraud. During these two years, the company can seek to be released from the contract if it discovers that the applicant made false statements.

Policy Loans

In any policy with cash reserves, the conditions under which policy loans are available will be stated somewhere in the policy. Related to these conditions is the automatic premium loan, which provides that if a policyholder fails to pay the premiums or take any other action, the company will use the cash surrender value to pay the premium, repeating the process as required until the cash value has been exhausted.

Ownership Rights and Assignment

The rights of the life insurance policy owner include the right to name and change the beneficiary, to use the cash value, to receive any dividends, and to dispose of any of these rights. If one person holds all of these rights, that person is the sole owner of the policy; if ownership is shared with someone, each becomes a part or joint owner. Usually the person insured and the owner are the same. Like other contracts, a life insurance policy is assignable—that is, its ownership may be transferred. For example, when a policy is used as collateral for a loan, the policy is assigned to the creditor.

Beneficiary

The beneficiary clause identifies who is intended to receive the proceeds of the insurance on the policyholder's death. In most cases, the insured may alter the designation of beneficiary by signing a declaration to be filed with the insurance company. Sometimes people forget to do this when family conditions change, leaving the insurance payable to an estranged, divorced, or deceased spouse. Insurance proceeds payable to a named beneficiary are not distributed through the deceased's will, but go directly to the person designated, free from claims that creditors or others may have on the estate.

If the primary beneficiary dies before the person whose life has been insured, and no alternative (secondary) beneficiary has been named, the company may pay the proceeds to the estate of the deceased. Only rarely will a policyholder name a beneficiary irrevocably, which means that the designation of beneficiary cannot be changed without the consent of the beneficiary. In such instances, the policyholder cannot assign the cash surrender value of the policy to a third party without the consent of the named **irrevocable beneficiary**.

Settlement Options

The way in which the proceeds of a life insurance policy will be paid to the beneficiary may be settled by the insured, prior to death, or can be left to the beneficiary's discretion. Some of the ways in which life insurance can be paid, other than as a lump sum, will be outlined here. The interest option involves leaving the principal sum on deposit with the insurance company and receiving the interest regularly. In the instalment option, the proceeds are paid in instalments over a selected period of time by various arrangements, all involving payment of principal and interest. The proceeds can be used to purchase a single payment annuity (life income) with payments to begin either immediately or at a later date; this is sometimes referred to as the life income option. (Annuities are explained in the chapter on retirement income.)

USES FOR THE CASH RESERVES

The policy reserve, also known as cash value or cash surrender value, has a number of possible uses during the lifetime of the policyholder; five of them will be reviewed here.

(a) Surrender of the policy

(b) Policy loan

(c) Automatic premium loan

(d) Collateral for a loan

(e) Paid-up policy

Surrender the Policy

One obvious use of the cash value is to cancel or surrender the policy and take the cash value, effectively terminating the insurance coverage. The table of cash values in the policy shows how much the cash value is according to the number of years the policy has been in force (Figure 6.8).

Policy Loan

It is possible to arrange a **policy loan,** or to borrow from the cash surrender value, at an interest rate that is usually lower than the rate on loans from other sources. There is no pressure to repay a policy loan, but in the meantime the interest continues to accumulate. If the insured should die before the loan is repaid, the unpaid balance and outstanding interest will be deducted from the face value of the policy before the proceeds are paid to the beneficiary.

MIMI TAKES OUT A POLICY LOAN

As she reviewed her finances in preparation for buying a new car, Mimi remembered that she had a whole life insurance policy that she bought 20 years ago. Since her children are now independent and her need for life insurance protection has declined, it occurred to her that a policy loan might be appropriate. On calling her insurance agent, she discovered that the current rate on policy loans was 8%, with interest calculated annually on the anniversary date of the policy. The maximum cash value available for a loan on this policy was $6850.

Mimi decided to request a policy loan and to let the interest accumulate as a claim against the policy. Five years later when Mimi died, the insurance company paid her beneficiary the face value of the policy less the outstanding debt. The amount was determined as follows:

Face amount of policy:.....................................$25 000.00

Amount of loan: 6 850.00

Compound interest factor:

(8%, for 5 years) 1.47

> Principal + interest due:
> $$\$6850 \times 1.47 \dots\dots\dots\dots\dots = \$10\,069.50$$
> Amount payable to beneficiary:
> $$\$25\,000 - 10\,069.50 \dots\dots\dots\dots = \$14\,930.50$$

Automatic Premium Loan

The cash surrender value may be used to pay the premiums if for some reason the policyholder does not do so. This is essentially the same as a policy loan, because the face value will be reduced by the amount used for this purpose. It is called an **automatic premium loan** because the company will use the cash value to pay the premiums rather than let the policy lapse if the policyholder takes no action. Policyholders who assumed that their policy had lapsed because they had stopped paying premiums might be surprised to learn how much longer their coverage was extended. If the insured should die, the face amount would be diminished by the amount of any policy loan.

Collateral for a Loan

The cash surrender value may also be used as collateral for a loan. This involves transferring the right to the cash surrender value to the creditor until the loan is repaid. If the insured defaults on the loan, the creditor can cash in the policy and retain whatever is owed. This would effectively terminate the policy. Should the insured die during the term of the loan, the outstanding balance would have to be paid from insurance proceeds or the estate.

Paid-up Policy

Instead of cancelling the policy and taking the cash surrender value, another option is to use the cash value to purchase a **paid-up policy** with a smaller face value. This is, in effect, a single premium purchase of life insurance. The amount of the face value will depend on the amount of the cash surrender value at that time. Policies usually include tables that show the cash value each year the policy is in force and the amount of paid-up insurance the cash value will purchase. Alternatively, the policyholder could use the cash surrender value to purchase term insurance with a larger face value.

DAVID CHOOSES A PAID-UP POLICY

Assume that David Hill (Figure 6.8) decided at age 60 he no longer required $50 000 life insurance coverage, now that his children had

grown up. He looked at the Table of Guaranteed Values in his policy and found that the paid-up value of his policy was $805 per $1000 of face amount (805 × 50 = $40 250). This means that he could convert his present policy to one with a face value of $40 250, which would be paid up for life. He would have somewhat less life insurance coverage but pay no more premiums. Another option would have been to cancel the policy and take out the cash value of $20 100.

ENDORSEMENTS OR RIDERS

An insurance policy may be modified by the addition of **endorsements** or **riders,** that specify various supplementary benefits to be included or omitted without affecting the rest of the policy. Such additions can be worthwhile, but they may change the risk to be covered, thus adding to the cost. Some riders in common use are: guaranteed renewability, waiver of premium, guaranteed insurability, conversion privilege, and accidental death benefit. These features may be available as riders in some instances, or written into policies, depending on the practices of the company.

Guaranteed Renewability

Term insurance buyers may find it desirable to have the option of renewing the policy at the end of the term without providing evidence of insurability with another medical examination. Guaranteed renewability adds another risk for the life insurance company, but the extra cost may be worthwhile to the insured.

Waiver of Premium

A waiver of premium rider usually releases the policyholder from paying premiums when disabled, while keeping the policy in force. A precise definition of what constitutes disability is generally included, and there is often a waiting period of several months. Inspect very closely the definition of disability.

Guaranteed Insurability

A rider that permits the policyholder to purchase additional life insurance at specified future dates, without evidence of insurability, can be useful. The option may be restricted to persons aged 37 or younger, and the maximum face amount that may be added will probably be specified.

Conversion Privilege

A rider may be added to a term policy, giving the insured the option of converting the policy to another type of insurance without evidence of insurability at any time prior to the end of the term. There may be an age limit on this privilege, such as age 60 or 65.

Accidental Death Benefit

Another rider frequently added to basic policies is the accidental death benefit. It provides an additional benefit that may be as much as the face amount of the policy if the insured dies as a result of an accident prior to some specified age, such as 65 or 70. The additional premium for this rider is usually small because the majority of deaths are not considered accidental. A buyer of life insurance needs to remember that the amount of insurance bought should be determined by the expected needs of dependents, not by the cause of death. Also, careful note should be taken of the definition of accidental death as far as the life insurance company is concerned. Accidental death coverage, like travel insurance, should not be necessary if the insurance program is carefully planned.

BUYING LIFE INSURANCE

National Trends

How much life insurance do Canadians buy, do they prefer individual or group policies, and who buys life insurance? From national life insurance industry data it is possible to get a general picture of coverage, characteristics of the insured, and their policy preferences.

REASONS FOR TERMINATION   It is well known that some buyers of life insurance change their minds and surrender policies or let them lapse. From the limited information available it is obvious that many people buy insurance that they are unable, or do not want, to keep in force. Some whole life policies are surrendered by policyholders who prefer to take the cash value and cancel the coverage. Other policies are allowed to lapse through non-payment of premiums. The surrender and lapse rate is climbing and far exceeds the rate for termination by death and maturity. For instance, in 1987 less than one percent of face value was terminated by death, maturity, disability, or expiry but about 12 percent was terminated because of surrender or lapse. The obvious question is why is this so? It is interesting to consider to what extent this problem is related to the way life insurance is sold.

LIFE INSURANCE OWNERSHIP   Canadians are the second most insured people in the world (Japanese are first), with an average per capita coverage of $46 640 in 1991. The total amount of life insurance in force per capita has increased nearly seventy times in the last 60 years. Some of that increase can be explained by inflation and the increased population, but it is clear from Figure 6.10 that the amounts of life insurance owned between 1930 and 1991 grew significantly, regardless of changes in population or price levels.

FIGURE 6.10 LIFE INSURANCE OWNERSHIP PER CAPITA (1981$), 1930–1991

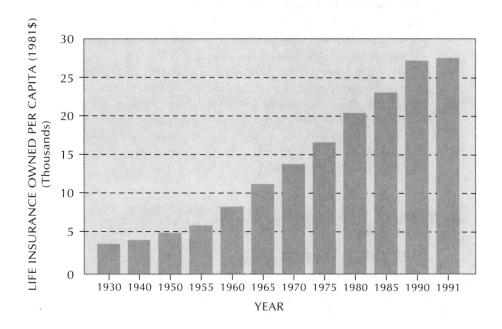

SOURCE OF DATA: *Canadian Life and Health Insurance Facts.* Toronto: Canadian Life and Health Insurance Association Inc., 1992 (p. 9). Reproduced and edited with permission from the Canadian Life and Health Insurance Association Inc.

We have been examining the trends in per capita life insurance ownership, but not every individual needs or owns coverage. It is important to look also at the average amounts owned per policyholder and per household. In 1991, the average per insured individual was $81 300, with about $123 500 per household. Although the figures may seem high, frequently families are not adequately covered: too often the wrong amounts of the wrong kinds of insurance are bought on the lives of the wrong persons. The combination of uninformed buyers and high pressure sales techniques can be disastrous for some families.

INDIVIDUAL OR GROUP POLICIES On examining the total value of life insurance owned in Canada, it is evident that the long-term trend, until recently, has been towards an increasing share for group insurance (Figure 6.11). Group insurance, not available in 1900, represented nearly 60 percent of all insurance owned in 1980 but dropped somewhat by 1991.

CHARACTERISTICS OF THE INSURED   The decision to buy life insurance is influenced by a number of variables, but most logically by the presence of dependents. The available industry data do not mention dependents, but do include gender, age, and income of the insured. Each pie graph in Figure 6.12 represents how the total face value of individual life insurance policies purchased in 1991 was distributed, by selected characteristics. For instance, there was more coverage on the lives of males (66 percent) than on females (34 percent). Looking at age, nearly one-half of coverage was on those aged 25–34. Buyers of life insurance tended to have incomes in the $25 000 – $50 000 range. One might conclude that young males with average incomes are most likely to buy life insurance.

FIGURE 6.11   **PERCENTAGE DISTRIBUTION OF INDIVIDUAL AND GROUP LIFE INSURANCE OWNED, 1900–1991**

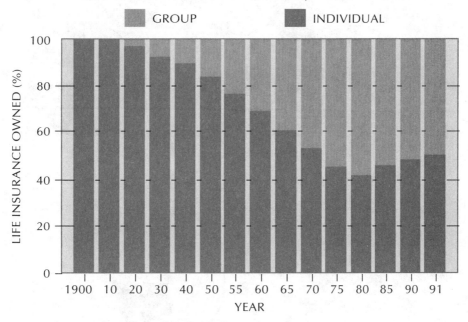

SOURCE OF DATA: *Canadian Life and Health Insurance Facts.* Toronto: Canadian Life and Health Insurance Association Inc., 1992 (p. 9). Reproduced and edited with permission from the Canadian Life and Health Insurance Association Inc.

FIGURE 6.12 PERCENTAGE DISTRIBUTION OF TOTAL FACE AMOUNT OF INDIVIDUAL LIFE POLICIES PURCHASED, BY SELECTED FACTORS, CANADA, 1991

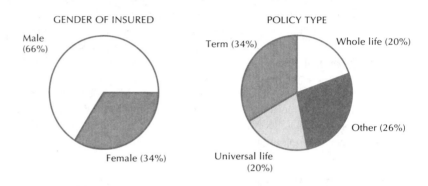

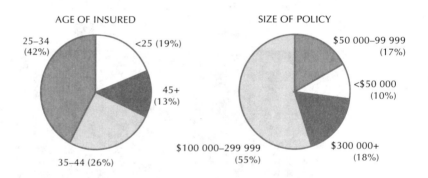

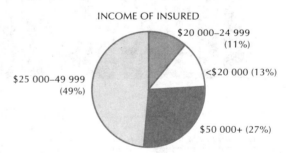

* Includes other combination policies and limited payment life.

SOURCE OF DATA: *Canadian Life and Health Insurance Facts.* Toronto: Canadian Life and Health Insurance Association Inc., 1992 (p. 14). Reproduced and edited with permission from the Canadian Life and Health Insurance Association Inc.

TYPE AND SIZE OF POLICY   Although, historically, whole life policies have been the leading type sold to individuals (as opposed to groups), it is interesting to note that by 1991 whole life represented about one-fifth of face value purchased individually (Figure 6.12). There was more term coverage (34 percent) than any other type, with the balance spread among universal life and various other combination policies. Over one-half of the coverage was for face values of $100 000 or more.

How Much to Buy

The following five steps provide a simplified way of estimating how much life insurance you may need. First, assume that your death could occur tomorrow. Who would need financial support and for how long?

1. Estimate needs of dependents for as long as they would need support. Call this total A.

2. Estimate the sources of income your dependents would receive independent of your estate, e.g., Canada or Quebec Pension, family allowances, employment income, investment income. This will be total B.

3. Subtract: A – B = C. This may be either a negative or a positive number. If the result is negative—and your estimates are realistic—it appears that your dependents could manage financially without help from your estate. If the result is positive, continue.

4. List all your assets, estimating their present value. Include life insurance, individual and group policies, pension benefits, Canada Pension death benefit, deposits in savings accounts, term deposits, Canada Savings Bonds, and other bonds. Estimate the value of your stocks and your equity in any real estate that would be sold.

    From this total, subtract your debts (not mortgages on property, because you counted equity only) to find the net worth of the estate that could be used to support dependents. This will be total D.

5. Finally, compare C and D. Is the net worth of your estate large enough to cover the net needs of your dependents? If so, their financial security seems assured; if not, more life insurance may be in order.

A more sophisticated estimate of insurance requirements would apply a discount factor, because all the funds estimated to be needed by your dependents would not have to be available to them immediately. The bulk of the estate could be invested, and this yield should be taken into consideration. Consult some of the references at the end of this chapter for information on forecasting life insurance needs.

Selecting a Policy

Buyers of life insurance are advised to first define their needs and then obtain quotations from several companies. Often, it may be difficult to make meaningful comparisons because different companies are offering dissimilar insurance packages which protect against different risks. The more clearly you can specify your requirements before approaching an insurance agent the greater the probability that you will be able to get comparable quotations.

TERM OR WHOLE LIFE?

Tina, who is 30 years old with two dependents, has decided that she requires $100 000 of life insurance coverage but she wonders which type of policy to buy. With the information she collected from agents she plotted the annual premium costs (Figure 6.13). She was surprised to find that five-year term insurance, much cheaper than whole life initially, would increase in cost at each renewal. This graph clarified for her the difference between the level premium for whole life and the increasing premiums for term. It illustrated that, until she was 55, even the increasing premiums for term coverage would be significantly less than those for whole life. She realized that since her children should be independent in fifteen years she did not need whole life coverage and decided on five-year renewable term insurance.

Selling Methods

Individual life insurance policies are sold by sales persons who depend on commissions for their livelihood, thus creating a possible conflict of interest when they act as advisers to buyers. When companies pay higher commissions on certain types of policies, sales people may attempt to sell these kinds over others. Generally, it has been possible to earn higher commissions from selling cash value policies than term policies. A recent development is that agents are presenting themselves more as general financial planners than as insurance agents. If remuneration comes from commissions rather than fees, conflicts of interest are bound to arise.

Another difficulty for consumers is the rapid turnover among life insurance sales people; after three years, only 20 percent of agents remain in the business. Although some do make a career in insurance sales, the large number of new entrants lowers the overall knowledge and skill level. This situation, combined with the pressure on agents to sell, makes it essential that prospective buyers of life insurance be as well informed as possible.

FIGURE 6.13 ANNUAL PREMIUMS FOR FIVE-YEAR RENEWABLE TERM AND WHOLE LIFE INSURANCE, BY AGE

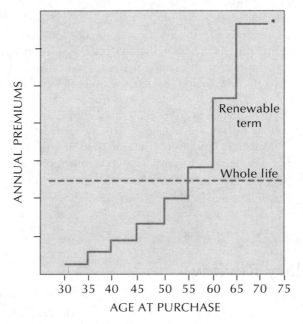

* 5-year renewable term no longer available after age 65.

Protection for Buyers

Although there have been few instances of life insurance companies going out of business and leaving policyholders unprotected, the industry has set up a compensation fund for such a contingency. For holders of RRSPs with life insurance companies, the fund provides protection to a maximum of $60 000, as the Canada Deposit Insurance Corporation does for banks, trust companies, and credit unions. Insurance policyholders are protected to a maximum of $200 000, and annuitants to $2000 per month. This plan is similar to one established a few years previously to protect clients of general insurance companies.

Summary

Life insurance, which may appear very confusing at first glance, is based on a few fundamental principles, such as pooling risk, the pure cost of insurance and the level premium. By sharing or pooling the risk of an untimely death with many people, individuals may obtain life insurance protection at reasonable cost. The pure cost of life insurance is determined by the mortality curve, rising with age. Premiums are made level for the term of the policy in order to provide lifelong insurance protection at a predictable cost.

Like most other financial sectors, insurance has some specific vocabulary that a competent consumer should understand, but the problem is compounded by a lack of common terminology in naming policies. Companies may add numerous special features to the few basic types of insurance policies and call the combinations whatever they wish. It is necessary to understand the fundamental types and principles of insurance to make an informed choice.

Before making any market comparisons, identify your need for life insurance, remembering that it is primarily a method of risk management. Rarely is life insurance needed as a form of savings. Unfortunately, there is a tendency for uninformed buyers to make poor choices. The sums of money involved are not small, and the need for greater awareness on the part of consumers is great.

Vocabulary Review

automatic premium loan (p. 163)

back-loaded (p. 158)

beneficiary (p. 140)

cash reserve (cash surrender value) (p. 150)

credit life insurance (p. 150)

dividend (p. 145)

endorsement (rider) (p. 164)

endowment life insurance (p. 156)

face amount (face value) (p. 140)

family income policy (p. 158)

family policy (p. 158)

front-loaded (p. 158)

grace period (p. 160)

incontestability clause (p. 160)

insurable interest (p. 140)

irrevocable beneficiary (p. 161)

level premium (p. 142)

limited payment policy (p. 156)

loading charge (p. 144)

non-participating policy (p. 145)

paid-up policy (p. 163)

participating policy (p. 145)

policy (p. 140)

policy loan (p. 162)

premium (p. 140)

pure cost of life insurance (p. 141)

term insurance (p. 146)

universal life insurance (p. 157)

whole life insurance (p. 150)

Problems

1. Bert, a 30-year-old chemist, is wondering whether he has enough life insurance, especially since a second child is due to arrive in a few months. His wife Mira,

27, is busy looking after young John and does not work outside the home. In reviewing his financial situation, Bert estimated that, if he should die tomorrow, he would need to leave a sum of $300 000 in his estate to support his children until they are independent, and his wife for her lifetime. His list of assets and debts is as follows:

Life insurance, five-year renewable term $100 000

Deposits in bank 2 700

Canada Savings Bonds 700

Equity in home. 44 000

Mutual funds 2 400

Consumer debts. 12 400

Funeral expenses 3 000

(a) If Bert were to die tomorrow, what would be the net worth of his estate? Would it be sufficient to provide the support he desires for his family? Should the equity in the house be included in this analysis? Give your reasons.

(b) What recommendation would you make to Bert regarding amount and type of life insurance?

(c) Assuming that Bert could purchase five-year renewable term insurance for $2.80 per $1000 and whole life for $8.50 per $1000, how much would your recommendation cost him per year?

(d) Assume that Mira acquires a full-time job. Should she have life insurance also? Would this change Bert's need for life insurance?

2.   George, a 49-year-old dentist practising in a small northern town, is active in sports and flies his own plane. His wife, who is 43, worked as a research assistant in Toronto before her marriage, but now is at home raising their four children. At this stage in his life, George has put all spare cash into buying property since he has sufficient current income for the needs of the family. George does not believe in life insurance and has not bought any. His reasons are that: (i) his wife has professional training and could support the children, (ii) his property has been appreciating in value, and (iii) he has a registered retirement savings plan.

(a) Do you think George needs any life insurance? Consider the family's need for readily available cash and how they would obtain it. Consider the possibilities for long-term support of his dependents.

(b) What recommendations would you make to George, and what arguments would you advance to support your suggestions?

3.   When Dave, 25, got married, he thought about his new responsibilities and decided to buy some life insurance. He consulted agents, read books on life

insurance, and selected a whole life policy. The agent presented him with an application form to be completed and a medical report to be filled in by his doctor. When the life insurance company had studied the information provided by Dave and by the agent, checked with the credit bureau, and made other investigations they felt necessary, Dave was accepted. He then received a copy of his policy (Figure 6.8).

The company examined Dave's finances, his occupation, and his health, among other things. Why did they need to have so much information about him?

4. Decide whether you AGREE or DISAGREE with the following statements.

   (a) If George, Bert, and Dave applied to the same company for the same type of life insurance policy and all were accepted, they would pay the same annual premiums.

   (b) If they chose whole life, all would pay level premiums for life, or until they reached an age limit such as 85.

   (c) If Bert purchases decreasing term insurance, his premiums will decrease each year during the term of the contract.

   (d) If Bert changes his job, his present group insurance coverage will continue as long as he pays the premiums.

   (e) If Dave chooses a participating policy, he can expect to receive dividends.

   (f) Five-year renewable term insurance means that the contract can be renewed after five years at the same premium.

   (g) For a given annual expenditure, an endowment policy will provide less insurance protection than other types of insurance.

   (h) A dividend may be regarded as interest earned by the money you paid the insurance company.

   (i) A group policy is the same as a participating policy.

5. Who needs insurance most? When is it most necessary?

6. What difference does it make in the distribution of property after the death of a policyholder whose life insurance is payable to his estate rather than to a named beneficiary, if (a) he dies intestate, or (b) he leaves a will?

7. Analyze each of the following situations and decide whether you AGREE or DISAGREE with the conclusions.

   (a) A single woman of 35, without dependents, who has $35 000 of group insurance in association with her employment, has been called on by a life insurance agent. He encourages her to take out a whole life policy of $50 000. His arguments are: (i) the premium will increase if she postpones buying insurance, and (ii) she should have permanent insurance and not depend on the group policy that covers her only as long as she stays with that employer. She decides that he is right.

    (b) A woman widowed at 35 returns to work as a professional librarian to support her four school-age children because her husband's estate was small. She asks an insurance agent for a renewable term policy. He recommends that she buy permanent whole life insurance so that she will have something for her old age. She tells him that she doesn't want a small amount of permanent life insurance, but a large amount right now.

    (c) A young couple with three small children wonders what kind of life insurance to buy. He earns $38 000 a year, and she stays at home to look after the children. They are thinking of taking out a family policy that would put $10 000 on his life, $4000 on hers and $2000 on each child. That way the couple would cover the major risks.

    (d) A retired couple of 75 and 73, who have a whole life policy for $10 000 on the husband's life, wonder whether to keep paying the annual premium of $175 or to cash in the policy and take the cash surrender value of $7200. They are living on Old Age Security, Canada Pension, employer's pension, and the income from their modest investments. They decide not to cash in the policy now but to keep it for the wife's protection in case she should be widowed.

8. Referring to the life insurance policy in Figure 6.8, decide whether you AGREE or DISAGREE with each of the following.

    (a) Dave bought a limited-pay whole life policy.

    (b) Dave should have requested an accidental death rider as better protection for his family.

    (c) Dave chose a participating policy.

    (d) If Dave decided to cancel the policy one year after purchasing it, he would receive a $130 cash value.

    (e) If Dave decided to surrender his policy 10 years after purchase, he could apply for the cash value of $3350 plus accumulated dividends.

    (f) Dave could buy a paid up policy that would have a face value of $15 500 if he surrendered his policy after 10 years.

    (g) After the children arrived, Dave had difficulty in making ends meet; then his union went on strike for four months. It was impossible for him to pay the premium due on August 7, 1996. Failure to make this payment meant that his policy was cancelled.

    (h) In 1988, Dave could have applied for a policy loan of $300.

    (i) Dave should select a lump-sum settlement option for his wife because this will leave her free to elect the settlement option best suited to her situation at the time.

    (j) If Dave selects a life income plan as the settlement option for his wife, he is in effect asking that the face value of his policy be used to buy a single-payment life annuity.

(k) If Dave's wife, his named beneficiary, should predecease him and if he neglected to change the beneficiary, on his death the company would pay the face value to his wife's heirs.

(l) When Dave dies, the payment of the face value of this policy is determined by the conditions of his will. His widow will not receive it automatically, even if she is the named beneficiary.

(m) If Dave used his life insurance policy as collateral to obtain a loan but died before it was repaid, his wife would not receive any life insurance benefits, but Dave's estate would not have to pay the balance outstanding on the debt.

9. Examine the following statements and identify those that are myths or involve faulty reasoning. Explain the error.

(a) Buying life insurance is a good way to build up savings.

(b) A policyholder's savings in a whole life insurance policy drop to zero on his death.

(c) You should buy life insurance while you are young, when the premiums are less.

(d) The cash surrender value of a whole life policy is your own money and the company should not charge interest when you borrow your own money.

(e) Term insurance is not a good buy because the coverage is temporary but the problem is permanent.

(f) At your death your beneficiary should receive the cash value as well as the face value.

10. Why is it said that "life insurance is sold but not bought"?

11. At retirement a person needs to review his or her insurance coverage in light of future needs. What are some reasons for (a) cashing in or cancelling all life insurance, or (b) retaining some coverage?

References

BOOKS

AMLING, FREDERICK and WILLIAM G. DROMS. *The Dow Jones-Irwin Guide to Personal Financial Planning*. Second Edition. Homewood, Illinois: Dow Jones-Irwin, 1986, 549 pp. Although written for American readers, much of the discussion of financial planning, life insurance, retirement planning, and investments is relevant for Canadians.

BELTH, JOSEPH M. *Life Insurance, A Consumer's Handbook*. Second Edition. Bloomington, Indiana: Indiana University Press, 1985, 216 pp. Examines life insurance from a consumer's point of view.

BUDD, JOHN, CLAUDE RINFRET, RICHARD DAW, and DANIELLE BRIEN. *Canadian Guide to Personal Financial Management*. Scarborough, Ontario: Prentice-Hall Canada, annual, 225 pp. Accountants provide guidance on a broad range of topics, including planning finances, estimating insurance needs, managing risk, and determining investment needs. Instructions and the necessary forms for making plans are provided.

BULLOCK, JAMES and GEORGE BRETT. *Insure Sensibly: A Guide to Life and Disability Insurance*. Markham, Ontario: Penguin Books, 1991, 182 pp. Offers practical tips on different kinds of life and disability insurance and how to determine the right policy and best price.

CANADIAN LIFE AND HEALTH INSURANCE ASSOCIATION. *Canadian Life and Health Insurance Facts*. Toronto: Canadian Life and Health Insurance Association, annual, 68 pp. Provides industry data on purchases and ownership of life and health insurance, and annuities. (Booklet free from the Association at Suite 2500, 20 Queen Street West, Toronto, Ontario, M5H 3S2.)

FLEMING, JAMES. *Merchants of Fear, An Investigation of Canada's Insurance Industry*. Markham, Ontario: Penguin Books Canada, 1986, 409 pp. An investigative report on the life and general insurance industries.

MATHESON, G. F. and JOHN TODD. *Information, Entry, and Regulation in Markets for Life Insurance*. Toronto: University of Toronto Press, 1982, 117 pp. A detailed analysis of Canadian life insurance.

MCQUEEN, ROD. *Risky Business, Inside Canada's $86 Billion Insurance Industry*. Toronto: Macmillan, 1985. An investigation into the operation of the insurance industry.

SELECT COMMITTEE ON COMPANY LAW. *The Insurance Industry—Fourth Report on Life Insurance*. Toronto: Ontario Legislative Assembly, 1980, 525 pp. A detailed study of life insurance with special attention to selling practices.

ZIMMER, HENRY B. *Making Your Money Grow, A Canadian Guide to Successful Personal Finance*. Third Edition. Toronto: Collins, 1989, 260 pp. The focus of this book is on basic calculations needed for personal financial decisions, as applied to compound interest, future and present values, investment returns, RRSPs, annuities, and life insurance.

CHAPTER SEVEN

Retirement Income

9. *To distinguish among these types of annuities: refund annuity, escalating annuity, joint and last survivorship annuity, and variable annuity.*

10. *To identify factors that affect the cost of an annuity.*

11. *To explain how the use of before-tax or after-tax dollars affects the tax treatment of annuity income.*

12. *To examine costs and benefits of buying a life annuity.*

13. *To explain how the use of an RRSP can enhance financial security in retirement.*

14. *To outline the rules regarding contribution limits, spousal plans, the number of RRSPs per person, borrowing from an RRSP, withdrawals before maturity, and the death of the RRSP owner.*

15. *To examine costs and benefits of RRSP maturity options.*

Introduction

For the student concerned about getting started in a career, retirement certainly seems like an abstraction for later consideration. It is not, however, only the young who defer thinking about retirement. People of all ages postpone retirement planning in the belief that retirement can best be dealt with when the time comes. We also expect that, somehow, there will be enough money for us to live comfortably after retiring, although we may not have any idea about how this will happen. The intent of this chapter is to increase awareness of financial planning for retirement and to emphasize the importance of getting an early start.

The two key questions in financial planning for retirement are:

(a) Where will the money come from for the retirement years?

(b) Will there be enough money to support the desired level of living?

It is usual to expect a change in sources of income at retirement: from employment earnings to pensions and investment income. What can be done to maximize this pension and investment income? It is important, first of all, to recognize the impact on later economic well-being of financial decisions taken during pre-retirement years. Attention to pension plans and disciplined saving can make a significant difference. Although individual employees may not have much influence on the terms of employment-related pensions, they are more likely to maximize their potential pension credits if they keep well informed about pension plans. Investment income is the result of saving and investing in income-producing assets.

Determining how much retirement income will be needed is difficult. The younger a person is the more uncertainty about future economic conditions and probable lifestyle. Fortunately, predictions about retirement income needs will increase in accuracy as retirement gets closer. Some of the references listed at the end of this chapter outline methods of making estimates of future needs.

How to save and invest to acquire the necessary assets to generate income for retirement will be discussed in some detail in later chapters. Here, the emphasis is on why savings will be needed. This chapter is concerned with identifying sources of retirement income, outlining public and private pension plans, and examining annuities and registered retirement savings plans.

FINANCIAL PLANNING FOR RETIREMENT

Retirement planning requires a long-term perspective on personal finances. As explained in Chapter 1, over a lifetime there is likely to be more variability in income than in living costs, and the positive gap between income and expenditures will usually be greatest in the middle years (Figure 1.1, Chapter 1). When earnings cease at retirement, pensions and investments will be the main sources of income. What is done about pensions and investments during the working years will have a significant bearing on the amount of income for retirement.

The basic rule in planning for retirement income is to begin saving early. To achieve financial independence and be able to maintain the preferred lifestyle in retirement, net worth must grow steadily during the working years. It is truly amazing how, due to the magic of compounding, small amounts saved regularly over a long period of time, can result in a substantial sum (Figure 9.1, Chapter 9). Generally, this gradual saving is preferable to attempting to save a great deal during the last few years of working life (Figure 1.2, Chapter 1). Since it is difficult to predict the exact time of retirement (there may be illness or a decision to retire early), it can be unwise to leave saving for retirement until the last few years.

SOURCES OF RETIREMENT INCOME

Where will retirement income come from? Those who have been in the labour force can expect to receive retirement benefits from the Canada or the Quebec Pension Plan and perhaps a pension from their employer. At age 65, there may be the Old Age Security pension if that program is still in effect. The total of these three pensions will surely be less than pre-retirement income. How can the gap be filled? Most people will need income from personal investments to maintain their accustomed level of living.

The major sources of retirement income may be summarized as:

Public Pensions

   Old Age Security (OAS)

   Guaranteed Income Supplement (GIS)

   Canada or Quebec Pension Plans (CPP, QPP)

Private Pensions

   Employment-related pensions

Investment Income

   RRSP funds

   Annuities

   Interest, dividends

   Rent

   Business income

There are certain eligibility requirements for pension benefits, such as age, residence, or membership in the plan during working years. Those who decide to retire early have to wait until age 65 for the Old Age Security pension, and until at least age 60 for the Canada/Quebec Pension. Members of an employment-related pension plan will probably take a reduced pension if they retire before age 65.

FIGURE 7.1 INCOME COMPOSITION OF PERSONS WITH TAXABLE INCOME, AGED 60 AND OVER, BY GENDER AND AGE, CANADA, 1990

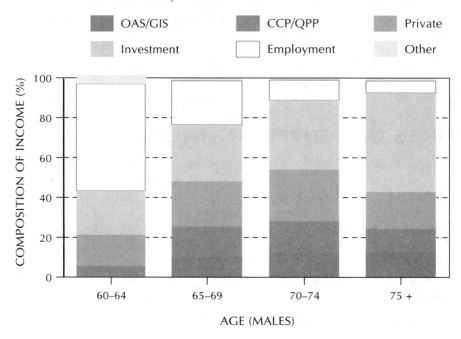

AGE (MALES)

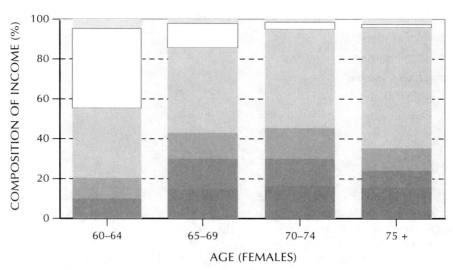

AGE (FEMALES)

SOURCE OF DATA: *Taxation Statistics*. Ottawa: Revenue Canada, Customs, Excise and Taxation, 1992 (pp. 189–192). Reproduced with the permission of the Minister of Industry, Science and Technology, 1993.

Income Patterns

What are the major sources of income for those who have already retired? The data presented in Figure 7.1, collected from 1990 taxation statistics, illustrate the income pattern by age and gender for people aged 60 and over. Each bar represents the percentage distribution of the total income of one age and gender group. There is a bias toward higher income individuals in these data because only those who filed income tax returns and had taxable income that year are represented.

Although the pattern of income sources differed by age and gender, there are some noticeable similarities. Both men and women, for example, were dependent on investment income for 22 to 60 percent of their incomes. Public pensions (OAS, GIS, CPP, QPP) comprised around a quarter of income in most cases. Males were more likely to have private (employment-related) pensions than were females, and were also more apt to have employment income. The lack of extensive labour force involvement among older women may explain their lower share of income from private pension plans, but some of them would receive survivor benefits from their spouses.

We will review some highlights of public and private pension plans before looking more closely at two ways to create retirement income from investments: (i) annuities that convert funds into a lifetime income, and (ii) registered retirement savings plans that accumulate funds in a tax shelter.

PUBLIC PENSIONS

The federal, provincial, and municipal governments provide a variety of social security programs, some of which are intended to provide benefits for older or retired persons. The major source of public retirement pensions is federal programs, but most provinces and the territories provide income supplements for those in financial need.

Public Retirement Pensions

Federal	Eligibility Criteria
Old Age Security	age, residence
Guaranteed Income Supplement	age, residence, need
Spouse's Allowance	age, residence, need
Canada Pension Plan	age, contributor
Provincial	
QPP for Quebec residents	age, contributor
Income support programs	need

Old Age Security(OAS)

The two eligibility criteria for Old Age Security pensions are age and residence: the applicant must be aged 65 and must have lived in Canada for a substantial period of time. Details of the residence requirements are rather complex, but essentially require at least ten years' residence in Canada prior to application. The pension is paid to eligible persons if they apply for it, regardless of any other income they may have, and is taxable.

CLAWBACK OF OAS   Since 1989, Old Age Security has been targeted to those in greatest need. Although all eligible citizens receive OAS cheques, some must repay all or a portion of the benefits. For instance, in 1993 recipients were required to pay back either all the benefit received or 15 percent of their net income in excess of $53 215, whichever was less.

INDEXATION   The OAS is fully indexed and adjusted quarterly, which means that every three months the pension amount is increased by the inflation rate of the previous quarter. At the beginning of 1993 the OAS was $378.95 per month, or about $4 547 a year.

Supplements to Old Age Security

Persons who receive Old Age Security but have little or no other income may apply for the Guaranteed Income Supplement (GIS). The amount received depends on other income and marital status. A sliding scale is used to reduce the supplement by $1 a month for each $2 of other income received. To simplify matters for the recipient, OAS and GIS benefits are combined in one monthly cheque. Like the OAS, the GIS is adjusted quarterly by the inflation rate. Unlike the OAS, the GIS is not taxable.

The Spouse's Allowance pays a pension to the spouse of an Old Age Security pensioner if the spouse is between the ages of 60 and 64, meets residency requirements, and is otherwise eligible for the GIS. This allowance is payable if the combined income of the couple is below a certain amount. The Spouse's Allowance is not taxable.

Canada Pension Plan (CPP)

This federal plan was established in 1966 to provide a measure of economic security for three categories of people: the retired, the disabled, and the dependent survivors of contributors. The Province of Quebec, which decided not to participate in the Canada Pension Plan, set up the companion Quebec Pension Plan instead. There is complete portability between the two plans for those who move into or out of Quebec.

CONTRIBUTIONS   Both the employee and the employer are required to make contributions to either the Canada or the Quebec Pension Plan. Upon retirement, the employee will receive a lifetime pension. The amount of the pension depends on the length of time the employee spent in the labour force and the amount contributed to the plan. The information that follows applies to the Canada Pension Plan; those who live in Quebec are advised to investigate the specific details of the Quebec Pension Plan.

Rules for contributions require that each employee contribute a certain portion of earnings, which is matched by the employer. The self-employed must contribute both the employee and the employer shares. The terminology used in calculating contributions is shown in Figure 7.2. For the purpose of calculating contributions to the Canada Pension Plan an individual's earnings are divided into three parts. The first part, the **year's basic exemption**, is an amount excluded when calculating the annual contribution. For example, if the year's basic exemption if $3 300, the first $3 300 earned is exempt from contributions to CPP. The contribution rate is applied to the second portion, called the **contributory earnings**. The contribution rate for employees, which was 2.45 percent of contributory earnings in 1993, is being escalated annually by .075 percent until 2011. The third portion is wages in excess of the year's **maximum pensionable earnings** and is excluded from the calculation.

FIGURE 7.2 TERMINOLOGY ASSOCIATED WITH CPP/QPP CONTRIBUTIONS (1993 AMOUNTS)

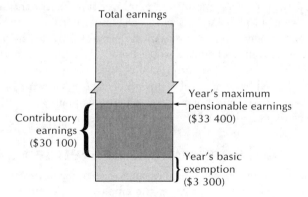

The maximum pensionable earnings figure has been changing annually in recent years in response to public demand that we be allowed to make larger contributions in order to qualify for larger pensions. Using 1993 figures, the following example shows how an employee's contributions are calculated.

CONTRIBUTIONS TO CANADA PENSION

Alice's earnings in 1993 . . . . $52 000
Year's basic exemption 3 300
Year's maximum pensionable earnings 33 400
Contributory earnings ($33 400 – 3 300) 30 100

In 1993 Alice paid 2.45 percent of $30 100 or $737.45 into the CPP, and her employer paid the same.

BENEFITS   The exact amount of a Canada Pension retirement benefit depends on prior contributions and the inflation rate (pensions are adjusted annually by the previous year's inflation rate). The benefits are taxable. To suggest the scope of benefits from public pensions, a person retiring in 1993 could receive a maximum of about $7 992 from CPP and $4 547 from OAS, making a total of $12 539 a year.

PRIVATE PENSIONS

Private retirement pensions may be arranged from personal savings, but generally when we speak of private pensions we mean employment-related ones. Look upon the following terms as synonyms: registered pension plans (RPP), company pension plans, private pension plans, and employer-sponsored pension plans. Essentially, private pension plans are a way of deferring a portion of wages until retirement. There is, however, no uniformity in the benefits provided by private pension plans, nor is there coverage of all paid workers in Canada. Slightly more than half of all full-time workers are members of private pension plans, the majority of these workers being employed by some level of government or by Crown corporations. This means that many workers are not in private pensions plans and will have to depend on public pensions and their own savings when they retire.

Defined Contributions or Defined Benefits

Contributory pension plans require employees to pay a percentage of their wages to the plan in addition to whatever the employer contributes. Some employers offer non-contributory plans where they provide all funds.

There are two main types of private pension plans: defined contribution and defined benefits plans. A **defined contribution** (or money purchase) **pension plan** has rules about the amount to be contributed by the employer and employee, but makes no promises about the size of the retirement pension. The contributions credited to an employee's pension account, plus interest, will be available at retirement to purchase an annuity. A **defined benefits pension plan**, by contrast, has a formula for calculating a retirement pension that usually depends on years of service and average wages earned during the last five working years. With this plan, the employer promises a certain level of retirement benefits. For the long-service employee, the defined benefits plan is usually preferable to the defined contributions plan. Not surprisingly, some employers prefer defined contributions because with such a plan they have no pension liability to fund as they do with defined benefits; they have not promised employees a certain level of pension.

Although the majority of private pension plans have been of the defined-benefit type, the trend is changing. Some employers, finding the new pension regulations onerous, are shifting the risk to employees by setting up defined contribution plans or group RRSPs. Thus, contributions are made to a retirement fund for employees, but the employer does not promise any particular level of pension. The employer also has less obligation to compensate for the effects of future inflation rates, or to maximize the yield from the invested pension funds.

Pension Terminology

Important issues related to pensions involve vesting, portability, survivor benefits, and indexation. We will examine each in turn.

VESTING   It is usual for employees not to have vesting rights until they have worked for the employer for a specified number of years (traditionally ten, but this is being reduced). **Vesting** refers to the time when employees have the right to receive a future pension or when they become entitled to the employer's contributions paid into the plan on their behalf. For instance, vesting occurs after one year in Saskatchewan; two years in Quebec, Ontario, and for federal employees; and five years in Alberta and Manitoba. Employees leaving a job before acquiring vesting rights will receive a refund of their contributions to the pension fund with interest, but no rights to the amounts contributed by their employer. If they leave their job after they have vesting rights, however, they may have a choice between a refund or retirement benefits, as explained in the next paragraph.

PORTABILITY   Formerly, when employees changed jobs they could not take their pension credits with them. **Pension portability** is the right to transfer pension credits from one employer to another. The lack of portability in private pensions has long been a serious problem. Recent legislation has, however, made some improvement. Now workers with vesting rights have three options when they change jobs: (i) leaving their pension credits with their former employer and receiving a pension at retirement; (ii) transferring their credits to their new employer's pension plan if that plan permits it; or (iii) transferring their benefits to a locked-in registered retirement savings plan. But if they did not stay long enough for vesting, all too often a change of job means a loss of pension rights and having to start over in another pension plan. Some of the options listed above for handling the pension credits for those with vesting rights offer a partial solution to the portability problem. It is important to analyze the costs and benefits of the various options to see which would make a better contribution to one's retirement income.

SURVIVOR BENEFITS   Provision of a pension for a surviving spouse has been more common in pension plans for government employees than for those employed in private industries. However, pension plans for federal employees and private pensions in Ontario, Alberta, and Nova Scotia are required to pay 60 percent of benefits to a surviving spouse. Also, if a pensioner should die before retirement, his or her spouse would be eligible for a 60 percent pension.

INDEXATION   Although public pensions have been fully indexed, many occupational plans do not have either full or partial indexing. A **fully indexed** pension is adjusted regularly to reflect changes in the Consumer Price Index. **Partial indexation** means that the pension is adjusted for part of the change in the Consumer Price Index. There has been more partial or full indexation of pensions in the public than in the private sector. The limiting factor is the unknown cost. Employers have been reluctant to promise fully indexed pensions to retirees because of uncertainty about future pension liabilities. Many employees, more oriented to the present than to the future, may also be reluctant to reduce their current take-home pay by making larger contributions to the pension plan to cover future indexing. Among those not yet retired, there may be a lack of awareness about how a fixed pension can be eroded by inflation. For example, with inflation of only four percent per year, an unindexed pension will lose about a third of its purchasing power in ten years, and about one-half in 18 years. If inflation is six percent, purchasing power will be reduced by one-half in only 12 years. However, at current low levels of inflation, indexation of pensions has become less of a public issue than it once was.

Know Your Plan

An employee may not have much influence on the benefits offered by an employment-related pension plan. Nevertheless, it is in the employee's interest to be informed about the plan. Pension benefits vary so widely that it is wise to ask the following questions:

(a) Is the plan defined-benefit or defined-contribution?

(b) If it is a defined-benefit plan, what formula will be used to calculate pension benefits?

(c) If it is a defined contribution plan, who makes the investment decisions, and what retirement options are there?

(d) Are there provisions for early retirement?

(e) What happens if an employee should become disabled?

(f) What are the survivor benefits?

(g) Will the employee's estate receive any of the employer's contributions?

(h) Is it possible to split pension credits in the case of marriage breakdown?

LIFE ANNUITIES

At retirement, there may be a need to transform life savings into an income stream. One way to accomplish this is by purchasing an annuity. For instance, pension funds or RRSPs may be invested in annuities to produce a monthly income for life. The following discussion of annuities will explain the basic annuity principle and the various ways in which annuities may be bought and paid out to the **annuitant.**

Retirees, not knowing how long they may live, face the question of whether to use some of their capital for living expenses. If they do use their capital, they must decide at what rate to spend it. If they spend too rapidly, they may outlive their resources; if they are too cautious, they may scrimp more than necessary. A method has been devised to ensure that one's savings last for a lifetime; it is called a life annuity. The process of liquidating a sum of money through a series of regular and equal payments is called an **annuity.** References to annuitizing a sum of money means converting it into a monthly income. Originally annuity payments were annual (hence the name annuity) but now they may be monthly, semi-annual, or annual. It is usually safe to assume that the income payment will be monthly, unless stated otherwise.

The Annuity Principle

There are two possible ways of protecting against the risk of outliving one's savings: either by (i) acquiring sufficient net worth to support the desired lifestyle, or (ii) buying a life annuity. A life annuity, like insurance, is a way of pooling resources with others to ensure that all will be protected against a given risk, in this case that of outliving one's income. Life insurance companies, the only financial institutions authorized to sell life annuities, accept the savings of many people and in return promise each annuitant a life income. Those who live a very long time will receive more from the pooled funds than those who die sooner, but all will receive an income for as long as they live. It must be emphasized that insurance companies do not promise annuitants that they will receive as much as they have contributed, as is illustrated in Figure 7.3. A life annuity can be useful for a person with modest means who is more concerned about protecting his or her level of living than in creating an estate for heirs. Some misconceptions about annuities stem from not understanding the annuity principle. Do not think of an annuity as a way of making money, but rather as *a way of converting a sum of money into a lifetime income.* This principle is illustrated in the example, "Should He Use Some of His Capital?"

FIGURE 7.3 EXPERIENCES OF TWO LIFE ANNUITANTS

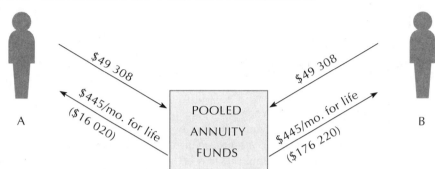

ACCUMULATION PERIOD: At age 65, both A and B purchased immediate, straight life annuities with lump sums of $49 308.

LIQUIDATION PERIOD: Immediately A and B began receiving payments of $445 a month, which would continue for life.

A died at age 68 after receiving payments for three years or a total of 36 x $445 = $16 020.

B died at age 98 after receiving payments for 33 years or a total of 33 x 12 x $445 = $176 220.

SHOULD HE USE SOME OF HIS CAPITAL?

George, who has just reached age 65, is considering ways of converting his savings of about $220 000 into an income stream for his retirement. He is looking at two possibilities which are illustrated in Figure 7.4. Option A is to deposit the funds and live on the interest, which, based on a prediction of four percent return on average, would generate $733 per month. At his death the capital would be intact for his heirs, and in the meantime he would have control over the investment.

Option B is to buy a life annuity with the $220 000, providing George with a guaranteed income of about $2 000 a month for life. Why is this annuity income larger than the interest he could earn from depositing the same sum of money? The answer is that annuity payments are a combination of interest and capital, since annuities are a way of gradually liquidating capital. Of course, at George's death the annuity payments would cease and none of this capital would be available for his heirs.

If a comfortable life in his old age is more important to George than is leaving an estate, he should use some of his capital. But the problem is how fast to use it when he cannot predict his life expectancy. He could use his capital too quickly and perhaps face some lean years in his old age, or he could be too cautious, making do with less. However, if George buys an annuity, his savings are added to those of others, creating a fund that can provide life incomes for all.

The two options George considered are shown diagrammatically in Figure 7.4.

FIGURE 7.4 OPTIONS FOR GENERATING RETIREMENT INCOME

OPTION A
Invest capital in securities and use return (interest, dividends)

Retirement income
(interest, dividends)

Capital
preserved

T_r TIME T_d

OPTION B
Purchase life
annuity

Retirement income
(annuity payments of
capital and interest)

Capital
liquidated

T_r TIME T_d

T_r = date of retirement
T_d = date of death

Characteristics of Annuities

Some important characteristics of annuities that should be clearly understood are:

(a) the distinction between the accumulation and liquidation periods,

(b) the method of paying the purchase price,

(c) when the liquidation period is to start,

(d) the number of lives covered,

(e) the refund features.

ACCUMULATION AND LIQUIDATION PERIODS   There are two stages associated with life annuities: (i) the **accumulation period** or the interval during which the annuitant pays the insurance company for the annuity, and (ii) the **liquidation period** during which the insurer makes payments to the annuitant (Figure 7.5). The accumulation period may last for many years if the annuity is bought by instalments, or may be very brief if purchased with a lump sum. Regardless of the method chosen for buying an annuity, the accumulation period must be completed before the liquidation period may start.

FIGURE 7.5 PAYMENT OPTIONS DURING THE ACCUMULATION AND LIQUIDATION PERIODS OF A LIFE ANNUITY

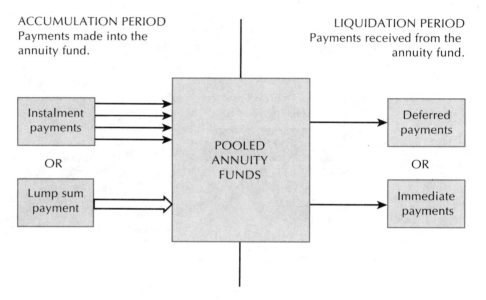

ACCUMULATION PERIOD
Payments made into the
annuity fund.

LIQUIDATION PERIOD
Payments received from the
annuity fund.

METHOD OF PAYING   If an annuity is purchased with a lump sum, it will be a **single payment annuity**. The other alternative is to buy the annuity gradually, over a number of years, by a series of regular instalments or premiums. The instalment method is useful for a person who finds saving difficult and therefore needs a contractual savings plan, but others may prefer the flexibility of accumulating capital under their own control and deciding later whether to buy an annuity.

STARTING THE LIQUIDATION PERIOD   The payout from an annuity may begin immediately upon purchase or deferred until a later date. An **immediate annuity** will start regular payments to the annuitant at once. By definition, an immediate annuity must be bought in a single payment, since all payments for an annuity must be completed before the liquidation period begins. With a **deferred annuity** the liquidation period is some time after purchase, but the annuity may be bought by either a single payment or by a series of premiums. For instance, a young person who has inherited a sum of money could decide to buy a single payment, deferred annuity that would begin payments when he or she is older.

NUMBER OF LIVES COVERED   The simplest and cheapest form of life annuity is the **straight life annuity,** that pays an income for the life of the annuitant and ceases at death, with no further payments to beneficiaries. An annuity may be designed, however, to produce a life income for more than one person, quite commonly for two. A couple, for example, may buy a **joint-life-and-last-survivorship annuity**. The name of this annuity is derived from "joint life," which pays as long as both are alive, and from "last survivor," meaning that the annuity will continue during the lifetime of the survivor. These points are illustrated in Figure 7.6.

FIGURE 7.6 LIQUIDATION PAYMENTS BY NUMBER OF LIVES COVERED

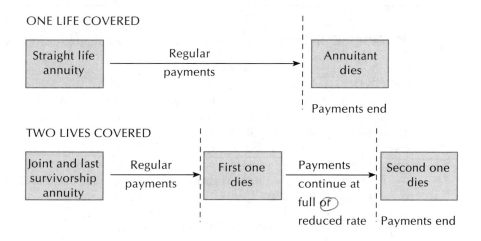

Not surprisingly, a joint-and-survivor annuity (to use the abbreviated name) is the most expensive of all annuities. The rates for the couple will be based on the woman's age because of her longer life expectancy and the possibility that she may be younger than her husband. The purchaser must decide whether, after the death of the first spouse, the survivor will continue to receive the full payment or some proportion of it, such as two-thirds or one-half. The cost of the joint-and-survivor annuity can be reduced if the payments are planned to decrease after the first death. Another possibility is to buy two separate life annuities, one on each life. Table 7.1 illustrates the costs of both alternatives.

TABLE 7.1   TWO LIFE ANNUITY OPTIONS FOR A COUPLE

Annuitant	Purchase price	Income per month
A. **STRAIGHT LIFE ANNUITY;** no certain period		
(Each has separate life annuity)		
Husband, age 65	$110 110	$1 000
Wife, age 62	126 229	1 000
Total, while both alive	236 339	2 000
B. **JOINT AND LAST SURVIVORSHIP ANNUITY;** no certain period		
(Survivor to receive 50% of monthly income)		
Husband and wife	$236 339	2 021
Survivor		1 010

ANNUITY CONTRACT   A sample annuity contract is presented in Figure 7.7. What type of annuity is it?

REFUND FEATURES   An annuitant may be interested in the refund features available during either the accumulation period or the liquidation period of the annuity. If the annuitant should die during the accumulation period, or decide to discontinue payments, it would be desirable to have the amount that has already been paid, plus interest, refunded. Or, an annuitant who does not wish to continue payments may be given the option of converting to a smaller paid-up annuity.

Refund features during the liquidation period are very popular with buyers who worry that they may not live long enough to receive as much as they contributed. In response to this concern, life insurance companies have created annuity plans that include payments for a guaranteed length of time, or to a guaranteed minimum amount, regardless of whether the annuitant lives or dies. Because of these provisions, these plans are called **refund annuities.**

A very popular type of refund annuity is one with a minimum number of instalments guaranteed. A life annuity with ten years "certain," for example, promises to make payments as long as the annuitant lives, but for a minimum of ten years even if the annuitant dies. If the annuitant should die within the first ten years of the payout period, a named beneficiary will receive a lump sum equivalent to the balance of payments the annuitant would have received if he or she had lived until the end of the ten-year period. Note that the certain period refers to the minimum payment period, not the maximum. These ideas are summarized below.

FIGURE 7.7 ANNUITY POLICY

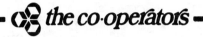

Policy Data

POLICY NUMBER   *350005*

POLICY DATE   *August 7, 1986*

ANNUITANT   *Melvin McDonald*
JOINT ANNUITANT   *Sharon McDonald*

AGE OF ANNUITANT   *65*
AGE OF JOINT   *65*
ANNUITANT

BENEFICIARY   as stated in the application unless subsequently changed

PLAN   *Joint & Last Survivor Annuity Guaranteed 10 Years,*
Immediate Annuity

AMOUNT OF ANNUITY   *$ 334.10 payable on the 23rd day of each month*
commencing July 23, 1986. These payments will
continue monthly until the later of August 23, 1996,
or the death of the last Annuitant.

PREMIUM   Amount $ *40,000.00*

Policy Data   SPECIMEN

FIGURE 7.7 ANNUITY POLICY (CONTINUED)

PROVISIONS

The Contract

The policy and the application are part of the contract. The contract also includes documents attached at issue and any amendments agreed upon in writing after the policy is issued. The policy may not be amended nor any provision waived except by written agreement signed by authorized signing officers of the Company.

Participation

This policy participates in the surplus distribution of the Company. Any distribution of excess charges or surplus shall remain at the credit of the contract and be used to increase the annuity.

Payment of Premium

The premium is payable either at the Head Office or at any Branch Office or through an authorized representative of the Company.

Currency

All payments to be made in connection with this policy shall be in the lawful money of Canada.

Age

The Company shall be entitled to proof of age of the annuitant before making any payment under this policy. If the age has been misstated, any amount payable hereunder shall be that which the premium would have purchased at the correct age.

Beneficiary

The annuitant may appoint a beneficiary. The annuitant may change the beneficiary unless the appointment was irrevocable. The interest of any legally designated beneficiary who shall die before the Annuitant, or before the surviving Annuitant or Annuitants, if there be more than one Annuitant, shall vest in the Annuitant or the surviving Annuitant or Annuitants, as the case may be, in the absence of any statutory provision as to the disposition thereof and if there be no other legally designated beneficiary.

No Assignment

The policy or annuity payments thereunder cannot be assigned.

SPECIMEN

SOURCE: The Cooperators Life Insurance Company. Reproduced with the permission of The Cooperators Life Insurance Company.

REFUND FEATURES DURING THE ACCUMULATION AND LIQUIDATION PERIODS

Situation	Refund
Accumulation Period:	
Annuitant decides to stop paying.	Contributions refunded.
Annuitant dies before completing purchase of annuity.	Contributions refunded.
Liquidation Period:	
Annuitant has policy with 10 years certain but dies before 10 years	Sum equivalent to balance of payments remaining in the 10-year period are paid to the beneficiary or the estate.

The Cost of an Annuity

Six factors influence the cost of an annuity:

(a) the size of the monthly payments desired,

(b) life expectancy (as influenced by age, gender, and health),

(c) interest rates,

(d) the length of the accumulation period,

(e) refund, or inflation protection features,

(f) number of lives covered.

SIZE OF PAYMENTS   There are two ways to approach the purchase of an annuity: either put a certain amount of money into an annuity and accept the income it will generate, or determine the specific monthly income desired and pay the necessary amount to generate this. Most buyers of annuities are in the first group: they buy as much monthly income as their limited funds permit, and are well aware of the relationship between cost and expected income.

LIFE EXPECTANCY   Although the price of an annuity is based on a number of factors, life expectancy is a critical one. Three variables used to predict life expectancy are gender, age, and health. Females, younger persons, and healthy persons are expected to live longer than males, older persons, or sickly persons, and therefore the company expects to make annuity payments to them for a longer time. Since this is more costly for the insurance company, individuals in this former group will receive a smaller monthly income from a given amount put into an immediate life annuity. The difference gender makes is shown in Figure 7.8.

FIGURE 7.8 **MONTHLY ANNUITY INCOME BY AGE AT PURCHASE AND GENDER (SINGLE PAYMENT, IMMEDIATE, STRAIGHT LIFE ANNUITY. ALL PURCHASERS PAY THE SAME PRICE.)**

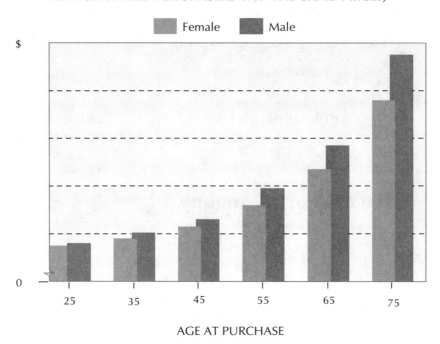

AGE AT PURCHASE

INTEREST RATES   The cost of an annuity is greatly influenced by the expected return that can be earned on annuity funds while they are held by the insurance company. When interest rates are high, a sum of money can be turned into a higher level of annuity income than when interest rates are low. That is why financial advisors suggest choosing the time carefully when converting capital into an annuity.

LENGTH OF ACCUMULATION PERIOD   The total cost of an annuity bought by instalments over many years will be reduced because of the additional interest the company earns during the longer time the premiums are on deposit. For instance, let us compare the total cost of two ways of buying a certain level of annuity income. A single payment immediate annuity will cost more than an instalment annuity bought over 30 years (Table 7.2). Looked at another way, a person could have invested the premiums, let the interest compound, and bought an immediate annuity when it was needed.

TABLE 7.2. PURCHASE PRICE AND MONTHLY INCOME BY METHOD OF PURCHASE

Method of Purchase	Purchase Price	Monthly Income
Single payment, immediate annuity bought at age 60	$256 483	$2 000
Instalment annuity; premiums paid from age 30 to 60. ($2 100/yr.)	63 000	2 000

Straight life annuity bought by a female with income to start at age 60.

REFUND FEATURES   If you wish to have an annuity with a guaranteed period, this will add to the cost because it changes the probabilities regarding the number of years the insurance company will have to make payments. This is illustrated in Table 7.3. The cost differences reflect the certainty of having to make payments for ten years, regardless of the annuitant's life expectancy.

TABLE 7.3 PURCHASE PRICE BY GUARANTEED PERIOD

Type of Annuity*	Purchase Price
Straight life; no certain period	$71 805
Life annuity; ten years certain	$75 845

*Immediate annuity to provide a life income of $650 per month for a male, aged 65.

The same point is made in Figure 7.9, which shows that, in general, a lump sum used to buy an immediate annuity will produce a lower monthly income if there is a refund feature. However, if the annuity is bought before age 45, the difference is small.

NUMBER OF LIVES COVERED   It will cost more to buy a life annuity to provide an income for the lifetimes of two people rather than for just one. In the case of a couple, the cost is related to gender and the age of the younger partner. A younger wife is expected to live longer than her husband.

FIGURE 7.9 Annuity Income by Age at Purchase and Guaranteed Period (Single payment, immediate life annuity.)

BUYING AN ANNUITY

In preparation for her forthcoming retirement, Mrs. Alvarez is thinking of converting her three RRSPs to a life annuity to generate a dependable income. With no dependents and a distaste for investment management, she feels that an annuity would be her best choice. Her first thought was to ask her life insurance agent to make all the arrangements. However, Mrs. Alvarez talked about her plans to several friends, who advised her to consult an annuity broker who could perhaps give her some help. She learned that an annuity broker can obtain quotations from many life insurance companies for a client. Since brokers get their commissions from the companies issuing annuities, there would probably not be a charge for this service.

On talking to a broker, she discovered that there was more to buying an annuity than she had supposed. The broker first familiarized himself with Mrs. Alvarez' financial situation, considering aspects such as other sources of retirement income, predicted marginal income tax rate, and needs of any dependents; then he presented several options to be considered. He mentioned that if a person's health was poor, she might, with the support of medical evidence, qualify for an impaired health annuity that would pay a higher income for the same premium. Mrs. Alvarez asked the reason why and was told that the insurer's liability is reduced if the annuitant is not expected to live long, making it possible for the company to pay a higher rate.

Two possible ways of preserving purchasing power were presented to her by the broker. She could investigate the escalating annuities offered by some insurance companies, or she could plan to buy a series of annuities in various years. The escalating annuity would pay a lower monthly income initially, but would be adjusted annually according to prevailing interest rates. Since an inflationary period would probably cause interest rates to rise, she would receive higher annuity payments. If interest rates were to fall, the company would not lower payments, but would instead increase them more slowly. Such escalating annuities are an example of one way insurers have modified annuities to help preserve purchasing power in inflationary times.

Some brokers suggest that a client buy a series of annuities in different years to take advantage of changing interest rates. The premiums for annuities are very sensitive to the interest rates companies expect to receive on invested funds. Mrs. Alvarez could deregister one of her RRSPs to buy an annuity now, and do likewise with the other two in later years. She realizes that she must have all her RRSPs deregistered by the time she is seventy-one to comply with the income tax laws. In a period of rising interest rates this plan of buying a series of annuities could be advantageous, but if rates are falling, the reverse could be true.

Mrs. Alvarez knew that she wanted an immediate annuity, but she was undecided about the refund feature. She discovered that for a given premium, she could obtain a somewhat larger annual income with a straight life annuity than one with a ten-year guarantee. The broker asked her whether she would rather have the higher income, or the assurance that should she die before ten years elapsed, her estate would receive payments for the balance of the decade.

She was advised to make up her mind on the kind of annuity she wanted before the broker obtained quotations for her because annuity prices change rapidly, even daily. For this reason some companies will guarantee their quotations for only one to three days. Since rates vary, not only from time to time, but also among companies, the broker would seek quotations from quite a number of firms for Mrs. Alvarez.

Variable Annuities

Annuities usually provide a fixed income, an unattractive feature to annuitants during periods of inflation. For instance, in 1950, a person may have thought that a deferred life annuity, paying $200 per month starting in 1975 would be adequate preparation for retirement. What she could not have predicted was that by 1975 a 1950 dollar would have lost half of its purchasing power, reducing the $200 per month to the equivalent of $100, and that by 1990 it would be worth only $32.

In response to this problem, life insurance companies developed the variable annuity, which does not guarantee a specific income. Rather, it promises that the money paid in premiums will be invested in stocks and bonds, with the annuity payments varying according to the investment return. The higher expected return in inflationary times will be reflected in higher annuity payments.

BUYING A VARIABLE ANNUITY

Marg purchased a variable, deferred annuity at a premium of $50 a month. This money was used to buy accumulation units, the price of which varied from time to time. When Marg's first payment was received, the units were $5 each. Therefore, after subtracting $1.50 for expenses, she was credited with 9.7 units.

$$\$50 - \$1.50 = \$48.50$$

$$\frac{\$48.50}{5} = 9.7 \text{ units}$$

If the price of the units had risen to $5.30, her next month's payment would buy

$$\$50 - \$1.50 = \$48.50$$

$$\frac{\$48.50}{5.3} = 9.1 \text{ units}$$

When the accumulation period has been completed and Marg decides to start receiving annuity payments, her accumulation units will be converted to annuity units. This conversion takes place only once, the rate of conversion depending on mortality rates and the return on the company's annuity portfolio.

Suppose that Marg has acquired an entitlement to 100 annuity units per month, and that the value of an annuity unit is $2.10 at that time. Marg would then receive a monthly income of $210 for the first year, after which the company may revise the value of an annuity unit depending on the success of the annuity portfolio. Marg's annuity

income will fluctuate as the value of the portfolio supporting it does. Variable annuities are designed so that the annuitant's income varies with investment yields, which, ideally, reflect changes in living costs resulting from inflation.

Annuities and Income Tax

The recipient of annuity payments will discover that the income tax treatment of this income is dependent on whether the annuity was bought with before-tax or after-tax dollars. Since each payment includes both capital and interest, they may be treated separately for tax purposes. If the annuity was purchased with before-tax dollars (they would have been in a tax shelter, such as an RRSP) both the capital and the interest components of the income payments are now exposed to income tax. On the other hand, if the annuity was purchased with after-tax dollars (the annuity was not in a tax shelter) the capital portion is not taxable when received. The issuing company will provide the annuitant with annual statements that separate the capital and interest portions they have received. Income tax rules require that, during the accumulation period of a deferred annuity, the owner report the accrued interest at least every three years.

Whether to Buy an Annuity

Before deciding to buy an annuity, various costs and benefits of annuities should be reviewed. A major advantage of an annuity is the guaranteed, usually fixed, lifetime income without the concern of having to manage any investments. On the other hand, the flexibility to manage one's own money is lost; once funds are put into an annuity they are committed. If a more beneficial investment opportunity should arise it will not be possible to take advantage of it; conversely, an annuity offers protection against a depressed investment climate. In an inflationary period a fixed income loses purchasing power, but this would be an advantage should prices fall. There is no way to guarantee that an annuitant will receive as much or more than was paid into an annuity, but that should be of little concern. The annuitant will have a guaranteed life income, even if his or her heirs do not receive an estate. Of course, it is possible to put only a portion of one's capital into an annuity, leaving a part to bequeath to others.

Annuities are not for everyone, but they are a useful way to make a small estate last for a lifetime. Those who are in poor health, concerned about an estate for heirs, or have the time and inclination to manage their own investments, may be wise to put their money elsewhere. However, a deferred annuity is a reasonable possibility for anyone who needs a contractual savings plan to ensure that money is saved for their retirement. This discussion of annuities is intended to illustrate basic principles, not to describe all variations of annuities that may become available. Financial institutions are quite inventive in constantly creating new services for consumers.

REGISTERED RETIREMENT SAVINGS PLANS

What is an RRSP?

A registered retirement savings plan (RRSP) is an investment used to shelter savings from income tax. Anyone who invests savings outside a tax shelter is using after-tax dollars; any income those investments earn, such as interest or dividends, is taxable. If, however, the money is put into an RRSP, no tax is payable when the investment is made, and the yield is not taxable while in the RRSP. Tax-exempt funds going into an RRSP are referred to as before-tax dollars. The diagram in Chapter 2 illustrates this point. Since an RRSP is only a means of tax deferment, all funds become taxable whenever they are removed from the tax shelter. The ideal strategy is to put money into an RRSP at a time of high marginal tax rate and take it out later when the rate is lower, such as when retired. The example in Chapter 2, "Should She Use a Tax Shelter," demonstrates how income tax may be deferred by an RRSP.

Two widely-held misconceptions associated with RRSPs are: (i) that everyone needs an RRSP, and (ii) that an RRSP is a specific type of investment. With such energetic promotion of RRSPs, investors may forget that income tax deferment is a major reason for putting money into an RRSP. It is a way of sheltering savings from tax to allow them to grow at a faster rate than otherwise, and to thus accumulate a fund for retirement or other purpose. Anyone who pays little or no income tax does not need an RRSP because they can invest their savings without the restrictions imposed on RRSPs. *An RRSP is not a specific type of investment, but a way of registering a variety of investments to shelter them and defer income tax.* As we will see, many kinds of investments may be put in an RRSP.

To repeat, the chief reason to put money into a registered retirement savings plan is to defer income tax. Savings grow faster inside a tax shelter than outside and if the money is taken into income in future years, when marginal tax rate is lower, income tax may be reduced. Refer to Chapter 2 for an explanation of marginal tax rate. The money in an RRSP is taxable eventually, whenever the plan is deregistered. Since RRSP funds are not quite as accessible as other savings, this may help some people build a retirement fund.

Since putting money in an RRSP is investing, as much care should be taken in choosing an RRSP as in selecting any investment. It can be a mistake to become so caught up in the prospect of deferring income tax that little attention is paid to the quality and appropriateness of the investment. The principles of investing that are discussed in Chapters 9 to 11 apply to all RRSP decisions.

Types of RRSPs

Under the Income Tax Act, a broad range of investments may be registered as RRSPs. Although some of these types may be unfamiliar, that should not matter at this stage. The focus of this chapter is on the tax shelter aspect of RRSPs, not on the specifics of the various types of investment, each of which is treated in some detail in other chapters. Major types of investments acceptable for RRSPs may be categorized as follows:

A. **Guaranteed funds**   These funds promise the return of the principal with a guaranteed rate of return; they are available from most banks, trust companies, credit unions, and life insurance companies.

1. savings accounts

2. term deposits or guaranteed investment certificates

B. **Mutual funds**   These funds make no promises about rate of return or safety of principal; they are available from mutual funds companies and agencies, trust companies, life insurance companies, investment dealers, and banks.

1. equity funds

2. bond funds

3. balanced funds

4. money market funds

C. **Self-administered RRSPs**   The investor makes the investment decisions. Self-administered RRSPs are available from various financial institutions, and may include any combination of the following:

1. cash

2. treasury bills

3. bonds, including Canada Savings Bonds

4. mortgages

5. mutual funds

6. stocks

D. **Life insurance or life annuity**   These products are sold by life insurance companies.

GUARANTEED FUNDS   These are the safest places to put RRSP money as long as the investor is prepared to accept the lower return associated with the low risk. The institutions promise a return of the principal with interest, and deposits (up to $60 000 per institution) are insured against loss. It is wise to inquire whether the plan is covered by deposit insurance, since there may be some exclusions.

Savings accounts in an RRSP, like any savings account, pay interest regularly at the prevailing rate without locking in the funds for a certain term. Higher interest is usually paid on term deposits or guaranteed investment certificates that promise a given interest rate and lock up the money for a stated term.

When choosing a guaranteed plan, check the following features:

(a) the interest rate,

(b) the frequency of compounding interest,

(c) when interest rates may be adjusted,

(d) the minimum deposit,

(e) the annual fees,

(f) registration, withdrawal, or other fees.

Many banks and trust companies have discontinued fees on guaranteed funds RRSPs. It is worthwhile to do some comparison shopping before selecting a plan and an institution.

MUTUAL FUNDS Without going into a detailed explanation of mutual funds (see Chapter 11), suffice it to say that mutual funds pool the funds of many investors. Instead of actually buying stocks, bonds, or mortgages, the investor buys a share in the mutual fund, which in turn invests in such securities. Professional fund managers make the investment decisions for the investors. There are over 700 different mutual funds sold in Canada and they are designed to achieve a range of investment objectives. Some funds are invested in common stock or equities, some in bonds or mortgages, and yet others, called money market funds, in treasury bills and other debt instruments.

Mutual funds are sold directly by some mutual funds companies, by mutual funds sales agents, and also by banks, trust companies, and life insurance companies which have their own funds. There may be costs the buyer has to pay, such as sales commissions (up to nine percent of the initial investment), annual management fees (one to two percent), and sometimes withdrawal fees.

An investor would use mutual funds for an RRSP only if prepared to accept more risk than with guaranteed funds. Mutual funds do not give the investor any assurance that he or she will get back the investment or any income from it; they do, however, offer the prospect of greater gain (or loss) to those willing to accept the risk. Nevertheless, within mutual funds there is a wide spectrum of risk levels, so it is possible to find an appropriate fund for almost any objective.

SELF-ADMINISTERED PLANS For those who have the time, expertise, and enough money to make it worthwhile, a self-administered RRSP has the advantage of allowing the investor to make the investment decisions. A wider range of investment types may be held in a self-directed plan, such as Canada Savings Bonds, other bonds, stocks, treasury bills, or mortgages. Funds can be shifted from one form of investment to another as desired, and the investor can decide how much risk to assume.

Institutions that handle self-directed RRSPs, such as most investment dealers and some banks, trust companies, and life insurance companies, charge an annual fee of about $100, as well as commissions on some transactions.

LIFE INSURANCE PLANS   In addition to offering guaranteed funds and mutual funds, life insurance companies provide a combination of life insurance coverage and retirement saving, whereby the cash value is registered as an RRSP. Think carefully before having RRSP money tied to life insurance coverage. The contract may require fixed annual payments that limit flexibility in annual contributions and in moving RRSP money around. Since the fees and commissions tend to be heaviest in the early years, an investor who cancelled the contract after a short time would lose money.

Various types of annuities available from life insurance companies are eligible for RRSPs. The schedule of payments may be fixed or flexible. As with life insurance, there will be commissions payable in the early years.

Criteria for Selecting an RRSP

The stiff competition among financial institutions to sell RRSPs has resulted in considerable variety in the characteristics of the offerings. Before making a selection, as with any investment, the investor should be clear about his or her objectives. Some questions to ask yourself are:

1. **Does the RRSP fit with my investment objectives?**

   How well will it complement my other investments in regard to risk, return, and liquidity?

2. **How much flexibility in contributions do I want?**

   Some RRSPs are contractual with an agreement at the outset to contribute a set amount at regular intervals. Such a plan does not permit a change in the contribution if circumstances change. Other plans require a minimum payment to keep the plan open, but otherwise are flexible; still others may not require an annual payment. When considering flexibility, it is important to remember that there is a maximum limit on annual RRSP contributions. If my income changes, my contribution limit will also change. Having only contractual plans could restrict my flexibility too much.

3. **Will the plan accept transfers of lump sums?**

   If I should change jobs and receive a refund of my pension contributions, I may be interested in "rolling over" this lump sum into an RRSP in order to postpone paying income tax.

4. **Will there be a penalty if the fund is cashed in before maturity?**

   Suppose I find the performance of a fund to be unsatisfactory and wish to transfer the money to another RRSP. I need to know in advance whether this will be possible and, if so, whether the institution will exact a penalty or charge a fee.

5. **How much risk and return can be expected?**

There is usually a trade-off between risk and return, with less risk associated with a lower return. What level is appropriate for me? Generally, the more distant the retirement date, the more the risk that can be handled. As I near retirement I will want to reduce risk.

6. **What will the administrative charges be?**

Is there a sales charge taken off contributions, or a management fee that is charged initially, annually or at maturity? Are there redemption fees, or any other charges? What is the relationship of the charges to the predicted yield? Looking for the lowest administrative charges may not always be the wisest move.

Contribution Limits

Anyone with earned income (salary, wages, royalties, business income, rental income, alimony) may contribute to a RRSP. The maximum annual contribution depends on: (i) membership in a employer-sponsored registered pension plan (RPP), and (ii) the type of plan. Those not in registered pension plans can contribute 18 percent of the previous year's earned income up to a specified maximum. This amount, which has been changed a number of times in recent years, is currently as follows:

1994	$13 500
1995	14 500
1996	15 500

In the following years, the maximum is to be indexed or adjusted according to changes in the Consumer Price Index.

For members of registered pension plans, the maximum annual contribution is 18 percent of the previous year's earned income to the limits shown above, less a pension adjustment. The pension adjustment is calculated by employers and Revenue Canada Taxation and notification is sent to employees late in the year. The calculation differs for defined benefit plans and defined contribution plans. The intent of these rules is to adjust RRSP limits to ensure that there is equity for employees who are in different pension plans. Members of plans with generous benefits will not be able to contribute as much to their RRSPs as those with more restricted benefits.

RRSP CARRY FORWARD Anyone who cannot use their RRSP maximum in a particular year may carry forward the allowance for up to seven years. Therefore, there is no penalty for a person who wants to invest in RRSPs but is short of money one year but has more the next.

Spousal Plans

Anyone may contribute to an RRSP for their spouse, provided that the total contributed to a personal plan and the spousal plan is within their personal limits. The reason for setting up a spousal plan is the expectation that when the funds are taken out, one spouse will have a marginal tax rate lower than the other. This can be a significant advantage at retirement if one spouse has little pension income. Not only does the family income become split between two people and thus reduce taxes, but the spouse can make use of the pension income deduction. Common law partners are now allowed to have spousal plans. There is a penalty if a spousal RRSP is deregistered a short time after it was set up. The spouse must wait three years before taking out funds. Otherwise, the contributor is taxed on the withdrawals.

SPOUSAL RRSP AND INCOME SPLITTING

Mike is retiring this year and his income will come from his company pension, Old Age Security, Canada Pension, dividends and interest, and RRSP funds. Sarah, who has not been in the labour force for many years, has no CPP or company pension benefits, but does have some interest and dividend income in addition to Old Age Security. Over the years, Mike has contributed to a spousal RRSP for Sarah. Mike is looking at ways of splitting his income with Sarah to lower his marginal tax rate and take advantage of her lower tax rate. He has requested that his Canada Pension benefits be split with her.

How does having a spousal RRSP affect the income tax this couple pays? Splitting their retirement income to decrease Mike's income and increase Sarah's can have several benefits. First, Sarah, with a lower marginal tax rate than Mike, will pay less tax on the RRSP income than Mike would have paid. Second, Sarah's RRSP income makes her eligible for the pension income tax credit. Third, Mike may repay less of his Old Age Security benefits (the clawback) because of his income reduction.

It is generally not possible for a person to transfer funds retroactively from his or her RRSP to a spouse's RRSP. Therefore, contributions to a spousal RRSP must be made from current income. The two situations when funds can be transferred from one spouse's RRSPs to the other's RRSP without attracting income tax are: (i) at death, if the spouse is named as beneficiary, and (ii) after a marriage breakup, if the court orders a division of RRSPs.

Other RRSP Rules

LOCKED-IN RRSPS   To facilitate the portability of pensions, new pension rules make use of locked-in RRSPs. One of the options becoming available to employees leaving an employer is to transfer pension credits to a locked-in RRSP. Also, some employers are sponsoring locked-in RRSPs for employees rather than registered pension plans. At retirement, the funds in a locked-in RRSP will be used to purchase an annuity.

HOW MANY RRSPS?   There is no limit to the number of RRSPs a person may have. Because of the variation in the types of plans and their yields, it may be wise to establish more than one RRSP to diversify assets.

BORROWING FROM AN RRSP   Generally, it is not possible to borrow from an RRSP. An exception was the home purchase plan of 1993-4 that allowed RRSP funds to be withdrawn to buy a home. RRSP funds may be used, however, as security for a loan but the exact procedure is complex because of the way in which it must be reported on the income tax return.

WITHDRAWALS BEFORE MATURITY   Funds may be withdrawn from an RRSP before maturity but they will be subject to income tax, including any interest or dividends earned by the plan to date.

DEATH OF THE RRSP OWNER   If the owner of an RRSP dies before the plan matures, contributions to the plan plus any accumulated yield will be refunded to a beneficiary or to the estate. The income-tax treatment of this refund varies depending on the beneficiary. A spouse named as beneficiary has the option of rolling the refund over into his or her own RRSP without incurring any income tax, or of accepting the refund as a lump sum and paying the tax. For any beneficiary other than the spouse or certain categories of dependents, refunds from RRSPs will be treated as income of the deceased in the year of death and taxed accordingly.

Who Needs An RRSP?

An RRSP is a good idea for anyone who has earned income and is paying a significant amount of income tax. On the other hand, a person with money to invest but who pays very little income tax can forego the restrictions of an RRSP. The financial press regularly publishes articles on RRSPs that emphasize the amount of tax deferred and the increase in savings possible with RRSPs. Whether this will be true in any particular case depends on the person's marginal tax rate and the yield from their RRSP.

IS AN RRSP WORTHWHILE?

Peter plans to save $2 000 a year in anticipation of his retirement in 30 years' time. He wonders about the advantages of using an RRSP instead of simply investing the money outside a tax shelter. For the comparison, he made the following assumptions:

Average interest rate	5%
Combined marginal tax rate	46%
After-tax interest rate	$5\% - (5 \times .46) = 2.7\%$

Annual investments for 30 years of:
$2 000 before-tax dollars in an RRSP
$1 080 after-tax dollars outside an RRSP
$[2\ 000 - (2\ 000 \times .46) = 1\ 080]$

Using the formula for the future value of a series of deposits (explained in Chapter 8), he discovered that the tax-sheltered investment would grow to $132 878 and the non-sheltered one to $48 956. Assuming that he pays the maximum tax rate when withdrawing the RRSP funds, the tax on the lump sum would be $61 124, leaving $71 754. Clearly, he will have more money for his retirement if he uses a tax shelter.

Maturity Options

All RRSPs must be deregistered sometime before the end of the year in which the owner turns 71. Deregistering means a change from accumulating savings to either (a) removing funds from the tax shelter and paying income tax, or (b) initiating a liquidation plan to provide income. You can choose one or any combination of these options:

Removal from tax shelter

(1) withdraw the funds and pay the income tax,

Income plan

(2) purchase a single-payment life annuity,

(3) purchase a fixed-term annuity,

(4) set up a registered retirement income fund (RRIF).

WITHDRAW THE FUNDS   The first of these options differs from the others in that funds are moved from the RRSP tax shelter to the owner's control. Money taken out of an RRSP is subject to tax in the year it is withdrawn. However, once the tax has been paid, no more restrictions are imposed by Revenue Canada. Unfortunately, a complete withdrawal of all RRSP funds at one time could result in a large tax bill. The taxes can be minimized by making a series of withdrawals over a number of years or in a year when income is lower than usual.

The other options provide various ways to convert RRSP funds into income gradually, over a number of years, thus spreading out the income tax liability. With these options, RRSP funds do not come into the owner's hands as a lump sum, but are transferred directly into an income plan. When an RRSP matures, there is no restriction in moving the funds to other firms, if desired. It is wise to do some comparison shopping before choosing an income plan and the company to handle it.

LIFE ANNUITY   With a single-payment life annuity the funds are transferred directly from an RRSP to a life insurance company to buy a life annuity. There is choice among a variety of annuity products, some of which were mentioned earlier in this chapter. An annuity converts funds into a lifetime income, with income tax payable each year on the amount received. This effectively spreads the tax burden over a lifetime.

FIXED TERM ANNUITY   Fixed term annuities are available from life insurance and trust companies, and are a way of gradually converting RRSP funds into income. A fixed term annuity differs from a life annuity in that it is unrelated to life expectancy; there is no pooling of funds with others. Funds are converted into an income stream that will continue until a specific age. However, if the annuitant does not live that long, the balance in the account will be refunded to a beneficiary or to the estate. The monthly payment will be dependent on the term, the amount invested in the annuity, and interest rates. With fixed term or life annuities there is the option of cancelling the contract and taking the commuted value of the remaining payments. These can be taken out of the shelter and the tax paid, or can be rolled over into a RRIF.

REGISTERED RETIREMENT INCOME FUND   RRIFs are similar to a self-directed RRSPs; the owners can make their own investment decisions if desired. RRIFs may also be set up so that little management is required, if, for instance, all funds are invested in fixed income securities. The same firms that handle RRSPs also look after RRIFs. The choice of possible investments includes savings accounts, term deposits, bonds, stocks, and mutual funds. It is a good idea to do some comparison shopping when deregistering RRSPs to find a RRIF with the most suitable terms.

Once a RRIF has been set up, payments may begin at any time. There is a requirement to take out a minimum amount each year, but there is no maximum. This allows flexibility in managing the funds so that income is available when needed, but care must be taken not to deplete the RRIF so quickly that there is a shortage in later years. The minimum annual withdrawal from a RRIF depends on age. For instance, at age 71 at least 7.38 percent of the plan's value at the beginning of the year must be withdrawn. The withdrawal rate gradually increases to 8.99 percent at age 81.

Since it is possible to have more than one RRIF, there is the possibility of diversifying RRSP funds by using different firms or financial products. For instance, some funds could be put in bank deposits and other funds into equity mutual funds held elsewhere. Funds can be transferred from one RRIF to another, but it would be wise to find out any restrictions or fees that may be involved. The advantage of a RRIF over annuities is the freedom to choose the type of investment and to determine the amount to be withdrawn each year.

Summary

This chapter was intended to increase awareness of possible sources of retirement income and the need to make preparations early in our working lives. At present, there are public pension programs, such as Old Age Security and the Guaranteed Income Supplement, that provide benefits to eligible people from the general revenue of the federal government. Those who have been in the labour force contribute to either the Canada or the Quebec Pension Plans, which pay benefits to the retired, to survivors of contributors, and a lump sum death benefit. About one-half of all full-time employees are members of employment-related private retirement pension plans, which vary widely in their benefits.

Life annuities are a way of stretching a sum of money over a lifetime, providing protection against the risk of outliving one's savings. By gradually liquidating the principal and interest, a lifetime income can be created, but will leave no estate for heirs. There are various modifications of the basic life annuity to cover several lives, or to provide a refund if the annuitant dies shortly after starting to receive payments.

At retirement, most people will find public and private pensions inadequate to support the lifestyle to which they have become accustomed. They need income from their own investments. RRSPs offer a way to invest tax-sheltered funds, permitting the income to compound tax-free until the plan is deregistered. A lower marginal tax rate after retirement makes it beneficial for most people to accumulate funds in RRSPs.

Vocabulary Review

accumulation period (p. 191)

annuitant (p. 189)

annuity (p. 189)

contributory earnings (p. 185)

deferred annuity (p. 192)

defined benefits pension plan (p. 186)

defined contribution pension plan (p. 186)

full indexation (p. 188)

immediate annuity (p. 192)

joint-life-and-last-survivorship annuity (p. 193)

liquidation period (p. 191)

maximum pensionable earnings (p. 185)

partial indexation (p. 188)

pension portability (p. 187)

refund annuity (p. 194)

single payment annuity (p. 192)

straight life annuity (p. 193)

vesting (p. 187)

year's basic exemption (p. 185)

Problems

1. Use the following annuity quotations for this question. For each $1 000 premium, monthly incomes are as follows:

    Male, aged 65:

    >   straight life annuity $8.99

    >   10 years certain $8.50

    Female, aged 62:

    >   straight life annuity $7.79

    >   ten years certain $7.64

    Joint and last survivor, male 65, female 62:

    >   no years guaranteed, 100% to survivor $7.29

    >   no years guaranteed, 50% to survivor $8.35

    (a) When Richard retires next year at age 65, he expects to have $70 000 to invest in immediate life annuities. His objective is to provide supplementary retirement income for himself and his wife, who will be 62, as well as income for her if he should predecease her. List three alternatives he might consider. Compare these options by making a chart with the following headings:

      (i) principal invested

     (ii) annual income

    (iii) advantages

    (iv) disadvantages.

    (b) Would Richard be better advised to invest the $70 000 in guaranteed income certificates at seven percent for a five-year term? Analyze the consequences of this alternative.

2. Irma is due to retire in one year, and she is giving some thought to her retirement income. Her assets, in addition to her bungalow, are $20 000 in Canada Savings Bonds that pay annual interest, a five-acre piece of land that does not yield any income but may be sold sometime for building lots, a small portfolio of common stocks invested for capital gain that do not pay much income, and a registered retirement savings plan that has grown to $68 000. She is wondering how to arrange her financial affairs in order to obtain the maximum income during her retirement years.

    (a) Do you think she should sell her property and reinvest the money?

    (b) She wonders whether to add any more money to the registered retirement savings plan. What information is needed to answer this question?

    (c) Why does impending retirement require some review of her finances?

3. (a) Ian earned $43 000 in 1994. Did he have to contribute to the Canada Pension Plan? If so, how much? How much did his employer contribute for him? What is the contribution rate in 1996?

    (b) If Ian should die at age 55, will Ann, his widow and beneficiary, receive anything from CPP, his company pension plan, or his RRSPs?

    (c) If Ian dies during the accumulation period, will Ann receive anything from the deferred annuity he had been buying?

    (d) If Ian used his RRSP funds to purchase an immediate life annuity at age 65, with ten years certain, and lived to age 70, would his wife receive anything from this annuity?

    (e) If Ann buys a variable annuity, when will she learn the amount of her monthly retirement income from it?

4. Ella, aged 67, receives a private pension, the Canada Pension, and Old Age Security, as well as $11 000 a year from part-time employment and return on her investments. Last year she received a lump sum of $15 000 that did not qualify as capital gains. Can you suggest some alternatives for her, as she faces a heavy tax bill? Are there any tax shelters she could use?

5. Decide whether you AGREE or DISAGREE with each of the following statements.

    (a) More than 80 percent of people now employed are members of occupation-related (private) pension plans.

    (b) If you have been a member of a private pension plan long enough to have obtained vesting rights, your pension automatically becomes portable if you should change jobs.

    (c) Canada Pension Plan benefits are not taxable.

    (d) If you are a contributor to a private pension plan you cannot also put money in an RRSP.

    (e) When an RRSP is deregistered, the funds must be taken out as an annuity.

    (f) You can avoid paying income tax on funds in an RRSP if you take the money out after you are 65; after that age, RRSP funds become tax-exempt.

    (g) An annuity with a refund feature is cheaper to buy than a straight life annuity, other things being equal.

    (h) The liquidation period of an annuity cannot start until the accumulation period is completed.

    (i) The more lives covered by an annuity, the more it will cost, other things being equal.

6. How does the annuity principle differ from the life insurance principle?

7. Analyze the costs and benefits of buying an annuity to provide retirement income.

8. Suggest some pros and cons for contractual RRSPs.

9. These questions refer to the annuity contract in Figure 7.7.

   (a) Is this a deferred annuity or an immediate one?

   (b) Was it purchased by instalments?

   (c) How much did it cost?

   (d) How much will the monthly income be?

   (e) How many lives are covered? What type of annuity is it?

   (f) When will payments end?

   (g) Are payments guaranteed for a certain number of years?

10. Use Figure 7.1 as a reference in deciding whether you AGREE or DISAGREE with each of the following statements.

    (a) Regardless of age, females received higher payments from Old Age Security than males.

    (b) Public pensions were a more significant source of income for women who had taxable income than for men.

    (c) Compared to other elderly persons, women over age 75 (who had taxable income) had a greater dependence on benefits from the Canada and Quebec Pension Plans.

    (d) Males (with taxable income) received a larger share of income from private pension plans than females because of their greater labour force involvement and greater probability of being in jobs that had pension plans.

    (e) For elderly persons with taxable income, investments provided an important source of income, generally over 20 percent.

    (f) Regardless of gender, employment income represented a declining share of total income as age increased.

    (g) Among persons over age 65, women were less likely than men to have employment income.

References

BOOKS

BEACH WAYNE and LYLE R. HEPBURN. *Are You Paying Too Much Tax?* Toronto: McGraw-Hill Ryerson, annual, 206 pp. A tax planning guide for the general reader that includes a discussion of capital gains, RRSPs, and investment income.

BIRCH, RICHARD. *The Family Financial Planning Book, A Step-by-Step Moneyguide for Canadian Families.* Revised Edition. Toronto: Key Porter, 1989, 216 pp. An easy-to-read guide to taking control of your personal finances that discusses budgets, income tax, insurance, RRSPs, mortgages, and investments.

BIRCH, RICHARD. *The Canadian Price Waterhouse Personal Tax Advisor*. Toronto: McClelland-Bantam, annual, 199 pp. A non-technical guide prepared by tax accountants that outlines how the tax system works and explains the basics of personal income tax, including RRSPs.

COHEN, DIAN. *Money*. Scarborough, Ontario: Prentice-Hall Canada, 1987, 270 pp. An economist suggests strategies for coping with personal finances in the context of changing economic conditions. Topics include financial plans, buying a home, insurance, income tax, retirement, estate planning, and investments.

CÔTÉ, JEAN-MARC and DONALD DAY. *Personal Financial Planning in Canada*. Toronto: Allyn and Bacon, 1987, 464 pp. A comprehensive personal finance text that includes financial planning, income tax, annuities, pensions, investments, credit, mortgages, and wills, with particular attention to the banking and insurance industries.

DELANEY, TOM. *The Delaney Report on RRSPs*. Toronto: McGraw-Hill Ryerson, annual, 280 pp. In addition to a comprehensive treatment of RRSPs (types, how to select, and maturity options), private and public pensions plans are explained and suggestions given for planning financial security.

DRACHE, ARTHUR B. C. and SUSAN WEIDMAN SCHNEIDER. *Head and Heart, Financial Strategies for Smart Women*. Toronto: Macmillan, 1987, 348 pp. Recognizing the needs and perspectives of women, a tax lawyer and journalist have collaborated to present basic financial information, taking into account women's concerns at different stages in their lives.

FINLAYSON, ANN. *Whose Money is it Anyway? The Showdown on Pensions*. Markham, Ontario: Penguin Group, 1989, 278 pp. Examines the issues related to retirement pensions for Canadians.

HEALTH AND WELFARE CANADA. *Basic Facts on Social Security Programs*. Ottawa: Supply and Services Canada, annual, 91 pp. Booklet that summarizes federal income security programs, with recent statistics.

HEALTH AND WELFARE CANADA. *Inventory of Income Security Programs in Canada*. Ottawa: Supply and Services Canada, annual, 247 pp. Compendium of basic information and statistics regarding: federal and provincial programs for the elderly and children; provincial and municipal social assistance programs; provincial taxation and shelter assistance programs; workers' compensation; unemployment insurance; veterans' programs.

HUNNISETT, HENRY S. and DENISE LAMAUTE. *Retirement Guide: An Overall Plan for a Comfortable Future*. Vancouver: International Self-Counsel Press, 1991, 280 pp. A general guide to retirement planning that includes some chapters on financial aspects.

KELMAN, STEVEN G. *Financial Times Guide to RRSPs: The Authoritative Guide to the Best Retirement Savings Strategies*. Toronto: Financial Times, annual, 193 pp. A detailed guide to selecting an RRSP, with comparisons between financial institutions.

LONGHURST, PATRICK and ROSE MARIE EARLE. *Your Pension. The Complete Guide to Pension Planning in Canada*. Toronto: Doubleday Canada, 1991, 178 pp. Explains how pension plans work and provides helpful tips on how to make the most of government and private pension plans. Includes new tax rules.

MACINNIS, LYMAN. *Get Smart! Make Your Money Count in the 1990s.* Second Edition. Scarborough, Ontario: Prentice-Hall Canada, 1989, 317 pp. A book for the general reader that includes financial planning and income tax principles, but gives major attention to investing in the stock market.

MCCARLEY, BRUCE D. *Retirement Planning, a Guide for Canadians.* Toronto: Key Porter, 1993, 208 pp. Examines the critical issues involved in financial planning for retirement: how much to save and invest; when and where to retire.

MCLEOD, WILLIAM E. *The Canadian Buyer's Guide to Life Insurance.* Seventh Edition. Scarborough, Ontario: Prentice-Hall Canada, 1989, 276 pp. A comprehensive guide to the various life insurance products, including annuities.

OJA, GAIL. *Pensions and Incomes of the Elderly in Canada, 1971–1985.* Statistics Canada, Ottawa: Supply and Services Canada, 1988, 118 pp. Statistical analysis of income data.

PAPE, GORDON. *Building Wealth in the '90s.* Scarborough, Ontario: Prentice-Hall Canada, 1992, 294 pp. An easy-to-read guide for the novice financial manager and investor which considers interest rates, credit cards, mortgages, RRSPs, mutual funds, and the stock market.

PAPE, GORDON. *Gordon Pape's 1993 Buyer's Guide to RRSPs.* Scarborough, Ontario: Prentice-Hall Canada, 1992, 202 pp. Provides basic rules for contributions, rollovers, transfers, kinds of instruments, and asset mix strategy.

POLSON, KIRK and GEORGE BRETT. *Retire Right: The Practical Guide to RRIFs, Annuities and Pensions.* Markham, Ontario: Penguin Books, 1989, 159 pp. Focuses on financial life after retirement and provides an easy-to-understand explanation of government securities, employer pensions and retirement income options.

WYLIE, BETTY JANE. *The Best is Yet to Come, Planning Ahead for a Financially Secure Retirement.* Toronto: Key Porter, 1989, 206 pp. Emphasis is on financial planning for retirement, but other aspects are also mentioned.

WYATT, ELAINE. *The Money Companion, How to Manage Your Money and Achieve Financial Freedom.* Markham, Ontario: Penguin Books, 1991. A guide to personal financial management that focuses on planning, investment strategy, and retirement needs.

ZIMMER, HENRY B. *Making Your Money Grow, A Canadian Guide to Successful Personal Finance.* Third Edition. Toronto: Collins, 1989, 260 pp. The focus of this book is on basic calculations needed for personal financial decisions, as applied to compound interest, future and present values, investment returns, RRSPs, annuities, and life insurance.

ZIMMER, HENRY B. *The Canadian Tax and Investment Guide.* Toronto: McClelland and Stewart, 1993, 301 pp. Comprehensive treatment of income tax as it relates to such topics as RRSPs, investment income, separation and divorce, retirement, and estate planning.

CHAPTER EIGHT

Interest

OBJECTIVES

1. To understand the concept of interest and how it is related to the time value of money.

2. To distinguish between simple and compound interest and to demonstrate the calculation of each.

3. To distinguish between nominal interest rate and effective annual yield.

4. To understand the process of calculating a repayment schedule for a loan to be repaid in equal instalments, with each payment a blend of interest and principal.

5. To explain how frequency of compounding interest affects the effective annual yield.

6. To understand the process of determining the total interest charge on loan contracts for either simple or compound interest.

7. To identify factors that influence the total interest charged on a loan.

8. To understand the concepts of future and present values.

9. To determine future and present values of a single payment, using either formulae or compound interest tables.

10. To calculate the future and present values of a uniform series of deposits made or a uniform series of payments received.

11. To explain the following terms: principal, maturity date, term of a loan, sinking fund, blended payment.

Introduction

Interest, the subject of this chapter, has important implications for lenders as well as borrowers and is therefore relevant to a variety of transactions. If you think that all lenders are people with a great deal of money, keep in mind that when you make deposits in banks or other financial institutions you are a lender. Borrowers pay for the use of other people's money and this goes to lenders (depositors) as interest. This chapter presents some basic principles applicable to interest, or the time value of money, and several ways of calculating interest.

The **time value of money** is based on the assumption that money can be lent to others for a rent, called interest, and that funds invested for a time will grow in value. Therefore, a dollar you invest for ten years will be worth more at the end of the decade, but a dollar promised to you in five years' time is worth less than a dollar given to you now. An understanding of interest and how to calculate present and future values should assist you, whether as a borrower or a lender, to make informed choices in various financial transactions.

This chapter is composed of two major sections: the first is concerned with interest, and the second with future and present values. A thorough understanding of the basic principles of interest and methods of calculation will be helpful for problems found in later chapters on credit, mortgages, and investments. Some acquaintance with the concepts of future and present values, which are applications of compound interest, can be useful in a variety of situations. However, this knowledge is not required for comprehension of later chapters and may be treated as reference material.

This chapter includes an explanation of interest, definitions of basic terms, and illustrations of simple and compound interest calculations. Borrowers are often mystified by repayment schedules used for consumer loans and mortgages, involving blended payments of principal and interest; examples illustrate how this works. We will demonstrate how to calculate future and present values using formulae or compound interest tables. Because the tables referred to in the examples and problems are quite detailed, you will find them at the end of the chapter rather than interspersed within the text.

THE CONCEPT OF INTEREST

Interest, which is payment for the use of someone else's money, is viewed as a cost by borrowers and as income by lenders. For the borrower, interest is the cost of doing something now that otherwise would have to wait. For the lender, interest provides compensation for: (i) foregoing the use of the money for the period of the loan, (ii) the risk that the loan will not be repaid, and (iii) the administrative costs of making the loan.

The rate of interest, which can be defined in a general way as the ratio of the interest payable at the end of a year to the money owed at the beginning of the year, is illustrated in the example, "Annual Interest Rate." This definition will be refined later when the concepts of nominal rate and effective annual yield are explained. It should be remembered that when an interest rate is quoted, it is assumed to be an annual rate unless specified otherwise.

ANNUAL INTEREST RATE

What is the interest rate on a $5000 debt, with interest of $500 payable annually?

$$\frac{500}{5000} = .10 \text{ (or 10\% per annum)}$$

The total interest charge, a most important component of any loan transaction, is the amount that must be repaid in addition to the **principal**, or the amount borrowed. It represents the lender's total return or the borrower's total carrying cost. Five factors that determine the magnitude of the total interest charge are: (i) rate of interest, (ii) frequency of compounding, (iii) term or length of time the loan is outstanding, (iv) principal, and (v) method of repayment. The effects of these factors will become apparent as various ways of calculating interest are explained in this chapter or illustrated in mortgage applications in Chapter 15.

Simple Interest

Simple interest is used when the total principal and all interest due are to be repaid as a lump sum at a specified time. The date when a loan is due is called the **maturity date,** and the length of time the loan is to be outstanding is the **loan term**. The amount of interest due may be calculated with this formula:

Interest = principal × annual rate × time (in years)

SIMPLE INTEREST

Principal: $3000
Annual interest rate: 8%
Term of loan: 2 years
Interest = principal × rate × time
= $3000 × .08 × 2
= $480

At maturity, the borrower will pay the lender:
$3000.00 (principal returned)
480.00 (total interest charge)
$3480.00 (total payment)

Compound Interest

Compound interest is paid on most savings accounts and charged on many loans, including home mortgages. **Compounding** simply means that, at specified intervals, the accumulated interest is added to the principal; in the next period, interest is earned on the new balance. Thus, interest is reinvested to earn more interest. Compounding may be done as often as daily, monthly, semi-annually, or annually. Naturally, the more frequently interest is compounded, the faster the investment grows. Assuming there is no repayment of principal or interest on a regular basis, the calculation of compound interest is exactly like simple interest, but it is repeated at each compounding interval, using a larger principal each time.

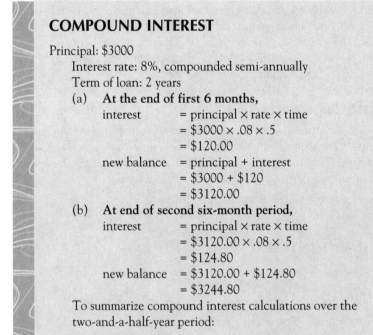

COMPOUND INTEREST

Principal: $3000
    Interest rate: 8%, compounded semi-annually
    Term of loan: 2 years
    (a) **At the end of first 6 months,**
        interest   = principal × rate × time
                    = $3000 × .08 × .5
                    = $120.00
        new balance = principal + interest
                    = $3000 + $120
                    = $3120.00
    (b) **At end of second six-month period,**
        interest   = principal × rate × time
                    = $3120.00 × .08 × .5
                    = $124.80
        new balance = $3120.00 + $124.80
                    = $3244.80
To summarize compound interest calculations over the two-and-a-half-year period:

Time period (months)	Balance of principal and interest at beginning of period	Interest at end of period	Outstanding balance at end of period
6	$3000.00	$ 120.00	$3120.00
12	3120.00	124.80	3244.80
18	3244.80	129.79	3374.59
24	3374.59	134.98	3509.58

At maturity, the borrower pays $3000.00 (principal returned)
                                                      509.58 (total interest charge)
                                              $3509.58 (total payment)

Compound interest is important to the saver because income (interest) is being reinvested regularly and begins earning additional interest. Banks calculate interest on savings accounts at different intervals, depending on the type of account. With a traditional savings account, interest may be calculated monthly on the minimum balance that was in the account during the month, but this interest is not added to the principal until the compounding date, which may be every six months. If you are planning to make a large withdrawal, consider doing so just after the end of the calendar month to avoid losing a month's interest. If you withdraw it too soon, it will not earn any interest for that month.

With a daily interest account, interest is calculated daily on the minimum balance and compounded perhaps monthly. Although the interest on such accounts is usually slightly lower than on the traditional savings account, a daily interest account can be worthwhile if you have a fluctuating balance in your account. Understandably, the interest rate paid by deposit institutions varies with the type of account: the interest rate may be depressed somewhat by chequing privileges, ready access to the deposit, or more frequent compounding.

RULE OF 72   If you would like to know how fast your money will double, you can use the Rule of 72, which gives an approximation of annual compounding. Divide 72 by the compound interest rate to find the number of years it will take to double your money. Alternatively, the compound interest rate can be approximated by dividing 72 by the number of years necessary to double your money.

COMPOUND INTEREST TABLES   To determine how much a sum of money will increase at various rates of interest, compounded annually, and left on deposit for various lengths of time, you may consult a compound interest table such as Table 8.1.

USING COMPOUND INTEREST TABLES

What will be the value of $1000 in 15 years, invested at 6% compounded annually?
From Table 8.1, find the compound value of 1, at 6%, for 15 years to be 2.40.

$$\$1000 \times 2.40 = \$2400.00$$

FREQUENCY OF COMPOUNDING AND YIELD   Whenever you lend or invest money, you expect some return. This return is called **yield** and may be expressed as an annual rate or as the total dollar amount received over some time period. The rate of return or **effective annual yield** is not necessarily the same as the quoted interest rate or nominal rate. **Nominal interest rate** is an annual rate that does not take account of the compounding effect. The more frequently interest is compounded, the faster your savings will grow and the higher the effective annual yield will be. To determine the effective annual yield, use the formula shown below.

$$\text{Effective annual yield (\%)} = \frac{\text{total annual interest}}{\text{principal}} \times 100$$

Working out the annual amount of interest for various compounding periods can become tedious, and therefore it is helpful to know the formula to use or to have convenient tables. If the interest is compounded m times a year at a nominal rate of r, then the effective annual yield can be defined as

$$\text{Effective annual yield} = \left(1 + \frac{r}{m}\right)^m - 1$$

EFFECTIVE ANNUAL YIELD

If the nominal interest rate (r) is 7% and the frequency of compounding (m) is quarterly, then

$$\text{Effective annual yield} = \left(1 + \frac{.07}{4}\right)^4 - 1$$

$$= 0.0719$$
$$= 7.19\%$$

Examine Table 8.2 to observe the effect of compounding frequency on effective annual yield. Would you prefer an investment paying 7.25% compounded monthly, or one at 7.5% compounded semi-annually? Which has the higher effective annual yield?

Compound Interest on Instalment Loans

BLENDED PAYMENTS   Very often loans are repaid in equal monthly instalments, composed of both principal and interest. Each payment will include one month's interest on the amount of principal outstanding, plus a return of some principal. In the succeeding months, as the outstanding principal gradually decreases, payments contain changing proportions of principal and interest. This is illustrated graphically in Figure 8.1. You will observe that the first payment includes a larger share of interest than later payments. As time goes on, the interest component declines and the principal component increases. Such payments, with changing proportions of principal and interest, are called **blended payments**. The example, "Blended Payments" shows how the changing proportions of principal and interest are calculated and the payments made level.

FIGURE 8.1   PROPORTIONS OF PRINCIPAL AND INTEREST IN EACH PAYMENT OF A 24-MONTH CONTRACT

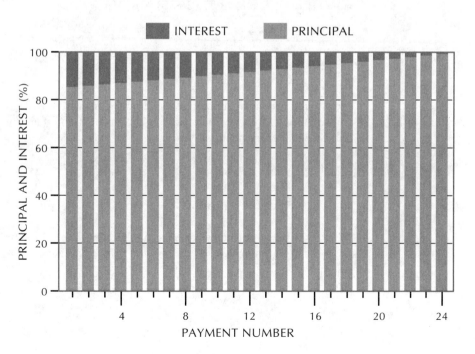

Finally, there are a couple of points to note regarding compounding and terminology. Although payments on instalment loans are paid monthly, interest is probably compounded at some other interval—often semi-annually. You may encounter the term, **amortization,** which simply means repayment of a loan over a period of time. For instance, a loans officer might say that the loan will be amortized over three years.

BLENDED PAYMENTS

Principal: $3000
Annual interest rate: 8% compounded semi-annually
Amortization period: 2 years
Equal monthly blended payments

(a) **How much will each monthly payment be?**
The monthly payment on a loan of $3000, at 8%, for 2 years is $135.51 (Table 8.3)

(b) **How much interest will be paid the first month?**
Refer to a table of interest factors, used to calculate monthly interest on instalment loans (Table 8.4). In this example, the appropriate interest factor is .006 558 1970

interest for 1 month	=	outstanding principal	×	appropriate interest factor
	=	$3000	×	.006 558 1970
	=	$19.68		

(c) **How much principal will be repaid the first month?**
Interest for 1 month must come out of the payment and then the balance will be repayment of principal.

payment on principal	=	monthly payment	–	interest for 1 month
	=	$135.51	–	$19.68
	=	$115.83		

(d) **What will be the principal balance outstanding after the first payment has been made?**

principal still owing	=	principal owing before payment	–	payment on principal
	=	$3000	–	$115.83
	=	$2884.17		

(e) **How much interest will be paid the second month?**

interest for one month	=	outstanding principal	×	appropriate interest factor
	=	$2884.17	×	.006 558 1970
	=	$18.91		

The process of calculating the monthly interest and then determining the size of the repayment on the principal will continue each month until the principal has been reduced to zero, as illustrated in "Excerpts from Payment Schedule for a $3000 Loan." (You may note small discrepancies in amounts between the above calculations and the table below because of differences in numbers of decimal points used in the calculations.)

(f) **How much will the total interest be?**

To find the total interest paid in a blended payment contract, use the following formula:

monthly payment	×	number of months	=	total amount repaid	–	principal borrowed	=	total interest charge
$135.51	×	24	=	$3252.24	–	$3000	=	$252.24

EXCERPTS FROM PAYMENT SCHEDULE FOR A $3000 LOAN (8% FOR 2 YEARS)

Payment number	Monthly payment	Principal owing before payment made	Interest paid per month	Principal repaid per month	Principal owing after payment
1	$135.50	$3000.00	$19.68	$115.82	$2884.18
2	135.50	2884.17	18.92	116.58	2767.60
3	135.50	2767.60	18.15	117.35	2650.25
4	135.50	2650.25	17.38	118.12	2532.13
5	135.50	2532.13	16.61	118.89	2413.24
6	135.50	2413.24	15.83	119.67	2293.57
12	135.50	1683.33	11.04	124.46	1558.87
18	135.50	924.22	6.06	129.44	794.78
24	135.50	134.74	0.88	134.62	0.12

To recapitulate, a loan that is amortized using blended payments, as in this last example, will have changing proportions of interest and principal in each payment. As the principal owing is gradually reduced there is less interest to pay, leaving an ever-increasing share for repayment of principal. The relation between the interest and principal portions of each payment will vary with such factors as interest rates, the term of the loan, and the size of the monthly payment. Home mortgages work the same way but the rate of principal repayment can be discouragingly slow if the loan is large, the payments modest, and the term 25 years or longer.

Total Interest Charges

The three previous examples used the same principal, interest rate, and time, but they differed in method of repayment and whether or not interest was compounded. How do these two differences affect the total amount of interest paid? With an instalment loan that has blended payments, the total interest charge is less apparent than in the examples of simple and compound interest with a single repayment.

The total interest charge on each of the examples is:

(a) simple interest $480.00
(b) compound interest   509.58
(c) compound interest, blended payments   252.24

       Can you suggest reasons for the variation?

Five factors that influence the total interest charge, as indicated at the beginning of this chapter, are:

(a) rate of interest,

(b) frequency of compounding,

(c) term of the loan,

(d) principal borrowed,

(e) method of repayment.

       It is fairly obvious that higher interest rates will increase the cost of borrowing. On a small, short-term loan, small differences in rate do not change the cost very much; however, when the principal is very large and the term long, as in a home mortgage, a quarter of a percentage point difference in interest rate can make a substantial difference in the total interest charge.

       The second factor, the frequency of compounding, is an important one for the borrower to keep in mind. If the interest on a mortgage is to be compounded quarterly instead of semi-annually, the difference in the total interest charge will be significant. The effect of the third factor, the term of the loan or the amortization period, is fairly obvious; the longer your loan is outstanding, the more you will have to pay. Likewise, the larger the principal borrowed, the more the interest charge.

Finally, the method of repayment has an effect on the total interest charge. If you have the use of the total principal for the whole term of the loan, you will have to pay more interest than if you start repaying the principal right away. Most mortgages and consumer loans are instalment loans with blended payments, composed of principal and interest. Since the very first payment includes some return of the principal to the lender this will reduce the total interest charge. Consequently, the method of payment affects the amount of principal outstanding at various times during the term of the loan. Did you notice that the total interest charge was lowest for the instalment loan example with blended payments? The reason is that the borrower did not have the use of the total principal for the entire term.

FUTURE VALUES AND PRESENT VALUES

Two questions investors may ask are: How much will a sum of money increase if left on deposit for a period of time? How much must I invest to have a certain sum at a future date? The answers involve applications of the concept of compound interest in estimating future or present values. Let us suppose that you have $1000 that you can invest today at nine percent for ten years. You want to know the **future value** of $1000 or what the total of principal and interest will be in ten years' time. A different question is, how much will you have to invest now, at nine percent, to have $5000 in five years' time for a down payment on a house? In the latter case, you want to know the **present value** of $5000.

In the two examples above it was assumed that a lump sum would be invested and a single payment received at a later date. These are fairly simple situations but sometimes investments are made in a series of deposits, or receipts may be received in a series of payments. For instance, what is the future value of depositing $500 a year for ten years? Or, what is the present value of an annuity of $800 a month that will continue for seven years? For the sake of simplicity, we will examine instances of single payments first, and later explain how to determine future and present values when serial payments are involved.

Single Payments

FUTURE VALUE OF A LUMP SUM   What will a present sum of money (P) be worth (i.e., its future value F) if the money is to be deposited at interest rate i for a period of n years? A time line will be used to help in visualizing such a problem. On the time line, receipts are shown by the upward-pointing arrow and payments by the downward-pointing arrow.

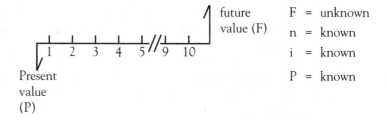

The unknown future value (F) can be found using the following formula which is applicable to a single payment compound amount.

$$F = P(1 + i)^n$$

Another way of expressing $(1 + i)^n$ is F/P at a given rate (i) and number of years (n), where F/P is the compound amount factor. Conveniently, there are tables of compound amount factors (F/P) for various combinations of interest rates and number of interest periods. Excerpts may be found in Tables 8.5 and 8.6. When tables are used to solve a problem, the equation may be expressed as:

$$F = P(F/P, i\%, n)$$

FUTURE VALUE OF $1000

You have $1000 and wish to know its future value, if invested for 5 years, at 10% compounded annually.

Set up a time line, indicating the knowns and unknowns.

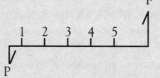

Payments

Calculate F, using the formula:

$$F = P(1 + i)^n$$
$$F = 1000(1 + .10)^5$$
$$= 1000 \times 1.6105$$
$$= 1610.51$$

Or, use Table 8.6 to find the value for F/P:

$$F = P(F/P, 10\%, 5)$$
$$= 1000 \times 1.6105$$

= 1610.51

Therefore, the future value of $1000 in 5 years' time will be $1610.51.

PRESENT VALUE OF A LUMP SUM   In this case, we want to know what the present value (P) is of a future sum of money (F) if it can be invested at interest rate i for a period of n years. By cross-multiplying the formula used for future values we get:

P   = F
    (1 + i)^n

Or, using tables:

P   = F (P/F, i%, n)
    = F × present worth factor (P/F) (Table 8.5 or 8.6)

PRESENT VALUE OF $2000 IN THREE YEARS

Sarah wonders how much she needs to invest now (P), to have a future sum (F) of $2000 saved for a trip in 3 years, if the interest rate is 6% compounded annually. The time line will be:

Receipts

F = 2000
n = 3
i = .06
P = unknown

Payments

Using the formula:

$$P = \frac{F}{(1 + i)^n}$$

$$= \frac{2000}{(1 + .06)^3}$$

$$= \frac{2000}{1.191016}$$

$$= 1679.24$$

Or, using Table 8.5:

P = F(P/F, 6%, 3)
  = 2000 × 0.8396
  = $1679.24

Therefore, if Sarah invests $1679.24 now at 6%, in 3 years she will have $2000 for her trip. Or, the present worth of $2000, invested at 6%, is $1679.24.

Uniform Series of Deposits

An interesting question is finding the future value of a series of deposits. For example, if you know how much you can afford to save each year (P) and for how many years (n), you can find out the future value (F) of this savings program.

A practical method to save for a trip or a down payment on a house would be to make regular deposits for several years. If you know how much will be needed (F), and how long you have to save (n), you can calculate the present value (P) in terms of the amount to be deposited each year. The problem is to determine the present value of a series of deposits.

FUTURE VALUE OF A SERIES What will be the future value (F) of a series of annual deposits (A) for **n** years at interest rate **i**? The time line will be as follows:

Receipts

```
                          F
    |   |   |  //|   |
    1   2   3    6   7
    A   A   A    A   A
```

F = unknown
n = known
i = known
A = known

Deposits

The appropriate formula is:

$$F = A \left(\frac{(1 + i)^n - 1}{i} \right)$$

Or, using compound interest tables:

$$F = A \times \text{compound amount factor (F/A)}$$
$$= A(F/A, i\%, n)$$

FUTURE VALUE OF A SERIES OF DEPOSITS

If Frank and Eva can set aside $500 a year for the next 10 years to create a fund for their son's education, how large will the fund be if the interest rate is 6%, compounded annually?

The time line will be:

Receipts

F = unknown
n = 10
i = 0.6
A = 500

A A A A A A A A A A

Deposits

$$F = 500 \left(\frac{(1 + 0.6)^{10} - 1}{.06} \right)$$
$$= 500 \times 13.181$$
$$= \$6590.50$$

Or, using tables:

$$F = A(F/A, 6\%, 10)$$
$$= 500 \times 13.181 \text{ (from Table 8.5)}$$
$$= \$6590.50$$

They will accumulate \$6590.50 in 10 years. Therefore, the future value of the series of \$500 deposits is \$6590.50.

PRESENT VALUE OF A SERIES   How much must be deposited in a uniform series to accumulate a future sum of money at a given date? This question is relevant for those planning to retire a debt and is often referred to as a sinking fund problem. A **sinking fund** is a sum being accumulated to retire a debt. The formula is:

$$A = F \left(\frac{i}{(1 + i)^n - 1} \right)$$

Using compound interest tables:

$$A = F \times \text{sinking fund factor (A/F)}$$
$$= F(A/F, i\%, n)$$

PRESENT VALUE OF A SERIES OF DEPOSITS

Since Ed wants to pay off his mortgage as fast as possible, he has decided to make a lump-sum payment of \$5000 in 4 years' time. At 6% interest, how much should he put aside annually for the next 4 years to reach his objective?

The time line will be:

Receipts

F = 5000
n = 4
i = .06
A = unknown

A A A A

Deposits

$$A = 5000 \left(\frac{.06}{(1 + .06)^4 - 1} \right)$$
$$= 5000 \times .2286$$
$$= \$1142.95$$

Or, using tables:

$$A = F(A/F, 6\%, 4)$$
$$= 5000 \times 0.22859 \text{ (from Table 8.5)}$$
$$= \$1142.95$$

If Ed invests $1142.95 a year at 6%, he will be able to reduce his mortgage debt by $5000 in 4 years' time.

Uniform Series of Payments Received

The previous two examples involved the present and future values of a uniform series of deposits. Now we will consider the present and future values of a uniform series of payments. Often a financial institution faces the question of converting a series of future payments into an equivalent lump sum, known as the **commuted value.** One instance of this occurs at the death of an annuitant who had an annuity with a guaranteed period. A lump sum may be paid to the beneficiary instead of making payments for the balance of the guaranteed period.

Another problem is deciding how much can be spent each year to exhaust a known sum in a certain length of time. This is called recovery of capital in a uniform series of payments.

PRESENT WORTH OF A SERIES OF FUTURE PAYMENTS What is the present worth of a property that is now renting at (A) each year, at a given interest rate (i)? The time line will be:

Receipts

A = known
n = known
i = known
P = unknown

Payments

The appropriate formula is:

$$P = A \left(\frac{(1 + i)^n - 1}{i (1 + i)^n} \right)$$

Or, if using compound interest tables:

P = A × present worth factor (P/A)

PRESENT VALUE OF A SERIES OF ANNUITY PAYMENTS

After Ted's death, the insurance company representative called on Magda to tell her that she would receive a lump sum, equivalent to the annuity payments due to her husband. He had been receiving annual payments of $8000 from an annuity that was guaranteed for 6 more years. When commuting the series of payments to a lump sum, the company assumed an interest rate of 10%. The time line would be:

Receipts

$$\begin{array}{cccccc} A & A & A & A & A & A \end{array}$$

| | | | | | |

1   2   3   4   5   6

P

Payments

$A =$ 8000
$n =$ 6
$i =$ $.10$
$P =$ unknown

Using the formula:

$$P = A \left(\frac{(1 + i)^n - 1}{i (1 + i)^n} \right)$$

$$= 8000 \left(\frac{(1 + .10)^6 - 1}{.10 (1 + .10)^6} \right)$$

$$= \$34\ 840$$

Using Table 8.5:

$$P = A(P/A, 10\%, 6)$$
$$= 8000 \times 4.355$$
$$= 34\ 840$$

Magda received a lump sum of $34 840 instead of 6 annual payments of $8000. Why did she not receive $48 000?

CAPITAL RECOVERY IN A UNIFORM SERIES OF PAYMENTS   How much can be withdrawn per year (A) from a capital fund with a present value (P) if it is invested at interest rate i so that the fund will be exhausted in n years? The time line will be:

Receipts

A = unknown
n = known
i = known
P = known

Payments

The appropriate formula is:

$$A = P\left(\frac{i(1+i)^n}{(1+i)^n - 1}\right)$$

Or, using compound interest tables:

$$A = P \times \text{capital recovery factor (A/P)}$$
$$= P(A/P, i\%, n)$$

GRADUAL WITHDRAWAL OF CAPITAL

Jeanne has a $20 000 travel fund that she plans to use up over the next 10 years. She is wondering how much to spend each year, assuming that she can invest the $20 000 at 10%, compounded annually. The time line will be:

Receipts

A = unknown
n = 10
i = .10
P = $20 000

Payments

Using Table 8.6:

$$A = P \times A/P$$
$$= P(A/P, i\%, n)$$
$$= 20\ 000 \times 0.162\ 75$$
$$= \$3255$$

If Jeanne uses $3255 per year for 10 years, her travel fund of $20 000 will be exhausted.

Multiple Compounding Periods Per Year

Thus far, we have explained how to calculate present and future values when interest is compounded annually, but very often interest is compounded more frequently. There is a simple way to adapt the formulae and procedures given in this chapter to accommodate various frequencies of compounding. Simply change the annual interest rate to the semi-annual or quarterly or whatever rate, and change the number of years to the number of compounding periods. For example, if the interest rate is 10% per year for 6 years, compounded quarterly, it will be expressed as 2.5% per quarter. The number of compounding periods will be 4×6 years = 24. When using the formula or tables, i = .025 and n = 24.

SEMI-ANNUAL COMPOUNDING

You wish to know the future value of $1000 in 3 years if the interest rate is 12%, compounded semi-annually.

First, put the interest rate into the same time frame as the compounding period. Thus, the rate will be 6% per half year. The total number of compounding periods will be 2 per year × 3 years = 6. Therefore n = 6, and i = .06.

$$
\begin{aligned}
F \quad &= P(F/P, i\%, n) \\
&= 1000 \times 1.4185 \text{ (Table 8.5)} \\
&= \$1418.50
\end{aligned}
$$

The future value of $1000, compounded semi-annually at 12% for 3 years, will be $1418.50.

Summary

This chapter has demonstrated the concept of interest as applied to a variety of situations, including compound interest with either a single payment or a series of blended payments. An important consideration in many transactions is the total interest charge, which is dependent on interest rate, frequency of compounding, term, principal, and method of repayment.

The next time you encounter a problem that involves future or present values, you should first draw a time line and list your knowns and unknowns. This will permit you to clarify the problem and to classify it as one involving single payments or a series of payments, and to decide whether it is a present or future value that is unknown. By comparing your problem statement and time line with the examples given in this chapter, you can find the appropriate formula to use.

Vocabulary Review

amortization (p. 226)

blended payments (p. 225)

commuted value (p. 234)

compounding (p. 222)

effective annual yield (p. 224)

future value (p. 229)

loan term (p. 221)

maturity date (p. 221)

nominal interest rate (p. 224)

present value (p. 229)

principal (p. 221)

sinking fund (p. 233)

time value of money (p. 220)

simple interest (p. 221)

yield (p. 224)

Problems

1. Calculate the amount of interest due in each of the following cases:

    (a) $500 @ 9% for 6 months, simple interest.

    (b) $850 @ 10% for 1 year, compounded semi-annually.

    (c) The interest component of the first monthly instalment on a loan of $1000 @ 12% compounded semi-annually.

2. Assume an instalment loan with the following terms:

    Principal: $5000, monthly blended payments of $158.62

    Interest rate: 9%, compounded semi-annually

    Term: 3 years

    Would the total interest on this loan be calculated as follows?
    $5000 × .09 × 3 = $1350

    Explain why you agree or disagree with this method. If you disagree, show how it should be done.

3. You have several options for investing $1000 at various interest rates and frequencies of compounding. Which one would you choose from each of the following sets of alternatives, based on the effective annual yield?

    (a) 4.75% compounded daily or 5.75% compounded semi-annually.

    (b) 7.75% compounded annually, 7.50% semi-annually, or 7.25% monthly.

4. Following are pairs of alternative loan arrangements. Calculate the total interest charge for each alternative and identify the preferred choice for the borrower.

    (a) Instalment loan of $3500 at 8% compounded semi-annually. To pay it off completely in 2 years or 3 years? (The monthly payments would be $158.10 for 2 years and $109.47 for 3 years).

(b) Single-payment loan of $4000 for 2 years. To borrow at 7.75% compounded semi-annually or at 7.25% compounded monthly?

(c) Loan of $5000 for 3 years. Instalment loan with monthly blended payments at 8% or single-payment loan at 7.5% ?

5. You have a piece of antique furniture that you are thinking of selling and have received two offers from an interested buyer: $1500 now or $2000 in 2 years' time. Assuming an interest rate of 9% compounded annually, which offer would you accept? Did you make your comparison based on present values or future values?

6. Recently, Fred won $10 000 in a lottery. He would like to spend this sum on holidays, over a five-year period, and is wondering how much he can withdraw annually to make it last 5 years. Assume an interest rate of 10% compounded annually.

7. As the owner of an company that rents office furniture, you have received two offers from one of your clients: $3000 per year for the use of the equipment over the next 3 years, or $9000 at the end of 3 years. Which offer will you accept, assuming 6% interest, compounded annually?

8. John wants to know what sum of money he has to save each year in order to have $15 000 available in 5 years' time to buy a new car.

(a) Assume that the money will be invested at 6% compounded annually.

(b) Assume that the money will be invested at 9% compounded semi-annually.

9. If you were receiving $3000 a year in rent from 50 acres of farm land, what is the present worth of this land if the interest rates are 10%, compounded annually? (Assume that the rent will be paid at the beginning of the year for the next 3 years.)

10. Lou has determined that his young family should have an educational fund of $10 000 to become available in 8 years' time. If he died tomorrow, how much money would be needed from an insurance settlement to provide this sum if the money could be invested at 8%, compounded annually?

References

BOOKS

ANDERSON, HUGH. *Money for Rent: A Guide to Earning Top Interest on Your Savings.* Markham, Ontario: Penguin Books, 1991, 170 pp. A comprehensive guide to investment, tax, legal, and accounting information.

CÔTÉ, JEAN-MARC and DONALD DAY. *Personal Financial Planning in Canada.* Toronto: Allyn and Bacon, 1987, 464 pp. A comprehensive personal finance text that includes financial planning, income tax, annuities, pensions, investments, credit, mortgages, and wills, with particular attention to the banking and insurance industries.

ESTES, JACK C. *Compound Interest and Annuity Tables*. New York: McGraw-Hill, 1976, 248 pp. A book of tables with a wide range of interest rates.

Financial Payment Tables for Canadian Mortgages. Toronto: Stoddart, 1983, 255 pp. Includes mortgage payment tables, loan progress charts, monthly interest factors.

Interest Amortization Tables. New York: McGraw-Hill, 1976, 246 pp. Uses interest rates from 5 to 25 percent.

ZIMMER, HENRY B. *Making Your Money Grow, A Canadian Guide to Successful Personal Finance*. Third Edition. Toronto: Collins, 1989, 260 pp. The focus of this book is on basic calculations needed for personal financial decisions, as applied to compound interest, future and present values, investment returns, RRSPs, annuities, and life insurance.

TABLE 8.1 COMPOUND VALUE OF 1 AT VARIOUS INTEREST RATES FROM 1 TO 40 YEARS (COMPOUNDED ANNUALLY)

Yrs.	4%	5%	6%	7%	8%	9%	10%	11%	12%	13%	14%	15%	16%
1	1.04	1.05	1.06	1.07	1.08	1.09	1.10	1.11	1.12	1.13	1.14	1.15	1.16
2	1.08	1.10	1.12	1.14	1.17	1.19	1.21	1.23	1.25	1.28	1.30	1.32	1.35
3	1.12	1.16	1.19	1.23	1.26	1.30	1.33	1.37	1.40	1.44	1.48	1.52	1.56
4	1.17	1.22	1.26	1.31	1.36	1.41	1.46	1.52	1.57	1.63	1.69	1.75	1.81
5	1.22	1.28	1.34	1.40	1.47	1.54	1.61	1.69	1.76	1.84	1.93	2.01	2.10
6	1.27	1.34	1.42	1.50	1.59	1.68	1.77	1.87	1.97	2.08	2.19	2.29	2.44
7	1.32	1.41	1.50	1.61	1.71	1.83	1.95	2.08	2.21	2.35	2.50	2.61	2.83
8	1.37	1.48	1.59	1.72	1.85	1.99	2.14	2.30	2.48	2.66	2.85	2.98	3.28
9	1.42	1.55	1.69	1.84	2.00	2.17	2.36	2.56	2.77	3.00	3.25	3.40	3.80
10	1.48	1.63	1.79	1.97	2.16	2.37	2.60	2.84	3.11	3.39	3.71	3.87	4.41
11	1.54	1.71	1.90	2.10	2.33	2.58	2.85	3.15	3.48	3.84	4.23	4.45	5.12
12	1.60	1.80	2.01	2.25	2.52	2.81	3.14	3.50	3.90	4.33	4.82	5.12	5.94
13	1.67	1.89	2.13	2.41	2.72	3.07	3.45	3.88	4.36	4.90	5.50	5.89	6.89
14	1.73	1.98	2.26	2.58	2.94	3.34	3.80	4.31	4.89	5.53	6.26	6.77	7.99
15	1.80	2.08	2.40	2.76	3.17	3.64	4.18	4.78	5.47	6.25	7.14	7.79	9.27
16	1.87	2.18	2.54	2.96	3.43	3.97	4.59	5.31	6.13	7.07	8.14	8.96	10.75
17	1.95	2.30	2.69	3.16	3.70	4.33	5.05	5.90	6.87	7.99	9.28	10.30	12.47
18	2.03	2.41	2.85	3.38	4.00	4.72	5.56	6.54	7.69	9.02	10.58	11.85	14.46
19	2.11	2.53	3.03	3.62	4.32	5.14	6.12	7.26	8.61	10.20	12.06	13.62	16.78
20	2.19	2.66	3.21	3.87	4.66	5.60	6.73	8.06	9.65	11.52	13.74	15.67	19.46
21	2.28	2.79	3.40	4.14	5.03	6.11	7.40	8.95	10.80	13.02	15.67	18.02	22.57
22	2.37	2.93	3.60	4.43	5.44	6.66	8.14	9.93	12.10	14.71	17.86	20.72	26.19
23	2.46	3.07	3.82	4.74	5.87	7.26	8.95	11.03	13.55	16.63	20.36	23.83	30.38
24	2.56	3.23	4.05	5.07	6.34	7.91	9.85	12.24	15.18	18.79	23.21	27.40	35.24
25	2.67	3.39	4.29	5.43	6.85	8.62	10.83	13.59	17.00	21.23	26.46	31.51	40.87
26	2.77	3.56	4.55	5.81	7.40	9.34	11.92	15.08	19.04	23.99	30.17	37.24	47.41
27	2.89	3.73	4.82	6.21	7.99	10.25	13.10	16.74	21.32	27.11	34.39	41.78	55.00
28	3.00	3.92	5.11	6.65	8.63	11.17	14.42	18.58	23.88	30.63	39.20	47.93	63.80
29	3.12	4.12	5.42	7.11	9.32	12.17	15.86	20.62	26.75	34.62	44.69	55.12	74.01
30	3.24	4.32	5.74	7.61	10.06	13.27	17.45	22.89	29.96	39.12	50.95	63.38	85.85
31	3.37	4.54	6.09	8.15	10.87	14.46	19.19	25.41	33.56	44.20	58.08	72.89	99.59
32	3.51	4.76	6.45	8.72	11.74	15.76	21.11	28.21	37.58	49.95	66.21	83.82	115.52
33	3.65	5.00	6.84	9.33	12.68	17.18	23.23	31.31	42.09	56.44	75.48	96.40	134.00
34	3.80	5.25	7.25	9.98	13.69	18.73	25.55	34.75	47.14	63.78	86.95	110.86	155.44
35	3.95	5.52	7.69	10.68	14.79	20.41	28.10	38.57	52.80	72.07	98.10	127.48	180.31
36	4.10	5.80	8.15	11.42	15.97	22.25	30.91	42.82	59.14	81.44	111.83	146.61	209.16
37	4.27	6.08	8.64	12.22	17.25	24.25	34.00	47.53	66.23	92.02	127.49	168.60	242.63
38	4.44	6.39	9.15	13.08	18.63	26.44	37.40	52.76	74.18	103.99	145.34	193.89	281.45
39	4.62	6.70	9.70	13.99	20.12	28.82	41.14	58.56	83.08	117.51	165.69	222.97	326.48
40	4.80	7.04	10.29	14.97	21.72	31.41	45.26	65.00	93.05	132.78	188.88	256.42	378.72

TABLE 8.2   EFFECTIVE ANNUAL YIELD BY NOMINAL RATE AND FREQUENCY OF COMPOUNDING

Nominal Rate %	Semi-annually %	Quarterly %	Monthly %	Weekly %	Daily %
3	3.02	3.03	3.04	3.04	3.05
3 1/4	3.28	3.29	3.30	3.30	3.30
3 1/2	3.53	3.55	3.56	3.56	3.56
3 3/4	3.79	3.80	3.82	3.82	3.82
4	4.04	4.06	4.07	4.08	4.08
4 1/4	4.30	4.32	4.33	4.34	4.34
4 1/2	4.55	4.58	4.59	4.60	4.60
4 3/4	4.81	4.84	4.85	4.86	4.86
5	5.06	5.09	5.12	5.12	5.13
5 1/4	5.32	5.35	5.38	5.39	5.39
5 1/2	5.58	5.61	5.64	5.65	5.65
5 3/4	5.83	5.88	5.90	5.92	5.92
6	6.09	6.14	6.17	6.18	6.18
6 1/4	6.35	6.40	6.43	6.45	6.45
6 1/2	6.61	6.66	6.70	6.71	6.72
6 3/4	6.86	6.92	6.96	6.98	6.98
7	7.12	7.19	7.23	7.25	7.25
7 1/4	7.38	7.45	7.50	7.51	7.52
7 1/2	7.64	7.71	7.76	7.78	7.79
7 3/4	7.90	7.98	8.03	8.05	8.06
8	8.16	8.24	8.30	8.32	8.33
8 1/4	8.42	8.51	8.57	8.59	8.60
8 1/2	8.68	8.77	8.84	8.86	8.87
8 3/4	8.94	9.04	9.11	9.14	9.14
9	9.20	9.31	9.38	9.41	9.42
9 1/4	9.46	9.58	9.65	9.68	9.69
9 1/2	9.73	9.84	9.92	9.96	9.96
9 3/4	9.99	10.11	10.20	10.23	10.24
10	10.25	10.38	10.47	10.51	10.52
10 1/4	10.51	10.65	10.74	10.78	10.79
10 1/2	10.77	10.92	11.02	11.06	11.07
10 3/4	11.03	11.19	11.29	11.33	11.34
11	11.30	11.46	11.57	11.61	11.63
11 1/4	11.57	11.73	11.84	11.89	11.90
11 1/2	11.83	12.00	12.12	12.17	12.19
11 3/4	12.10	12.28	12.40	12.45	12.47
12	12.36	12.55	12.68	12.73	12.74
12 1/4	12.62	12.82	12.96	13.01	13.03
12 1/2	12.89	13.10	13.24	13.29	13.31
12 3/4	13.15	13.37	13.52	13.58	13.60
13	13.42	13.65	13.80	13.86	13.88
13 1/4	13.69	13.92	14.08	14.15	14.18
13 1/2	13.95	14.20	14.36	14.43	14.45
13 3/4	14.22	14.47	14.65	14.72	14.74
14	14.49	14.75	14.93	15.01	15.02
14 1/4	14.75	15.03	15.22	15.30	15.31
14 1/2	15.02	15.30	15.50	15.58	15.60
14 3/4	15.29	15.58	15.79	15.87	15.89
15	15.56	15.87	16.08	16.16	16.18
15 1/4	15.83	16.14	16.36	16.44	16.47
15 1/2	16.10	16.42	16.65	16.74	16.76
15 3/4	16.37	16.70	16.94	17.03	17.00
16	16.64	16.98	17.23	17.32	17.34

TABLE 8.3   AMORTIZATION TABLE:
MONTHLY PAYMENT NECESSARY TO AMORTIZE A LOAN AT 8%

Term Amount	1 Year	2 Years	3 Years	4 Years	5 Years	6 Years	7 Years	8 Years	9 Years	10 Years	11 Years	12 Years	13 Years
$100	8.70	4.52	3.13	2.44	2.03	1.75	1.56	1.41	1.30	1.21	1.14	1.08	1.03
200	17.39	9.04	6.26	4.88	4.05	3.50	3.11	2.82	2.60	2.42	2.27	2.16	2.06
300	26.08	13.56	9.39	7.31	6.07	5.25	4.66	4.23	3.89	3.62	3.41	3.23	3.08
400	34.78	18.07	12.52	9.75	8.09	6.99	6.21	5.63	5.19	4.83	4.54	4.31	4.11
500	43.47	22.59	15.64	12.18	10.11	8.74	7.77	7.04	6.48	6.04	5.68	5.38	5.13
600	52.16	27.11	18.77	14.62	12.13	10.49	9.32	8.45	7.78	7.24	6.81	6.46	6.16
700	60.85	31.62	21.90	17.05	14.15	12.23	10.87	9.85	9.07	8.45	7.95	7.53	7.19
800	69.55	36.14	25.03	19.49	16.18	13.98	12.42	11.26	10.37	9.66	9.08	8.61	8.21
900	78.24	40.66	28.15	21.92	18.20	15.73	13.97	12.67	11.66	10.86	10.22	9.68	9.24
1000	86.93	45.17	31.28	24.36	20.22	17.47	15.53	14.08	12.96	12.07	11.35	10.76	10.26
2000	173.86	90.34	62.56	48.71	40.43	34.94	31.05	28.15	25.91	24.13	22.70	21.51	20.52
3000	260.79	135.51	93.83	73.06	60.65	52.41	46.57	42.22	38.86	36.20	34.04	32.26	30.78
4000	347.72	180.68	125.11	97.41	80.86	69.88	62.09	56.29	51.81	48.26	45.39	43.02	41.04
5000	434.65	225.84	156.39	121.76	101.08	87.35	77.61	70.36	64.76	60.33	56.73	53.77	51.30
6000	521.57	271.01	187.66	146.12	121.29	104.82	93.13	84.43	77.71	72.39	68.08	64.52	61.55
7000	608.50	316.18	218.94	170.47	141.50	122.29	108.66	98.50	90.66	84.45	79.42	75.28	71.81
8000	695.43	361.35	250.22	194.82	161.72	139.76	124.18	112.57	103.62	96.52	90.77	86.03	82.07
9000	782.36	406.52	281.49	219.17	181.93	157.23	139.70	126.64	116.57	108.58	102.11	96.78	92.33
10000	869.29	451.68	312.77	243.52	202.15	174.70	155.22	140.71	129.52	120.65	113.46	107.54	102.59

TABLE 8.3 AMORTIZATION TABLE: (CONTINUED)
MONTHLY PAYMENT NECESSARY TO AMORTIZE A LOAN AT 8%

Term Amount	16 Years	17 Years	18 Years	19 Years	20 Years	21 Years	22 Years	23 Years	24 Years	25 Years
$100	.92	.90	.87	.85	.83	.82	.80	.79	.78	.77
200	1.84	1.79	1.74	1.70	1.66	1.63	1.60	1.58	1.55	1.53
300	2.76	2.68	2.61	2.54	2.49	2.44	2.40	2.36	2.33	2.29
400	3.67	3.57	3.47	3.39	3.32	3.25	3.20	3.15	3.10	3.06
500	4.59	4.46	4.34	4.24	4.15	4.07	3.99	3.93	3.87	3.82
600	5.51	5.35	5.21	5.08	4.98	4.88	4.79	4.72	4.65	4.58
700	6.43	6.24	6.07	5.93	5.80	5.69	5.59	5.50	5.42	5.35
800	7.34	7.13	6.94	6.78	6.63	6.50	6.39	6.29	6.19	6.11
900	8.26	8.02	7.81	7.62	7.46	7.32	7.19	7.07	6.97	6.87
1000	9.18	8.91	8.68	8.47	8.29	8.13	7.98	7.86	7.74	7.64
2000	18.35	17.82	17.35	16.94	16.57	16.25	15.96	15.71	15.48	15.27
3000	27.52	26.72	26.02	25.40	24.86	24.37	23.94	23.56	23.21	22.90
4000	36.70	35.63	34.69	33.87	33.14	32.49	31.92	31.41	30.95	30.53
5000	45.87	44.53	43.36	42.33	41.42	40.62	39.90	39.26	38.68	38.17
6000	55.04	53.44	52.03	50.80	49.71	48.74	47.88	47.11	46.42	45.80
7000	64.22	62.34	60.70	59.26	57.99	56.86	55.86	54.96	54.15	53.43
8000	73.39	71.25	69.37	67.73	66.27	64.98	63.84	62.81	61.89	61.06
9000	82.56	80.15	78.04	76.19	74.56	73.11	71.81	70.66	69.62	68.69
10000	91.74	89.06	86.72	84.66	82.84	81.23	79.79	78.51	77.36	76.33

TABLE 8.4   MONTHLY INTEREST FACTORS AT NOMINAL ANNUAL RATES, INTEREST COMPOUNDED SEMI-ANNUALLY

Rate %	Factor	Rate %	Factor	Rate %	Factor
4	.003 305 8904	8 7/8	.007 262 6831	13 3/4	.011 143 2522
4 1/8	.003 408 3260	9	.007 363 1231	13 7/8	.011 241 7802
4 1/4	.003 510 7094	9 1/8	.007 463 5130	14	.011 340 2602
4 3/8	.003 613 0406	9 1/4	.007 563 8530	14 1/8	.011 438 6923
4 1/2	.003 715 3196	9 3/8	.007 664 1431	14 1/4	.011 537 0764
4 5/8	.003 817 5466	9 1/2	.007 764 3832	14 3/8	.011 635 4128
4 3/4	.003 919 7215	9 5/8	.007 864 5735	14 1/2	.011 733 7014
4 7/8	.004 021 8445	9 3/4	.007 964 7141	14 5/8	.011 831 9423
5	.004 123 9155	9 7/8	.008 064 8049	14 3/4	.011 930 1355
5 1/8	.004 225 9347	10	.008 164 8461	14 7/8	.012 028 2811
5 1/4	.004 327 9021	10 1/8	.008 264 8377	15	.012 126 3791
5 3/8	.004 429 8178	10 1/4	.008 364 7797	15 1/8	.012 224 4297
5 1/2	.004 531 6818	10 3/8	.008 464 6722	15 1/4	.012 322 4327
5 5/8	.004 633 4941	10 1/5	.008 564 5152	15 3/8	.012 420 3883
5 3/4	.004 735 2549	10 5/8	.008 664 3089	15 1/2	.012 518 2966
5 7/8	.004 836 9642	10 3/4	.008 764 0532	15 5/8	.012 616 1575
6	.004 938 6221	10 7/8	.008 863 7482	15 3/4	.012 713 9712
6 1/8	.005 040 2285	11	.008 963 3940	15 7/8	.012 811 7377
6 1/4	.005 141 7837	11 1/8	.009 062 9906	16	.012 909 4570
6 3/8	.005 243 2875	11 1/4	.009 162 5381	16 1/8	.013 007 1292
6 1/2	.005 344 7401	11 3/8	.009 262 0365	16 1/4	.013 104 7543
6 5/8	.005 446 1416	11 1/2	.009 361 4858	16 3/8	.013 202 3325
6 3/4	.005 547 4919	11 5/8	.009 460 8863	16 1/2	.013 299 8636
6 7/8	.005 648 7912	11 3/4	.009 560 2378	16 5/8	.013 397 3478
7	.005 750 0395	11 7/8	.009 659 5404	16 3/4	.013 494 7852
7 1/8	.005 851 2369	12	.009 758 7942	16 7/8	.013 592 1758
7 1/4	.005 952 3834	12 1/8	.009 857 9993	17	.013 689 5196
7 3/8	.006 053 4791	12 1/4	.009 957 1557	17 1/8	.013 786 8166
7 1/2	.006 154 5240	12 3/8	.010 056 2634	17 1/4	.013 884 0670
7 5/8	.006 255 5182	12 1/2	.010 155 3225	17 3/8	.013 981 2708
7 3/4	.006 356 4617	12 5/8	.010 254 3331	17 1/2	.014 078 4280
7 7/8	.006 457 3546	12 3/4	.010 353 2952	17 5/8	.014 175 5387
8	.006 558 1970	12 7/8	.010 452 2088	17 3/4	.014 272 6030
8 1/8	.006 658 9889	13	.010 551 0740	17 7/8	.014 369 6208
8 1/4	.006 759 7303	13 1/8	.010 649 8909		
8 3/8	.006 860 4214	13 1/4	.010 748 6596		
8 1/2	.006 961 0622	13 3/8	.010 847 3799		
8 5/8	.007 061 6527	13 1/2	.010 946 0522		
8 3/4	.007 162 1929	13 5/8	.011 044 6762		

Interest for one month on any amount may be obtained by multiplying that amount by this factor.

TABLE 8.5 6% COMPOUND INTEREST FACTORS

	Single Payment		Uniform Series				
n	Compound Amount Factor F/P	Present Worth Factor P/F	Sinking Fund Factor A/F	Capital Recovery Factor A/P	Compound Amount Factor F/A	Present Worth Factor P/A	n
1	1.0600	0.9434	1.00000	1.06000	1.000	0.943	1
2	1.1236	0.8900	0.48544	0.54544	2.060	1.833	2
3	1.1910	0.8396	0.31411	0.37411	3.184	2.673	3
4	1.2625	0.7921	0.22859	0.28859	4.375	3.465	4
5	1.3382	0.7473	0.17740	0.23740	5.637	4.212	5
6	1.4185	0.7050	0.14336	0.20336	6.975	4.917	6
7	1.5036	0.6651	0.11914	0.17914	8.394	5.582	7
8	1.5938	0.6274	0.10104	0.16104	9.897	6.210	8
9	1.6895	0.5919	0.08702	0.14702	11.491	6.802	9
10	1.7908	0.5584	0.07587	0.13587	13.181	7.360	10
11	1.8983	0.5268	0.06679	0.12679	14.972	7.887	11
12	2.0122	0.4970	0.05928	0.11928	16.870	8.384	12
13	2.1329	0.4688	0.05296	0.11296	18.882	8.853	13
14	2.2609	0.4423	0.04758	0.10758	21.015	9.295	14
15	2.3966	0.4173	0.04296	0.10296	23.276	9.712	15
16	2.5404	0.3936	0.03895	0.09895	25.673	10.106	16
17	2.6928	0.3714	0.03544	0.09544	28.213	10.477	17
18	2.8543	0.3503	0.03236	0.09236	30.906	10.828	18
19	3.0256	0.3305	0.02962	0.08962	33.760	11.158	19
20	3.2071	0.3118	0.02718	0.08718	36.786	11.470	20
21	3.3996	0.2942	0.02500	0.08500	39.993	11.764	21
22	3.6035	0.2775	0.02305	0.08305	43.392	12.042	22
23	3.8197	0.2618	0.02128	0.08128	46.996	12.303	23
24	4.0489	0.2470	0.01968	0.07968	50.816	12.550	24
25	4.2919	0.2330	0.01823	0.07823	54.865	12.783	25
26	4.5494	0.2198	0.01690	0.07690	59.156	13.003	26
27	4.8223	0.2074	0.01570	0.07570	63.706	13.211	27
28	5.1117	0.1956	0.01459	0.07459	68.528	13.406	28
29	5.4184	0.1846	0.01358	0.07358	73.640	13.591	29
30	5.7435	0.1741	0.01265	0.07265	79.058	13.765	30
31	6.0881	0.1643	0.01179	0.07179	84.802	13.929	31
32	6.4534	0.1550	0.01100	0.07100	90.890	14.084	32
33	6.8406	0.1462	0.01027	0.07027	97.343	14.230	33
34	7.2510	0.1379	0.00960	0.06960	104.184	14.368	34
35	7.6861	0.1301	0.00897	0.06897	111.435	14.498	35
40	10.2857	0.0972	0.00646	0.06646	154.762	15.046	40
45	13.7646	0.0727	0.00470	0.06470	212.744	15.456	45
50	18.4202	0.0543	0.00344	0.06344	290.336	15.762	50

TABLE 8.5 6% COMPOUND INTEREST FACTORS (CONTINUED)

	Single Payment		Uniform Series				
n	Compound Amount Factor F/P	Present Worth Factor P/F	Sinking Fund Factor A/F	Capital Recovery Factor A/P	Compound Amount Factor F/A	Present Worth Factor P/A	n
55	24.6503	0.0406	0.00254	0.06254	394.172	15.991	55
60	32.9877	0.0303	0.00188	0.06188	533.128	61.161	60
65	44.1450	0.0227	0.00139	0.06139	719.083	16.289	65
70	59.0759	0.0169	0.00103	0.06103	967.932	16.385	70
75	79.0569	0.0126	0.00077	0.06077	1300.949	16.456	75
80	105.7960	0.0095	0.00057	0.06057	1746.600	16.509	80
85	141.5789	0.0071	0.00043	0.06043	2342.982	16.549	85
90	189.4645	0.0053	0.00032	0.06032	3141.075	16.579	90
95	253.5463	0.0039	0.00024	0.06024	4209.104	16.601	95
100	339.3021	0.0029	0.00018	0.06018	5638.368	16.618	100

TABLE 8.6 10% COMPOUND INTEREST FACTORS

	Single Payment		Uniform Series				
	Compound Amount Factor	Present Worth Factor	Sinking Fund Factor	Capital Recovery Factor	Compound Amount Factor	Present Worth Factor	
n	F/P	P/F	A/F	A/P	F/A	P/A	n
1	1.1000	0.9091	1.00000	0.10000	1.000	0.909	1
2	1.2100	0.8264	0.47619	0.57619	2.100	1.736	2
3	1.3310	0.7513	0.30211	0.40211	3.310	2.487	3
4	1.4641	0.6830	0.21547	0.31547	4.641	3.170	4
5	1.6105	0.6209	0.16380	0.26380	6.105	3.791	5
6	1.7716	0.5645	0.12961	0.22961	7.716	4.355	6
7	1.9487	0.5132	0.10541	0.20541	9.487	4.868	7
8	2.1436	0.4665	0.08744	0.18744	11.436	5.335	8
9	2.3579	0.4241	0.07364	0.17364	13.579	5.759	9
10	2.5937	0.3855	0.06275	0.16275	15.937	6.144	10
11	2.8531	0.3505	0.05396	0.15396	18.531	6.495	11
12	3.1384	0.3186	0.04676	0.14676	21.384	6.814	12
13	3.4523	0.2897	0.04078	0.14078	24.523	7.103	13
14	3.7975	0.2633	0.03575	0.13575	27.975	7.367	14
15	4.1772	0.2394	0.03147	0.13147	31.772	7.606	15
16	4.5950	0.2176	0.02782	0.12782	35.950	7.824	16
17	5.0545	0.1978	0.02466	0.12466	40.545	8.022	17
18	5.5599	0.1799	0.02193	0.12193	45.599	8.201	18
19	6.1159	0.1635	0.01955	0.11955	51.159	8.365	19
20	6.7275	0.1486	0.01746	0.11746	57.275	8.514	20
21	7.4002	0.1351	0.01562	0.11562	64.002	8.649	21
22	8.1403	0.1228	0.01401	0.11401	71.403	8.772	22
23	8.9543	0.1117	0.01257	0.11257	79.543	8.883	23
24	9.8497	0.1015	0.01130	0.11130	88.497	8.985	24
25	10.8347	0.0923	0.01017	0.11017	98.347	9.077	25
26	11.9182	0.0839	0.00916	0.10916	109.182	9.161	26
27	13.1100	0.0763	0.00826	0.10826	121.100	9.237	27
28	14.4210	0.0693	0.00745	0.10745	134.210	9.307	28
29	15.8631	0.0630	0.00673	0.10673	148.631	9.370	29
30	17.4494	0.0573	0.00608	0.10608	164.494	9.427	30
31	19.1943	0.0521	0.00550	0.10550	181.943	9.479	31
32	21.1138	0.0474	0.00497	0.10497	201.138	9.526	32
33	23.2252	0.0431	0.00450	0.10450	222.252	9.569	33
34	25.5477	0.0391	0.00407	0.10407	245.477	9.609	34
35	28.1024	0.0356	0.00369	0.10369	271.024	9.644	35
40	45.2593	0.0221	0.00226	0.10226	442.593	9.779	40
45	72.8905	0.0137	0.00139	0.10139	718.905	9.863	45
50	117.3909	0.0085	0.00086	0.10086	1163.909	9.915	50

TABLE 8.6 10% Compound Interest Factors (continued)

	Single Payment		Uniform Series				
n	Compound Amount Factor F/P	Present Worth Factor P/F	Sinking Fund Factor A/F	Capital Recovery Factor A/P	Compound Amount Factor F/A	Present Worth Factor P/A	n
55	189.0591	0.0053	0.00053	0.10053	1880.591	9.947	55
60	304.4816	0.0033	0.00033	0.10033	3034.816	9.967	60
65	490.3707	0.0020	0.00020	0.10020	4893.707	9.980	65
70	789.7470	0.0013	0.00013	0.10013	7887.470	9.987	70
75	1271.8952	0.0008	0.00008	0.10008	12708.954	9.992	75
80	2048.4002	0.0005	0.00005	0.10005	20474.002	9.995	80
85	3298.9690	0.0003	0.00003	0.10003	32979.690	9.997	85
90	5313.0226	0.0002	0.00002	0.10002	53120.226	9.998	90
95	8556.6760	0.0001	0.00001	0.10001	85556.760	9.999	95
100	13780.6123	0.0001	0.00001	0.10001	137796.123	9.999	100

CHAPTER NINE

Saving and Investing

OBJECTIVES

1. To distinguish between the following pairs of terms:

    (a) saving and investing,

    (b) investing and speculating,

    (c) liquidity and marketability,

    (d) debt and equity securities,

    (e) income and capital gain,

    (f) total and liquid assets,

    (g) nominal and real interest rates,

    (h) income and wealth.

2. To categorize reasons for saving and to explain how these reasons affect the choice of investments.

3. To identify reasons why people find saving difficult and investing overwhelming.

4. To examine the trends in the savings rate in Canada.

5. To analyze the effects of age and income on the amount that Canadians save.

6. To explain these terms: portfolio, term, investment pyramid.

7. To distinguish among the different types of risks to which investments are exposed.

8. To identify the types of risk associated with various kinds of investments.

9. To explain why there are trade-offs between risk and return, return and liquidity, term and return, current income and capital gain.

10. To explain the principle of diversification and why it is significant in investment planning.

11. To examine ways of handling risk in an investment portfolio.

12. To identify conflicting investment objectives.

13. To explain how to make an investment plan.

Introduction

Are you a saver? If not, why not? If you do save, do you invest profitably? While it is quite possible to save without investing, it is rather difficult to be an investor without any savings. Although often linked together, the terms saving and investing are not synonyms: saving simply means not spending; investing means using your funds with the expectation of yield. For instance, putting money in your sock or under the mattress would be considered saving, but not investing. You would be investing if you deposited the money in a savings account, or bought Canada Savings Bonds, stocks, property, or treasury bills, because these give some prospect of a return. Although savings accounts and term deposits are forms of investment, you may find little discussion of them in the investment literature, probably because it is assumed that their characteristics are well understood.

The range of possible investments is broad. The only characteristic that savings accounts, real estate, stocks, bonds, and precious metals have in common is the investor's expectation of gain. Even if, in a particular instance, the yield turned out to be nonexistent or less than anticipated, it would still be considered an investment, although an unfortunate one, as long as gain was the intent. Unless you are lucky enough to receive an inheritance or other windfall, you will find it impossible to become an investor without first saving. For that reason, this chapter begins with a consideration of ways to become a better saver, followed by an introduction to investing, including characteristics of investments, identification of investment objectives, and the process of developing an investment plan and portfolio.

In this overview of investments many points are introduced that will be treated in more detail in later chapters, particularly Chapters 10 and 11. Your understanding will be enhanced if you reread this chapter after studying the next two.

SAVING

Why Save?

Anyone who receives an income has to make daily decisions about how much of it to spend and how much to save. In our society there is every incentive to spend, but not much pressure to save. Usually we feel that it is more urgent to pay bills or buy some new thing than to save. Saving is for the future, we tell ourselves, and the future is far away. Furthermore, we may feel that our purchases will provide more immediate gratification than a growing balance in a savings account.

To put the need for savings in perspective, it may be helpful to project income and economic needs over a life span (Figure 1.1 in Chapter 1). On average, earnings can be expected to increase until about age 55 or 60, then level off or start to decline. During their working years, most people's wages increase to reflect their growing skill and experience as well as to accommodate price changes, but in late middle age some choose early retirement while others must leave the labour force because of ill health or job loss. At retirement, which often occurs by age 65, earnings stop and must be replaced by pension and investment income. Investment income is dependent, of course, on first having had some savings to invest.

Long-term consumption needs, as shown in Figure 1.1, generally do not follow the curvilinear pattern of income; most of us want a fairly steady, but perhaps gently rising, level of living throughout our life span. How can this be accomplished? Knowing that expenditure is likely to be more constant than income flow, you can take steps to smooth out the cash flow over your lifetime. This means basing your financial planning on a longer time horizon than just this month or this year. If you are to achieve and maintain financial independence you will have to save some of your income during your working years, and invest it to create retirement income. In addition, you will need savings for short-term needs, for smoothing out any unevenness in cash flow, and for specific goals.

There are at least four important reasons to save. Funds are needed for: (i) emergencies, (ii) liquidity, (iii) short-term goals, and (iv) long-term goals. We will consider each in turn.

EMERGENCY FUND   Since most people start out their working lives with very little net worth, the first need is to create an emergency fund—money that is readily accessible to handle the unexpected expenses that we all have. It is often suggested that several months' take-home pay, perhaps three, should be set aside as the emergency fund. Expect that it will take some time to achieve this goal. Emergency funds could be kept in a savings account, term deposits, Canada Savings Bonds, or any savings instrument that pays interest without locking in the money. In addition, obtaining adequate insurance to cover risks to your property or dependents is a matter for serious consideration, as was discussed in previous chapters.

LIQUIDITY NEEDS   You will need to have some funds available to cope with any unevenness in your cash flow and to pay for infrequent large expenses. Ready access to about one month's take-home pay may be adequate. Put these funds where they will earn as much interest as possible but remain readily accessible, possibly in an interest-bearing deposit account that permits chequing.

SHORT-TERM GOALS   How can you distinguish a short-term from a long-term goal? When you review your financial goals, you will find some that can be accomplished within the next five years and others that will take longer. You can decide what time frame best fits your situation, but do make a distinction between short-term and long-term goals. It is best to segregate the funds for short-term goals from those for longer-term goals, either by accounting or keeping the funds in separate accounts. The money being saved for next year's holiday should not get mixed with that being saved for retirement.

Short-term goals might include holidays and trips, vehicles, furniture, appliances, and education for yourself or your children. If your children are very young, planning for their post-secondary education will be a long-term goal. Those interested in becoming home owners may want to start saving for a down payment or, if they already have a house, to reserve funds for mortgage prepayments.

Home ownership, you may have observed, is the single most important investment for many Canadian families. In general, house prices change in response to both the prevailing inflation rate and the demand for housing. During periods of rapid inflation, the prices of houses tend to appreciate as much or more than the inflation rate, making property an effective and tax-free storehouse of value. At other times, house prices may fall to the disadvantage of those who must sell.

In spite of some uncertainty about future house prices, there are advantages to home ownership. Any capital gain realized on your home has long been excluded from taxation. From an investment perspective, buying a house is a form of forced saving. The discipline of regular mortgage payments not only results in a place to live but eventually in the ownership of an asset.

Depending on how soon they will be required, funds being saved for short-term goals may be invested in low-risk securities with appropriate maturities. The discussion that follows in this and later chapters should give you some ideas.

LONG-TERM GOALS   A key long-term goal of most people is to increase their net worth so that their financial security will be enhanced, financial independence achieved, and financial support for their retirement years ensured. To have a comfortable lifestyle during retirement, planning must start early in the working years. By the magic of compounding, small amounts will grow to large sums if left invested for long periods. For instance, if you invested $1000 each year at an average annual compound rate of only three percent, your deposits of $30 000 would grow to $47 575 in 30 years. At five percent interest you would have doubled your money to $66 439, and at seven percent nearly tripled it to $94 461 (Figure 9.1). If saving for retirement is put off until within a few years of retirement, there will be little time for savings to grow (Figure 1.2). Acquiring capital to fund retirement is a long-term savings goal, and the funds can be invested with a longer time horizon than those intended for short-term goals. That is, they can be invested in securities that are not readily accessible but have prospects for long-term growth.

FIGURE 9.1   COMPOUND VALUE OF ANNUAL INVESTMENTS OF $1000, INVESTED AT 3%, 5%, AND 7%

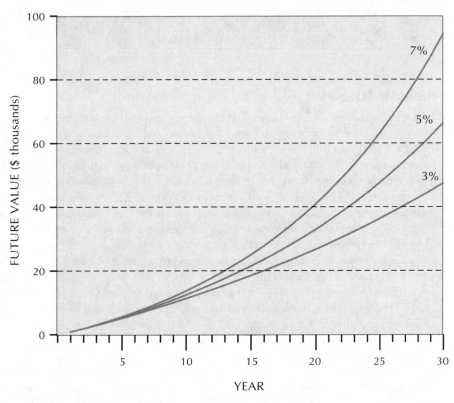

HOW MUCH CAPITAL WILL BE NEEDED?

Deirdre estimates that she will need an income of about $600 a month ($7200 a year) from her investments to supplement her pensions when she retires. She wonders how much capital (principal) she will need, based on a conservative return of 5% on average. She makes the following calculations by converting the formula:

Interest   = principal × rate × time

Principal   = $\dfrac{\text{interest (required income)}}{\text{rate} \times \text{time}}$

= $\dfrac{600 \times 12}{.05 \times 1}$

= $144 000

Deirdre has not made any adjustment for inflation because she anticipates that a higher inflation rate will push up interest rates correspondingly. Now that she has a long-term goal of building up a net worth of $144 000, she will make plans for saving and investing.

How to Save

In spite of the widely-held belief that everyone should save some money, these good intentions tend to be given low priority. Saving can be difficult, easy to postpone, and not that much fun. To ensure success, there must be a firm commitment with definite plans. There will always be demands on your income that seem most urgent and require saving to be postponed. You may reason that it will be easier to save later when there will be no unexpected expenses, but eventually you will discover that this pattern is repetitive and that no time ever seems the right time to save. The only solution is to set up an automatic savings plan now and follow it determinedly.

There are two basic approaches to saving—taking savings off the top of each paycheque before spending anything, or waiting to see what will be left at the end of the pay period. Those who follow the first system will accumulate savings and will have funds to invest; the others will never get around to it. Which approach will you take? The best plan is to establish a certain amount or percentage to be set aside from each pay, e.g., five to ten percent.

When developing a savings strategy, be aware of your strengths and weaknesses. If you are an impulsive spender, you will need a system to make your savings unavailable. Look into payroll savings plans and automatic saving methods at financial institutions and arrange that a certain portion of your income be directed into these plans before it reaches you. For example, each autumn Canada Savings Bonds become available by payroll deduction, some credit unions have automatic savings plans, and a number of mutual funds offer regular investment plans.

AN AUTOMATIC SAVINGS PLAN

Peter found saving very difficult. His intention was to bank whatever money was left at the end of the month, but more often than not, nothing was left. A friend who belonged to a credit union told him about an automatic savings plan by which he saves $200 a month. He authorized the credit union to deduct funds on each pay day from the account into which his employer deposited his pay, and to transfer the funds to his savings account.

Peter decided that he would give this plan a try, but when he

inquired at his bank, he found that they had no such system in effect. An alternative, they suggested, was for Peter to write a year's supply of post-dated cheques and, at the appropriate time, the bank would transfer funds from his chequing to his savings account. He tried this method, and was very pleased at the end of the year to find that he had saved $2400.

RULES FOR SAVING   The key rules for becoming a successful saver are:

(a) have a purpose or goal for which you are saving,

(b) make a plan for accomplishing your goal,

(c) save regularly.

You have to be committed to a plan for increasing your net worth, or nothing will be accomplished. It would be ridiculous, of course, to go to the other extreme and become a miser; letting saving become an end in itself is also a mistake. A balance between present and future consumption is the objective. Some financial experts suggest that if you save 10 percent of your salary throughout your working years and invest it carefully, you can become financially independent by the time of retirement.

HOW MUCH DO CANADIANS SAVE?

National Savings Rates

To determine how much Canadians save, we examine the macro-economic data from the national accounts, where savings is defined as those sums in the hands of individuals that were not spent for income tax or current consumption. By this definition, Canadians have been saving from 5 to 15 percent of their disposable income (after income tax and CPP and UI premiums) during the past four decades (Figure 9.2). Savings rates are quite variable and much affected by economic conditions, but in recent years the rate rose to the historically high level of 15 percent, then fell back to around 10 percent.

Why do savings rates become so high at times? Uncertainty created by economic conditions, high rates paid on deposits, and encouragement of RRSPs and other pension plans are factors. Our present income tax system offers incentives to put money in RRSPs. In addition, contractual savings in the Canada Pension Plan and private pension plans have been growing. It is estimated that in 1982, when the savings rate was 15 percent, our savings were split about evenly between contractual and discretionary saving. By 1991, the rate had fallen to 10 percent, mostly contractual savings in life insurance plans, trusteed pension plans, and RRSPs.

FIGURE 9.2 SAVINGS RATE*, CANADA, 1950–1992

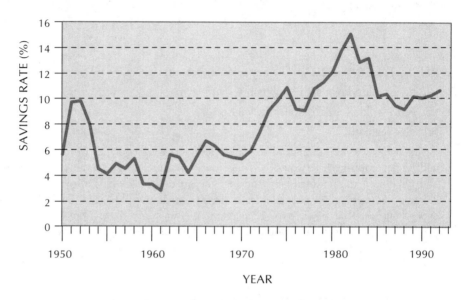

YEAR

* Personal savings as a percentage of personal disposable income.

SOURCE OF DATA: *Historical Statistical Supplement, 1991/2,* and *Canadian Economic Observer.* Ottawa: Statistics Canada, various issues. (Catalogue No. 11-210 and 11-010.) Reproduced with the permission of the Minister of Industry, Science and Technology, 1993.

Household Surveys of Wealth

Another important source of information about the savings patterns of Canadians is from household surveys in which people are asked how much they have saved. These surveys provide an estimate of household wealth at a given date (stock) in contrast to the macro data on the rate of saving per year (flow). Recall the difference between a stock and a flow discussed in Chapter 1. Statistics Canada conducts such surveys infrequently; the last two were in 1977 and 1984. Although the levels of income and wealth are no longer up-to-date, we can still analyze these data for patterns; such behaviour patterns change much more slowly than the averages or medians.

It will be helpful in interpreting these survey results to be aware of some definitions. **Net worth** (total assets less debts) and **wealth** are used as synonyms.

Total assets refers to all the items of monetary value of the household, including property. In the figures presented in this chapter, a distinction is made between families and households: families have two or more members and households include families and unattached individuals.

WEALTH OF FAMILIES   It is not unexpected to find that wealth increases with income, but the difference between the mean and the median levels may be a surprise (Figure 9.3). The median (the mid-point in the distribution) is a more useful measure because a few households with very high wealth levels distort the averages. Generally, wealth is distributed less equally than income. Can you suggest reasons for the large differences between mean and median wealth in the lowest and highest income groups?

FIGURE 9.3 MEDIAN AND MEAN WEALTH OF FAMILIES BY 1983 INCOME GROUP, CANADA, 1984.

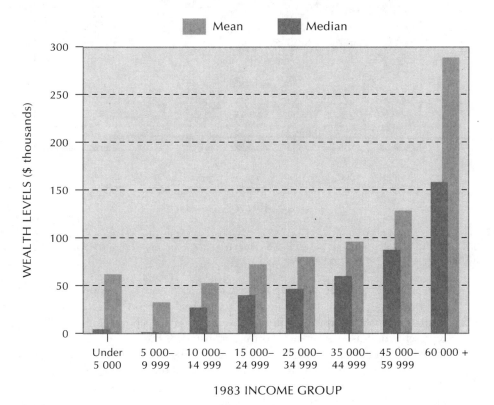

SOURCE OF DATA: *The Distribution of Wealth in Canada, 1984.* Ottawa: Statistics Canada, 1986, Table 1 (p. 26). (Catalogue No. 13-580.) Reproduced with the permission of the Minister of Industry, Science and Technology, 1993.

NEGATIVE NET WORTH Although most households have some wealth, there are those with negative net worth; that is, they owe more than they own. The distribution of these households by income shows that as income increases, the probability of having a negative net worth declines (Figure 9.4). Are you surprised to find households with negative net worth at all income levels?

FIGURE 9.4 Percentage Distribution of Households with Negative Net Worth, Canada, 1984

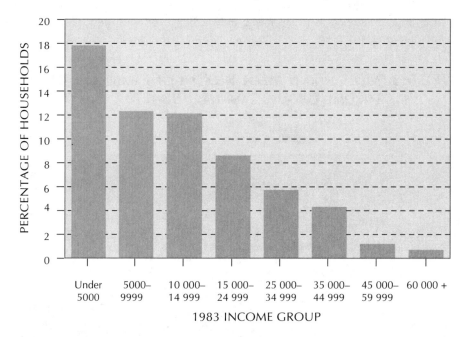

Source of data: *The Distribution of Wealth in Canada, 1984.* Ottawa: Statistics Canada, 1986, Table 1 (p. 26). (Catalogue No. 13-580.) Reproduced with the permission of the Minister of Industry, Science and Technology, 1993.

DISTRIBUTION OF ASSETS What relation do you see between income level and the significance of various kinds of assets? Each bar in Figure 9.5 represents the distribution of total assets within one income group. Keep in mind that these data represent total assets, not net worth. For instance, the market value of homes is included, without subtracting the outstanding mortgage debt. Ownership of a home is usually the single most important asset of a household, regardless of income level. Looking at other assets, it is apparent that income influences the forms in which families hold their wealth. **Liquid assets** are those that can be converted to cash quite readily with little loss of principal, such as deposits, cash, savings certificates,

Canada Savings Bonds, other bonds. These are the funds we depend on for emergencies or liquidity. Why do you think liquid assets form a larger share of wealth at lower income levels, and stocks, RRSPs, and miscellaneous financial assets form a larger share at higher income levels?

FIGURE 9.5 PERCENTAGE COMPOSITION OF TOTAL ASSETS OF CANADIAN HOUSEHOLDS BY INCOME CLASS, SPRING 1984

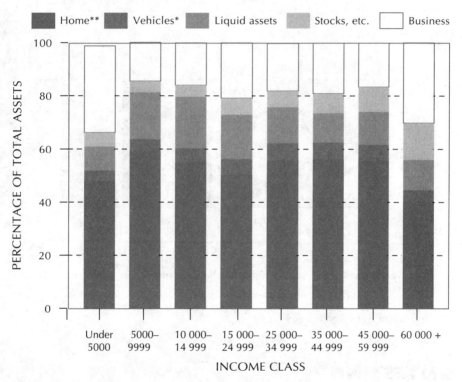

* Includes cars, trucks, and selected recreational vehicles.
** Market value of home, vacation home, and equity in other real estate.

SOURCE OF DATA: *The Distribution of Wealth in Canada, 1984.* Ottawa: Statistics Canada, 1986, Table 24 (p. 64). (Catalogue No. 13-580.) Reproduced with the permission of the Minister of Industry, Science and Technology, 1993.

AGE AND WEALTH One way of looking at the age effect on wealth is to observe the pattern of wealth-to-income ratios (Figure 9.6). You will note that, on average, households are in their mid-thirties before they have a net worth equivalent to a year's income. At peak earning (ages 45–64) the average household has a net worth about two or two and one-half times income. The higher ratio after age sixty-five is influenced by the drop in income after retirement and the fact that this age category is much broader than the others.

FIGURE 9.6 WEALTH TO INCOME RATIOS* BY AGE OF HOUSEHOLD HEAD, CANADA, 1984

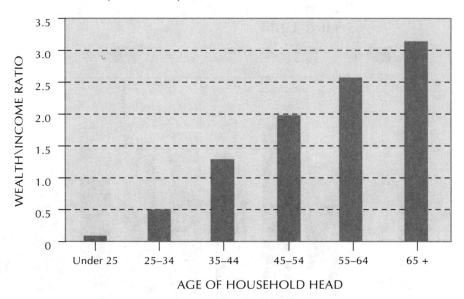

* Median wealth divided by mean income. Median income figures were not available.

SOURCE OF DATA: *The Distribution of Wealth in Canada, 1984.* Ottawa: Statistics Canada, 1986, Table 5 (p. 32). (Catalogue No. 13-580.) Reproduced with the permission of the Minister of Industry, Science and Technology, 1993.

INVESTING

Why Invest?

The primary reason for investing is self-evident: your savings must grow to make your financial goals possible. A secondary reason may be that you enjoy investing and see the possibilities for an interesting hobby. There are excellent savers who have no idea how to invest their money profitably. They may be quite cautious and apprehensive about investing; they deposit their money at the credit union, bank, or trust company, or buy Canada Savings Bonds because they want safety and ready access to their funds at all times. The cautious ones probably do not realize that they may be sacrificing much in terms of yield, inflation protection, and tax reduction, or that all investments are exposed to some risk.

In many cases, fear of the unknown and lack of information are the impediments to wise investing, rather than unwillingness to assume some risk. Do not confuse fear of investing with risk. If you do nothing about investing because of anxiety, confusion, and uncertainty, this inaction can be costly. You may pay more income tax than necessary, forego higher yields, and see your savings eroded by inflation.

Investing or Speculating

Assuming that you have been successful at saving, what can you do to make your net worth grow? The first thing is to have patience. Investing is not speculating or gambling; you do not want to risk your hard-earned savings, you want them to increase gradually. Although it is erroneously believed that investing is putting your money in a safe place and speculating is buying stocks, **investing** can be defined as committing funds in a way that minimizes risk yet protects capital, while earning a return that is satisfactory for the degree of risk. This can be accomplished in a variety of ways.

Investors are not in a hurry; speculators, on the other hand, look for large profits from a small layout of funds within a short time. **Speculation** tends to be based on a shorter time horizon and involves more risk than investing. Speculators use money with the expectation of capital gain through a change in market value and are primarily motivated by short-term gains.

Unless you have several hundred thousand dollars in assets and can afford to hire an investment counsellor, you will have to manage your own investments. The choices are either to become knowledgeable and devote some time to monitoring your portfolio, or to choose investments that require minimal attention. Having a portfolio may sound very grand, but a **portfolio** is simply a list or collection of assets. If money matters are distasteful to you and there seems to be no likelihood of change, find ways to put your savings where they will grow without your efforts. Most of the discussion that follows is based on the assumption that you are interested in learning more about investing.

When you have finished reading this book, you will have been introduced to the basics of investing and should have the vocabulary to understand the articles in the financial press that you need to read to keep up-to-date. As mentioned before, lack of knowledge and fear of the unknown deter many people from making wise investment decisions. Since you need an understanding of the basic characteristics of investments before you can make a personal investment plan, these will be examined next.

DEBT AND EQUITY INVESTMENTS

Debt Securities

There are two basic ways to invest: (i) by lending money, or (ii) by acquiring ownership. Lenders become creditors and are said to possess **debt securities.** The income from debt instruments is called interest. The borrower promises to repay the principal with interest at some specified time. Perhaps you had not thought of yourself as a creditor when you deposited funds at a bank, trust company, or credit union. Were you aware that you were lending money to a government or corporation when you bought a bond or a treasury bill? Deposit accounts, term deposits, guaranteed investment certificates, mortgages (you are the lender), bonds, and treasury bills are types of debt securities. Their characteristics will be reviewed in the next chapter.

Equity Securities

Instead of becoming a creditor, you could become an owner or part-owner by purchasing real estate, goods of various sorts— including art, jewellery, and antiques—stocks, or part of a business. In the ownership role you receive some rights regarding the management of the goods or property, but you obtain no guarantee that the sum you invested will be returned to you, or that it will generate any income. You have acquired an **equity** because you are an owner, with opportunities for gains or losses but no promises. Although more risk is generally associated with equities than with debt securities, it is also possible to find equities that are less risky than some debt instruments. For instance, there is less risk in owning common shares in certain utilities than in lending mortgage money to a person who has a poor record of repayment. Equities are usually chosen because of the expectation of greater gain than is possible from debt securities.

A comparison of average annual yields from three-month treasury bills and common stocks over a 15-year period will illustrate the difference in risk and return from debt and equity securities (Figure 9.7). The salient point is the steady rate of return from the treasury bills and the variability in common stock yields. Between 1975 and 1992, the average annual return was 10 percent on treasury bills, and about 16 percent on stocks. However, to achieve the higher return the stock investor had to be prepared to wait out the down swings in the stock market.

Investment Returns

INCOME   The return on an investment may take the form of either: (i) income (interest, dividends, rent, profit) or (ii) capital appreciation (capital gain). The type of return received will vary with the investment. Those who lend money expect interest; those who own shares in stocks expect dividends; those who own property and rent it to others will receive rent; owners of shares in a business hope to receive profit. In addition to the income generated by ownership, the purchase may increase in value and generate capital gain.

FIGURE 9.7 **AVERAGE ANNUAL RATES OF RETURN ON THREE-MONTH TREASURY BILLS, AND THE STOCKS IN THE TORONTO STOCK EXCHANGE INDEX, 1975–1992**

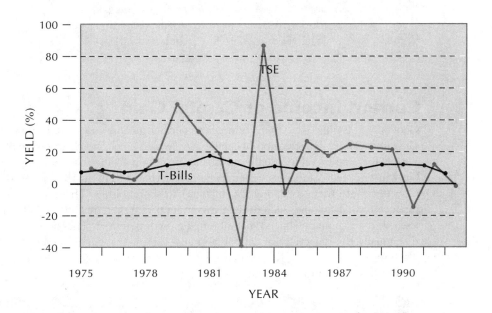

CAPITAL GAIN The difference between the purchase price of an asset and the selling price represents capital gain. For example, something purchased at $2700 and sold for $3500 would result in a capital gain of $800. **Capital gain** is the windfall accruing to an investor, by virtue of ownership, during a change in prices caused by increased demand or inflation. If an asset, such as a house, was improved and then sold, the value of the improvements would not be counted as capital gain. It should be remembered that the expectation of capital gain always carries with it the possibility of capital loss.

TYPE OF INVESTMENT	FORM OF RETURN
Debt investments	
Deposits, loans	interest
Mortgage loans	interest
Canada Savings Bonds	interest
Treasury bills	interest
Bonds	interest, capital gain (loss)
Equity investments	
Real property	rent, capital gain (loss)
Business	profit, capital gain (loss)
Stocks (shares)	dividends, capital gain (loss)
Gold, silver	capital gain (loss)

Current Income or Capital Gain?

Generally, it is impossible to maximize both current income and capital gain from the same investment. The creation of capital gain, which comes from ownership of assets as they increase in value, usually takes time if you are an investor, not a speculator. Growth-oriented companies generally re-invest their profits in the business rather than distribute them as dividends (income) to shareholders. Those securities that produce regular income, such as debt investments and preferred shares (which carry less risk than common shares), have limited growth potential. Therefore, we can say that usually the objectives of capital gain and current income are inversely related. To improve the possibility of capital gain, current income would have to be sacrificed, as shown in the example below.

THE CURRENT INCOME/CAPITAL GAIN TRADE-OFF

After her husband died, Selima found herself handling investments for the first time, and decided that she needed some help. She consulted a financial planner who asked her what her investment objectives were. She was confused by the question, so the planner asked whether it was more important to her that the $50 000 she planned to invest provide a regular income or that the capital have an opportunity to grow to increase her net worth and provide a hedge against future inflation.

She replied that, since she was 55 and not in the labour force, income was very important, but some provision should be made to cope with any inflation in the future. She was given a card, like the one shown below, with two sets of numbers, zero to ten, and asked to circle the relative importance to her of current income versus future capital gain. The total of the two circled numbers must equal ten. After much thought, she gave seven to current income and three to capital gain. Her financial planner now had a better idea about possible investments that might be appropriate for Selima.

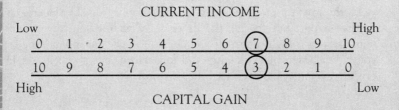

CURRENT INCOME

Low   High

0   1   2   3   4   5   6   ⑦   8   9   10

10   9   8   7   6   5   4   ③   2   1   0

High   Low

CAPITAL GAIN

Selima's son Jai, who is in his mid-thirties, unmarried, and well-paid, has a small portfolio of growth stocks. He ranks capital gain as ten and return as 0 for his stock portfolio. His emergency funds are in Canada Savings Bonds and guaranteed investment certificates. Taking all of Jai's assets together, the balance between capital gain and income is about 50–50.

CHARACTERISTICS OF INVESTMENTS

Six characteristics of investments are particularly relevant to investors as they endeavour to decide among alternatives:

(a) the risk/return trade-off,

(b) liquidity,

(c) marketability,

(d) term,

(e) management effort required,

(f) income tax treatment.

Risk, the most important factor in investment decisions, will be examined in more detail than the others and discussed further in Chapter 11. The significance of the other five factors will be considered next.

Liquidity

In the strictest sense, **liquidity** means that an investment can be converted into cash readily and without loss of principal. There are degrees of liquidity, ranging from cash which is the most liquid asset, to property which tends to be the least liquid. Savings accounts, term deposits, and Canada Savings Bonds can be liquidated during banking hours without loss of principal and thus are considered to be very liquid. Corporate bonds, stocks, and real estate are not very liquid because it may take time to sell them without a loss. Since very high liquidity is associated with an expectation of lower yield, the investor must decide what compromise to make (Figure 9.8). What is the relative importance to you, the investor, of having your investment provide high liquidity versus high return? If you decide to put your money in a savings account, you have chosen high liquidity and low return, but if you invest in a business or property, you may have reversed the situation.

FIGURE 9.8 THE LIQUIDITY/RETURN TRADE-OFF

Examine your priorities in relation to a specific investment. Circle the numbers that represent your compromise between liquidity and return. The two numbers must add up to ten; as you increase one characteristic, you have to accept less of the other.

Low					RETURN					High
0	1	2	3	4	5	6	7	8	9	10

10	9	8	7	6	5	4	3	2	1	0
High					LIQUIDITY					Low

Marketability

The popular usage of the term liquidity, when marketability is what is really meant, can be confusing. Marketable assets are those for which there is an active market. Certain stocks are in greater demand than others, trade more often, and thus are more marketable. Some houses are easier to sell than others and thus are more marketable. An asset may be highly marketable but not very liquid because of price fluctuations. At the time you wish to sell the asset, the prices of all houses, or stocks, for example, may be in a slump, making it impossible to recover your capital totally. Although any asset can be sold if the price is lowered enough, that is not what is meant by marketability; the aim is to get no less than a fair market price.

Term

Those investments that mature at a specified date are said to have a **term,** which is the time until maturity. Some kinds of investments are not accessible until maturity, others can be sold before the term ends. You can find investments with terms from a few days to many years. Choose investments appropriate to your savings goals. There tends to be a direct relation between term and return because of increasing uncertainty as the maturity date lengthens. Investors demand a higher return in exchange for making a longer-term commitment of their funds. Therefore, short-term investments tend to yield less than long-term ones, although the relationship does become inverted at times.

Personal Management Effort

How much time and attention are you prepared to give to your investments? This is an important consideration in choosing securities. If you are not prepared to put time and effort into supervision, you should select investments that require minimum attention; choose debt securities rather than equities, or buy mutual funds. If you decide not to become involved with investing, you may have to accept a lower return. The relation between effort and return tends to be direct; those who get the highest returns invest their time as well as money. On the other hand, the relation between management effort and liquidity is inverse. Usually the most liquid investments require the least attention and likewise, more attention may be required for less liquid investments.

Tax Considerations

Comparisons of potential yield from investments should be done in after-tax dollars because the various types of investment return are taxed differently: interest is taxed at a higher rate than dividends and some capital gain is exempt from tax. If income can be deferred until a time when you expect to have a lower marginal tax rate, two advantages can be gained. Not only will the total tax be less, but funds put in a tax shelter, an RRSP for instance, grow faster because tax on the yield is deferred. Later chapters will have more about income tax in connection with investments.

INVESTMENT RISKS

Every investor wants maximum return with minimum risk, but unfortunately there are no risk-free investments. Any investment carries some risk: the possibility of (i) losing all or part of the principal, (ii) losing some of the principal's purchasing power, or (iii) receiving a return that is less than anticipated. Unfortunately, these are not generally insurable risks. Nevertheless, you can attempt to reduce risk by being as well-informed as possible about investment alternatives and by having some diversity in your choice of assets so that all will not be lost in a single setback. Since investments are not risk-free, it is essential to understand the different types of risks and to know which assets are most subject to which kinds of risks.

Types of Risks

Four risks associated with investments are:

(a) **inflation risk,** or the possibility that invested funds will lose purchasing power,

(b) **interest rate risk,** or the likelihood that interest rates will fall, adversely affecting either the return or the price of the asset,

(c) **market risk,** or the chance that the demand for the asset will drop, lowering its value,

(d) **business risk,** or the possibility that the firm invested in will do poorly or fail.

INFLATION RISK   Inflation is measured by the annual percentage change in the Consumer Price Index. To put the high inflation of the early 1980s in perspective, look at the long-term trend in the annual inflation rate from 1952 to 1992 (Figure 9.9). After many years of relative stability, prices began rising rapidly in 1974 and again in 1980, but by 1992 the rate had fallen to around two percent.

Inflation decreases the purchasing power of money. With inflation at 10 percent, $1000 saved one year will buy 10 percent less the next. Although you still have a nominal $1000, it has become less valuable. If you were paid 13 percent interest, however, you would have gained enough to compensate for inflation and would also receive three percent real return. **Real rate of return** is the nominal or quoted rate of return less the inflation rate.

INTEREST RATE COMPARISONS

Bjorn, who remembered receiving 15.5% interest when inflation was 11.8 %, was disturbed to find one year that Canada Savings Bonds were paying only 7 3/4%. What he forgot was that the inflation rate had dropped to 4.1%. The comparison he should have made was in real rates of return, or 3.7% versus 3.65%.

In some years, such as in the mid-1970s, the real interest rate was negative, meaning that the inflation rate exceeded interest rates. When investors are receiving a negative real rate of return on investments, they are not getting enough to compensate for inflation, let alone receiving a reward for lending. A comparison of the inflation rate with the average interest rate on three-month treasury bills shows the variation in real interest rates between 1956 and 1992 (Figure 9.10). In 1982 with nominal interest rates at 13.6 percent and inflation at 10.8 percent, the real rate was only 2.8 percent. By contrast, in 1990 the high real rates of seven percent were a result of a nominal rate of 12 percent and inflation at five percent. These examples illustrate how misleading it can be to look at the nominal rates only. Generally, high real rates reflect uncertainty in the investment sector. Over the long term, an investor might look for about three percent real return, on average, as minimum compensation for lending.

FIGURE 9.9 INFLATION RATE*, CANADA, 1952–1992

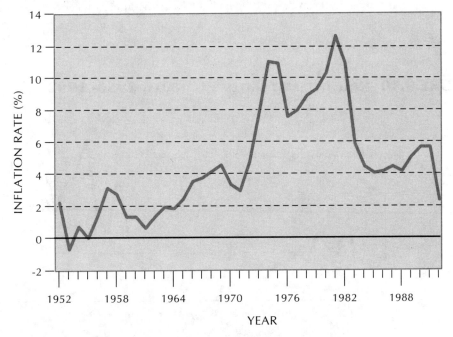

* Average annual change in the Consumer Price Index.

SOURCE OF DATA: *Consumer Prices and Price Indexes.* Ottawa: Statistics Canada, various years. (Catalogue No. 62-010.) Reproduced with the permission of the Minister of Industry, Science and Technology, 1993.

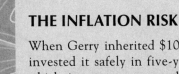

THE INFLATION RISK

When Gerry inherited $100 000 from his grandfather in 1955 he invested it safely in five-year guaranteed investment certificates which, in most years, earned a positive real rate of return. He found it

very convenient to use the interest to supplement his salary, and so he did not re-invest it.

At his retirement in 1990 Gerry took a look at this capital and considered ways to generate as much income as possible. At a possible 10% rate, he would receive about $10 000 a year, and less if interest rates fell. He had always assumed that this large sum would provide a much better retirement income. What had happened to it?

By adjusting the $100 000 for the effect of inflation at five-year intervals, it is possible to see how inflation eroded the purchasing power of this capital over 35 years (Figure 9.11). Would his retirement income have been better if he had not spent the interest but left it to compound?

FIGURE 9.10 REAL INTEREST RATES*, CANADA, 1956–1992

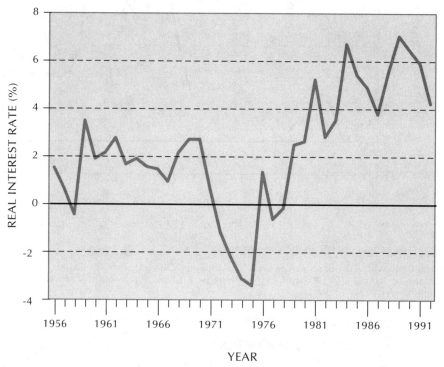

* Difference between the three-month Treasury Bill rate and the inflation rate.

SOURCES OF DATA: *Consumer Prices and Price Indexes*. Ottawa: Statistics Canada, various years. (Catalogue No. 62-010.) Reproduced with the permission of the Minister of Industry, Science and Technology, 1993. *Bank of Canada Review*. Ottawa: Bank of Canada, various issues. Reproduced and edited with the permission of the Bank of Canada.

FIGURE 9.11 PURCHASING POWER OF $100 000 (1955$), CANADA, 1955–1990

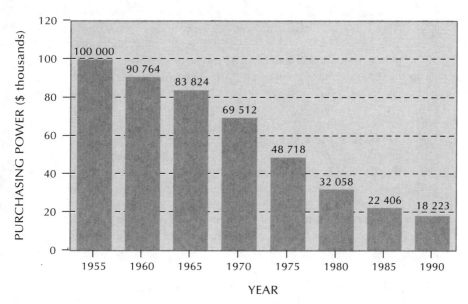

SOURCE OF DATA: *Consumer Prices and Price Indexes.* Ottawa: Statistics Canada, various years. (Catalogue No. 62-010.) Reproduced with the permission of the Minister of Industry, Science and Technology, 1993.

INTEREST RATE RISK   There is always the risk that a change in interest rates will adversely affect investments. If interest rates rise after a long-term bond has been purchased, the bond will drop in price and create a capital loss if sold (more about this in the next chapter). If funds are locked up in a five-year guaranteed investment certificate at six percent and interest rates later rise to 11 percent, an opportunity to benefit from the new higher rates will be lost. If, as is likely, the inflation rate also rises, the return may not cover purchasing power losses. The only protection is to try to diversify holdings, and have debt securities with a range of maturities. Debt securities are not the only assets affected by changes in the general level of interest rates. Common stocks are influenced indirectly because high interest rates discourage business expansion, but may push up the dividend rate; low rates do the opposite.

HOW COULD SHE LOSE ON A GIC?

Tina invested $5000 in a five-year guaranteed investment certificate (GIC) in 1973, when interest rates were close to historically high levels at 5.5%. She did not want to miss the opportunity to lock her money in at this unusually high interest rate (Figure 9.12). For the next five years she received annual payments at 5.5%. But what happened to interest rates during this time? From the graph you can see that nominal interest rates rose to nearly 9% then fell and rose again.

Look at the real rate of return. During most of this time it was close to zero or negative. Tina did not receive enough interest from this GIC to cover the depreciation of her capital by inflation. Not being able to forecast the future, what could Tina have done?

One way to protect assets from such situations is to invest in debt securities with a range of maturities so that some will come due each year, providing the opportunity to re-invest at prevailing rates.

Although they do not follow each other exactly, there is a link between interest rates and inflation. Generally, lenders require interest rates high enough to more than compensate for inflation. A lack of stability in interest rates complicates matters for investors. When interest rates are volatile, it is difficult to make wise investment decisions because there is so much uncertainty about future rates. When investors feel uncertain, as in the early 1980s, they demand higher real interest rates as compensation.

MARKET RISK   General economic conditions may change the demand for one of your assets, resulting in lower prices just when you wish to sell. For instance, if you bought a house in Calgary at the height of economic activity, when work was plentiful and houses were in short supply, the price would have been high. Suppose that you had to sell your house and move to another city at a time when economic activity had slowed down and house prices were in a slump. You would face the effects of a market risk, not because your house had any less quality but because a lower demand for houses caused prices to fall. Similarly, your shares in a gold mining company could drop in price because of a reduction in the demand for gold.

BUSINESS RISK   There is a risk that the business you invest in might fail totally, but more often the risk is that earnings from the business will decline, thus reducing not only your equity but also your return. Investors are attracted to companies with growing or stable earnings and usually pay a higher price for investing in them. As an investor, your risk is that you may pay too high a price for the security.

FIGURE 9.12 RETURN FROM A FIVE-YEAR GIC, NOMINAL AND REAL
INTEREST RATES, CANADA, 1973–1978
(GIC INVESTED AT 5.5% IN 1973)

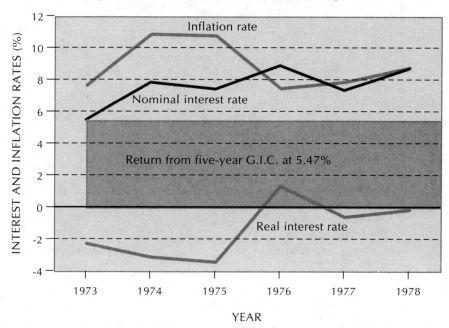

How to Reduce Risk

Since uncertainty about the future creates investment risk, the further into the future
you try to predict the quality of an investment, the greater the uncertainty—hence,
the greater the risk. Risk is thus related to both time and knowledge. This
relationship is summarized in Figure 9.13, which shows that risk exposure increases as
knowledge about the future decreases. The best defence against risk in your
investment portfolio is an understanding of current economic conditions, knowledge
of particular investments, and diversification.

KNOWLEDGE   There is a wide range of investment alternatives to consider,
some of which will be discussed in later chapters.

A successful investor should be well-informed about the securities he or she
holds. Anyone who plans to invest in real estate must learn a great deal about the
real estate market; to make money in the stock market it is necessary to take an
interest in the market in general and some specific stocks in more detail. Leaving
money in deposits requires less of the investor. A compromise might be to buy mutual
funds and leave investment decisions to the fund manager.

FIGURE 9.13 DEGREE OF RISK AND KNOWLEDGE ABOUT THE FUTURE

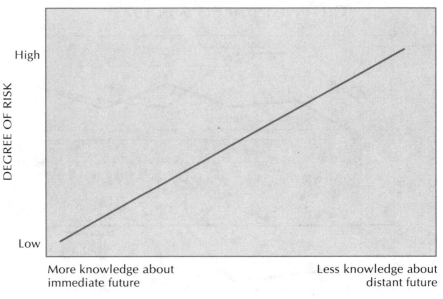

More knowledge about immediate future
Less knowledge about distant future

KNOWLEDGE OF FUTURE

THE RISK/RETURN TRADE-OFF Everyone wants the highest return and the lowest risk, but most will accept somewhat more risk if the expected return is greater. This brings up the risk/return trade-off. How much safety will you give up in the expectation of an additional unit of return? This inverse relationship is illustrated in Figure 9.14.

Once you know what your priorities are with respect to risk and return, look for investments that provide the desired qualities. It is difficult to generalize about classes of investments and risk because there are always exceptions and qualifications. Figure 9.14 is intended as a general illustration of the relation between risk and return.

RISK MANAGEMENT

What are Your Risks?

Analyze the various kinds of assets you have or might acquire, to identify which risks apply to them. Plan to avoid concentration in any one risk category. If most of your assets are fixed-income debt securities, you are more exposed to interest rate and inflation risks, but much less to market and business risks. Try to diversify by choosing investments with different risks. A portfolio with a balance between debt and equities should offer protection against a broad range of risks.

FIGURE 9.14 EXPECTED RETURN AND ESTIMATED RISK OF SELECTED INVESTMENTS

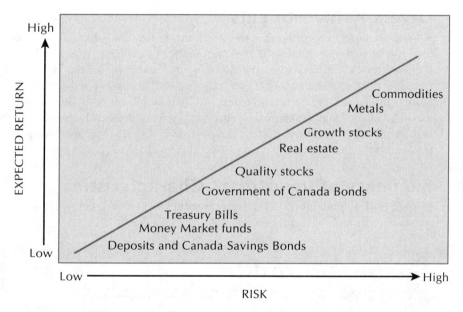

Balance Investment and Other Risks

LIFE CYCLE AND RISK The amount of risk that will be acceptable will likely vary with the stage in the life cycle. A young single person who has an adequate income and no dependents may be in a position to handle more risk than will be possible a few years later when starting a family. The middle years, when income is more than enough to handle expenses, permit a higher proportion of risk than during retirement. A young person has time to recoup a loss, but retired persons should not put their retirement income at risk unless their net worth is very large.

INCOME AND RISK Some people have more risk associated with income than others. A civil service employee can usually count on more security than a person who is self-employed, or who is in a cyclical industry that often lays off workers. Farmers and other self-employed people often invest in their businesses instead of the stock market. To balance the high risk associated with their equity-based income, they may put some savings in very low-risk debt securities.

At this first level of diversification, look at total net worth as well as the income source. If, for instance, your income is dependent on the real estate market, you would not want to put your savings into the same sector. In addition to planning for a balance among a broad range of risks, attention should also be given to spreading the risk within an investment portfolio by diversifying the types of assets.

Diversify Investments

A basic principle in portfolio management is **diversification,** which means reducing total risk by choosing securities that are not subject to the same types of risk. If there is enough money to work with, the risk to your whole portfolio can be reduced by spreading the risk over a variety of investments. Small investors can diversify by using mutual funds, a topic to be discussed in Chapter 11. Since it is impossible to maximize safety, yield, and growth in any one portfolio, decide which of these is the highest priority, but do not neglect the other two. Expect to adjust your portfolio from time to time as needs and economic conditions change.

Summary of Investment Characteristics

In spite of the difficulties in classifying investments by various characteristics, the summary chart in Table 9.1 is presented as a general guide.

DIVERSITY IN PORTFOLIOS

Three investors, Ann, Bob, and Carl, are at different stages in life and have different attitudes toward investments, as you can see from this summary of their portfolios.

Investment	Ann	Bob	Carl
	%	%	%
Canada Savings Bonds	0	50	15
Guaranteed investment certificates	0	25	10
Mutual fund (balanced)	0	25	30
Corporate bonds	0	0	15
Common stocks	60	0	25
Gold	40	0	5
TOTAL	100	100	100

Which one is probably young, single, and not averse to risk? Who likely spends the least time looking after his or her portfolio? Who seems to have spread the risk most widely?

Bob, who appears to be the most conservative in this group, as he has three-quarters of his portfolio in debt securities, is exposed to interest rate and inflation risks. This is offset by the balanced mutual fund (invested in stocks and bonds) which offers some opportunity for growth and protection from inflation without very high risk. Perhaps he is retired, has a lower marginal tax rate, and needs income-producing securities.

Ann, with no debt securities, has the most risk in her portfolio. She is very heavily exposed to market and business risks but should be protected against inflation. But what will she use for emergency funds or short-term goals? If she should need funds when the market is low, she might be forced to take a capital loss.

Carl, the seasoned investor, may have the largest net worth. At any rate, he has diversified his holdings more than the others, and thus has protection against a range of risks.

TABLE 9.1 INVESTMENT CHARACTERISTICS BY ASSET CATEGORY

Asset category	Investment characteristics				
	Safety	Liquidity	Income/ capital gain	Mgt. effort	Inflation protection
DEPOSITS: (savings accounts, CSBs, term deposits)	Exc.	Exc.	Fixed income	Very little	None
GICs	Exc.	Poor	Fixed income	Very little	None
Treasury bills, money market funds	Exc.	Very good	Fixed income	Little	None
High quality bonds	Exc. to good	Varies	Fixed income, gain possible	Not much	Not much
High quality preferred shares	Good to fair	Varies	Both possible	Some	Some
Common stock	Good to poor	Poor	Both possible	Some to much	Good in long run
Real estate (income property)	Good to poor	Poor	Both possible	Necessary	Usually Good
Mutual funds	Good to poor	Poor	Both possible	Not much	Varies

PERSONAL INVESTMENT PLANS

Investment Objectives

Within the general framework of an overall aim of maximizing investment return with minimum risk and effort, you must establish personal priorities with respect to your total portfolio before considering specific investments. What is your personal preference for risk, and for spending time and effort managing investments? At your stage in the life cycle, what are your needs for current income? Use Table 9.2 to record your preferences, on a scale of zero to ten. With paired characteristics, the combined values must equal ten to reflect the trade-off involved.

TABLE 9.2 PRIORITIES FOR YOUR TOTAL PORTFOLIO

Objectives Priorities

1. Return	0	1	2	3	4	5	6	7	8	9	10
Safety	10	9	8	7	6	5	4	3	2	1	0
						(combined value = 10)					
2. Current income	0	1	2	3	4	5	6	7	8	9	10
Capital gain (growth)	10	9	8	7	6	5	4	3	2	1	0
						(combined value = 10)					
3. Liquidity	0	1	2	3	4	5	6	7	8	9	10
Return	10	9	8	7	6	5	4	3	2	1	0
						(combined value = 10)					
4. Inflation protection	0	1	2	3	4	5	6	7	8	9	10
Safety	10	9	8	7	6	5	4	3	2	1	0
						(combined value = 10)					
5. Management effort	0	1	2	3	4	5	6	7	8	9	10
6. Tax reduction	0	1	2	3	4	5	6	7	8	9	10

Analyze Present Portfolio

Make a list of the assets you now own, their values, their share of the total, and their annual rate of return. Use Table 9.3 to classify each according to its prime investment objective.

Compare your investment priorities with this asset analysis, but do not be surprised if you find that your expressed preferences do not exactly correspond to your current holdings. You might have indicated that you gave a high priority to inflation protection but discover that you have mostly fixed-income assets. This analysis of your objectives will be a guide in planning changes to your portfolio and in choosing additional investments.

TABLE 9.3 ANALYSIS OF PRESENT PORTFOLIO

	Present Value	% of total	Annual rate of return	Investment objective
Savings Account				
GIC				
Term Deposits				
Canada Savings Bonds				
RRSPs				
Mutual Funds				
Bonds				
Stocks				
Real Estate				

Investment Pyramid

A widely used guide to investment planning is the investment pyramid, which summarizes an individual's portfolio (Figure 9.15). As the pyramid rises, so does the risk; those investments at the base of the pyramid carry the least risk. If drawn to scale, each slice of the pyramid would represent the distribution of the portfolio among the various risk categories. The order of priority is from bottom to top. First, ensure that you have invested money for emergencies, liquidity needs, and short-term goals in secure but accessible securities. For those who choose home ownership, investment in a home property will be the next priority. After taking care of these needs, investments can be made in good quality securities to fund long-term goals. The top slices of the pyramid are high-risk securities that should not represent a significant share of most portfolios and should be considered only if other investment goals have been adequately funded.

FIGURE 9.15 THE INVESTMENT PYRAMID

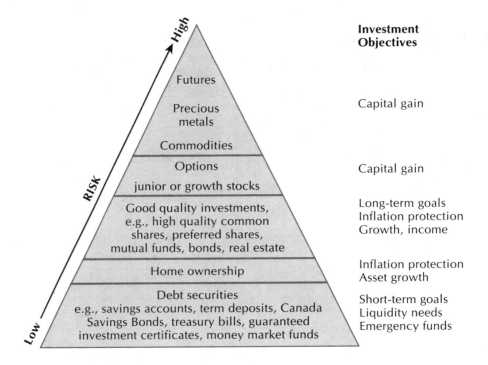

Make a drawing of your own portfolio pyramid to see how well you have implemented your priorities. There is no one right way to divide the pyramid; it will depend on your stage in the life cycle, your personal objectives, and your financial situation. Those who are very young or very wealthy may be more aggressive than older or retired investors. Nevertheless, everyone needs a safety cushion of funds for short-term needs before moving into other types of investments. The purpose of this pyramid exercise is to become more aware of portfolio planning and to avoid haphazard investing, which may not be the best way to achieve your financial goals.

What Will Your Next Investment Be?

Once you have a clear picture of your overall objectives, you will be in a position to determine the specific objectives of an additional investment. If your portfolio is largely low-risk, low-return, fixed-income securities, you would probably want your next investment to offer more inflation protection, more return, and somewhat less safety.

An Investment Plan

A well-designed plan for saving and investing is the road to financial independence. As we saw in Chapter 4, financial security is the assurance that you can maintain your desired level of living now and in the future. In spite of public income security programs and personal insurance, a significant component of financial security is dependent on individual net worth. Should you wish to retire early from the labour force to pursue other interests, or to have a comfortable life after the conventional retirement age, the size of your net worth will be a determining factor. Furthermore, a saving and investment plan is a good defence against impulse spending or social pressure to buy things.

Earlier in this chapter there was discussion of the need to save for emergency funds, liquidity needs, and short-term and long-term goals. This money should be invested in securities with appropriate maturities and with characteristics that match your priorities. Your investment plan will include a forecast of the total amount required, the amount to be saved each pay period, and indications as to how these savings will be invested.

Summary

This general discussion of investment provides an introduction to chapters on the specifics of debt securities and stocks. This chapter emphasized that you must save money if you wish to invest. You should devise ways to give saving a high priority, examine reasons for investing and, finally learn how to make an investment plan. All investors want to maximize their return and minimize risk, the effects of inflation, and income tax. To accomplish these objectives it is necessary to have clear investment goals, and some knowledge about securities, and to be prepared to invest time as well as money in the process. Although there are no risk-free investments, the wise investor understands the risk inherent in various types of securities and uses diversification to reduce overall risk.

Vocabulary Review

capital gain (p. 265)

debt securities (p. 264)

diversification (p. 278)

equity (p. 264)

investing (p. 263)

liquid assets (p. 260)

liquidity (p. 268)

portfolio (p. 263)

net worth (wealth) (p. 258)

real rate of return (p. 270)

speculation (p. 263)

term (p. 269)

total assets (p. 259)

Problems

1. Decide whether you AGREE or DISAGREE with each of the following statements. State reasons for your decision.

   (a) Do not invest your emergency funds in common stocks because the liquidity is too high.

   (b) Investing means putting money in high-risk assets.

   (c) A savings account is not really a type of investment.

   (d) If you lend money to someone to buy a house and take back a mortgage, you have acquired an equity security.

   (e) If you own rental property, the rent you receive is not considered capital gain.

   (f) Interest is one form of income received from equity securities.

   (g) Accumulating enough money to pay the annual taxes on the house is an example of a need for a liquidity fund.

2. (a) When do you think a person should start saving for retirement?

   (b) What kind of retirement saving would you suggest, if any, for a person who is 25 and in their first job?

   (c) What are some of the costs and benefits of leaving retirement saving until about age 50?

   (d) Look at Figure 1.1 (Chapter 1) and identify the life cycle stage(s) when you think the financial pressures will be the greatest.

3. Suppose that a young couple consulted you about their financial affairs. They claimed that it was impossible for them to save anything at all because they had credit card bills to pay each month for a wide range of necessities. In fact, the amount outstanding on the two credit cards was gradually increasing. What suggestions might you make?

4. Decide whether you AGREE or DISAGREE with each of the following statements, based on the information provided in this chapter.

   (a) Most Canadian families have some wealth.

   (b) For most families, their home is their single largest asset.

   (c) The lower the income level, the more the diversity in the average family's portfolio.

   (d) Stocks and miscellaneous financial investments are more significant forms of assets for higher-income families than for low-income or middle-income households.

   (e) All low-income or middle-income families have a positive net worth.

(f) With age, a household's wealth exceeds its average annual income because of an increasing propensity to save.

(g) In the Statistics Canada survey of assets, stocks were classified as liquid assets.

(h) On average, families with heads under age 45 have enough wealth to replace their income for a couple of years if they faced unemployment or illness.

(i) Those who own stocks are more likely to have high incomes.

(j) The savings rate in Canada has been rising steadily for a decade or more.

(k) The aggregate savings rate in Canada has varied but has rarely exceeded 10 percent.

5. (a) It is apparent from Figure 9.2 that, on average, Canadians are successful savers. However, the results of a household survey indicate that only around 10 percent of Canadians invest in the stock market. Suggest reasons for this.

   (b) Do you think many people equate buying stocks with speculating?

6. (a) List four factors that are inversely related to return on investments.

   (b) Why is there usually an inverse relation between income and capital gain?

   (c) Why is more risk generally associated with equity than with debt investments?

7. Which of the following pairs of investments is more liquid?

   (a) Canada Savings Bond or five-year guaranteed investment certificate.

   (b) common stock or a term deposit.

8. In the example about Gerry and his $100 000 inheritance (Figure 9.11), safety of principal was apparently given the highest priority.

   (a) Identify some risks he failed to protect against.

   (b) How would you have invested such a sum if you wanted it to be a source of retirement income?

9. Refer to Figure 9.12. This investor locked in funds in 1978 when interest rates were close to a historical high, a decision that seemed very rational at the time.

   (a) Did the investor receive enough return during this period to compensate for inflation and also to gain from having lent the money?

   (b) If you planned to invest several thousand dollars in debt securities, is there any way to hedge against a sudden change in interest rates?

10. Why do we say that stocks are not liquid investments?

11. Assume that a friend, who has just inherited $40 000, asked your advice on investing it. Before offering any ideas you need to know something about your friend's situation. Write out five essential questions you would ask your friend.

12.

WHAT ARE HIS INVESTMENT OBJECTIVES?

Jim admits he is a spendthrift and generally unable to save money. At 28 he has plans to marry within the year and possibly to build his own house. As a welder-fitter, he finds his income more than sufficient for his needs. Jim owes $7000 on a car loan, which is life-insured. When asked how he would invest a windfall of $11 000, he said he was not averse to taking some risk. He recognizes that inflation can erode capital and thinks that perhaps he should try for capital gain. He wants this investment to be highly liquid and invested for a short term in a safe place. He does not want to risk the capital.

(a) From this limited information, make a list of Jim's investment priorities.

(b) How do you suggest he should invest this money to achieve all of his goals?

(c) If you were Jim's investment adviser, what advice would you have for him?

13.

INVESTMENT PRIORITIES

Sid, 45, has grown, independent children; his house is paid for and he is the owner of a well-established business. He has a large margin between his current income and his expenses. He owns bonds and common stock, and is saving for his retirement. When asked how he would invest his next $6000 of savings, he listed his highest priorities as safety of principal, current income, capital appreciation; liquidity and inflation protection were less essential. He thinks he might invest in mining stock and a second mortgage as soon as his savings build up enough.

(a) Examine Sid's investment objectives in light of what you know about his financial situation.

(b) Identify any inconsistencies between his stated objectives and his plans.

(c) It is not uncommon to find such inconsistencies. Why is that?

14.

HOW MUCH RISK?

Claude and Janet are consulting you about their investments. They are in their mid-40s, with two teen-age daughters. Claude is employed as a computer programmer with a large company, and Janet is a teacher. They have a mortgage on their house, but no other debts. Their assets include Canada Savings Bonds and term deposits, but they are now thinking of buying some common stocks.

In conversation you discover that they want their investment to be a hedge against inflation. They would prefer an investment that does not require much attention from them, and that offers the prospect of capital gain. They are nervous about assuming risk and want their funds readily available in case of an emergency.

(a) What would you say to this couple about their investment goals?

(b) What kind of investment would you suggest for them?

References

BOOKS

AMLING, FREDERICK and WILLIAM G. DROMS. *The Dow Jones-Irwin Guide to Personal Financial Planning.* Second Edition. Homewood, Illinois: Dow Jones-Irwin, 1986, 549 pp. Although written for American readers, much of the discussion of financial planning, life insurance, retirement planning, and investments is relevant for Canadians.

BIRCH, RICHARD. *The Family Financial Planning Book, A Step-by-Step Moneyguide for Canadian Families.* Revised Edition. Toronto: Key Porter, 1989, 216 pp. An easy-to-read guide to taking control of your personal finances that discusses budgets, income tax, insurance, RRSPs, mortgages, and investments.

BUDD, JOHN, CLAUDE RINFRET, RICHARD DAW, and DANIELLE BRIEN. *Canadian Guide to Personal Financial Management.* Scarborough, Ontario: Prentice-Hall Canada, annual, 225 pp. Accountants provide guidance on a broad range of topics, including planning finances, estimating insurance needs, managing risk, and determining investment needs. Instructions and the necessary forms for making plans are provided.

CHAKRAPANI, C. *Financial Freedom on $5 a Day.* Fifth Edition. Vancouver: International Self-Counsel Press, 1991, 183 pp. Presents a method of increasing net worth by consistently saving and investing small sums.

COHEN, DIAN. *Money.* Scarborough, Ontario: Prentice-Hall Canada, 1987, 270 pp. An economist suggests strategies for coping with personal finances in the context of changing economic conditions. Topics include financial plans, buying a home, insurance, income tax, retirement, estate planning, and investments.

COSTELLO, BRIAN. *Your Money and How to Keep It.* Fifth Edition. Toronto: Stoddart, 1990, 248 pp. Particular emphasis on investments and income tax.

CÔTÉ, JEAN-MARC and DONALD DAY. *Personal Financial Planning in Canada.* Toronto: Allyn and Bacon, 1987, 464 pp. A comprehensive personal finance text that includes financial planning, income tax, annuities, pensions, investments, credit, mortgages, wills, with particular attention to the banking and insurance industries.

DRACHE, ARTHUR B. C. and SUSAN WEIDMAN SCHNEIDER. *Head and Heart, Financial Strategies for Smart Women.* Toronto: Macmillan, 1987, 348 pp. Recognizing the needs and perspectives of women, a tax lawyer and journalist have collaborated to present basic financial information, taking into account women's concerns at different stages in their lives.

DRACHE, ARTHUR B. C. and PEGGY WATERTON. *Dollars and Sense, The Complete Canadian Financial Planner.* Toronto: Grosvenor House, 1987, 207 pp. An overview of a range of financial topics, including budgets, credit, investing, taxes, insurance, retirement planning, estates, and effects of changes in family status.

FORMAN, NORM. *Mind Over Money, Curing Your Financial Headaches with Moneysanity.* Toronto: Doubleday Canada, 1987, 248 pp. A psychologist examines the effects money has on behaviour, looking at the origin of money problems and suggesting therapies to help us to better understand ourselves.

FRIEDLAND, SEYMOUR and STEVEN G. KELMAN. *Investment Strategies, How to Create Your Own and Make it Work for You.* Markham, Ontario: Penguin Canada, 1991. Offers guidance for the general reader in defining objectives and establishing an investment program.

GOHEEN, DUNCAN. *Planning for Financial Independence, Choose Your Lifestyle, Secure Your Future.* Vancouver: International Self-Counsel Press, 1988, 128 pp. Detailed guidance for making a financial plan, including the necessary charts and tables.

HATCH, JAMES E. and MICHAEL J. ROBINSON. *Investment Management in Canada.* Toronto: Prentice-Hall Canada, 1988, 836 pp. A technical university text with in-depth coverage of many aspects of investing.

MACINNIS, LYMAN. *Get Smart! Make Your Money Count in the 1990s.* Second Edition. Scarborough, Ontario: Prentice-Hall Canada, 1989, 317 pp. A book for the general reader that includes financial planning and income tax principles, but gives major attention to investing in the stock market.

MOTHERWELL, CATHRYN. *Smart Money, Invesing for Women.* Toronto: Key Porter, 1989, 192 pp. A financial journalist explains how to get started investing, how to evaluate the products and how to build a portfolio.

PAPE, GORDON. *Building Wealth in the '90s.* Scarborough, Ontario: Prentice-Hall Canada, 1992, 294 pp. An easy-to-read guide for the novice financial manager and investor. Considers interest rates, credit cards, mortgages, RRSPs, mutual funds, and the stock market.

PAPE, GORDON. *Low-Risk Investing*. Scarborough, Ontario: Prentice-Hall Canada, 1989, 244 pp. A book written to encourage the novice investor to get started on saving and investing. Outlines the basics of investing in debt and equity investments.

WYATT, ELAINE. *The Money Companion, How to Manage Your Money and Achieve Financial Freedom*. Markham, Ontario: Penguin Books, 1991. A guide to personal financial management that focuses on planning, investment strategy, and retirement needs.

WYLIE, BETTY JANE and LYNNE MACFARLANE. *Everywoman's Money Book*. Fourth Edition. Toronto: Key Porter, 1989, 223 pp. A journalist and a stock broker have collaborated on this wide-ranging treatment of a variety of personal finance topics, including women and credit; the budget; insurance; retirement; children and money.

PERIODICALS

Canadian Money Saver. Monthly. Canadian Money Saver Inc., Box 370, Bath, Ontario, K0H 1G0. Includes short articles on a range of personal finance topics, with special emphasis on investments.

Financial Times. Weekly. Suite 500, 920 Yonge Street, Toronto, Ontario, M2W 3L5. Provides current information on a range of business and economic topics.

Report on Business. Daily. A section of *The Globe and Mail*. Important source of information on the financial markets.

The Financial Post. Daily and weekly. The Financial Post Company, 777 Bay Street, Toronto, Ontario, M5G 2E4. Up-to-date information on business, economics, income tax, and investments.

The Financial Post Magazine. Monthly. The Financial Post Company, 777 Bay Street, Toronto, Ontario, M5G 2E4. Includes a section on personal finance.

CHAPTER TEN

Debt Securities

1. To understand the significance of the following features when comparing deposits offered by financial institutions:

    (a) term,

    (b) interest rate and frequency of compounding,

    (c) minimum deposit,

    (d) accessibility of invested funds.

2. To explain the purpose and coverage of deposit insurance.

3. To distinguish among the following types of debt securities: term deposits, guaranteed investment certificates, commercial paper, Treasury Bills, money market funds, mortgage-backed securities.

4. To outline the process of underwriting and selling a bond issue and to identify factors that affect the interest rates of new bond issues.

5. To distinguish between the following pairs:

    (a) bearer and registered bonds,

    (b) mortgage and collateral trust bonds,

    (c) nominal rate and yield to maturity,

    (d) an investment dealer acting as a principal and as an agent in the distribution of bonds,

    (e) the money market and the bond market,

    (f) bonds and debentures,

    (g) extendible and retractable bonds,

    (h) interest on a cash basis and on a receivable basis.

6. To explain these terms: maturity date, term, call feature, denomination, par, discount, premium, redemption, coupon, underwriter, bank rate, bond certificate, convertible bond, floating rate, sinking fund, stripped bonds, spread.

7. To calculate the approximate yield to maturity on a marketable bond.

8. To explain how changing bond prices affect yield to maturity.

9. To explain why and when accrued interest is added to the price of a bond.

10. To explain the differences in the tax treatment of two types of bond yield: interest and capital gain.

11. To explain in what ways Canada Savings Bonds are more like savings certificates than bonds.

Introduction

This chapter is about debt securities, in which the investor becomes a lender rather than an owner. As a result, there is generally less risk assumed and less management required. Five groups of debt securities will be discussed:

(a) deposits,

(b) money market securities,

(c) mortgage-backed securities,

(d) bonds and debentures,

(e) Canada Savings Bonds.

Most of these are low-risk, very liquid investments, appropriate as a base for any portfolio. Deposits and Canada Savings Bonds are not transferable to other investors, but money market securities, mortgage-backed securities, and bonds may be traded in the financial markets. It is important to distinguish between Canada Savings Bonds, which are more like savings certificates, and other types of bonds.

This chapter provides an introduction to basic principles and terminology associated with debt securities, but does not address portfolio management strategies. It may be helpful to consult other references for further study of debt securities.

DEPOSITS

The easiest and simplest way to invest is to lend capital to financial institutions by placing it in deposit securities. Savings accounts, term deposits, and guaranteed investment certificates are all examples of deposit securities. Although these savings vehicles may differ in interest rates, term, minimum deposit, and accessibility, most are very low risk, pay interest regularly, and require minimal attention from the investor.

Savings Accounts

Banks, trust companies, and credit unions offer a bewildering array of accounts, which may or may not permit chequing. Institutions generally pay higher interest rates on accounts that require the least service. If funds are to be left relatively untouched in a savings account, look for an account that combines the best interest rate with the most frequent compounding. If the account balance tends to fluctuate, it might be advantageous to have a daily interest account, in spite of the lower interest rate. With such accounts, interest is paid on the daily balance and compounded monthly. On regular savings accounts, interest is paid on the minimum monthly balance and compounded semi-annually. The highly competitive markets of today force financial institutions to make frequent changes in the types of accounts they offer; it is best to do some comparison shopping to find the best account for any particular purpose. Some factors to be considered when comparing accounts are shown in "Criteria for Comparing Banking Services."

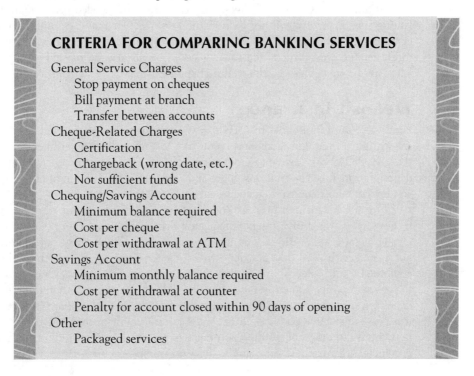

CRITERIA FOR COMPARING BANKING SERVICES

General Service Charges
    Stop payment on cheques
    Bill payment at branch
    Transfer between accounts
Cheque-Related Charges
    Certification
    Chargeback (wrong date, etc.)
    Not sufficient funds
Chequing/Savings Account
    Minimum balance required
    Cost per cheque
    Cost per withdrawal at ATM
Savings Account
    Minimum monthly balance required
    Cost per withdrawal at counter
    Penalty for account closed within 90 days of opening
Other
    Packaged services

Term Deposits

As the name implies, **term deposits** are for a specified term at a guaranteed interest rate and, in some cases, require a minimum investment. Savings accounts, by contrast, have no guaranteed interest rate, no minimum deposit, and no set term that the funds are required to be on deposit. The rate of return on term deposits is usually higher than on savings accounts and, although the money is invested for a specified term, funds can usually be withdrawn before maturity by sacrificing some interest. Since the frequency of interest payments affects the interest rate, expect a lower rate if interest is to be paid monthly.

Guaranteed Investment Certificates

Guaranteed investment certificates (GICs) have terms ranging from one to five years, during which time the interest rate is guaranteed and the money is usually locked in until maturity (settling an estate after death is an exception). For certain rates and maturities, a minimum deposit may be required. Some certificates provide regular interest payments and others offer automatic compounding. Generally, the interest rate will be slightly less if interest payments are to be made more often than once a year. If funds in a guaranteed investment certificate are needed before maturity, the issuing trust company will not redeem the certificate. It may be possible to sell the certificate, however, through some brokerage houses. The price will depend on interest rates prevailing at the time; it could be discounted or sold at a premium. These terms are explained later in this chapter.

Deposit Insurance

Funds deposited in a bank, trust company, or credit union are insured against loss if the institution should become insolvent. In 1967, the federal government established the Canada Deposit Insurance Corporation (CDIC) as a Crown corporation to insure deposits in member institutions. Signs indicating membership are often seen on the windows of banks and trust companies.

The CDIC insures savings and chequing accounts, money orders, deposit receipts, guaranteed investment certificates, debentures, and other obligations issued by the member institutions. The maximum coverage is changed from time to time, but is currently $60 000 per depositor for each institution, which applies to a combined total of deposits at all branches of the same institution. One restriction is that term deposits, to be insurable, must be redeemable no later than five years after deposit. Joint accounts are insured separately from individual accounts, meaning that it is possible to have both a personal and a joint account in the same bank, with the maximum coverage of $60 000 on each account. Credit unions, through their provincial organizations, offer similar deposit insurance.

MONEY MARKET SECURITIES

Periodically, corporations and governments need to borrow money to support their various activities. The federal government borrows by selling Canada Savings Bonds, Treasury Bills, or Canada bonds; provincial and municipal governments borrow by selling debentures. Corporations borrow from banks, or borrow by selling bonds, debentures, or short-term commercial paper. These various types of loans are usually classified as either short-term (money market instruments) or long-term (bonds or debentures). We will look first at money market securities, which include Treasury Bills, commercial paper, and money market funds.

The Money Market

A large pool of cash moves from lenders to borrowers for short periods through a mechanism known as the **money market.** The major actors in this market are the banks, other financial institutions (trust companies, small loan and sales finance companies), corporations, governments, and the Bank of Canada. The lenders are usually corporations or institutions with spare cash that can be invested for a short period, and the borrowers are those who temporarily need extra funds. There is no physical site where money market transactions take place; there is only a communication system. Because of the large minimum investment required, few individual investors are aware of all this money market activity.

The money market, as has been mentioned, deals with short-term loans, mostly for 30, 60, 90, or 365 days, but occasionally for as long as three to five years. Commercial paper and Treasury Bills are two widely used instruments in the money market. **Commercial paper** (discounted paper) is the name used for short-term loans or promissory notes. Instead of borrowing a principal sum and repaying it with interest at maturity, the lender may invest a discounted sum and at maturity receive an amount equivalent to the loan plus interest. For instance, a 30-day note for $50 000 might be purchased for $49 600 by the lender, who would receive $50 000 at maturity. The difference between the amount invested and the amount received is the interest on the loan, which in this instance is 9.6 percent.

Treasury Bills

Short-term promissory notes, issued principally by the federal government, but also by other levels of government, are called **Treasury Bills.** The usual denominations are $1 000, $5 000, $25 000, $100 000, and $1 000 000, with terms up to 365 days (the majority are for 91 or 182 days). Treasury Bills, like commercial paper, do not carry specific interest rates but sell at a discount and mature at par. The purchaser's yield is determined by the difference between the price paid and the maturity (par) value. Treasury Bills are marketable securities since investors can sell them before maturity, at a price determined by current interest rates.

Each Tuesday, Government of Canada Treasury Bills are auctioned in Ottawa by the Bank of Canada. Prior to the auction, the Bank of Canada announced the amounts and maturities of the Bills to be auctioned, and interested investors (i.e. banks and investment dealers) submitted bids. At the auction, Bills are sold to the highest bidders, with the Bank of Canada possibly tendering reserve bids. This Treasury Bill auction is a mechanism whereby the federal government exerts influence on all interest rates. The bank rate, the rate at which the Bank of Canada lends funds to the chartered banks, is tied to the weekly auction; for instance the bank rate may be 1/4 percent higher than the market yield on 91-day Treasury Bills. Usually, the evening news on Tuesdays includes an item on the change in the bank rate as a result of this weekly auction. Changes in the bank rate eventually influence most other interest rates. Most of the Treasury Bills are bought by banks, to be kept as part of their reserves, or by investment dealers who sell them on the secondary market.

Investment dealers provide an active secondary market offering outstanding Treasury Bills with shorter maturities than the new issues. In recent years, some investment dealers have made Treasury Bills available to small investors with a minimum purchase of $1 000, in increments of $1 000. Anyone who wishes to invest for the short term in a top quality, low-risk, very liquid investment, might consider Treasury Bills. To buy Treasury Bills, it may be necessary to open an account with a stock broker. Usually Treasury Bills pay somewhat higher interest than savings accounts or term deposits, as noted in Table 10.1.

TABLE 10.1 Costs and Benefits of Several Debt Securities

Debt Security	Interest Rate %	Costs and Benefits
Savings Accounts (daily interest)	1.25	Liquid, less interest
T-Bill Account	1.60	Liquid, minimum balance required (e.g., $5 000)
Term Deposit	3.75	Locked in (e.g., 3 months), higher interest rate
Treasury Bill	4.38	Liquid, need broker's account, minimum purchase required (e.g., $5 000), highest interest rate

BUYING A T-BILL

When Ivan inherited $27 000, he needed a short-term investment until he made other plans. His broker offered him a 36-day Treasury Bill, quoted at a price of 99.627. Note that the quoted price is the amount he will pay for each $100 that he buys. The amount he invested was 270 × 99.627 = $26 899.29. When the T-bill matures, Ivan will receive $27 000, including interest of $100.71.

To calculate the yield on his T-bill, Ivan used this formula:

$$\text{Yield} = \frac{100 - \text{price}}{\text{price}} \times \frac{365 \times 100}{\text{term}}$$

$$\text{Yield} = \frac{100 - 99.627}{99.627} \times \frac{365 \times 100}{36}$$

$$\text{Yield} = \frac{0.373}{99.627} \times \frac{36500}{36}$$

$$\text{Yield} = .0037439 \times 1013.888 = 3.8\%$$

If Ivan had needed to sell the Treasury Bill before it matured, the return would have been re-calculated to reflect the current T-bill rate at the time of the sale.

Money Market Funds

Savings accounts are not the only low-risk, highly liquid, interest-earning securities available for small sums. When there is not enough money to buy Treasury Bills directly from a broker, savings can be put in the money market through a **money market fund**, which is a way of pooling contributions from many small investors. A money market mutual fund accepts small amounts from many people. A paid manager invests these funds in a portfolio of Treasury Bills and commercial paper. The return from money market funds, in the form of interest, may be received regularly by the investor, or reinvested in additional shares of the fund. The investor's shares in a money market fund can be sold at any time.

Money market funds differ in selling practices and commission fees. Some funds are sold directly to customers, while others are available through brokers. Some funds do not charge a fee but require a large initial deposit; others charge an acquisition fee of two to nine percent, depending on the size of the investment (the larger the deposit, the smaller the rate). Most money market funds charge annual management fees, which are deducted before any return is paid to the investor. Fees for mutual funds will be discussed in detail in Chapter 11.

KATALIN INVESTS IN A MONEY MARKET FUND

Katalin has $5 000 that she wants to invest in a money market fund because she likes the combination of liquidity and reasonably high interest rates. On making inquiries, she discovered that the acquisition fee for her modest investment would probably be two percent, or about $100; in future years this fee would not recur. There would also be an annual management fee of about one-half of one percent, which is subtracted from earnings before interest is paid to shareholders.

From the financial papers, Katalin discovered that the average return paid by the more conservative companies last year was about eight percent. Interest rates had dropped considerably since then, however, and now the annualized return was about 4.25 percent. At that rate, first year interest would amount to $212.50.

Katalin decided to invest in this money market fund and have the interest reinvested automatically so that her liquid assets would grow but still be readily accessible.

MORTGAGE-BACKED SECURITIES

Direct investment in home mortgages requires expertise, time, and willingness to accept risk. However, these difficulties can be overcome by using mortgage-backed securities. A buyer of **mortgage-backed securities** acquires a share in a large pool of residential mortgages that are secured by the Canada Housing and Mortgage Corporation. Each pool of mortgages has its own interest rate and maturity date, which could be as short as six months. Mortgage-backed securities are available from stock brokers in units of $5 000 and trade on the public market where they may be sold before maturity. Generally, the yield is higher than that of Treasury Bills.

There are two types of mortgage-backed securities: prepayable and non-prepayable (terms that will be more meaningful after studying the chapter on mortgages). In essence, the terms mean that some pools of mortgages permit home buyers to make prepayments in order to repay their mortgages faster. Investors in mortgage-backed securities are affected by this because they may find their principal being repaid faster than they anticipated; investors therefore have to re-invest their capital at a faster rate. However, there may be a bonus of some extra money for investors because of penalties paid by those making prepayments.

The holders of mortgage-backed securities do not have to be concerned with either managing this investment or its safety. Each month, they simply receive a cheque that includes a combination of interest and principal. What they do have to remember, however, is that some of their capital is being returned in each cheque; if they want to preserve their capital, a plan for continual reinvestment is needed. However, if the goal is to gradually spend some of the capital, this is one way to do it.

BONDS

Bonds and Debentures

Debt securities with longer-term maturities include bonds and debentures, which may have terms up to 25 years or more. There is a distinction between bonds and debentures, although often the terms are used interchangeably. Technically, **bonds** are secured with property, while **debentures** are unsecured loans. To further confuse matters, Government of Canada bonds are really debentures. In this chapter, bonds will be used as the generic term to include both bonds and debentures. Bonds are issued by the federal, provincial, and municipal governments, by public utilities, and by private corporations when they need to borrow money. Those who buy their bonds become their creditors and receive a promise that interest will be paid on specific dates and that the principal will be repaid at maturity.

How Bonds Are Issued

A government or corporation that wishes to float a new bond issue usually makes use of an investment dealer as an underwriter. The **underwriter** agrees to purchase all of the bonds offered at a stated price, then endeavours to sell them at a slightly higher price. With large bond issues, there may be a consortium of investment dealers acting as underwriters. In the initial stages, the underwriter will be consulted for advice on terms (interest rate, maturity, etc.). After an agreement is reached, the bonds will be printed and transferred by the issuer (borrower) to the underwriters. Underwriters, therefore, are involved not only in designing the terms of the issue, but also in its sale and distribution. The **par value** is the face value of the bond or other security and is printed on the bond itself; for example, $1 000. Investment dealers advertise each new issue of bonds and sell them to buyers at a price that may be either at par or slightly below, depending on the market at the time.

BOND ISSUE ANNOUNCEMENT Examine the announcement of a new bond issue reproduced in Figure 10.1. It gives the name of the bond issuer (Newfoundland and Labrador Hydro) and the total value of the bond issue ($40 million). The terms of the issue are: interest at 10 percent of the face value will be paid for 25 years from June 27, 1978 to June 27, 2003; Hydro will not recall these bonds before June 27, 1998; and the principal and interest are guaranteed by the Province of Newfoundland. Note that when first issued, the bonds could be purchased for 99, which means that a $1 000 bond cost $990. It is a convention to list bond prices in hundreds of dollars, although a $1 000 bond is frequently the lowest denomination available. Although the bonds described in such an announcement (known as "tombstones" in the industry) may have already been sold to investors by the time it appears in the papers, they will be trading on the bond market at the going price.

The investment dealers, listed at the bottom of the advertisement (Figure 10.1), underwrote this issue and initially may have bought all the bonds from Hydro. However, once sold by the investment dealers, the bonds trade on the bond market. Bondholders who no longer wish to keep their bonds cannot redeem them from Hydro until 1998, but may sell them to another investor. It might be interesting to find out from a broker the price at which these bonds are currently selling. Later in this chapter, it will be explained why they may be priced at less or more than 100.

FACTORS AFFECTING INTEREST RATES Three significant factors affecting the interest rate on a new bond issue are: (i) the general level of interest rates in the country at the time, (ii) the length of time to maturity, and (iii) the credit rating of the issuer. At a time when general interest rates are quite high, bond issuers will have to offer equivalent rates to attract investors. Since money has a time value, the longer the term the more uncertainty about the future and, consequently, the higher the rate needed to interest investors in very long-term bonds.

FIGURE 10.1 ANNOUNCEMENT OF A BOND ISSUE

New Issue

$40,000,000

NEWFOUNDLAND AND LABRADOR HYDRO

**10% Sinking Fund Debentures, Series L
to be dated June 27, 1978 and mature June 27, 2003**
(Non redeemable before June 27, 1998)

Guaranteed unconditionally as to principal and interest by
Province of Newfoundland

We, as principals, offer these Debentures, subject to prior sale and change in price, if, as and when issued by Newfoundland and Labrador Hydro and accepted by us and subject to the approval of Counsel. Subscriptions will be received subject to rejection or allotment in whole or in part and the right is reserved to close the subscription books at any time without notice. It is expected that definitive Debentures will be ready for delivery on or about June 27, 1978.

A copy of the circular will be furnished upon request.

PRICE: 99 to yield approximately 10.11%

A. E. Ames & Co. Limited   Burns Fry Limited

Wood Gundy Limited	Greenshields Incorporated	Dominion Securities Limited
McLeod Young Weir Limited	Morgan Stanley Canada Limited	Merrill Lynch, Royal Securities Limited
Richardson Securities of Canada	Nesbitt Thomson Securities Limited	Pitfield Mackay Ross Limited
Midland Doherty Limited	Walwyn Stodgell Cochran Murray Limited	Bell, Gouinlock & Company, Limited
Lévesque, Beaubien Inc.	Scotia Bond Company Limited	Pemberton Securities Limited
Tassé & Associés, Limitée	René T. Leclerc Incorporée	Mead & Co. Limited
	Molson, Rousseau & Cie Limitée	

The Bank of Nova Scotia   Bank of Montreal

Canadian Imperial Bank of Commerce	The Toronto-Dominion Bank	The Royal Bank of Canada

May, 1978

The credit rating of a bond issuer is dependent on its financial status and its revenue base. The federal government, considered to have the highest credit rating, can borrow more cheaply than the provinces. Municipalities are considered to be in the third level of safety and must pay somewhat more interest than the two senior governments. Generally, corporations rank below all governments and must pay somewhat higher interest rates on their bonds. However, corporations vary considerably in their credit ratings. This ranking of credit status from the federal government at the top to corporations at the bottom is a useful generalization, but does not cover all cases.

BOND RATINGS   Bond ratings published in Canada by the Canadian Bond Rating Service or the Dominion Bond Rating Service may be consulted to find the credit rating of a government or corporation. Moody's and Standard and Poor's are two American agencies that rate Canadian bond issues sold in the United States. The ratings go from AAA at the top to AA, A, BBB, and so on.

Bond Certificates

A bondholder receives a bond certificate that states the terms of the issue and the **denomination** or par value of the bond, which may be $500, $1 000, $10 000 or more. Usually, the smallest denomination is $1 000. The terms of the bond issue include the maturity date, the interest rate, and how the interest will be paid. The maturity date is the date when the issuer promises to repay the principal, a process known as **bond redemption**. Interest payments are usually made twice a year on the dates indicated on the bond. A typical bond certificate is shown in Figure 10.2.

INTEREST PAYMENTS   Interest on bonds may be paid either by cheque or coupon. A **coupon bond** has a series of coupons attached to the bond certificate. Each coupon has a value printed on it, as well as the date when it may be cashed (Figure 10.2). For example, a bond with a ten-year term will have 20 coupons, dated at six-month intervals, each worth a half year's interest. It will be stated on either the coupons or the certificate at which financial institutions the coupons may be cashed. When the specified date arrives, the coupon is cut off and exchanged for cash at the bank or brokerage house. Coupons should be cashed in promptly and the interest reinvested, since no interest is earned on uncut coupons. Bond coupons are the equivalent of cash and care should be taken to safeguard them.

BOND REGISTRATION   Some bonds have registered owners, while others do not. There are: (i) bearer bonds, (ii) bonds registered as to principal, and (iii) fully registered bonds. **Bearer bonds** have no proof of ownership; as with currency, whoever possesses them can sell them or cash in the coupons. Bearer bonds always have coupons because the bond issuer has no way of knowing to whom the interest cheques should be sent. These bonds should never be left in an unsecured place, since there would be no way to trace them. **Bonds registered as to principal** have the name

FIGURE 10.2 FACSIMILE OF A BEARER BOND AND COUPON

$1000

THE TELEPHONE COMMISSION OF QUEBEC
9¼% Bond Due February 1, 1995
(Subject to Prior Redemption)

$1000

Guaranteed as to Principal and Interest by the Province of Quebec

The TELEPHONE COMMISSION OF QUEBEC (hereinafter called the "Commission") for value received hereby promises to pay to the bearer or if registered to the registered holder hereof on the 1st day of February 1995, or on such earlier date as this bond may be redeemed in accordance with the provisions for redemption hereinafter set forth, on presentation and surrender of this bond, the sum of

ONE THOUSAND DOLLARS

in lawful money of Canada at any branch of any chartered bank in Quebec, or in any of the cities of Saint John, Quebec, Montreal, Winnipeg, Regina, Calgary, Edmonton, Vancouver, or Victoria, Canada, at holder's option, with interest thereon from the 1st day of February 1995 at the rate of nine and one-quarter per centum (9¼) per annum payable half-yearly in like money at any of the said places at holder's option on the 1st days of February and August in each year of the currency of this bond on presentation and surrender of the interest coupons hereto annexed as they severally become due.

The Commission shall have the right at its option to redeem the bonds of this issue, either in whole or in part, in advance of maturity, on any interest payment date on or after the 1st day of February 1991, at the places where and in the money in which the said bonds are expressed to be payable, upon payment of the principal amount thereof together with interest accrued thereon to the date of redemption, and upon giving previous notice of such redemption. In the event that less than all of the said bonds shall be redeemed, the bonds to be redeemed shall be chosen by lot in such manner as the Commission may deem equitable, and for the purpose of redemption and selection for redemption, each bond of a denomination greater than $1,000 each and any part of the principal amount of such bond comprising one or more of such units may accordingly be selected and called for redemption. In the event of the selection for redemption of a portion only of the principal amount of any coupon bond, payment of the redemption price of such portion will be made only upon surrender of such bond with all unmatured unredeemed balance of such principal amount, with all unmatured interest coupons attached. In the event of the selection for redemption of a portion only of the principal amount of any fully registered bond, payment of the redemption price of such portion will be made only upon surrender of such bond in exchange for a fully registered bond or bonds of this issue for the unredeemed balance of such principal amount.

This bond is subject to the conditions endorsed hereon which form part hereof.

This bond is issued under the authority of the Telephone Commission Act and of an order of the Lieutenant Governor in Council.

In witness whereof the Commission has caused its corporate seal and the engraved facsimile signature of its chairman or a vice-chairman to be affixed hereto and this bond to be duly signed by an authorized signing office of the Commission and to be dated the 1st day of February 1975.

GUARANTEE by QUEBEC

By virtue of the powers conferred by the legislature of Quebec and of an order of the Lietenant-Governor in Council, Quebec hereby guarantees to the holder for the time being of this bond and to the holder for the time being of any of the coupons attached thereto, due payment of the principal of this bond and of the interest thereon according to the tenor of the said bond and of the coupons attached thereto.

Thomas Carlyle
Chairman

Officer of the Treasury Department

Authorized Signing Officer

Specimen

FIGURE 10.2   FACSIMILE OF A BEARER BOND AND COUPON (CONTINUED)

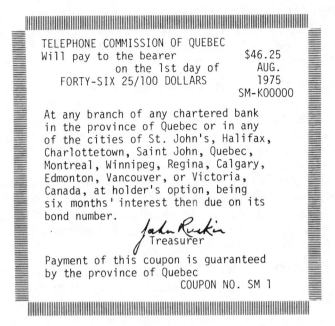

of the owner typed on them, but they carry coupons which, if detached, may be cashed in by anyone. Other bonds are **fully registered**, which means that not only is the owner's name on the bond certificate but the interest is paid directly to the owner by cheque. Coupons are therefore not required. When bonds are sold from one owner to another, the coupon bonds can be simply handed over, but the two registered types require a transfer-of-ownership form to be signed and witnessed. Therefore, it is difficult for anyone but the registered owner to redeem a registered bond.

Bond Issuers

GOVERNMENT OF CANADA   Debt securities issued by the federal government are considered to be of the highest quality and to be safer than those of any other Canadian borrower. With its broad taxing powers the government is unlikely to fail to pay interest or redeem the "Canadas," or Government of Canada bonds. In the Canadian market, the federal government is the largest issuer of bonds, and the frequent trading of "Canadas" makes them very marketable. In addition to its own bonds, the Government of Canada guarantees bonds issued by various Crown corporations. Although the federal government also issues Canada Savings Bonds, they are more like savings certificates than bonds and will be considered separately.

PROVINCIAL GOVERNMENTS   The provinces also issue bonds in their own right and guarantee bond issues of those commissions, hydro-electric corporations, and school boards under their jurisdiction. As previously mentioned, provincial bonds are usually considered to be a notch or two below the "Canadas" in security.

MUNICIPALITIES   Local governments issue debentures to pay for costly but long-lasting public projects such as streets, waterworks, schools, and hospitals. By issuing bonds, the cost is spread over a number of years. The fact that the provinces usually exert some regulatory control over the borrowing of municipalities may be a comfort to investors. Municipal debentures do not trade as frequently as the more senior provincial and federal debentures and, therefore, are generally less marketable. The quality of municipal securities is dependent on the tax base: municipalities with a broader range of industries are preferable to single-industry towns or regions. Generally, municipal debentures are ranked below provincial and federal issues, but it is difficult to generalize because the budgets of some large Canadian cities exceed those of the smallest provinces.

CORPORATIONS   When long-term funding is needed, corporations issue a variety of bonds and debentures, a few of which will be mentioned here. If the corporation's credit rating is high enough, unsecured debentures may be issued; otherwise, their bonds are backed by some type of security. As a loan secured by property, a **mortgage bond** is similar to any mortgage. However, because the sums corporations borrow are so large, the loan is divided into smaller units enabling a number of investors to be involved. Property put up as security will be used to compensate bond holders if the corporation should default. Among mortgage bonds, as in home mortgages, there are first mortgage bonds and second mortgage bonds, which are an indication of the order in which creditors would rank in the case of compensation claims.

If a corporation does not have a high enough credit rating to borrow with unsecured debentures, and has no property to offer as security, it may issue **collateral trust bonds** which are secured with financial assets the company holds, such as bonds and stocks.

Special Features

Bonds and debentures are often issued with special characteristics. They may be callable, convertible, extendible, or retractable. Some of these features are intended to make an issue more attractive to investors.

CALLABLE   Some bond certificates state that the issuer can recall the bond before the maturity date, making them **callable bonds.** If borrowers wish to reserve the right to pay off bond debt before maturity, they issue callable bonds. The call or redemption feature usually includes an agreement to give the bondholder a month's notice of the intention to call them in. The issuer may agree to pay the owner somewhat more than the face value of the bond as compensation for the early recall, although the Government of Canada usually does not do so. Bonds are assumed to be non-callable unless indicated otherwise. With a call feature, the initiative remains with the issuer; bondholders do not have the option of redeeming a callable bond whenever they wish. Unless the bond is called by the issuer, investors wanting to sell a callable bond must find a buyer or wait until the maturity date. The example, "A Bond Redemption," illustrates the recall of a bond issue.

A BOND REDEMPTION

The paper of June 25, 1990 contained the announcement that, on July 25th, the Consolidated Group would be redeeming certain 10.5 percent sinking fund debentures due to mature on June 1, 1997. The company would pay a redemption price of 102.05 plus accrued interest. The announcement listed the serial numbers of all the debentures to be called. Bondholders were asked to redeem the bonds being called in at any branch of CIBC. After the redemption date no more interest would be paid on these bonds.

CONVERTIBLE   Bonds with a clause giving the holder the option of exchanging the security for a specified number of common shares of the company are called **convertible bonds**. The terms of the conversion are established when the bonds are issued, and do not change. This feature gives the holder of a debt security the possibility of capital gain. The investor would profit if, in the future, the price of the common stock should rise above the set conversion price. The option of converting to common stock may help support the price of a bond, which might otherwise drop. The terms of one series of convertible debentures are shown in the example, "Conversion Terms."

CONVERSION TERMS

A corporation issued convertible debentures with the following conversion terms:
"The conversion rate will be approximately 85.11 shares per $1 000 debenture. The right of conversion may be exercised at any time prior to the close of business on July 15, 1999."

> At this conversion rate, the bond holder would be getting common shares for about $11.75 each. If the common shares were trading above this price at the time of conversion, the bond holder would make a capital gain.

EXTENDIBLE   Sometimes bonds or debentures with short maturities carry an extendible feature that allows the bond holder to extend the maturity date, perhaps for ten years, at the same or a slightly higher interest rate.

RETRACTABLE   Long-term bonds that carry an option permitting the holder to shorten the maturity are called **retractable bonds**. This feature may attract investors willing to accept a slightly lower interest rate in exchange for this flexibility. An example of a debenture series with a retraction privilege is shown in Figure 10.3.

FLOATING RATE   **Floating interest rate** bonds were issued a few years ago in a period of rapidly changing interest rates. The interest rate on these bonds is periodically adjusted in relation to the Treasury Bill rate. With this feature, neither the lender nor the borrower is locked into a set interest rate. Whether the lender or the borrower benefits in the long run depends on which way interest rates move. The price of floating rate bonds fluctuates very little.

SINKING FUND PROVISION   Many debt securities carry a **sinking fund** provision, meaning that the issuer will be setting aside sums of money each year to provide for their redemption. These funds are held in trust by a trustee, usually a trust company, until needed. A sinking fund provision is useful to the corporation as a way of reducing debt, but not particularly helpful to the investor who may not want to have the bonds recalled before maturity. Note that the bond announcement in Figure 10.1 carries a sinking fund provision.

Buying and Selling Bonds

An investor who has a bond that will not mature for many years, but needs the cash now must find a buyer. Bonds are bought and sold on the **bond market** or over the counter, which is not a physical place but a communication system linking investment dealers and brokers. When an investor informs a broker that he or she has a bond to sell, this information is sent to other brokers who may have a client interested in buying that very bond. Alternatively, the investment dealer may purchase the bond from the investor. In the distribution of bonds, investment dealers may act as principals or as agents. They are said to act *as principals* when they buy bonds for resale to the public. When investment dealers act *as agents* they do not buy the bonds for their own account but attempt to link buyers and sellers.

FIGURE 10.3 ANNOUNCEMENT OF A RETRACTABLE DEBENTURE

This advertisement is not to be construed as a public offering in any province of Canada unless a prospectus relating thereto has been accepted for filing by a Securities Commission or similar authority in such province. The offering is made by prospectus only, copies of which may be obtained from the undersigned.

New Issue

UNION GAS
LIMITED

$75,000,000
$10\frac{5}{8}\%$ Debentures, 1986 Series
(unsecured)

To be dated February 26, 1986   To mature December 15, 2005

Multiple Retraction Privilege and Interest Rate Adjustment
The Debentures will be retractable at the option of the holder on December 15, 1995 and on December 15 each year thereafter at par plus accrued interest thereon to the date of retraction. Prior to each retraction date, Union Gas Limited may, at its option, increase the interest rate. Any increase in interest rate will be effective for a period of one year from such retraction date.

Price: 100

Nesbitt Thomson Bongard Inc.	Gordon Capital Corporation	Merrill Lynch Canada Inc.
Midland Doherty Limited	Dominion Securities Pitfield Limited	McLeod Young Weir Limited

February 1986

Commission is not charged on bonds, but instead the dealers add their profit to the buying or selling price; this difference is sometimes called the **spread**. The spread will be greater for bonds that are less frequently traded, or for small orders of bonds.

SPREAD IN BOND PRICES

Bond Quotation:

"Bell Canada 8.58 percent due 15 February 2002, bid 94.5, ask 95.5"

This $1 000 bond may be sold to a broker for $945 or purchased for $955. The spread between these two prices represents the broker's commission. The amount of the spread depends on both the trading activity in a particular bond and the size of the transaction. If a certain issue of bonds trades thinly, the broker may have more difficulty in finding a buyer or seller and thus may take a larger spread. Investors who place large bond orders are able to negotiate a smaller spread per bond than a small investor. Usually the minimum spread is about $10.

BOND PRICE FLUCTUATION   When a bond is issued, the interest rate is fixed for the entire term, which may be 10, 20, or more years. But economic conditions generally cause interest rates to change during that period. This creates a problem for anyone wishing to sell a bond paying 5 percent when rates on other, more recently issued debt securities are closer to 10 percent. To interest a purchaser, the seller will have to lower the price of the bond below par, or sell it **at a discount.** Likewise, if interest rates have fallen since this bond was issued, it can be sold for a price greater than par, or **at a premium.**

YIELD TO MATURITY   In the financial world, yield usually means the annual return from an investment expressed as a percentage of its market price. In the case of bonds, the time value of future interest and of principal payments are taken into account. Payments received in the near future are worth more to the investor than those received in the uncertain, distant future. A precise calculation of bond yield to maturity takes into account the present value of coupon payments and the present value of the principal repayment at maturity. Bond traders use a complex formula to make this calculation. The simple method used in the example below serves to show how the nominal interest rate and the potential capital gain or loss can influence the yield. The results using this method will be somewhat different from those found in bond yield quotations; here we have made no adjustment for the time value effect.

If a bond is held until maturity, the owner expects to receive the face value of the bond regardless of the price paid for it. However, if the bond is sold prior to maturity, there may be a capital gain or loss. Therefore, when buying a bond the investor takes into account the possibility of capital gain or loss, in addition to the amount of interest the bond will pay.

BOND PRICES AND YIELDS

Maria bought a 10.9 percent Royal Bank bond due January 15, 1999. After a few years she needed the money and decided to sell the bond. By then, interest rates were around 12 percent. When she asked a broker what price she might get for the bond, she was quoted 97.65. This meant a selling price of $976.50 for a bond which had originally cost her $1 000, or a capital loss of $23.50. Why would anyone buy such a bond paying a lower rate of interest than term deposits? The attraction is the approximately 11.35 percent yield to maturity; part of this yield is capital gain that is taxed at a lower rate than interest.

Bela bought an Alberta Energy bond at a purchase price of 95.80. The yield he would receive if held to maturity can be approximated by the following calculation.

Face value	$1 000.00
Amount paid	$958.00
Nominal interest rate	10.5 percent
Maturity date	30 June 1996
Time to maturity	5.5 years
Date of purchase	31 Dec. 1990

The average annual return from this bond, if held to maturity, consists of interest and capital gain.

Annual interest	$105.00
Capital gain over 5.5 years	$42.00
Average annual capital gain	$42.00/5.5 = $7.64
Total average annual return	$105.00 + 7.64 = $112.64
(*Add capital gain, deduct capital loss*)	

$$\text{Annual yield to maturity} = \frac{\text{ave. annual return} \times 100}{\text{purchase price}}$$

$$= \frac{112.64 \times 100}{958}$$

$$= 11.76$$

Why is Bela's yield to maturity higher than Maria's?

ACCRUED INTEREST Bond interest is paid on fixed dates, usually every six months from the date of issue. This presents problems for buyers and sellers of bonds who may transfer ownership at any time. Whoever owns the bond on the interest payment date will receive six months' interest, but perhaps this person has held the bond for only two months. The seller should not lose four months' interest because the bond was sold to someone else. The solution is to charge the buyer **accrued interest,** which is the amount owing but not yet paid. Bonds, therefore, are sold at a certain price plus accrued interest. The buyer pays the seller for the interest due to date, and recovers this in the next interest payment. The example, "Accrued Interest," clarifies this process.

ACCRUED INTEREST

Bond denomination	$1 000
Interest rate	10.5 percent
Interest payment dates	March 15, September 15
Sale date	June 15

George sold a bond at par to Elizabeth on June 15. The previous interest payment had been on March 15 and there would not be another until September 15. At the time of the sale, three months' interest was due to George, so Elizabeth paid him 1 000 × .105 × 3/12 = $26.25. In September when the next interest payment is sent to bondholders, Elizabeth will receive six months' interest or $52.50. Thus, the system of paying the seller for accrued interest adjusts for the inflexibility of bond interest payments.

BOND QUOTATIONS Financial papers do not provide as much information about bond quotations as they do about stock prices because of the difficulty in collecting the information; bond trades are not concentrated on a few exchanges as are stock transactions. Bond quotations may be found in *The Financial Post* or the *Globe and Mail's Report on Business* (on Mondays). In these quotations, bond prices are given in hundreds and bonds of the same issuer are distinguished by the interest rate and the maturity date. Thus we speak of the "10 percent Canadas of 1 May 02," meaning that this issue of Government of Canada bonds carried an interest rate of 10 percent and will mature on May 1, 2002. The quotation will also give a recent price at which these bonds traded, and the yield to maturity (Table 10.2).

TABLE 10.2 BOND QUOTATIONS, JULY 1993

Issuer	Maturity	Coupon	Quote	Yield
Canada	1 Dec 21	4.25	98.50	4.34
Canada	1 Oct 06	14.00	150.80	7.78
Nova Scotia	1 Mar 98	9.88	110.70	7.13
Montreal Urban	15 Dec 98	10.38	113.50	7.32
Imperial Oil	15 Dec 99	9.88	113.00	7.30
3-month T-Bills				4.38

Stripped Bonds

Stripped bonds are another way of investing in debt securities. Investment dealers buy large denomination bonds, issued by federal or provincial governments or Crown corporations, and strip off the coupons. Long-term bonds with maturities of at least 20 years are usually selected for coupon stripping. With a **stripped bond** the interest has been separated from the principal (bond residue) and each is sold separately. Each coupon, with a fixed payment date, becomes a little bond that may be sold at a discount price dependent on the prevailing interest rates. For example, in 1990 $4 079 would have bought a stripped bond maturing at $10 000 in 1998. No payments would be paid until maturity when the investor will receive $10 000 that includes interest of $5 921.

Dealers usually pool the stripped bond funds and give a deposit receipt or certificate. These go by a variety of names depending on who issues them, such as TIGRs (term investment growth receipts), Cougars, and Sentinels. In the latter case, the investor has a share in a pool of coupons or residuals that are held in trust. These certificates are registered in the name of the investor, who may sell them at any time on the secondary market. The sale price, which changes with general interest rates, will generally fluctuate more than bond prices. The purchase price of stripped bonds reflects current interest rates and the time value of money, or the time the investor has to wait to receive the yield. The market offers investors discounted coupons that mature every six months.

A STRIPPED BOND HELD TO MATURITY

In the newspaper, Adrian saw an offering of stripped bonds maturing in five years with an asking price of $560 per $1 000 face value. He knew that because the bonds had been stripped of their coupons, there would

be no semi-annual interest payments. Instead, he would receive $1 000 in five years' time. Adrian's yield will be $440 on an investment of $560, which works out to about 10.25 percent per annum. This was slightly higher than current rates for some other five-year debt securities.

Taxation of Bond Yield

Bond yield is composed of interest income and the possibility of capital gain or loss if they are traded before maturity. Interest and capital gain are taxed differently. Interest is added to taxable income and taxed accordingly, while net capital gain (capital gain less any capital loss) is exempt from tax to a maximum of $100 000 over a lifetime. The tax treatment of capital gains has become most complex and will not be explained here. Books on income tax may be consulted for details.

The differential tax treatment of interest and capital gain provides an incentive for some investors to prefer their bond return in the form of capital gain rather than in interest. The yield from stripped bonds is considered by Revenue Canada Taxation to be interest, not capital gain, and for this reason they are often selected for self-administered RRSP accounts where the return is tax-sheltered. If these bonds are not in a tax shelter, accrued interest must be reported annually, even if it is not received.

WHAT HAS HAPPENED TO OUR INCOME?

Jan and Paul are worried about their falling income. Interest rates in 1993 are the lowest they have been in twenty years and about one-third of their retirement income comes from interest-bearing securities. When they retired in 1981, these investments were paying around 18 percent. Although rates have gradually fallen since then, the rapid drop in 1992-3 has been most upsetting. Will they have enough to live on?

The financial advisor they consulted suggested that Jan and Paul look at real interest rates, not only nominal rates. She made a graph to show what has been happening since their retirement (Figure 10.4). First she plotted the nominal interest rate, using the three-month Treasury Bill rate. Next, she assumed a combined federal and provincial marginal tax rate of 40 percent and took 60 percent of the nominal interest rate to obtain the after-tax rate of return. Finally, the real after-tax rate of return was calculated by subtracting the annual change in the Consumer Price Index. This shows how much yield the couple was receiving after adjusting for income tax and inflation. They were surprised to find that they were getting a negative real after-tax return in 1981. They did remember one compensating factor, which was that the first $1000 of interest income had been exempted from income tax before 1987.

We will assume that Jan and Paul had capital of $200 000 in 1981, all invested in interest-bearing securities. At 18 percent return, they had an income of $36 000 a year from these investments. Did they notice the 12.5 percent inflation rate in 1981 and did they realize that their capital had lost 12.5 percent in purchasing power that year? Although in 1982 they still had a nominal investment of $200 000, the purchasing power of that sum had been reduced by $25 000 to

FIGURE 10.4 NOMINAL INTEREST RATES, AFTER-TAX RATES, AND REAL AFTER-TAX RATES, CANADA, 1981–1993

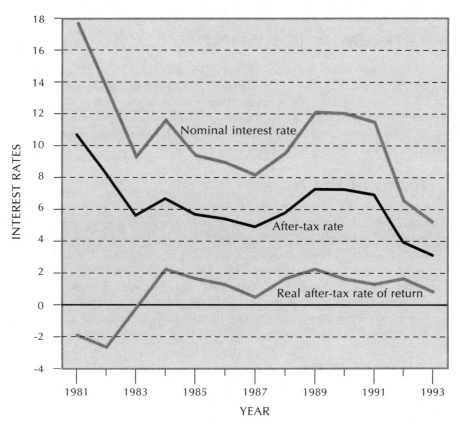

$175 000. Each successive year their capital was eroded by inflation so that by 1993 it had a purchasing power of only $115 246. As compensation for this loss, they were receiving high interest rates. They had two choices: (i) they could spend all the interest income and let the capital erode in value, or (ii) they could spend about two percent of the interest and re-invest the balance. In other words, if this couple wanted to preserve the value of their capital, they should have reinvested some of their income. What they were doing was living partially on their capital. Now, with very low inflation, their capital will lose less value each year.

Immediate alternatives for Jan and Paul are: (i) accept a little more risk and invest some of their funds in preferred shares that have beneficial tax treatment, or (ii) reduce expenses to make them more in line with their real after-tax income.

CANADA SAVINGS BONDS

Although they are called bonds, Canada Savings Bonds (CSBs) are more like savings certificates and do not have many of the attributes of bonds or debentures. Since they cannot be traded but only redeemed, their value does not fluctuate. Canada Savings Bonds, developed from the Victory bonds which were so successful in raising funds for the war effort between 1940 and 1944, have become a significant part of federal government borrowing for the past 50 years.

Terms of the Issues

Once each year in November (and often for a limited time), a new issue goes on sale and is available only to Canadian residents. In addition, there are restrictions on the amount an individual may purchase in any one year. Issues may be bought at the face value in denominations of $100, $300, $500, $1 000, $5 000, and $10 000 from banks, trust companies, credit unions, and investment dealers. No commission is paid by the buyer at the time of either purchase or redemption. Although the bonds are not transferable, except in the case of death, the government will redeem them at face value on any business day. Consequently, CSBs are not only very low risk, but also very liquid investments.

Types of CSBs

Bonds issued since 1977 carry no coupons, are fully registered, and are available in two forms: (i) regular interest bonds, and (ii) compound interest bonds. Interest is mailed each November to holders of regular interest bonds, and left to compound until maturity or redemption on compound interest bonds.

Interest

CSB issues have no coupons or any guaranteed rate for the whole term. Instead, each autumn the federal government announces the interest rate to be paid for the coming year on both the new and all outstanding issues. The rate on CSBs, previously slightly higher than on savings accounts, has been lowered in recent years to encourage Canadians to invest in other securities. Nevertheless CSBs are popular because of their safety and high liquidity.

Income Tax

Before 1991, holders of compound interest bonds were allowed to choose whether to report interest: (i) as received, on a cash basis, or (ii) as earned, on a receivable basis. Revisions to the Income Tax Act require that interest on bonds purchased since 1990 be reported annually, whether or not it has been received.

Savings Bonds Versus Other Bonds

In spite of their name, Canada Savings Bonds lack many of the attributes of bonds. Instead, think of them as a type of savings certificate. Unique features of CSBs are listed below.

1. **Sale** They are sold directly to investors, are not traded on the bond market, are not transferable, and carry no commission charges.
2. **Eligibility** Distribution is limited to Canadian residents.
3. **Redemption** Face value is available on any business day.
4. **Denominations** They are available in smaller denominations than other bonds.
5. **Types** There are two types: regular interest bonds (interest mailed annually), and compound interest bonds (interest paid at redemption or maturity).
6. **Annual interest** Interest is paid each November on regular interest CSBs.

CSBS OR PREFERRED SHARES?

It is November and you have $5 000 to invest. Should you buy some of the current issue of Canada Savings Bonds, which carry a 5 percent rate for the first year, or put your money into preferred shares of B.C. Telephone with a return of 7.5 percent? To answer the question, the following assumptions are made: your combined federal and provincial marginal tax rate is 44 percent, and the income tax on share dividends is reduced by the tax dividend credit (explained in Chapter 11).

Annual return on the CSBs:
$5 000 × .05   = $250 before tax
$250 × .44   = $110 income tax
$250 – 110   = $140, or an after-tax yield of 2.8 percent

Annual return on the preferred shares:
$5 000 × .075   = $375 before tax
Income tax   = $66.47 (see Chapter 11 for method)
$375 – 66.47   = $308.53, or an after-tax yield of 6.2 percent

Thus, preferential tax treatment of dividends from Canadian corporations results in a higher after-tax rate of return for the preferred shares than for the CSBs. Investment decisions require other considerations but this example illustrates the importance of comparing yields on an after-tax basis.

Summary

Debt securities represent not only a very large share of the financial transactions in the country, but also a significant portion of the portfolios of individual investors. As a lender of funds, the investor does not acquire either the opportunity to influence management decisions or the potential for gain that is possible with equities. On the other hand, there is generally less risk with debt securities, which are considered senior to equity in the case of company failure. Deposits, money market instruments, Canada Savings Bonds, mortgage-back securities, and bonds and debentures promise regular interest payments and the return of the principal at some specified time. Capital gain or loss is a possibility with bonds and debentures if traded prior to maturity, but is not the case with the other debt securities discussed in this chapter.

Canada Savings Bonds are very secure, liquid investments. They have more attributes of savings certificates than they do of bonds because they do not trade on the bond market, are redeemable at par at any time, do not carry an interest rate fixed for the term, are available in small denominations, and are sold only to Canadian residents.

Vocabulary Review

accrued interest (p. 310)

at a discount (p. 308)

at a premium (p. 308)

bearer bond (p. 301)

fully registered bond (p. 303)

floating interest rate bond (p. 306)

money market (p. 304)

money market fund (p. 297)

bond (p. 298)

bond market (p. 306)

bond redemption (p. 301)

bond registered as to principal (p. 301)

callable bond (p. 304)

collateral trust bond (p. 304)

commercial paper (p. 295)

convertible bond (p. 305)

coupon bond (p. 301)

debenture (p. 298)

denomination (p. 301)

mortgage bond (p. 304)

mortgage-backed security (p. 298)

par value (p. 299)

retractable bond (p. 306)

sinking fund (p. 306)

spread (p. 308)

stripped bond (p. 311)

term deposit (p. 293)

Treasury Bill (p. 295)

underwriter (p. 299)

Problems

1. On July 10, 1993, the *Report on Business* of *The Globe and Mail* reported the following information about interest rates:

   CANADIAN ADMINISTERED RATES

Bank of Canada	4.73 percent
Prime	5.75 percent

   MONEY MARKET RATES

   (for transactions of $1-million or more)

Three-month Treasury Bills	4.38 percent
30-day commercial paper	4.52 percent
60-day commercial paper	4.56 percent
90-day commercial paper	4.62 percent

   (a) Look in the financial section of a recent paper to find current interest rates, and update the above table.

   (b) Why is the bank rate lower than the prime rate?

   (c) Why is the rate higher on commercial paper than on Treasury Bills?

   (d) Do the interest rates on commercial paper increase as the term increases? If not, why so?

   (e) What is commercial paper and who would buy and sell it?

   (f) If you had $5 000 to invest in the money market, would the interest rate quoted be the same as those above? Explain.

   (g) How would you go about investing the $5 000 in the money market?

2. Try to find a newspaper advertisement announcing a new bond issue. (These are usually found in the financial section, but occur irregularly.) Otherwise, analyze the announcement in Figure 10.1.

Look for the following information in the advertisement:

(a) Name of the bond issuer,

(b) Names of the underwriters,

(c) Offering price,

(d) Maturity date,

(e) Interest rate,

(f) Special features, eg, callable, retractable, extendible, convertible.

(g) Denominations available,

(h) Size of the issue (amount to be borrowed).

3. Examine these two bond quotations:

Issuer	Maturity	Coupon	Quote	Yield
Imasco	28 Apr 98	10.50	112.50	7.36
Canada	15 Mar 98	3.75	90.25	6.18

(a) Are these bonds selling at par, at a discount or at a premium? Suggest reasons why.

(b) What is the probable minimum denomination available in these bonds?

(c) Calculate the yield to maturity if purchased in 1994 at the quoted price on June 15 and July 11, respectively. How does your result compare with the published yield?

(d) Suggest reasons why the Canada bond has a lower yield to maturity than the Imasco bond.

4. Assume that you bought a 12 percent Canadian Utilities $1 000 debenture, maturing 15 October 2007, on March 15, 1995.

(a) How much accrued interest would you have paid?

(b) Will you get this interest back? If so, when?

(c) Why did you have to pay accrued interest?

(d) If you could buy this debenture at a price $122.63, how much capital loss would you suffer at maturity?

5. The following questions refer to Figure 10.5.

(a) How do dealers distinguish among the various issues of Canada bonds, only a few of which are listed here?

(b) Why is there one Ontario bond quoted at 97.63 and another at 113.85?

(c) Suggest two reasons for such a wide range of coupon interest rates on the bonds. (In June 1993 the bank prime rate was about 5.75 percent.)

(d) Are some of these bonds really debentures? If so, which ones?

(e) In this list of bonds there seem to be more bonds selling at a discount than there are at a premium. Can you suggest any reasons why this is the case?

FIGURE 10.5 EXCERPTS FROM BOND QUOTATIONS, JUNE 1993

Issuer	Maturity	Coupon	Quote	Yield
Canadas				
Canada	15 Oct 99	9.00	107.60	7.47
Canada	1 Dec 99	9.25	109.00	7.47
Canada	1 Dec 99	13.50	129.05	7.73
Canada	15 Mar 00	13.75	130.75	7.82
Canada	1 May 00	9.75	111.10	7.65
Canada	1 Jul 00	10.50	114.90	7.72
Cahada	1 Jul 00	15.00	137.85	7.91
Canada	1 Sep 00	11.50	120.30	7.78
Canada	15 Dec 00	9.75	111.35	7.73
Canada	1 Feb 01	15.75	143.95	7.97
Canada	1 Mar 01	10.50	115.15	7.85
Canada	1 May 01	13.00	129.10	7.97
Canada	1 Jun 01	9.75	111.30	7.82
Canada	1 Oct 01	9.50	109.80	7.87
Canada	1 Dec 01	9.75	111.80	7.82
Canada	1 Feb 02	8.75	105.60	7.84
Canada	15 Mar 02	15.50	146.65	8.00
Canada	1 Apr 02	8.50	104.95	7.71
Canada	1 May 02	10.00	113.50	7.86
Canada	15 Dec 02	11.25	121.95	7.92
Municipals				
Dartmouth HS	15 Feb 99	13.00	117.13	9.08
Guelph	30 Oct 93	12.38	102.50	5.97
Halton Reg	6 Dec 05	12.13	122.75	9.05
M.F.A. of BC	30 Jul 97	10.00	108.50	7.57
M.F.A. of BC	27 Oct 98	10.88	112.75	7.92
M.F.A. of BC	5 Dec 04	13.00	121.63	9.82
Montreal Urb	15 Dec 98	10.38	109.50	8.20
Peel Region	30 Oct 01	9.88	107.88	8.54
Toronto	15 May 95	11.50	107.88	7.09
Toronto	15 Dec 97	10.38	109.50	7.84
Toronto	20 Mar 01	10.25	109.38	8.57
York Region	8 Jan 01	11.38	114.88	8.66
Provincials				
Ont Hydro	15 Oct 21	10.13	110.70	9.07
Ont Hydro	18 Aug 22	8.90	98.00	9.09
Ontario	1 May 96	10.75	109.05	7.24
Ontario	16 Apr 97	8.75	104.13	7.50
Ontario	27 Aug 98	10.20	110.30	7.76
Ontario	10 Jan 01	10.88	113.85	8.37
Ontario	12 Dec 01	10.50	112.45	8.42
Ontario	11 Mar 03	8.00	97.63	8.36
Ontario	22 Apr 03	8.75	102.25	8.41
Ontario	13 Jul 22	9.50	104.38	9.07
P.E.I.	15 Dec 93	12.00	103.13	5.92
P.E.I.	26 Nov 97	11.38	112.30	8.05
P.E.I.	30 Apr 02	9.75	105.38	8.86
P.E.I.	4 Jul 02	9.75	104.13	8.83
P.E.I.	12 Dec 04	12.75	122.50	9.50
P.E.I.	3 Apr 06	10.63	109.50	9.34
P.E.I.	15 Jan 07	9.88	103.00	9.35
P.E.I.	22 Jun 08	11.38	116.25	9.34
P.E.I.	1 Dec 08	10.75	111.35	9.35
Que (Hydro)	30 Sep 93	12.50	102.13	5.66
Que (Hydro)	16 Aug 94	14.25	108.63	6.64
Que (Hydro)	15 Oct 94	13.00	108.13	6.65
Que (Hydro)	25 Sep 95	10.75	107.65	7.09
Que (Hydro)	16 Sep 96	17.50	127.75	7.75
Que (Hydro)	2 Dec 96	9.25	105.45	7.45
Que (Hydro)	1 Jun 97	10.00	100.38	9.88
Que (Hydro)	16 Jul 97	9.75	107.35	7.63
Que (Hydro)	1 Feb 99	10.75	112.25	8.05
Que (Hydro)	6 Feb 00	9.75	104.40	8.86
Que (Hydro)	10 Oct 00	11.25	115.65	8.35

Issuer	Maturity	Coupon	Quote	Yield
Utilities				
Bell Canada	15 Oct 11	11.00	113.75	9.41
Bell Canada	15 Feb 15	10.55	110.38	9.42
Bell Canada	15 Dec 32	9.70	106.13	9.12
Cdn Util	1 Jun 94	13.10	106.13	6.62
Cdn Util	15 Jul 00	12.00	110.00	10.01
Cdn Util	1 Oct 06	9.85	105.00	9.19
Cdn Util	12 Dec 06	10.25	107.75	9.23
Cdn Util	15 Oct 07	12.00	118.63	9.58
Cdn Util	30 Nov 09	10.20	110.38	8.98
Cdn Util	15 Aug 10	11.40	119.88	9.09
Cdn Util	30 Nov 20	11.77	126.00	9.17
Cmrs Gas Co	1 May 99	10.45	104.50	9.43
Cmrs Gas Co	15 Jul 05	10.88	109.63	9.52
Cmrs Gas Co	1 Jun 06	9.88	105.63	9.13
Gaz Metro	1 Dec 97	11.25	111.50	8.14
Gaz Metro	15 Nov 05	11.75	120.00	9.04
Gaz Metro	15 Dec 06	10.75	114.00	8.94
Gaz Metro	31 Oct 16	10.45	110.25	9.36
I.P.L.	1 May 96	10.13	100.55	9.90
I.P.L.	15 Dec 06	10.00	106.45	9.16
I.P.L.	15 Apr 08	10.80	110.80	9.43
I.P.L. NW	1 Apr 04	13.40	120.75	10.19
I.P.L. NW	15 Nov 04	12.70	119.13	9.87
Maritime T&T	15 Jun 99	10.38	104.75	9.33
Maritime T&T	1 Aug 06	10.25	107.25	9.28
Maritime T&T	1 Mar 13	10.45	109.00	9.43
Nfld Tel	6 May 06	9.75	103.13	9.33
Nfld Tel	5 Jul 10	11.40	116.00	9.49
Nfld Tel	12 Jun 14	10.75	112.63	9.36
Nova Corp	15 Jul 93	12.13	100.75	5.22
Nova Corp	1 Dec 94	10.95	105.13	7.26
Nova Corp	14 Apr 99	10.75	109.13	8.72
Corporations				
Bank NS Prop	3 Feb 97	9.38	104.00	8.09
Bank Of NS	19 Jul 01	10.35	109.88	8.63
C.I.L.	15 Dec 93	12.38	103.50	5.57
Cad Fairview	1 Nov 94	10.00	101.00	9.21
Cdn Oil Debc	31 Oct 00	11.00	101.60	10.68
CIBC	15 Oct 96	9.50	101.00	9.14
CIBC	15 Feb 98	9.25	101.50	8.85
CIBC	1 Dec 00	12.45	120.25	8.71
CNR	15 Nov 04	13.00	106.90	11.88
CNR	1 May 05	12.25	106.50	11.24
Four Seasons	25 Mar 96	11.05	98.63	11.62
Imasco	15 Feb 96	11.85	109.88	7.72
Imasco	20 Nov 96	10.50	108.50	7.65
Imasco	28 Apr 98	10.50	109.63	8.08
Imasco	18 Dec 01	10.25	109.38	8.67
Imperial Oil	15 Dec 99	9.88	109.13	8.05
Markbor Wood	15 Jan 97	10.45	102.25	9.69
Novacrp Rlty	31 Dec 97	11.25	108.00	9.07
Provigo	15 Mar 01	11.25	107.88	9.77
Royal Bank	1 Jun 98	10.80	110.88	8.11
Royal Bank	15 Jan 99	10.90	111.88	8.21
Royal Bank	14 Oct 99	10.20	109.25	8.30
Royal Bank	31 Jan 01	11.75	116.88	8.68
Royal Bank	15 Aug 01	10.75	112.25	8.63
Royal Bank	11 Jan 02	11.00	114.13	8.64
Royal Bank	1 Mar 02	10.50	111.50	8.60
Suncor	1 Jun 03	12.00	113.50	9.85
TD Centre	12 May 98	10.70	110.50	8.08
TD Centre	22 Nov 99	10.35	109.13	8.23
TD Centre	15 Sep 03	13.15	111.00	11.31
Thomson Corp	2 Dec 98	9.15	105.00	8.01
Thomson Corp	10 May 01	10.55	111.25	8.56
Tor Eaton C	1 Feb 00	9.50	97.25	10.07
Wardair Fin	31 Oct 99	11.20	99.88	11.22

6. Decide whether you AGREE or DISAGREE with each of the following statements:

   (a) Bonds are a form of equity security.

   (b) Bond prices vary inversely with changes in general interest rates.

   (c) All coupon bonds are bearer bonds.

   (d) Fully registered bonds have no coupons.

   (e) Both Canada Savings Bonds and Government of Canada bonds trade on the bond market.

   (f) The price of a bond quoted at 93.5/8 is always $1 000, but the face value can vary.

   (g) All bond interest is exempt from income tax.

   (h) Most bonds pay interest annually.

   (i) As a bondholder, you have no promise from the issuer of the bond regarding payment of interest or repayment of the principal.

7. Explain why you have to pay more than the face value if you buy a Canada Savings Bond by payroll deduction. Is this extra sum called interest? Can it be used as an income tax deduction?

8. Assume that you decide to redeem three $1 000 Canada Savings Bonds on March 1. You will receive the face value and accrued interest. These bonds are paying five percent interest at the moment. Calculate the amount of accrued interest you will receive.

9. Look at bond quotations in a recent newspaper.

   (a) How do bond yields compare with the current rate on Treasury Bills?

   (b) Are most bonds selling at a discount or a premium? Why?

10. In 1991, Kase invested $5 000 in a compound series of Canada Savings Bonds. For income tax purposes, should he report interest on the receivable basis?

11. How might a high marginal tax rate affect a decision to buy a discounted bond?

12. Why would anyone buy a bond selling at a premium when there would be a capital loss if held to maturity?

13. Why would anyone want to buy stripped bonds instead of regular bonds?

References

BOOKS

ANDERSON, HUGH. *Money for Rent: A Guide to Earning Top Interest on Your Savings* Markham, Ontario: Penguin Books, 1991, 170 pp. A comprehensive guide to investment, tax, legal, and accounting information.

BEACH, WAYNE and LYLE R. HEPBURN. *Are You Paying Too Much Tax?* Toronto: McGraw-Hill Ryerson, annual, 206 pp. A tax planning guide for the general reader that includes a discussion of capital gains, RRSPs, and investment income.

BIRCH, RICHARD. *The Family Financial Planning Book, A Step-by-Step Moneyguide for Canadian Families*. Revised Edition. Toronto: Key Porter, 1989, 216 pp. An easy-to-read guide to taking control of your personal finances that discusses budgets, income tax, insurance, RRSPs, mortgages, and investments.

BUDD, JOHN, CLAUDE RINFRET, RICHARD DAW and DANIELLE BRIEN. *Canadian Guide to Personal Financial Management*. Scarborough, Ontario: Prentice-Hall Canada, annual, 225 pp. Accountants provide guidance on a broad range of topics, including planning finances, estimating insurance needs, managing risk, and determining investment needs. Instructions and the necessary forms for making plans are provided.

CANADIAN SECURITIES INSTITUTE. *How to Invest in Canadian Securities*. Third Edition. Toronto: Canadian Securities Institute, 1984, 251 pp. Provides detailed explanations of various types of bonds and stocks.

COSTELLO, BRIAN. *Your Money and How to Keep It*. Fifth Edition. Toronto: Stoddart, 1990, 248 pp. Particular emphasis on investments and income tax.

CÔTÉ, JEAN-MARC and DONALD DAY. *Personal Financial Planning in Canada*. Toronto: Allyn and Bacon, 1987, 464 pp. A comprehensive personal finance text that includes financial planning, income tax, annuities, pensions, investments, credit, mortgages, and wills with particular attention paid to the banking and insurance industries.

DRACHE, ARTHUR B. C. and SUSAN WEIDMAN SCHNEIDER. *Head and Heart, Financial Strategies for Smart Women*. Toronto: Macmillan, 1987, 348 pp. Recognizing the needs and perspectives of women, a tax lawyer and journalist have collaborated to present basic financial information, taking into account women's concerns at different stages in their lives.

FRIEDLAND, SEYMOUR and STEVEN G. KELMAN. *Investment Strategies, How to Create Your Own and Make it Work for You*. Markham, Ontario: Penguin Canada, 1991, 168 pp. Offers guidance for the general reader in defining objectives and establishing an investment program.

HATCH, JAMES E. and MICHAEL J. ROBINSON. *Investment Management in Canada*. Toronto: Prentice-Hall Canada, 1988, 836 pp. A technical university text with in-depth coverage of many aspects of investing.

HOGG, R. D. *Preparing Your Income Tax Returns*. Toronto: CCH Canadian, annual, 589 pp. A complete and technical guide to income tax preparation.

HUNTER, W. T. *Canadian Financial Markets*. Third Edition. Peterborough, Ontario: Broadview Press, 1991, 193 pp. An economist gives an overview of the workings of the bond market, the mortgage market, and the stock market.

MACINNIS, LYMAN. *Get Smart! Make Your Money Count in the 1990s*. Second Edition. Scarborough, Ontario: Prentice-Hall Canada, 1989, 317 pp. A book for the general reader that includes financial planning and income tax principles, but gives major attention to investing in the stock market.

MOTHERWELL, CATHRYN. *Smart Money, Investing for Women*. Toronto: Key Porter, 1989, 192 pp. A financial journalist explains how to get started investing, how to evaluate the products and how to build a portfolio.

PAPE, GORDON. *Building Wealth in the '90s*. Scarborough, Ontario: Prentice-Hall Canada, 1992, 294 pp. An easy-to-read guide for the novice financial manager and investor that considers interest rates, credit cards, mortgages, RRSPs, mutual funds, and the stock market.

PAPE, GORDON. *Low-Risk Investing*. Scarborough, Ontario: Prentice-Hall Canada, 1989, 244 pp. A book written to encourage the novice investor to get started on saving and investing. Outlines the basics of investing in debt and equity investments.

SPITZ, WILLIAM T. *Get Rich Slowly, Building Your Financial Future Through Common Sense*. New York: Macmillan, 1992, 271 pp. The thesis of this book is that the investor who takes control of personal finances, is one who has clear goals, selects risk carefully, and accepts that slow but steady gains can increase wealth.

WYATT, ELAINE. *The Money Companion, How to Manage Your Money and Achieve Financial Freedom*. Markham, Ontario: Penguin Books, 1991, 203 pp. A guide to personal financial management that focuses on planning, investment strategy, and retirement needs.

ZIMMER, HENRY B. and JEANNE V. KAUFMAN. *Your Investment Strategies for the 1990s*. Toronto: Collins, 1988, 249 pp. The authors, with backgrounds in accounting and taxation, discuss financial planning and a wide range of investment possibilities, including RRSPs, insurance, real estate, stocks, mutual funds, and metals.

PERIODICALS

Canadian Money Saver. Monthly. Canadian Money Saver Inc., Box 370, Bath, Ontario, K0H 1G0. Includes short articles on a range of personal finance topics, with special emphasis on investments.

Financial Times. Weekly. Suite 500, 920 Yonge Street, Toronto, Ontario, M2W 3L5. Provides current information on a range of business and economic topics.

Report on Business. *Daily*. A section of *The Globe and Mail*. Important source of information on the financial markets.

The Financial Post. Daily and weekly. The Financial Post Company, 777 Bay Street, Toronto, Ontario, M5G 2E4. Up-to-date information on business, economics, income tax, and investments.

The Financial Post Magazine. Monthly. The Financial Post Company, 777 Bay Street, Toronto, Ontario, M5G 2E4. Includes a section on personal finance.

CHAPTER ELEVEN

Stocks and Mutual Funds

OBJECTIVES

1. To evaluate advantages and disadvantages of investing in the stock market.

2. To distinguish between floor trading and electronic stock trading.

3. To interpret a stock quotation.

4. To compare long-term and short-term trends in stock prices.

5. To identify characteristics that differentiate common from preferred shares.

6. To explain the limited liability of a stockholder.

7. To distinguish between

   (a) stock exchange and stock exchange index,

   (b) board and odd lots,

   (c) market and stop loss orders,

   (d) full-service and discount brokers,

   (e) bid and ask prices,

   (f) rights and warrants,

   (g) cumulative and non-cumulative preferred shares,

   (h) redeemable and retractable preferred shares,

   (i) stock split and stock dividend,

   (j) open-end and closed-end investment funds,

   (k) acquisition and redemption fees,

   (l) sales and management fees,

   (m) expense ratio and variability rating of mutual funds.

8. To explain how objectives and portfolios differ among equity, debt, and balanced mutual funds.

9. To explain how information on mutual fund performance is relevant to choosing or monitoring the investment.

10. To identify advantages and disadvantages of investing in mutual funds.

11. To identify the kinds of risks associated with different types of investments.

12. To explain how diversification reduces the risk in a portfolio.

13. To outline the different income taxation of interest, dividends, and capital gain.

Introduction

This chapter is an introduction to the complexities of investing in the stock market. The intent is to explain how stocks are bought and sold, and to indicate the distinguishing characteristics of common shares, preferred shares, and mutual funds. Studying this chapter should make it easier to understand articles on equity investing found in the financial papers and other literature, since many assume readers understand essential terminology and know how the stock market functions. An important topic for further study, not addressed in this book, is how to evaluate the quality of stocks. You are encouraged to research this topic independently.

INVESTING IN THE STOCK MARKET

Before investing in the stock market, it is generally prudent to have funds set aside in debt securities for emergencies, liquidity needs, and short-term goals. It is also important to recognize that, while stocks offer potential for greater gain than do debt securities, there is a trade-off between return and safety, as explained in Chapter 9. Although shareholders are promised neither the return of their capital nor any income from their investments, the stock market does encompass a sufficiently broad spectrum of stocks ranging from quite low-risk, preferred stocks to very high-risk, speculative stocks so that even very conservative investors can find appropriate choices.

Comparative Returns

Over the long term, stocks have proven a better hedge against inflation than have debt securities. For instance, between 1975 and 1992, when consumer prices increased an average of 6.7 percent a year, Treasury Bills paid 10.4 percent interest on average. This 3.7 percent real rate of return, less income tax, did not leave a great deal for the investor. During the same period, stocks in the Toronto Stock Exchange Composite Index produced an average annual return of 15.7 percent, an annual real return of nine percent. Since income from stocks is taxed at a lower rate than is interest (as will be explained later), the after-tax return on stocks was quite attractive. This higher return was, however, associated with more risk and price volatility. The greater variability in the yield from common stocks compared to that from Treasury Bills is illustrated in Figure 9.7 in Chapter 9.

Price Volatility

Even though stocks have been more profitable over the long term than have been debt securities, their price fluctuations can be a drawback. Stock prices are affected by business cycles that may last four years or more. During a business cycle, business activity tends to expand and then contract, causing stock prices to move up and then down. It is normal for stock prices to fluctuate, but the result can be low liquidity for the investor who cannot be sure of selling without a loss on any given day. Those who are investors as opposed to speculators, however, look upon stocks as relatively long-term investments and choose carefully the times to buy and sell.

Need For Knowledge

To become a successful investor in the stock market one needs to be reasonably well-informed. Two common problems arise because of a lack of understanding of price volatility and of the breadth of choice within the stock market. Inexperienced investors may become pessimistic when stock prices are low and be reluctant to invest in the market. Rising prices leads to optimism, however, and by the time the market has reached a high level, these people decide to buy. Later, when stock prices invariably fall, they panic and sell, vowing never again to invest in the market. Unfortunately, they cannot make money by buying high and selling low. Also, they have made the mistake of thinking of stocks as short-term investments. Another difficulty arises for those with limited knowledge of investment alternatives. They may feel their choices are restricted either to depositing their funds in safe, low-yielding debt securities or to speculating in the stock market. They do not realize that there are many intermediate possibilities.

STOCK TRADING

Stock Exchange

A **stock exchange** is an organized marketplace for buying and selling shares in corporations. Businesses that require working capital can obtain it by selling shares to investors who become part owners of the corporation. These companies are known as publicly-owned corporations. A new offering of shares may be put on the market at the start of a new business or whenever the company requires additional capital. Once the new offering has been sold, the shares usually trade in the secondary market where they change owners frequently. Investors, however, cannot sell their shares back to the corporation whenever they wish. For instance, an owner of Canadian Pacific shares who no longer wishes to keep them must find a buyer. It is the function of stockbrokers and stock exchanges to link buyers and sellers of securities, and to facilitate transactions between them.

Stocks may be traded at stock exchanges or on the **over the counter market,** which is not a place but a communication system. Generally, stocks that do not meet the listing requirements for a major stock exchange (referred to as unlisted stocks) are traded on the over the counter market. On the stock exchange, only members can execute orders for clients. Each member of an exchange has purchased one of the limited number of seats or member trading permits entitling them to trade listed securities on that exchange. A firm of investment dealers, wishing to trade on a certain stock exchange, must either purchase one of these seats or work through a dealer who has one.

With the advent of computer technologies, there has been a move towards electronic selling through a communication system rather than by the physical presence of representatives of buyers and sellers on the floor of an exchange. The Vancouver and Montreal Stock Exchanges have already converted to computerized trading, the Toronto Stock Exchange is in the process of doing so, while the New York Stock Exchange still prefers traditional floor trading. If the exchange is computerized, the order to buy shares is handled by traders in offices who can see bids and ask quotations on their computer screens, then execute a trade with the touch of a button.

Whether a trade is executed on the floor of an exchange or electronically, information about the transaction is transmitted immediately to the stock exchange's computer, becoming widely available across the nation and the world. Details of the trade are quickly sent to the broker, who in turn can inform the client of the results. All this activity may be accomplished within very few minutes. After an order has been executed, the client has five business days to pay for the shares.

MAKING A STOCK TRADE

When Anya decided to buy 100 shares of Bank of Montreal she telephoned her stockbroker. He sent her order directly to the trading department at his investment dealer's head office, where it was passed to their agent at the stock exchange. At the exchange, which was using floor trading, the order went to the firm's floor trader, who moved to the post where Bank of Montreal stock is traded to look at posted recent prices. When the floor trader called out that he wanted to buy 100 shares of Bank of Montreal he attracted the attention of traders who had sell orders. Two traders agreed on a price, the sale was made and recorded on a slip of paper, and the information relayed to the exchange's computer. Anya's broker telephoned her to confirm the purchase of 100 shares of Bank of Montreal.

Trading Quantities

Just as "one dozen" is the basic unit for buying eggs, shares can be purchased in convenient quantities known as **board lots**. Board lots facilitate trading because it is more difficult to match buy and sell orders for odd numbers of shares. The number in a board lot is related to the share price, as shown below, but most shares are priced to sell in board lots of 100.

Price of Shares	Number in a Board Lot
Under 10 cents	1000
From 10 to 99 cents	500
From $1 to under $99	100
$100 and over	10

When fewer shares than a board lot are traded, they are referred to as an **odd lot.** Since it is more difficult to find buyers or sellers for odd lots, the price may be somewhat higher or the trade less quickly executed than for board lots.

Kinds of Orders

Various kinds of orders may be placed with a broker. A **market order** is executed immediately at the best available price. Any order without a specific price is handled as a market order; it is left up to the trader to get the best price. An **open order** specifies a price and remains open until it is either executed or cancelled. An investor who wants to buy a specific stock if the price falls to a certain level gives the broker an open order to execute if and when that price is reached. A **stop loss order** gives the broker authority to sell the shares if the price falls to a named level. A stop loss order is used to ensure that the shares will be sold at a set price should prices fall, but makes it unnecessary to sell if the price keeps rising.

Stock Brokers

Stock brokers, or registered representatives as they are often called, may be classified as full service brokers or discount brokers. **Full service brokers** charge higher commission rates, but also offer advice, research reports on companies, and other information. By contrast, **discount brokers** charge less than full-service brokers and may offer no information at all.

Stock brokers charge a commission for arranging either a sale or a purchase of securities. Each firm sets its own fee schedule, usually on a sliding scale, with lower rates for larger orders. Anyone planning to place a small order should inquire about the minimum commission charge, which may be $50.

Transactions involving large sums of money are carried out by verbal agreement, dependent solely on trust. The client simply telephones an order to the broker, who then executes it. Consequently, a broker will not conduct business for a client until an account has been opened. This usually involves a meeting of the client and the broker to discuss the objectives and financial status of the investor. The broker may also check with the credit bureau to verify the creditworthiness of the client. (The credit bureau is explained in Chapter 16.)

JANE SELLS SHARES

Jane telephoned her full service broker and asked her to sell 300 shares of Power Corporation at the market price, which that day was 26 3/8. The confirmation of the sale that arrived in the mail a few days later gave this information:

Sold 300 shares Power Corp.	@ 26.375
Gross amount	$7 912.50
Commission	147.41
Net amount	$7 765.09

Jane received a cheque for $7 765.09 as a result of this transaction.

Stock Quotations

Considerable information about the stock trades of the previous day is carried in the financial press. Stock quotations give the price range within which the stock traded, the share price as at the closing of the exchange, and how many shares traded. In addition, the high and low prices of the past year and the amount of the most recent dividend are usually included. (The income from a stock is known as a **dividend**.) Some newspapers provide still more information in their weekly summaries. Newspapers differ somewhat in the way stock quotations are presented; one example is shown below in "Reading Stock Quotations." Some newspapers quote bid and ask prices. The **bid price** is what a buyer is willing to pay and the **ask price** is what the seller is willing to accept. Unless buyer and seller can reach an agreement there will be no transaction. Prices of stocks are quoted in dollar amounts, except for those trading for less than five dollars which are quoted in cents. Those priced around three dollars or less are often referred to as **penny stocks**.

READING STOCK QUOTATIONS

On August 25, 1993, Royal Bank common stock was quoted as follows:

52-week								
High	Low	Stock	Div	High	Low	Close	Ch'ge	Vol (hundreds)
20 1/4	19 1/8	RylBk	1.45	20 3/8	20 1/4	20 1/4	–1/8	2 800

This quotation means that over the previous 52 weeks, the common stock of Royal Bank traded as high as $20.25 and as low as $19.125. The most recent dividend rate was $1.45 per share, per annum. During trading the previous day, 280 000 shares of Royal Bank changed hands

at prices as high as $20.375 and as low as $20.25, ending the day at $20.25. This closing price was $0.125 lower than the previous day.

An announcement on the evening news that Royal Bank was "down an eighth" meant that the closing price was 12.5 cents less than the previous day.

Stock Exchange Indexes

Since on any trading day some stocks rise in price while others fall, investors need a measure of the overall trend in prices. A **stock exchange index** is a statistical measurement of the percentage change in the prices of a group of representative common stocks. The Toronto Stock Exchange Composite Index (TSE Index) is the market average of 300 stocks actively traded on that exchange. Within this index there are 14 sub-groups representative of major sectors, including metals and minerals, oil and gas, paper and forest products, transportation, utilities, and financial services. Each business day, the change in the overall index and in each sub-index is reported. A graph showing recent changes in the Toronto Stock Exchange Composite Index often accompanies newspaper stock quotations (Figure 11.1).

FIGURE 11.1 TORONTO STOCK EXCHANGE COMPOSITE INDEX MONTHLY CLOSE, JULY 1990 – JUNE 1991

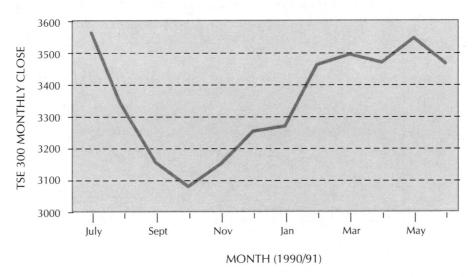

MONTH (1990/91)

SOURCE OF DATA: Index Section, Toronto Stock Exchange. © 1993. Reprinted with the permission of the Toronto Stock Exchange.

Shareholders find stock exchange indexes useful in measuring the progress of their personal portfolios against that of the stocks represented in the index. Investors whose stocks consistently under-perform the market may want to make some changes.

There are many stock market indexes, but in Canada we hear most frequently about the TSE Composite Index, the TSE 35 Index, and the Dow Jones Index (New York). In 1987, the Toronto Stock Exchange introduced the TSE 35 Index to track the price changes of thirty-five of the most actively traded stocks. In the United States, there are several stock indexes, including the well-known Dow Jones Industrial Index, which is based on 30 stocks.

Although the TSE Composite Index fluctuates all the time, the long-term trend has been upward (Figure 11.2). It is apparent that the timing for buying and selling stocks is critical. Stocks are considered to be low in liquidity because there is no assurance that the investor can sell on a given date without incurring a loss. Nevertheless, many stocks are highly marketable. The marketability of a particular stock can be seen from the volume of shares traded; those that trade actively are more marketable.

FIGURE 11.2   TORONTO STOCK EXCHANGE COMPOSITE INDEX, YEARLY CLOSE, JANUARY 1925 – DECEMBER 1992

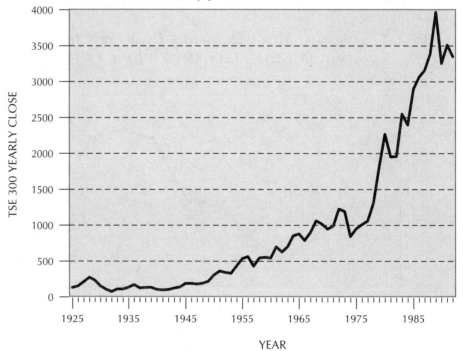

SOURCE OF DATA: Index Section, Toronto Stock Exchange. © 1993. Reprinted with the permission of the Toronto Stock Exchange.

COMMON SHARES

Corporations, especially large ones, often have many owners who provide capital for the business. These owners, or shareholders, may hold common or preferred shares. Common shareholders take greater risk and may gain or lose more than preferred shareholders. Owners of preferred shares usually accept a smaller voice in the management of the enterprise in exchange for greater safety of principal and assurance of income. The characteristics of common shares will be examined first.

Characteristics of Common Shares

An investment in common stock has two attributes that differentiate it from a debt security: (i) equity (ownership) with its associated rights, and (ii) uncertainty of return. **Common shareholders** become part owners in a corporation with certain rights that include:

(a) a vote at annual meetings,

(b) an opportunity to share in the profit of the company (dividends or capital gain),

(c) regular financial statements from the company,

(d) a claim on the company's assets in case of dissolution.

Buying common stock represents a decision to give up some measure of safety in favour of prospects for greater return. As mentioned earlier, an equity investment carries neither a promise that the investor's capital will be returned to him or her, nor a guarantee of income from that investment. When a company does well the shareholders benefit, but when it does poorly some or all of the investment can be lost. Fortunately, a shareholder has a limited liability for the losses of the corporation: if the firm should become bankrupt the maximum loss is limited to the funds invested.

Rights and Warrants

Sometimes shareholders are offered **rights**, which are privileges to buy additional shares directly from the company. Rights can be an effective way for a firm to raise more capital while offering the shareholder the oportunity to obtain more shares at a price often below market price without paying commission. The recipient of rights has the choice of either exercising them to buy more shares, or of selling them on the market. There is usually a short period during which rights may be exercised before they expire and become valueless.

A RIGHTS OFFER

Acme Corporation has been cleared for a rights offering to shareholders of record July 28 on the basis of one right for each share held. Five rights and $2.25 will be needed to purchase three additional shares. The offer expires August 25.

The term **warrant** has more than one application, the most common referring to a certificate that can be attached to bonds and new issues of common or preferred shares to make them appeal to investors. A warrant allows the owner to buy shares of the issuing company at a set price within a specified period of time. Warrants do not usually expire as quickly as rights but, like rights, may be detached and sold separately.

PREFERRED SHARES WITH WARRANTS

On July 6, 1990, BCE announced a new issue of preferred shares with attached warrants. Each preferred share carried one common share purchase warrant. These warrants could be exercised until the close of business on April 28, 1995, and each warrant could be used to buy one common share at a price of $45.75.

The examples "A Rights Offer" and "Preferred Shares With Warrants" illustrate that rights and warrants are similar in some ways. Both, for example, offer the holder the opportunity to buy shares from the company under certain conditions. Whereas rights may be offered to existing shareholders with a limited time to exercise them, warrants tend to be attached to new issues of bonds or stocks and do not expire as quickly. Since warrants do not cost as much as shares, an investor can buy warrants as an inexpensive way to make a capital gain. If the underlying stock rises in price, so will the warrants; the warrants can then be sold at a profit.

BUYING WARRANTS

Tim feels that Zenith Pipe Line is a company in which he should invest. Currently the common shares are trading at $19 and the warrants at $3.40. Each warrant gives the right to purchase one common share at $19.25 before July 13 1996, when the warrants will expire. Tim is prepared to forego the dividends he would receive as a Zenith common shareholder in expectation of capital gain from this small investment in warrants. If the common share price rises, the warrants will also increase in price. Then, Tim can make a capital gain from selling the warrants without exercising them. If, however, Zenith prices fail to rise above $19.25 before the warrants expire, Tim will lose his investment.

Stock Splits

Sometimes corporations split their stock by exchanging each share for several shares. For example, when CIBC common shares were trading around $40, the directors decided to split the stock, two-for-one. That meant that a shareholder who previously had 200 shares became the owner of 400 shares, now trading around $20 each. The new lower price made the stock more attractive to investors: instead of paying $4 000 to buy a board lot of 100 shares, the price became a more manageable $2 000. In addition, by doubling the number of outstanding shares, the bank increased the possibility of its shares being more widely held.

PREFERRED SHARES

Characteristics of Preferred Shares

In addition to common stock, companies often issue a class of shares called **preferred shares**, which represent limited ownership in a corporation. Investors usually choose preferred shares over common shares because of their lower risk and greater assurance of income. There is, however, such a broad spectrum of both common and preferred shares that it is possible to find common shares that offer less risk than some preferred shares. If, however, the company prospers, its common shares will probably rise in price more than its preferred shares. Most preferred shares promise a certain rate of return in contrast to common shares which have no set dividend rate. Issues of preferred shares can vary considerably, but in general their characteristics may be summarized as follows:

(a) part ownership in the company,

(b) no voting rights,

(c) a set dividend rate,

(d) a risk level lower than the common shares of the company.

When a company has financial difficulties its first obligation is to pay interest on its bonds and then to pay dividends on the preferred shares. Only then can dividends be declared on the common shares. This puts the security of preferred shareholders midway between bondholders and common shareholders. Any company that does not pay dividends on its preferred shares will be looked upon with disfavour by investors. If a company closes down, bondholders (who are creditors not owners) have claims on assets that take precedence over those of both preferred and common shareholders.

Special Features

Issues of preferred shares often carry features intended to attract investors. Such preferred shares may be cumulative, redeemable, retractable, or convertible.

CUMULATIVE Most Canadian preferred shares are **cumulative preferred shares** which means that if the company does not pay the dividends due each quarter, the unpaid dividends accumulate in arrears. All arrears of cumulative preferred shares must be paid before any common dividends are paid. Whenever the financial condition of the company improves, dividends in arrears are paid to the current shareholders without any interest for the period they were in arrears. In stock quotations, companies with dividends in arrears are shown with an "r" or other designation. The existence of unpaid dividends usually causes the market price of the shares to drop.

Dividends on non-cumulative preferred shares are not paid automatically but must be declared each quarter by the board of directors. If a decision is made not to declare a dividend in some particular quarter, the shareholder has no future claim.

REDEEMABLE Redeemable preferred shares give the issuer the right to redeem them at a future date. Like callable bonds, redeemable preferred shares may be called in by the company at its discretion, usually at a price slightly higher than the par value.

RETRACTABLE If the shareowner has the right to sell the shares back to the company at a specific date, they are called retractable preferred shares. The option to exercise this privilege belongs to the stockholder. This contrasts with redeemability, in which the issuing company has the right to call in shares.

CONVERTIBLE Convertible preferred shares give the investor the option of converting the shares into other stock of the company, often common stock, at a specified price and within a certain period. The shareholder has the opportunity to decide at a later date whether it will be more beneficial to hold common or preferred stock.

NEW ISSUE OF PREFERRED SHARES

Issued at the end of 1984, these shares had the following features:

Cumulative, with a par value of $25.

Dividends, to be paid in equal amounts on the fifteenth of February, May, August, and November at an annual rate of 9.125 percent, until Feb. 15 1990. Thereafter, at a floating rate, equal to one-quarter of 70 percent of the average prime rate of a specified Canadian chartered bank.

Redeemable at the option of the company on Feb. 15 1995, or at any time afterwards, on 30 days' prior notice, at $25 per share plus accrued and unpaid dividends. Not redeemable before 1995.

Retractable at the option of the holder by advance notice given on or before Feb. 6 1995, for payment on Feb. 15 1995 at $25 per share plus accrued and unpaid dividends.

Convertible into another class of preferred shares of the company on Feb. 15 1995, if notice given 30 days prior.

INVESTMENT RETURN

Investors in the stock market expect a return on their capital in one or more forms: cash dividends, stock dividends, or capital gain. The return from ownership of common shares will be examined first, then that of preferred shares.

Common Share Dividends

Common stock dividends are not promised in advance or paid automatically as is interest on debt securities. The board of directors of the corporation decides whether a dividend will be paid, when it will be paid, and how large the dividend will be. As may be expected, the amount paid out in dividends varies with the profitability of the company. At times, the directors may decide not to declare any dividend at all because of: (i) low profits in the past quarter, (ii) a decision to invest most of the profit back in the business, or (iii) the need to conserve cash flow. Dividends, when declared, are usually paid quarterly.

Since common shares are continually trading, there must be a way to determine who receives dividend cheques. Whenever a dividend is declared, a record date is set to determine ownership. For instance, notices appear in the financial press stating that a dividend will be paid to **shareholders of record**, or those who owned shares at the close of business on a certain date. This date may be two weeks before the payment date to give the company time to prepare dividend cheques. During this two-week interval the stock will continue to trade, but the corporation will send dividends to those who were shareholders on the dividend record date.

The stock exchange sets a date, known as the ex-dividend date, on or after which the stock sells **ex-dividend**, or without a dividend for that quarter. During this time, it is sellers and not buyers who receive the dividend. For example, an investor who purchased 100 shares of Noranda trading ex-dividend would not receive the next dividend.

DIVIDEND NOTICE

The Board of Directors of ABC Corporation has declared the following dividends of the company payable on December 2 to the shareholders of record at the close of business on October 31:

Class A common shares	10 cents per share
Class B common shares	12.5 cents per share

By Order of the Board
John A. Doe, Secretary
Dated this 17th day of October.

STOCK DIVIDENDS   Instead of cash dividends, companies may offer shareholders new shares in the company, known as **stock dividends**. These new shares are allotted to shareholders in proportion to the number of shares already held. Recipients of stock dividends may add them to the shares already owned or sell them on the market. The tax treatment of stock dividends is the same as that of cash dividends.

AUTOMATIC DIVIDEND REINVESTMENT PLANS   Some major companies have **automatic dividend reinvestment plans**, whereby dividends are not paid in cash but are reinvested in more stock in the firm. This can be arranged directly with the company without the assistance of a broker. One advantage for the investor is not having to pay commission on the new shares; another is the possibility of purchasing new shares below the current market price. These plans are not only a useful way to increase net worth with little effort, but are also a disciplined way of reinvesting dividend income instead of spending it.

Preferred Share Dividends

When preferred shares are first issued, each has a stated value, known as the **par value** or face value. Investors can buy the new issue at par, but afterwards the shares will trade at the market price which is not necessarily the par value. Most Canadian preferred shares have a par value of $20 or $25 and carry a fixed dividend rate that may be expressed either as a percentage of par value or as an amount per share. The issue of preferred shares described in Figure 11.3 has a par value of $20 per share, and promises an annual dividend of $2.70 per share (a return of 13.5 percent a year). In the example "A New Issue of Preferred Shares," Nova issued preferred shares with a par value of $25 and dividends of 9.125 percent.

FIGURE 11.3 A NEW ISSUE OF PREFERRED SHARES

$225,000,000

Bell Canada

11,250,000 shares

**$2.70 Cumulative Redeemable Convertible Voting Preferred Shares, Class E, Series I,
of the par value of $20 each**

*This offering may be increased, at the option of the underwriters by up to $11,250,000
(562,500 shares).*

Conversion Privilege

Each $2.70 Preferred Share will be convertible into one common share of Bell Canada on or before March 15, 1992.

Price: $20 per share to yield 13.50%

It is interesting to note that the 1982 issue of Bell preferred stock (Figure 11.3), which had a par value of $20, was trading at $41.75 per share by 1987 and had been redeemed by 1990. Why did the share price rise so much? It rose because these shares were convertible into common stock, and the rising price of Bell common increased the demand for the preferred shares. Why was this issue redeemed by the company? Bell redeemed the stocks because interest rates, which were very high in 1982 and influenced the dividend rate set by Bell, have not been as high since. This made the 13.5 percent dividend rate very attractive to investors but too expensive for the company.

Preferred shares are indicated in newspaper stock quotations by such designations as *p*, *pfd.*, or simply by the dividend rate appearing after the name of the corporation. The various issues of Bell Canada Enterprises preferred stock, for example, may be shown as BCE 1.84, BCE 1.94, and so on.

Capital Gains

Most investors in common stock are looking for capital gains in addition to dividends or, in the case of growth stocks, in lieu of dividends. They hope to sell the shares at a higher price than they paid but face the possibility of a capital loss. Capital gain (loss) is calculated as follows:

$$\text{Total receipts from sale} - \left(\text{selling commission} + \text{purchase cost} \right) = \text{capital gain (loss)}$$

The term **growth stocks** is usually applied to companies thought to have very good prospects for increasing their business and thus their profits. Growth companies tend to invest profits back in the business instead of paying them out as large dividends to shareholders. Investors who choose growth stocks are hoping the price of the shares will rise and they can make a capital gain. Those who want current income and low or moderate risk would not choose growth stocks.

INVESTMENT FUNDS

For some investors there are two obstacles to investing in the stock market. One is the management effort required. The second is the impossibility of achieving diversity in a small portfolio. One solution is to invest in pooled funds, known collectively as **investment funds**. The monies of many investors are gathered together by investment funds companies which, in turn, hire professional managers to invest the pooled funds in a portfolio comprised of many securities. Each investor acquires shares in the investment fund but not in the individual securities that make up the fund's portfolio (Figure 11.4). The investor pays fees to the investment fund company to make the investment decisions and, in return, receives whatever interest, dividends, or capital gain the fund earns.

FIGURE 11.4 BUYING AN INVESTMENT FUND

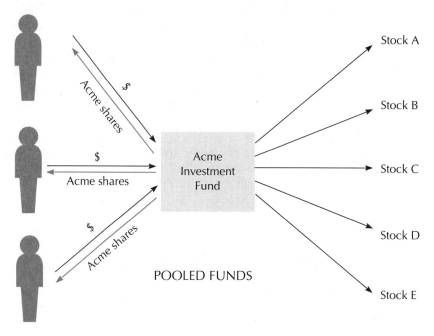

INVESTORS   FUND PORTFOLIO

Closed-End and Open-End Funds

Investment funds are either (i) closed-end, or (ii) open-end funds (Figure 11.5). **Closed-end investment funds** issue a fixed number of shares. After the initial share offering, anyone wishing to invest in a closed-end fund must find someone with shares to sell. The shares of about 20 closed-end funds trade on the TSE and recent trades are listed in daily stock quotations. BGR Precious Metals and Germany Fund of Canada are examples of closed-end funds. There is the usual broker's commission to buy or sell a closed-end fund but no entry or exit fees as exist with open-end funds. Management fees tend to be less than those of open-end funds which spend more on marketing.

Open-end investment funds, commonly known as **mutual funds**, are much more numerous than closed-end funds. These funds do not have a fixed number of shares and will accept as much money as investors wish to put into them. Therefore, the total assets in a mutual fund portfolio are constantly changing and are therefore known as open-ended. Investors buy shares directly from the mutual fund company which promises to redeem them at any time. Unlike closed-end funds and common or preferred stock, mutual fund shares are not sold from investor to investor. A mutual fund, then, is an ever-changing common pool of funds, which belongs to many investors who have arranged for professional managers to invest in a portfolio on their behalf.

FIGURE 11.5 CLOSED-END AND OPEN-END FUNDS

1. CLOSED-END FUND

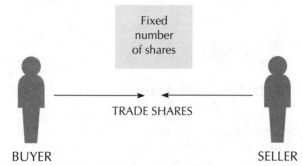

2. OPEN-END FUND—MUTUAL FUND

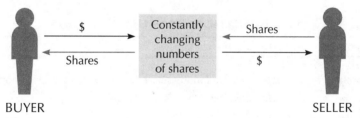

Net Asset Value Per Share

The value of individual shares of investment funds is called the **net asset value per share** (NAVPS) and is based on the net worth of the fund's total portfolio on any given date. The NAVPS is calculated by subtracting liabilities and management costs from the estimated value of the total portfolio, and dividing the answer by the number of outstanding shares. The calculation is as follows:

$$\text{Net asset value of portfolio} = \text{Total value of fund portfolio} - \left(\text{Liabilities} + \text{Management charges} \right)$$

$$\text{Net asset value per share} = \frac{\text{Net asset value of portfolio}}{\text{Total number of shares outstanding}}$$

The net asset value per share of mutual funds is determined frequently (daily for most funds, but weekly or quarterly in some cases) and published regularly in the financial papers. While mutual funds are bought and sold at their NAVPS, closed-end funds trade on the stock market at prices that may be at either a premium or a discount to their net asset value; the price depends on the demand for the shares. For instance, Central Fund of Canada, with net asset value per share of $5.89, was trading at $6.63 (at a premium) on the same day that BGR Precious Metals, with a NAVPS of $12.49, was trading at $11.63 (at a discount). The NAVPS of closed-end funds are published occasionally in the financial papers.

MUTUAL FUNDS

Types of Mutual Funds

The 750 or so mutual funds being sold in Canada are intended to meet a wide variety of investment objectives. Mutual funds can be categorized in a variety of ways but, for our purposes, can be divided into four major groups according to the kinds of securities they hold: (i) debt funds, (ii) equity funds, (iii) balanced funds, and (iv) specialty funds. A summary of this classification is shown in Table 11.1

TABLE 11.1 CLASSIFICATION OF MUTUAL FUNDS

Category	Description
1. Debt Funds	
A. *Money market funds*	Invested in treasury bills, commercial paper, short-term bonds.
B. *Fixed income funds*	Invested in bonds, mortgages.
C. *Guaranteed income funds*	Invested in various deposits.
2. Balanced Funds	
Invested in a combination of debt and equity securities.	
3. Equity Funds	
A. *Dividend Funds*	Invested in dividend-paying stocks.
B. *Growth Funds*	Invested in common stocks.
(a) Broad spectrum funds. Invested in a variety of growth companies.	
(b) Market segment funds. Invested in a specific sector of the market (e.g., oils, energy, high technology).	
(c) International funds. Invested in specific countries (e.g., Japan, USA).	
4. Specialty Funds	
A. *Gold funds*	Invested in gold bullion or gold certificates.
B. *Real estate funds*	Invested in property.

DEBT FUNDS   The objective of debt mutual funds is to generate income with low or moderate risk. Among the funds specializing in debt securities are: (i) money market funds that are low-risk and highly liquid, (ii) fixed income funds that invest in mortgages or bonds, and (iii) guaranteed income funds that invest in deposits that are often sponsored by banks or trust companies. Although the portfolios of these funds earn interest, the payments to shareholders are called dividends. Nevertheless, these dividends are not eligible for the tax dividend credit (explained later in this chapter) but are treated as interest income for tax purposes. Also, some debt funds, such as bond funds, may generate capital gains. Receipts provided for tax purposes will separate these different kinds of return.

BALANCED FUNDS   The purpose of balanced funds is to maximize a balance of capital appreciation and income, yet preserve capital. These funds maintain a fairly conservative level of risk by investing in a variable mixture of securities; the proportions of each type of security are adjusted according to economic conditions. There are many balanced funds with different types of portfolios. Some are restricted to Canadian bonds and stocks, while others use a broader range of securities.

EQUITY FUNDS   Although all equity funds invest in stocks, they differ widely in risk levels. Dividend funds are conservative investments with limited opportunities for capital gain. They maximize income by specializing in stocks that pay high dividends; this allows investors to take advantage of the dividend tax credit. Growth funds concentrate on capital appreciation, not income. Their fortunes go up and down with the stock market, making large gains in some years and losses in others. Over the long term, however, growth funds often report the highest gains of any type of mutual fund. Equity funds also include those that specialize in particular segments of the market or in the stocks of a particular country or group of countries. Some of these can be identified by their names, such as Canadian Resources Fund, Energy Fund, American Fund, or Global Fund.

SPECIALITY FUNDS   Specialized funds, such as real estate funds or gold funds, do not invest in the stock market but do invest directly in specific commodities. Although they do not offer diversity they make it possible for the small investor to have exposure to a selected portion of the market.

Risk Levels

The investor can estimate the risk of a particular mutual fund by examining the type of securities held in its portfolio and by comparing its past performance with others in the same fund category. The financial press rates mutual funds according to their risk or volatility based on the stability of the rates of return of the stocks in the fund's portfolio. The somewhat different measures of volatility, used by various financial papers are explained in the report each paper publishes on mutual funds.

For instance, the Report on Business from the *Globe and Mail* reports volatility on a scale of 1 (low) to 10 (high). Volatility data show how the monthly return of a fund has fluctuated in recent years, compared to other funds within the same category. When comparing one category of funds against another, money market funds are usually at the low end of the scale and growth funds are at the high end. High-variability funds make great gains when the stock market is rising but, conversely, lose rapidly in a falling market. The low-risk funds will neither make nor lose as much money.

Fees

The fees charged for investing in mutual funds not only vary considerably among funds but have also become increasingly difficult for the investor to assess. The sales commissions charged either when shares are purchased or redeemed are made quite explicit. Annual fees for management and other expenses, however, are less well explained.

ACQUISITION FEES   If a sales fee is imposed at the time mutual fund shares are purchased, it is called an **acquisition fee** or **front-end loading charge** and may be from two to nine percent of the amount invested. This fee tends to be higher for funds managed by companies that hire their sales force directly. Independent brokers, who handle the funds of many companies, may be willing to negotiate a lower commission fee.

REDEMPTION FEES   Another way of covering sales commissions is to charge a **redemption fee** or **rear-end loading charge** that is paid at the time money is withdrawn from the fund. Redemption fees may be a set amount per transaction (e.g., $15 to $25), or a percentage (e.g., five to ten percent) of either the amount of the initial investment or the current market value of the holding. Redemption fees often have a sliding scale structure: the longer the funds are held, the lower the redemption fee. After nine years or so the fee may fall to zero. Some investors are attracted by redemption fees as a way of postponing costs. However, a mutual fund should not be selected only by the timing of fees; other factors, such as risk and performance, need to be considered as well. It is apparent, however, that the length of time the investor expects to hold the shares is an important consideration when choosing between a front-load and a back-load fund.

NO-LOAD FUNDS   Funds that do not charge sales fees are called **no-load funds**. However, the fee may be disguised. Some supposedly no-load funds impose a distribution fee of one percent a year, which is added to the management fee for the first few years as a way of compensating sales people. The no-load funds, most of which have no sales force, use other methods of finding investors, such as advertising, direct mail, and arrangements with stockbrokers. Sometimes, there is a system of reciprocal commissions whereby managers of mutual funds, who need the services of stock brokers, agree to send business to a broker who, in return, will promote sales of that particular mutual fund. In these instances, the investor does not pay a sales fee, but may receive somewhat biased advice.

MANAGEMENT FEES Management fees represent a significant cost for both closed-end and mutual funds. While acquisition and redemption fees are visible, management fees are less so. Charges of .5% to two percent a year are deducted from the assets of the fund before calculating return to investors. Management fees cover a variety of costs, including investment advice, annual reports, legal services, brokerage commissions, sales commissions, and the goods and services tax. A useful means of comparing the management fees of various funds is the **expense ratio**. This ratio, expressed as a percentage, is an annual ratio of all fees (excluding sales fees) and expenses to the average net assets of the fund. A cursory examination of newspaper reports on mutual funds indicates how widely funds vary in their expense ratios, even within a similar group of funds. Some of the factors that affect fund expense ratios are the marketing and distribution costs of a fund, and whether or not the fund pays trailer fees. Some funds pay their agents annual commissions, called **trailer fees**, in addition to the initial sales commission. A broker receives trailer fees on an ongoing basis as encouragement to continue to provide services to the client.

Buying Mutual Funds

Buying shares in a mutual fund is easy. The investor merely contacts the fund company directly or contacts a mutual funds agent and indicates how much money is to be invested. The cost will be the net asset value per share plus any sales fees. Likewise, selling mutual fund shares is simply a matter of informing a representative of the fund. The investor will receive the current net asset value per share less any exit fees.

INVESTING IN A MUTUAL FUND

With $1000 to invest and no time to look after it, Michelle decided to buy shares in a mutual fund. The fund she chose had a sales fee of five percent and a net asset value per share of $6.53. How many shares did she buy?

Sales commission	$1000 × .05	=	$50.00
Sum to invest	$1000 − $50	=	$950.00
Number of shares bought	$950/$6.53	=	145.482

Some months later a dividend of .30 per share was declared.

Dividends received	145.482 × .30	=	$43.64

> Michelle had arranged to have her dividends automatically reinvested in more shares of the mutual fund, which now had a net asset value per share of $7.04. This would give her 6.199 more shares.
>
> | Dividends to reinvest | | = | $43.64 |
> |---|---|---|---|
> | Number of shares received | $43.64/$7.04 | = | 6.199 |
> | Total shares owned | 145.482 + 6.199 | = | 151.681 |

Although the market is very competitive and many agents are anxious to sell mutual fund shares, the investor needs to give the matter careful consideration when making a choice. The following four steps are presented as a guide to mutual fund investors.

(a) Determine your personal objectives for this investment.

(b) Find a fund that matches these personal objectives.

(c) Investigate the fees that will be charged.

(d) Analyze the past performance of several possible funds.

OBJECTIVES The names of mutual funds often indicate their different objectives, e.g., growth, income, dividend, and money market funds. More information about the objectives of a fund is found in the fund prospectus that lists the securities currently held in the portfolio. Since many mutual fund companies operate a number of funds with different objectives, investors can contact a few companies, state their desired objectives, and request the prospectuses of any appropriate funds. Addresses of mutual fund companies may be found in the financial papers or in books that rate mutual funds. Also, agents acting for a number of mutual funds agents can supply prospectuses.

FEES The various fees already described can have a very significant effect on the gains made from a mutual fund investment. It is best to make careful comparisons before choosing a fund.

PERFORMANCE Information about a mutual fund's past performance can be useful to prospective mutual fund buyers. How does its historical return compare to that of similar funds? The financial papers publish regular surveys of mutual fund performance over a number of years. The yield figures are based on annual compound rates of return, assuming dividends and capital gain are re-invested in the fund. However, the reported returns exclude direct charges, such as acquisition or redemption fees. Hidden fees for management costs have been taken into account, but the effect of sales fees on reported investment return needs to be considered. Past performance, of course, is not a sure indication of future success but is one factor to consider.

ADVANTAGES AND DISADVANTAGES To conclude this discussion of mutual funds, some of the advantages and disadvantages of mutual funds are summarized. First, advantages of mutual funds are:

(a) professional management,

(b) wide variety of funds available,

(c) diversification,

(d) marketability.

Mutual funds may also present disadvantages for the investor but generalizing is difficult because of the great variety of funds. The following list does not apply to all funds, but suggests factors to consider.

(a) low liquidity,

(b) high fees,

(c) long-term nature of the investment,

(d) variable skill of fund managers.

Equity mutual funds are low in liquidity because share values fluctuate as the whole market rises and falls. The optimum time for selling may not coincide with the need for funds. The fees attached to mutual funds are significant and, in the short term, may reduce the net yield on the investment. With the exception of money market funds, most mutual funds are poor short-term investments, best selected for the long term. The success of a particular fund is dependent upon the skill of the managers.

INVESTMENT RISK

Types of Risk

All investments are exposed to some degree of risk, but the kind of risk varies with the type of investment. It is essential that the investor be aware of the risks associated with any proposed investment and be willing to accept them. As explained in Chapter 9, investors face risks caused by: (i) inflation, which causes the value of cash and debt securities to fall, (ii) interest rates, which have differential effects on various investments, (iii) the stock market, where the demand for a security rises and falls, and (iv) a particular business, which may do poorly. Ownership of stocks is subject to market, business, and interest rate risks.

MARKET RISK   This is the possibility that, an asset may lose favour among investors from factors other than the profitability of the company or economic conditions. The price of equity assets is dependent on demand in a stock market that is variable (Figure 11.1). It is normal for stock prices to fluctuate for many reasons, some of which may be unrelated to earnings or dividend changes. Since a great deal of emotion is associated with stock ownership, irrational factors influence prices. It is difficult to predict the direction or magnitude of change in stock prices in the short run, but over the long run stock prices have produced real gains (in excess of inflation). The problem for the investor is timing. The investor who is in a position to wait until an opportune time to sell has an advantage. Funds for emergencies or short-term goals are best not invested in equities.

BUSINESS RISK   Although it is possible for the business in which one has invested to fail totally, the more likely risk is a decline in the earnings of the firm. Lower earnings often result in lower dividends and a drop in the price of the security. Paying too high a price for a stock is also a risk. For instance, anyone who invested $24 a share in Inco, the nickel mining company, when the demand for metals was high, received regular dividends. Later, an oversupply of nickel caused profits to fall, dividends to be cut, and share prices to drop to $14. This is an example of a business risk where investors could lose some of their invested capital if shares were sold, and received less dividend income than anticipated. However, those patient investors who waited until the market for nickel improved saw Inco shares rise to $35.

INTEREST RATE RISK   Rising interest rates, beneficial for investors in debt securities, are not helpful for stockholders. High interest rates restrict business activity and tend to affect profits and share prices adversely. When interest rates are low, people decide to buy cars and houses, and businesses borrow to expand. This activity is reflected in rising stock prices.

Risk Reduction

Since there is no way to pick investments that will do well under all circumstances or to avoid some possible bad results, the rational approach is to take steps to reduce risk. At best, some risk will always remain because the future may not turn out as expected. Some people are more averse to risk than others, that is, they are less comfortable with uncertainty. The most risk-averse people are uneasy with any but the most secure fixed-income investments. They prefer certainty to the possibility of greater yield.

Since it is impossible to avoid all risk, the wise investor decides on an acceptable risk level and tries to spread this risk by diversification. Diversification can be applied at several levels: to the total portfolio of the investor and to elements within in it. For example, on one level a portfolio might be balanced between debt and equity investments. Within both the debt and equity portions, further diversity is desirable. For example, a well-constructed stock portfolio is not concentrated on any one sector. Instead of buying shares in oil companies only, some funds would be invested in transportation, utilities, or industrial products. The odds are that, in a diversified portfolio, some securities will do better than expected, which will balance those that did not do as well as hoped. If a portfolio is well-balanced, the overall risk will be less than that associated with any particular investment. Diversity reduces risk because the poor performance in one sector will be offset by successes in another, as individual companies react differently to economic and other conditions.

Finally, diversification can be excessive. No one investor can effectively monitor a portfolio of too many kinds of assets. For a small stock portfolio, six to ten stocks may be appropriate. A rule of thumb is that with less than $50 000 (excluding a residence), each asset should be limited to about 10 percent of the total. Those with a larger net worth may be able to handle 20 securities.

INCOME TAX

Investment return may be interest, dividends, or capital gain. Generally, these three types of income are taxed differently. Each will be reviewed in turn.

Interest

All interest must be added to taxable income and taxed accordingly. This has made debt securities less attractive than equities for some investors, as will be illustrated in the following examples.

Marginal federal tax rate		=	26%.
Provincial tax rate		=	52%
Total interest earned		=	$2 000.00
Federal income tax	$2 000 × .26	=	$520.00
Provincial income tax	$520 × .52	=	$270.40
Total income tax	$520 + $270.40	=	$790.40
After-tax return	$2 000 − $790.40	=	$1 209.60

The Dividend Tax Credit

Dividends from Canadian corporations are eligible for the tax dividend credit. This preferential treatment of dividends is designed to encourage investment in Canadian corporations.

The rules for calculating the dividend tax credit require that the actual amount of dividends received be *grossed-up* or increased by a specific percentage (25 percent in 1993). The following example illustrates how the dividend tax credit is calculated.

Marginal federal tax rate	=	26%
Provincial tax rate	=	52%
Gross-up rate	=	25%
Tax on grossed-up dividends	=	16 2/3%
Total dividends received	=	$2 000.00

Grossed-up by 25%	2 000 × 1.25	=	$2 500.00
Federal income tax (26%)	2 500 × .26	=	$650.00
Dividend tax credit			
(16 2/3% × grossed-up amount)	$2 500 × .167	=	$417.50
Federal tax payable			
(federal tax – dividend credit)	$650.00 – 417.50	=	$232.50
Provincial tax			
(52% of federal tax)	$232.50 × .52	=	$120.90
Total tax (federal + provincial)		=	$353.40
After-tax return	$2 000 – 353.40	=	$1 646.60

The two previous examples illustrate that the after-tax return from $2 000 in interest or dividends is $437 greater for dividend income. A quick way to estimate the after-tax differences between interest and dividend income is to multiply the dividend rate by 1.27. For instance, an investor choosing between shares paying a dividend of five percent and a debt security with six percent interest would multiply the dividend rate by 1.27 (.05 × 1.27 = 6.35). The comparison now becomes between 6.35 percent and 6.0 percent with a slight advantage for dividends.

Capital Gains

Each person has a lifetime exemption of $100 000 in net capital gains. (Net capital gain is gross capital gain less any capital loss.) After this exemption has been used, three-quarters of net capital gains must be added to taxable income and taxed along with other income. Recent tax reform has added considerably to the complexity of capital gains taxation. Details are not given here but are well explained in many income tax publications.

Summary

This overview of stocks and mutual funds introduced the specific vocabulary of the stock market and outlined the process of stock trading. This should make the financial section of the newspaper easier to understand. Some knowledge of the stock market and the risks involved is essential for those planning to invest in stocks. Differences between common and preferred shares were explained, as were rights, warrants, stock splits, and special features attached to some preferred shares. Investors in the stock market may receive various kinds of returns, including cash dividends, stock dividends, and capital appreciation.

Investment funds may be closed-end or open-end, but the vast majority are of the latter type, and are known as mutual funds. The net asset value per share is the price of mutual funds, but not of closed-end funds. Mutual funds, classified as debt, balanced, equity and specialty funds, offer enough diversity to suit a wide range of investment objectives. It is important to choose a fund to match personal objectives, and to be aware of the various sales and management fees.

The discussion of investments concluded with an identification of the kinds of risk associated with equity investing, such as market, business and interest rate risks, and the importance of portfolio diversification. Taxation of investment return varies with the type of income earned; it is therefore wise to compare yield on an after-tax basis.

Vocabulary Review

acquisition fee
  (front-end loading charge) (p. 344)

ask price (p. 330)

automatic dividend reinvestment
  plan (p. 338)

bid price (p. 330)

board lot (p. 328)

closed-end investment fund (p. 340)

common shareholders (p. 333)

convertible preferred share (p. 336)

cumulative preferred share (p. 335)

discount brokers (p. 329)

dividend (p. 330)

ex-dividend (p. 337)

expense ratio (p. 345)

full service broker (p. 329)

growth stock (p. 339)

investment fund (p. 339)

market order (p. 329)

net asset value per share (p. 341)

no-load fund (p. 344)

odd lot (p. 329)

open order (p. 329)

open-end fund investment
  (mutual fund) (p. 340)

over the counter market (p. 327)

par value (p. 338)

penny stock (p. 330)

preferred share (p. 335)

redeemable preferred share (p. 336)

redemption fee
  (back-end load) (p. 344)

retractable preferred share (p. 336)

right (p. 333)

shareholder of record (p. 337)

stock dividend (p. 338)

stock exchange (p. 327)

stock exchange index (p. 331)

stop loss order (p. 329)

trailer fee1 (p. 345)

warrant (p. 334)

Problems

1. Use stock quotations from a recent newspaper to answer the following questions. Look at the legend for an explanation of the footnotes.

    (a) How much was the most recent dividend per share, in annual terms, on Noranda common stock? On Bell Canada Enterprises (BCE)?

(b) Try to find an example of a preferred share for which the dividend is in arrears.

(c) Look at the volume figures and find a stock that traded very actively.

(d) Find a quotation for stock warrants. It may be indicated by a "w" after the name of the corporation.

(e) Examine the quotations for Transalta preferred shares to find out how many issues are listed.

(f) Look for a stock that has issued stock dividends recently.

2. Decide whether you AGREE or DISAGREE with each of the following statements:

(a) If the primary objective of an investor is safety of principal, common stock should be considered.

(b) Preferred stocks have some attributes of both bonds and common shares.

(c) An investment firm must have a seat on the stock exchange if it is to trade on that exchange.

(d) All mutual funds are highly speculative.

(e) If you wish to buy shares in a mutual fund, you or your broker must find someone with shares to sell.

(f) All mutual funds have sales fees.

(g) A no-load mutual fund will not have any management fees.

(h) A mutual fund is a type of investment fund.

(i) The main reason for investing in mutual funds, rather than directly in the stock market, is to obtain the highest possible return on your money.

(j) If you sell common shares and use the money to buy more shares of another company immediately, your broker will charge you commission on one transaction only.

(k) An open-end investment fund offers new shares without limit to the investing public, but does not offer to redeem the shares.

(l) An investor who buys shares in a mutual fund with a front-end load and decides to sell them within a few months may lose money.

3.

RIGHTS OFFERING

A news report states that Consolidated Trustco plans to raise approximately $80 million in new capital through an issue of rights to shareholders, who will receive one right for every four common shares

> held. With one right and $12, the holder can buy another share of
> Consolidated Trustco. The offer will be mailed to shareholders in late
> October, and will expire 21 days later. With this new issue, rights will
> be offered to shareholders of record on October 15.
>
> At the time of this announcement, Consolidated Trustco shares
> were trading at $12. By Nov. 1, they were up to $13. Over the
> previous year the shares had traded between 7 1/4 and 14.

(a) is the company making this offer?

(b) As a shareholder, would you be interested in this offering? Comment.

(c) If you were a shareholder, what choices would you have in regard to this rights offering?

(d) If you bought Consolidated Trustco stock on October 30, would you be eligible for rights? Explain whether you would be considered a shareholder of record as far as this offering is concerned.

4. An investor with a high marginal tax rate is interested in planning her investments to minimize her income tax. What would be the relative merits for her of interest, dividends, and capital gain?

5. Bell Enterprises Inc. announced that, on Nov. 4, the $1.80 preferred shares would be redeemed at $21.365 each unless the shareholder wished to convert them to common shares at the rate of .67 common share for each preferred. At the time this notice appeared, the preferred shares were trading at $24.50 and the common at $37.50.

(a) Assume that you held 100 of the preferred shares. Calculate the amount you would receive if you accepted the redemption offer, and the value of your holdings if you converted to common shares. Which is higher?

(b) What are some reasons for accepting the redemption offer?

6. Identify the type of investment risk that seems to predominate in each of these cases.

(a) Shares of a lumber company dropped in price after news of a duty on wood products to be imposed by the United States.

(b) Stock market prices, which had been rising for several years, continued to fall for months.

(c) An investor who inherited $100 000 invested it all in five-year GICs at 8 percent, then interest rates moved to 11 percent.

7. A survey of mutual funds, published in the financial press reported the following information about several mutual funds.

MUTUAL FUNDS

	Industrial Equity Fund	Group Average	Investors Mutual Fund	Group Average
Type of fund	equity		balanced	
Assets	286 234		429 500	
Fees	F5% or R5%		F5% + R1%	
Expense ratio	2.63%		2.04%	
Rate of return (%)				
6 months	48.56	21.0	16.37	12.76
1 year	87.08	23.8	18.63	14.17
5 years	6.81	9.3	8.58	9.19
10 years	9.14	8.7	8.59	9.90

	Dynamic Dividend Fund	Group Average	Industrial Cash Management	Group Average
Type of fund	dividend		money market	
Assets ($ millions)	1 627		188 461	
Fees	D or R4.5%		F2%	
Expense ratio	1.80		.5%	
Volatility	2		1	
Rate of return(%)				
6 months	11.11	13.44	2.59	2.45
1 year	12.15	13.47	5.49	5.11
5 years	6.69	7.49	9.52	9.10

Fees:

"F" indicates the maximum front-end load.

"D" indicates a redemption fee on the original invested capital.

"R" indicates a redemption fee on the entire amount withdrawn.

Expense ratio:

The ratio includes all management and operating fees (excluding GST) as a percentage of the fund's total net assets.

Volatility:

The rating shows how the monthly return on the fund has fluctuated over the past three years, compared with other funds in all groups on a scale of 1 to 10. A rating of 1 means the return is steady; a rating of 10 is very high volatility.

Return:

The rate of return includes reinvestment of dividends and adjustments for management fees and expenses, but excludes sales fees.

SOURCE: "Report on Mutual Funds," *The Globe and Mail*, August 19, 1993.

(a) Which fund has the larger sum of money to invest?

(b) Among these funds, do there appear to be any relationships among expense ratios, fees, and volatility? Comment.

(c) Compare the past performance of each fund to the group average. What is your conclusion? Were some funds successful over the short-term as well as over the long-term?

(d) Which fund had the best five-year rate of return? Is this a comparison between interest and dividends? If so, how would that affect the after-tax return?

(e) Which fund had the highest six-month rate of return? In what form was this return? How does the six-month rate of return compare with the five-year average? How reliable is the return from this fund?

References

BOOKS

ANDERSON, HUGH. *Bulls and Bears*. Markham, Ontario: Penguin, 1990, 172 pp. A guide for the investor that explains the language of the stock market, the functions of analysts and brokers, the difference between fundamental and technical analysis, and a variety of investment possibilities.

BEACH WAYNE and LYLE R. HEPBURN. *Are You Paying Too Much Tax?* Toronto: McGraw-Hill Ryerson, annual, 206 pp. A tax planning guide for the general reader that includes a discussion of capital gains, RRSPs, and investment income.

CÔTÉ, JEAN-MARC and DONALD DAY. *Personal Financial Planning in Canada*. Toronto: Allyn and Bacon, 1987, 464 pp. A comprehensive personal finance text that includes financial planning, income tax, annuities, pensions, investments, credit, mortgages, and wills, with particular attention to the banking and insurance industries.

THE FINANCIAL POST. *Preferred Shares and Warrants*. Toronto: The Financial Post, annual. Provides details about all outstanding issues of preferred shares and warrants.

FRIEDLAND, SEYMOUR and STEVEN G. KELMAN. *Investment Strategies, How to Create Your Own and Make It Work for You*. Markham, Ontario: Penguin Canada, 1991, 168 pp. Offers guidance for the general reader in defining objectives and establishing an investment program.

GRAHAM, BENJAMIN. *The Intelligent Investor, A Book of Practical Counsel*. Fourth Edition. New York: Harper & Row, 1973, 318 pp. A classic guide to investing in the stock market.

HUNTER, W. T. *Canadian Financial Markets*. Third Edition. Peterborough, Ontario: Broadview Press, 1991, 193 pp. An economist gives an overview of the workings of the bond market, the mortgage market, and the stock market.

KELMAN, STEVEN G. *Understanding Mutual Funds*. Markham, Ontario: Penguin, 1990, 214 pp. Explains different types of mutual funds, how to select a fund, and how to analyze performance. Provides a detailed directory of funds with dates of establishment, historical rates of return, fees, and addresses.

MACINNIS, LYMAN. *Get Smart! Make Your Money Count in the 1990s.* Second Edition. Scarborough, Ontario: Prentice-Hall Canada, 1989, 317 pp. A book for the general reader that includes financial planning and income tax principles, but gives major attention to investing in the stock market.

MOTHERWELL, CATHRYN. *Smart Money, Investing for Women.* Toronto: Key Porter, 1989, 192 pp. A financial journalist explains how to get started investing, how to evaluate the products, and how to build a portfolio.

PAPE, GORDON. *Building Wealth in the '90s.* Scarborough, Ontario: Prentice-Hall Canada, 1992, 294 pp. An easy-to-read guide for the novice financial manager and investor that considers interest rates, credit cards, mortgages, RRSPs, mutual funds, and the stock market.

WYATT, ELAINE. *The Money Companion, How to Manage Your Money and Achieve Financial Freedom.* Markham, Ontario: Penguin Books, 1991, 202 pp. A guide to personal financial management that focuses on planning, investment strategy, and retirement needs.

ZIMMER, HENRY B. *Making Your Money Grow, A Canadian Guide to Successful Personal Finance.* Third Edition. Toronto: Collins, 1989, 260 pp. The focus of this book is on basic calculations needed for personal financial decisions, as applied to compound interest, future and present values, investment returns, RRSPs, annuities, and life insurance.

PERIODICALS

Canadian Money Saver. Monthly. Canadian Money Saver Inc., Box 370, Bath, Ontario, K0H 1G0. Includes short articles on a range of personal finance topics, with special emphasis on investments.

Canadian Shareowner. Bimonthly. Canadian Shareowner Magazine Inc., Suite 204, 1090 University Avenue West, Windsor, Ontario, N9A 5S4. Intended for investors who wish to become knowledgeable about managing their own stock portfolio. Special attention to growth stocks.

Financial Times. Weekly. Suite 500, 920 Yonge Street, Toronto, Ontario, M2W 3L5. Provides current information on a range of business and economic topics.

Report on Business. Daily. A section of *The Globe and Mail.* Important source of information on the financial markets.

The Financial Post. Daily and weekly. The Financial Post Company, 777 Bay Street, Toronto, Ontario, M5G 2E4. Up-to-date information on business, economics, income tax, and investments.

PART THREE

CREDIT

This section presents a comprehensive treatment of consumer and mortgage credit, beginning with a review of trends in the use of consumer credit in Canada, followed by two chapters on consumer loans and vendor credit that examine the various institutions that provide credit, the types of credit available, terminology used, and the contracts that borrowers sign. Although consumer credit contracts are sometimes difficult to understand, it is important that borrowers understand what they are signing. Therefore, samples of credit contracts are included to familiarize the reader with them.

It is a convention to make a distinction between consumer credit and mortgage credit and, following this practice, there is a separate chapter on home mortgages. The chapter on credit reporting and debt collection explains processes that are mysterious and challenging to many. In the final chapter, strategies are outlined that debtors may use to handle their problems with debt.

CHAPTER TWELVE

The Use of Consumer Credit

1. To distinguish between consumer debt, mortgage debt, and total debt.

2. To distinguish between macro and micro sources of information about consumer credit and debt.

3. To suggest explanations for trends in the national use of consumer credit.

4. To interpret trends in family income, using both current and constant dollars.

5. To formulate generalizations that apply at the household level, about relations between the following pairs of variables:

   (a) income and probability of having consumer debt,

   (b) income and average consumer debt,

   (c) stage in the life cycle and incidence of consumer debt,

   (d) age and average consumer debt.

6. To identify several ways of measuring use of consumer credit.

7. To examine major reasons for using credit.

8. To examine, from the borrower's perspective, some advantages and disadvantages of using credit.

9. To understand the following terms: debtor, creditor, principal, interest, total consumer credit outstanding, current dollars, constant dollars, flexibility cost of credit, debt burden, personal disposable income, discretionary income.

Introduction

To set the stage for this study of consumer credit, empirical information on the amounts of credit used in Canada over several decades will be examined. The data on consumer credit come from two sources: macro or national data obtained from creditors, and micro data from household surveys. These micro surveys are not conducted very often but they do provide information about variables associated with the use of consumer debt. Finally, some reasons for using credit will be considered.

WHAT IS CREDIT?

Credit and Debt

Every borrowing transaction has two actors. There is the lender (creditor) who supplies money for a loan in exchange for a credit, and who looks upon the transaction in terms of the amount of credit that has been extended. The other actor is the borrower (debtor) who receives the money and views the transaction as an accumulation of debt. Therefore, that which is *consumer debt* to you, the borrower, is *consumer credit* to the lender or creditor. Information about this transaction may be reported as debt or credit, depending on the perspective of the reporter. Although it is really the same phenomenon, data obtained from households about their borrowing are usually reported as consumer debt, while the statistics gathered from lenders are referred to as consumer credit. In this chapter both kinds of data will be examined.

The debtor in a credit/debt transaction accepts a commitment to repay the debt some time in the future, and thus must be prepared to give up future purchasing power in order to have extra resources available at present. The debtor, making the decision that it is more important to have extra funds now than to wait until the money can be saved, should realize that a cost of using credit is the commitment of future income to interest payments; these funds will not be available for other uses. The debtor makes a promise to repay, not only the principal, or the sum borrowed, but also the interest, which is the charge for borrowing. Thus, the lender or the creditor holds a claim that the borrower will repay interest and principal as promised.

It is a convention to make a distinction between consumer debt and mortgage debt; **total debt** is the sum of these two. **Consumer debt** is defined as all the personal debt incurred by households, exclusive of mortgage debt or business debt. **Mortgage debt** is debt secured by real property, such as buildings and land. To summarize:

$$\begin{matrix} \text{consumer} \\ \text{debt} \end{matrix} \quad + \quad \begin{matrix} \text{mortgage} \\ \text{debt} \end{matrix} \quad = \quad \begin{matrix} \text{total debt of} \\ \text{households} \end{matrix}$$

For analytical purposes, it is useful to make a distinction between mortgage debt and consumer debt. Mortgage debt generally involves much larger amounts and for much longer terms than consumer debt; combining these statistics would obscure trends in consumer debt. From the household's perspective, mortgage debt can be viewed as the ongoing cost of housing—a regular expense—in contrast to short-term debt. Also, borrowing to invest in property can be an effective way to accumulate assets, but borrowing for current consumption is not. For a discussion of mortgages see Chapter 15.

NATIONAL CONSUMER CREDIT DATA

Sources of Information

Lenders are required to make regular reports to Statistics Canada about the amount of credit they have extended; this is called the **total consumer credit outstanding.** These statistics, collected at the national level (macro data), show the amounts of credit held by various lenders, but provide no information about individual borrowers. Such macro data are, however, quite useful in giving a picture of national trends. These data were not available before 1951, which is probably an indication of the increasing significance of consumer credit in our society.

How Much Credit Do We Use?

You may have heard people say that Canadians now use more consumer credit than ever before. To verify this statement, we will examine the trends in the total consumer credit outstanding since 1951 (Figure 12.1). It is clear that since 1951 the increase in total credit outstanding has been dramatic. Look at one decade at a time to find when the rate of increase (slope of the line) changed significantly. What are some possible explanations for the great increase in the use of consumer credit? It may be that: (i) the population grew rapidly and thus more credit was needed in Canada, or (ii) prices of goods rose substantially necessitating larger loans, or (iii) each person used more credit. Each of these possibilities will be examined in turn.

POPULATION CHANGES The data shown in Figure 12.1 make no allowance for any changes in the population of Canada. This can be corrected by dividing the total credit figures by the population of Canada for each year. Examine the line in Figure 12.2 labelled "current dollars," showing the amounts of consumer credit outstanding per capita. Generally the slope of this line matches that in Figure 12.1, indicating about the same rate of increase. Apparently, the rapid increase in total consumer credit outstanding cannot be explained by a change in the population of Canada. Another possible cause is inflation.

INFLATION Perhaps rising prices caused people to use increasing amounts of consumer credit. For example, as the prices of cars rose, the size of each car loan necessarily increased. In this case, it would mean that inflated prices increased loan amounts, rather than more people buying more cars. To check whether the rapidly rising amounts of consumer credit were caused by inflation, the credit outstanding per capita will be adjusted for changes in consumer prices. The statistical procedure for doing this is to convert the values that were in **current dollars** (that is, the dollar amounts recorded in each year) into **constant dollars** which estimate the values if

FIGURE 12.1   TOTAL CONSUMER CREDIT OUTSTANDING, CANADA, 1951–1992

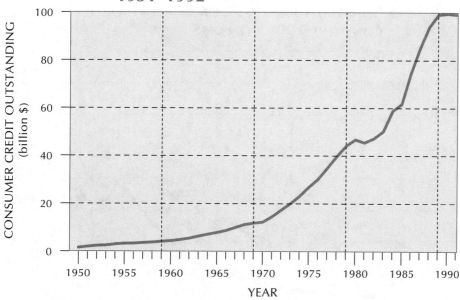

SOURCES OF DATA: *Bank of Canada Review*. Ottawa: Bank of Canada, various issues; *Canada Year Book, Canadian Statistical Review, Canadian Economic Observer, and Historical Statistical Supplement*. Ottawa: Statistics Canada, various issues. Reproduced with the permission of the Bank of Canada and the Minister of Industry, Science and Technology, 1993.

prices had remained constant. The numbers plotted in Figure 12.1 were in current dollars, but may be converted to constant dollars by using the following formula:

$$\frac{\text{Value in current dollars in Year X}}{\text{Consumer Price Index in Year X}} \times 100 = \frac{\text{Constant \$}}{\text{in Year X}}$$

This is a way of eliminating, statistically, the effect of changes in prices. In other words, if consumer prices had remained unchanged since 1951, the amount of consumer credit extended would be approximately that shown in constant dollars in Figure 12.2.

If the increase in consumer credit outstanding had been entirely due to population changes and rising prices, the constant dollar line in Figure 12.2, which has been corrected for both, should be perfectly horizontal. On the contrary, it shows a rising trend and therefore we can conclude from these data that, regardless of any changes in population or consumer prices, Canadians did use more consumer credit. Much of the difference between the two lines in Figure 12.2 can be attributed to the effects of inflation; as prices of goods and services rose, so did the amounts borrowed.

It is clear from these data that the recession of 1982–3 was a turning point in the use of consumer credit. Economic events such as the slowdown in the economy, escalating interest rates, and high unemployment combined to create uncertainty and a natural reluctance to incur more debt. Many of those with debts found it very

FIGURE 12.2 CONSUMER CREDIT OUTSTANDING PER CAPITA, CANADA, 1951–1992 (IN CURRENT AND CONSTANT 1981 DOLLARS)

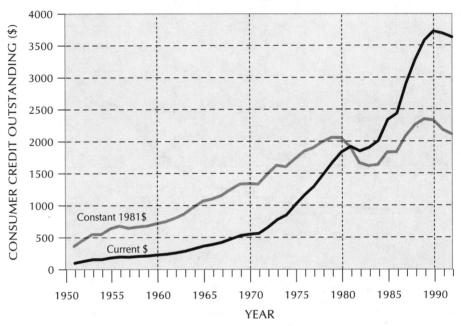

SOURCES OF DATA: *Bank of Canada Review*. Ottawa: Bank of Canada, various issues; *Canada Year Book, Canadian Statistical Review, Canadian Economic Observer, and Historical Statistical Supplement*. Ottawa: Statistics Canada, various issues. Reproduced with the permission of the Bank of Canada and the Minister of Industry, Science and Technology, 1993.

difficult to maintain their payment schedules, and bankruptcies were common. For a while, attitudes toward using consumer debt became more cautious. How long did these effects last? What has been the trend since 1983?

By 1985, Canadians began to increase their use of consumer credit, slowly at first, then more rapidly between 1987 and 1990. Predictably, the recession of 1990–92 resulted in another downturn in consumer credit use.

Debt Burden

Another way of analyzing the use of consumer credit is to relate it to income levels. If about the same proportion of income is committed to the repayment of debt year after year, it is reasonable to conclude that the burden of debt is unchanged. **Debt burden** is often measured as a ratio of debt or credit to income. Continuing to use macro data, a comparison will be made between the ratio of total consumer credit outstanding to total personal disposable income in each of the years since 1951. **Personal disposable income** is all the income received by Canadians after income tax was paid.

Debt burden, which was less than 10 percent in 1951, more than doubled to 22 percent in 1980, then declined for a few years before rising again (Figure 12.3). To understand debt burden, it is helpful to consider what was happening to family incomes in the same period. Between 1951 and 1980, the real incomes (adjusted for inflation) of Canadians increased substantially, leaving most families with more **discretionary income,** which is income left after paying for such necessaries as food, clothing, and shelter. This new prosperity made it possible to buy more consumer durables and recreational goods, which are the items most frequently bought on credit. In this period of steadily rising incomes, it became easier to repay debt because incomes tended to increase annually while most debt contracts remain fixed for several years. Thus, the combination of fixed debt commitments and rising income was beneficial for borrowers. However, in times of slower economic growth a reduction in debt burden is wise. By 1990, the ratio of debt to income had dropped somewhat.

FIGURE 12.3 RATIO OF TOTAL CONSUMER CREDIT OUTSTANDING TO PERSONAL DISPOSABLE INCOME, CANADA, 1951–1992

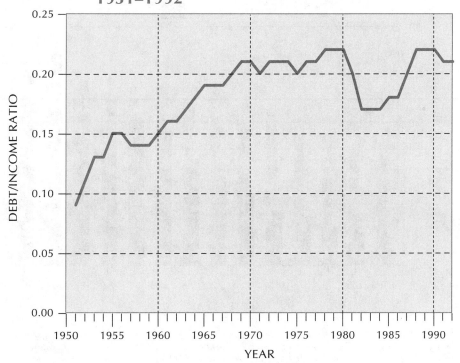

SOURCES OF DATA: *Bank of Canada Review*. Ottawa: Bank of Canada, various issues; *Canada Year Book, Canadian Statistical Review, Canadian Economic Observer, and Historical Statistical Supplement*. Ottawa: Statistics Canada, various issues. Reproduced with the permission of the Bank of Canada and the Minister of Industry, Science and Technology, 1993.

A look at what has been happening to family incomes may be helpful in interpreting trends in the use of consumer credit. According to the current dollar bars in Figure 12.4, median incomes of Canadian families increased seven-fold, or on average about 26 percent a year between 1965 and 1990. However, this rapid increase in household incomes does not mean that economic welfare grew at the same rate. By converting these data to constant 1986 dollars it is possible to estimate the purchasing power of each year's income. Assuming that the prices of goods and services had remained unchanged for these 25 years, the constant dollar figures give an estimate of the changes in purchasing power of family incomes, also known as **real incomes.** Note the steady increase in real incomes from 1965 to 1981, until the downturn in 1983. How do you think this affected the use of credit? After 1983 real incomes increased slightly, then dropped somewhat in 1990.

FIGURE 12.4 MEDIAN INCOMES OF CANADIAN FAMILIES, 1965–1990 (IN CURRENT AND CONSTANT 1986 DOLLARS)

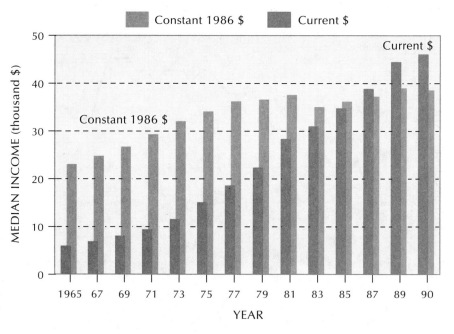

SOURCES OF DATA: *Income Distributions by Size in Canada, 1975.* Ottawa: Statistics Canada, 1977, Table 1 (p. 25); *Income Distributions by Size in Canada, 1977.* Ottawa: Statistics Canada, 1979, Table 1 (p. 39); *Income Distributions by Size in Canada, 1990.* Ottawa: Statistics Canada, 1991, Table 1 (p. 39). (Catalogue No. 13-207); *Canadian Economic Observer, Historical Statistical Supplement,* 1989/90. Ottawa: Statistics Canada, 1990, Table 3.2 (p. 4) (Catalogue No. 11-210.) Reproduced with the permission of the Minister of Industry, Science and Technology, 1993.

CONSUMER DEBT USE AT THE HOUSEHOLD LEVEL

The information examined thus far has been macro data from national statistics that give a general picture of credit use in Canada over a number of years. Another source of information about credit or debt is micro data obtained by interviewing householders. Statistics Canada has conducted infrequent surveys of consumer debt; the last three were conducted in 1969, 1977, and 1984. By asking people about their debts, incomes, and other variables, it is possible to explore relationships between debt levels and variables such as income, age, education, and occupation. Here the relation between the use of consumer debt and both income and age is examined. It is important to be aware of the exact definitions of credit and debt being used in any report. Although debt can generally be classified as consumer debt or mortgage debt, a somewhat different terminology is used in Statistics Canada household surveys where "personal debt" refers to all non-mortgage debt. For our purposes, consider personal debt and consumer debt as synonyms.

Income and Consumer Debt

Are people with higher incomes more likely to incur consumer debt than those with lower incomes? Each bar in Figure 12.5 divides all households according to whether or not they have any personal debt. What pattern do you see here? Low income families may wish to use credit, but usually are denied it because of their lack of ability to repay. From these data one may generalize that the probability of having consumer debt increases with income. Were you surprised to find a significant proportion of Canadian households with no consumer debt at all? Middle- or high-income households have the greatest probability of incurring consumer debt.

Another way of looking at the relation between income and debt is illustrated in Figure 12.6, which shows how average debt load varies by income group. Compare Figures 12.5 and 12.6. Why is the difference between the bottom and top income groups more marked in Figure 12.6? Keep in mind that these data are for all Canadian households, not only those with debts. If information were available for debtors only, the average debts would of course be much higher.

Stage in the Life Cycle and Consumer Debt

Is the stage in the life cycle (or age) associated with the probability of having certain kinds of debt? A curvilinear relation between age and the incidence (probability) of personal and mortgage debt is clearly shown in Figure 12.7. It appears that those who are 35 to 44 years old are most likely to have both kinds of debt, and those over 65 to have neither. This is consistent with the needs at different stages in the life cycle. Younger families start buying houses and collecting household durables, and by retirement they have usually discharged these debts.

FIGURE 12.5 PERCENTAGE DISTRIBUTION OF CANADIAN HOUSEHOLDS BY STATUS OF CONSUMER DEBT AND BY INCOME GROUPS, SPRING 1984

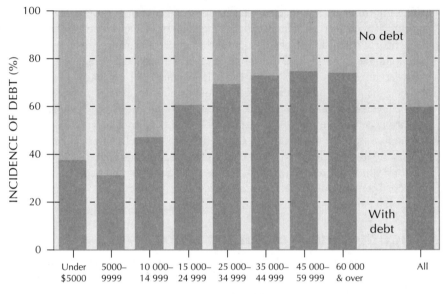

SOURCE OF DATA: *The Distribution of Wealth in Canada, 1984.* Ottawa: Statistics Canada, 1986, Table 25 (p. 67). (Catalogue No. 13-580.) Reproduced with the permission of the Minister of Industry, Science and Technology, 1993.

The relation between average debt and the age of the household head follows a pattern similar to the incidence data. Those aged 35 to 44 have the highest levels of consumer debt (Figure 12.8). Again these data are for all households, not only debtors.

Debt/Income Ratio

The data examined thus far show how income and stage in the life cycle (age) affect (i) the probability that households will use consumer debt, and (ii) how much debt they use. Another way to analyze the use of consumer debt is to look at the ratio of consumer debt to income, or debt burden. No recent data are available, but in the past it has been found that middle-income households had a higher propensity to incur a heavy debt burden. This is quite understandable, considering that low-income families are often very young or very old, and not usually seen as good candidates for consumer credit. Those with high incomes, while heavy users of credit, have large enough incomes to make the burden manageable.

FIGURE 12.6 AVERAGE TOTAL PERSONAL DEBT OF CANADIAN HOUSEHOLDS BY INCOME GROUPS, CANADA, SPRING 1984

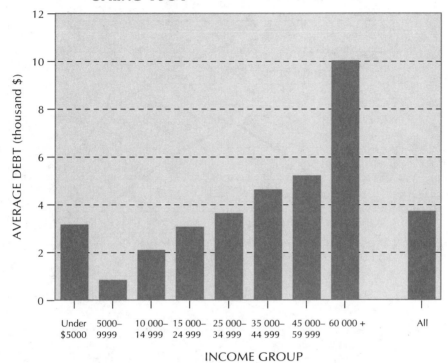

SOURCE OF DATA: *The Distribution of Wealth in Canada, 1984.* Ottawa: Statistics Canada, 1986 Tables 1 and 24 (pp. 26, 64). (Catalogue No. 13-580.) Reproduced with the permission of the Minister of Industry, Science and Technology, 1993.

Measuring Use of Consumer Credit

To determine which population segments use more credit, it is necessary first to decide how to measure consumer credit activity. Three possible ways are: (i) the probability that any consumer credit will be used (Figures 12.5 and 12.7), (ii) the average amount of consumer debt carried by the household (Figures 12.4 and 12.6), or (iii) the debt burden.

WHY DO WE USE CREDIT?

Undoubtedly, there are many reasons why we use credit, but most can be classified into four main categories. Credit is used: (i) for convenience, (ii) to obtain

FIGURE 12.7 INCIDENCE OF CONSUMER AND MORTGAGE DEBT OF CANADIAN HOUSEHOLDS, BY AGE OF HEAD, SPRING 1984

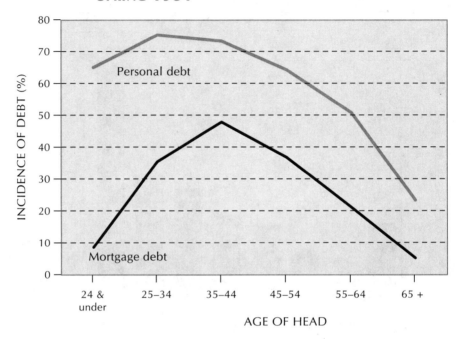

SOURCE OF DATA: *The Distribution of Wealth in Canada, 1984.* Ottawa: Statistics Canada, 1986, Table 27 (p. 73). (Catalogue No. 13-580.) Reproduced with the permission of the Minister of Industry, Science and Technology, 1993.

something before saving enough to pay for it, (iii) to bridge the gap if income is insufficient, infrequent, or irregular, and occasionally (iv) to consolidate debts. Each of these reasons may have costs as well as benefits.

Convenience

It is very handy to use a credit card instead of carrying cash, and to be able to use one cheque to pay for a number of bills. As long as the amount outstanding is paid monthly, it is an interest-free convenience. Some charge accounts require that the total bill be paid monthly, but there are others, such as bank credit cards and retail revolving accounts, that offer a choice of paying all or a portion of the debt. This option makes it quite easy to let bills accumulate and the interest rates charged on unpaid balances are usually high. Another disadvantage is that a credit card tends to encourage impulsive shopping; having to pay in cash is a more effective restraint.

FIGURE 12.8 AVERAGE TOTAL PERSONAL DEBT OF CANADIAN HOUSEHOLDS BY AGE OF HEAD, SPRING 1984

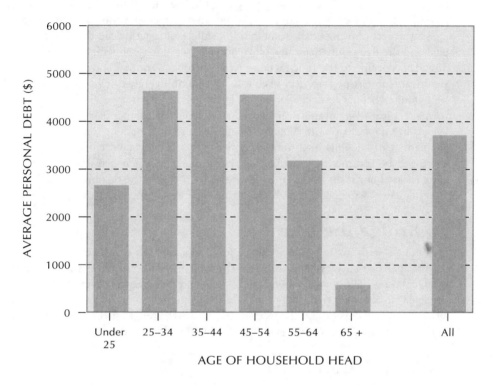

SOURCE OF DATA: *The Distribution of Wealth in Canada, 1984.* Ottawa: Statistics Canada, 1986, Tables 5 and 26 (pp. 32, 70). (Catalogue No. 13-580.) Reproduced with the permission of the Minister of Industry, Science and Technology, 1993.

Immediacy

As advertisers eagerly point out, credit allows us to have things immediately and pay later. This is a very successful means of selling high-priced goods and services because buyers do not have to consider whether they can afford the selling price, but merely whether they can manage the monthly payments. Each individual must decide whether or not the benefits outweigh the costs. Sometimes, the opportunity to have a good or service immediately can be worth the cost. When you take into account the costs of being without a car or certain equipment, you may discover monetary benefits in using credit.

Most of the benefits of using credit for this reason, however, are not monetary. It is very appealing to have something we want as soon as we see it, but whether the resulting satisfaction offsets the cost is a personal decision. There are people who find it almost impossible to save enough to accumulate the purchase price of expensive items; using credit is the only way they can acquire such things. In such instances, credit becomes a form of forced saving, although an expensive one.

Two costs of using credit to obtain immediate satisfaction are the interest to be paid and the loss of financial flexibility. Interest is a direct monetary cost that varies directly according to the time taken to repay the debt. Another cost that can be very significant, but is perhaps less visible, is the **flexibility cost** of having committed some future income to debt repayment. Using credit means accepting an obligation to make future payments that may curtail freedom to spend in other ways. If something happens to the income stream because of illness or loss of a job, debt payments can become a substantial burden. Or, if unexpected emergencies occur, there will be less money available for large expenses. When consumer durables or vehicles are bought on credit, one must consider not only the flexibility cost but also whether it is possible to handle the recurring expenses of operation and maintenance.

To Bridge the Gap

Individuals with an irregular income, such as many self-employed persons, may require loans to pay regular costs until the next income cheque. Until a sufficient reserve fund is built up, loans to bridge this gap may be necessary. Even with a regular income, on occasion there may not be enough money to cover reasonable needs. When income prospects appear good, it may be worthwhile to incur debt to furnish a first home, to support a growing family, or to obtain education.

Consolidation Loans

When all the bills and debts exceed income, some people borrow enough to repay all outstanding debts and then owe a larger amount to one lender for a longer time, through a consolidation loan. Such a loan is one way to reduce the financial pressure, but it tends to lock a person into continual debt. This will be discussed in more detail in the chapter on debt strategies.

Inflation

In inflationary periods, borrowers tend to benefit at the expense of lenders. As prices rise and incomes tend to increase, borrowers pay back loans that have fixed payments. This makes it comparatively easy to handle debt. The lender, on the other hand, is paid back in dollars that will buy less than when they were lent. Another aspect of very rapid inflation is the advantage of making a purchase before the price goes up any more. Under these conditions it may be quite rational to use credit rather than accumulate savings. However, doing so may leave you vulnerable if economic conditions change, as they did in the early 1980s and the early 1990s.

Summary

Consumer debt and consumer credit are synonyms, with the choice of term dependent on one's perspective. By convention, data on mortgage debt are kept separate from consumer debt. Canadians have significantly increased their use of consumer credit during the past several decades, but only a small portion of the increase may be attributed to population growth. Inflation had a significant effect on the total amount of credit extended, but when the data are corrected for price change, it is apparent that we have been making greater use of consumer credit. Information about consumer credit use may be obtained from lenders or from borrowers themselves. In this chapter, we examined data from both macro and micro sources.

Three measures of the use of consumer credit by households are (i) the proportion of families that make some use of credit (or incidence of credit use) (ii) the average debt level of the household, and (iii) the ratio of consumer debt to income. Income level tends to be positively related to the probability of using consumer credit and there is a curvilinear relation between credit use and age. Middle-income families that use consumer credit tend to carry the heaviest debt burdens.

Vocabulary Review

constant dollars (p. 360)

consumer debt (p. 359)

current dollars (p. 360)

debt burden (p. 362)

discretionary income (p. 363)

flexibility cost (p. 370)

mortgage debt (p. 359)

personal disposable income (p. 362)

real income (p. 364)

total consumer credit outstanding (p. 360)

total debt (p. 359)

Problems

1. Refer to Figures 12.1 and 12.2 when answering these questions

   (a) What numbers were plotted to make Figure 12.1? Who supplied these credit figures to Statistics Canada?

   (b) Do these data refer to all Canadians, only those with debts, or to whom?

   (c) Is it possible to tell from these data how many people had large debts and how many had no debts?

   (d) Do these figures include mortgage credit?

   (e) Why is the slope of the line in Figure 12.1 steeper each decade? Suggest several possibilities.

(f) Why is the constant dollar line in Figure 12.2 the more meaningful one?

(g) Suggest two or three reasons why Canadians have increased their levels of debt since 1951.

(h) Why did we convert the data from current dollars into constant dollars?

(i) Why did the constant dollar line in Figure 12.2 curve downward in the early 1980s? What has been happening more recently?

2.   These questions relate to Figure 12.3.

(a) What adjustment was made to the total consumer credit outstanding figures to create the ratios plotted in this graph?

(b) How are the data presented in Figure 12.3 different from those shown in the two previous graphs?

(c) Explain how debt burden was measured.

(d) What would it have meant if the line in the graph had been perfectly horizontal?

(e) Write a sentence that summarizes Figure 12.3.

(f) Is it true that the debt burden of Canadians in 1992 was about the same as 20 years before?

3.   What is the difference between

(a) total debt and consumer debt?

(b) consumer debt and personal debt?

(c) current and constant dollars?

(d) consumer debt and consumer credit?

(e) personal disposable income and personal discretionary income?

(f) debt burden and average debt?

(g) principal and interest?

4.   (a) Why is it important to use constant dollars when comparing the trend in family incomes?

(b) What is the significance of the information presented in Figure 12.4 in explaining use of consumer credit?

5.   Is it true that in 1984,

(a) slightly over one-half of Canadian households had some personal debt?

(b) about one-fifth of households in the lowest income class had consumer debt?

(c) the probability of having consumer debt exceeded that of having mortgage debt at all stages in the life cycle?

(d) those households headed by a person aged 24 or under were very much more likely to have consumer debt than mortgage debt?

(e) the probability of having mortgage debt is highest when the head of the household is between the ages of 35 and 44?

6. (a) What is the difference between the kinds of information plotted in Figures 12.7 and 12.8?

   (b) How can the information in Figure 12.7 be used in interpreting that in Figure 12.8?

7. Suggest some examples or situations in which the flexibility cost of credit could be so high that borrowing might be unwise.

8. In this chapter, four reasons for using consumer credit were advanced. Can you suggest others? In your opinion, which reason is the most common?

9. Do you think Canadians should use less credit? Comment.

10. Have you observed any difference between your parents' or grandparents' generations and your own in their attitudes toward using credit? Comment.

REFERENCES

STATISTICAL REPORTS

STATISTICS CANADA. *Canadian Economic Observer*. Ottawa: Supply and Services Canada, monthly. (Catalogue No. 11-010.)

STATISTICS CANADA. *The Distribution of Wealth in Canada, 1984*. Ottawa: Supply and Services Canada, 1986. (Catalogue No. 13-580.)

STATISTICS CANADA. *Income Distribution by Size in Canada*. Ottawa: Supply and Services Canada, annual. (Catalogue No. 13-207.)

Consumer Loans

(c) the penalties for late payments,

(d) the conditions under which a creditor may enforce security and the means that may be used.

10. To explain these terms: spread, common bond, fiduciary, living trust, testamentary trust, term of a loan, loan terms, fully secured loan, collateral, maturity date, skip, seize or sue law.

11. To compare the cost of various types of consumer loans.

Introduction

This chapter and the next are about various forms of consumer credit, who the chief lenders are, and the lending process. One way to organize this subject is to classify credit transactions as either: (i) obtaining a loan from a financial institution, or (ii) making a purchase and arranging with the vendor for credit financing. This chapter will focus on **consumer loans,** where credit is obtained separately from a purchase. Although a person may borrow from the bank and use the funds to buy a car, these are separate transactions with two different firms. **Point-of-sale credit,** the subject of the next chapter, occurs when the purchase and the extension of credit occur in the same transaction.

READING CREDIT CONTRACTS   Generally, it is difficult to obtain credit without signing a contract. Some contracts cover all future purchases or loans (e.g., for a credit card or line of credit) while others apply to a specific transction. Many people, intimidated by the legal terminology and small print, sign their acceptance of terms they do not understand. To help you to develop skill in reading credit contracts, several samples are presented in this and the next chapters. Read them carefully and do the related problems. Although the contracts may seem forbidding at first glance, your ability to understand them will grow with practice. It is hoped that in future you will never sign an agreement that you have not read and do not fully understand.

MAJOR CONSUMER LENDERS

Funds can be borrowed from a number of places, but four financial institutions particularly active in providing consumer loans are banks, credit unions, trust companies, and small loan companies. Funds may also be borrowed against the cash value of life insurance if you happen to own the right kind of policy. Other possibilities, which do not fit this discussion, are family and friends, the pawnbroker, and the loan shark.

Market Shares

In the previous chapter, we saw that the long-term trend in Canada was towards an increase in the use of consumer credit. Here, we will examine how the consumer credit market is shared by various creditors. In Figure 13.1 each bar represents all the consumer credit outstanding in Canada in a given year, and the divisions show how the business was divided among lenders. These data include both consumer loans and point-of-sale credit, and since some creditors offer both, the data are difficult to separate. Bank consumer lending, which includes personal loans and credit cards, represents a mixture of loan and point-of-sale credit.

FIGURE 13.1   SHARE OF TOTAL CONSUMER CREDIT OUTSTANDING BY SOURCE,* CANADA, 1951–1992

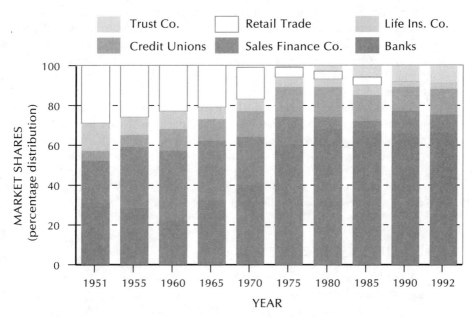

* These data show estimated amounts of consumer credit on the books of selected lenders. The data collected have not been completely consistent over the 40-year period. Since 1978, the data do not include credit held by TV and appliance stores, other retail outlets, motor vehicle dealers, public utilities, credit card issuers not included elsewhere in the data, and charge card accounts of oil companies.

** Retail trade no longer shown separately.

*** In 1992, finance companies included other institutions; in previous years only sales finance and small loan companies were combined.

SOURCES OF DATA: *Bank of Canada Review*. Ottawa: Bank of Canada, various issues. *Canada Year Book*. Ottawa: Statistics Canada, various issues. (Catalogue No. 11-402.) Reproduced with the permission of the Bank of Canada and the Minister of Industry, Science and Technology, 1993.

It is clear from Figure 13.1 that significant changes in market shares have occurred over past decades. The most striking point is the shift to banks as the major creditors; they have taken market shares from retail trade, and also from sales finance and small loan companies. Credit unions have slightly increased their share of the consumer credit business while life insurance policy loans have shown a decline. Trust companies entered the consumer credit business more recently, but have been gaining an increasing market share. Keep these trends in mind as we review the major consumer lenders and think about possible reasons for the changes.

Financial Institutions

At one time banks, credit unions, trust companies, and small loan companies were distinctly different in structure and in the services they provided but now the trend is towards greater similarity. Changes in legislation have removed many of the barriers that once kept banks, brokers, trust companies and insurers operating distinctly different businesses. Although consumers may find little changed on the surface, behind the scenes things are very different. Banks have bought much of the brokerage industry, become active in mutual funds, are moving into the trust business and are endeavouring to get into the life insurance industry. What does this mean for consumers? For one thing, there is less competition in the market place, now dominated by a few giant companies.

In the present period of rapid change, it is difficult to find clear distinctions among financial institutions. Soon, we may be going to one place to do banking, buy insurance, order mutual funds and set up trusts. Credit unions have changed also, but so far, have not merged with other financial institutions.

LIFE INSURER OPENS BANK

In late 1992, Manufacturers Life Insurance Company announced that it would become the first insurer to open a bank under new federal rules. The new Manulife Bank intends to build a commercial and retail business with offices across Canada, beginning with 14 Ontario branches converted from three tiny trust companies it owns. The company is considering offering mutual and money market funds, credit cards, an automated teller network, and RRSPs.

Banks

The chartered banks, many of which have large systems of branch offices, borrow from depositors to lend to those who need money. They charge sufficient interest on the money they lend to pay interest to their creditors, the depositors. The difference between the rate charged on loans and the rate paid on deposits is called the **spread,** and covers the cost of operation and profit for bank shareholders. Chartered banks are regulated by the federal Bank Act which is revised about once a decade. Until the 1967 revision, banks were restricted in their consumer loan activity by the act. Afterwards banks became very active in consumer loans as can be seen in Figure 13.1. Although they once concentrated on banking, now they are the most powerful Canadian financial institutions.

Trust Companies

Trust companies, active in Canada since the latter part of the nineteenth century, provide financial and trustee services to individuals and corporations. A **trustee,** which may be a person or a trust company, manages financial affairs for others—either during their lifetime or after death. Sometimes people stipulate in their wills that a trust fund be set up on their death, naming a person or trust company as trustee to handle the funds. In Canada, trust companies have been the only corporations that may act as trustees. Previously, banks and other financial institutions were not permitted to conduct **fiduciary** business, that is, to act as trustees, but this may be changing.

Trust companies have certain advantages over individuals acting in a trustee role because they can provide continuous service over a long period of time. In addition, the expertise of trust companies may be invaluable if the trust is a complex one and involves large sums of money. In exchange for their services, trust companies charge an annual fee, which is usually a percentage of the capital being managed. For individuals, trust companies handle both **living trusts,** which have been established by persons still alive, and **testamentary trusts,** which are created by a will, on a person's death. A large part of the business of trust companies is acting as trustees for other corporations in handling pension funds, bond issues, and the like.

Because the charters of trust companies do not limit them to fiduciary business, they are active financial intermediaries, taking in deposits and making loans of various kinds. Generally, only the larger trust companies are in the consumer loan business, but mortgage lending is a different matter. In recent years, trust and mortgage loan companies have provided significant amounts of mortgage funds. As many small trust companies go out of business or are bought by larger ones, we see fewer and larger trust companies dominating the scene. The survivors are competing directly with banks in the services they offer.

Small Loan Companies

Many small loan companies and money lenders are affiliated with other financial institutions, especially sales finance companies. It is not uncommon for a firm to operate both a small loan and a sales finance business from the same premises; because of this close affiliation their statistics are often combined. The principal distinction is that small loan companies and money lenders make cash loans, while sales finance companies buy credit contracts arranged by retailers (as will be explained in Chapter 14). The cost of credit at these small loan companies tends to be high because of such factors as their acceptance of higher risk borrowers, the cost of processing small loans, and the fact that they are not deposit-taking institutions but must borrow from other sources. Note that before 1975 they had a significant share of the consumer credit business which has since diminished (Figure 13.1). Consequently, there are fewer small loans or sales finance companies in business these days.

Life Insurance Policy Loans

Loans may be made against life insurance policies that have a cash surrender value, such as whole life, but not against term or most group policies that have no cash value. It takes two or three years for cash surrender value to build up enough to make the policyholder eligible for a loan. The cash value of the policy grows each year that the policy is in force and the amounts are shown in the policy. Generally, policies permit about 90 percent to 100 percent of the cash value to be borrowed.

The interest rate on life insurance policy loans is usually lower than from other commercial sources. Before 1968 the maximum loan rate was 6 percent, but policies written since are not so restricted and now the usual practice is not to state a lending rate in the policy. There is no difficulty in obtaining the loan because the policyholder borrows from the cash value of his or her own policy. Also, there is no time limit for repaying the loan; interest due will automatically be added to the loan. A loan on a policy does not invalidate life insurance coverage. When the policyholder dies, the policy remains intact, but any outstanding debt is subtracted from the payment to the beneficiary. The terms of the loan are stated in the life insurance policy. Look at the sample life insurance policy in Chapter 6 to find out what the terms are for a policy loan.

As a share of all consumer credit outstanding in Canada, life insurance policy loans are not very significant and, in fact, are decreasing. In 1955, policy loans represented less than nine percent of all consumer credit, but by 1992 this share was down to three percent. Some possible reasons are that the demand for consumer credit has increased at a much faster rate than the purchase of life insurance, more life insurance without cash value is being sold now than previously, and loans are readily available elsewhere. It is quicker and simpler to charge things on a credit card than to negotiate a life insurance loan. Life insurance companies do not especially promote policy loans and many people have so little understanding of their life insurance coverage that they may not be aware of this source of credit.

CREDIT UNIONS

The financial cooperatives in the consumer lending and saving business are the **credit unions,** originally created to offer services to low-income families whose only alternative was a loan shark. By pooling the funds of savers, money could be lent at reasonable rates to those who needed to borrow, resulting in an arrangement advantageous to both savers and borrowers. Early credit unions were small, members knew one another, and personal needs received careful attention. When a debt to one's credit union was seen as a personal obligation to friends or associates, social pressure to repay loans was strong and losses minimized, but this has now changed considerably.

History

The credit union movement began in 1847 when mayor and lay preacher, Friedrich Raiffeisen, became concerned about the peasants of southern Germany, who were hopelessly in debt following a series of crop failures. The only sources of loans available to them were banks, which required gilt-edged security, or loan sharks who exacted punitive interest rates. He was instrumental in establishing credit societies, using the small savings of members to create funds to be borrowed by others. By the time of his death in 1888, 423 credit unions were flourishing in Germany.

At the turn of the century a legislative reporter, Alphonse Desjardins of Lévis, Quebec, noted the high rates being charged by money lenders to the poor people of the region. Using some of Raiffeisen's ideas, Desjardins started **La Caisse Populaire de Lévis** with an initial membership of 80 people and assets of $26. This venture was so successful in meeting a widespread need that credit unions were organized in many Quebec parishes. As the credit union idea spread, first from Lévis to Boston, then to Nova Scotia, Saskatchewan, and across the continent, it was adapted to meet local requirements. Few credit unions were established in Ontario before 1945, when the move towards industrial credit unions began.

Organization

COMMON BOND   To do business with a credit union one must be a member and, furthermore, it is a legal requirement that members share a **common bond,** which may be the same place of employment; membership in the same church, labour union, or fraternal organization; or residence in a community or on a military base. Potential members must meet the common bond requirement and buy a share in the credit union, which may cost as little as five dollars. Recently, as a result of mergers, larger credit unions with residential common bonds have replaced small credit unions with their very specific common bonds (such as place of employment or church membership).

MEMBER INVOLVEMENT   As part of a non-profit cooperative, members have a say in the credit union's operation through the elected board of directors, which determines general policy and either handles operating decisions or delegates them to a paid manager. The net earnings of credit unions are returned to members, both borrowers and depositors, in a variety of ways, such as dividends on the share accounts, higher interest rates on deposits, lower charges for loans, or additional services.

PROVINCIAL DIFFERENCES   The credit union movement is strongest in Quebec (over 60 percent of the population are members) and in Saskatchewan (more than half of the population are members). In most other provinces, credit union members represent less than a third of the population. The Quebec credit unions, or caisses populaires, have nearly one-half of all the Canadian credit union assets. Saskatchewan and Quebec far outrank the other provinces in credit union assets per capita.

NETWORK All credit unions are linked into regional, provincial and national networks. Starting at the top, there is the World Council of Credit Unions, made up of national associations such as the Credit Union Central of Canada. In Canada, the three-tiered structure is composed of provincial chapters or centrals, regional groupings, and local credit unions. This leaves credit unions with much local autonomy but with connections to the larger organization. Local credit unions, with their separate boards of directors, are more independent than the branches of large banks. Nevertheless, there is a move to coordinate services so that a member of one credit union can conduct business at another credit union.

The provincial centrals offer important assistance to credit unions, including: investing their surplus funds or lending them additional money; supplying legal assistance, lobbying power, and educational services; and providing central purchasing of supplies. Deposit insurance, which is very important to savers, is arranged through the provincial centrals.

SECURITY Borrowers at credit unions may be asked to provide several forms of security. For example, they may be required to maintain the equivalent of ten percent of the outstanding balance on their loans in a deposit account, and in addition to sign a promissory note, a wage assignment and, if appropriate, a chattel mortgage. In some instances a co-signer may be required. These terms will be explained later in this chapter.

Recent Trends

NUMBERS OF CREDIT UNIONS Historically, most credit unions were operated by volunteers in premises that were often rent-free. These small, amateur operations were low cost and intimate, but eventually, they became unable to compete with the larger-scale and more professional activities of banks and trust companies. As a consequence, many small credit unions merged to form fewer, larger unions, and hired staff to run them, making them into more efficient and impersonal institutions. The pattern of change in numbers of credit union locals is illustrated in Figure 13.2, which shows the gradual growth of credit unions in the early years, their rapid expansion between 1950 and 1960, and the effects of the mergers after 1970.

SERVICES Credit unions vary considerably in size and in the range of services offered. All receive deposits and make loans, but some offer a variety of deposit accounts and savings vehicles, chequing services, mortgage loans, and automatic tellers. The larger credit unions have become quite competitive with banks and trust companies in interest rates and services offered.

With the creation of larger credit unions, volunteer staff have been replaced with paid professional managers, loan officers, and independent auditors. These changes were necessary if credit unions were to become competitive with other financial institutions. Interestingly, credit unions were the leaders among financial institutions in offering weekly payment mortgages, daily interest savings accounts, and exploring the use of debit cards. To expedite the blurring of distinctions among

FIGURE 13.2   NUMBER OF CREDIT UNIONS IN CANADA, 1920–1992

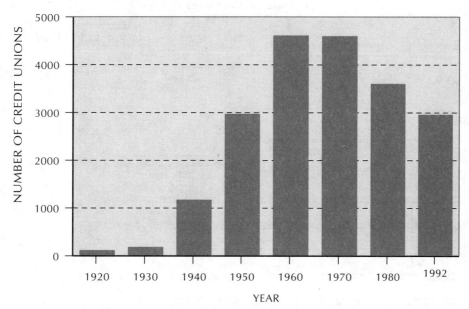

SOURCE OF DATA: Canada Year Book. Ottawa: Statistics Canada Various issues: 1948–49 (p. 1051); 1961, Table 18 (p. 1130); 1962, Table 18 (p. 1108); 1972, Table 17 (p. 1245); 1990, Table 18.14, (p. 18–17); 1992, personal communication. (Catalogue No. 11-402.) Reproduced with the permission of the Minister of Industry, Science and Technology, 1993.

financial institutions, British Columbia revised its Financial Institutions Act making credit unions subject to the same rules as other institutions and giving them the right to sell equity shares to members. In 1992, the national trade association, the Credit Union Central of Canada, announced plans to introduce a new group of ethical mutual funds across Canada.

OBTAINING A LOAN

Loan Application

The procedure for obtaining a loan is about the same at any lender. The credit manager will request the completion of a loan application form (Figure 13.3), which requires considerable detail about the applicant's past financial activities. On the basis of this and other information that may be obtained in a credit report, the loan officer will decide whether or not to grant the loan. (Discussion of credit reports, credit bureaus, and how lenders evaluate the creditworthiness of customers is found in Chapter 16.) If the decision is favourable, the next step is to settle the **terms of the**

FIGURE 13.3 PERSONAL LOAN APPLICATION

Bank of Montreal

Personal Loan Service Application
(including Mortgages and MasterCard)

Application No. 2,3,4,1,2,3,5,6,7,3,4,5

Domicile
NOTE — COMPLETE ALL APPLICABLE CODE BOXES

– – – – –IDENTIFIES INFORMATION NOT ENTERED ON CCAPS

Own Transit D | Sale Transit | PLC Designation No. H | Priority if other than standard | Priority Code | Language Preference: English E / French F | Source Description | Business Gained/Source Code

Interviewing Officer — Name: Nancy King — I.D. No. 2,1,2,1 — Dealer — I.D. No.

Realtor Referral — Name of Realty Office — Name of Agent — Area Code — Telephone No.

SECTION 1 — Application Details / Customer Identification

Application for — RECORD DETAILS OF PURPOSE ON PAGE 3

	Product Code	Required Amount/Limit	Purpose Code	Term (Months)	Amortization Period (Months)	Interest Rate	Payment Frequency	Payment Amount
1	automobile	$ 16,000		12	60	7¼	bi-weekly	$ 158.95
2		$						$
3		$						$
4		$						$
5		$						$

Present/Previous Borrower? ☐ Yes ☒ No (If yes complete this section in full)

Original Loan Date M M Y Y | Original Loan Amount $ | Current Balance $ | Customer Since?

Branch — Transit No. — Address | Refinance? ☐ Yes ☐ No

Application Type Code | Related Application (Use only with APP Types JO or IO) Name | Reference No.

ALSO COMPLETE FIELDS AS APPROPRIATE FOR MORTGAGE APPLICATIONS AND OTHER REAL ESTATE FINANCING
Owner Occupied ☐ Yes ☐ No | Purchase Price $ | Interest Rate % (P.A.) ☐ Fixed ☐ Variable
Portable Mortgage Option ☐ Yes ☐ No | If yes, existing Mortgage No.

IF THIS APPLICATION IS NOT JOINT WITH SPOUSE, IT IS NOT NECESSARY TO COMPLETE THE SPOUSAL INFORMATION SECTIONS MARKED WITH AN ASTERISK*

	Title	First Name	Middle Initial	Last Name	Date of Birth D D M M Y Y	Identification Code	Number
Primary Applicant	Mrs	Jill	A	Dubois	31 05 45	SIN	234 567 890
*Spouse	Mr	Peter	D	Dubois	06 03 40	SIN	342 756 908

Marital Status Code: ☒ Married M ☐ Single S | ☐ Separated P ☐ Divorced D | ☐ Widow(er) W ☐ Unknown U | No. of Dependents (Excluding Spouse): 2

Present Address — No. Street: 44 Niska Rd. | Street Type Code | Apt./Suite Box | City/Town: Salem | Province Code: Ont.
Postal Code: N I M 2 W 3 | Area Code Telephone No.: 519 846 3121 | How Long? 6 0 2 Y Y M M | Occupancy Code ☒ Own O ☐ Rent R | ☐ Room and Board B ☐ Other X | ☐ Live with Parents or Relatives P

Previous Address — No. Street | Street Type Code | Apt./Suite Box | City/Town | Province Code
Postal Code | How Long? Y Y M M

Prod. 1090554 - Form. 3004 AIR (1/92) Litho. CANADA - 514915

FIGURE 13.3 PERSONAL LOAN APPLICATION (CONTINUED)

SECTION 2 — Employment Customer Name _____

Present Employer			
Company Name: **Gorge Pottery**		Area Code **519**	Telephone No. **846-9,222**
Address: **5 Main St.**	City/Town: **Elora**		Province: **Ont.**
Occupation: **Potter**		Occupation Code	How Long? **05** Y/Y **08** M/M
Employment Type Code: ☐ Full-Time 00, ☐ Part-Time 01, ☒ Self Employed 02, ☐ Unemployed 03, ☐ Retired 04, ☐ Other 05, ☐ Seasonal 06			Business For Self? ☒ Yes ☐ No

Previous Employer		
Company Name	Address	How Long? Y/Y M/M

*Spouse's Employer			
Company Name: **University of Guelph**		Area Code **519**	Telephone No. **824-4,120**
Address	City/Town: **GUELPH**		Province: **Ont.**
Occupation: **Electrician**		Occupation Code	How Long? **10** Y/Y **04** M/M
Employment Type Code: ☒ Full-Time 00, ☐ Part-Time 01, ☐ Self Employed 02, ☐ Unemployed 03, ☐ Retired 04, ☐ Other 05, ☐ Seasonal 06			Business For Self? ☐ Yes ☒ No

*Spouse's Previous Employer		
Company Name	Address	How Long? Y/Y M/M

SECTION 3 — Gross Monthly Income

Applicant	From Employment	Pension	Other	Total Income
	$ **24,500**	+ $	+ $	= $ **24,500**
	Source/Details of Other Income			

*Spouse	From Employment	Pension	Other	Total Income
	$ **52,000**	+ $	+ $	= $ **52,000**
	Source/Details of Other Income		Was income provided by the customer? ☐ Yes ☐ No	

SECTION 4 — Assets ENSURE ACCURATE, DETAILED DESCRIPTIONS & BALANCES ARE PROVIDED FOR ANY ASSETS LISTED

Type	CODE	Description			Estimated Value
Residence	RES	Registered in Name(s) of **PETER + JILL DUBOIS**	Purchase Price $ **85,000**	Purchased **05** M/M **84** Y/Y	$ **135,000**
Vehicles 1	VEH 1	Year **1991**	Make **Suzuki Swift**	Model	$ **12,000**
Vehicles 2	VEH 2	Year **1984**	Make **Honda Civic**	Model	$ **7,000**
Investments 1		Type			$
2					$
Other Assets 1		Description **RRSP**			$ **7,500**
2		**Canada Savings Bonds**			$ **1,500**
3		**Bolton Tremblay Money Fund**			$ **10,000**
4					$
5					$
Savings Account		Name and Address of Financial Institution	Account No.		Balance $
Chequing Account		Name and Address of Financial Institution **Bank of Montreal**	Account No. **2500-000**		Balance $ **1,235**
				TOTAL ASSETS	$ **174,235**

FIGURE 13.3 PERSONAL LOAN APPLICATION (CONTINUED)

Customer Name _____

SECTION 5 – Liabilities   ENSURE ACCURATE, DETAILED DESCRIPTION & BALANCES ARE PROVIDED FOR ANY LIABILITIES LISTED

Type	CODE	I/J	Description			Balance	Monthly Payment	R (Rating)	Is this Liab. to be Consolidated? If yes enter "C"	Payout
Mortgage Holder/ 1	MTG __		Name Bank of Montreal Address Guelph		Mtg. (P.I.T.)					$
			Telephone No. 519-824 2112	Account No. 12-321-02	Maturity Date 05/04	$38800	$507.82			
2nd Mortgage Holder 2	MTG __		Name Address							$
			Telephone No.	Account No.	Maturity Date	$	$			

Type	CODE	I/J	Name / Address & Account No.	Credit Limit (revolving only)	Balance	Monthly Payment	R (Rating)	Is this Liab. to be Consolidated? If yes enter "C"	Payout
M/C 3	MC __			$	$	$			$
Visa 4	VCO		VISA R/B	$1000	$ 0	$ 30			$
Landlord if Applicable 5	RENT					$			
6			SEARS CARD INC.	$1000	$235	$ 50			$
7				$	$	$			$
8			Property taxes	$	$	$125			$
9				$	$	$			$
10				$	$	$			$
11				$	$	$			$
			TOTALS		$39035	$712.82			

Is applicant willing to provide security?
☐ NO ☒ YES – DESCRIPTION: automobile   Security Code
Purpose Details/Comments personal and business use

Security on Present Advances

FIGURE 13.3 PERSONAL LOAN APPLICATION (CONTINUED)

Customer Name _____

Personal References (Relatives or Friends not living with Applicant)

	Name	Address	Area Code	Telephone No.	Relationship
1	John French	St. Jacobs	519	664 1212	father
2	Pamela Smith	Salem	519	846 9999	friend

Please read and sign below *If a Co-Applicant signs below, the words "I" and "me" refer to each of the Applicant and Co-Applicant.*
I authorize the Bank to obtain personal and credit information about me from any source.
This information, as well as that provided by me on this application, will be referred to in connection with this loan/credit and other banking relationships we may establish from time to time. **I also authorize the Bank to disclose from time to time to other lenders, credit bureaux or other credit reporting agencies personal and credit information about me.** I certify that the information in this application is true and correct.

If this application is for a loan other than a mortgage, I authorize the Bank to debit the following account with all amounts payable under the requested loan including any costs involved in arranging/maintaining security.

Transit   Account No.

Deposit Proceeds to |0|0|2|3| |2|5|0|0| |0|0|0|

Debit Payments to ☒ Same Account No.

Transit   Account No.

OR |_|_|_|_| |_|_|_|_| |_|_|_|

If this application is for a MasterCard card, please indicate your preferred choice of card :

APPLICANT'S INITIALS	SPOUSE'S INITIALS (IF CARD REQUESTED)	
		Standard MasterCard card for which there is no annual fee.*
		Standard AIR MILES MasterCard card for which there is a $35.00 annual fee.*
		Gold MasterCard card for which there is a $60.00 annual fee.* If this application for a gold MasterCard card is not approved, please treat this application as a request for your standard MasterCard card and applicable card services for which there is no annual fee.*
		Gold AIR MILES MasterCard card for which there is a $95.00 annual fee.* If this application for a gold AIR MILES Master-Card card is not approved, please treat this application as a request for your standard AIR MILES MasterCard card and applicable card services for which there is a $35.00 annual fee.*
		Prime Plus MasterCard line of credit for which there is an $18.00 annual fee* and a $10.00 annual fee* for any additional cards.

* Current fees available on request. Annual fee as of January 1, 1992.

I request a Bank of Montreal MasterCard card and renewals or replacements thereof from time to time at the Bank's discretion. I also request a Personal Identification Number (PIN) in order to allow use of the card in Bank of Montreal Instabank units, and, if available, other automated banking machine systems. If a MasterCard card is issued, I agree to abide by the terms and conditions of the applicable Bank of Montreal MasterCard Cardholder Agreement accompanying the MasterCard. If there is an annual fee, I agree that the fee is for the card and for other available plan services and will be billed directly to the card account. If an additional card is requested in Co-Applicant's name, each of the undersigned agrees to be jointly and severally liable for indebtedness and obligations incurred through use of the cards issued pursuant to such request and authorizes through use of such cards, deposits to and withdrawals from bank accounts designated by either of the undersigned.

If this application is for a mortgage, I also authorize the Bank to disclose to mortgage insurers, solicitors, notaries and real estate agents information about the mortgage that it considers appropriate. I understand that the actual granting of a mortgage loan is conditional upon an appraisal of the property satisfactory to the Bank. I acknowledge that if the mortgage loan requested exceeds 75% of the property value, a mortgage insurance premium will be payable by me to a mortgage insurer and that such premium may be added to the loan amount. I authorize the Bank to debit the following account with all amounts payable under the requested mortgage.

Transit   Account No.

|_|_|_|_| |_|_|_|_| |_|_|_|

at Bank _____

Address _____

NOTE : If payments are to be made more frequently than monthly, the above account must be maintained with and be satisfactory to Bank of Montreal. For other than Bank of Montreal accounts chequing privileges must be permitted. Please attach a specimen cheque.

APPLICABLE IN PROVINCE OF QUEBEC ONLY
It is the express wish of the Parties that this agreement and any related documents be drawn up and executed in English. Les parties conviennent que la présente convention et tous les documents s'y rattachant soient rédigés en anglais.

Signature of Applicant	Signature of Co-Applicant	Date
		May 25 19 XX

Interviewing Officer's Comments/Recommendations
Use to record additional information on security, marketing, existing loan requirements and/or financial information. Refer to individual Information Addendum for details required for specific loan situations.

Employment & Income Verification

	Employment	Income		Employment	Income	
Direct verification with employer	☐	☐	Applicant's employment known first hand, by branch management (min. req. 2 years)	☐	☐	I recommend ☐ Approval or ☐ Decline. I also have verified the Applicant's Income and Employment as indicated.
Current pay stub	☐	☐	Current security pass or work badge	☐	N/A	Branch Lender/Manager (Signature)
Current letter from employer	☐	☐	Other (Please specify)	☐	☐	
Evidence of internal direct deposit payroll	☐	☐				

loan, i.e., the principal to be lent, the interest rate, the length of time to repay, and the security required. The date when the loan must be completely repaid is known as the **maturity date**, and the length of time the loan is to be outstanding is called the **term of the loan**. Notice the distinction between the "terms" of the loan and the "term" of the loan.

Types of Loans

The kinds of loans available to individuals at financial institutions differ in their terms and conditions. Interest rates are dependent on the risk level presented by the borrower and the services provided. Some arrangements provide funds on an ongoing basis and others are contracts drawn up for a specific instalment loan. Examples of the ongoing types of loans are: (i) line of credit, (ii) overdraft protection, and (iii) cash advances on a bank credit card. All of these give the borrower advance permission to borrow within set limits if the need arises. The advantage of these arrangements is that the funds are available if needed, but there are no interest charges if they are not used. At other times, a sum may be borrowed for a specific purpose with a set repayment schedule, such as: (i) a demand loan or (ii) an instalment loan.

PERSONAL LINE OF CREDIT   Banks, trust companies, and credit unions may offer their creditworthy customers a personal line of credit as a convenient substitute for personal loans. A personal line of credit is a flexible way to use credit because the financial institution makes funds available to a customer up to a set limit, whenever they are needed. There is no interest charge until some or all of the funds are used.

Once the application has been approved, a customer is granted a line of credit up to a specified maximum amount. There is usually a minimum monthly payment required in addition to interest on the outstanding monthly balance. A line of credit could be as low as $2500 or $5000, with payments of at least three to five percent of the outstanding balance. The interest rate on a line of credit is related to the prime rate and is adjusted monthly. Sometimes it is possible to arrange a line of credit that requires interest payments only. For those eligible, a line of credit may be a cheaper alternative to a personal loan.

OVERDRAFT PROTECTION   The difference between a personal line of credit and overdraft protection may be blurred by some financial institutions. Overdraft protection, available at banks, trust companies, and credit unions allows deposit accounts to become overdrawn to a set limit, for instance, $1000. The overdraft becomes a loan and is subject to interest rates as high or higher than those charged on credit card loans. The rates on a personal line of credit may be six to seven percent lower than on overdraft protection so, clearly, it is worthwhile to check this.

CREDIT CARD CASH ADVANCES   Anyone with a credit card issued by a financial institution (bank, credit union, trust company) has the option of obtaining a loan, called a cash advance, without making a special application each time funds are needed. The original contract and the previously established loan limit cover the situation. Interest, calculated daily, begins at once at rates usually higher than a line of credit or a personal loan.

DEMAND LOAN   Rather than flexible credit, customers with a good credit rating may arrange for a demand loan by signing an agreement to repay the loan in full at a certain date, with interest due monthly. The lender has the right to recall a demand loan at any time. Holders of demand loans often renegotiate them at maturity. Interest charges will be set slightly above the prime rate and will fluctuate according to the prevailing rate. The **prime rate** is the lowest interest rate that financial institutions charge their best corporate customers and is the guide for setting other interest rates.

INSTALMENT LOANS   Instalment loans usually have a set interest rate, a maturity date, a repayment schedule, and certain security requirements, as will be explained shortly. The contract signed varies with the kind of security pledged.

APPLYING FOR A PERSONAL LOAN

When Sarah and Matt applied at the bank for a personal instalment loan of $10 000 to buy a sailboat, they had outstanding balances on several credit and charge cards but their credit rating was well established. After the loans officer heard about their debts of $1100 to Mastercard, $500 to American Express, and $950 to Sears she strongly recommended that they consolidate these debts into one loan with the bank, and have only one payment to make. The bank would be happy to lend them the $10 000 they asked for and, in addition, enough to pay off all their debts.

Sarah and Matt were not keen to consolidate their credit card debt with the bank loan, but they got the impression that their loan application would be looked at more favourably if they did.

What factors should they consider before deciding to consolidate their debts?

SECURITY FOR LOANS

Lenders must consider the risk of not being repaid and take steps to minimize the consequences. They can choose to accept as borrowers only those who appear to be good risks, or can lend to a wider range of people but ask them for certain assurances. It is common practice to require a borrower to sign documents that give the lender permission in advance to take over specified possessions or assets of the borrower, should the latter fail to make the payments as agreed. These various claims on the borrower, which are arranged at the time the loan is taken out, are referred to as the security for the loan.

SECURITY AND COLLATERAL It is sometimes difficult to make a clear distinction between security and collateral. It may help to consider security as a claim or right that the borrower has voluntarily assigned to the lender in order to reduce the lender's risk. The term collateral is applied to certain tangible assets used as security, such as financial assets or durable goods. Therefore, the signature of a guarantor or co-signer is a form of security for the lender, but is not a tangible object and therefore not collateral. Promises may have some security value but are not collateral.

Fully and Partially Secured Loans

Loans may be fully or partially secured. If the borrower signs over to the lender assets equal in value to the total loan, that loan is said to be **fully secured**. Naturally, very few consumer loans are fully secured, because those with enough assets would buy the goods for cash. There are occasions, however, when requesting a fully secured loan is a reasonable decision. For instance, if funds are needed for a few months only, it may be preferable to use assets as security rather than sell the assets to pay in cash. If these assets are already invested and producing a higher yield than is available in the current market, it might be better to retain the assets and take a loan for a short time. By using bonds or similar assets as security for the loan, the borrower can expect to be charged a very favourable interest rate because the lender is taking no risk at all.

More often, loans are **partially secured** because buyers do not have sufficient assets to obtain fully secured loans. A car buyer may use the car as security for the loan, but this debt will not be fully secured because cars and some other durables depreciate faster than loans are repaid.

Signature Loans

A borrower considered to present little risk to the lender may be asked for nothing more than a signature on a **promissory note,** which is an unconditional promise to repay the loan. Such a loan, also called a signature loan, is considered to be unsecured by the lender. In other words, if the borrower does not repay the loan as promised, the lender has nothing of value belonging to the borrower that can be liquidated to pay the debt. The legal contract used for signature loans is the promissory note, which is simply a promise to repay the loan. A sample promissory note used for a personal loan is shown in Figure 13.4.

Many people are not eligible for signature loans and those who are may choose a personal line of credit because of its greater flexibility. Long-time customers of financial institutions, whose character and credit record are judged to be exemplary,

FIGURE 13.4 PERSONAL LOAN PROMISSORY NOTE

Bank of Montreal   Personal Loan Plan - Promissory Note

Branch Domicile Stamp

PLEASE PRINT

Full Name of Borrower(s)
Peter D. Dubois and Jill A. Dubois

PLP Account No. *2 5 0 0 - 0 0 0*   Date *September 5* 19

In this promissory note the words "I" and "me" mean the borrower, or if more than one, all borrowers jointly and severally.
In return for lending me money I promise to pay to the order of Bank of Montreal at the branch named above the principal sum of

$ *850.00 —* . I promise to pay interest on that sum at the rate of *7.25* % per year calculated on the dates payments are due as set out below.

I will pay the principal sum and interest by paying $ *73.61 —* on *October 5* , 19 *92* and then by paying

$ *73.61 —* every *month* _____ starting on *November 5* , 19 *92* through and including
          (specify frequency)

September 5 , 19 *93* when I will pay any balance owing.
(specify date of maturity**)

If I fail to pay any amount when it is due I will pay interest at the rate shown above on the amount until it is paid. This interest will be calculated and

payable on the dates payments are due until the maturity date and every _____ *month* _____ after that date.
                (specify frequency)

If I fail to make any payment when it is due, Bank of Montreal may require me to pay immediately the entire balance of what I owe.

If the term of the loan evidenced by this note, original or as extended, is not equal to the amortization period and if there have been no default of payments on their due dates nor any default under any security given to secure the loan evidenced by this note, I shall have the right to extend the term of the loan evidenced by this note for the balance owing on the Maturity Date to a new Maturity Date and at the interest rate required by Bank of Montreal at the time of such extension. If I do not exercise this right of extension on or before the Maturity Date or any subsequent new Maturity Date by advising Bank of Montreal of my intention to extend, Bank of Montreal may extend or further extend the term of the loan evidenced by this promissory note to a new Maturity Date and at an interest rate as required by Bank of Montreal and advise me accordingly. If Bank of Montreal does not receive from me before the 15th day after such advice has been mailed to my last known address (as shown by Bank of Montreal's records) my written advice that I do not accept such extension I shall be deemed to have accepted the same.

Peter Dubois   *Jill Dubois*
Signature of Borrower   Signature of Borrower

Prod. 2243014 · Form LF 275 (7/91) Litho. CANADA - 508975

SOURCE OF DATA: Reproduced with the permission of the Bank of Montreal.

are permitted signature loans with no other security, but most borrowers are required to provide a tangible form of security in addition to their promise. For this reason, promissory notes are often incorporated into more complex credit contracts of the sort to be discussed below. Four frequently used forms of security for loans are: (i) co-signers, (ii) future wages, (iii) financial assets, and (iv) durable goods.

Co-signer

The lender may require that the borrower find another person to sign the loan agreement. By signing, the **co-signer** (guarantor) agrees to repay any outstanding balance on the loan if the borrower fails to do so. Sometimes, people agree to co-sign loans as a gesture of friendship, without fully realizing the commitment they have made. The extent of their responsibility becomes evident when the lender requires them to make restitution for the friend or relative who cannot repay or has disappeared without repaying the loan. People who can't be found are referred to in the credit business as skips.

Future Wages

Sometimes borrowers sign an agreement that if they do not maintain the repayment schedule, the lender has permission to collect a portion of their wages directly from their employers. This contract is called a **wage assignment.** To protect borrowers from abuses of this system which have occurred in the past, the use of wage assignments has been curtailed. For instance, in Ontario credit unions are the only creditors that are permitted to use wage assignments. Note in Figure 13.5 that the borrower voluntarily agrees that, if the debt is not repaid, the credit union may collect 20 percent of his wages directly from his employer. Whether the 20 percent is based on gross or net wages varies according to jurisdiction.

In practice, the credit union would not enforce a wage assignment until less drastic measures had failed. The debtor would, of course, be informed that this was about to happen, giving him time to repay the debt or to petition for a reduction in the amount of wages to be taken. The decision to enforce the wage assignment is made

FIGURE 13.5 ASSIGNMENT OF WAGES

ASSIGNMENT OF WAGES

TO: GUELPH and WELLINGTON CREDIT UNION LIMITED
(hereinafter called the "Credit Union")

I, Michel Gélinas
(Name of Assignor)

for Valuable Consideration hereby assign, transfer and set over unto the Credit Union, (i) 20 per cent of all wages, (as defined in the Wages Act of Ontario), but excluding any amount that an employer is required by law to deduct from any such wages and (ii) all other monies owing to me, or hereafter to become owing to me by my employer: Wellington County Board of Education or any other person, firm, corporation or entity by whom I may be hereafter employed.

AND I HEREBY AUTHORIZE AND DIRECT my said employer or any future employer to pay the 20 per cent of all such wages and all such other monies to the Credit Union, and I hereby irrevocably authorize the Credit Union to take all proceedings which may be proper and necessary for the recovery of any amount or amounts above assigned and to give receipts for same, or any part thereof, in my name, and I hereby release and discharge my said employers and each of them from all liability to me for or on account of any or all monies paid in accordance with the terms hereof. Nothing herein shall prevent the Credit Union from exercising any other right of recovery available in law of any amount lawfully owing to the Credit Union in excess of the amounts assigned above.

Signed, Sealed and Delivered this 25th day of August 19 94
at GUELPH Ontario in the presence of:
WITNESS:

(FORM O.L.-D 1923/5-92 REV)

(Signature of Assignor)

Reproduced with the permission of Credit Union Central of Ontario Limited.

by the loan officer or the Board of Directors, who may grant an exemption or reduction if the borrower's situation seems to warrant it.

Financial Assets

To secure a loan, a lender may require a borrower to lodge in the lender's possession some form of **collateral,** such as bonds, stock certificates, life insurance policies, or deposits. These types of collateral are financial assets that can be readily converted to cash, which is what the lender will do if the borrower fails to maintain the terms of the loan agreement. With each form of collateral offered, the borrower will be asked to sign an appropriate agreement giving the lender the power to realize these assets in case of default on the loan. Different contracts are used, depending on the nature of the asset pledged.

A borrower who has a life insurance policy with sufficient cash surrender value may assign it to a lender as security for a loan. This process is discussed in more detail in the chapter on life insurance. Essentially it means that the policy is held by the lender until the debt is cleared, but the policyholder must continue to pay the premiums. If the borrower defaults on the loan, the lender can cash in the policy.

Durable Goods

When consumer durables such as vehicles, appliances, and furniture are bought with credit, these articles are usually offered as security. If the consumer obtains a loan from a bank, credit union, small loan, or trust company, a **chattel mortgage** will be signed that transfers the ownership of the goods to the lender (Figure 13.6). Note that the term **chattel** applies to moveable goods, but not to land or buildings (called real property), which are used as security in home mortgages. The borrower has possession of the goods and full use of them, but agrees to maintain them in good condition and, in most cases, to insure them.

During the term of the chattel mortgage, which is the time until the debt is repaid, the borrower does not have the right to sell the pledged goods without the permission of the lender. If the borrower defaults on the loan, the lender has prior permission to repossess the goods and sell them. In some provinces, Ontario for instance, the creditor may have the right to repossess and also to sue for any balance outstanding if the proceeds from the sale are insufficient to extinguish the debt. However, there has been a trend toward "seize or sue" laws (in British Columbia, Alberta, and Newfoundland) that give the creditor the option of repossessing the goods or suing the debtor, but not both.

It is important to take careful note that chattel mortgages are the contracts used by lenders when taking the title to goods as security. Vendors of goods, who already have title to the goods they are selling, are in a position to retain the title until the total cost is paid; for these transactions a different contract, called a conditional sales contract, is used. In the case of default, the vendor enforces his security by repossession. Credit sales are discussed in the next chapter.

FIGURE 13.6 CHATTEL MORTGAGE

Bank of Montreal

Chattel Mortgage - Personal Loans

(For use in all provinces except Quebec, British Columbia and Yukon)

A

THIS INDENTURE made (in duplicate)

BETWEEN

Jill A. Dubois
(First Name - Middle Name - Last Name - No Abbreviations)

31/05/45
Date of Birth - DD - MM - YY

Show full name and address

of 44 Niska Drive in the city of Salem
(Street Address) (City, etc.) (Name of City)

in the Province of Ontario , N1M 2W3
Postal Code

(hereinafter called the "Mortgagor")

— and —

BANK OF MONTREAL

of any street in the city of Guelph
(Street Address) (City, etc.) (Name of City)

in the Province of Ontario

(hereinafter called the "Mortgagee").

Insert net amount of note

WITNESSETH that in consideration of the sum of sixteen thousand —
——————————————— Dollars ($ 16,000 —),
lent and paid to the Mortgagor by the Mortgagee, (the receipt of which the Mortgagor hereby acknowledges)

Insert gross amount of note

and to secure payment of — nineteen thousand seventy four —
——————————————— Dollars ($ 19,074 —) (hereinafter called the

Insert amount of interest

"said amount owing") being the said sum so lent and paid together with — three thousand
seventy four ——————— Dollars ($ 3,074 ——), being the cost of the said

sum so lent and paid, the Mortgagor by these presents grants, bargains, sells and assigns to the **Mortgagee** the following chattels and all proceeds thereof and accessions thereto, namely :

1993 Toyota Camry
Serial No. IFBAP320J200 10714
Licence No.

Insert detailed description of chattels

(hereinafter sometimes called the "property") all of which are now owned by the Mortgagor and are located at

44 Niska Drive, Salem Ontario
(Address) (City or Town) (County or District) (Province)

TO HAVE AND TO HOLD the same unto the Mortgagee forever :

Insert gross amount of note

PROVIDED that if the Mortgagor shall pay to the Mortgagee the said amount owing of nineteen thousand
seventy four ———— Dollars ($ 19,074 —) and interest according to the terms of and as evidenced by a promissory note of even date herewith and any and all renewals thereof, and upon the due and timely performance by the Mortgagor of all the terms and covenants on the Mortgagor's part to be performed hereunder, then this mortgage shall be void.

The Mortgagor covenants with the Mortgagee as follows :

1. THAT the Mortgagor will pay to the Mortgagee the said sum of money and interest thereon as in the above proviso mentioned.

FIGURE 13.6 CHATTEL MORTGAGE (CONTINUED)

3.   THAT if the property is at the time of the making of the loan, or thereafter becomes, subject to any charge in favour of any person other than the Mortgagee, the Mortgagee may pay such charge and the amount so paid shall, together with interest thereon at the rate specified in the said promissory note, become a charge on the property in favour of the Mortgagee and be added to the sum secured hereby and the sum secured hereby, including the amount so added, shall, at the option of the Mortgagee, forthwith become due and payable.

4.   THAT the Mortgagor will insure and keep insured the property for its full insurable value against loss or damage by fire or theft and if the property includes a motor vehicle, collision, and hereby assigns to the Mortgagee all such policies of insurance and all amounts payable thereunder. If the Mortgagor fails to effect or maintain such insurance, the Mortgagee may effect and maintain the same and all moneys expended by it for such purpose, together with interest thereon at the rate specified in the said promissory note, from the time the same has been expended, shall become a charge on the property and be added to the sum secured hereby.

5.   THAT the Mortgagor will not sell or dispose of or part with the possession of the property or any part thereof and will not permanently remove it from the premises where it now is without first obtaining the written consent of the Mortgagee.

6.   THAT if the Mortgagor fails to pay any of the moneys mentioned in the proviso in accordance with the terms there set out, or fails to observe or perform any of the covenants contained herein, or institutes or does anything which permits to be instituted any proceedings leading to the Mortgagor becoming a bankrupt, or if the Mortgagor dies, then all the moneys secured hereby shall, at the option of the Mortgagee, forthwith become due and payable and the Mortgagee, its servants or agents, may, with or without legal process, take possession of the property (and may for that purpose enter upon the premises where the property is located) and sell the same at public auction or private sale or otherwise realize on the property by any method not prohibited by law, including by lease or by sale for deferred payment, with or without notice to the Mortgagor, and after payment out of the net proceeds of such sale of all amounts due to the Mortgagee hereunder the Mortgagee shall pay over to the Mortgagor or such other person who may be entitled thereto any surplus but if such proceeds are not sufficient to pay all amounts due to the Mortgagee hereunder the Mortgagor will pay the deficiency to the Mortgagee.

7.   That the Mortgagor will pay on demand to the Mortgagee all costs (including legal costs as between a solicitor and his own client) incurred by the Mortgagee in realizing on the property and enforcing the covenants in this Mortgage and the promissory note, all of which sums shall be secured hereunder and bear interest at the rate specified in the note.

8.   THAT the Mortgagee may, in order to recover any amount owing to it, hereunder, pursue either singly or concurrently the remedy of action and the remedy of taking possession and selling given to it hereby and shall not be precluded by the exercise of either remedy from proceeding to exercise the other remedy. The Mortgagee shall not be responsible for any loss or damage to the property, whether caused by the negligence or fault of the Mortgagee, its servants or agents, or a sheriff or receiver, and the Mortgagee shall not be obliged to preserve rights against other persons or prepare the property for disposition, and shall only be liable to account for funds (net of costs of collection, realization and sale, including solicitor and his own client legal costs), actually received by the Mortgagee.

Applicable in Alberta only

9.   The Mortgagor waives receipt of any financing statement registered by the Bank and any confirmation of registration.

10.   The Mortgagor acknowledges receipt of a copy of this Chattel Mortgage.

ALL grants, warrants, covenants, agreements, rights, powers, privileges and liabilities contained in this indenture shall enure to the benefit of and be binding upon the heirs, executors, administrators, successors and assigns of the parties hereto respectively ; all covenants and agreements on the part of the Mortgagor shall be construed as both joint and several and when the context so requires the singular number shall be read as if the plural were expressed.

This mortgage was executed on the   25ᵗʰ   day of   May   19 XX

IN WITNESS whereof the Mortgagor has hereunto set his hand and seal.

SIGNED, SEALED AND DELIVERED

In the presence of

Nancy King   *Jill Dubois*   (SEAL)

SOURCE OF DATA: Reproduced with the permission of the Bank of Montreal.

Lien

In popular usage, the term **lien** is often used as a synonym for a chattel mortgage, but there is a distinction in law. A lien is a claim registered against certain property, generally in cases where the goods or service provided cannot be seized. For example, if a contractor paved a driveway, but payment is overdue, the creditor may register a lien against the house. This would represent a claim against the property that must be settled before the owner can obtain a clear title. If a service station has not been paid for repairing a car, an automobile lien could be registered against the car. This gives the proprietor of the garage the right to retain the car until the debt is satisfied, or, if the default continues, to sell the car.

COST OF BORROWING

Insurance

On signing a credit contract, the borrower assumes not only the responsibility of repaying the debt, but also the risk that something will happen to make it impossible or difficult to carry out this intent. Unexpected illness, unemployment, disability, or death may disrupt a payment schedule. It is possible to obtain insurance to give protection against two of these risks—death or disability.

CREDIT LIFE INSURANCE   Lenders often require that their consumer loans be life-insured. They do this by having a group life insurance policy that covers the lives of their borrowers against the risk of someone dying before their debts have been repaid. This insurance on the life of the borrower is often called credit life insurance. When an insured borrower dies, the insurance company will pay the lender the outstanding balance due on the debt. The borrower's estate does not receive anything, but the survivors may be relieved that the debt has been paid.

Some lenders automatically include credit life insurance without an additional charge; others offer it as an option with a specific cost. Either way, the borrower ultimately pays for this service. If it is optional, a borrower might give some thought to the need for it. When a borrower with an outstanding debt dies without credit life insurance, the balance of the debt is a charge on the estate, which must be paid before any funds are distributed to the heirs. If the estate is adequate there may be no difficulty; however, if the family has many needs and few assets, a large debt could create hardship for the survivors.

DISABILITY INSURANCE   Not all lenders offer disability insurance, but credit unions often do. For an additional fee, disability insurance covers the borrower for the risk of being unable to make payments because of a personal disability. It is important to find out what the conditions of such insurance are as well as what it will cost. How does the insurance company define disabled? How long must one be disabled before the insurance will take effect? If the borrower meets the criteria for disability, the insurance company will assume responsibility for the debt payments as long as the disability lasts.

BANK OFFERS NEW INSURANCE PROGRAM

Late in 1992, when many people were unemployed, CIBC announced insurance coverage for borrowers that covered loss of a job as well as disability. A month after a borrower loses a job, loan payments are postponed and the insurance pays the interest for up to six months.

Interest Charges

The cost of borrowing depends on the lender's cost of money, the assessment of the risk of the loan not being repaid, and the services offered. Deposit-taking institutions, with a ready supply of funds to lend, can charge lower rates than small loan companies which have to borrow funds to lend. To cover their costs, banks, trust companies, and credit unions allow a one to three percent spread between the rate paid to depositors and the rate they charge borrowers.

On receipt of a loan application, a creditor assesses the degree of risk involved. Some lenders, notably small loan companies who will lend to higher risk borrowers, charge higher rates to cover losses on bad debts. Most lenders establish the level of risk they will accept and refuse loans to those who do not qualify.

INTEREST RATES   At the present time, there is little variation in rates between financial institutions for the same type of loan but there are significant differences in the rates charged for different types of loans. These differences are illustrated in Figure 13.7.

ENFORCEMENT OF SECURITY

In Arrears

When a debtor does not adhere to the repayment schedule originally agreed on, the account is first considered to be **in arrears** (delinquent) because the payments are somewhat behind. However, if the borrower contacts the lender and explains the problem, it is usually possible to make some adjustments. If the borrower is ill or unemployed, the lender may agree to freeze loan payments, or ask for interest only. An account in arrears, provided that it does not last too long, is not as serious a blot on the debtor's record as an account that is in default.

FIGURE 13.7 INTEREST RATES BY TYPE OF LOAN, 1992

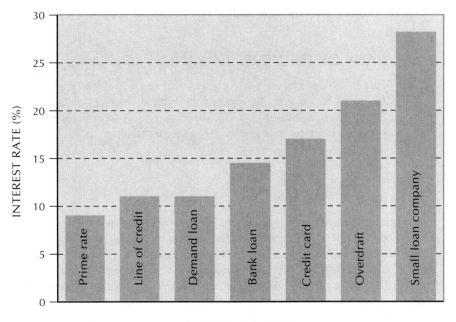

TYPE OF LOAN

In Default

The difference between an account in arrears and one in default is largely a matter of degree. In both cases the regular payment schedule has not been maintained. An account is **in default** if payments are hopelessly behind, and the lender is not having any success in collecting the debt. Such an account may be turned over for collection to a special department within the firm or to an outside collection agency. Default has a negative effect on one's credit record. The leniency of lenders varies; in recessionary times creditors may take action faster than in periods of prosperity and high employment.

Enforcing Security

When a debtor defaults, the lender is in a position to **enforce security,** that is, to realize funds from whatever was put up for security by the borrower before the loan was granted. If there was a co-signer, the lender will attempt to collect from this person, using various amounts of pressure. If the creditor is a credit union, a decision may be made to exercise the wage assignment, which means directing the debtor's employer to deduct up to 20 percent of wages due on each payday and send it to the creditor. If financial assets such as bonds, stocks, deposits, and life insurance were used as security, the lender can now convert these into cash to cover as much of the debt as possible. If consumer durables were the security, the lender can take possession and offer them for sale.

Enforcement of security is limited to whatever the particular credit contract specifies; it means taking steps to obtain funds from goods, assets, or co-signers according to the pledges made when the loan was initially arranged. At this stage, the creditor cannot seize goods unless they were listed as security in the credit contract. A creditor may choose not to enforce his or her security, especially in the case of chattel mortgages or conditional sales contracts, if the pledged goods have been in use for some time. Whether exercised or not, the possibility of repossession serves as a powerful threat to debtors.

ENFORCEMENT OF SECURITY VERSUS COURT ACTION There is a distinction between enforcing security and using the courts to collect debts. In the first instance, the lender exercises a right given by the borrower at the time the loan was arranged, and as explained above, the creditor can take any of the steps specified in the contract without resorting to the courts. If the creditor does not realize enough from the sale of the pledged assets, or if a decision is made not to enforce the security, the debtor can be sued in the appropriate court. The court will determine the validity of the creditor's claim on the debtor and make a decision about the amount owed. If the creditor wins the case, there are ways to coerce the debtor to make payment. Court collection of debts is discussed in Chapter 16.

REGULATIONS AND POLICIES

Consumer credit practices are governed by federal laws and provincial statutes, as well as by the policies of lenders. It may be difficult at first to distinguish among these. Laws can be changed only by legislatures, regulations by order-in-council, but lender policies can be altered more readily and often are modified in response to the pressures of competition. For instance, determining levels of acceptable risk or when a loan is in default are policy decisions that firms make.

Federal Regulation

The power to regulate consumer credit is shared between the federal and provincial governments. The federal government has jurisdiction over banks, promissory notes, bills of exchange, interest, and bankruptcy. In general, there is no legislated ceiling on interest rates on consumer loans. The Small Loans Act does state that it is an indictable offense to charge more than the criminal rate of interest, which is 60 percent.

Provincial Regulation

All provinces have consumer credit laws requiring that borrowers be informed about the cost of credit, expressed both as an annual rate and as a total dollar cost. Also, all provinces have an Unconscionable Transactions Relief Act, which permits a debtor to apply to court for a review of a loan contract. If the court finds, considering the circumstances, that the cost of the loan is excessive and the contract harsh and unconscionable, the transaction may be reopened and all or part of the contract set aside. There is more about the regulation of consumer credit in the next chapter.

Summary

This chapter focused on consumer loans obtained from financial institutions such as banks, credit unions, trust companies, and life insurance companies. The market shares of these creditors have changed over the years, with the banks now the major suppliers of consumer credit. Differences among these institutional lenders have become blurred as all have attempted to broaden their range of services. Credit unions, the financial cooperatives, have changed considerably as they became competitive members of the financial community.

Financial institutions, anxious to make loans, offer a bewildering range of credit options, including personal lines of credit, overdraft protection, credit card cash advances, demand loans, and instalment loans. The security required for a loan differs with the borrower's financial status and the type of loan requested, but may include promissory notes, co-signers, wage assignments, or pledges of financial assets or durable goods. There is not much regulation of consumer loans, other than to require full disclosure of the cost, leaving it to competition to maintain economic rates.

Vocabulary Review

chattel (p. 393)

chattel mortgage (p. 393)

co-signer (p. 391)

collateral (p. 393)

common bond (p. 381)

consumer loan (p. 376)

credit union (p. 380)

enforce security (p. 398)

fiduciary (p. 379)

fully secured loan (p. 390)

living trust (p. 379)

maturity date (p. 388)

partially secured loan (p. 390)

point-of-sale credit (p. 376)

prime rate (p. 389)

promissory note (p. 390)

spread (p. 378)

term of a loan (p. 388)

terms of a loan (p. 383)

testamentary trust (p. 379)

in arrears (delinquent) (p. 397)   trustee (p. 379)

in default (p. 398)   wage assignment (p. 392)

lien (p. 396)

Problems

1. Suggest some reasons for the shift in consumer credit market shares from small loan companies, sales finance companies, and retail vendors to the banks.

2. What are the responsibilities of a person who co-signs a loan?

3. Do you AGREE or DISAGREE with the following statements?

    (a) If you borrowed $1500 from a small loan company, the lender could charge any rate the market will bear (excepting the criminal rate) since there is no maximum set by law.

    (b) The provincial government sets a maximum interest rate on loans from banks.

    (c) Being a good credit risk is important in obtaining a policy loan from your life insurance company.

    (d) Using a life insurance policy as collateral for a loan is essentially the same thing as getting a policy loan.

    (e) Life insurance policies issued in recent years state the rate to be charged on policy loans.

    (f) There has been a trend among Canadians to prefer to obtain credit from vendors of goods and services rather than cash lenders.

    (g) Banks now supply more than two-thirds of all consumer credit, which is double their share in 1965.

4. Which of the following forms of security would be considered collateral? What is the distinguishing criterion?

    (a) wage assignment,

    (b) bonds,

    (c) life insurance with cash value,

    (d) promissory note,

    (e) durable goods, such as cars,

    (f) deposits in a savings account.

5. (a) Try to find out from local lenders whether they offer disability insurance with most loans.

    (b) When do you think it is worth the extra cost to have a consumer loan insured for disability?

6.

BORROWING TO BUY A CAR

The Dubois have had two experiences with consumer loans. First, they borrowed money from the bank to buy a washing machine. By using Jill's Canada Savings Bonds as collateral, they were able to obtain a fully secured loan at a low interest rate.

A year later, Peter and Jill realized that they needed a new car but could not pay cash for it. They thought about approaching the credit union in Guelph where Peter worked, but since he had never joined it, he wasn't sure how their request would be received. Remembering how easy it had been to borrow at the bank, they went back for a larger loan. The loan officer asked them to sign a chattel mortgage on the car and gave them the loan. (The forms and contracts signed by the Dubois may be found earlier in this chapter.)

(a) Why did the Dubois pay a lower rate of interest on the fully secured loan?

(b) Was the loan for the car fully or partially secured? How can you tell?

(c) The loan officer at the bank told the Dubois that credit life insurance would be included at no additional cost. Does that mean if Peter dies, Jill will receive some money from the insurance? Explain.

(d) There are real estate mortgages and chattel mortgages. What characteristics of the security pledged differentiate these mortgages?

(e) Must the Dubois carry insurance on this car? Does it matter to the bank?

(f) If they wish to trade in the car and get another before the debt is repaid, do they need to consult the bank, as long as they maintain their payments?

(g) Does the chattel mortgage contract make mention of any penalties for late payments? What do you think might happen if the Dubois made a payment a month late?

(h) According to the contract they signed, does the bank have the right to seize anything but the car if the Dubois should default on the loan?

(i) If the Dubois defaulted, and the bank repossessed and sold the car, but failed to realize enough to cover the outstanding debt, could the bank sue the Dubois for the balance owing? If the bank incurs costs in the repossession and sale of the car, who pays this?

(j) If the loan officer at the bank had reservations about the ability of the Dubois to repay the loan on schedule, would she:

(i) offer them a signature loan?

(ii) offer them a loan without credit life insurance?

(iii) require more security before making the loan?

7.

MICHEL JOINS THE CREDIT UNION

When Michel began his new teaching job in the city, a friend told him to consider joining a credit union where he could obtain similar, but more personal, services than at a bank. The credit union officer, Mrs. Stein, explained that as a result of several mergers with small credit unions, this was now a community credit union with a common bond requirement that members live or work in the city or surrounding county. Michel was thus eligible to become a member if he opened a share account with a small deposit.

Mrs. Stein told him about the services available to members of the credit union, which included the option of having his paycheque deposited in the credit union account by his employer and the opportunity to authorize the credit union to deposit a portion of each cheque into a true savings account and a portion into a chequing account.

Later, when Michel applied for a loan to buy a car, he found that he had to sign not only a promissory note, but also a wage assignment (Figure 13.5) and a chattel mortgage. Feeling very healthy, he declined the disability insurance. However, as luck would have it, he fractured his leg very badly in a skiing accident the next winter. His income was reduced while he was unable to work, but his living costs and debt payments continued as before. In these circumstances, Michel was unable to make his loan payments to the credit union. Fortunately, he called to tell them of his problem, and the credit union arranged for him to make interest payments only until he returned to work.

(a) What are some common bond requirements used by credit unions?

(b) What will be the consequences for Michel of paying interest only for a couple of months?

(c) If Michel disappeared without repaying his loan, what security would the credit union be able to enforce? If he defaulted, but failed to disappear, what further security could be enforced?

(d) If Michel had decided to get his car loan from a bank, would he have signed a wage assignment? Why or why not?

(e) Does the credit union offer Michel any benefit he could not get from other financial institutions?

8. If a person arranged to have loan payments deducted monthly from a chequing account at a credit union or bank, would this be considered a wage assignment? Explain.

9. Distinguish between the following pairs:

(a) enforcement of security and taking a debtor to court to collect a debt,

(b) a demand loan and a credit card cash advance,

(c) a living trust and a testamentary trust,

(d) term of a loan and terms of a loan,

(e) collateral and security,

(f) a personal line of credit and overdraft protection.

10. Who makes the decision to use a wage assignment? Can the amount of money taken from a paycheque be reduced? If so, how?

11. Why are some loans cheaper than others?

REFERENCES

BOOKS

Canadian Commercial Law Reports. Don Mills, Ontario: CCH Canadian, subscription service. Two-volume reporting service with up-to-date federal and provincial laws regarding sales contracts, conditional sales, instalment sales, chattel mortgages, and consumer protection.

CÔTÉ, JEAN-MARC and DONALD DAY. *Personal Financial Planning in Canada.* Toronto: Allyn and Bacon, 1987, 464 pp. A comprehensive personal finance text that includes financial planning, income tax, annuities, pensions, investments, credit, mortgages, and wills with particular attention to the banking and insurance industries.

DYMOND, MARY JOY. *The Canadian Woman's Legal Guide.* Toronto: Doubleday, 1989, 449 pp. Includes a section on women and credit.

FORMAN, NORM. *Mind Over Money, Curing Your Financial Headaches with Moneysanity.* Toronto: Doubleday Canada, 1987, 248 pp. A psychologist examines the effects money has on behaviour, looking at the origin of money problems and suggesting therapies to help us to better understand ourselves.

PARKER, ALLAN A. *Credit, Debt, and Bankruptcy.* Eighth Edition. Vancouver: International Self-Counsel Press, 1990, 128 pp. A handbook on Canadian credit law for credit users.

WYLIE, BETTY JANE and LYNN MACFARLANE. *Everywoman's Money Book.* Fourth Edition. Toronto: Key Porter, 1989, 223 pp. A journalist and a stock broker have collaborated on this wide-ranging treatment of a variety of personal finance topics, including women and credit, the budget, insurance, retirement, children and money.

CHAPTER FOURTEEN

Point-of-Sale-Credit

1. To outline trends in the use of credit cards.

2. To distinguish among the following and to identify an appropriate situation for using each:

   (a) debit card,

   (b) charge card,

   (c) credit card,

   (d) conditional sales agreement,

   (e) chattel mortgage.

3. To suggest reasons for the spread between credit card interest rates and the bank rate.

4. To explain how these factors affect credit card interest costs:

   (a) frequency of calculation,

   (b) when charges apply,

   (c) size of a partial payment.

5. To explain why comparing nominal rates is an inadequate basis for evaluating credit card costs.

6. To ascertain by reading a conditional sales contract:

   (a) the security offered,

   (b) who holds title to the goods,

   (c) who has possession of the goods,

   (d) the penalties for late payment or default,

   (e) whether a promissory note is included,

   (f) whether there is an acceleration clause,

    (g) whether the name of a financial institution that may buy the contract from the vendor is included,

    (h) whether provincial disclosure rules were followed.

7. To distinguish between

    (a) point-of-sale credit and consumer loans,

    (b) variable credit and conditional sales,

    (c) credit card transaction fees and annual fees.

8. To explain the main provisions of the legislation regarding:

    (a) disclosure of information about credit transactions,

    (b) supervision of itinerant sellers,

    (c) repossession of goods when the borrower defaults,

    (d) advertising credit,

    (e) unsolicited credit cards and unsolicited goods.

9. To evaluate to what extent the consumer's interest is protected by each of the following:

    (a) "cooling-off" period legislation,

    (b) content of credit contracts,

10. To identify some current issues of concern to credit card users.

11. To explain the following terms: revolving charge account, variable credit, grace period, conditional sales contract (executory contract), acceleration clause, itinerant (direct) seller, discounted paper.

Introduction

This chapter is about credit extended at the time a purchase is made, using a charge card, a credit card, or a conditional sales contract. Consumer loans, the subject of the previous chapter, are obtained directly from financial institutions rather than arranged at a retailer's. Instead of approaching a financial institution for a loan, you are primarily involved in a purchase transaction with a retailer, but choose to use credit rather than cash. Debit cards, which are not a form of credit, are mentioned in this chapter to demonstrate their difference from credit and charge cards. The extension of credit usually involves application forms and contracts, some samples of which are included to give you further practice in reading and understanding such documents. Legislation regulating certain aspects of credit varies somewhat by province but the general outline given here will serve as an introduction; check your provincial legislation for details. Finally, particular issues and problems of concern to credit users are reviewed.

ECONOMIC SIGNIFICANCE

As everyone knows, our society depends on credit for much economic activity and from the data presented in the two previous chapters it is evident that our use of consumer credit has been accelerating quite rapidly. The most recent change is our dependence on credit cards: approximately two-thirds of Canadians have at least one credit card and indeed it is not uncommon to have more than one. This trend towards greater use of consumer credit cards is reflected in the increasing value of sales charged to cards issued by Visa and Mastercard between 1977 and 1991 (Figure 14.1). In fourteen years, sales increased about eleven times, or, if converted to constant dollars (explained in Chapter 12), about four and one-half times. During this same period, the number of Mastercard and Visa cards in circulation tripled to about 24.3 million cards. The Canadian credit card market is dominated by these two cards: over one-half of all the credit cards in circulation and three-quarters of the total outstanding balances on credit cards are from Visa and Mastercard.

DEBIT CARDS

Although debit cards are not used for credit, they are included in this chapter to prevent confusion with credit cards. A **debit card,** also called a payment card, differs from a credit card in that purchases are immediately deducted from the purchaser's regular chequing account, possibly with a line of credit to handle overdrafts. Debit cards may also be used as a means of access to automatic teller machines.

Credit unions initiated the use of debit cards, most often at the local level. More recently, other financial institutions, especially banks, have been working on a nationwide electronic system that would allow payment for goods and services

FIGURE 14.1 DOLLAR SALES USING MASTERCARD AND VISA, CANADA, 1977–1991 (IN CURRENT AND CONSTANT 1981 DOLLARS)

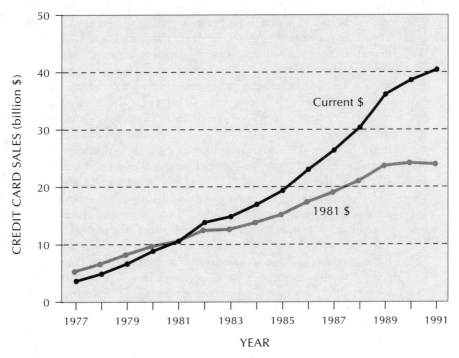

SOURCE OF DATA: *Credit Cards in Canada in the Nineties,* Report of the Standing Committee on Consumer and Corporate Affairs and Government Operations (p. 3). Ottawa, 1992.

without the use of cash or cheques. Once such an electronic payments system is put in place, you may be able to use a plastic card to instantly debit your bank account for the week's groceries right at the check out counter. Pilot testing of debit cards in several regions of Canada has been sufficiently successful that the system is gradually being expanded. In September 1992, this direct payment system was introduced in Quebec and British Columbia and very likely we will soon see it becoming available in other regions.

LUKE USES A DEBIT CARD FOR GROCERIES

Last week when the grocery stores in town advertised that they were now equipped to handle debit-card shopping, Luke was keen to try out this new system. At the checkout counter, his grocery bill was tallied then he was asked for his debit card (which in Luke's case was his automated banking card). After the cashier put his card through her machine, he was handed a small hand-held "PIN pad" that showed the amount of his grocery bill. He had to select which of his accounts was to be debited and punch in his personal identification number (PIN). Magically, his bill was paid as funds were transferred from his account to that of the grocery store. Luke left with his groceries, the usual sales slip, and a transaction record of the debit.

At home, Luke told the family about his new experience, starting a discussion about the merits of debit cards. Undoubtedly, he observed, the system is good for financial institutions, which are concerned about the rising costs of handling cheques and cash. The store, which no longer has to cope with NSF cheques and handle as much cash and cheques, pays a small fee for the electronic terminal. "But what about the shopper?" Jane asked. "What are the advantages and disadvantages for us?" Luke explained that they would not have to carry cash or produce identification in order to pay by cheque; they would have access to funds at the bank without going there; their money on deposit could earn daily interest until it was needed; and they would have a more accurate record of their spending than if they had used cash. On the other hand, he noted, there is a transaction fee to be paid by the shopper—about the same as for a cheque—as well as concerns about privacy and lost cards.

POINT-OF-SALE CREDIT ARRANGEMENTS

If credit is obtained in connection with a purchase it is considered **point-of-sale credit** in contrast to loan credit, which is obtained separately from purchases. Three of the most common kinds of point-of-sale credit will be the focus of our attention. They are: charge cards, credit cards, and conditional sales. Note the distinction between a **charge card,** used for accounts that require payment in full each month and a **credit card,** used for accounts that permit instalment payments.

Charge Cards

Charge cards are provided for short-term credit (about a month) primarily by oil companies and travel and entertainment clubs such as American Express or Diner's. They offer charge accounts requiring full payment within a specified **grace period,** or the number of days after the statement date before a late payment penalty becomes effective. The grace period varies but may be from 21 to 45 days. After that, late payments will attract a penalty at a fairly high rate of interest.

Credit Cards

REVOLVING ACCOUNTS   Credit cards are used for **revolving charge accounts,** so named because it is possible to continue charging purchases to the account as long as a portion of the bill is paid each month. There are two major types of credit cards: (i) those issued by banks, trust companies, credit unions, and other financial institutions (often called "bank cards") and (ii) those issued by retailers. The credit card accounts at financial institutions and retailers differ in two respects: (i) whether the institution is providing a loan or selling goods, and (ii) how credit charges are calculated.

To open a revolving charge account, referred to in legislative documents as **variable credit,** an application form similar to the one in Figure 14.2 must be completed. The credit department evaluates the information provided in the application and sometimes obtains a credit report from the credit bureau (explained in Chapter 16). On the basis of the applicant's current financial situation and previous credit record, the credit manager assesses the individual's credit-worthiness and establishes a ceiling on the amount of credit that may be outstanding at any one time.

Once the account has been opened, credit purchases may be made within the set limit. Monthly statements will report the status of the account, including the minimum payment, the outstanding balance, and the credit limit. Whenever the balance reaches the established limit on the account, the use of the card is supposed to cease until the debt has been reduced. However, in some instances the credit card issuer may simply increase the limit, without consulting the cardholder; the new credit limit will, of course, be shown on the next statement.

GRACE PERIOD   Most credit card issuers offer the cardholder a certain number of days after the statement date, called a grace period, in which to make full payment without interest charges. There are, however, some low-interest rate accounts that have no grace period. Generally, bank, trust company and credit union accounts have a grace period of 21 days and retailer accounts from 21 to 30 days. There is no grace period on amounts carried over from previous months, nor on cash advances.

CASH ADVANCES   Credit cards issued by financial institutions permit cash advances, within limits, as well as retail purchases. These advances are treated as small daily loans, with daily interest charged from the date the funds are advanced.

COMPARATIVE INTEREST RATES   It is instructive to compare the relation between the bank rate (defined in Chapter 10) and the rates charged on retail and bank cards over the past decade (Figure 14.3). Most of the time there has been a substantial spread between the bank rate and credit card rates; note that interest rates for retail cards were the highest and the most infrequently adjusted. One reason for high interest rates on credit cards is the substantial risk associated with them; credit card issuers lose millions of dollars each year through uncollectible debts and fraudulent use of these cards.

FIGURE 14.2 CREDIT CARD APPLICATION

CIBC *Convenience Card with* VISA *Application*

1

PLEASE TELL US ABOUT YOURSELF

1 MR. 2 MS. 3 MISS [X] MRS. 5 OTHER

YOUR NAME AS YOU WOULD LIKE IT TO APPEAR ON VISA CARD
FIRST NAME/INITIAL/LAST NAME (INCLUDE TITLE IF APPLICABLE): LIIVI J. KASAK

PRESENT ADDRESS

ADDRESS	APT. NO.
RR #6	
CITY, PROVINCE: NEW HAMBURG, ONT.	POSTAL CODE: N2J 2Z4

HOW LONG HAVE YOU LIVED THERE? YEARS: 6 MONTHS: 3 HOME TELEPHONE: (519) 662 1100

[X] OWN YOUR HOME [ ] BOARD [ ] RENT [ ] LIVE WITH PARENTS

OTHER PROPERTY OWNED? [ ] YES [X] NO

TOTAL MONTHLY HOUSING PAYMENT: $ 925.38 [ ]

PREVIOUS ADDRESS (IF LESS THAN 2 YEARS)

ADDRESS	APT. NO.
CITY, PROVINCE	POSTAL CODE

SOCIAL INSURANCE NUMBER (OPTIONAL):

DATE OF BIRTH: DAY 14 MONTH 08 YEAR 64

[ ] SINGLE [X] MARRIED [ ] DIVORCED [ ] SEPARATED [ ] WIDOW(ER)

SPOUSE'S NAME: ANDRAS T. KASAK

PLEASE TELL US THE NAME, ADDRESS AND TELEPHONE NUMBER OF YOUR NEAREST PERSONAL REFERENCE

NAME: Mr. BEN TOTH	TELEPHONE: (519) 882 3311
ADDRESS: 202 Columbia st.	APT. NO.
CITY, PROVINCE: Waterloo, Ontario	POSTAL CODE: N2H 5W4

2

YOUR SOURCES OF INCOME

EMPLOYER — SELF-EMPLOYED? [ ] YES [X] NO

EMPLOYER NAME: New Hamburg Community Services	DEPARTMENT (IF APPLICABLE)
ADDRESS: 175 Waterloo St. New Hamburg	TELEPHONE: (519) 662 2731
HOW LONG? — GROSS MONTHLY INCOME: $2520	POSITION/OCCUPATION: social worker [ ]

PREVIOUS EMPLOYER (IF LESS THAN TWO YEARS):

EMPLOYER NAME	TELEPHONE ( )
HOW LONG? — POSITION/OCCUPATION	[ ]

SPOUSE NOW EMPLOYED BY

EMPLOYER NAME: University of Waterloo	DEPARTMENT (IF APPLICABLE)
ADDRESS: 200 University W. Waterloo	TELEPHONE: (519) 885 1211
HOW LONG? 4 — GROSS MONTHLY INCOME: $2450	POSITION/OCCUPATION: librarian

OTHER INCOME SOURCES AND AMOUNTS (PLEASE SPECIFY SOURCE)

GROSS MONTHLY INCOME $

FIGURE 14.2   CREDIT CARD APPLICATION (CONTINUED)

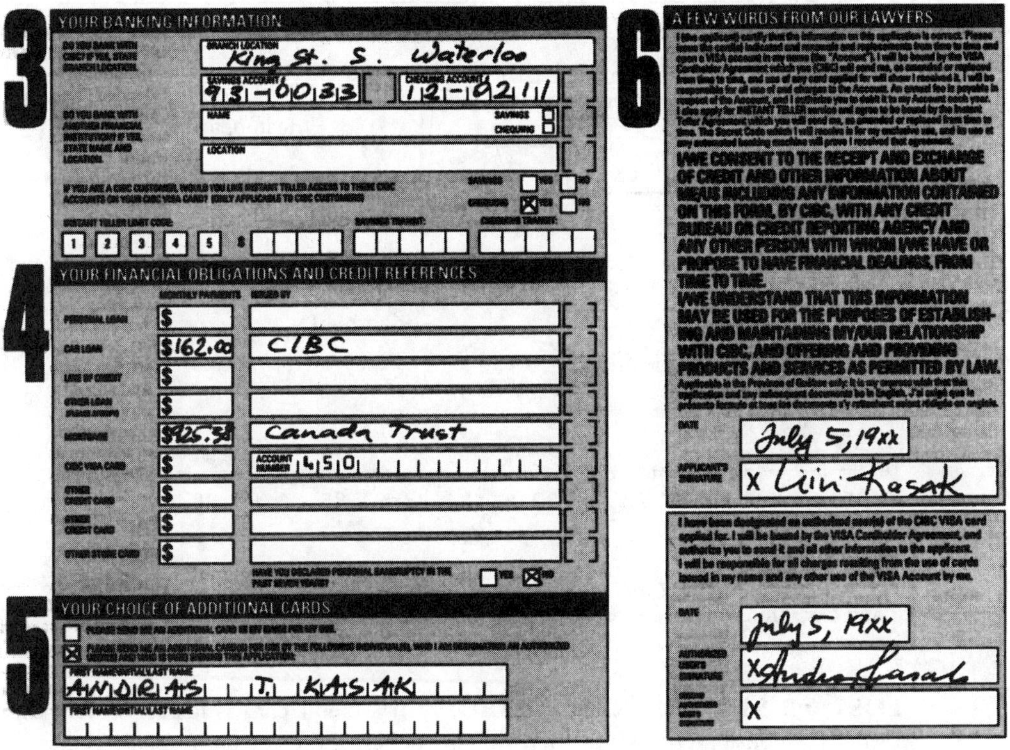

Reproduced with the permission of CIBC.

Note that credit card rates changed slowly in response to changes in the bank rate. Two contributing factors that make credit card rates "sticky" are the requirement that they give cardholders at least a month's notice (six months in some provinces) of a change and the large fixed costs of running a credit card operation. Before concluding that it will cost more to use a retail card than a bank card for instalment credit, you should examine the different methods of calculating interest charges, which will be demonstrated later in this chapter.

FIGURE 14.3 REPRESENTATIVE CREDIT CARD RATES VERSUS THE BANK RATE, CANADA, 1973–1991

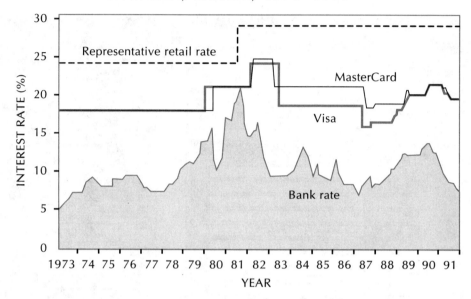

SOURCE OF DATA: *Credit Cards in Canada in the Nineties.* Report of the Standing Committee on Consumer and Corporate Affairs and Government Operations (p. 5). Ottawa, 1992.

LOST OR STOLEN CREDIT CARDS If a credit card is lost or stolen, the owner's responsibility tends to vary with the policy of the company issuing the card. However, in Alberta, Manitoba, or Quebec cardholders have no legal obligation for any debts incurred after they have notified the company of the loss. If there should be any bills charged after the loss and before notification, the cardholder's responsibility in Alberta and Manitoba is limited to about $50. All the banks limit the cardholder's liability to $50 after notification. Some firms offer insurance protection against lost or stolen credit cards in return for an annual fee.

PREMIUM CREDIT CARDS Nowadays, you can get more than credit with a credit card. For an additional fee it is possible to have a super credit card, called a premium card, that provides such features as a higher credit limit, travel insurance, guaranteed hotel reservations, collision insurance on rental cars, health insurance, credit card registry, airline points, travellers' cheques, etc. Whether or not such a card will be beneficial to you will depend on an evaluation of your need for these additional services in relation to the extra cost involved. The annual fee may be in the range of $100 to $130.

LOST AND STOLEN CREDIT CARDS

In 1991, of the about 25 million bank credit cards in use in Canada, more than 600 000 were reported lost or stolen. Of the 37 000 that were used fraudulently, 8000 were taken from an unattended purse, jacket, or locker, and 6000 from automobiles. Some were stolen from lockers at recreational facilities and about 5000 lost cards were left behind in restaurants and bars. A few cards are pilfered from the mail.

Before reporting a card as lost, it is well to check with family members. When a credit card is reported as lost or stolen and someone uses it, this becomes a criminal matter. If a family member should inadvertently use your lost card, you may be surprised to find yourself caught up in the justice system.

DO YOU NEED A CREDIT CARD?

Consumer and Corporate Affairs Canada has developed the following questions to help you decide whether or not you need a certain credit card and whether you can afford it.

1. Why do you want this credit card?
2. What inconveniences are you experiencing by not having this credit card?
3. When would you use this credit card rather than cash, debit card, cheque, line of credit, or existing credit cards and why?
4. What types of purchases would you be making with this credit card, and how often?
5. How much new credit do you feel you require, and why?
6. What portion of your current average monthly expenses is related to the use of existing credit cards?
7. How would the use of this credit card affect your monthly expenditures?
8. Would you expect to pay your monthly balance in full? If not, what repayment schedule would you meet?
9. Can you afford new debt and how will you budget for it?
10. Should you, in fact, be trying to cut back on your use of credit cards?

Conditional Sales Agreements

For the sale of high-priced items—such as vehicles, appliances, and furniture—that are paid for in instalments, the retailer may use a conditional sales contract rather than a revolving charge account in order to increase the vendor's security in case of default. With a credit card sale, the vendor has no security claim on the merchandise purchased, only the borrower's signature with a promise to repay. A **conditional sales agreement,** however, permits the creditor to retain title of the goods until they are paid for, with the option of repossessing them if the buyer defaults. There is more about conditional sales agreements later in this chapter.

Rates for Point-of-Sale Credit

There is no regulation of rates charged on revolving charge accounts or conditional sales because it is expected that competition among creditors will keep rates in line with other forms of consumer credit. At present, a comparison between lenders shows interest rates to be about the same for similar forms of credit. There is, however, variation among types of credit at any given source (Figure 14.4). Although the interest rates move up and down, the relationship among rates for different types of credit remains fairly stable.

CREDIT CARD COSTS

Credit card holders may be charged for two types of costs: (i) transaction or annual fees, and (ii) interest. Each will be examined in turn.

Transaction or Annual Fees

Some financial institutions, such as banks, trust companies, and credit unions may impose either an annual fee ($8–$14) or a transaction fee (15 cents). Travel and entertainment cards have much higher annual fees, perhaps in the range of $30 to $55. Retailers usually do not charge fees for their credit cards. With this much variation in costs, it is worthwhile to check out the fees before applying for a credit card.

Interest Charges

Interest charges are not a concern for the 50 percent of credit cardholders who pay their total outstanding balances each month, but are of some significance to the rest of us. Two important factors affecting interest costs on partial or instalment payments are: (i) frequency of interest calculation, and (ii) timing in the application of interest charges. Since lenders can change their methods of calculating interest at any time, it is difficult to generalize. The point to be made is that methods of determining interest charges can be quite complex and consumer information is often hard to obtain and difficult to understand.

FIGURE 14.4   CREDIT AND CHARGE CARD INTEREST RATES, CANADA, 1992

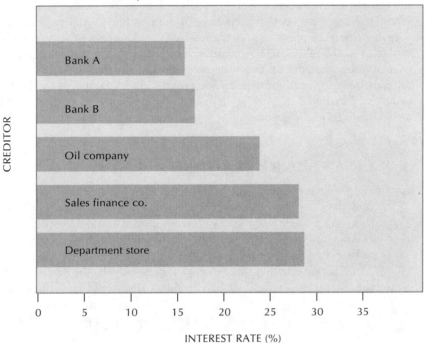

SOURCE OF DATA: *Credit Card Costs.* Consumer and Corporate Affairs Canada, Ottawa, September 1992.

FREQUENCY OF INTEREST CALCULATION   Banks, trust companies and credit unions calculate interest on the daily outstanding balance. For example, assume that a bank card was used to charge three purchases that were posted to the account on March 2, March 12, and March 23 and a partial payment was made after the first statement was received. Daily interest charges on Purchase A would begin March 2, on Purchase B March 12, and on Purchase C March 23. This makes it virtually impossible for the cardholder to figure out the interest charges on bank cards. Retailers, on the other hand, are more apt to charge interest on the monthly balances.

TIMING OF APPLICATION OF INTEREST CHARGES   When a credit card holder receives a statement, he or she has the option of paying the balance in full without interest, or making a partial payment. The person who chooses the latter option may be surprised to find that some financial institutions charge interest for three periods: (i) from the date the credit card office posted the transaction to the next statement date, (ii) from one statement date to the next, and (iii) from the second statement date to the payment date (called **residual interest**). The amount of residual interest due appears on the second statement.

Retailers, on the other hand, generally charge interest on a monthly basis, starting from the statement date, not the purchase date (except in Quebec, where all interest must be calculated daily). Usually, they do not charge residual interest; interest charges are on the balance outstanding after partial payment is made, accruing from the previous statement date. One example of such complexity is explained in "Gina's Charge Accounts" and illustrated in Figure 14.5. However, by changing the assumptions about the proportion of the debt repaid each month, a different result may be obtained. The point of this example is to illustrate the complexity involved in interest charges on credit cards rather than to present a model that is generally applicable.

GINA'S CHARGE ACCOUNTS

Soon after she started her first job, Gina got two credit cards—a bank card and a department store card. She made purchases using each card that were posted to her accounts on March 2, 12, and 23. At the end of the month, statements arrived from the bank and the retailer and it so happened that both were dated March 30.

When she settled down to pay bills on April 11 she knew that if she paid these credit card bills in full, there would be no interest charges. However, she was a bit short of funds and decided to pay half of each bill. Each statement indicated the minimum payment but did not show any interest charges.

On April 30, new statements arrived from both credit cards, showing how much she had paid and how much interest had accrued.

She knew that there was a difference in interest rates (16.75 percent on the bank card and 28.8 percent on the store card) but she did not understand how the interest was calculated. After some investigation she learned that the retailer had charged interest on the unpaid portion of her bill for the month between statement dates. The bank card interest charges had begun from the date of posting her purchases and were divided into three periods: (i) from the posting date to the statement date, (ii) from one statement date to the next, and (iii) residual interest as shown in Figure 14.5. After her partial payment on April 11, the bank charged her interest on the new balance.

On May 13 she paid the total outstanding balance shown on the April 30th statement. Although she did not charge anything more to her bank card in the meantime, she was surprised to find a charge for interest on the May 30th statement. That, she found out, was a residual interest charge for the period between April 30 and May 13.

FIGURE 14.5 BANK AND RETAIL CREDIT CARD INTEREST CHARGES ON ACCOUNTS WITH PARTIAL PAYMENTS

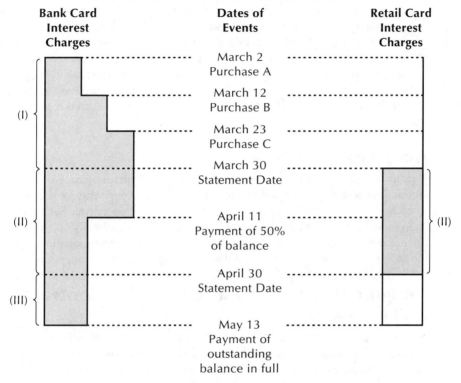

EFFECT OF SUBSTANTIAL PAYMENT   If the partial payment is 50 percent or more of the balance owing, credit card issuers differ in when they apply interest charges. Retailers usually subtract the partial payment from the outstanding balance before calculating the new interest charges. Financial institutions, however, calculate interest on the previous total balance and then subtract the partial payment. When the partial payment is less than 50 percent of the balance, retailers do not subtract the payment before the interest is calculated.

NOMINAL AND EFFECTIVE INTEREST RATES   Nominal interest rates on revolving credit accounts can vary significantly; recently the range was from 16.75 to 28.8 percent. From Chapter 8 you will recall that nominal interest rate is the quoted rate but it may not be the same as the more significant effective rate. Unfortunately, it is quite difficult to compare effective annual interest rates on credit cards because of the complex calculation methods.

CONDITIONAL SALES CONTRACTS

When you examine the sample contract in Figure 14.6 you will notice that a conditional sales agreement is quite similar to a chattel mortgage in that both provide a statement of the terms of the credit agreement, a description of the security pledged, and penalties for failing to keep the terms of the contract. The main difference is that the former is a sales rather than a loan agreement. The vendor retains title to the goods until complete payment has been received, reserving the right to repossess the pledged goods if the buyer does not make payments as scheduled.

Acceleration Clause

A statement indicating that the lender can demand immediate payment of the total outstanding debt if the borrower is late with one or more payments, or does anything to make the lender feel "insecure," is called an **acceleration clause**. Such a clause is often included in credit agreements for the benefit of the lender. By making the total balance due at once, the lender is in a position to initiate court proceedings to collect the debt without waiting for each monthly instalment to become in arrears.

Assignment of a Conditional Sales Contract to a Third Party

Signing a conditional sales agreement gives a purchaser the opportunity to buy and enjoy the use of a high-priced durable good by distributing the cost over a number of months or years. Retailers find this encourages sales, but ties up working capital that they need to buy new stock. This difficulty is solved by sales finance companies and some banks, which make a business of buying conditional sales contracts from retailers—a transaction sometimes referred to as selling credit paper.

Careful examination of most conditional sales contracts may reveal a statement specifying that the contract may be assigned to a third party, a named financial institution. The blank contract forms, often supplied to the retailer by the sales finance company, may bear the name of that company. The arrangements made between retailers and sales finance companies vary, but usually the sales finance company will buy the contract from the retailer for a sum equal to the purchase price of the item; this makes it equivalent to a cash sale from the retailer's perspective. The purchaser now makes payments directly to the sales finance company that holds the contract.

The sales finance company makes its profit from the interest part of the contract. Depending on competition and economic conditions, the sales finance company may offer the retailer an additional premium or charge a discount.

FIGURE 14.6 CONDITIONAL SALES CONTRACT

 **Bencharge**
CREDIT SERVICE

CONDITIONAL SALE CONTRACT

SELLER: Keyboards Plus
Name

23 Lindsay St.
Address

Peterborough, Ont. P5T 2K8
City · *Province* · *P.C.*

BUYER(S): Kimberley Travinski
Name(s)

1611 Princess St.
Address

Peterborough, Ont. P6T 1O1
City · *Province* · *P.C.*

Dear Customer:
We are writing this Contract in easy-to-read language because we want you to understand its terms. Please read your Contract carefully and feel free to ask us any questions you may have about it. We are using the words, *you, your* and *yours* to mean all persons signing the Contract as the Buyer. The words *we, us* and *our* refer to the Seller.

Contract Coverage: We sell and you buy the following Property and/or Services:

Description of Goods	Make	Model	Serial No.	Price
Piano	Yamaha	YH252	23Y3467	#3560

Disclosure of your credit costs:

Cash Price	$ 3560.00
Less Trade-In	$ —
Net Cash Price	$ 3560.00
Provincial Sales Tax +GST	$ 534.00
Fees for Registration	$ 10.00
Total Cash Price	$ 4104.00
Cash Down Payment	$ 304.00
Amount Financed	$ 3800.00
Scheduled Finance Charge	$ 1216.18
Total Amount of Contract	$ 5016.18
Annual Percentage Rate 28.22 %	

Payment Schedule: Your payment schedule is ___24___ payments of $ _209.03_, except the last which shall be the balance owing. Each payment shall be due on the _first_ day of each month beginning _June 1_, 19 XX, or one month from the date of this Contract if not otherwise specified.

Date of Contract ___May 18th___, 19 XX

SEE REVERSE SIDE FOR TERMS OF THIS CONTRACT

Notice to Buyer: Do not sign this Contract before you read it, or if it contains any blank spaces.

1. Please note that in connection with this credit application a consumer report containing credit information or personal information may be obtained by the prospective creditor. If you so request the creditor will inform you of the name and address of the consumer reporting agency supplying the report. Any information obtained in connection with this credit application may be divulged to other credit grantors or to a consumer reporting agency. 2. When you sign this Contract, you acknowledge that you have read and agreed to all its terms. 3. Be sure and read the terms and conditions contained on the reverse side of this Contract as they are binding on you as well. 4. All copies must be individually signed in ink.

_____
Seller's Signature

I hereby guaranty payment of the total of payments of this Contract:

_____
Guarantor's Signature

You confirm receiving a completed copy of this Contract with disclosures of your credit costs.

_____
Buyer 1's Signature

_____
Buyer 2's Signature

FIGURE 14.6 CONDITIONAL SALES CONTRACT (CONTINUED)

TERMS AND CONDITIONS

1. Promise to Pay: You promise to pay the total amount of contract according to your payment schedule.

2. Interest Rate: The rate shown on the front page as Annual Percentage Rate shall be the rate agreed upon for the computation of pre-judgment and post-judgment interest and shall be used in the computation of any such interest by a Court of Justice when making an order or granting a judgment to enforce this contract.

3. Credit Statement: You certify that all statements in your credit statement are true and complete and were made for the purpose of obtaining credit.

4. Warranties: Unless you have been given a written warranty, there is no warranty on the goods purchased and no statements or promise made by any party shall be valid or binding.

5. Title: Title, and therefore legal ownership, to the goods which you have purchased by this Contract does not pass to you until payment in full of this Contract. You understand and acknowledge that the Seller, and any assignee of the Seller, retains a continuing security interest in the goods which you have purchased until payment in full of this Contract. Furthermore, you agree not to transfer possession or control of the property to any other person without first notifying us by registered mail of your intention to do so.

6. Location: You agree that the goods are to remain at the address indicated on the front of this Contract. If you wish to move the goods, you must notify us by registered mail before you do so. The registered letter can be sent to the same address where you send you payments If you move from the address shown on the reverse side, you must notify us of your new address without delay.

7. Insurance: It is your obligation to keep the property insured against fire and theft. You acknowledge that any loss, injury or destruction of the property covered by this Contract does not relieve you of your obligation to pay the full amount owed on the Contract.

8. Default: You will be considered in default under the terms of this Contract if:

a)   you fail to make any payment on time;
b)   you fail to meet any promise you have made in this Contract;
c)   you become insolvent or bankrupt;

d)   the property is lost or destroyed;
e)   the property is seized in any legal proceeding.

9. Remember: If you are in default under this Contract, we have certain legal remedies available to us. We may, at our election,

a)   demand that the full balance owing be paid immediately;
b)   take possession of the goods according to law;
c)   commence legal proceedings for recovery of the balance owing.

Where we have taken possesion of the goods, you will be sent the required notice which will explain how you may regain possession of the goods. If you do not do so, we will be entitled to dispose of the goods at a public or private sale, or at an auction. We may exercise our rights at any time. Where a deficiency has resulted from such a sale, we may commence legal proceedings for recovery of the deficiency, if permitted by law.

10. Additional Charges on Default: You agree to pay a delinquency charge of 5¢ per each $1.00 of any instalment which is not paid within 5 days after the instalment due date. You agree to pay interest at the same annual percentage rate as stated in this contract after maturity on any unpaid balance which remains.

11. Insufficient Funds Charge: In the event a cheque tendered for payment is returned for insufficient funds, we may collect a $10.00 charge as a reasonable charge for expenses incurred, over and above any other charges.

12. Refund: If you repay in full one month or more before the maturity date of this Contract, a portion of the Total Amount of Contract shall be refunded to you, calculated according to the Consumer Protection Act of Ontario and the regulations. We are entitled to retain an additional amount of $20 or one half of the refund, whichever is less. You are not entitled to the rebate if after deducting the amount we can retain, the rebate is less than two ($2.00) dollars.

13. Assignment: You understand that this Contract may be assigned by the Seller. The assignee will then be entitled to all the rights which the Seller may have had.

14. Applicable Law: Any part of this Contract which is contrary to the laws of any province shall not invalidate the other parts of this Contract.

THIS CONTRACT CONTAINS THE ENTIRE AGREEMENT BETWEEN THE PARTIES

Reproduced with the permission of Beneficial Canada.

CREDIT REGULATION

Historical Background

The proliferation of consumer protection legislation, which began in the mid-1960s, continued until all provinces had one or more acts confirming the rights of consumers in credit transactions. The reason for this legislative activity is not difficult to find. You will recall that the rate of increase in the use of consumer credit was fairly gradual in the 1950s but accelerated in the 1960s (Figure 12.1). Many consumers with little expertise in the credit market were at a disadvantage in their dealings with large corporate creditors. Consequently, provincial governments attempted to come to the aid of consumers with consumer protection legislation.

Historically, most credit transactions had been conducted between businesses experienced in the credit market, and except for informal charge accounts at the local store, most consumers did not enter the credit market. This changed after 1950 with the advent of mass production of high-priced consumer durables, which were merchandised on a "buy now, pay later" arrangement. Unsophisticated buyers, unversed in credit or contracts, entered the market and enlarged the demand for both the durables and the credit, but unfortunately many signed contracts they did not understand, waiving rights they did not know they held.

Not surprisingly, some borrowers got into difficult situations for which they had no legal defense. This prompted provincial legislatures to entrench certain rights of consumers in law and to set up ministries of consumer affairs. The aims were laudable, but the budgets were rarely sufficient to provide help on the scale that was needed. Although consumers acquired rights that lawyers and creditors knew about, most consumers were unaware of them. Insufficient resources were allocated for public information or law enforcement. Nevertheless, consumers benefited from the legislation because lenders knew the rules and endeavoured to follow them.

Provincial statutes regulating credit have many similar provisions. The very general discussion that follows is limited to some of the highlights; for greater detail or precision the relevant statutes should be consulted. These statutes are called the Consumer Protection Act in most provinces; the equivalents are the Cost of Credit Disclosure Act in New Brunswick and Saskatchewan, and the Consumer Credit Transactions Act in Alberta.

Disclosure of Credit Charges

One of the main achievements of the consumer protection legislation was to require creditors to disclose all the costs of credit, both as total dollar amounts and as annual percentage rates. Because of divided federal-provincial jurisdiction regarding the regulation of consumer credit—interest is a federal matter and trade is provincial— there was uncertainty about exactly which costs of borrowing could be called interest. Consequently, the provincial acts usually avoid the use of the word interest, and substitute the broader term, credit charges. This disclosure of the cost of credit, both as a rate and as an amount (referred to as "truth in lending" in the United States) is now mandatory in all provinces and states.

After the disclosure laws had been in effect for a number of years, some research was done to determine whether consumers make use of this information to comparison shop for credit. Many borrowers were found to be generally insensitive to interest rates and more concerned with the size of their monthly payments. Apparently, users of consumer credit are often more interested in shopping for the purchase than for the financing.

The disclosure requirements for variable credit or revolving charge accounts are that the borrower must be told in advance what the interest rate will be and that, after extending the credit, the lender will provide a statement showing the outstanding balances at the beginning and end of the period, amounts and dates of each transaction, and the cost of borrowing expressed in dollar amounts.

The conditional sales agreement, when used for a consumer purchase, is subject to provincial consumer protection legislation regarding disclosure of credit charges and the content of the contract. The statutes concerned with conditional sales agreements may refer to them as a type of **executory contract**, that is, one in which both parties have made promises regarding future action, but have yet to act.

The rules for disclosure of credit costs apply to conditional sales contracts whether signed at the vendor's premises or in the customer's home. The method of calculating credit charges on conditional sales is set forth in the regulations that accompany the various provincial acts. Included in the disclosure legislation is a list of information that must be included in an executory contract (e.g., a conditional sales contract) if the total cost of the purchase exclusive of credit charges is above a specified amount, which may be around $50. Essentially, the contract must contain names and addresses of the buyer and seller, a description of the goods being purchased, and details about the financial transaction.

Supervision of Itinerant Sellers

Do door-to-door sellers exert undue pressure on people to buy their products? Perhaps. At any rate, each province has legislation that allows consumers time to change their minds about contracts signed in their own homes. In fact, the consumer's right to cancel the agreement can apply to any sales contract signed at a location other than the company's place of business. The length of this "cooling-off" period varies from province to province, but within the specified time, a consumer may cancel the contract simply by informing the company of that intention. This is best done by registered mail, but verbal notice is acceptable in some provinces. Usually the postmarked date on the letter is considered to be the time the notice was received by the company. The "cooling-off" period does not include Sundays or statutory holidays. When a contract is cancelled, the consumer is expected to return any goods received and possibly to pay compensation for the use of them; the seller is expected to return any down payment. A summary of this legislation by province is shown in Table 14.1.

TABLE 14.1 COOLING-OFF PERIODS BY PROVINCE

Province	Legislation	Length of cooling-off period	Notification of cancellation	Minimum amount of sale
Newfoundland	*The Direct Sellers Act*	Within 10 days of date on which contract was signed.	Written, personally delivered, or sent by registered mail; in which case it is deemed effective on the day after it is mailed.	no min.
Prince Edward Island	*The Direct Sellers Act*	Within 7 days of date on which contract was signed.	In writing or by personal delivery, telegram, or registered mail to vendor's last known address. When sent registered mail, it is deemed effective on the day after it is mailed.	$40
Nova Scotia*	*Direct Sellers Licensing and Regulation Act*	Within 10 days of date on which contract was signed.	Written or by personal delivery to direct seller or one of his salesmen or by registered mail to address shown on contract, in which case it is deemed at time of mailing.	$25
New Brunswick	*Direct Sellers Act*	Within 5 days of date on which contract was signed.	Written, to direct vendor or one of his salesmen or by personal deliveryor registered mail to address incontract in which case it is deemedeffective at time of mailing.	$25
Quebec*	*The Consumer Protection Act*	Not later than 10 days after buyer receives copy of contract.	By returning goods to vendor's address or by written notice.	$25
Ontario*	*The Consumer Protection Act*	Within 2 days after duplicate original copy of contract is received by buyer.	Written, by personal delivery or by registered mail to address stated in the contract, in which case it is effective at time of mailing.	$50
Manitoba*	*The Consumer Protection Act*	Within 4 days of date on which contract was signed.	Written, by personal delivery, or by registered mail to address of vendor stated in contract.	no min.

TABLE 14.1 COOLING-OFF PERIODS BY PROVINCE (CONTINUED)

Province	Legislation	Length of cooling-off period	Notification of cancellation	Minimum amount of sale
Saskatchewan	*The Direct Sellers Act*	Within 10 days of date on which contract was signed.	Written, or by personal delivery, telegram or registered mail to vendor's last known address. In case of registered mail, it is deemed effective on date of postmaster's receipt.	no min.
Alberta	*The Direct Sales Cancellation Act*	Not later than 4 days after date on which purchaser received his copy of contract by personal delivery or mail.	Written, by personal delivery or mailed to vendor named in contract. If no contract, notice sent to any addressof salesman known to buyer. It is deemed effective at time of mailing.	$25
British Columbia*	*Consumer Protection Act*	Not later than 7 days after date when buyer receives copy of contract.	Written, by personal delivery or mailed to seller's address stated in contract or any address of seller known to buyer.	*$20*

*In some provinces, legislation is only effective when the purchase exceeds a minimum dollar price.

1. In Manitoba and Nova Scotia, if the contract does not include rescission rights the cooling-off period is 30 days after the goods or services were delivered.

2. All provinces, except Ontario and Quebec, provide for cancellation after longer periods if certain conditions are not met.

Prepayment of Credit Contracts

Most creditors arrange the repayment of accounts by calculating the credit charges on the outstanding balance at the end of each month, as discussed in the chapter on interest. Less frequently, a precomputed schedule of credit charges may be used. In both instances, the monthly payments will be of equal size, composed of varying amounts of principal and interest. The difference is that the proportions of interest and principal are established in advance in the precomputed schedule, instead of being computed for each payment period. The monthly computation offers more flexibility to a borrower who may wish to repay the debt faster than scheduled. In such a case, the lender simply charges interest on whatever principal sum is outstanding at the end of the month, subtracts this amount from the payment, and uses the remainder to reduce the principal. (You may wish to review the calculation of compound interest on instalment loans in Chapter 8.) Precomputed charges create more complexity if the borrower wishes to repay early but we will not go into the detail here since this practice is becoming less common.

Unsolicited Credit Cards and Goods

Provincial legislation sets limits on your responsibility for unsolicited goods or credit cards you may receive.

UNSOLICITED CREDIT CARDS   Five provinces prohibit the issuing of unsolicited credit cards (Table 14.2). Other provinces do not make it illegal to send out such cards, but they make it quite clear that if a credit card was not requested, the intended recipient has no legal responsibility for transactions made with it unless some indication of acceptance was made, such as signing the card and presenting it to a vendor.

UNSOLICITED GOODS   Prince Edward Island is the only province that prohibits sending unsolicited goods. In British Columbia, Newfoundland, Nova Scotia, Ontario, and Saskatchewan, the recipient of unsolicited goods has no responsibility to return, pay for, or take any special care of such goods. However, if residents of British Columbia or Saskatchewan acknowledge the receipt of such goods, they lose their immunity from responsibility.

Advertising the Cost of Credit

All provinces regulate advertising the cost of credit. This became necessary when retailers and lenders deceived potential customers by advertising their credit arrangements in such a way as to be misleading. For instance, an advertisement might have stated that there would be no down payment without telling the rest of the story. Lenders who advertise the cost of credit must indicate the cost of borrowing

TABLE 14.2 PROVINCIAL LAWS REGARDING UNSOLICITED CREDIT CARDS

The law states that...	Provinces where this law applies
issuing of unsolicited credit cards is forbidden.	Alberta, Manitoba, New Brunswick, Prince Edward Island, Quebec.
if an unsolicited credit card is received, the recipient has no legal obligation for transactions made with it, unless he writes to the issuer of the card stating his intention of accepting it.	Alberta, British Columbia, Newfoundland, Nova Scotia, Ontario, Saskatchewan.
signing and using an unsolicited credit card is considered to be acceptance of responsibility for the card.	Alberta, Newfoundland, Nova Scotia, Ontario.
if the unsolicited credit card has not been accepted, the intended recipient has no responsibility if the card is lost or misused.	Alberta, Ontario, British Columbia, Newfoundland, Nova Scotia, Saskatchewan.

expressed as an annual percentage rate. If other information about the credit terms is to be advertised, lenders are required to present all relevant information, which includes the number of instalments, the amount of the down payment, and the size of each instalment.

Repossession of Secured Goods

If a debtor is in default, the creditor can usually seize the secured goods without a court judgment. However, provincial laws place some restrictions on this process. In practice, most creditors prefer to press for payment of the debt rather than become involved in the complications of repossession. Although threat of repossession is a powerful weapon for encouraging borrowers to make payments, it is not worthwhile for creditors unless the pledged goods are of significant value. The creditor usually has the right to repossess the goods, sell them, and claim against the debtor for any balance not covered by the sale. However, because some unscrupulous creditors would sell the goods at a lower price to friends and then sue the debtor for the difference, some provinces have "seize or sue" laws that allow the creditor to repossess secured goods or to sue, but not both (British Columbia, Alberta, and Newfoundland).

Promissory Notes on Conditional Sales Agreements

A promissory note is not only an unconditional promise to repay a debt, it is also a negotiable instrument. Like a cheque, it can be endorsed and made payable to a third party. There is usually a promissory note implied in a conditional sales agreement but in such cases there are some restrictions to protect borrowers. The reason is that a person who holds the usual type of promissory note can demand payment regardless of any responsibilities for delivery, quality of goods, and so on. However, anyone who buys a conditional sales agreement from a retailer shares responsibility with the retailer for ensuring that obligations associated with the goods are met. The vendor and the third party, usually a sales finance company or bank, share in the responsibility for ensuring that the goods or service are satisfactory for the intended purpose.

ISSUES AND PROBLEMS

Credit Cards

NEED FOR STANDARDIZED DISCLOSURE   In spite of the widespread use of credit cards, their costs are not well understood. The available cards differ significantly in two kinds of costs: (i) non-interest costs such as annual or transaction fees, and (ii) terms and conditions associated with interest charges. To make rational choices consumers must understand the terms and conditions of each credit card.

However, that is not possible with the present state of information disclosure. Although the nominal interest rates are readily available, as you have seen they are not an accurate basis for comparing costs.

Some of the information card issuers do provide is not presented in an easily understandable form. For instance, it is commonly believed that a partial payment will proportionately reduce the interest charges but this is not the case with all credit cards. There is a need for a standardized set of terms and conditions for calculating interest charges on credit cards, as is the case for consumer loans.

In 1987, in response to a demand for better information about credit card costs, Consumer and Corporate Affairs Canada began to issue a brief release called "Credit Card Costs" three times a year. It includes a chart comparing credit cards by fees, grace periods, interest rates, and the period when interest charges apply. Contact the department if you wish to be on the mailing list.

DISPUTES WITH RETAILERS   A complicating aspect of purchases made with bank cards is that if there is a dispute about goods or services purchased with them, one has to deal with a retailer who has already been reimbursed by the financial institution. The bank or other institution, which specifically stated in the cardholder agreement that it does not take responsibility for merchandise or services, will not be interested in hearing about the dispute (Figure 14.7). Payments to the issuer of the credit card must be kept up-to-date; withholding payment will not succeed, since more credit charges will be added to the unpaid amount. The problem will have to be handled in the same manner as an unsatisfactory cash purchase.

Some consumers have faced a quite different problem. They have had the unfortunate experience of having their credit cards rejected at the point of sale, in spite of a good payment record. The cause could be an employee error or it could be that the card issuer's computer has detected unusual purchasing patterns. When this occurs, it is difficult to get the problem resolved in a store or hotel lobby. One alternative is to have another method of payment available, such as cash or another credit card.

CREDIT CARD COSTS   There is no restriction on interest rates charged on credit card debt. It is assumed that cardholders can compare costs between sources of credit and make rational choices. An estimated 70 to 80 percent of cardholders pay interest charges at least some of the time. Banks claim that they need high interest rates to cover losses from fraud and default. However, the delinquency rate on bank cards is about 1.5 percent compared to 2 percent on other bank personal loans.

Contracts

Two significant problems consumers have to face when they sign credit contracts are their weak bargaining position and the difficulty of understanding the legal terminology used in the contracts. Chattel mortgages and conditional sales agreements have been drawn up by lawyers hired to protect the interests of creditors,

FIGURE 14.7 CREDIT CARDHOLDER AGREEMENT

VISA CARDHOLDER AGREEMENT

In this Agreement, the words "you" and "your" mean "Canadian Imperial Bank of Commerce" and the words "I", "me" and "my" mean the person in whose name you have opened a VISA* account (the Account) and whose name is embossed on one or more of your charge cards which carry the Chargex* and/or VISA name ("Cards"). "Authorized User" means each person whose name is embossed on a Card or Convenience Cheque at my request.

I and each Authorized User agree with you as follows:

1. Use of Cards and Convenience Cheques

I will ensure that each Card is signed immediately upon receipt. I will not use a Card or Convenience Cheque prior to any validation date embossed on a Card or after the expiry date embossed on a Card. Cards and Convenience Cheques are your property. They may be used to purchase goods and services and to obtain cash advances, and the Account may be used in any other way you may permit (a "Transaction"). I can not stop payment on any Transaction (except a Convenience Cheque).

2. Liability for Indebtedness

The purchase price of goods and services, the amount of cash advances and Convenience Cheques and all other amounts payable under this Agreement, except interest, are called Indebtedness. I am liable for all Indebtedness and interest on it (including Indebtedness incurred by each Authorized User, any family member or any other person, to whom I have given either express or implied authority to use the Account (an "Authorized Person")). If I or any Authorized Person sign a sales or cash advance draft or give the Account number to make a purchase or obtain a cash advance without presenting the Card (such as for a mail order or telephone purchase), the legal effect shall be the same as if the Card was used by me and a sales or cash advance draft was signed by me. Each Authorized User is jointly and individually liable with me for all Indebtedness and interest on it incurred by such Authorized User or with such Authorized User's Card.

3. Credit Limit

I will not permit the Indebtedness to exceed the credit limit established by you from time to time. However you may (but are not required to, even if you have done so before) permit the Indebtedness to exceed the credit limit established from time to time. The credit limit appears on the document which accompanies a Card when it is issued and also appears on the monthly statement. I am liable for all Indebtedness, whether or not it exceeds the credit limit.

4. Payment

I will pay the Indebtedness and interest on it by the Payment Due Date on the monthly statement as follows:

(a) in full, or

(b) by a part payment equal to the greater of $10.00 or 5% of the unpaid balance shown on the statement, or

(c) by any payment greater than (b).

In addition, I will immediately pay any Indebtedness exceeding the credit limit, and if the balance shown on a statement is less than $10.00, I will pay it in full by the statement's Payment Due Date. Payments received at your VISA Center, or by 3:00 p.m. on a banking day at any of your Canadian branches, will be applied to the Account as of the day of receipt. I will not use the Account to pay the Indebtedness.

5. Interest

(a) **Payment in Full.** There is a benefit to me if I pay my Account in full by the Payment Due Date. If I pay the entire balance in full by the Payment Due Date shown on the statement, interest is charged only,

   (i) on cash advances from and including the date they are obtained

   (ii) on Convenience Cheques from the date they are charged to the Account, and

   (iii) on Indebtedness shown on the statement which also appeared on the previous statement.

(b) **Partial Payment.** If I do not pay the entire balance in full by the Payment Due Date then interest is charged;

   (i) on cash advances from and including the date they are obtained, and

   (ii) on all other Indebtedness from the date they are charged to the Account.

(c) **Interest Rate.** Interest is charged at the rate specified in the Disclosure Statement which accompanies this Agreement. The

FIGURE 14.7   CREDIT CARDHOLDER AGREEMENT (CONTINUED)

interest rate is subject to change in accordance with paragraph 14, and the current rate at any time appears on the monthly statement. Interest is calculated by totalling the interest bearing Indebtedness owing at the end of each day in the period in question and multiplying the result by the daily interest rate.

6. Application of Payments

Payments are applied, in accordance with paragraph 4, in the following order: previously billed interest; previously billed cash advances and Convenience Cheques; previously billed purchases, fees and charges which are interest-bearing; previously billed purchases, fees and charges which are not yet interest-bearing; unbilled cash advances and Convenience Cheques; and, at the end of a billing period, any unapplied payments are applied to unbilled purchases.

7. Special Services

You may make available to me and/or to any Authorized User special services or benefits (a "Service"). The Services shall be subject to the terms and conditions applicable to them (which may vary from time to time) and may be cancelled with or without notice. You are not liable for any Service not directly supplied by you.

8. Fees and Charges

I will pay the fees and charges described in the Disclosure Statement and those described in any notice or monthly statement sent to me from time to time.

9. Monthly Statements

The number of days covered by each monthly statement will vary as a result of several factors, including holidays, weekends and the different number of days in each month, and will normally be between 28 and 33 days.

10. Loss or Theft of Card

If a Card is lost or stolen, I will immediately notify you and you may take whatever steps you consider necessary in order to recover the Card including reporting the lost or stolen Card to the appropriate authorities to facilitate its recovery. Until notification, I am liable for up to $50 for unauthorized use.

11. Failure to Honour Cards or Accept Convenience Cheques; Claims Against Merchants

You will not be liable if a Card is not honoured, a Convenience Cheque is not accepted, or the Account cannot otherwise be used. I will settle all claims and disputes regarding any Transaction or any credit voucher issued by a merchant directly with the merchant. You will credit the Account upon receipt of a merchant's credit voucher for a purchase made with a Card. If you have not received a credit voucher when a monthly statement is prepared, I will pay the balance shown on the statement as required by this Agreement, and any credit will appear on a subsequent statement following your receipt of the voucher.

12. Foreign Currency

I will pay Indebtedness incurred in a foreign currency in Canadian dollars. If you convert the Indebtedness to Canadian currency, you will use a conversion rate no higher than your selling rate in effect at the time that the Transaction is processed by you or by your agents. If you are charged in Canadian currency, you will use the conversion rate billed to you plus a service charge based on the converted amount.

13. Errors in Statement; Copies of Documents

If I or an Authorized User do not notify you in writing within 30 days after the date of a monthly statement of any error or omission, the statement will be conclusively settled to be complete and correct except for any amount improperly credited to the Account. A microfilm or other copy of a sales draft, cash advance draft, Convenience Cheque or other document relating to a Transaction will be sufficient to establish liability.

14. Changes

You may change this Agreement and/or any Disclosure Statement from time to time, by mailing a notice (or sending it in any other way) to me at the most recent address appearing in the records of your VISA Center. The notice will bind the Authorized User if it is also mailed or sent to the Authorized User at my address. The Authorized User directs you to use that address for such purposes. A change may apply both to existing Indebtedness and to Indebtedness arising after the change is made. I will give your VISA Center prompt written notice of any change in my address.

15. Termination of Agreement

I may terminate this Agreement at any time without notice. You may terminate this Agreement at any time without notice if I am in breach of this Agreement, if I am in default in respect of any other loan arrangement I may have with you, or if you receive information about me which leads you to believe that I may be unable to repay the Indebtedness.

If this Agreement is terminated, you may do any or all of the following without notice;

(a) refuse to honour any Convenience Cheques (whether made before or after such termination),

(b) require that all Indebtedness and interest be paid immediately,

(c) debit any bank account I have with you and apply the funds against the Indebtedness and interest owing under this Agreement,

(d) request that all Cards and unused Convenience Cheques be returned to you,

(e) take possession of all Cards and unused Convenience Cheques.

If this Agreement is terminated, I will continue to be liable for Indebtedness and interest and I am responsible for returning the Cards and unused Convenience Cheques to you. If a Card or a Convenience Cheque is used after this Agreement is terminated I will be liable for the Indebtedness and interest incurred even though the Agreement was terminated.

I will pay to you all legal fees and expenses (on a solicitor and client basis) incurred by you to recover any Indebtedness or interest and all expenses incurred by you to take possession of a Card.

CIBC VISA Cards are owned and issued by Canadian Imperial Bank of Commerce.

*CIBC Registered User of Marks

CX 921E - 4/89

Reproduced with the permission of CIBC.

not those of consumers. A borrower has the choice of accepting the contract as it stands or rejecting it and going elsewhere for credit. The sales person or credit manager usually lacks the authority to renegotiate the terms to suit the borrower and rarely understands the contract any better than the customer does. It is encouraging, however, to find that some creditors have started to rewrite these contracts in language that is much easier to understand.

Summary

Point-of-sale credit, which may take the form of charge cards, credit cards, or conditional sales, plays a significant part in consumer transactions. The use of credit cards has accelerated in recent years but consumer understanding of the associated terms and conditions has not kept pace. Charge cards are for short-term credit and do not attract interest unless payment is overdue. Credit cardholders have the option of paying monthly balances in full without interest or making partial payments with interest. The methods used to determine interest charges on partial payments are very complex, making it virtually impossible to use nominal interest as a basis for comparing costs. There is a need for a standardized method of calculating interest charges and a improved means of communicating this to consumers.

In view of the weak bargaining position of most consumer borrowers in relation to corporate creditors, provincial consumer legislation has been enacted to redress the balance, but some problems still remain. Generally, consumers are unaware of their rights. The legislation requires full disclosure of credit costs and terms, but borrowers tend to be insensitive to interest rates. "Cooling-off" laws are intended to assist those who sign credit contracts at home and who may have been subject to undue sales pressure, but in most cases they do not know of this right.

Vocabulary Review

acceleration clause (p. 420)

charge card (p. 410)

conditional sales agreement (p. 416)

credit card (p. 410)

debit card (payment card) (p. 408)

executory contract (p. 424)

· grace period (p. 410)

point-of-sale credit (p. 410)

residual interest (p. 417)

revolving charge account (p. 411)

variable credit (p. 411)

Problems

Note: You must consult the appropriate consumer protection legislation for your province to find the information needed to answer these questions.

1. Kim is frustrated because the lawn mower she purchased from Handy Appliances, using her Visa card, has been defective from the time she brought it home. She took it back to the store but was not able to get satisfaction. At first they said, "Bring it in, we'll look it over," but it turned out that the store was a sales business only, without any service personnel. The sales clerks commented that the lawn mower looked to be in order and suggested that Kim try it again. In the meantime the Visa bill arrived. Since she was contesting this sale, she wrote Visa to say that she wasn't paying the bill until the lawn mower was fixed or replaced. Time passed and along came another Visa statement. The bill for the lawn mower was on it as well as a credit charge for the delay in paying.

   (a) Where can Kim find out what her rights are in her dispute with Visa?

   (b) What are these rights?

   (c) What is your opinion of the situation? What would you do?

   (d) What rights does Kim have in her dispute with the retailer?

   (e) What interest rate would Kim pay if she obtained a cash loan with her Visa card? How does this compare with the rates that banks charge for personal loans? (Refer to Chapter 13 or call a financial institution.)

2. Kim also bought a piano using a conditional sales agreement. Her partner, Paul Wong, co-signed the contract (Figure 14.6).

   (a) At the time she signed the contract was it possible for her to predict that it might be sold to a third party?

   (b) Explain who will have possession and who will have the title to the piano during the payment period.

   (c) Will there be additional costs if Kim misses a few payments and has her contract extended?

   (d) If the couple's house is damaged by fire and the piano destroyed, can Kim cancel the contract since she no longer has a piano?

   (e) Is there an acceleration clause in Kim's contract? What does an acceleration clause usually say?

   (f) If, after she has paid two-thirds of the purchase price of the piano, Kim is unable to make further payments, can the holder of the contract repossess the piano? Explain.

   (g) If the piano has been repossessed, but not sold, and Kim has found some money to make up the payment, will she have to pay any extra charges? If so, for what?

   (h) If the holder of the conditional sales contract uses the services of a lawyer to enforce some aspect of the contract, who pays the lawyer's fee?

   (i) Could Kim have saved money by obtaining credit from another source?

   (j) From Kim's perspective, what difference is there between a chattel mortgage and a conditional sales contract? What is the legal distinction?

3. Susan and David are about to book a vacation to Puerto Vallarta through the travel section of a major department store. They want this, their first real holiday, to be special so they have been looking at packages costing about $1500 each. Knowing that they will be rather short on cash with the trip coming right after Christmas, they are planning to use either a bank card or the store's credit card to pay for the trip. The store accepts either, leaving them in a quandary as to which card to use. The nominal interest rate is 28.8 percent on the store card and 17 percent on the bank card.

   (a) Their first thought is that the decision is easy; it seems obvious that the bank card would be the best choice. What other factors beside the nominal interest rate might they consider before making a choice?

   (b) Susan and David realize that there will be other things that they will need before the trip. If they spend an additional $750 on gifts and clothes at various times during the second month, could this influence their decision about which account to choose?

   (c) David might get a bonus of about $1600 in three months' time. Should they use all of it to reduce their credit card balance or put it in a savings account?

   (d) Are there other possibilities you think this couple should explore before making their final decision?

4. (a) What minimum monthly payment is required on a Visa account?

   (b) If you obtain a cash advance and repay it all when the bill arrives, will you pay any credit charges?

5. How is an itinerant seller defined in the consumer protection legislation of your province? Can you think of examples of door-to-door selling that are not regulated by this legislation?

6. The "cooling-off" legislation is intended to provide consumers with some protection from itinerant sellers.

   (a) What are the conditions regarding a door-to-door sale that make the "cooling-off" legislation applicable?

   (b) How much and what kinds of protection from itinerant sellers do you think consumers need?

   (c) How effective do you think the present legislation in your province is in meeting these needs?

   (d) Do you think the right to cancel the contract should be written on the contract? Why or why not?

7. Make a list of arguments for and against this statement: "In the area of point-of-sale credit, consumers have enough protection in law; what they need is more education about their rights and responsibilities."

8. What is your responsibility regarding:

    (a) debts charged against you by someone who found or stole your credit card?

    (b) paying for unsolicited goods you received in the mail?

    (c) an unsolicited credit card received in the mail?

9. Decide whether you AGREE or DISAGREE with each of the following statements:

    (a) There is a provincial law that regulates the maximum rates that retailers can charge on revolving accounts.

    (b) There is no legal limit to the credit rate that sales finance companies may charge on conditional sales agreements.

    (c) The contract will be void if a conditional sales agreement omits any of the following:

        (i) the total cost of credit in dollar amounts,

        (ii) a guarantee of the quality of the merchandise,

        (iii) the credit rate expressed as an annual rate,

        (iv) the name and address of the manufacturer of the goods.

10. Make inquiries to find out if bank credit cardholders are charged a fee. If there is one, is it by the month or by the transaction?

11. Assume that you have a choice between buying a television set with a credit card or with a conditional sales agreement. In either case you plan to pay for it over 12 months. Identify some of the costs and benefits for you of each alternative.

12. Suppose that you made a purchase using a debit card, and a friend made a similar purchase with a credit card. From your perspective, what differences would there be between the two transactions?

13. You have saved $11 000 to buy a new car. Is it better to buy the car for cash or, as the sales person suggested, put $1500 down, use credit for the balance, and invest the $9500? The credit terms are 11 percent with payments of $244.42 for 48 months. Your money could be invested at 5 percent compounded annually in a guaranteed investment certificate.

    (a) Calculate the total cost of credit if you choose the first option.

    (b) Find the total interest that you could earn from the guaranteed investment certificate. (Remember to use a compound interest table or formula.)

    (c) How much tax would you pay on the interest income from the GIC? Assume a combined federal and provincial marginal income tax rate of 40 percent.

    (d) Subtract the income tax from the GIC income to find the after-tax return. Compare this with the cost of borrowing.

(e) Look at this situation in another way. Suppose that you had bought the car for cash, and then had invested $244 a month for 48 months. How much would this amount to in four years? To find the answer use the formula for the future value of a uniform series of deposits, but adapt it for semi-annual compounding by using an interest rate of 4.5 percent and change n=4 to n=8 to reflect the eight compounding periods.

REFERENCES

BOOKS

Canadian Commercial Law Guide. Don Mills, Ontario: CCH Canadian, Topical Law Reports. Subscription service in two volumes on federal and provincial law regarding the sale of personal property and consumer protection.

DYMOND, MARY JOY. *The Canadian Woman's Legal Guide*. Toronto: Doubleday, 1989, 449 pp. Includes a section on women and credit.

FORMAN, NORM. *Mind Over Money, Curing Your Financial Headaches with Moneysanity*. Toronto: Doubleday Canada, 1987, 248 pp. A psychologist examines the effects money has on behaviour, looking at the origin of money problems and suggesting therapies to help us to better understand ourselves.

PARKER, ALLAN A. *Credit, Debt, and Bankruptcy*. Eighth Edition. Vancouver: International Self-Counsel Press, 1990, 128 pp. A handbook on Canadian credit law for credit users.

ARTICLES AND REPORTS

Charge It, Credit Cards and the Canadian Consumer. Ottawa: Consumer and Corporate Affairs Canada, 1989, 53 pp. Minutes and proceedings of a House of Commons Committee that reviewed the background to the problems with credit card costs, the extent of market competition, and current disclosure practices, and made proposals for legislation. Data in appendix.

Credit Cards in Canada. Ottawa: Queen's Printer, 1987, 58 pp. Minutes and proceedings of a House of Commons Committee that examined credit card operations in Canada (including pricing, calculation of interest charges, disclosure requirements, and competition) and made recommendations.

Credit Cards in Canada in the Nineties. Ottawa: Consumer and Corporate Affairs Canada, 1992, 40 pp. Bilingual. Report of the Standing Committee on Consumer and Corporate Affairs and Government Operations. Reviews developments in the credit card market in Canada and the United States since 1987, identifies current issues, and makes recommendations for change.

Discussion Paper on Credit Card Interest Charges. Ottawa: Consumer and Corporate Affairs Canada, 1988, 24 pp. An analysis of the pricing of credit cards that examines how interest is calculated and recommends more standardization.

STEVENSON, DEREK. "Playing Your Cards Right." *Canadian Consumer*, 19, No. 10, 1989, 8–16. Explains the complexities of selecting credit cards and how the various charges are calculated.

PERIODICAL

Credit Card Costs. Ottawa: Consumer and Corporate Affairs Canada, three times a year, 5 pp. Lists fees, interest rates, grace periods, and date from which interest is calculated by name of creditor. Free copy on request.

CHAPTER FIFTEEN

Home Mortgages

OBJECTIVES

1. To explain why opportunity cost and non-money income are considerations when deciding to buy a house.

2. To compare the costs and benefits of these sources of mortgage funds:

    (a) private individuals,

    (b) vendor take-back mortgage,

    (c) assumption of an existing mortgage,

    (d) mortgage broker.

3. To explain the differences between a conventional mortgage and an insured mortgage regarding:

    (a) down payment,

    (b) special costs,

    (c) constraints on the borrower.

4. To explain how lenders determine whether a potential borrower qualifies for a loan.

5. To calculate the size of loan for which an applicant is eligible, given income, debts, and the taxes on the prospective property.

6. To distinguish between these methods of repayment:

    (a) equal instalments of principal,

    (b) blended payments.

7. To calculate the interest and principal components in a mortgage payment.

8. To identify the following components in a mortgage contract:

    (a) description of the property,

    (b) identification of the parties,

    (c) the covenants,

    (d) repayment terms, including prepayment restrictions.

9. To explain the effect of each of the following variables on the total cost of a house:

    (a) interest rate,

    (b) amortization period,

    (c) frequency of compounding interest,

    (d) size of down payment.

10. To identify costs associated with a house purchase (other than the down payment and the monthly mortgage payments).

11. To distinguish between:

    (a) mortgagor and mortgagee,

    (b) chattel mortgage and real estate mortgage,

    (c) term and amortization period,

    (d) first and second mortgages (consider risk, interest rate, and term from both the lender's and the borrower's perspectives),

    (e) mortgage insurance and mortgage life insurance,

    (f) lending value and purchasing price,

    (g) repayment and prepayment,

    (h) open and closed mortgages.

12. To explain how a reverse income mortgage may be used to turn a non-liquid asset into an income stream.

13. To explain the links between the National Housing Act, the Canada Mortgage and Housing Corporation, and lenders in the provision of home mortgages.

14. To explain these terms: gross debt service, total debt service, closing costs, closing date, appraisal, mortgage discharge, interest penalty, prepayment privilege, capital gain, commitment period, equity, maturity date, amortize, mortgage broker, equity of redemption, high ratio mortgage, non-money income, pre-approved mortgage, interest adjustment date, variable rate mortgage, interest rate differential.

Introduction

This chapter explains the basic process of using credit to buy personal real estate; it is not about how to choose a house, but rather about how to understand mortgages. There is, of course, much more to buying a house than the financing and many books have been written on whether to buy or rent, and how to select a house. Such issues are important but are beyond the scope of this book, which focuses on financial issues, rather than all aspects of consumer decision making.

Sometimes prospective buyers are so enthusiastic about their new house that they leave all the financial arrangements to the real estate agent. Perhaps they feel overwhelmed by the terminology and mathematics associated with mortgages. After studying this chapter, it should be possible to talk intelligently with mortgage officers, ask knowledgeable questions, and do some comparison shopping.

THE ECONOMICS OF HOME OWNERSHIP

To Buy or Rent

For most families, the decision whether to buy or rent is not strictly an economic one, but a choice between two different lifestyles. However, the economics of this question involve consideration of the opportunity costs of ownership as well as any differences in regular monthly expenditures. (An **opportunity cost** is anything that was foregone in order to do something else.) A decision to buy a house means tying up funds that otherwise could have been invested in an income-producing asset. To find the financial opportunity cost of buying a house, estimate how much interest has been foregone by not investing the money at current interest rates and leaving it to compound. There are, however, other opportunity costs of home ownership such as the time commitment to home maintenance.

The house you live in does not usually generate money income but provides services or non-money income, in the form of shelter. **Non-money income** is a flow of services that are available for use as a result of our own efforts or gifts, but not purchased in the market. For instance, a home owner gets a place to live without paying rent. In addition to a stream of non-money income, home ownership has the potential for capital gain. When a house is sold for more than it cost, the difference is called **capital gain**. In times of rising prices, houses may appreciate faster than they wear out, thus creating a potential capital gain.

Finally, the income-tax implications of buying a house need to be considered. If savings are invested in a house, any capital gain will not be taxable because of the tax exemption on principal residences. If, instead, funds are invested in deposits, bonds, or stocks, the income will be taxable.

How Much to Spend

How much should a family spend on a house? Some financial advisers suggest that a house should not cost more than two or three times one's annual salary, but these guidelines are much too imprecise to be helpful. The rules do not specify gross income or take-home pay, and the difference can be quite significant. Families live so differently and have such varied financial goals that general rules are often not applicable. It is preferable to work out what is affordable based on consideration of each unique situation.

One way to start is to determine how much can be spared for a down payment and add on the amount that can be borrowed; this will give an approximation of the maximum purchase price that can be afforded. The next step is to find out what all the costs would be on a monthly basis.

HOW MUCH CAN THEY AFFORD?

The Martens decided that they could afford a down payment of $12 000 on a house. Their banker agreed to lend them $88 000 at 10 percent, amortized (repaid) over 25 years. They found their expenses for a $100 000 house might be as follows:

	Per month
Mortgage payment	$787.60
Taxes	95.00
Insurance	25.00
Utilities	150.00
Maintenance and repairs (annually 2% value of house)	200.00
Total	$1257.60
Monthly interest foregone on $12 000 at 8% per annum	80.00
Grand Total	$1337.60

The Martens must now examine their income and expenditures to determine if they can afford $1257.60 a month for housing. If they are paying $975 a month for rent at present, the additional cost of buying a home is about $282.60 a month or $3391.20 a year.

Financing a Home

Most buyers of homes or other real estate need credit to finance the purchase, but because the loan is likely to be large and the repayment period long, the borrowing process is somewhat more complex than for the usual personal loan. To obtain such a large loan the buyer must pledge security of some significance, usually the property being purchased.

When real estate (immovable property) is used to secure a loan, the borrower signs a contract called a **mortgage,** distinguished from a chattel mortgage, which is used for movable goods. The mortgage contract refers to the borrower as the **mortgagor** because this person is giving the mortgage to the lender, who in turn becomes the **mortgagee,** or the one who receives the mortgage as security for the loan. Alternative terms, chargor and chargee, may be used, as in the mortgage contract shown in Figure 15.1 in the Appendix. The gradual repayment of a mortgage by periodic payments of principal and interest is referred to as **amortizing** the debt.

MORTGAGE DEBT   Most of the total debt of households is mortgage debt, although the pattern varies somewhat with income level (Figure 15.2). Single individuals, who are less likely to be home owners, are not included in this graph. Each bar, which represents the average total debt of households in one income class, shows how the total is divided, on average, between consumer and mortgage debt. It is perhaps not surprising to find that, regardless of income level, mortgage debt represents the largest component of total family debt. There appears to be a tendency for mortgage debt to represent a larger proportion of total debt among higher income households, which can afford more expensive houses and may also have vacation homes.

Equity in Real Estate

Equity refers to the value that the owner has in a property, and can be estimated by finding a fair market price and subtracting the outstanding mortgage debt. If house prices fall, equity falls too, as people living in areas that have experienced severe economic down turns have discovered.

HOW MUCH EQUITY?

Jim and Marie bought a $125 000 house with a down payment of $20 000 and a mortgage of $105 000. At this time, they had equity of $20 000 and debt of $105 000. A year later similar houses were selling for $135 000. How has their equity changed?

If they could sell at $135 000, they would perhaps have about $30 000 left after discharging the mortgage, assuming that the small amount they had repaid on the principal during the first year would probably not cover the costs of the sale. Their new equity value of $30 000 is the total of the down payment and the $10 000 that resulted from an increase in house prices. Assuming stable house prices and that they continue to pay down the mortgage, their equity will slowly increase.

FIGURE 15.2 PERCENTAGE COMPOSITION OF TOTAL DEBT OF CANADIAN FAMILIES BY INCOME GROUPS, SPRING 1984

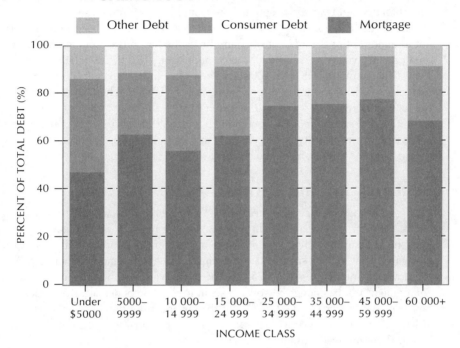

SOURCE OF DATA: *The Distribution of Wealth in Canada, 1984.* Ottawa: Statistics Canada, 1986, Table 24 (p. 65). (Catalogue No. 13-580.) Reproduced with the permission of the Minister of Industry, Science and Technology, 1993.

TYPES OF MORTGAGES

First and Second Mortgages

A particular property may have more than one mortgage on it, which will be ranked as first, second, etc., according to the order in which they were recorded at the local Registry Office. If the first mortgage on a property is discharged, the second mortgage automatically becomes the first mortgage. This does not happen often, because first mortgages are usually for larger sums and longer terms than second mortgages.

The distinguishing characteristic between first and second mortgages is their priority ranking in claims against the property. In the event that the buyer defaults on the mortgage payments and the property must be taken back and sold, the holder of the **first mortgage** would have first claim on the proceeds from the sale. After this has been paid, the claims of the holder of the **second mortgage** would be settled. If there were insufficient funds to pay all claims, the second mortgagee might have to accept a loss. This is the reason why second mortgages are considered to be higher risks than first mortgages, and consequently carry higher interest rates.

From the home owner's perspective, the number of mortgages on the property is not as important as the amount of equity he or she has in the property. For instance, on a property valued at $200 000, the owner's equity of $30 000 would be the same with a first mortgage of $150 000 and a second mortgage of $20 000, or a first mortgage of $160 000 and a second mortgage of $10 000. The interest rate paid on the second mortgage depends on the owner's equity. From the lender's point of view, if the first and second mortgages combined are less than 75 percent of the appraised value (the owner's equity is 25 percent), the second mortgage is nearly as secure as the first and the interest rate should reflect this.

Security for the Lender

Mortgage money may be obtained privately or from financial institutions such as banks, trust companies, and credit unions. As a mortgage is a large loan, the lender must have assurance that it is a sound investment. To protect the lender, the mortgagor must make a sizeable down payment or have the mortgage insured. When the down payment is less than 25 percent of the value of the property, the buyer's equity might not be enough to cover costs if, in the case of default, the lender had to take back the property and sell it. When the buyer cannot provide a downpayment of at least 25 percent of the property's value, an institutional mortgagee will not offer a loan without mortgage insurance.

Mortgage insurance covers the risk to the lender that the borrower will default on the loan. Canada Mortgage and Housing Corporation is the Crown corporation that provides full loan insurance to mortgage lenders. CMHC reimburses the lender for loss in cases of default but, correspondingly, imposes a number of restrictions on the granting of the mortgage, as will be explained later. First, the differences between conventional mortgages and insured mortgages will be examined.

Conventional Mortgages

A **conventional mortgage** is not usually insured, but the down payment is at least 25 percent of the value of the property. A number of financial institutions, notably banks, trust, and mortgage companies, offer conventional mortgages. Privately arranged mortgages are always conventional mortgages, in that they are not insured, and the down payment can be whatever the parties involved agree on.

Insured Mortgages

At one time, all mortgages were conventional mortgages, but in 1954 the federal government established a system to guarantee mortgage loans made by approved financial lenders as a means of increasing the mortgage money available to home buyers and builders. The legislation is the National Housing Act, and the Crown corporation that administers it is the Canada Mortgage and Housing Corporation, usually known as CMHC. A lender making a mortgage loan approved by CMHC can extend a mortgage that is more than 75 percent of the value of the property. These **insured mortgages** permit the buyer to obtain a mortgage with less than 25 percent of the value of the property as a down payment. If the buyer defaults on the mortgage, the lender applies to CMHC for any losses incurred.

To finance this mortgage insurance program, the buyer pays a fee, from one-half of a percent to two and one-half percent of the total loan, which is added to the principal at the outset. The fee is based on a sliding scale, depending on the ratio of the down payment to the loan. The lender deducts the mortgage insurance premium and forwards it to the insurer (CMHC). This insurance, which protects the lender in case of default, may not seem to offer much benefit to the borrower. However, without it, mortgages with low down payments would not be available at all, or purchasers would have to resort to a more expensive second mortgage. These insured first mortgages, which represent a high proportion of the value cost of the house, are sometimes referred to as **high ratio loans.**

Finding a Mortgage

There are a number of ways to obtain a mortgage. It may be possible to arrange a private mortgage with a relative or other individual who has money to lend. In this case, a lawyer would draw up a contract stating the terms agreeable to both borrower and lender. Most mortgages, however, are obtained from financial institutions: banks, trust companies, and credit unions.

In some cases, it is possible to arrange a **vendor take-back mortgage** for all or part of the required financing, which means that the seller lends part of the selling price to the buyer. Perhaps the buyer has found a desirable house and the vendor offers to sell it for $150 000, with the arrangement that the buyer pay $50 000 on closing and the rest in monthly instalments. Since the vendor is providing the loan of $100 000, it is called a vendor take-back mortgage. Sometimes, this takes the form of a second mortgage.

Assumption of an Existing Mortgage

At times it is advantageous to take over a mortgage already existing on the property. If the vendor has a mortgage with four more years remaining in the term, with a lower interest rate than that currently available for a new mortgage, the buyer may wish to take over the vendor's mortgage. The buyer should investigate whether the mortgagee's approval would be required for such a transfer and if it can be obtained. Mortgage contracts vary in this regard. If an existing mortgage is assumed, the buyer replaces the original mortgagor by taking responsibility for the agreements in the mortgage contract; in case of default the original borrower may still be bound by the personal covenant, which is the promise to repay the debt. In practice, when the purchaser has been approved to assume the existing mortgage, the vendor often obtains a written release of this covenant from the lender as protection from this contingency.

Mortgage Brokers

Mortgage brokers specialize in making contact between those who have funds to invest in mortgages and those who need a mortgage. The rates charged for arranging a mortgage vary, depending on the amount of work involved, but are payable by the borrower at the time of closing. As with any mortgage, the property in question has to be satisfactory to the lender. Sometimes, home buyers will ask a broker to find them a mortgage because they do not qualify at the local bank or trust company. A borrower might need the services of a broker because of his or her poor credit rating, previous bankruptcy, very short employment history, or seasonally fluctuating income.

QUALIFYING FOR A MORTGAGE

The rules and procedures that govern the mortgage-granting process originate from three sources: (i) legislation, both federal and provincial, (ii) insurers' requirements for high ratio mortgages, and (iii) the policies of each financial institution. Essentially, two criteria for determining whether or not to grant a mortgage relate to the quality of the property as security, and the creditworthiness of the borrower.

The Property

Before agreeing to arrange a mortgage on a property, a lender will have it appraised to determine its **lending value** (appraised value), that is, the value the lender's appraiser assigns the property, which is not necessarily the same as the selling price. It is conceivable that a buyer may be prepared to pay $150 000 for a much desired property that the lender considers to be worth $143 000. In such a case, the mortgage loan is based on the lending value, not the selling price.

CMHC has rules that vary from time to time and from place to place relating to the proportion of the lending value that may be lent for an insured mortgage. For example, CMHC insured loans could be as large as 95 percent of the first $180 000 of the lending value, plus 80 percent of the remainder (for a first time home buyer).

The Borrower

A potential lender will want a full report on the buyer's credit history as well as complete details about income, assets, and debts. The applicant will be asked to provide statements from an employer verifying current income and employment history of the applicant and spouse, and from a banker about funds available for a down payment.

From these facts, the lender will calculate two ratios to determine the client's capacity to handle the proposed mortgage: the gross debt service and total debt service. **Gross debt service** is the percentage of the buyer's annual gross income needed to cover the mortgage payments plus municipal taxes, and sometimes heating costs also. If a condominium is to be purchased, 50 percent of the condominium fee is usually included in the calculation. Lenders have guidelines, which change from time to time, about the maximum gross debt service that is acceptable to them; it may range from 25–32 percent.

A quick way to determine the maximum mortgage that can be afforded is to find 30 percent (or whatever the ratio is) of gross annual income, subtract the estimated annual property taxes, and divide by 12. The resulting amount is the monthly payment one can presumably afford for principal and interest. For a given interest rate and amortization period, the size of the loan can be found from an amortization table.

Another measure of capacity to handle a mortgage is **total debt service,** the percentage of annual income needed to cover mortgage payments, taxes, heating costs, and consumer debt payments. This should not exceed 37–38 percent, or 40 percent if heating costs are included. Lenders may use this rule for any type of mortgage, conventional or insured.

GROSS AND TOTAL DEBT SERVICE

The Kuprowskys have three questions about financing the house they have selected: (i) How much is the gross debt service? (ii) How much is the total debt service? (iii) What is the largest mortgage they can afford?

In order to find answers to their questions they made the following assumptions:

Husband's income	$56 900 (wife not employed)
Property taxes	$1450/yr.
Heating cost	$450/yr.
Mortgage	$105 000
Interest	9.5%
Amortization	25 years
Payments	$905.10/mo.; $10 861.20/yr.
Consumer debt	$3600/yr.
Lender's maximum TDS	38%

1. How much will the gross debt service (GDS) be?

$$\text{GDS} = \frac{\text{payments/yr. + taxes/yr.+ heating/yr}}{\text{gross annual income}} \times 100$$

$$= \frac{10\,861.20 + 1450 + 450}{56\,900} \times 100$$

$$= \frac{12\,761.20}{56\,900} \times 100$$

$$= 22.43\%$$

2. How much will their total debt service (TDS) be?

$$\text{TDS} = \frac{\text{payments/yr. + taxes + heating + consumer debt}}{\text{gross annual income}} \times 100$$

$$= \frac{10\,861.20 + 1450 + 450 + 3600}{56\,900} \times 100$$

$$= \frac{16\,361.20}{56\,900} \times 100$$

$$= 28.75\%$$

3. What is the largest mortgage for which they are eligible?

Since their total debt service is well below the lender's maximum, they wonder how large a mortgage they could get if they had a TDS of 38%.

Transpose the formula for total debt service to find the annual payment, then insert 38% as the TDS.

$$\frac{\text{Payments + taxes + heating + consumer debt}}{\text{gross annual income}} \times 100 = \text{TDS}$$

$$\text{Payments + (taxes + heating + consumer debt)} = \frac{\text{TDS} \times \text{gross income}}{100}$$

$$\text{Payments} = \left(\frac{\text{TDS} \times \text{gross income}}{100}\right) - (\text{taxes + heating + consumer debt})$$

$$= \left(\frac{38 \times 56\,900}{100}\right) - (1450 + 450 + 3600)$$

= 21 622 − 5500

= $16 122.00 per year (or $1343.50 a month)

With a TDS of 38%, the monthly payment would be $1343.50. The next step is to find the principal of such a loan. Table 15.1 shows the monthly payment per $1000 for mortgages at various rates; at 9.5% and 25-year amortization, the monthly payment per $1000 is $8.62. Multiply this amount by the number of thousands of principal to find the monthly payment. The formula is as follows:

$$\text{Monthly payment} = \frac{\text{principal}}{1000} \times \text{payment per } \$1000 \text{ [x\%] (Table 15.1)}$$

Transposing the formula,

$$\text{Principal} = \frac{\text{monthly payment} \times 1000}{\text{payment per } \$1000 \text{ (Table 15.1)}}$$

Assuming payments of $1343.50 per month,

$$\text{Principal} = \frac{1343.50 \times 1000}{8.62 \text{ [interest 9.5\%, 25 years]}}$$

= $155 858.47

Based on a total debt service ratio of 38%, the Kuprowskys would be eligible for a maximum mortgage of $155 858.47 providing the property qualified.

In addition to gross debt service and total debt service, a third requirement for most mortgages is that the buyer have enough personal funds to make a down payment that is some minimum proportion of the selling price. For a conventional mortgage this would be 25 percent, for a high ratio mortgage it might be as low as five percent. If the total available for a down payment combined with the maximum mortgage is less than the price of the house, a second mortgage might be a consideration. However, the cost of servicing the second mortgage would have to be included in the gross and total debt service ratios. In qualifying purchasers for a mortgage, some conservative lenders may wish to satisfy themselves that the down payment is actually from the borrower's own resources and not a gift or undisclosed loan. To this end, the lender may require evidence of the source of the funds, such as the history of a savings account.

TABLE 15.1 MONTHLY PAYMENTS REQUIRED TO AMORTIZE A $1000 LOAN, INTEREST COMPOUNDED SEMI-ANNUALLY

Nominal interest rate	Amortization period (years)						
	5	10	15	20	25	30	35
%			(dollars per thousand)				
6	19.30	11.06	8.40	7.12	6.40	5.94	5.65
6 1/4	19.41	11.19	8.53	7.26	6.55	6.10	5.82
6 1/2	19.53	11.31	8.66	7.40	6.62	6.26	5.98
6 3/4	19.64	11.43	8.80	7.55	6.85	6.42	6.15
7	19.75	11.56	8.93	7.69	7.00	6.59	6.32
7 1/4	19.87	11.68	9.07	7.84	7.16	6.75	6.49
7 1/2	19.98	11.81	9.20	7.99	7.32	6.91	6.66
7 3/4	20.10	11.94	9.34	8.13	7.47	7.08	6.83
8	20.21	12.06	9.48	8.28	7.63	7.25	7.01
8 1/4	20.33	12.19	9.62	8.43	7.79	7.42	7.18
8 1/2	20.44	12.32	9.76	8.58	7.95	7.58	7.36
8 3/4	20.56	12.45	9.90	8.74	8.12	7.76	7.54
9	20.68	12.58	10.05	8.90	8.25	7.93	7.72
9 1/4	20.08	12.71	10.19	9.05	8.45	8.11	7.90
9 1/2	20.92	12.84	10.34	9.21	8.62	8.28	8.08
9 3/4	21.04	12.98	10.48	9.36	8.78	8.46	8.26
10	21.15	13.11	10.63	9.52	8.95	8.63	8.45
10 1/4	21.27	13.24	10.77	9.68	9.12	8.81	8.63
10 1/2	21.39	13.37	10.92	9.84	9.29	8.99	8.81
10 3/4	21.51	13.51	11.07	10.00	9.46	9.17	9.00
11	21.63	13.64	11.22	10.16	9.63	9.34	9.18
11 1/4	21.74	13.78	11.37	10.32	9.80	9.52	9.37
11 1/2	21.86	13.91	11.52	10.49	9.98	9.71	9.56
11 3/4	21.98	14.05	11.67	10.65	10.15	9.89	9.74
12	22.10	14.19	11.82	10.81	10.32	10.07	9.93
12 1/4	22.22	14.32	11.97	10.98	10.50	20.25	10.12
12 1/2	22.34	14.46	12.13	11.15	10.68	10.43	10.31
12 3/4	22.46	14.60	12.28	11.31	10.85	10.62	10.50
13	22.59	14.74	12.44	11.48	11.03	10.80	10.69
13 1/4	22.71	14.22	12.59	11.65	11.21	10.99	10.88
13 1/2	22.83	15.02	12.75	11.82	11.39	11.17	11.07
13 3/4	22.95	15.16	12.90	11.99	11.56	11.36	11.26

THE MORTGAGE CONTRACT

Equity of Redemption

In the mortgage document, the mortgagor agrees to transfer the ownership of the property to the mortgagee (a financial institution or an individual lender) as security for the loan until such time as it is repaid. The mortgagor will receive a copy of the signed mortgage and the mortgagee will retain the original. The mortgage leaves the mortgagor with an interest in the property, called the **equity of redemption,** which is the right to redeem the property and have the ownership transferred back when the mortgage is discharged. It states that the mortgagor will retain possession of the property and may enjoy the use of it, but must take good care of it and keep it insured, with the mortgagee as joint beneficiary of the insurance policy. If there is a fire while the mortgage is outstanding, the insurance money would be paid to the mortgagee, who can decide what to do about the repairs.

The exchanges involved when using real property as security for loans are summarized in Figure 15.3. The purchaser briefly acquires title to and possession of the property, but on giving the first mortgage, legal title is surrendered to the first mortgagee; the mortgagor retains the equity of redemption. Should the mortgagor give a second mortgage on this property, the equity of redemption would be transferred to the second mortgagee as security.

The Contract

The essential features of a mortgage are:

(a) a description of the property,

(b) identification of the mortgagor and mortgagee,

(c) the amount of the mortgage with terms of repayment,

(d) an agreement that the mortgagor will give a charge on the property to the mortgagee, but will keep the right of possession and the right to redeem the property when the mortgage is discharged,

(e) certain promises or covenants.

A sample mortgage contract is reproduced in the Appendix (Figure 15.1). This lender gives the borrower a mortgage contract written in legal language as well as a version in plain English. The legal version is not reproduced in this book. This contract uses the alternative terms, chargee and chargor, instead of mortgagee and mortgagor.

Mortgage Covenants

Apart from the main contract, every mortgage contains a number of **covenants**, or promises made by the borrower or mortgagor, which are binding. Particularly important is the personal covenant, which is the mortgagor's promise to pay principal and interest. It is called a personal covenant because the mortgagee can sue the mortgagor personally to obtain repayment in full or those payments that are in arrears. The mortgagee can take a number of other actions to recover the loan, as will be mentioned later.

FIGURE 15.3 EXCHANGES WHEN REAL PROPERTY IS SECURITY FOR A LOAN

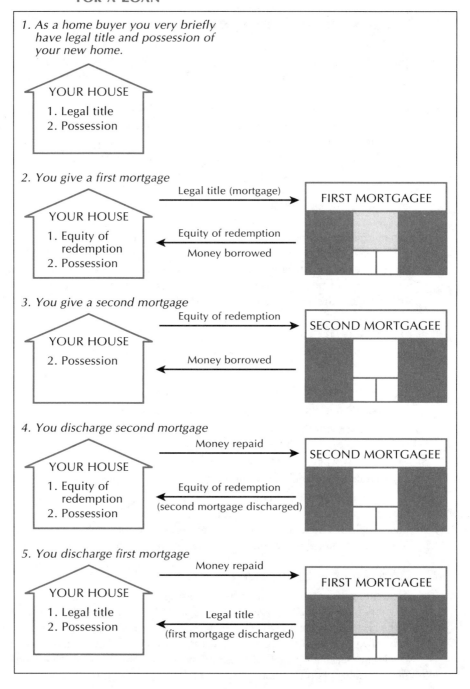

TAXES   Other covenants bind the mortgagor to pay the taxes, to insure the property, and to maintain it in good repair. It is important that taxes be paid on time, because taxes are a prior claim on property, taking precedence over a first mortgage. If taxes are allowed to fall into arrears the mortgagee's security may be impaired, as in the case of a property being sold for taxes. Some lenders require that the mortgagor pay one-twelfth of the annual taxes with each monthly mortgage payment, in order to build up a fund to pay the taxes when they become due. This saves the mortgagee the annual bother of finding out if the taxes have been paid. Interest on this tax fund may be credited to the mortgagor or it may not, depending on the agreement. Penalties for inadvertent late payment of taxes by the lender are usually debited to the borrower's account.

PROPERTY INSURANCE   Before mortgage money is advanced, the mortgagor may be required to insure the property against fire and other possible risks, and to have the policy made in favour of the mortgagee. The insurance policy will be endorsed to ensure that the mortgagee's interest in the property is known to the insurer.

Sale of Mortgages

A person or institution who holds a mortgage (mortgagee) may decide that they would prefer to have the cash at once instead of receiving a monthly income stream for the term of the mortgage. They can sell the mortgage without asking the mortgagor's permission, although the mortgagor would be informed. Mortgages may be sold at their face value, or for more or less (at a premium or at a discount) depending on interest rates at the time. Refer to Chapter 10, to review how changing interest rates affect the price of a security. For the mortgagor, one of the risks of assuming a vendor take-back mortgage is that if the vendor sells the mortgage the mortgagor will have to deal with another person or institution. This is the principal reason why all of the terms of the loan should be written into the mortgage document, especially any terms favourable to the mortgagor.

Breach of Mortgage Contract

If the mortgagor fails to carry out any of the promises agreed to in the mortgage contract, this failure is considered a default and he or she may be subject to a variety of penalties. The mortgage contract stipulates that the mortgagor must: (i) make payments on time, (ii) pay the taxes, (iii) keep the property insured, (iv) keep the property in good condition, and (v) not sell the property without the mortgagee's written approval.

Anyone who finds it impossible to make a mortgage payment on time should immediately contact the mortgagee to search for a solution to the problem before it gets worse. The mortgagor is usually liable for late interest charges, which would be added to the outstanding principal and thus cause interest to be paid on interest. A mortgagee has a number of options to force a defaulting mortgagor to pay, which may include taking possession of the property, suing the borrower under the personal covenant, exercising the acceleration clause, selling the property, and foreclosure. Before any of these actions begin, the mortgagor would receive notice of the mortgagee's intentions and have an opportunity to take some preventative steps if desired. The details of procedures that follow default are explained in several of the references listed at the end of this chapter.

Discharge of Mortgages

When a mortgage has been repaid in full, steps are taken to obtain a legal **mortgage discharge** and transfer the property ownership back to the mortgagor. Either the mortgagor or the lawyer will take a signed statement, which indicates that the debt has been paid, from the mortgagee to the local land registry office. For a small fee the claim against the property is removed and the title cleared.

MORTGAGE REPAYMENT

Term and Amortization Period

Repayment of a mortgage can take as long as 25 or 30 years. The time to completely repay a mortgage, established when the mortgage is arranged, is called the **amortization period.** The length of time before the lender can demand repayment of all the outstanding principal is the **mortgage term.** In most cases, the interest rate and monthly payments are fixed for the term. Although it has not always been so, nowadays mortgage terms are usually much shorter than amortization periods. Mortgage terms can now be as short as six months or as long as ten or more years. At the end of the term, or at the **maturity date,** the lender can demand full payment for all the outstanding balance, but usually will offer to renew the mortgage at the prevailing rate. There have been times in the past when the term and amortization period were the same, but in recent years the high variability in interest rates has made it less likely for lenders to offer mortgages with interest rates fixed for 20 to 25 years.

SHORT TERM, LONG AMORTIZATION

When Tom and Sandra were buying a house, they were told that the mortgage would be amortized over 25 years, but that the term would be five years. That meant that the monthly payments were worked out so that, at current interest rates, the mortgage would be completely repaid in 25 years.

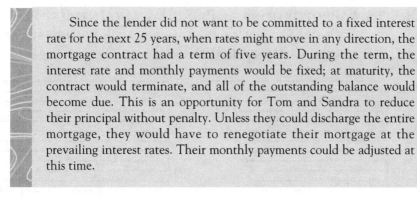

Since the lender did not want to be committed to a fixed interest rate for the next 25 years, when rates might move in any direction, the mortgage contract had a term of five years. During the term, the interest rate and monthly payments would be fixed; at maturity, the contract would terminate, and all of the outstanding balance would become due. This is an opportunity for Tom and Sandra to reduce their principal without penalty. Unless they could discharge the entire mortgage, they would have to renegotiate their mortgage at the prevailing interest rates. Their monthly payments could be adjusted at this time.

Methods of Repayment

Mortgage loans may be repaid in a number of ways as long as an agreement can be reached between the mortgagor and the mortgagee. Since it is not practicable for most people to repay an entire mortgage with interest in a lump sum, most mortgages are amortized, that is, the debt is extinguished by regular payments of interest and principal.

Two methods of repayment will be explained in this chapter: (i) equal instalments of principal, and (ii) blended payments. The difference between them is in the proportions of interest and principal in each payment, as illustrated schematically in Figure 15.4. Each horizontal bar represents one payment and the way it is divided between principal and interest. These diagrams show the proportions in a general way; an exact plot of blended payments would result in a curved line rather than a straight one dividing interest and principal. As will be explained below, if a mortgage is repaid with equal instalments of principal, the amount of interest owing declines, making succeeding payments smaller. By contrast, if all payments are level, as in blended payments, the proportions of interest and principal must vary over the repayment period.

Equal Instalments of Principal

In this repayment schedule, the principal is repaid at a constant rate but each consecutive payment becomes smaller because, as the principal owing is reduced, the interest due also decreases (Table 15.2 and Figure 15.4). This arrangement is used for various payment intervals—for instance, annually, semi-annually, or quarterly—but seldom monthly. Mortgages with equal instalments of principal are much less common than those with blended payments.

FIGURE 15.4 PROPORTIONS OF PRINCIPAL AND INTEREST PER PAYMENT, EQUAL INSTALMENTS OF PRINCIPAL, AND EQUAL BLENDED PAYMENTS

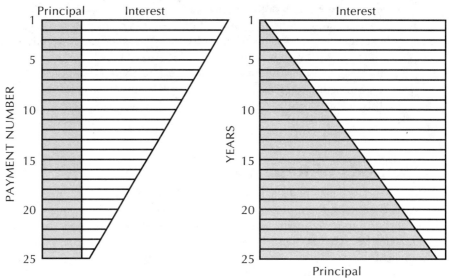

EQUAL INSTALMENTS OF PRINCIPAL   EQUAL BLENDED PAYMENTS

TABLE 15.2 MORTGAGE REPAYMENT SCHEDULE, EQUAL INSTALMENTS OF PRINCIPAL

Principal		$100,000		
Term		20 years		
Interest		9% annually on outstanding balance		
Annual payment		$5000 plus interest		

| Payment | Payment to consist of | | Total | Balance |
number	Principal	Interest	payment	outstanding
1	$5000	$9000	$14 000	$95 000
2	5000	8550	13 550	90 000
3	5000	8100	13 100	85 000
4	5000	7650	12 660	84 000
5	5000	7200	12 200	75 000
6	5000	6750	11 750	70 000
7	5000	6300	11 300	65 000
8	5000	5850	10 850	60 000
19	5000	900	5 900	5 000
20	5000	450	5 450	nil

Total interest paid in 20 years = $94 500

Equal Blended Payments

Repaying a loan in equal instalments of principal is quite easy to understand but is not a widely used method because of the very large unequal payments. Most people prefer to repay loans with smaller and more frequent level payments that fit more easily into their budgets. To accomplish this, the arithmetic becomes somewhat complicated. Essentially, each payment will include one month's interest on the total outstanding balance, with the remainder of the payment used to reduce the principal. As the principal owing slowly drops each month, the interest component declines, allowing more of each payment to be used to reduce the principal, as is illustrated in Figure 15.4 and Table 15.3.

CALCULATING THE REPAYMENT SCHEDULE FOR EQUAL BLENDED PAYMENTS The procedure for calculating the repayment schedule for mortgages is identical to that used for instalment loans as described in Chapter 8. (Refer to Table 15.4 in the Appendix for a complete mortgage schedule.) The steps in calculating interest and principal components in each payment are reviewed in the following example.

TABLE 15.3 PORTION OF MORTGAGE REPAYMENT SCHEDULE, EQUAL BLENDED PAYMENTS

Principal	$100 000
Interest rate	9 percent compounded semi-annually
Amortization period	20 years
Monthly payment	$889.20

Payment number	Monthly payment	Principal portion	Interest portion	Balance outstanding
First year				
1	$889.20	$152.89	$736.31	$99 847.11
6	889.20	158.60	730.60	99 065.60
12	889.20	165.74	723.46	98 089.14
Final year				
230	889.20	820.33	68.87	8533.49
239	889.20	876.32	12.88	873.33

Total interest $113 392.30

CALCULATIONS FOR BLENDED PAYMENTS

Mortgage terms:

Principal	$120 000
Interest rate	7.25%
Compounding	semi-annual
Amortization period	25 years
Term	5 years
Monthly payment	$859.20 (Table 15.1)
Interest factor	.005 952 3834 (Table 8.4)

(a) **Amount of monthly payment:**

Consult an amortization table (Table 15.1) to find the monthly payment for a loan of $1000, at 7.25%, for 25 years. Calculate the monthly mortgage payments for a loan of $120 000.

$$\text{Monthly payment} = \frac{\text{principal}}{1000} \times \text{payment/\$1000 [7.25\%] (Table 15.1)}$$

$$= \frac{120\ 000}{1000} \times \$7.16$$

$$= 120 \times 7.16$$

$$= \$859.20$$

(b) **Interest at end of first month:**

Interest for one month	=	outstanding principal	×	appropriate interest factor (Table 8.4)
	=	120 000	×	0.005 952 3834
	=	$714.28		

(c) **Principal component of the first month's payment:**

Repayment of principal	=	monthly payment	−	interest for one month
	=	859.20	−	714.28
	=	$144.92		

(d) **Principal outstanding after first payment:**

Principal outstanding	=	principal owing before payment	−	payment on principal
	=	120 000	−	144.92
	=	$119 855.08		

(e) **Second month's interest:**

$$\begin{array}{rcl} \text{Interest for} \\ \text{1 month} \end{array} = \begin{array}{c} \text{outstanding} \\ \text{principal} \end{array} \times \begin{array}{c} \text{appropriate interest} \\ \text{factor (Table 8.4)} \end{array}$$

$$= \quad 119\ 855.08 \quad \times \quad 0.005\ 952\ 3834$$

$$= \quad \$713.41$$

(f) **Mortgage schedule for the first six months:**

Payment number	Date of payment	Monthly payment	Interest portion	Principal portion	Outstanding balance
1	June 1	$859.20	$714.28	$144.92	$119 855.10
2	July 1	859.20	713.42	145.78	119 709.30
3	August 1	859.20	712.55	146.65	119 562.70
4	September 1	859.20	711.68	147.52	119 415.10
5	October 1	859.20	710.80	148.40	119 266.70
6	November 1	859.20	709.92	149.28	119 117.50

Renewing a Mortgage

If a mortgage has a term of five years and an amortization period of 25 years, every five years the contract will have to be renewed. At the maturity date, all the outstanding balance on the principal is due and must be repaid or renegotiated for a further term. At this time, the mortgage can be renewed with the same lender at the prevailing interest rate or changed to another lender. Changing lenders may result in a lower interest rate, but this gain may be offset by additional fees such as for a new appraisal or title search. Currently, some lenders are offering low or no-cost mortgage transfer promotions. The borrower needs to search out this information before making a decision to change lenders.

At the end of a term when the total outstanding balance becomes due, there is an opportunity to reduce the principal before renegotiating the mortgage. As illustrated in the examples included in this chapter, any reduction in principal will result in considerable interest savings over the long run.

PREPAYMENT OF PRINCIPAL

The difference between repayment and prepayment is that **repayment** means following the mortgage schedule in extinguishing the loan, while **prepayment** is a way to accelerate the reduction of the principal during the term. A mortgagor may wish to repay a mortgage faster than the original schedule, make lump sum payments to reduce the principal, or discharge the mortgage on selling the property, but the possibilities of doing so will be dependent on the terms established when the original mortgage contract was drawn up.

Open and Closed Mortgages

There tends to be some confusion about open and closed mortgages because of the degrees of openness and the fact that few are completely closed. A fully open mortgage permits prepayments without restriction or penalty and the loan may be paid off completely at any time. A totally closed mortgage, on the other hand, permits no prepayments. In practice, most so-called closed mortgages permit some prepayments without penalty under certain conditions, and mortgages referred to as open may actually be only partially open. Some mortgage contracts permit limited amounts to be prepaid at specified times, while others are more liberal. In summary, prepayment may be totally unrestricted, or restricted in the amount of prepayment allowed, or in the timing of the prepayment.

Prepayment Penalties

When you make a prepayment, the lender may charge a fee called a prepayment penalty. Having to pay a penalty to make a prepayment of principal is not unusual and is based on the rationale that the mortgagee has invested money in this mortgage for a regular income and is inconvenienced by having to reinvest unexpected repayments. The penalty may be three months' interest on the amount of the prepayment. When interest rates are such that the lender must reinvest the prepaid funds at a rate of interest less than the contract rate of the mortgage, the lender may charge an amount, in addition to the prepayment penalty, representing the interest rate differential for the remainder of the term. There is more discussion of interest rate differential in the section, "Mortgage Features and Options."

Since mortgage lenders change their policies about prepayment from time to time, it is important to find out the prepayment opportunities being offered by competing lenders. Regardless of verbal representations made by the lending officer, it is important that a mortgage contract be read carefully to find out exactly what the prepayment conditions are. There may be a requirement not only to give the lender notice of intention to repay, but also to pay a penalty.

When prepayments are made, it is common practice for the lender to make no change in the size of the monthly payments, thus shortening the time that the loan will be outstanding. The reduced amortization period will result in less total interest.

To calculate the savings in making a prepayment, it is necessary to use an amortization schedule, showing the principal and interest components of each payment (Table 15.4 in the Appendix). A prepayment eliminates a number of payments from the schedule, thus reducing both principal and interest for the mortgagor. Consequently, the mortgage will be repaid in less time than originally expected.

COSTS AND BENEFITS OF A PREPAYMENT

The Changs, who had a CMHC-insured mortgage for $100 000 at 9%, amortized over 20 years, were in a position to repay an additional $11 000 two years later. The mortgage stated that they could make a prepayment of 10% of the original loan at the end of the second year with 3 months' interest penalty. In their case, the maximum prepayment would be:

Prepayment   = $100 000 × .10
              = $10 000

How much interest penalty would they have to pay?

Penalty   = prepayment × interest rate × time
              = $10 000 × .09 × 3/12
              = $225

What are some of the costs and benefits of making this prepayment?

Costs

(a) *Penalty of three month's interest = $225.*
(b) *Foregone interest on prepayment:*

The Changs had a choice of leaving the $10 000 invested to earn interest or using it to reduce the principal outstanding on the mortgage. Assuming they could have earned interest at 6% on $10 000 for 18 years (the time remaining in their amortization period), what is the opportunity cost of this prepayment?

$10 000 invested at 6%, compounded annually for 18 years would grow to:

Future value = principal × compound value of $1 [6%, 18 years]
              = $10 000 × 2.85 (Table 8.1)
              = $28 500

Interest
component   = $28 500 – 10 000
              = $18 500

Assuming 30% average income tax rate:

Income tax   = $18 500 × .30
              = $5550

After-tax income = $18 500 – 5550
                  = $12 950

Total cost	= $225 + 12 950
	= $13 175

Benefits

(a) *Reduction in total mortgage interest:*

Use the Chang's amortization schedule (Table 15.4 in the Appendix). Figures taken from the schedule are marked with an asterisk.

Balance outstanding:

after payment #24 = $96 002.43*
after prepayment = 96 002.43 – 10 000
= $86 002.43

after payment #70 = $86 063.18*

$$\text{Interest saved} = \text{accumulated interest at payment #70} - \text{accumulated interest payment #24}$$

= $48 307.28* – 17 343.27*
= $30 964.01

(b) *Reduction in time:*
Number of payments
eliminated = 70 – 24
= 46

Mortgage discharge is nearer by 46 months (3 years, 10 months).

Conclusion

The results will, of course, vary with the interest rates on mortgage loans and deposits, and one's marginal tax rate. In this case, looking at after-tax dollars, the prepayment would have saved $30 964 compared to a potential investment return of $13 175, and the mortgage would be discharged nearly four years sooner. In this example, no allowance was made for the opportunity to invest the interest savings resulting from the prepayment.

What are some other factors you would want to consider in making a decision to prepay or not?

Total Interest

Not infrequently the total interest paid during the life of a mortgage greatly exceeds the purchase price of the house. For example, a mortgage of $80 000 at 10 percent for

25 years would result in total interest charges of $134 677. Consult the mortgage schedule in the Appendix to find out the total interest on that $100 000 loan. Three influential and interrelated factors affecting total interest are: (i) the principal, (ii) the interest rate, and (iii) the amortization period. If it is possible to reduce any of them, the total interest will be decreased. (You may wish to refer to Chapter 8 to review the method of calculating total interest.)

The first opportunity to reduce total interest is when the mortgage is being arranged. If you can lower the principal of the loan by making a larger down payment, you will pay less total interest (Figure 15.5). A second factor is the interest rate. If you can find a loan at a lower rate, that will be to your advantage. What appear to be quite small differences in interest rates can have a significant effect on the total interest. Using the example above, a 1/4 percent reduction in interest rate on the $80 000 loan would mean $4026 less in total interest. Finally, the shorter the amortization period, the less total interest, as illustrated in Figure 15.5; it is, of course, necessary to make larger monthly payments to accomplish this.

CLOSING COSTS

When a property is purchased, the agreement to purchase is often signed some time before the date for closing the deal. When the closing date arrives the buyer must pay: (i) the seller for the property, (ii) the lawyer for services and disbursements, such as registration of the transaction at the registry office, (iii) taxes (where applicable) such as land transfer or property purchase tax, goods and services tax, provincial sales tax, and (iv) adjustment costs. With or without a mortgage, there are sure to be closing costs when property is purchased.

Statement of Adjustments

Sometime before the closing date for the house purchase, the lawyer will send the buyer a **statement of adjustments,** which sets forth the accounts between buyer and seller relating to this sale. It will include purchase price, deposit, property taxes, and possibly insurance, and fuel. Since the vendor has been paying property taxes and insurance, the buyer will have to reimburse the vendor for any prepaid taxes and insurance when ownership changes. For example, if a house was bought in June, the insurance may have been paid until September and the taxes until November. The buyer would pay three months' insurance and five months' taxes to the vendor. Sometimes there is fuel oil in the tank to be paid for.

The new property must be insured against fire, as noted in the mortgage contract. At this stage, the buyer can decide whether to take over the vendor's property insurance policy, convert a previous policy to fit this new property, or take out a new one.

FIGURE 15.5 TOTAL COST OF A HOUSE, VARYING DOWN PAYMENT AND AMORTIZATION PERIOD (PURCHASE PRICE AND INTEREST RATE HELD CONSTANT)

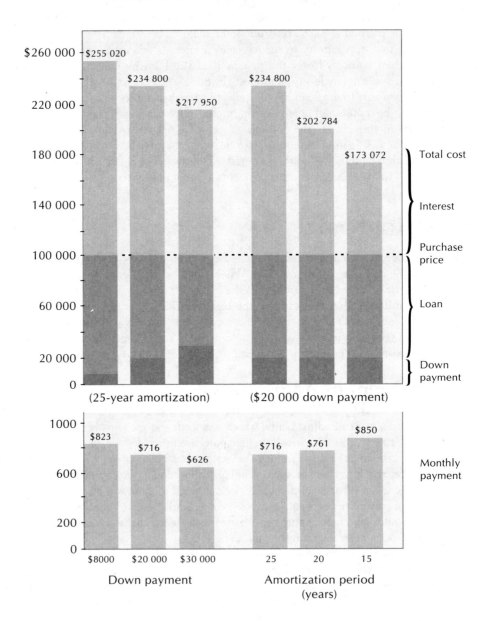

Legal Fees and Taxes

The lawyer's bill usually includes fees for services and any expenditures made on the buyer's behalf, such as fees for title searches, registration of various documents, and any federal or provincial taxes. The lawyer's fee is dependent on the complexity of the transaction and the local guidelines for fees.

Some provinces impose a land transfer or property-purchase tax on real property at the time of registration of the deed. In 1992, the Ontario land transfer tax rates were:one-half of one percent of value up to and including $55 000 and one percent of the remainder. In British Columbia, the property-purchase tax is one percent of the first $200 000 and two percent of the balance. Find out if there is a land transfer tax where you live and what the current rates are.

A copy of an up-to-date land survey is usually required by all lenders. The vendor or the vendor's mortgagee may provide a copy of the survey. Otherwise, the purchaser may be liable for significant surveyor fees in conjunction with placing a new mortgage on the property.

The goods and services tax and provincial sales tax are applied to some aspects of property purchases (e.g., mortgage insurance, legal fees, and certain disbursements) and thus add to closing costs.

LIFE INSURANCE AND MORTGAGES

If they so wish, home buyers may arrange a decreasing term life insurance policy with their own insurance company to make provision for enough funds to discharge the mortgage in the event of their death. Initially, the life insurance policy will be for approximately the same amount as the mortgage loan, with periodic reductions in value to roughly correspond to the declining debt on the property. If the person whose life is insured should die before the mortgage is fully repaid, the beneficiary of the life insurance will have some funds to discharge the mortgage debt, but is not obligated to do so.

Some lenders, who have group policies covering the lives of a number of borrowers, offer mortgage life insurance as part of the mortgage package. If this coverage is selected, the survivors have no choice in the use of the insurance money, since the policy is not a personal one. In such cases, the outstanding balance on the mortgage is repaid by the insurer directly to the lender. If the income of the two persons purchasing a residence is required for debt servicing, it is important to determine whether the lives of both wage earners are covered. If not, additional private life insurance may be prudent. In any event, it is always wise to compare the cost of optional group life insurance offered by the mortgagee with similar coverages available in the market place.

This reducing term insurance is sometimes called mortgage life insurance, but it should not be confused with the mortgage insurance that lenders use to cover the risk of losing money if the borrower defaults. This latter type of insurance is mandatory for mortgages insured by CMHC.

MORTGAGE FEATURES AND OPTIONS

From the previous discussion of basic mortgage principles, one might think that choosing a mortgage would not be too difficult. However, keen competition among financial institutions has created a rapidly changing mortgage market with little variation in interest rates but intense competition in a fascinating and often confusing array of mortgage features and options. These company policies are readily changed, making it impossible to predict which special features or options will be available at any given time or place. However, those to be discussed here are:

   (i) pre-approval
   (ii) interest rate adjustments
   (iii) early renewal, and
   (iv) accelerated payment opportunities.

Pre-approved Mortgages

It is not unusual for home buyers to select a property, sign an offer to purchase conditional on obtaining financing, and then start looking for a mortgage. In the excitement of choosing a new house they neglect to give as much attention to the financing as they do to finding the property. This method has two significant disadvantages: the buyers have to do their mortgage shopping under time pressure and they have made a commitment to a property before determining how large a loan they may qualify for.

Lenders are now offering **pre-approved** (or pre-arranged) mortgages, which give tentative approval for a mortgage amount based on an assessment of the borrower, with final approval dependent on an appraisal of the property. By applying for a pre-arranged mortgage, buyers can shop around for the best financing terms before making a commitment to a property, and at the same time find out how much lenders are willing to lend them. Armed with this knowledge, they will be in a position to make a more attractive offer on a property, one not conditional on obtaining financing, but rather only on a satisfactory appraisal.

Pre-approved mortgages give the buyer an opportunity to apply to several lenders, with usually no fee for the assessment and no obligation to deal with any particular institution. However, the guaranteed interest rate period may be quite short—usually no more than three months. The tendency of borrowers to accept the first institution's terms rather than comparison shop for a mortgage works very well for lenders trying to increase their market share, but not so well for borrowers. Applicants may feel so pleased to receive approval that they do not look any further.

MORTGAGE SHOPPING STRATEGY   A better strategy for the prospective borrower is to first make an estimate of how much debt can be handled, given current interest rates, then to visit lenders to find out what terms and options are currently being offered. After determining which features are most desirable, a list can be made of the most essential ones before applying for a pre-approved mortgage from the lender who offers the best combination of the preferred options.

Interest Rate Adjustments

COMMITMENT PERIOD   After a mortgage is approved, there is usually a period of weeks or months before the closing date. The day when the purchase transaction is completed—the buyer pays the vendor and receives possession of the property—is known as the **closing date.** If interest rates are changing frequently, will the borrower be charged the rate prevailing at the time of approval or at the closing date? Some lenders will make a commitment to an agreed upon rate at the time of approval with the option that if rates drop in the interim, the mortgage rate will be reduced accordingly. Find out the lender's policy and how long their commitment period is.

INTEREST ADJUSTMENT DATE   Mortgage payments are usually made at the end of each month, "not in advance." That means if mortgage money was advanced on February 21 the first payment would be due a month later, on March 21. This seems straightforward, but some institutional lenders prefer to collect all mortgage payments on the first of each month. Since closing dates can be any business day, the lender solves this problem by collecting interest for the period from closing to the beginning of the next month. When lenders refer to the **interest adjustment date** they mean the day the mortgage starts.

AN UNEXPECTED COST

When Tony and Maria bought their first house they closed the deal on March 12, getting their mortgage from a firm that collected mortgage payments on the first of every month. Their mortgage adjustment date became April 1, nineteen days later. They were surprised to find that their lender collected 19 days' interest on the whole mortgage ($105 000 ×.0875 × 19/365 = $478.25) at the time of closing. This amount was subtracted from the mortgage funds being advanced to them, forcing them to find the extra money to complete the house purchase. Later they discovered that some lenders calculate this interest with daily compounding, making an even higher interest payment. Their first regular mortgage payment will be made on May 1, a month after the interest adjustment date.

VARIABLE RATE MORTGAGES Variable or floating rate mortgages were devised in the early 1980s to reduce uncertainty for lenders in a period of rapidly changing interest rates. Financial institutions had difficulty matching the interest rates and maturities of the deposits they accepted with those of the mortgage funds they lent. With variable rate mortgages, lenders pass the risk of fluctuating rates on to the borrower, who has the advantage of a fully open mortgage that can be discharged at any time. On this type of mortgage, the interest rate is adjusted frequently, usually monthly. A payment schedule, based on 20-year or 25-year amortization, is drawn up for a specified period, usually one year, during which the borrower is committed to regular payments of a predictable amount. The rate quoted on variable rate mortgages, which may be half a percent lower than for other types, may look especially attractive, but you should remember that the interest is compounded monthly rather than semi-annually.

While reducing uncertainty for lenders, variable rate mortgages can create problems for borrowers by making it difficult for them to accurately predict their future liabilities. If interest rates rise, a mortgagor could find that the fixed monthly payment is composed entirely of interest with no reduction in principal. It is conceivable that some payments would be insufficient to cover all the interest due, and that the balance of the interest owing could be added to the unpaid principal. In such a case, the home buyer would be increasing liabilities rather than assets.

In times of more stable interest rates, borrowers are less interested in variable rate mortgages. Recently lenders offered short term, fully open mortgages with the interest rate guaranteed for a period of, for example, six months.

Early Renewal

With falling interest rates, mortgagors may be anxious to refinance their mortgages before the end of the term at the new lower rates. Mortgagees, however, are not as keenly interested in receiving the smaller income stream and consequently may charge an interest rate differential. The **interest rate differential** is based on the present value of the difference between the lender's income stream under the old mortgage rate and the new lower rate; this is to compensate the lender for giving up future income. The mortgagor makes a lump-sum payment in return for a renegotiated mortgage at a reduced rate.

The amount of the interest rate differential depends on the spread between the existing contract rate and current mortgage rates as well as the time remaining in the mortgage term. Predictably, the greater the spread and the longer the time, the greater the penalty. Also, lenders use different methods of calculating the interest rate differential. It is wise for the mortgagor to do some calculations before deciding on refinancing. It may be better to make a prepayment to reduce the principal than to try to obtain a lower interest rate.

Accelerated Payment Opportunities

Repayment of the principal may be accelerated by: (i) lump-sum prepayments (as was discussed earlier), (ii) increases in monthly payments, or (iii) more frequent payments.

INCREASING MONTHLY PAYMENTS   Lenders may permit mortgagors to increase their monthly payments, once a year or on any payment date, by as little as 10 percent or as much as 100 percent.

WEEKLY PAYMENTS   Weekly or bi-weekly payment mortgages are a way of shortening the amortization period by making payments more frequently. If the usual monthly payment is divided by four and paid each week, the borrower will make 52 weekly payments in a year. The usual 12 monthly payments are equivalent to only 48 weekly ones. The effect of making four extra weekly payments a year will be a reduction in total interest and in the time needed to repay the mortgage. The bi-weekly mortgage scheme is similar, except that payments are made fortnightly, or 26 times a year, instead of the equivalent of 24.

The mortgagor should be aware of the method being used to calculate the payments. If the monthly payment is divided by four or two and paid weekly or bi-weekly, the mortgage will be reduced faster than by 12 monthly payments. However, if the annual amount of interest and principal is divided by 52 or 26 this will not happen.

MONTHLY OR WEEKLY PAYMENTS?

Mike plans to take out a $70 000 mortgage, but cannot decide what frequency of payment best suits him. He is aware that a monthly payment schedule is the most common one, but would like to know what difference weekly payments would make. The mortgage officer gave Mike the following figures.

	Conventional amount paid monthly	Monthly amount paid in 52 weekly payments
Mortgage	$70 000	$70 000
Interest rate	10.5%	10.5%

Amortization	25 years	19.5 years
Payment	$649.84/mo.	$162.46/wk.
Payment/yr.	$7798.08	$8447.92
Total repaid	$194 952	$164 734
Total interest	$124 952	$94 734

When comparing these options, two points stood out. First, with weekly payments, the total interest charge would be less by over $30 000. Second, the rate of repayment would not be exactly the same. The weekly payment was arrived at by dividing the monthly payment by 4, but since there are 52 weeks in a year, he would be making payments equivalent to 13 months. If he can handle the weekly payments he will extinguish his mortgage 5 1/2 years sooner. Mike decided he preferred a weekly payment plan.

Comparison Shopping for a Mortgage

The following chart can be used to record information gained when shopping for a mortgage.

Item	Lender 1	2	3
Interest rates			
First mortgage			
Second mortgage			
Fixed for term or variable			
Frequency of payment			
Monthly, bi-weekly, or weekly			
Flexibility			
Charges			
Appraisal fee			
Application fee			
Qualification guidelines			
GDS			
TDS			
Prepayment privileges			
Amount			
Time			
Penalty			

Flexibility _____

Renewal conditions
   Fee _____
   Time before maturity _____

After the borrower selects a mortgage, it is important to insist that any special features be written in the mortgage contract.

REVERSE INCOME MORTGAGES

Most people spend years paying off their mortgage debt and are very relieved when it has been discharged, looking forward to living in a debt-free house in their retirement years. However, some find that in their old age they are short of income, but have a significant asset tied up in the house. There is a way to live in the house but also get some income from it—the **reverse income mortgage.** Essentially, a financial institution takes a claim on the property in return for monthly payments to the owners. Eventually, the debt must be paid, perhaps by selling the house after the death of the owners.

Several strategies have been used to implement reverse income mortgages, including a simple reverse mortgage, a reverse annuity mortgage, and a reverse mortgage line of credit. These are described in some of the references listed at the end of this chapter. At present, there is no legislation governing reverse mortgages, and without standardization of terms and documents it is difficult to compare the various options. There has not been much demand for such mortgages, probably because people who have saved for years to buy a house do not find the idea of re-mortgaging it very appealing. Doing so may seem to threaten their financial security, since no one knows what his or her life span will be.

Summary

Although a mortgage is simply a large loan, secured by real property, the magnitude of the sum borrowed, the long repayment period, and the nature of the security create considerable complexity. There are two major types of mortgages, depending on the proportion of the property cost used for a down payment: conventional and insured. To qualify for a mortgage, a prospective home buyer must be considered a satisfactory credit risk and have selected property that is acceptable security for the lender. The terms, conditions, and obligations associated with the loan are set forth in a mortgage contract signed by lender and borrower. To safeguard their investment, mortgage lenders have regulations regarding down payments, insurance of the property, insurance against default, and prepayments.

The most common way of repaying a mortgage is with a series of equal blended payments that have changing proportions of principal and interest. Mortgage financing involves four interrelated factors: principal, interest rate, amortization period, and monthly payment. Often the total interest paid over the life of the mortgage is much greater than the price of the house, but this may be reduced by decreasing the principal, the interest rate, or the amortization period. The opportunity to do this, once the mortgage has been signed, depends on the rules of the lending institution. It is worthwhile to investigate the mortgage conditions offered by various institutions to find those best suited to your needs. Special attention should be given to prepayment privileges, payment frequency, and renewal policies.

Vocabulary Review

amortization period (p. 454)

amortize (p. 442)

capital gain (p. 440)

closing date (p. 467)

conventional mortgage (p. 444)

covenant (p. 451)

equity (p. 442)

equity of redemption (p. 451)

first mortgage (p. 443)

gross debt service (p. 447)

high ratio loan (p. 445)

insured mortgage (p. 445)

interest adjustment date (p. 467)

interest differential (p. 468)

lending value (appraised value) (p. 446)

maturity date (p. 454)

mortgage (p. 442)

mortgage broker (p. 446)

mortgage discharge (p. 454)

mortgage insurance (p. 444)

mortgage term (p. 454)

mortgagee (p. 442)

mortgagor (p. 442)

non-money income (p. 440)

opportunity cost (p. 440)

preapproved (prearranged) mortgage (p. 466)

prepayment (p. 459)

repayment (p. 459)

reverse income mortgage (p. 471)

second mortgage (p. 444)

statement of adjustments (p. 463)

total debt service (p. 447)

vendor take-back mortgage (p. 445)

Problems

1. Assume that you bought a house for $135 000 with a $20 000 down payment and $115 000 mortgage.

   (a) Sometime later, when you are considering selling the house, you have an unpaid balance on the mortgage of $42 500. How much would your equity be if you could sell it for $153 000?

(b) If you are making mortgage payments of $978 per month, do your payments add to your equity in the property? Explain.

(c) Does the down payment represent part of your equity in the property?

2. Rick and Jean paid $187 000 for a house in Vancouver when prices were very high, financed with a down payment of $30 000 and a mortgage for $157 000. Now that Rick has been moved to a job in Toronto, they must sell the house at a time when the outstanding balance on the mortgage is $135 000 and the best offer on the house is $125 000. Explain what happened to Rick and Jean's equity.

3. Refer to the mortgage contract signed by Paul and Louise McCartney (Figure 15.1 in the Appendix).

(a) Who is the mortgagee (chargee) in this contract?

(b) How long is the term of this mortgage? What will happen at the maturity date?

(c) What are some property rights that the McCartneys have given up for the duration of the mortgage?

(d) What is required of Paul and Louise by the insurance covenant?

(e) Six months after they gave this mortgage, the McCartneys won $5000 in a lottery, which they would like to use to reduce their mortgage. When can they make a repayment? How much can it be? What will the penalty be?

(f) If Paul dies before the mortgage is discharged, and Louise does not have enough income to maintain the payments, will she lose her equity in the house?

(g) How much did Paul and Louise pay for mortgage insurance? If you can't find this figure in the contract, assume 2%.

(h) When is this mortgage insurance paid?

(i) What protection does this insurance offer the mortgagors?

(j) Did Paul and Louise have a choice about taking this insurance?

4. (a) Why would a person obtain a mortgage loan instead of a personal bank loan to buy a house?

(b) Would you expect a bank to charge a higher rate on a loan secured by a chattel mortgage than on one secured by a real estate mortgage? Why?

5. A mortgage officer suggested to Duncan, a prospective client, that he could save on legal fees by engaging the same lawyer to look after his interests in the transaction as the lending institution is employing to look after their interests. Would there be a possible conflict of interest involved here? What would you do?

6.

THEIR FIRST HOUSE

Tiep and Vinh finally located a house they really liked, with an asking price of $145 000, which seemed reasonable. They recognized that the house would require redecorating as soon as possible in two downstairs rooms, and that they would have to buy major appliances. The taxes on the property had been $1350 the previous year and the heating costs amounted to $550. Their offer to purchase the house for $135 000 was conditional upon the arrangement of financing.

At the bank, the mortgage officer inquired about the family income and how much money they could use as a down payment. Tiep explained that his annual income was $48 000 and Vinh's part-time earnings came to $18 900; their only debt was for their car, which cost $280 a month. They had accumulated $16 000 for a down payment.

The mortgage officer calculated their gross debt service and their total debt service for a mortgage of $119 000 at 8.75% amortized over 25 years, and suggested they apply for a CMHC-insured mortgage. They were told that the application would cost $100 and that an appraiser would be looking at the house they wanted to buy and would determine its lending value. The appraisal fee would be $150.

In a few days' time they learned that the house had a lending value of $132 500 and that they were eligible for a mortgage for $119 000.

(a) List the criteria that the lender would use to determine the eligibility of (i) Vinh and Tiep, and (ii) the property.

(b) Would this couple be eligible for a conventional mortgage?

(c) How much would the monthly payments be on this mortgage?

(d) Calculate the gross debt service and the total debt service.

(e) Work out the interest and principal components of the first payment.

(f) How much total interest will this couple pay over 25 years, assuming no change in interest rates and no prepayments?

(g) How much would the total interest be reduced if they could get a mortgage for 1/2% less?

(h) How much interest could they save if they amortized this mortgage over 20 years instead of 25?

(i)   Use the chart below to estimate some of the costs (in addition to the down payment and mortgage) that Tiep and Vinh will probably encounter as they complete the purchase and move from their apartment. How much is the total?

SOME COSTS ASSOCIATED WITH HOME BUYING

The numbers used here are estimates; find out current costs.

		Totals
Mortgage Fees		
Appraisal fee	$_____	
Mortgage insurance fee (added to mortgage; assume 2%)	$_____	$_____
Statement of Adjustments		
Tax adjustments (allow six months)	$_____	
Fire insurance	$200.00	
Fuel oil (part of a tank)	$100.00	$_____
Goods and Services Tax (if applicable)		$_____
Lawyer's Account		
Disbursements by lawyer for land transfer tax (if applicable)	$_____	
Deed registration	$16.00	
Legal fees	$750.00	$_____
Moving and Related Costs		
Moving (two men and a truck, five hrs. @ $55/hr.)	$_____	$_____
Connection of utilities		
Telephone	$28.50	
Cable TV	$54.42	
Electricity	$8.50	
Others	$25.00	$_____
Appliances, Repairs		
Purchase of major appliances	$2900.00	
Decorating supplies	$600.00	
Repairs	$1000.00	$_____
Grand total		$_____

What are some other costs that might be anticipated but are not included here?

7. The Baileys' offer to purchase a house has been accepted. Now they are considering ways of financing it. The purchase price is $187 000 and they have $18 000 for a down payment. The alternatives they are considering are:

Down payment	First mortgage	Second mortgage
(i) $18 000	$169 000 @ 9%, 25 yrs.	none
(ii) $18 000	$169 000 @ 9%, 20 yrs.	none
(iii) $10 000	$169 000 @ 9%, 25 yrs.	$8000 @10% for 5 yrs. ($169.19/mo.)

   (a) Which of these alternatives would result in the lowest monthly cost?

   (b) Which of these alternatives would result in the lowest total interest?

   (c) What are some factors the Baileys should consider when making their choice?

8. When the Karlovs bought their house, they took over the vendor's mortgage because it was at 8.5% and had 4 more years to maturity. The purchase price was $109 000, the down payment $16 000, and the vendor's mortgage was $72 640. How will they raise the balance of the purchase price? What interest rate will they probably have to pay?

9. Barbara and George have decided to buy a house, but before looking they would like some information on the size of mortgage they might be able to obtain. They have monthly credit payments of $250 on the car and $150 for furniture. Their joint income is $48 000 a year. They found out that the annual taxes on houses of the type they would like are about $900 and the heating costs $480. (Assume the guideline for total debt service was 38%.)

   (a) How much might they expect to borrow at 7.5%, amortized over 25 years?

   (b) If they would prefer a 20-year mortgage, what will the maximum loan be?

   (c) With a down payment of $10 000, and the mortgage amortized over 20 years, what price of home could they purchase if the mortgage was:

   (i) conventional?

   (ii) insured?

10. Use the Chang's amortization schedule (Table 15.4 in the Appendix) to answer this question.

   (a) How much principal and how much interest will they pay in the first five years?

   (b) How much principal and how much interest will they pay in the last five years?

   (c) Compare the difference in total interest saved, and the effect on the time to repay the mortgage, if a prepayment of $10 000 is made after five years.

   (d) Compare the difference in total interest saved, and the effect on the time to repay the mortgage, if a prepayment of $10 000 is made after ten years.

(e) If they made two prepayments of $10 000—after five years and after ten—when would the mortgage be extinguished?

11. Find out if there is a property tax credit for taxpayers in your province. If so, what are the eligibility criteria? This information will be included in the federal income tax materials.

12. Sometimes mortgage lenders include property taxes and heating costs as well as principal, interest, and taxes (P.I.T.) in the monthly payments. What is the reason for this?

REFERENCES

BOOKS

BIRCH, RICHARD. *The Family Financial Planning Book, A Step-by-Step Moneyguide for Canadian Families*. Revised edition. Toronto: Key Porter, 1989, 216 pp. An easy-to-read guide to taking control of your personal finances that discusses budgets, income tax, insurance, RRSPs, mortgages, and investments.

COHEN, DIAN. *Money*. Scarborough, Ontario: Prentice-Hall Canada, 1987, 270 pp. An economist suggests strategies for coping with personal finances in the context of changing economic conditions. Topics include financial plans, buying a home, insurance, income tax, retirement, estate planning, and investments.

GOLDENBERG, DAVID M. *Mortgages and Foreclosure, Know Your Rights*. Sixth Edition. Vancouver: International Self-Counsel Press, 1992, 128 pp. Explains the legal terms found in a mortgage contract, the different types of mortgages, and how foreclosure law works.

PAPE, GORDON. *Building Wealth, Achieving Your Financial Goals*. Scarborough, Ontario: Prentice-Hall Canada, 1988, 246 pp. An easy-to-read guide for the novice financial manager and investor that considers interest rates, credit cards, mortgages, RRSPs, mutual funds, and the stock market.

ROSE, STANLEY M. *Real Estate Buying/Selling Guide for Ontario*. Ninth Edition. Vancouver: International Self-Counsel Press, 1992, 224 pp. A non-technical discussion of housing transactions with special emphasis on legal aspects.

SILVERSTEIN, ALAN. *Hidden Profits in Your Mortgage, The Smart-Money Guide to Canadian Home Ownership*. Toronto: Stoddart, 1985, 221 pp. A real estate lawyer offers suggestions for minimizing costs of mortgages and explains the details of some payment plans.

SILVERSTEIN, ALAN. *The Perfect Mortgage, Your Key to Cutting the Cost of Home Ownership*. Toronto: Stoddart, 1989, 136 pp. Explains, in non-technical language, basic mortgage terms, the most common options and how to make an informed choice.

SILVERSTEIN, ALAN. *Save! Alan Silverstein's Guide to Mortgage Payment Tables*. Don Mills: Stoddart, 1993, 160 pp. A practical guide that helps create your own customized payment schedule and helps keep track of mortgage payments. Features mortgage tables with rates starting at 4 percent.

STEACY, RICHARD. *Canadian Real Estate*. Seventh Edition. Toronto: Stoddart,1987, 456 pp. Includes a section on mortgages.

STEWART, GEORGE C. *Real Estate Buying/Selling Guide for Alberta*. Fifth Edition. Vancouver: International Self-Counsel Press, 1990, 159 pp. Explains the processes involved in real estate transactions for the general reader.

SYBERG-OLSEN, E. *Real Estate Buying/Selling Guide for British Columbia*. Ninth Edition. Vancouver: International Self-Counsel Press, 1990, 240 pp. An introduction to the general area of mortgages and buying real estate.

WYATT, ELAINE. *The Money Companion, How to Manage Your Money and Achieve Financial Freedom*. Markham, Ontario: Penguin Books, 1991. A guide to personal financial management that focuses on planning, investment strategy, and retirement needs.

ZIMMER, HENRY B. *Making Your Money Grow, A Canadian Guide to Successful Personal Finance*. Third Edition. Toronto: Collins, 1989, 260 pp. The focus of this book is on basic calculations needed for personal financial decisions, as applied to compound interest, future and present values, investment returns, RRSPs, annuities, and life insurance.

ARTICLE

PHILIP, MARGARET. "Mortgage Broker Scrutiny Urged." *The Globe and Mail*, April 17, 1993, A1 & A4.

PERIODICAL

Canadian Money Saver. May 1993. Canadian Money Saver Inc. Box 370, Bath, Ontario, K0H 1G0. Includes short articles on a range of personal finance topics, with special emphasis on investments.

CHAPTER SIXTEEN

Credit Reporting and Debt Collection

1. To explain the following aspects of credit bureaus:

    (a) how they are financed,

    (b) how they obtain information,

    (c) who has access to the information,

    (d) how they serve the interests of both debtors and creditors.

2. To identify:

    (a) factors considered in the assessment of an individual's credit rating,

    (b) the respective roles of the credit bureau and the creditor in assessing credit risk.

3. To explain the consumer rights provided in provincial credit reporting legislation with respect to:

    (a) prohibited information in credit files,

    (b) disclosure of information,

    (c) notice that a credit report may be obtained,

    (d) consumer access to own file.

4. To explain how collection agencies assist creditors.

5. To evaluate the protection provided debtors by the provincial regulation of collection agencies.

6. To explain ways in which debts may be collected without resorting to the courts.

7. To explain the process of suing a debtor to obtain a court judgment.

8. To explain how garnishees and execution orders are used to collect judgment debts.

9. To explain the differences and similarities between these pairs of terms:

   (a) wage assignment and wage garnishment,

   (b) wage garnishee and bank account garnishee,

   (c) demand on a third party and a wage garnishee,

   (d) family court garnishee and a wage garnishee,

10. To explain these terms: credit file (history), credit report, consumer information, personal information, information exchange, investigative agency, credit scoring, third-party collecting, judgment debt.

Introduction

This chapter sheds new light on a not-too-well understood aspect of credit: credit reporting, or providing information about an individual's credit history to creditors so that they may assess how much risk they are accepting when they grant a loan.

While credit reporting happens at the beginning of a credit transaction, debt collection, the other subject of this chapter, occurs at the other end of the process. Creditors try not to extend credit to anyone they think will be unable to repay, but sometimes predictions prove wrong or the debtor's situation changes. Those with overdue debts will discover that creditors have a variety of ways to collect debts and that they can be quite aggressive about it.

CREDIT REPORTING

When you apply for credit, the lender must estimate the probability that you will be able to repay the debt as scheduled. What does a lender need to know to predict your reliability and capacity to repay this debt? The creditor starts with an assessment of your application for credit in which you provided quite a bit of information about yourself: for instance, your residence, occupation, bank, salary, mortgage, and consumer debts (Figure 14.2). In addition, the lender may want to know how you handled previous credit transactions, information that can be obtained from the local credit bureau.

The Credit Bureau

A **credit bureau** is a business that sells information about credit transactions to its subscribers, who are mostly creditors and other businesses. There used to be many local, privately owned credit bureaus serving a specific geographic region, but gradually most of them became affiliated with or managed by larger firms. Now, the credit reporting business in Canada is dominated by a large multi-national company and a few smaller ones that are in competition with each other.

Credit bureaus obtain funds by selling memberships to firms that extend credit—especially financial institutions and retailers—as well as to a variety of other businesses that need information on the credit histories of customers. Employers and landlords have an interest in subscribing to the credit bureau, as do life insurance companies; however, in order to become a member, each must have a legitimate business interest in such credit information.

Credit bureau subscribers pay an annual membership fee in addition to a charge for each credit report that they obtain. Most credit reports are transferred electronically from the credit bureau to the member (computer to computer) instead of by telephone as in the past. Now, with electronic transmission of information, credit bureaus can easily send reports nearly anywhere in the world. The service contract signed by members binds them to using the information obtained from the credit bureau for strictly *bona fide* business purposes only, and also requires that they give the credit bureau any relevant credit information they have about their customers.

The Credit File

Anyone who has credit cards or charge accounts, has ever obtained a mortgage or other loan, has rented accommodation, or is connected to utilities such as telephone or hydro, probably has a file at a credit bureau. Most of the information in the file comes from three major sources: the individual, the individual's creditors, and public records. Each time an application is made for credit, the facts supplied on the application form will be transferred to the credit bureau file by the credit grantor when a credit report is drawn.

In addition, it is common practice for major credit grantors, such as bank credit card companies, large retailers, and financial institutions, to send their entire credit files to the credit bureau every month. These computer files, reporting the status of all their credit accounts, are electronically merged with those already in the credit bureau files, or new files are set up for anyone who does not already have one. The information in a credit bureau file includes the account number, the outstanding balance, and whether payment has been made on time. Items of public record, such as chattel mortgages and conditional sales agreements registered with provincial authorities, and reports on court judgments or bankruptcies, are obtained by the credit bureau and added to the files.

Nowadays, most credit bureaus store their files in computers where they are immediately accessible to other bureaus. The sample credit report (Figure 16.1) illustrates the types of information that may be kept in a credit bureau file. The record, entered in code or an abbreviated form for conciseness, includes the individual's usual manner of payment classified on a nine-point scale, as well as information from a number of sources.

CURRENT MANNER OF PAYMENT
(North American Standard)

Abbreviations for Type of Account:

O   Open account (30 or 90 days)

R   Revolving or option (open-end account)

I   Instalment (fixed number of payments)

Current Manner of Payment

(Using payments past due or age from due date)

0   Too new to rate; approved but not used.

1   Pays (or paid) within 30 days of payment due date or not over one payment past due.

2   Pays (or paid) in more than 30 days from payment due date, but not more than 60 days, or not more than two payments past due.

3   Pays (or paid) in more than 60 days from payment due date, but not more than 90 days or not more than three payments past due.

4   Pays (or paid) in more than 90 days from payment due date, but not more than 120 days, or four payments past due.

5   Pays (or paid) in more than 120 days but not yet rated 9.

7   Making regular payments under a consolidation order or similar arrangement.

8   Repossession.

9   Bad debt; placed for collection; skip.

INTERPRETING THE CREDIT FILE   The sample credit report in Figure 16.1, abbreviated to conserve space, is difficult to understand. Therefore, the following interpretation may be helpful. In February 1992 (reporting date, RPTD), the credit bureau received information about Jacob Zwinkle's account from T. Eaton Acceptance. Eatons' code for communicating with the credit bureau is 650DC32 (BUS/ID CODE). The account at Eatons was opened January 1991 (date opened, OPND), with a credit limit of $1000 (high credit, H/C) and current outstanding balance is $587 (BAL), all of which is past due (P/D). Mr. Zwinkle's method of payment is currently rated R9 (rating, RT). There are 22 monthly ratings (MR) in the history of this account at Eatons, indicating the level of activity in the account. The date of the last activity (DLA) at Eatons was July 1992. Jacob Zwinkle's account number at Eatons is 12345; his method of payment was rated R5 in May 1992, and R4 in April 1992.

In addition to the report from Eatons, the credit bureau has obtained information from public records. In January 1989 Zwinkle declared individual (personal) bankruptcy at the Court of Queen's Bench (CQB) in Winnipeg and was discharged from bankruptcy January 1990. At the time of bankruptcy he had liabilities of $10 345 and assets of $423. The firm of Smith and Smith acted as trustees in this bankruptcy.

In February 1992, Equifax Winnipeg Collectrite took over collection of a $330 debt on behalf of Canada Safeway for an NSF cheque. The account number at Safeway was 345789, the date of last activity February 1992; $30 was collected, leaving $300 outstanding.

FIGURE 16.1 SAMPLE CREDIT REPORT

NAME AND ADDRESS OF BUREAU MAKING REPORT

EQUIFAX CANADA INC. – TORONTO REGIONAL CENTER
60 Bloor Street West
TORONTO, ONTARIO
M4W 3C1

REPORT TYPE

☐ SUMMARY   ☐ SINGLE REF.   ☐ TRADE
☐ SHORT   ☐ FULL   ☐ PREV. RES

DATE RECEIVED	DATE MAILED	ACB REPORT
03/05/93	03/05/93	

DATE TRADE CLEARED	DATE EMPL. VERIFIED	INCOME VERIFIED
RE: D/RPTD		YES NO

CONFIDENTIAL REPORT   FOR   ,M,,YX3

IN FILE SINCE
01/04/72

This information is furnished in response to an inquiry for the purpose of evaluating credit risks. It has been obtained from sources deemed reliable, the accuracy of which this organization does not guarantee. The inquirer has agreed to indemnify the reporting bureau for any damage arising from misuse of this information, and this report is furnished in reliance upon that indemnity. It must be held in strict confidence, and must not be revealed to the subject reported on.

REPORT ON (SURNAME):	MR., MRS., MISS	SOCIAL INSURANCE NUMBER	SPOUSE'S NAME
ZWINKLE,JACOB,A.JR.		623-546-124	

ADDRESS:	CITY:	PROVINCE:	POSTAL CODE	RESIDENCE SINCE	SPOUSE'S SOC. INS. NO
55,SIMPLICITY,,WINNIPEG, MB,R2N4V7					

COMPLETE TO HERE FOR TRADE REPORT AND SKIP TO CREDIT HISTORY

PRESENT EMPLOYER AND KIND OF BUSINESS:	POSITION HELD:	MONTHLY INC.	SINCE
RAFFLERS RESTAURANT, WNNI,MB	CHEF	$	07/76

COMPLETE TO HERE FOR SHORT REPORT AND SUMMARY REPORT AND SKIP TO CREDIT HISTORY

DATE OF BIRTH	NUMBER OF DEPENDENTS INCLUDING SPOUSE →			
04/07/55		☐ OWNS	☐ BOARDS	☐ RENTS

FORMER ADDRESS:	CITY:	PROVINCE:	FROM:	TO:
124,SMITH ST,, WINNIPEG, MB,				

FORMER EMPLOYER AND KIND OF BUSINESS:	POSITION HELD:	MONTHLY INC.	FROM:	TO:
		$		

SPOUSE'S EMPLOYER AND KIND OF BUSINESS:	DATE VERIFIED	POSITION HELD:	MONTHLY INC.	FROM:	TO:
			$		

CREDIT HISTORY (Complete this section for all reports)

```
BUS/ID CODE    RPTD OPND  H/C    TRMS    BAL    P/D    RT    30/60/90    MR    DLA

T EATON ACCEPTANCE (416) 343-3375
  650DC32     02/93 01/91 1000            587    587    R9    04 03 01    22    07/92
ACCOUNT NUMBER 12345
        PREV HI RATES: R5   05/92, R4 04/92


PUBLIC RECORDS AND/OR SUMMARY OF OTHER INFORMATION
01/89  BKRPT CQB WNNI, INDIVIDUAL, SUBJECT, DISCHARGED 01/90, LIAB 10345, ASSET
0,423 89 SMITH    SMITH
02/92 UNPAID COLLECTION, EQUIFAX WINNIPEG COL, #330, GS,,,BRN-CANADA SAFEWAY
NSF, ACC-345789,DLA 02/92, BAL-$300
04/91  JUDG CQB WNNI,  $515, DEF-S, CASE NO- 4444,DECIBEL CREDIT UNION,
DISPOSITION UNKNOWN

INQS-
09/14/92  0094HT43      ADVANCE RADIO TV SAL  (204) 786-6541
08/30/92  009FC1177     VALLEY CR UN          (204) 746-2391
```

SOURCE OF DATA: Reproduced with the permission of Equifax Canada Inc.

In April 1991, there was a judgment in favour of Decibel Credit Union at the Court of Queen's Bench in Winnipeg for $515. The defendant was self (DEF-S), case number 4444, and the disposition of the case is unknown.

The credit bureau received inquiries regarding Jacob Zwinkle from: Advance Radio and TV Sales on September 14, 1992 and Valley Credit Union on August 8, 1992.

The Credit Check

Whenever an application is made for a loan, a credit card, to open a charge account, or to purchase an appliance with a conditional sales contract, the borrower is asked to complete an application form and then await the credit grantor's decision. The credit officer at the bank, trust company, or store may contact the credit bureau through a computer terminal or, less frequently, by telephone. Two conditions must be met before the credit officer can receive information about the individual's credit history: (i) the inquiring firm must be a member of the credit bureau, and (ii) the file that the credit bureau retrieves must apply to this person and not to someone else.

Safeguards are built into the credit reporting system to ensure that access to credit information is restricted to members of the credit bureau only. This is done electronically when the data are transferred from one computer system to another, or with a code for telephone requests. To be sure that the retrieved file is the right one, a comparison is made between the information on the application form and that in the file at the credit bureau. In addition to name and address, other information used to identify people are birth date, social insurance number, credit card account numbers, and place of employment.

Assuming that the credit application matches the file at the credit bureau, there will be an exchange of information between the lender and the credit bureau. The file at the credit bureau will be updated with any new facts from the application, and the creditor will find out how the individual has handled credit in the past.

Credit Rating

The decision whether or not to extend credit is made by the credit grantor, not the credit bureau. Credit bureaus collect and sell information, but do not make assessments of anyone's capacity to handle credit. In the interests of efficiency and cost, large retail firms are coming to depend heavily on an automatic assessment system, called **credit scoring,** whereby points are given for certain characteristics. The weight given to these characteristics may vary somewhat among companies and from time to time as credit is made easier or harder to obtain. There is general agreement that the traditional three Cs of capacity, character, and collateral play an important part. Higher scores are assigned to those who are owners of property, show stability in residence and in their jobs, possess several credit cards, have paid past obligations on time, do not write bad cheques, and have low debt/income ratios.

Lenders have programmed their computers to quickly score the information on the application form and indicate whether the applicant is a good risk, a bad risk, or an uncertain one. In the first two instances, the decision to grant or not grant credit is fairly obvious and may be made without contacting the credit bureau. Possibly, a firm may decide that the top 10 to 15 percent of applicants are automatically accepted and the bottom 30 percent rejected. That leaves about half of the applicants in the uncertain category, where more information is needed to reach a decision; credit bureau reports will be drawn for these people.

Since the assessment of creditworthiness depends on the creditor, an applicant may find that at any one time, some lenders will grant credit while others will not. Obviously, this is more apt to be true if the individual falls in the uncertain category, because creditors vary in the levels of risk they are willing to accept. Nevertheless, whether or not credit will be granted may be influenced by factors other than personal history. Lender policies are affected by conditions in the economy and the situation in the lender's own business. Sometimes a lender has surplus funds and is very anxious to lend, but at other times scarce funds or poor economic conditions, such as high unemployment, may discourage lending.

THE CONSUMER AND THE CREDIT BUREAU

Many users of consumer credit are unaware that some of their financial transactions are on file at the credit bureau; in fact, they may never have heard of the credit bureau. Often, they only discover its existence when there is a mix-up over their files or they are refused credit. It is the policy of the Associated Credit Bureaus of Canada, and a legal requirement in most provinces, that consumers be permitted to know what is in their files, if they ask.

Regulation of Credit Bureaus

All provinces except Alberta and New Brunswick have passed laws to regulate consumer reporting agencies, which include credit bureaus. The two basic concerns reflected in these laws are the consumer's privacy in regard to credit information and the right not to suffer from inaccurate credit or personal information.

CREDIT REPORTING LEGISLATION

Province	Title
British Columbia, Ontario, Nova Scotia, Prince Edward Island	Credit Reporting Act
Saskatchewan, Newfoundland	Credit Reporting Agencies Act
Manitoba	Personal Investigations Act
Quebec	Consumer Protection Act

INFORMATION IN FILES The provincial laws make a distinction between **consumer information,** which includes such details as name, address, age, occupation, residence, marital status, education, employment, estimated income, paying habits, debts, assets, and obligations, and **personal information,** which has little to do with financial transactions, e.g., character, reputation, and personal characteristics. Credit bureaus are restricted to consumer information only. Although the details differ, all of these acts set limits on the type of information that can be included in a consumer report; generally they must be restricted to consumer information. In addition, there are limits on the inclusion of detrimental information in a credit report. For example, information about previous bankruptcies may not be reported after 14 years (six years in British Columbia and Nova Scotia; and seven years in Ontario, Prince Edward Island and Newfoundland). Disclosure of other detrimental information more than seven years old is also prohibited. Restrictions are set on the situations in which consumer reporting agencies may make reports. Acceptable circumstances are court orders and requests from those who are concerned with extending credit, renting, employment, or insurance.

PERMISSION FOR CREDIT REPORT Consumer reports, also known as credit reports, may not be requested unless a consumer has either given written consent or is sent written notice that the report was obtained. Ontario and Newfoundland require that notice be given before the report is obtained; in Manitoba, notice must follow within ten days of granting or refusing credit. The permission to obtain a report may be included in a credit application, as in Figure 14.2.

In 1988 the Ontario government revised the Consumer Reporting Act in response to misuse of credit bureau files. Businesses were obtaining credit reports to identify consumers as possible targets in promotional campaigns, such as offers of new credit cards. If an individual has not made an application for credit, the credit bureau cannot give a credit report to a third party without informing the person of the request and providing him or her with the name and address of the third party.

ACCESS TO OWN FILE The consumer has the right to know what is in his or her file at a credit bureau, and if arrangements are made with the local bureau an individual will be told the contents of the record. Should the accuracy of information found there be questioned, the agency must make every effort to verify the record and to correct any errors.

OTHER CREDIT REPORTING AGENCIES

Although this chapter is about credit bureaus, brief mention should be made of two other types of reporting agencies. **Information exchanges** are formed by groups of creditors, such as small loan and sales finance companies, to share information about their debtors as a way of preventing the occurrence of bad debts. Information exchanges are interested in the same kinds of information as credit bureaus, but differ in their organizational structure. **Investigative agencies**, on the other hand, collect a wider range of information, including very personal data about family relations, addictions, and so on, and may visit neighbours for opinions on character.

DEBT COLLECTION

When debts are in arrears or default, initially the creditor is concerned with retrieving the money owed as quickly and cheaply as possible, with minimal destruction of the debtor's goodwill. If the first phase of debt collection—notices and reminders—is unsuccessful, difficult-to-collect debts may be handled more aggressively. They may be referred to a special collection division of the creditor's firm or to an independent collection agency. Finally, the debtor may be sued in court. All three stages will be reviewed here, leaving to the next chapter consideration of the ways in which a debtor may respond to debt problems.

Who Does the Collecting?

There is no simple answer to this question because creditors choose a procedure that is suitable for them and seems feasible for the particular debt. Usually, one finds that firms in the finance business, such as banks, small loan companies, or credit unions, tend to have collection facilities to collect their own overdue accounts. Large retailers also do much of their own collecting. Smaller companies and independent professionals, particularly, prefer to devote their energies to their specialties and tend to turn over delinquent accounts to a collection agency. Sometimes, a firm will pursue overdue accounts for a time, referring only the very difficult ones. For simplicity, a distinction will be made between a creditor's internal debt collection practices and third-party collecting.

INTERNAL COLLECTION PRACTICES   Collection practices vary, but it is usual to begin with polite reminder notices or telephone calls. At this stage, the bulk of the overdue accounts are collected without harassment or much personal contact. Debtors who are still resistant will find the techniques used becoming progressively more aggressive because, at this stage, maintaining goodwill is no longer a concern of the creditor. Although the debt may have been written off in the accounts of the business, it may yet be possible to collect a portion of the debt by referring the matter to a lawyer or an independent collection agency.

Collection Agencies

A **collection agency** is a provincially licensed business that specializes in collecting overdue accounts for others; that is, it does third-party collecting. Its income depends on success in collecting, because the collector may retain from 30 to 50 percent of the amounts collected, but no fees if unsuccessful. It is not surprising, then, that collection agencies are quite energetic in their efforts to collect.

In recent years, some collection agencies have started calling themselves "collection services" and are offering a wider range of services to creditors. A collection service may take over doing credit approvals for a company. Or, a bank credit card company or a large utility may arrange for the collector to send out the usual monthly statements to cardholders or households. The collectors' computers are programmed to identify any persons who are more than one day late with a payment so that they can be called to inquire if a cheque has been sent. If not, collection procedures may be put in place immediately. In this way, the card company or utility saves money by cutting down the time they have outstanding receivables.

THIRD-PARTY COLLECTION PRACTICES Since the staff of a collection agency work on commission they are under pressure to get funds coming in as soon as possible. Therefore, they usually demand immediate receipt of the money owed or at least evidence that it will be coming very shortly. Failing that, they will threaten to sue the debtor. In practice, the collector will sue only if there is a good chance of getting a return, for instance if they find that there are wages that may be garnisheed or assets that can be seized. Creditors who refer debts to collectors expect 20 to 25 percent recovery of funds within three months, on average. Collectors who cannot meet this target will lose business to those who can.

Collection procedures often depend heavily on psychological tactics in the early stages before it is taken to court. Measures are chosen that are hoped to be intimidating to some degree: for example, using legal-looking forms and letterheads, referring the debt to a lawyer or collection agency, or making threats that may not be enforceable but go unchallenged by uninformed debtors. At any time, the debtor can slow down or stop the collection process by making some payments.

A COLLECTING TECHNIQUE

Recently, a prominent Canadian company was reprimanded by the provincial law society because it was using stationery of a sham law firm to scare debtors into paying delinquent debts. The company had been sending out thousands of notices on the letterhead of the fake law firm, stating that the lawyers were acting on behalf of the company and threatening to sue the debtor unless payment was received within three weeks. In its defence, the company reported that debtors were more likely to pay if they received a legal-looking notice than one sent on their own letterhead and, furthermore, it was cheaper than hiring a real law firm to do the collecting.

Persuasive, intimidating, or dunning techniques will be ineffective if the debtor cannot be found. Nowadays, reporting networks of credit bureaus make it much more difficult for debtors to disappear. An alert is placed on the files of missing debtors. Whenever or wherever they next apply for credit and their credit history is examined the creditor making the inquiry will provide their most recent address, which will be forwarded to the creditor who is looking for the defaulter. Not all defaulters skip deliberately; some have moved, and never informed their creditors.

ENFORCEMENT OF SECURITY   Normally, a creditor will enforce any security considered worthwhile before beginning aggressive collection processes. When the creditor holds security in the form of assets, durables, or promise of future income, the creditor also has the debtor's prior permission to realize on any of these in the case of default. But sometimes the security is not sufficient to cover the balance owing, and alternate procedures are needed.

REGULATION OF COLLECTION AGENCIES   The legislation regulating collections does not apply to all those who collect debts, but in the main is directed at third-party collections, where the collector is not the creditor. Therefore, it is chiefly concerned with regulating collection agencies. The professions and institutions that are exempted from the requirements of this legislation vary among provinces. In British Columbia and Ontario, for instance, credit unions, banks, trust companies, barristers, real estate agents, and insurance agents, among others, are exempt. Refer to the appropriate provincial legislation to determine which collectors are regulated.

LEGISLATION REGULATING COLLECTION AGENCIES

Province	Title
British Columbia	Debt Collection Act
Alberta	Collection Practices Act
Saskatchewan	Collection Agents Act
Manitoba	Consumer Protection Act
Ontario	Collection Agencies Act, and Debt Collectors Act
Quebec	Act Respecting the Collection of Certain Debts
New Brunswick, Nova Scotia, Prince Edward Island	Collection Agencies Act
Newfoundland	The Collections Act

The Criminal Code of Canada prohibits indecent, threatening, or harassing telephone calls. This applies to all collection endeavours and, thus, provides some recourse for the consumer who is being pursued for payment by someone whose activities are not regulated under provincial legislation. Initiative in lodging a complaint with provincial authorities would rest with the consumer. Another difficulty may arise in determining what constitutes harassment.

Using the Courts to Collect Debts

As mentioned earlier, the creditor who has an account in default has the right to enforce security and use reasonable collection procedures. If these are not sufficient, the next alternative is to sue the debtor. The details of the procedure vary from province to province, but a general summary of the process will indicate the procedure for collecting debts through the courts.

The creditor files a claim at the appropriate court (this depends on the amount of the claim) giving names, addresses, and reasons for suing. The court clerk sends the claim and a summons to the debtor, who has three alternatives:

(a) try to settle the matter out of court, for instance, repaying the debt,

(b) file a defense if there seems to be grounds for dispute,

(c) do nothing.

When the first alternative is selected, the debtor and creditor may reopen negotiations about payment of the debt, and if an agreement is reached, the creditor will drop the claim. Should the second alternative be chosen, the debtor must file a defense in the same court within a specified number of days, stating his or her reasons for disputing the creditor's claim. Anyone who decides to ignore the summons may be surprised to discover that failure to file a defense may result in a judgment against the debtor by default.

When a defense has been filed, there may be a trial to hear both sides of the matter. On the date of the trial, all witnesses, the creditor, the debtor, and any lawyers for either party, will appear before the judge. Small claims courts are meant to be informal courts where legal counsel is not required. After both sides of the story have been heard, the judge will announce the decision. On very small claims no appeal may be permitted. The judge's decision or judgment has two possible outcomes: either the debtor does not owe the money and the case is dismissed, or the debtor does owe some or all of the money claimed by the creditor. In the latter instance the debtor is responsible for paying the amount owing, which becomes a **judgment debt.**

ENFORCEMENT OF JUDGMENT   If the debtor either cannot or will not repay the debt, the creditor has several possible courses of action to attempt to enforce the judgment. The creditor may choose to garnishee the debtor's wages or bank account, or seize some of the debtor's goods under an execution order.

GARNISHEES   Wages or bank accounts may be garnisheed to satisfy a judgment debt. **Wage garnishment** is a court order to an employer to pay into court some percentage of the debtor's wages. If a debtor has more than one garnishee order outstanding, the court will send them out one at a time. The debtor will not be taken by surprise but will receive a statement from the court that the creditor has requested a garnishee, with time to respond to the court. The debtor can plead for a reduction in the amount taken off his or her wages and can stop the garnishee if it can be shown that steps to handle the debt problems are being taken. Sometimes, when more than one creditor has judgment against a debtor, the court may divide the funds collected by each garnishee order among the creditors, rather than handle the claims sequentially.

Garnishment is governed by a number of regulations, including those regarding exemption of certain persons, exemption of a portion of wages, and protection of employees from dismissal when their wages have been garnisheed. The social security income of those receiving welfare, Unemployment Insurance, or Old Age Security is exempt from garnishment. The proportion of wages that may be garnisheed is specified in provincial legislation (70 to 80 percent of gross wages may be exempt) but can be reduced if the debtor can persuade the court of need. When an employer receives a garnishee order, there may be an inclination to dismiss the employee on the assumption that he or she is not very reliable. Provincial laws attempt to prevent this, but sometimes it is difficult to find out the real reason for dismissal. Sometimes, home owners are surprised to receive garnishee orders for temporarily-employed trades people who have outstanding judgment debts.

A **bank account garnishment** can be taken to obtain money from a debtor's account to satisfy a judgment debt. Like a wage garnishee, the process is initiated through the court. One difference is that a bank garnishee order may take 100 percent of an account to satisfy a debt. Bank account garnishees are sometimes used to collect debts of persons receiving welfare.

DEMAND ON A THIRD PARTY   A demand on a third party may be issued by the federal government for debts incurred against the federal government (such as income tax arrears and Unemployment Insurance benefit overpayments). The demand on a third party is like a garnishee in many ways, but it does not require a court judgment and does allow attachment (seizure) of a larger share of income. In the case of a self-employed individual, a demand on a third party may be issued against the person's bank account.

FAMILY COURT GARNISHEE   Whenever payments on a maintenance order are not kept up-to-date, the family court can also issue an attachment on wages, or **family court garnishee**, that has a continuing effect, similar to a demand on a third party. Again, the percentage of the wages that can be attached may exceed limits set under provincial wage legislation. In Ontario, the Director of Support Custody Enforcement can issue a garnishee for 50 percent of gross wages. To apply for relief, the person would have to file a dispute with the courts and await a hearing. At the hearing, the judge decides whether or not to reduce the percentage garnisheed.

EXECUTION ORDER   A creditor who has obtained a favourable judgment has the right to seize and sell some of the debtor's property to satisfy the debt. In legal terms, this process is called **executing against the debtor's property**. The goods seized must be completely owned by the debtor without liens or mortgages attached to them. The provincial Execution Acts exempt the seizure of certain possessions, such as essential household furnishings.

CONSUMER ISSUES

Two issues of great concern to users of consumer credit relate to protection of privacy of personal data and the handling of credit records of married women.

Privacy of Personal Data

Electronic means of storing and transferring personal data have made it possible for the police, the doctor, the credit reporting company, or the direct marketing firm to obtain personal profiles of individuals for whatever use they may wish. This explosion of activity in processing personal data is not restricted by geographic or political boundaries. In Canada and the United States privacy legislation applies only to the public sector, but in Europe there is regulation of how personal information is used in both the private and public sectors. At the time of writing, Quebec was preparing legislation to restrict private-sector use of personal information.

Credit Records of Married Women

Traditionally, when a woman married, the credit bureau combined her credit file with her husband's. Now that does not happen, or if it does, a woman can ask to have a separate file set up. The credit bureau normally maintains a separate file for each individual. However, when a couple co-signs a loan or mortgage, this information would be entered into both their credit files. Anyone who has any doubts about how their record is stored can make an appointment at the credit bureau to discuss the file. Some women make a special effort to develop an independent credit history by using credit in their own names, without a co-signer. A credit report cannot be drawn for the spouse of a person applying for credit unless the spouse also signed the application.

Summary

Our consumer credit system depends on reliable means for a lender to quickly assess the risk potential of each borrower. To meet this need, a network of credit bureaus that sell credit information about borrowers to the member lenders has been developed. As a control on credit bureaus in collecting and preserving information about consumers, provincial legislation has specified what types of information may be included in a credit report and how long detrimental facts may be kept. Credit bureaus provide information to creditors but do not determine credit ratings; each lender makes this decision in light of company policies.

Overdue debts may be collected by the creditor or turned over to a third party, such as a collection agency, for collection. Various forms of pressure may be exerted on delinquent debtors to encourage payment, including legal action. Provincial legislation tends to regulate the licensing of collection agencies without defining what undue harassment is, or exerting control over creditors who do their own collecting. However, there are provisions under the Criminal Code of Canada which prohibit certain threatening or harassing actions on the part of anyone trying to collect a debt.

Vocabulary Review

bank account garnishment (p. 493)

collection agency (p. 489)

consumer information (p. 488)

credit bureau (p. 482)

credit scoring (p. 486)

execution against property (p. 494)

family court garnishee (p. 493)

information exchanges (p. 488)

investigative agency (p. 489)

judgment debt (p. 492)

personal information (p. 488)

wage garnishment (p. 493)

Problems

Note: Consult the appropriate legislation for the province where you live in answering these questions.

1. With reference to legislation in your province regarding credit reporting, decide whether you AGREE or DISAGREE with the following statements:

   (a) Information about judgments that occurred more than seven years ago may be included in a credit report.

   (b) A credit report may indicate the race, creed, colour, or ethnic origin of the subject of a credit report.

   (c) A credit bureau is required to reveal the contents of a consumer's file, if requested by that consumer.

   (d) Prospective employers cannot obtain credit reports from a credit bureau.

   (e) A creditor must advise the consumer involved before obtaining a credit report.

(f) If a consumer makes a written request for the information on file and the sources of this information, the credit bureau can decide whether or not to respond.

2. What are the roles of the lender and the credit bureau in evaluating a consumer's credit-worthiness? What criteria are used?

3. Why might an individual be granted credit at one institution and refused it at another, on the same day and in the same town?

4. Find the section of the act regulating credit bureaus in your province that relates to "notice of intention to procure consumer report," and then examine the credit application form in Figure 14.2 to discover if the form complies with the Act.

5. Evaluate the benefits to the debtor of the provincial legislation regulating collection agencies.

   (a) What abuses does it control?

   (b) Do you see any problems in enforcing it?

   (c) Has the law specified what constitutes undue harassment?

   (d) Does the credit reporting legislation apply to the majority of debt collection activity?

6. Identify similarities and difference between these pairs of terms:

   (a) a credit file (history) and a credit report,

   (b) a collection agency and a collection department,

   (c) consumer information and personal information,

   (d) a credit bureau and a collection agency,

   (e) a garnishee and an execution order,

   (f) a demand on a third party and a family court garnishee,

   (g) a wage assignment and a wage garnishee.

7. Decide whether you AGREE or DISAGREE with the following statements:

   (a) Most debts can be collected without aggressive action.

   (b) Collection agencies and collection departments are essentially the same.

   (c) The amount a creditor can obtain through garnishment is limited by provincial legislation or a court decision.

8. If debtors learn that they are about to have their wages garnisheed, is there anything they can do to stop or alter the process?

9. Can a creditor garnishee the wages of a debtor before successfully suing the debtor? Can the creditor do this after the suit is started but before judgment is decided in the creditor's favour?

REFERENCES

BOOKS

BERGER, ESTHER M. and CONNIE CHURCH HASBUN. *Money Smart: Secrets Women Always Wanted to Know About Money*. New York: Simon and Schuster, 1993, 304 pp. Insight into money management and tips on dealing with financial professionals is offered by a financial planner.

Canadian Commercial Law Reports. Don Mills, Ontario: CCH Canadian, subscription service. Two-volume reporting service with up-to-date federal and provincial laws regarding sales contracts, conditional sales, instalment sales, chattel mortgages, consumer protection.

DYMOND, MARY JOY. *The Canadian Woman's Legal Guide*. Toronto: Doubleday, 1987, 449 pp. Includes a section on women and credit.

PARKER, ALLAN A. *Credit, Debt, and Bankruptcy*. Eighth Edition. Vancouver: International Self-Counsel Press, 1990, 128 pp. A handbook on Canadian credit law for credit users.

ARTICLE

FINKLE, KAREN. "See You in Court." *Canadian Consumer*, March/April 1993, pp. 21–23. Box 9300, Ottawa, Ontario, K1G 3T9.

CHAPTER SEVENTEEN

Strategies for Overcommitted Debtors

OBJECTIVES

1. To identify some major causes of overindebtedness.

2. To explain why it is difficult to prevent overindebtedness.

3. To explain what negotiation with creditors involves and when it may be appropriate for an overcommitted debtor.

4. To identify costs and benefits of a consolidation loan.

5. To outline the process of a debt repayment program.

6. To suggest reasons for the rising rate of consumer bankruptcies in Canada.

7. To distinguish between a consumer proposal and bankruptcy.

8. To explain why consumer proposals were included in the revised bankruptcy legislation of 1992.

9. To distinguish among the responsibilities of the five actors in the insolvency process.

10. To outline consequences of bankruptcy for:

    (a) creditors,

    (b) the discharged bankrupt.

11. To evaluate the potential benefits of a consumer proposal for the insolvent debtor.

12. To explain these terms: overindebtedness, debt management, bankrupt, discharged bankrupt.

Introduction

Within one generation, our society has made a major shift from paying cash for nearly everything to dependence on credit, a change that may have contributed to economic growth by increasing demand but has not been without attendant social costs. The combination of rising real incomes and easy credit made it seem unnecessary to postpone spending until sufficient money had been saved. For many people this worked quite satisfactorily, but for an increasing number the result was overindebtedness, followed by despair and crisis. As long as there were expectations of job security and steadily rising incomes, many found debt not too hard to handle. However, when economic conditions change, as in the recessions of the early 1980s and 1990s, those with heavy debt loads are very vulnerable if they become unemployed.

The purpose of this chapter is to understand why people become overindebted and to examine possibilities for resolving the crisis. You will find, as you read on, that overindebtedness is usually not a simple bookkeeping problem, but is bound up in the intricacies of human behaviour. Most strategies to help the overindebted begin with an assessment of the financial muddle to get a clear and complete picture of the situation, followed by identification of possible options. Any solution that will be effective for the long term usually requires significant behavioural change. Sometimes, a financial crisis sufficiently frightens debtors to motivate them to make changes. In other cases, the necessary changes are just too difficult to accomplish. Those strategies outlined in this chapter are biased toward economic solutions, with recognition of the possible need for other types of personal counselling. Some of the options considered are negotiation with creditors, a consolidation loan, credit counselling, filing a consumer proposal, and making an assignment in bankruptcy.

OVERINDEBTEDNESS—WHY DOES IT HAPPEN?

Overindebtedness

Overindebtedness is the condition of having more debts than one can or is willing to repay. Usually, an overindebted person is found to have several accounts in arrears, with creditors and collectors actively pressing for payment. Reneging on a promise to a lender may prompt gentle reminders, leading to more urgent requests, possible enforcement of security, and eventual referral of the debt to a collection agency or department. When these measures fail to obtain results, the lender may sue the debtor in court, as you will recall from the discussion in the previous chapter. A lender who wins a court case gains some additional means to collect a debt, such as garnisheeing wages or seizing property and possessions. Of course, at any stage of overindebtedness, the debtor can take the initiative by contacting the creditor to attempt to negotiate a new arrangement, by consulting a credit counsellor for assistance in identifying possible solutions to debt problems or by talking with a trustee in bankruptcy (or administrator).

SHOPPING WITH PLASTIC

Janet and George love credit cards; having cards makes them feel like they have money. Until quite recently, they had two bank cards, three department store cards, three gasoline cards, and two entertainment cards. As soon as their teen-age children were old enough, they got credit cards too. For this family, paying with plastic doesn't seem like using real money; it is so easy to block out the fact that the bills have to be paid sometime.

When the monthly statements arrive, they usually try to pay at least the minimum on each one. But, when Janet's job changed from full-time to part-time, there wasn't enough money to make all the minimum payments, so they got a bank loan to consolidate their debts and kept on shopping and charging. As their worries increased, they took out a second mortgage on their house.

When Janet lost her part-time job, they reached a crisis. They could not get more loans from anywhere and their creditors were hounding them. The pressure became intense. Were they going to go bankrupt? Would they lose their house? Someone suggested credit counselling.

The credit counsellor helped them to get a total picture of their income, expenses, and debts and to plan a new budget. Janet and George decided that they wanted to go on an agency-administered debt management plan. The counsellor insisted that they cut up all their credit cards in her office. The debt repayment plan required that they make regular payments to the agency for 4 years to clear the debt. Janet and George left the office feeling they had lost everything. Having credit cards in their pockets had made them feel they had money. Now what would they do?

Did this experience give Janet and George and their children a big enough scare to change their behaviour? Will they stick to the repayment plan and live without credit cards for 4 years?

What do you think?

Why Debtors Default

There are different degrees of overindebtedness, just as there are many reasons for becoming overindebted. Some people are unable to repay their debts because of an unexpected loss of income, unforeseen large expenses, personal difficulties, poor financial management, etc. A few are unwilling to pay because of disputes with creditors or retailers, or because of their own irresponsibility. Those with a small amount of overindebtedness and reasonable earning capacity have the potential to get their affairs under control, perhaps with some professional help. Others are too deeply in debt and have such limited capacity to repay that more drastic measures are necessary.

Recently, the Office of the Superintendent of Bankruptcy, investigating some of the causes of personal bankruptcy, discovered the issues associated with insolvency to be much more complex than previously imagined, and not simply due to mismanagement, unemployment, or overuse of credit (Wally Clare, "Repeat Bankruptcies of Consumer Debtors," *Insolvency Bulletin*, Consumer and Corporate Affairs Canada, No. 10, 1990, pp. 201–210) There is rarely a single cause of bankruptcy. Often, the difficulties are related to serious personal and lifestyle problems that, unless addressed, continue to influence household decision-making. Compulsive behaviour may be part of the problem, sometimes compounded by illiteracy. At least 24 percent of bankrupts are functionally illiterate, making it difficult for them to cope with the complexities of consumer credit.

Causes of insolvency, as identified in this research, may be conceptualized as follows:

(a) Deficiencies in early socialization or education,

(b) Problems with relationships,

(c) Early marriage or living relationships,

(d) Obsessive or compulsive behaviour,

(e) Severe medical problems or disabilities,

(f) Expenditures on cars or education,

(g) Loss of job income.

DEFICIENCIES IN SOCIALIZATION OR EDUCATION   Those children who do not have opportunities to learn basic financial skills at home or in school are vulnerable as young adults. Entering the market financially unskilled, they get into difficulty early in their lives, usually as soon as they start using consumer credit; the average age of a consumer bankrupt in Canada is 27. Perhaps related to family socialization is the problem of illiteracy. Many of the overindebted are functionally illiterate for various reasons: they have learning disabilities, left school early, or both. How can these people be expected to understand the responsibilities of a debtor or cope with the intricacies of consumer credit? Those without skills often get into a vicious cycle of high unemployment, little money, and too much debt, from which it is difficult to escape.

RELATIONSHIP PROBLEMS   The increased frequency of marriage breakdown has resulted in more people finding themselves with financial problems. When a two-income family breaks up, the situation changes from two people supporting one household to two people sustaining two households. There may not be enough income to make this possible, at least not in the style to which they had become accustomed. The causes of financial problems of separated families tend to be complex and closely related to the causes of their marital failure. If, as often happens, both spouses cosigned their loans, they remain jointly responsible for the debts, even after separation. Should one declare bankruptcy the other has to assume total responsibility for the debts or declare bankruptcy also.

Some people seem to drift from one self-defeating relationship to another. They tend to have low self-esteem and get involved with a partner who has a substance abuse problem, exhibits other compulsive behaviour (gambling, spending), or is violent. When the relationship breaks up, one partner often assumes the joint debts, usually because the other is unable or unwilling to do so. Although both men and women may get themselves into this situation, it is women who seem to be the most vulnerable. Some keep repeating the unhealthy relationships and financial problems, declaring bankruptcy more than once.

EARLY MARRIAGE OR LIVING RELATIONSHIPS   Those who marry or start living together when they are very young usually have so few economic resources that they must use credit to set up a household. Thus begins a pattern that can eventually lead to insolvency. They buy furnishings on credit, then struggle to make payments and cover living costs, resulting in a hand-to-mouth existence. Eventually, they borrow more to reduce the monthly payments, start to argue about money, and their family life begins to deteriorate. By constant juggling they may get along for a time if both are working, but when something happens to one income they can no longer cope.

OBSESSIVE OR COMPULSIVE BEHAVIOUR   Dependence on alcohol or drugs is a frequent cause of overindebtedness but, most often, the abuser does not admit that financial problems are related to this dependency. Sadly, unless the abuse problem is confronted, the financial problems will continue.

Some compulsive gamblers get into a cycle: they declare bankruptcy, get discharged, continue gambling, and declare bankruptcy again. In fact, some keep on gambling throughout the bankruptcy process. Since it seems that bankruptcy is rarely enough to stop gamblers from gambling, they often become repeat bankrupts.

Another group at risk of overindebtedness are compulsive spenders. They cannot resist shopping. Buying something gives them a lift and our consumer market is designed to encourage impulse spending. It is so easy in the excitement of a purchase to forget about the reality of future payments. Here again, there is no hope of solving the financial problems of compulsive shoppers until their behaviour is modified.

SEVERE MEDICAL PROBLEMS OR DISABILITIES   It is indeed unfortunate that persons who suffer severe medical problems can progress through reduced job income, to no job income, and finally to using savings in an effort to handle living costs. Although some of these people are forced to declare bankruptcy, they make up less than 10 percent of bankrupts.

EXPENDITURES ON CARS OR EDUCATION   The relationship between young men and their cars can lead to insolvency. When they buy cars, they must license them, insure them, run them, and repair them. If this is done with credit and more credit, it is not uncommon to find that the debts have grown much larger than the value of the car. Sometimes the car no longer works and they buy another before the debt on the first one has been cleared. If this pattern is combined with an early marriage or unemployment, a financial crisis is surely ahead.

Student loans work well for most who go to university or college but there are some who do not graduate, cannot find a job, or can find only a very low-paying one. Mature students who give up a full-time income may fail to realize how quickly they can get behind. Perhaps they had not thought about how difficult it would be to adapt to the lifestyle of a student. For various reasons, student loans can lead to bankruptcy for a few people.

LOSS OF JOB INCOME   It does not take long to get behind when a family loses its regular income; living costs do not stop. Anyone with a heavy debt load or who spends all they earn is particularly vulnerable. This kind of financial crisis is just as likely to happen to a high-income family as a low-income one. High-income earners find credit easier to get and their debt problems can compound very quickly.

As mentioned in the chapter on the use of credit, one of the costs of credit is the flexibility cost—with future income committed to repaying debts, fewer resources are available for other wants or needs, emergencies, or the unexpected. Any family with high debt commitments is especially vulnerable to any changes in their employment situation that reduce or stop their income. Although debtors may be insured against the possibility that death or disability may impair their ability to repay the debt, perhaps there is an equally compelling need to insure debtors against loss of income.

INSURANCE FOR JOB LOSS

Late in 1992, a major bank announced an insurance plan for borrowers who lose their jobs, with coverage becoming effective a month after the job loss. Debtors may postpone loan payments for up to 6 months and the insurance will pay the interest.

Symptoms of Insolvency

The conclusions of this research indicated that in most instances several interconnected causal factors are present in the lives of the insolvent. A combination of several of the following symptoms are usually present in cases of bankruptcy:

(a) debtors do not understand what went wrong or how they got into trouble,

(b) they do not know how to handle money or make wise purchase decisions,

(c) they do not understand basic consumer credit concepts,

(d) they have never saved money,

(e) they do not make budgets and do not believe that others do.

Having reviewed some of the causes of insolvency, we will turn our attention to possible strategies to resolve or alleviate the problem.

ALTERNATIVES FOR THE OVERCOMMITTED DEBTOR

A creditor has a number of options to try to force a debtor to repay a debt, some of which may be quite unpleasant. What rights does the debtor have and what steps can he or she take? If debt commitments exceed the debtor's capacity to repay them, the options include:

(a) negotiating new terms with creditors,

(b) obtaining a consolidation loan,

(c) seeking help from a credit counselling service,

(d) declaring insolvency and filing a consumer proposal,

(e) making an assignment in bankruptcy.

Unfortunately, from fear or ignorance some over-extended debtors do nothing at all, letting the situation worsen rapidly.

Negotiation With Creditors

Anyone who becomes overindebted should talk to creditors as soon as it is apparent that things are getting out of hand. Tell them what has happened and ask what adjustments can be arranged. Above all, creditors prefer to see their money returning, even if delayed slightly, rather than to be forced to take strong measures. The policies of the particular institution will determine which alternatives may be available to the debtor. The creditor may offer to freeze the loan—that is, to accept no payments at all for a time. Additional interest payments may or may not be charged for this period, but of course, the date for the completion of the credit contract will be moved forward.

TAKING THE PRESSURE OFF

Tim and Brenda found themselves in a bind when Tim was off work for several months because of ill health. There was no way they could make all their debt payments and meet basic living expenses. When a friend advised that they see a credit counsellor, they made an appointment right away.

After the counsellor assessed their financial situation, he suggested that it would be worthwhile to try to contact their creditors. He helped them to write a letter asking that collection procedures not be pursued for a time and requesting permission to delay payments until Tim goes back to work. Since this family had had no previous problems with debt repayment and had a good credit rating, the creditors were willing to help them to cope with a temporary loss of income.

Consolidation Loan

Some lenders offer consolidation loans to overcommitted debtors. A **consolidation loan** is a new loan used to discharge a number of existing debts and is usually requested when the debtor is unable to maintain previous repayment commitments. Advertisements often exhort credit users to borrow enough money to pay off all their debts and thus owe just one company. Unfortunately, this is not a perfect solution. To borrow sufficient funds to cover all outstanding obligations and yet make smaller monthly payments than before will have two predictable consequences—the loan will be for a longer term and the total interest charges may be increased. A consolidation loan may be a reasonable solution in some cases, but for many people it can be the beginning of a vicious cycle from which it is difficult to escape. Unfortunately, the smaller monthly payments may tempt a debtor to take on even more debt, and so the problem worsens.

Before deciding on a consolidation loan, examine the interest rate that will be charged and make a comparison with the rates on existing obligations. It is unwise to transfer to a consolidation loan those debts that now carry a lower interest rate or are not interest-bearing. Consolidation loans tend to carry quite high rates of interest because they are made to people who are not very good credit risks. In the case of a loan contract that is close to completion, the final payments are composed mostly of principal and very little interest. If such a contract were prepaid with funds obtained from a consolidation loan and the amount owing transferred to a new consolidation loan, the debtor would significantly increase the amount of interest to be paid.

During the recession of the early nineties, banks became less eager to offer consolidation loans because of the high number of defaults on such loans. Some people were getting consolidation loans to lower their monthly debt payments, then running up more debt on their credit cards.

KAREN CONSIDERS A CONSOLIDATION LOAN

When Bob lost his job, their monthly loan payments of $715 suddenly became more than they could handle. Karen visited the credit union to inquire about a consolidation loan to tide them over until Bob found work. She took along this list of their current debts:

Creditor	Balance outstanding	Interest rate (%)	Monthly payment	Term remaining	Total interest
Sears	$1 000	25	$50	26 mo.	$307.02
Canadian Tire	1 000	21	50	25	241.55
Mastercard	2 000	19	100	24	423.87
Visa	1 100	16.75	55	24	198.83
Beneficial	1 500	23	140	12	195.04
Avco	7 600	22	320	31	2 469.38
TOTALS	$14 200		$715		$3 835.69

At the credit union Karen was told that they could get a consolidation loan of $14 200, at 14% interest, with a choice of a 2-, 3-, or 4-year term.

Consolidation Loan Possibilities

	Option #1	Option #2	Option #3
Terms			
Term (years)	2	3	4
Monthly payment	$681.80	$485.32	$388.04
Total interest	$2162.73	$3271.62	$4425.66

Costs and benefits compared to present loans:

Change in monthly payment	−$33.20	−$228.68	−$326.96
Change in total interest cost	−$1672.96	−$564.97	+$589.97

Karen noticed an inverse relation between the term of the loan and the monthly payment: a longer term meant lower payments. At first they were attracted by the low payments of $388.04 with Option #3. Then, they realized that it would take 4 years to repay and the total interest cost would be $4425. Recognizing that the first option would not reduce their monthly payment enough, but the third one would be too costly, they finally decided on Option #2.

Credit Counselling

Another option for the overcommitted debtor is to approach one of the government- or community-sponsored credit or debt counselling services usually found in larger centres. Although their organizational structure varies from province to province, all of these agencies have the same objective, and may offer services without charge. They help clients to find an appropriate solution to their financial problems; in some instances this involves acting as a mediator between the overindebted family and their creditors to alleviate the crisis and to facilitate the eventual repayment of the debt. Credit counselling usually begins with an assessment interview, followed by a review of possible solutions.

ASSESSMENT INTERVIEW The first step the credit counsellor takes is to interview the debtor with his or her partner to obtain detailed information about the family's financial situation and consider the type of solution that might be appropriate. This financial analysis includes a complete listing of: (i) income, (ii) living expenses, and (iii) debts. If the family's monthly income is sufficient to cover living expenses and debt obligations, the counsellor may spend some time discussing ways of improving their financial management so that the family can make their income stretch from one pay day to the next. If there is a prospect of allocating a reasonable amount toward debt repayment, although less than the family's present commitment, a debt repayment plan may be developed. If, however, there is insufficient income to cover living expenses and partial debt payments, another solution may be needed, such as applying for insolvency protection under the Bankruptcy and Insolvency Act.

DEBT REPAYMENT PROGRAM The counsellor will work out with the family the amount that can be used to repay debts, and allocate this among their creditors in proportion to each creditor's share of the total outstanding debt (*pro rata*). This process is a debt repayment program, also known as debt management or a prorate. The creditor who is owed the largest part of the family's total debt will receive the largest share of any repayment. Once a debt repayment plan that is acceptable to both the debtor and creditors is set up, the debtor signs a contract specifying the amount to be forwarded to the counselling agency on a regular basis. The agency, acting as a trustee, handles the distribution of the funds to the creditors.

The success of a debt repayment program depends on the ability of the family to live within the budget drawn up in consultation with the counsellor, the stability of the family's circumstances, and also on the willingness of the creditors to participate in the plan. Often creditors will cooperate because they prefer to accept reduced but regular payments instead of trying more collection procedures or writing the account off as a bad debt. If the family fails to maintain the agreed payments, the agency will cancel the plan. The case study, "A Debt Repayment Plan," illustrates how a debt repayment program may be set up.

A DEBT REPAYMENT PLAN

Constant strife about bills made life so unpleasant that Michael and Susan decided to seek the help of a credit counselling service. With the counsellor's assistance, they began, for the first time, to get a picture of their financial situation. When the counsellor asked them to list all their expenses and all their income, they were surprised at the result. Their monthly living costs were exceeding their income before any consumer debt payments were made. The figures below show that they were short nearly $1250 per month.

MONTHLY CASH FLOW

Total family take-home pay $2750
    Living expenses.. $2865
    Debt commitment $1135
Total monthly expenses..................................... $4000
Difference between income and expenses .... –$1250

Michael and Susan were also surprised to discover how much their total debt was; they knew that their loan balance at the credit union was low but had never added up all they owed. They hadn't realized how quickly their credit card debts had mounted up. When the counsellor went over the monthly statements from their various credit cards with them, there was another surprise: the balances were increasing in spite of sporadic payments and recent purchasing restraints.

After a careful review of their financial affairs, several possible solutions were discussed and carefully analyzed. Michael and Susan decided that they would go on an agency-administered debt repayment program. The counsellor explained that this would require reductions in living expenses, an increase in income, or both. They thought the potential for augmenting their income was low but they felt that they could cut back on some of their expenses.

For a start, they decided to reduce their gift-giving and forego vacations until their situation improved. The effect of these changes on their deficit would be approximately $100 per month. They proposed a further cut in their expenses by dropping "Super Channel" on their TV cable package and also agreed to reduce the number of restaurant meals and "take-outs." The anticipated gain there was another $90 a month. Before making any more sacrifices, the counsellor suggested that they take more time to consider the implication of these suggestions and to decide what other appropriate action to take.

When Susan and Michael returned a week later they offered these ideas: to reduce the telephone bill by making fewer long distance calls and to lower child-care costs by having their eldest child take more responsibility. They estimated that this would save about $125 per month. However, they realized that they had been a little over-zealous the week before and decided even if they didn't go away for vacations, they would spend extra money while they were off work, probably $200 a year. The counsellor, also recognizing that such changes are easier to plan than to carry out, suggested that they allocate $650 per month toward repayment of their consumer debt.

The counsellor confirmed the outstanding balances with each creditor and was not surprised to find that the couple's debt was about $747 more than they had estimated—a total of $19 186. The counsellor's debt profile for this family shows the following list of creditors and amounts of debt, and the proportions of the total to be paid each month to each creditor.

Creditor	Reason for debt	Monthly payment	Confirmed balance	%	Prorate* payment
Credit union	cars	$295	$4917	25.6	$166.40
The Bay	stove, refrigerator, dishwasher, stereo	249	4023	21.0	136.50
Eatons	clothing, household goods Christmas gifts	227	3813	19.9	129.35
Sears	washer, dryer, clothes, gifts, VCR	228	3967	20.7	134.55
Visa	car repairs, vacuum, cash advances, misc.	136	2304	12.0	78.00
Esso	gas		162	0.8	5.20
Total		$1135	$19 186	100.0	$650.00

* To prorate is to distribute proportionally.

Susan and Michael will require approximately three-and-a-half to four years to repay these debts, and during this time they must refrain from assuming any new ones. If the family is successful in making the necessary adjustments in their lifestyle, they will probably eliminate their debt and become more effective financial managers. Unfortunately, some families cannot accept such a regimen, or their circumstances change and they do not complete the debt management program.

Consumer Proposals and Bankruptcy

Another solution to overindebtedness is to apply for insolvency protection under the federal Bankruptcy and Insolvency Act, either by filing a consumer proposal or making an assignment in bankruptcy. These procedures are discussed in some detail in the following sections.

BANKRUPTCY AND INSOLVENCY

This discussion is about procedures that relate to consumers under the federal Bankruptcy and Insolvency Act of 1992. It is a formal process of declaring insolvency by filing a consumer proposal or an assignment in bankruptcy and eventually obtaining a certificate indicating that the conditions of the consumer proposal have been met or being **discharged from bankruptcy**. Declaring insolvency, the last resort of the overindebted, is much dreaded because of the attached social stigma and detrimental effect on a credit rating. However, it may be the only alternative for families who do not have enough income to cover their regular living expenses and also repay their debts in full. A **consumer proposal** is a plan for paying creditors a portion of the total debt. **Bankruptcy** allows an insolvent debtor to obtain relief from a financial crisis, with any assets distributed in an orderly fashion among creditors. After the conditions of the proposal or bankruptcy are met, the insolvent debtor is free to start over.

The case study, "Bankruptcy or Asset Liquidation?" illustrates a situation in which a heavily overindebted family faces a choice between bankruptcy or a negotiated settlement with creditors.

BANKRUPTCY OR ASSET LIQUIDATION?

When a credit counsellor encounters a family whose debts are far in excess of its ability to repay, a consumer proposal or an agency-administered debt management plan may not be possible options. Sheila was such a case. Until her separation from her alcoholic husband, Sheila had managed to keep all the bills paid and the family lived well on a combined income of over $100 000. After the separation, she had hoped that with her salary as an executive secretary and substantial support payments for the two young children she would still be able to keep on top of her expenses. However, her ex-husband lost his middle-management job a few months after the separation and the sporadic support payments ceased.

Now, Sheila was behind on the mortgage and owed the gas company for fuel; the bank was threatening to take her car; her credit cards and charge accounts were at their limit. She still owed money to the lawyer for handling her separation. The pressures from these financial problems made Sheila sometimes wonder if she and the children were really better off living apart from her abusive husband. It seemed to her that things were always going wrong.

The situation that Sheila found herself in is not uncommon today with the frequency of marriage and relationship breakdowns and employment instability. What is manageable on two incomes is not always manageable on one. Sheila was so angry at what she felt to be the injustice of her circumstances that it was hard for her to take any kind of an objective look at her financial affairs. The counsellor tried to help Sheila focus on one problem at a time.

It soon became evident to both Sheila and the counsellor that keeping the house was not going to be possible nor, on her income alone, would she be able to meet her other monthly debt commitments. The counsellor suggested two alternatives. Since Sheila was insolvent, bankruptcy was one possibility. Another option to consider was to make use of the equity in her home and some valuable antiques by selling them and using the proceeds to offer her creditors a cash settlement. Neither solution was ideal. The credit counsellor also recommended that Sheila seek legal advice, particularly concerning her right to sell the house and antiques.

Sheila also was encouraged to seek counselling for herself and the children concerning their feelings about separation.

Bankruptcy in Canada

Bankruptcy is no longer an insignificant factor in our society. It is estimated that over one million Canadians have been touched by bankruptcy during their lifetimes—as individuals or as family members. A look at the changing rate of consumer bankruptcies in Canada demonstrates the need to give this matter more attention (Figure 17.1). For instance, in 1972 there were 14 consumer bankruptcies per 100 000 of population, but by the end of 1992 this had increased to 226.

Bankruptcy and Insolvency Act

The federal Bankruptcy and Insolvency Act, that became effective November 30, 1992 was welcomed because it offered more options for overindebted consumers. The earlier Act of 1949 was designed primarily for the needs of commercial organizations with assets to distribute, rather than those of consumers, who rarely have much to disperse. Meanwhile, the numbers of consumer bankruptcies were overtaking business bankruptcies; now, more than 75 percent of all bankruptcies are consumer bankruptcies.

FIGURE 17.1 CONSUMER BANKRUPTCIES PER 100 000
POPULATION, CANADA, 1966–1992

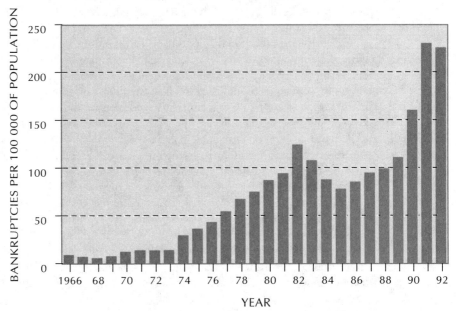

SOURCE OF DATA: Personal communication from the Office of the Superintendent of Bankruptcy

The 1992 legislation was designed to respond to some of the needs of the overindebted with a more streamlined process and an emphasis on rehabilitation. It is based on the premise that the best that the insolvency system can do for society is to return bankrupts to the marketplace as better informed and responsible citizens, with enhanced ability to contribute to the economy. Recovery of funds is less important. In most consumer bankruptcies, there are few assets, other than income tax refunds, to distribute and little potential for repaying debts from income. A bankrupt's family tends to have an income that is only 40 percent of the Canadian average.

In all provinces, both corporate and personal bankruptcies are regulated by the federal Bankruptcy and Insolvency Act. In the past, bankruptcy was managed by the federal Office of the Superintendent of Bankruptcy without provincial involvement. Trustees in bankruptcy are still federally appointed, but certain tasks are now delegated to the provinces if they wish to accept them. Those provinces already offering Orderly Payment of Debts programs have agreed to also handle consumer proposals. At the time of writing, Quebec had decided not to become involved with this Act, and Ontario had not announced a decision regarding the appointment of administrators of consumer proposals.

ORDERLY PAYMENT OF DEBTS The federal Bankruptcy and Insolvency Act provides for an Orderly Payment of Debts (OPD) program (i.e., debt repayment plan) to be administered by the provinces if they choose. Six provinces—British Columbia, Alberta, Saskatchewan, Manitoba, Nova Scotia, and Prince Edward Island—have implemented the OPD program, but there is no particular uniformity in procedures among these provinces. Essentially, this section of the Act permits a debt administration program to be established under provincial government sponsorship.

Basics of the Insolvency Process

A hopelessly indebted person who applies for insolvency protection under the Bankruptcy and Insolvency Act now has a new option not available in the past, that of filing a consumer proposal.

ELIGIBILITY An applicant for a consumer proposal must be insolvent and have less than $75 000 in debts (excluding a mortgage on the principal residence). To file for bankruptcy, a debtor must owe at least $1000.

INITIATING THE PROCESS Insolvency proceedings are usually started when a debtor makes an application to an administrator of consumer proposals or a trustee in bankruptcy.

INSOLVENCY ACTORS There are five main actors in the insolvency or bankruptcy drama:

(a) the **insolvent** who is unable to meet his or her debt obligations,

(b) the **creditors,** who are all those who can prove a claim against the bankrupt,

(c) the **official receiver,** the federal civil servant who oversees the insolvency process,

(d) the **trustee in bankruptcy,** a federally licensed official (usually a chartered accountant) who carries out the insolvency process,

(e) the **administrator of proposals,** who has more limited powers than a trustee. A trustee may handle consumer proposals and bankruptcies while an administrator is limited to consumer proposals and counselling.

RESPONSIBILITIES OF THE DEBTOR The insolvent person must reveal complete information about assets, debts, and income and may be asked to meet the official receiver and answer questions under oath. If there is a meeting of creditors, the debtor is expected to be there to provide information. There are several counselling sessions to be attended and regular statements about income and expenses to be submitted. The debtor is expected to cooperate with the insolvency officials.

RESPONSIBILITIES OF CREDITORS   In cases of bankruptcy, the creditors are invited to a meeting to consider the affairs of the debtor, to confirm the appointment of the trustee, and may appoint inspectors to act as their agents in the bankruptcy process. However, in a streamlined consumer bankruptcy process some of these steps may be unnecessary. Finally, the agreement of the creditors is necessary to effect the discharge of the insolvent person from bankruptcy. In the case of a consumer proposal, the creditors have to accept the plan before it can be put into effect.

DUTIES OF THE OFFICIAL RECEIVER   The receiver generally oversees the whole insolvency process which includes receiving petitions or proposals from the trustee or administrator, making decisions about holding meetings of creditors, and submitting applications to court.

DUTIES OF THE TRUSTEE IN BANKRUPTCY   On receiving an inquiry about insolvency protection, the trustee investigates the debtor's financial situation through an assessment interview and possibly by checking with creditors. The debtor decides whether to submit a consumer proposal or file for bankruptcy. If the debtor decides on a consumer proposal, the trustee changes to another hat and becomes an administrator of consumer proposals. Either a trustee or an administrator can handle the counselling sessions and the preparation of the consumer proposal but only a trustee looks after the bankruptcy process.

DUTIES OF THE ADMINISTRATOR OF CONSUMER PROPOSALS   An administrator of consumer proposals may be a trustee in bankruptcy or another person appointed to this task. The administrator can provide counselling, conduct an assessment interview, assist the debtor to file a consumer proposal, and handle the disbursement of funds to creditors. If, at the assessment interview, the debtor decides to file for bankruptcy, the client must be transferred to a trustee.

COST OF INSOLVENCY   Although the Act specifies charges for various tasks, the total cost associated with a bankruptcy or consumer proposal varies with the complexity of the case. As a rough estimate, the cost of a consumer proposal may be about $750 plus 5 to 10 percent of the funds distributed. As an example of personal bankruptcy costs, one firm has a policy of charging a minimum of $1275. In a bankruptcy, all assets are realized and held in trust by the trustee. Bankruptcy fees have first claim on the estate before other creditors.

Counselling Sessions

The legislation, with its focus on rehabilitation, offers the possibility of three counselling sessions. The first occurs when the overindebted person contacts a trustee or administrator to discuss possible solutions to the insolvency problem. The administrator or trustee examines the debtor's whole financial situation and reviews possible alternatives. The second counselling session takes place a month or two after filing a consumer proposal or an assignment in bankruptcy. At this time, the emphasis is on identifying the root causes of the financial difficulties and finding ways to change the situation. Failure to attend the second counselling session will result in a penalty of not being eligible for an automatic discharge from bankruptcy. The third, and optional, counselling session takes place within six months of filing a proposal or making an assignment. It is intended to provide the debtor and his or her family with further guidance in financial management or assistance with such personal problems as substance abuse, gambling, relationship difficulties, or compulsive shopping. The first counselling session must be done on an individual basis, but subsequent counselling may be done in groups.

The legislation requires that an administrator or trustee who agrees to assist an insolvent debtor must provide for at least two counselling sessions. The trustee or administrator can do the counselling or delegate it to a qualified person. The fees for counselling are paid out of the estate of the debtor before any distribution to creditors.

Consumer Proposals

As we have seen, a consumer proposal is a plan for reorganizing personal financial affairs for presentation to the creditors. The debtor, with help from an administrator, prepares a plan for repayment of all or part of the debt within five years. If the proposal is accepted by the court and the creditors, it becomes binding on the debtor and the creditors. Generally, a consumer proposal does not release a debtor from certain kinds of obligations, such as fines, penalties, alimony, maintenance agreements, or co-signer responsibilities. It does, however, protect the debtor from any claims for accelerated payments or discontinued service by public utilities; it nullifies the effect of any existing wage assignments; it prohibits an employer from taking any disciplinary action because the employee has made a consumer proposal. If the creditors accept a consumer proposal, bankruptcy can be avoided but if they do not, an assignment in bankruptcy may follow.

CERTIFICATE OF PERFORMANCE   When all the conditions of a consumer proposal have been met, the debtor receives a certificate to that effect.

Bankruptcy

The first step in bankruptcy is the assignment of all the debtor's assets to a licensed trustee. From this time, until he or she is released from debts by the court, the debtor is an undischarged bankrupt. Next, a meeting of creditors will be called, at which the appointment of the trustee will be affirmed and instructions given concerning the administration of the estate. The trustee will then proceed to liquidate the estate. All the property of the debtor is available for payment of debts, except that which is exempt from execution or seizure under the laws of the province. All creditors must prove their claims against the estate and secured creditors will be paid first because they have a claim on specific assets. Any remaining assets are then distributed in a specified order, with payment for the cost of the administration of the bankruptcy taking precedence over other claims.

ASSETS EXEMPT FROM SEIZURE IN ONTARIO

Provincial laws exempt some assets from seizure by the trustee in bankruptcy. In Ontario the most common exemptions are:

(a) Furniture, household furnishings, and appliances not exceeding a total value of $2000.

(b) All necessary and ordinary clothing of the bankrupt and family, not exceeding $1000 in value.

(c) Tools, implements, professional books, and other necessaries used in the practice of a business, trade, calling or profession, not exceeding $2000.

(d) A company pension plan.

(e) Cash surrender value of a life insurance policy if there is a designated irrevocable beneficiary (e.g., a spouse). (Refer to Chapter 6 for an explanation of irrevocable beneficiary.)

(f) Registered retirement savings plan with a life insurance company if there is a designated irrevocable beneficiary (e.g., a spouse).

(g) Monies received for pain and suffering, such as a claim for injuries received in an accident.

(h) Certain farm assets of those engaged in farming.

DISCHARGE FROM BANKRUPTCY   Once the existing assets have been distributed, the court may grant the bankrupt a discharge. This releases the debtor from all claims of creditors except those for court fines, bail bond, alimony or support payments and certain debts incurred by fraud. If there is no opposition from creditors and the counselling sessions have been attended, a first-time bankrupt is eligible for an automatic discharge nine months after declaring bankruptcy.

THE CASE OF PENNY AND TONY

Sometimes bankruptcy is not the panacea that people hope for. The case of Penny and Tony illustrates some of the problems that can be involved in a bankruptcy. Penny and Tony had been managing well on a government-sponsored debt repayment program for a year and a half. However, the birth of a seriously handicapped child left them both financially and emotionally drained. Weeks of commuting to a hospital in a larger centre, followed by the baby's death, seemed more than they could bear. When they contacted the agency handling their debt repayments they had made up their minds that they were filing for bankruptcy and nothing the counsellor said would dissuade them.

Several days after they signed the bankruptcy papers, the finance company, which had a chattel mortgage on their household goods, arrived with a truck and picked up most of their furniture leaving them without a washing machine and barely a chair to sit on. Ironically, they had to borrow money right away to get some furniture. To their surprise, they discovered that their debt was reduced by only $1100 through the bankruptcy. The bank was going to take possession of their car, but they were able to make arrangements with the bank to keep it so Tony could get to work when he was on the night shift. Tony's employer lent him the money and will deduct payments from his wages.

COMPLEXITIES OF OVERINDEBTEDNESS

The case study, "Debt Problems of a Blended Family," illustrates how interconnected family relations and financial matters can become. None of the alternatives identified appears to be a perfect solution, forcing the family to look for the least costly option.

DEBT PROBLEMS OF A BLENDED FAMILY

When the mail brought Robert a summons to appear in family court regarding arrears in his support payments, it was the last straw. He persuaded Denise that they had better get some help.

Robert and Denise were obviously feeling very overburdened and stressed by their financial situation when they approached the credit counselling agency. They were considering separating. In addition to their debt problems, Denise's recurring medical problem had flared up again and the school principal had called about some serious problems Denise's son, Tim, was having at school. Denise has been missing a fair amount of work recently and Robert's boss has told him to do something about his personal problems. It was apparent to the counsellor that the family needed relief from their financial problems soon.

The counsellor asked the couple to outline their family situation as necessary background for any new plans. Denise and Robert explained that they had been living common-law for several years, and were caring for Denise's 12-year-old son from a previous marriage. Robert, who had also been married before, was ordered by the court to make support payments of $1200 per month to his ex-wife for the support of their 3 teenage children. These children spend every other weekend with Denise and Robert, as well as much of the summer. Both Robert and Denise resent having to make such large support payments; Denise feels that she works for Robert's ex-wife. To aggravate matters, Denise's ex-husband is $2400 behind in support payments to her as he rarely sends his $300-a-month payments.

When Robert and his wife separated two-and-a-half years before, he had to assume their debts of approximately $12 000 ($7000 for the car and $5000 on charge accounts) because she went on long-term social assistance.

Anxious to establish her own credit rating after her separation, Denise borrowed $5000 to buy a car with her elderly parents as co-signers. Denise still owes about $3500 on that loan and has another $2500 in credit card debt. Cash advances on Robert's credit cards and loans from her family to keep up their commitments have added another $6500 to their debts.

Their resources for financial aid were exhausted months ago and now creditors are calling both Robert and Denise at work about their delinquent payments. Robert has received a summons to appear in family court regarding the $1050 owing in support payments. The arrears occurred when Denise was laid off earlier in the year. The only payment that is up-to-date is Denise's bank loan that her parents co-signed. She says that she would starve before she would let her parents use their old age pension to pay that debt.

Before the counsellor could help the couple look at possible solutions to their problems, everyone needed to have a clearer picture of their financial position. The counsellor's assessment revealed the following.

BALANCE SHEET

Assets

Small bank account, two cars, household furnishings	$9 500	
Support arrears owed to Denise	2 400	
Total Assets		$11 900

Liabilities

Robert's old debts	$12 000	
Robert's support payments in arrears	1 050	
Denise's loan	3 500	
Robert's current debts	6 500	
Total Liabilities		$23 050

Net Worth   –$11 150

MONTHLY CASH FLOW

Income		$3 022
Expenses		
Net living expenses	2 286	
Robert's support payments	1 200	
Consumer debt payments		
Charge accounts, credit cards	675	
Bank loans	502	

Total Expenses $4663

Deficit   –$1641

The counsellor helped the couple to look objectively at their situation, and together they drew up the following possible solutions.

1. **Both seek legal recourse regarding support payments in arrears.** Denise might be successful in obtaining a form of garnishee for support payments and those in arrears. This could increase the family's income by at least $300 a month. Robert could apply to the family court for a reduction in support payments, but it was unlikely that a judge would be sympathetic to his situation.

2. **Find cheaper living accommodation.** Robert and Denise are renting a 4-bedroom townhouse so there will be space for Robert's children when they come to visit. They could reduce their housing expenses by at least $300 a month if they moved into a 2-bedroom apartment. However, they would be very cramped when Robert's children came to stay.

3. **Consolidate their debts.** Charge account and credit card interest rates are usually higher than consumer loans. A consolidation loan might reduce their monthly debt load and the total amount owed. Since the couple had a negative net worth, it was doubtful that they could find a lender willing to give them a loan for the total owed.

4. **Arrange a debt repayment program** This may be done through a governmental or social agency and would allow the couple to repay their debts with more manageable monthly payments, over a longer period of time. There were risks involved in this choice. If the *pro rata* share on Denise's bank loan was less than the contractual amount, Denise's parents might be asked by the bank to make up the deficit. Unless interest concessions were negotiated, the total debt could increase substantially through accrued interest charges. It is possible that a creditor might decide to exercise rights to security, and thus take possession of household chattels or a car. And last, but not necessarily least, the family would have to make changes in their lifestyle to reduce living expenses, and exert considerable self-discipline over approximately four years for the program to be a success.

5. **Declare bankruptcy.** This would relieve the family of their monthly debt burden, with the exception of support arrears. They would, however, undoubtedly lose some of their possessions. There is also the stigma attached to bankruptcy and the limit it may place on the ability of an individual or family to get credit in the future. Denise's elderly parents would, no doubt, be forced to take over her bank loan if she were to file for bankruptcy.

What do you think they should do?

Summary

People may become overindebted through circumstances beyond their control that reduce the stream of income, or through careless and impulsive use of credit. There are those in our society who do not have the necessary expertise to handle all the easy credit that is offered to them. Anyone who becomes overindebted will find that they begin to have much more frequent contact with creditors who will use every possible tactic to collect the debts. A debtor in this situation has several options to consider, including negotiation with the creditors, obtaining a consolidation loan, going to a credit counsellor, or applying for insolvency protection under the Bankruptcy and Insolvency Act, either with a consumer proposal or a declaration of bankruptcy.

Vocabulary Review

administrator of proposals (p. 513)

bankruptcy (p. 510)

consolidation loan (p. 515)

consumer proposal (p. 510)

discharge from bankruptcy (p. 510)

official receiver (p. 513)

overindebtedness (p. 499)

trustee in bankruptcy (p. 513)

Problems

1. Examine Figure 17.1 to find if there is any relation between changes in the bankruptcy rate and the recessions of 1981–82 and 1991–92.

2. Refer to the case studies: "A Debt Repayment Plan" and "Bankruptcy or Asset Liquidation?"

   (a) In both instances, the families were referred to a credit counselling service. Which aspects of these cases were similar and which were different?

   (b) Do you think Sheila should file for bankruptcy, or try for a negotiated settlement? What are the pros and cons of each alternative?

   (c) How does a credit counsellor arrive at an expenditure plan for an overcommitted debtor?

   (d) Do you think Michael and Susan should continue to make their debt payments to the agency for four years, or do you think they should assume responsibility for their financial affairs before that time?

   (e) What would be the consequences for Susan and Michael if they failed to maintain the repayment schedule established by the agency?

3. Some books suggest that a debtor arrange a prorate or debt pooling plan directly with his or her creditors, without the use of a counselling agency. For whom would this work? What problems do you see arising?

4.

THE NOVICE COUNSELLOR

My first assignment in a student counselling practicum involved Glen and Mary. An administrator for the local housing authority wanted me to visit them because they had fallen behind in their rent payments. I made my first call at their house, confident that with a bit of help from me, this family would soon find itself able to cope with its financial problems.

When I arrived at their home at the appointed time, Mary was out shopping but returned within the hour. This friendly woman, in her mid-30s, was most cooperative, telling me that her husband was employed at a local factory, that she did part-time work at a nursing home, and that they have three children between the ages of 5 and 13. During this interview, I tried to determine the actual amount of their debts, but Mary was very vague about the amounts.

My second visit was very pleasant and Mary made every attempt to answer my questions. However, it appeared that she really did not know much about their financial situation. She wasn't sure what her husband's usual take-home pay was, but we made an estimate of their main debts, which were about $14 000 in total.

I was astonished to find two large television sets in the midst of a rather poorly furnished living room. Mary said they were both quite new and in working condition, and that they had bought the first one about a year ago and the second one last month. She said "The man that sold them to us is a very good friend of ours and whenever he gets a really good deal he calls us and we go down and look at it. He is awfully nice about letting us pay for the televisions when we can."

When I looked at the contracts for their television sets, I realized that they were paying a substantial amount of credit charges. I mentioned this to Mary and she was most surprised because she didn't realize that her friend was charging them anything extra. She said they are paying them off fairly quickly because every so often they use Glen's whole paycheque for some of the television debt. When I asked what they did about their other debts on these occasions, Mary said that frequently they let hydro, rent, and telephone bills accumulate for a few months. As we talked about their debts it became obvious that Mary really had no understanding of credit contracts or credit costs.

During the period of my visits to this household, Glen absolutely refused to meet me, although I was willing to go when he would be at home. I discovered that they have two cars although Mary doesn't drive. The whole family enjoys going out to eat once or twice a week, and Glen usually meets a friend to have a few drinks at their club every week.

My visits ended without meeting the husband, and with the wife repeatedly stating that unless Glen agreed to make some changes there was very little that she could do. I learned later that they will probably be evicted from their low-rental townhouse. From this experience, I realize that solving financial problems is more complicated than I had thought, and that simply providing this family with information would not change much. This particular couple did not seem anxious to make a change, and until they are motivated to review their goals and values in light of their resources, a counsellor cannot be of help. This experience was obviously more beneficial for me than for the family.

    (a) Why was the counsellor so unsuccessful?

    (b) Could a more experienced counsellor have assisted this family? What would you have done?

    (c) What changes would be necessary to improve this family's success in managing their finances?

5. Refer to "The Debt Problems of a Blended Family."

    (a) Do you think this family should declare bankruptcy? What would be some advantages for them?

    (b) Can they afford the cost of bankruptcy?

    (c) Will the creditors get anything at all?

    (d) Will they lose their household furnishings?

    (e) How will the bankruptcy affect their credit rating if they want another loan?

    (f) What could they have done to avoid their present predicament?

    (g) Are there other solutions to the family's financial problems that might have been discussed in a later interview? If so, what?

6. Why might a debtor choose to file a consumer proposal instead of making an assignment in bankruptcy?

7. Is it possible to be too poor to go bankrupt? What would such a person do?

8. Review the eight case studies included in this chapter and, from the information given, try to identify causes of their overindebtedness. How many of the reasons suggested by Wally Clare apply in each case? Refer to the section "Why Debtors Default."

REFERENCES

BOOKS

BENNETT, FRANK. *Bankruptcy and Insolvency Act with Draft Regulations 1992.* Toronto: CCH Canadian Limited, 1992, 334 pp. A technical reference.

LIPTRAP, PATRICIA R. and AMY E.G. COUSINEAU. *Manual for Credit Counsellors.* Second Edition. Grimsby, Ontario: Ontario Association of Credit Counselling Services, 1983. Provides guidance for credit counsellors. Available from the Association at Box 189, Grimsby, Ontario, L3M 4E3.

PARKER, ALLAN A. *Credit, Debt, and Bankruptcy.* Eighth Edition. Vancouver: International Self-Counsel Press, 1990, 128 pp. A handbook on Canadian credit law for credit users.

TOPHAM, MARK and PATRICIA LIPTRAP. *Guidelines and Standards for Credit Counsellors.* Second Edition. Grimsby, Ontario: Ontario Association for Credit Counselling Services, 1988, 64 pp. A listing of professional standards for credit counselling in Ontario. Available from the Association at Box 189, Grimsby, Ontario, L3M 4E3.

VAN ARSDALE, MARY G. *A Guide to Family Financial Counseling, Credit, Debt and Money Management.* Homewood, Illinois: Dow Jones-Irwin, 1982, 381 pp. Provides guidance for financial counsellors on such topics as building the relationship, obtaining client information, diagnosis, generating alternatives, and evaluation of results.

YOUNG, JENNIFER. *Small Claims Court Guide for Ontario.* Seventh Edition. Vancouver: International Self-Counsel Press, 1992, 176 pp. A complete manual to proceeding with or defending an action in small claims court.

ZINKHOFER, FRED. *Small Claims Court Guide for Alberta.* Fourth Edition. Vancouver: International Self-Counsel Press, 1985, 122 pp. A complete manual for proceeding with or defending an action in small claims court.

Appendix

FIGURE 15.1 SAMPLE MORTGAGE CONTRACT

Province of Ontario

Charge/Mortgage of Land
Form 2 — Land Registration Reform Act, 1984

Canada Trust   B

FOR OFFICE USE ONLY

New Property Identifiers

Additional: See Schedule ☐

Executions

Additional: See Schedule ☐

(1) Registry ☒ Land Titles ☐	(2) Page 1 of **3** pages

(3) Property Identifier(s)   Block   Property   Additional: See Schedule ☐

(4) **Principal Amount**

--ONE HUNDRED THOUSAND--   Dollars $ 100,000.00

(5) **Description**

Part of Lot Number One, Concession 15, Township of Middleton, County of Wellington.

(6) **This Document Contains**   (a) Redescription New Easement Plan/Sketch ☐   (b) Schedule for: Description ☒   Additional Parties ☐   Other ☒

(7) **Interest/Estate Charged**
Fee Simple

(8) **Standard Charge Terms** — The parties agree to be bound by the provisions in Standard Charge Terms filed as number **8544** and the Chargor(s) hereby acknowledge(s) receipt of a copy of these terms.

(9) **Payment Provisions**

(a) Principal Amount $ 100,000.00	(b) Interest Rate 8.75 % per annum	(c) Calculation Period **semi-annual not in advance**

	Y	M	D				Y	M	D
(d) Interest Adjustment Date	94	02	15	(e) Payment Date and Period	15th of each month	(f) First Payment Date	94	03	15
(g) Last Payment Date	99	02	15	(h) Amount of Each Payment	Eight hundred seventy three 90/100 Dollars $ 873.90				
(i) Balance Due Date	99	02	15	(j) Insurance	Full replacement cost Dollars $				

(10) **Additional Provisions**

Continued on Schedule ☐

FIGURE 15.1 (CONTINUED)

(11) Chargor(s) The chargor hereby charges the land to the chargee and certifies that the chargor is at least eighteen years old and that

I am a spouse. The person consenting below is my spouse.

The chargor(s) acknowledge(s) receipt of a true copy of this charge.

Name(s)	Signature(s)	Date of Signature Y M D
MCCARTNEY, Paul C.		

(12) Spouse(s) of Chargor(s) I hereby consent to this transaction.

Name(s)	Signature(s)	Date of Signature Y M D
ING-MCCARTNEY, Louise S.		

(13) Chargor(s) Address for Service

12 Maple Drive, Fergus, Ontario, N1F 4H6

(14) Chargee(s)

CANADA TRUSTCO MORTGAGE COMPANY

(15) Chargee(s) Address for Service

Wyndham Street, Guelph, Ontario

(16) Assessment Roll Number of Property

Cty.	Mun.	Map	Sub.	Par.
32	08	020	011	20300

	Fees	
FOR OFFICE USE ONLY	Registration Fee	25.00
	Total	25.00

(17) Municipal Address of Property

12 Maple Drive
Fergus, Ontario
N1F 4H6

(18) Document Prepared by:

Smith and Smith
100 Douglas Street
Guelph, Ontario

05-359 (1285)

FIGURE 15.1 (Continued)

SCHEDULE 1 A

1 TO 5 YEAR

All terms that are defined in the Standard Charge Terms referred to in box 8 of the attached Charge/Mortgage of Land have the same meaning when used in this Schedule.

PAYMENT PROVISIONS

Interest

Interest is payable on the balance of the principal amount outstanding from time to time as follows:

(a) from the date that any part of the principal amount is advanced until __**February 15**__ , 19 **99** , interest is payable at the rate of **8.75** percent (**8.75** %) per annum, calculated half-yearly, not in advance, before and after default, demand, maturity and judgment; and

(b) after **February 15** , 19 **99** , interest is payable at the rate which, on any day, is the greater of the rate specified in (a) and Canada Trust's Prime Demand Rate on such day, calculated half-yearly, not in advance, before and after default, demand, maturity and judgment. Canada Trust's Prime Demand Rate is subject to change from time to time without notice to you.

Interest is also payable at the rate payable on the principal amount on any amount not paid when due (including interest) and on any judgment. If interest on an overdue amount is not paid within six months of the date the amount was due, such interest will become due and payable at the end of such six months and, therefore, will itself bear interest at the same rate thereafter.

Payments

Canada Trust may, at its option, deduct from any advance of the principal amount the interest that has accrued on previous advances or any other amount payable to it. The principal amount and accrued interest will be payable by monthly instalments of $ __**873.90**__ on the __**15 th**__ day of each month beginning __**March 15**__ , 19 **94** , and ending __**February 15**__ , 19 **99** , on which date the balance of the principal amount and accrued interest become payable on demand. Any demand for payment made by Canada Trust may be delivered personally to you or may be mailed, postage prepaid, to your most recent address appearing in Canada Trust's records relating to the mortgage. ANY SUCH DEMAND SHALL BE CONCLUSIVELY DEEMED TO BE GIVEN AND RECEIVED ON THE DATE OF DELIVERY OR THE FIFTH DAY AFTER MAILING. All amounts paid to Canada Trust will be applied first to accrued interest and then to the principal amount, except that, if you fail to comply with any of your obligations under the mortgage, Canada Trust may apply any amount it receives to any amount secured by mortgage.

Weekly, Bi-Weekly or Semi-Monthly Payments

Canada Trust has agreed that instead of paying the regular monthly instalments stated above, you may, on written notice to Canada Trust, select one of the following payment options:

A. WEEKLY PAYMENTS equal to 1/4 of the regular monthly instalment stated above, payable on the 7th day after the final advance of the principal amount and on every 7th day thereafter,

or

B. BI-WEEKLY PAYMENTS equal to 1/2 of the regular monthly instalment stated above, payable on the 14th day after the final advance of the principal amount and on every 14th day thereafter,

or

C. SEMI-MONTHLY PAYMENTS equal to 1/2 of the regular monthly instalment stated above, payable on the 15th day and the last day of each month beginning with the first such day after the final advance of the principal amount,

until the balance of the principal amount and accrued interest become payable on demand.

However, if at any time your payments are in arrears in an amount which equals or exceeds the regular monthly instalment stated above, this privilege of making payments weekly, bi-weekly or semi-monthly will, at Canada Trust's option, cease to apply and you must pay the regular monthly instalment stated above on the regular monthly instalment date stated above until the balance of the principal amount and accrued interest become payable on demand.

FIGURE 15.1 (CONTINUED)

ADDITIONAL PROVISIONS

Prepayments

During each year of the mortgage (that is, each twelve-month period starting on the day the final advance of the principal amount is made or on an anniverary of that date), you may (provided you have complied with all of your obligations under the mortgage):

(a)   make one or more prepayments, which in aggregate total not more than fifteen percent (15%) of the principal amount; and/or

(b)   once in each year, increase the amount of your regular weekly, bi-weekly, semi-monthly or monthly payment by up to fifteen percent (15%) of the amount of such payment established above.

You may not, in any such year, prepay more than 15% of the principal amount or increase your regular payment by more than 15%, whether or not you prepaid less than 15% or increased a regular payment by less than 15% in previous years.

Early Renewal

If you have complied with all of your obligations under the mortgage, and Canada Trust receives a written notice (the "notice") that you wish to extend the period during which the balance of the principal amount is payable in regular instalments for an additional term commencing on a date (the "effective date") specified in the notice (which date may not be more than 12 months before the day your last regular payment under the mortgage is due), then such period will be so extended on the effective date. In such event, the rate at which interest is then payable under the mortgage (the "then existing mortgage rate") will be changed, commencing the effective date, to Canada Trust's rate on such date for mortgages having a term equal to the additional term specified in the notice (the "new rate"). The provisions of this paragraph will apply to a notice only if Canada Trust is, on the effective date, offering mortgages having a term equal to the additional term specified in the notice and only if you pay, prior to the effective date, an interest differential adjustment in an amount which is calculated in accordance with Canada Trust's then usual procedures and is based on the difference between the new rate and the then existing mortgage rate. You may, on the effective date, prepay any portion of the principal amount of the mortgage and you may also reduce the mortgage's remaining amortization period by specifying the reduced period in the notice. The amount of your regular weekly, bi-weekly, semi-monthly or monthly payment will be changed, commencing on the effective date, to the amount specified by Canada Trust as approximately reflecting the new rate, the balance of the principal amount and accrued interest outstanding on the effective date and the mortgage's remaining amortization period (as reduced, if applicable, in accordance with the notice).

Sale of Property

If you enter into a genuine agreement to sell the property to a person with whom you deal at arm's length, then you may pay off the mortgage from the proceeds of the sale provided you pay us, in addition, the greater of:

(a)   three months interest on the balance of the principal amount then outstanding, calculated at the rate that interest is then payable under the mortgage; and

(b)   an interest differential adjustment in an amount which is calculated in accordance with Canada Trust's then usual procedures and is based on the difference between (i) Canada Trust's then current rate for mortgages having a term equal to the remaining period during which the balance of the principal amount is payable in regular monthly instalments and (ii) the rate at which interest is then payable under the mortgage.

No Other Right of Prepayment

You shall have no right of premature repayment except as provided above. You agree that any right of prepayment given to you by the provisions of any present or future law (including the rights under Section 10 of the Interest Act and any similar provincial law) will not apply to the mortgage and you waive any such right.

FIGURE 15.1 (Continued)

Mortgage Portability

If you pay off the mortgage in full in connection with a genuine sale of the property to a person with whom you deal at arm's length and complete the purchase of a new residence within sixty days of paying off the mortgage, Canada Trust will, on application by you but subject to (c) below, provide financing for the purchase of your new residence on the security of a mortgage (the "new mortgage") on such residence, on the following basis:

(a)   if the amount to be advanced under the new mortgage (the "new principal") does not exceed the balance of the principal amount outstanding under the mortgage immediately before the mortgage was paid off (the "portable amount"), then, for the period during which the portable amount would have been payable in regular instalments if the mortgage had not been paid off, (rounded to the nearest full year) interest will be payable under the new mortgage at the last rate at which interest was payable under the mortgage and, at the end of such period, the balance of the portable amount then outstanding will become payable on demand and will bear interest at the rate determined in accordance with paragraph (b) above under the heading "Interest";

(b)   If the new principal exceeds the portable amount, then at the time you apply for the new mortgage, a blended rate and term will be determined using Canada Trust's then current procedure for blended rate and term financing.

(c)   Canada Trust's then current policies, procedures and documentation will apply to the new mortgage (including its terms) and your application for it and, in particular, Canada Trust's obligation to provide mortgage financing will be subject to your application meeting its approval criteria in effect at the time you make the application and you must pay Canada Trust's then standard processing fees, all legal and appraisal fees and all other expenses incurred in connection with the new mortgage.

FIGURE 15.1 (CONTINUED)

FORM 6

LAND REGISTRATION REFORM ACT, 1984

SET OF STANDARD CHARGE TERMS

FILED BY

FILING NO. 8544

THE CANADA TRUST COMPANY

— and —

CANADA TRUSTCO MORTGAGE COMPANY

The following set of standard charge terms shall be deemed to be included in every charge in which the set is referred to by its filing number, as provided in section 9 of the Act.

1. In this set of standard charge terms, "Mortgage form" means a Charge/Mortgage of Land which refers to the filing number of this set of standard charge terms and all schedules to it. "Mortgage" means the Mortgage Form and this set of standard charge terms, and includes the mortgage as amended from time to time. "You" and "your" refer to each person who signs the Mortgage Form as chargor and their heirs, executors, administrators, successors and assigns and "Canada Trust" refers to the chargee named in the Mortgage Form and its successors and assigns. "Principal amount" means the principal amount set out in the Mortgage Form and "property" means the land described in the Mortgage Form and all buildings, improvements and other structures now or later on it.

2. You own the property and have the right to charge it in favour of Canada Trust in accordance with the terms of the mortgage. Except as you have advised Canada Trust in writing, there are no mortgages, charges, liens or other encumbrances or claims on the property.

3. By signing the Mortgage Form, you agree to make the payments as and when required by it and to perform and observe all of your other obligations under the mortgage, and you charge all of your present and future interest in the property as security for the payment of all of amounts you are required to pay under the mortgage and the performance of all of your other obligations under it. However, Canada Trust is under no obligation to advance money to you even if the Mortgage Form is signed and registered and whether or not any money has previously been advanced. If more than one person signs the Mortgage Form, each is liable and all are jointly liable under the mortgage.

4. You agree not to demolish or make any major alterations, improvements or additions to any part of the property without Canada Trust's written consent. You agree to keep the property in good condition and repair and not to do, fail to do or permit anything to be done that might diminish its value. Canada Trust may enter and inspect the property and may (but does not have to) make and pay for any repairs it considers necessary.

5. You will pay all taxes assessed against the property and provide Canada Trust with evidence of such payment and with all tax bills, receipts, notices of assessment and other notices relating to property taxes. Canada Trust may (but does not have to) pay such taxes either before or after they are due. If you are required to make monthly payments under the mortgage, Canada Trust may, at its option, estimate the amount of taxes for the year in which case you will pay one-twelfth of the estimated taxes, and one-twelfth of any overdue taxes, to Canada Trust along with each monthly payment. If property taxes have or will become payable in the calendar year in which you are to receive the balance of the money advanced on the security of the mortgage, Canada Trust may pay such taxes and deduct the amount paid from the final advance.

FIGURE 15.1 (Continued)

6.   You will keep the property insured with an insurance company and for an amount acceptable to Canada Trust against loss or damage caused by fire, against other risks usually covered by fire insurance policies and against those risks requested by Canada Trust. You will provide Canada Trust with evidence that you have obtained the necessary insurance and, at least ten days before any insurance policy expires, evidence that the insurance coverage has been continued. If you do not, Canada Trust may (but does not have to) insure the property and pay the premiums. By signing the Mortgage Form, you transfer to Canada Trust your right to receive the proceeds of any insurance on the property, and Canada Trust may apply them to the amount you owe whether or not that amount is then due. Every policy of insurance on the property must include a mortgage clause acceptable to Canada Trust stating that the proceeds are payable to it.

7.   If you sell, transfer, dispose of, lease or otherwise deal with all or part of the property (or agree to do so), then Canada Trust may, at its option, require you to immediately pay all amounts payable under the mortgage.

8.   Canada Trust may pay or satisfy any existing or future mortgage, charge, lien or other encumbrance or claim against the property and may pay the fees and expenses of any receiver or of any real estate broker, realtor or agency (including Canada Trust Realtor) appointed or retained by Canada Trust in connection with the mortgage.

9.   You will immediately pay Canada Trust all amounts it is permitted to pay under the mortgage and all expenses (including legal costs as between a solicitor and his or her own client, allowances and expenses for the time and expense of Canada Trust employees, and management, real estate or leasing fees for services performed by Canada Trust charged at Canada Trust's normal rates for such services) that Canada Trust incurs in investigating title, evaluating the property, registering the Mortgage Form and any related documents, collecting the amounts secured by the mortgage, taking and keeping possession of and managing the property and taking any other proceedings or exercising any of its other rights under the mortgage. You will also pay interest at the rate set out on page 2 of the Mortgage Form on all such amounts and expenses from the date Canada Trust paid the amount or incurred the expense.

10.   If you fail to (i) make any payment required by the mortgage, (ii) comply with any of your other obligations under the mortgage, (iii) comply with any of your obligations under any charge which is entitled to priority over the mortgage or (iv) immediately discharge

any construction lien registered against the property, or if any statement contained in paragraph 2 above or any other part of the mortgage is untrue, then all amounts secured by the mortgage will, at Canada Trust's option and without notice to you, become payable immediately. In the event of any such failure, Canada Trust may do any one or more of the following, in any order and at any time:

A.   Canada Trust may enter on and take possession of all or any part of the property, repair or complete the construction of any buildings or improvements on the property, collect any rents and otherwise protect or manage the property.

B.   Canada Trust may sell and/or lease all or any part of the property after giving any notice required by law. For this purpose, Canada Trust may list the property with and sell or lease the property through a licensed real estate broker, realtor or agent (including Canada Trust Realtor). Any sale or lease may be for cash or credit (or partly for cash and partly for credit) and Canada Trust will only be accountable for proceeds received by it in cash. Canada Trust may cancel or change the terms of any sale or lease and will not be responsible for any resulting loss.

C.   Canada Trust may commence court proceedings to foreclose your right, title and equity of redemption to and in the property or to take possession of, sell, lease or otherwise deal with the property.

D.   Canada Trust may sue you for any amount secured by the mortgage. Any judgment Canada Trust obtains will provide that interest is payable at the rate payable under the mortgage and will not affect your obligations under the mortgage.

E.   Canada Trust may apply any amount paid to it for property taxes in satisfaction of any amount secured by the mortgage.

F.   Canada Trust may also exercise any other rights it may have.

You will not interfere with Canada Trust's possession of the property nor with the possession of anyone to whom it is sold or leased.

FIGURE 15.1 (CONTINUED)

11. Should you breach your obligations under the mortgage, Canada Trust does not have to exercise any rights it may have under the mortgage and may decide not to do so, but no such decision will be considered to have been made unless it is communicated to you in writing. Any decision by Canada Trust not to exercise its rights as a result of any particular breach of your obligations shall not be considered a waiver of compliance with any of your obligations in the future nor excuse any other breach.

12. Canada Trust's rights against you or any other person will not be affected by (i) any extension of the time for making payments under the mortgage or any consent to a change in the amount or frequency of payments or in the rate of interest payable under the mortgage or in any other provision of the mortgage given by Canada Trust to you or to anyone to whom the property is transferred or (ii) the release of any part of the property from the mortgage.

13. Canada Trust's charge on the property will terminate when all amounts secured by the mortgage have been paid in full and all other obligations secured by the mortgage have been performed. Within a reasonable time thereafter, Canada Trust will prepare or execute a discharge or, if you request, an assignment of the mortgage. You will pay Canada Trust's usual administrative fee for preparing, reviewing or signing either document and all of its related legal and other expenses.

14. The mortgage is in addition to and does not replace any other security Canada Trust may hold. Canada Trust may exercise its remedies under the mortgage or any other security in any order it chooses. Any judgment or recovery under the mortgage or under any other security shall not affect Canada Trust's right to realize upon the mortgage or any other security.

15. The mortgage may be amended from time to time pursuant to a written agreement between you and Canada Trust, and such amendments may extend the time for payment and change the frequency of payments or the rate of interest payable under the mortgage. Whether or not there are any subsequent encumbrances at the time of any such amendment, it will not be necessary to register the amendment on title in order to retain priority for the mortgage as amended over any instrument registered after the mortgage.

16. You will sign any document and do any other act or thing reasonably requested by Canada Trust to carry out the intent of the mortgage. You will tell Canada Trust if there is a change in your marital status or if you sell the property so that Canada Trust will be kept fully informed at all times of the name(s) and adddress(es) of the owner(s) of the property and of the spouse of each such owner.

17. The covenants deemed to be included in the mortgage by the Land Registration Reform Act, 1984 are excluded from the mortgage.

18. Clause 2 of this paragraph 18 only applies if you now or subsequently rent all or part of the property to a third party.

    (1) You agree that the following, whether now or later on the property, will be considered to be affixed to and to form part of the property: all fences, aerials, heating, lighting, ventilating and air conditioning apparatus, elevators and plant and machinery, whether movable or stationary, together with all gear, connections, appliances, gas pipes, wiring, gas, plumbing and electrical fixtures and fittings, cooling and refrigeration equipment, radiators and covers, fixed mirrors, window blinds, fitted blinds, storm doors, storm windows, window screens and screen doors, shutters and awnings, wall-to-wall floor covering and growing things.

    (2) If, pursuant to paragraph 10 above or any other provision of the mortgage, all amounts secured by the mortgage may become, or become, payable immediately at Canada Trust's option, then Canada Trust may do any one or more of the following, in any order and at any time, in addition to all other things it is permitted to do under the mortgage:

        A. Canada Trust may appoint in writing a receiver (which term wherever used in the mortgage includes a receiver and manager) or a new receiver to replace a receiver previously appointed to do any or all of the things Canada Trust is permitted to do under the mortgage. Any receiver appointed will be considered your agent and all actions taken by the receiver will be considered to be your actions. Nothing done by the receiver puts Canada Trust in possession of the property nor makes it accountable for any money not received by it. The receiver may apply any income received from the property to pay any amount Canada Trust is permitted to pay under the mortgage (including the receiver's fees and expenses) and the balance will be paid to Canada Trust to reduce the amount secured by the mortgage, whether or not such amount is then due.

        B. Canada Trust may distrain or attorn rents for overdue interest, principal or other payments and for overdue taxes (including interest and penalties payable because the taxes are overdue).

TABLE 15.4   Mortgage Amortization Schedule

Loan	$50000.00	Rate %11.0000		Compounded Semi-Annually	Term 300
Payment	$ 481.26	Paid Monthly		Factor 0.0089633939	

No.	Due Date	Interest	Principal	Payment	Accumulated Interest	Balance
1	0 0	448.17	33.09	481.26	448.17	49966.91
2	0 0	447.87	33.39	481.26	896.04	49933.52
3	0 0	447.57	33.69	481.26	1343.62	49899.84
4	0 0	447.27	33.99	481.26	1790.89	49865.85
5	0 0	446.97	34.29	481.26	2237.86	49831.56
6	0 0	446.66	34.60	481.26	2684.52	49796.96
7	0 0	446.35	34.91	481.26	3130.87	49762.05
8	0 0	446.04	35.22	481.26	3576.90	49726.82
9	0 0	445.72	35.54	481.26	4022.62	49691.28
10	0 0	445.40	35.86	481.26	4468.03	49655.43
11	0 0	445.08	36.18	481.26	4913.11	49619.25
12	0 0	444.76	36.50	481.26	5357.86	49582.74
13	0 0	444.43	36.83	481.26	5802.29	49545.91
14	0 0	444.10	37.16	481.26	6246.39	49508.75
15	0 0	443.77	37.49	481.26	6690.16	49471.26
16	0 0	443.43	37.83	481.26	7133.59	49433.43
17	0 0	443.09	38.17	481.26	7576.68	49395.26
18	0 0	442.75	38.51	481.26	8019.43	49356.75
19	0 0	442.40	38.86	481.26	8461.83	49317.89
20	0 0	442.06	39.20	481.26	8903.89	49278.69
21	0 0	441.70	39.56	481.26	9345.59	49239.13
22	0 0	441.35	39.91	481.26	9786.94	49199.22
23	0 0	440.99	40.27	481.26	10227.94	49158.96
24	0 0	440.63	40.63	481.26	10668.57	49118.33
25	0 0	440.27	40.99	481.26	11108.83	49077.33
26	0 0	439.90	41.36	481.26	11548.73	49035.97
27	0 0	439.53	41.73	481.26	11988.26	48994.24
28	0 0	439.15	42.11	481.26	12427.42	48952.14
29	0 0	438.78	42.48	481.26	12866.19	48909.65
30	0 0	438.40	42.86	481.26	13304.59	48866.79
31	0 0	438.01	43.25	481.26	13742.60	48823.54
32	0 0	437.62	43.64	481.26	14180.23	48779.91
33	0 0	437.23	44.03	481.26	14617.46	48735.88
34	0 0	436.84	44.42	481.26	15054.30	48691.46
35	0 0	436.44	44.82	481.26	15490.74	48646.64
36	0 0	436.04	45.22	481.26	15926.78	48601.42

This schedule has been processed with interest calculated not in advance.

TABLE 15.4 (CONTINUED)

Loan Payment	$48601.42 $ 481.26	Rate %11.0000 Paid Monthly		Compounded Semi-Annually Factor 0.0089633939		Term 300
No.	Due Date	Interest	Principal	Payment	Accumulated Interest	Balance
37	0 0	435.63	45.63	481.26	16362.41	48555.79
38	0 0	435.22	46.04	481.26	16797.64	48509.76
39	0 0	434.81	46.45	481.26	17232.45	48463.31
40	0 0	434.40	46.86	481.26	17666.85	48416.45
41	0 0	433.98	47.28	481.26	18100.82	48369.16
42	0 0	433.55	47.71	481.26	18534.37	48321.45
43	0 0	433.12	48.14	481.26	18967.50	48273.32
44	0 0	432.69	48.57	481.26	19400.19	48224.75
45	0 0	432.26	49.00	481.26	19832.45	48175.75
46	0 0	431.82	49.44	481.26	20264.27	48126.31
47	0 0	431.38	49.88	481.26	20695.64	48076.42
48	0 0	430.93	50.33	481.26	21126.57	48026.09
49	0 0	430.48	50.78	481.26	21557.05	47975.31
50	0 0	430.02	51.24	481.26	21987.07	47924.07
51	0 0	429.56	51.70	481.26	22416.63	47872.37
52	0 0	429.10	52.16	481.26	22845.73	47820.21
53	0 0	428.63	52.63	481.26	23274.36	47767.58
54	0 0	428.16	53.10	481.26	23702.52	47714.48
55	0 0	427.68	53.58	481.26	24130.20	47660.90
56	0 0	427.20	54.06	481.26	24557.41	47606.85
57	0 0	426.72	54.54	481.26	24984.13	47552.31
58	0 0	426.23	55.03	481.26	25410.36	47497.28
59	0 0	425.74	55.52	481.26	25836.09	47441.75
60	0 0	425.24	56.02	481.26	26261.33	47385.73
61	0 0	424.74	56.52	481.26	26686.07	47329.21
62	0 0	424.23	57.03	481.26	27110.30	47272.18
63	0 0	423.72	57.54	481.26	27534.02	47214.64
64	0 0	423.20	58.06	481.26	27957.22	47156.58
65	0 0	422.68	58.58	481.26	28379.90	47098.00
66	0 0	422.16	59.10	481.26	28802.06	47038.90
67	0 0	421.63	59.63	481.26	29223.69	46979.27
68	0 0	421.09	60.17	481.26	29644.78	46919.10
69	0 0	420.55	60.71	481.26	30065.34	46858.40
70	0 0	420.01	61.25	481.26	30485.35	46797.15
71	0 0	419.46	61.80	481.26	30904.81	46735.35
72	0 0	418.91	62.35	481.26	31323.72	46673.00

This schedule has been processed with interest calculated not in advance.

TABLE 15.4 (CONTINUED)

Loan	$46673.00	Rate %11.0000		Compounded Semi-Annually	Term 300
Payment	$ 481.26	Paid Monthly		Factor 0.0089633939	

No.	Due Date	Interest	Principal	Payment	Accumulated Interest	Balance
73	0 0	418.35	62.91	481.26	31742.07	46610.09
74	0 0	417.78	63.48	481.26	32159.85	46546.61
75	0 0	417.22	64.04	481.26	32577.07	46482.57
76	0 0	416.64	64.62	481.26	32993.71	46417.95
77	0 0	416.06	65.20	481.26	33409.77	46352.75
78	0 0	415.48	65.78	481.26	33825.25	46286.97
79	0 0	414.89	66.37	481.26	34240.14	46220.60
80	0 0	414.29	66.97	481.26	34654.43	46153.63
81	0 0	413.69	67.57	481.26	35068.12	46086.06
82	0 0	413.09	68.17	481.26	35481.21	46017.89
83	0 0	412.48	68.78	481.26	35893.69	45949.11
84	0 0	411.86	69.40	481.26	36305.55	45879.71
85	0 0	411.24	70.02	481.26	36716.79	45809.69
86	0 0	410.61	70.65	481.26	37127.40	45739.04
87	0 0	409.98	71.28	481.26	37537.37	45667.75
88	0 0	409.34	71.92	481.26	37946.71	45595.83
89	0 0	408.69	72.57	481.26	38355.40	45523.26
90	0 0	408.04	73.22	481.26	38763.45	45450.05
91	0 0	407.39	73.87	481.26	39170.83	45376.17
92	0 0	406.72	74.54	481.26	39577.56	45301.64
93	0 0	406.06	75.20	481.26	39983.61	45226.43
94	0 0	405.38	75.88	481.26	40389.00	45150.56
95	0 0	404.70	76.56	481.26	40793.70	45074.00
96	0 0	404.02	77.24	481.26	41197.72	44996.76
97	0 0	403.32	77.94	481.26	41601.04	44918.82
98	0 0	402.63	78.63	481.26	42003.66	44840.18
99	0 0	401.92	79.34	481.26	42405.58	44760.84
100	0 0	401.21	80.05	481.26	42806.79	44680.79
101	0 0	400.49	80.77	481.26	43207.28	44600.02
102	0 0	399.77	81.49	481.26	43607.05	44518.53
103	0 0	399.04	82.22	481.26	44006.09	44436.31
104	0 0	398.30	82.96	481.26	44404.39	44353.35
105	0 0	397.56	83.70	481.26	44801.95	44269.65
106	0 0	396.81	84.45	481.26	45198.75	44185.19
107	0 0	396.05	85.21	481.26	45594.80	44099.98
108	0 0	395.29	85.97	481.26	45990.09	44014.01

This schedule has been processed with interest calculated not in advance.

TABLE 15.4 (CONTINUED)

Loan Payment	$44014.01 $ 481.26		Rate %11.0000 Paid Monthly		Compounded Semi-Annually Factor 0.0089633939		Term 300
No.	Due Date		Interest	Principal	Payment	Accumulated Interest	Balance
109	0	0	394.51	86.75	481.26	46384.60	43927.26
110	0	0	393.74	87.52	481.26	46778.34	43839.74
111	0	0	392.95	88.31	481.26	47171.29	43751.43
112	0	0	392.16	89.10	481.26	47563.45	43662.33
113	0	0	391.36	89.90	481.26	47954.82	43572.44
114	0	0	390.56	90.70	481.26	48345.37	43481.73
115	0	0	389.74	91.52	481.26	48735.12	43390.22
116	0	0	388.92	92.34	481.26	49124.04	43297.88
117	0	0	388.10	93.16	481.26	49512.14	43204.72
118	0	0	387.26	94.00	481.26	49899.40	43110.72
119	0	0	386.42	94.84	481.26	50285.82	43015.88
120	0	0	385.57	95.69	481.26	50671.38	42920.18
121	0	0	384.71	96.55	481.26	51056.09	42823.63
122	0	0	383.85	97.41	481.26	51439.94	42726.22
123	0	0	382.97	98.29	481.26	51822.91	42627.93
124	0	0	382.09	99.17	481.26	52205.00	42528.76
125	0	0	381.20	100.06	481.26	52586.20	42428.70
126	0	0	380.31	100.95	481.26	52966.51	42327.75
127	0	0	379.40	101.86	481.26	53345.91	42225.89
128	0	0	378.49	102.77	481.26	53724.40	42123.12
129	0	0	377.57	103.69	481.26	54101.96	42019.42
130	0	0	376.64	104.62	481.26	54478.60	41914.80
131	0	0	375.70	105.56	481.26	54854.30	41809.24
132	0	0	374.75	106.51	481.26	55229.05	41702.73
133	0	0	373.80	107.46	481.26	55602.85	41595.27
134	0	0	372.83	108.43	481.26	55975.68	41486.84
135	0	0	371.86	109.40	481.26	56347.55	41377.45
136	0	0	370.88	110.38	481.26	56718.43	41267.07
137	0	0	369.89	111.37	481.26	57088.32	41155.70
138	0	0	368.89	112.37	481.26	57457.22	41043.34
139	0	0	367.89	113.37	481.26	57825.11	40929.97
140	0	0	366.87	114.39	481.26	58191.98	40815.58
141	0	0	365.85	115.41	481.26	58557.82	40700.16
142	0	0	364.81	116.45	481.26	58922.63	40583.71
143	0	0	363.77	117.49	481.26	59286.40	40466.22
144	0	0	362.71	118.55	481.26	59649.12	40347.68

This schedule has been processed with interest calculated not in advance.

TABLE 15.4 (Continued)

Loan	$40347.68		Rate %11.0000		Compounded Semi-Annually		Term 300
Payment	$ 481.26		Paid Monthly		Factor 0.0089633939		

No.	Due Date	Interest	Principal	Payment	Accumulated Interest	Balance
145	0 0	361.65	119.61	481.26	60010.77	40228.07
146	0 0	360.58	120.68	481.26	60371.35	40107.39
147	0 0	359.50	121.76	481.26	60730.85	39985.63
148	0 0	358.41	122.85	481.26	61089.25	39862.77
149	0 0	357.31	123.95	481.26	61446.56	39738.82
150	0 0	356.19	125.07	481.26	61802.75	39613.75
151	0 0	355.07	126.19	481.26	62157.83	39487.57
152	0 0	353.94	127.32	481.26	62511.77	39360.25
153	0 0	352.80	128.46	481.26	62864.57	39231.79
154	0 0	351.65	129.61	481.26	63216.22	39102.18
155	0 0	350.49	130.77	481.26	63566.71	38971.41
156	0 0	349.32	131.94	481.26	63916.03	38839.47
157	0 0	348.13	133.13	481.26	64264.16	38706.34
158	0 0	346.94	134.32	481.26	64611.10	38572.02
159	0 0	345.74	135.52	481.26	64956.84	38436.50
160	0 0	344.52	136.74	481.26	65301.36	38299.76
161	0 0	343.30	137.96	481.26	65644.65	38161.79
162	0 0	342.06	139.20	481.26	65986.71	38022.59
163	0 0	340.81	140.45	481.26	66327.52	37882.14
164	0 0	339.55	141.71	481.26	66667.08	37740.44
165	0 0	338.28	142.98	481.26	67005.36	37597.46
166	0 0	337.00	144.26	481.26	67342.36	37453.20
167	0 0	335.71	145.55	481.26	67678.07	37307.65
168	0 0	334.40	146.86	481.26	68012.47	37160.79
169	0 0	333.09	148.17	481.26	68345.56	37012.62
170	0 0	331.76	149.50	481.26	68677.32	36863.12
171	0 0	330.42	150.84	481.26	69007.74	36712.28
172	0 0	329.07	152.19	481.26	69336.80	36560.08
173	0 0	327.70	153.56	481.26	69664.50	36406.52
174	0 0	326.33	154.93	481.26	69990.83	36251.59
175	0 0	324.94	156.32	481.26	70315.77	36095.27
176	0 0	323.54	157.72	481.26	70639.30	35937.54
177	0 0	322.12	159.14	481.26	70961.43	35778.41
178	0 0	320.70	160.56	481.26	71282.12	35617.84
179	0 0	319.26	162.00	481.26	71601.38	35455.84
180	0 0	317.80	163.46	481.26	71919.18	35292.38

This schedule has been processed with interest calculated not in advance.

TABLE 15.4 (CONTINUED)

Loan	$35252.38	Rate %11.0000		Compounded Semi-Annually		Term 300
Payment	$ 481.26	Paid Monthly		Factor 0.0089633939		

No.	Due Date	Interest	Principal	Payment	Accumulated Interest	Balance
181	0 0	316.34	164.92	481.26	72235.52	35127.46
182	0 0	314.86	166.40	481.26	72550.38	34961.06
183	0 0	313.37	167.89	481.26	72863.75	34793.17
184	0 0	311.86	169.40	481.26	73175.62	34623.78
185	0 0	310.35	170.91	481.26	73485.97	34452.87
186	0 0	308.81	172.45	481.26	73794.78	34280.42
187	0 0	307.27	173.99	481.26	74102.05	34106.43
188	0 0	305.71	175.55	481.26	74407.76	33930.88
189	0 0	304.14	177.12	481.26	74711.89	33753.75
190	0 0	302.55	178.71	481.26	75014.44	33575.04
191	0 0	300.95	180.31	481.26	75315.39	33394.73
192	0 0	299.33	181.93	481.26	75614.72	33212.80
193	0 0	297.70	183.56	481.26	75912.42	33029.24
194	0 0	296.05	185.21	481.26	76208.47	32844.03
195	0 0	294.39	186.87	481.26	76502.87	32657.17
196	0 0	292.72	188.54	481.26	76795.59	32468.63
197	0 0	291.03	190.23	481.26	77086.61	32278.39
198	0 0	289.32	191.94	481.26	77375.94	32086.46
199	0 0	287.60	193.66	481.26	77663.54	31892.80
200	0 0	285.87	195.39	481.26	77949.41	31697.41
201	0 0	284.12	197.14	481.26	78233.53	31500.27
202	0 0	282.35	198.91	481.26	78515.88	31301.36
203	0 0	280.57	200.69	481.26	78796.44	31100.66
204	0 0	278.77	202.49	481.26	79075.21	30898.17
205	0 0	276.95	204.31	481.26	79352.16	30693.86
206	0 0	275.12	206.14	481.26	79627.28	30487.72
207	0 0	273.27	207.99	481.26	79900.56	30279.74
208	0 0	271.41	209.85	481.26	80171.97	30069.89
209	0 0	269.53	211.73	481.26	80441.49	29858.15
210	0 0	267.63	213.63	481.26	80709.12	29644.52
211	0 0	265.72	215.54	481.26	80974.84	29428.98
212	0 0	263.78	217.48	481.26	81238.62	29211.50
213	0 0	261.83	219.43	481.26	81500.46	28992.08
214	0 0	259.87	221.39	481.26	81760.33	28770.69
215	0 0	257.88	223.38	481.26	82018.21	28547.31
216	0 0	255.88	225.38	481.26	82274.09	28321.93

This schedule has been processed with interest calculated not in advance.

TABLE 15.4 (CONTINUED)

Loan	$28321.93	Rate %11.0000		Compounded Semi-Annually		Term 300
Payment	$ 481.26	Paid Monthly		Factor 0.0089633939		

No.	Due Date	Interest	Principal	Payment	Accumulated Interest	Balance
217	0 0	253.86	227.40	481.26	82527.95	28094.53
218	0 0	251.82	229.44	481.26	82779.77	27865.09
219	0 0	249.77	231.49	481.26	83029.54	27633.60
220	0 0	247.69	233.57	481.26	83277.23	27400.03
221	0 0	245.60	235.66	481.26	83522.83	27164.37
222	0 0	243.48	237.78	481.26	83766.31	26926.59
223	0 0	241.35	239.91	481.26	84007.66	26686.68
224	0 0	239.20	242.06	481.26	84246.87	26444.63
225	0 0	237.03	244.23	481.26	84483.90	26200.40
226	0 0	234.84	246.42	481.26	84718.75	25953.99
227	0 0	232.64	248.62	481.26	84951.38	25705.36
228	0 0	230.41	250.85	481.26	85181.79	25454.51
229	0 0	228.16	253.10	481.26	85409.95	25201.41
230	0 0	225.89	255.37	481.26	85635.84	24946.04
231	0 0	223.60	257.66	481.26	85859.44	24688.38
232	0 0	221.29	259.97	481.26	86080.73	24428.41
233	0 0	218.96	262.30	481.26	86299.69	24166.11
234	0 0	216.61	264.65	481.26	86516.30	23901.46
235	0 0	214.24	267.02	481.26	86730.54	23634.44
236	0 0	211.84	269.42	481.26	86942.39	23365.03
237	0 0	209.43	271.83	481.26	87151.82	23093.20
238	0 0	206.99	274.27	481.26	87358.81	22818.93
239	0 0	204.54	276.72	481.26	87563.34	22542.20
240	0 0	202.05	279.21	481.26	87765.40	22263.00
241	0 0	199.55	281.71	481.26	87964.95	21981.29
242	0 0	197.03	284.23	481.26	88161.98	21697.06
243	0 0	194.48	286.78	481.26	88356.46	21410.28
244	0 0	191.91	289.35	481.26	88548.37	21120.93
245	0 0	189.32	291.94	481.26	88737.68	20828.98
246	0 0	186.70	294.56	481.26	88924.38	20534.42
247	0 0	184.06	297.20	481.26	89108.44	20237.22
248	0 0	181.39	299.87	481.26	89289.83	19937.35
249	0 0	178.71	302.55	481.26	89468.54	19634.80
250	0 0	175.99	305.27	481.26	89644.53	19329.53
251	0 0	173.26	308.00	481.26	89817.79	19021.53
252	0 0	170.50	310.76	481.26	89988.29	18710.77

This schedule has been processed with interest calculated not in advance.

TABLE 15.4 (CONTINUED)

Loan Payment	$18710.77 $ 481.26	Rate %11.0000 Paid Monthly		Compounded Semi-Annually Factor 0.0089633939	Term 300

No.	Due Date	Interest	Principal	Payment	Accumulated Interest	Balance
253	0 0	167.71	313.55	481.26	90156.00	18397.22
254	0 0	164.90	316.36	481.26	90320.90	18080.86
255	0 0	162.07	319.19	481.26	90482.97	17761.67
256	0 0	159.20	322.06	481.26	90642.17	17439.61
257	0 0	156.32	324.94	481.26	90798.49	17114.67
258	0 0	153.41	327.85	481.26	90951.90	16786.82
259	0 0	150.47	330.79	481.26	91102.36	16456.02
260	0 0	147.50	333.76	481.26	91249.86	16122.26
261	0 0	144.51	336.75	481.26	91394.37	15785.51
262	0 0	141.49	339.77	481.26	91535.87	15445.75
263	0 0	138.45	342.81	481.26	91674.31	15102.93
264	0 0	135.37	345.89	481.26	91809.69	14757.05
265	0 0	132.27	348.99	481.26	91941.96	14408.06
266	0 0	129.15	352.11	481.26	92071.10	14055.94
267	0 0	125.99	355.27	481.26	92197.09	13700.67
268	0 0	122.80	358.46	481.26	92319.90	13342.22
269	0 0	119.59	361.67	481.26	92439.49	12980.55
270	0 0	116.35	364.91	481.26	92555.84	12615.64
271	0 0	113.08	368.18	481.26	92668.92	12247.46
272	0 0	109.78	371.48	481.26	92778.70	11875.98
273	0 0	106.45	374.81	481.26	92885.15	11501.17
274	0 0	103.09	378.17	481.26	92988.24	11123.00
275	0 0	99.70	381.56	481.26	93087.94	10741.44
276	0 0	96.28	384.98	481.26	93184.22	10356.46
277	0 0	92.83	388.43	481.26	93277.04	9968.02
278	0 0	89.35	391.91	481.26	93366.39	9576.11
279	0 0	85.83	395.43	481.26	93452.23	9180.69
280	0 0	82.29	398.97	481.26	93534.52	8781.72
281	0 0	78.71	402.55	481.26	93613.23	8379.17
282	0 0	75.11	406.15	481.26	93688.34	7973.02
283	0 0	71.47	409.79	481.26	93759.80	7563.22
284	0 0	67.79	413.47	481.26	93827.59	7149.75
285	0 0	64.09	417.17	481.26	93891.68	6732.58
286	0 0	60.35	420.91	481.26	93952.03	6311.67
287	0 0	56.57	424.69	481.26	94008.60	5886.98
288	0 0	52.77	428.49	481.26	94061.37	5458.49

This schedule has been processed with interest calculated not in advance.

TABLE 15.4 (CONTINUED)

Loan $5458.49	Rate %11.0000	Compounded Semi-Annually	Term 300
Payment $ 481.26	Paid Monthly	Factor 0.0089633939	

No.	Due Date	Interest	Principal	Payment	Accumulated Interest	Balance
289	0 0	48.93	432.33	481.26	94110.29	5026.15
290	0 0	45.05	436.21	481.26	94155.35	4589.95
291	0 0	41.14	440.12	481.26	94196.49	4149.83
292	0 0	37.20	444.06	481.26	94233.68	3705.76
293	0 0	33.22	448.04	481.26	94266.90	3257.72
294	0 0	29.20	452.06	481.26	94296.10	2805.66
295	0 0	25.15	456.11	481.26	94321.25	2349.55
296	0 0	21.06	460.20	481.26	94342.31	1889.35
297	0 0	16.93	464.33	481.26	94359.24	1425.02
298	0 0	12.77	468.49	481.26	94372.02	956.54
299	0 0	8.57	472.69	481.26	94380.59	483.85
300	0 0	4.34	476.92	481.26	94384.93	6.93

Daily Factor = .00029342   Balance Remaining on Loan   6.93

This schedule has been processed with interest calculated not in advance.

INDEX